Microsoft® Press

Microsoft®
BackOffice® Small Business Server 4.5 Resource Kit

PUBLISHED BY
Microsoft Press
A Division of Microsoft Corporation
One Microsoft Way
Redmond, Washington 98052-6399

Copyright © 1999 by Microsoft Corporation

All rights reserved. No part of the contents of this book may be reproduced or transmitted in any form or by any means without the written permission of the publisher.

Library of Congress Cataloging-in-Publication Data
Microsoft BackOffice Small Business Server 4.5 Resource Kit /
    Microsoft Corporation.
        p. cm.
    ISBN 0-7356-0577-7
    1. Microsoft BackOffice.   2. Client/server computing.
    I. Microsoft Corporation.
QA76.9.C55M522   1999
005.7'1376--dc21   99-13774
                                                                CIP

Printed and bound in the United States of America.

1 2 3 4 5 6 7 8 9   QMQM   4 3 2 1 0 9

Distributed in Canada by Penguin Books Canada Limited.

A CIP catalogue record for this book is available from the British Library.

Microsoft Press books are available through booksellers and distributors worldwide. For further information about international editions, contact your local Microsoft Corporation office or contact Microsoft Press International directly at fax (425) 936-7329. Visit our Web site at mspress.microsoft.com.

Macintosh is a registered trademark of Apple Computer, Inc. used under license. ActiveX, BackOffice, FrontPage, Microsoft, Microsoft Press, MS-DOS, MSN, NetMeeting, NetShow, Outlook, PivotTable, Visual Basic, Visual Studio, Windows, and Windows NT are either registered trademarks or trademarks of Microsoft Corporation in the United States and/or other countries. Other product and company names mentioned herein may be the trademarks of their respective owners.

The example companies, organizations, products, people, and events depicted herein are fictitious. No association with any real company, organization, product, person, or event is intended or should be inferred.

Acquisitions Editor: Juliana Aldous
Project Editor: Thom Votteler

User Education Group Manager
Stefan Sierakowski

User Education Project Managers
Mary Harris, Amy Michaels

Technical Writer
Greg Gille

Lead Technical Editor
Liz Halverson

Copy Editor
Jackie Rubino

Technical Consultants
Erin Dunphy, Ryan Waite, Lisa Butler, Brian Jeans, Nancy Williams, Klaus Diaconu, Wil Campbell, Ken Stanfield, Duane Craig, Sean Everhart, John Bay, Greg Winn, Ruben Cruz, Sean Marvin, Richard Pogonko, Scott Hay, Phil Clark, Samantha Smith, and William Harding.

Production Lead
Jessica Vu

Production Specialists
Egan Orion, Mark Anable

Graphic Designer
Blaine Carpenter

Print Production Specialist
Kat Liekhus

Indexers
Lee Ross, Tony Ross

Contents

Part 1 Introductory Information for the Technology Consultant

Chapter 1 Small Business Server Customer Profile 3
The Need for a Complete Business Solution 3
The Importance of Small Business Server to the Customer 4
    Advantages of the Client/Server Model Network 4
    Upgrading from an Existing NetWare Network 5

Chapter 2 Small Business Server Design Philosophy 7
Making Everything Easy to Use. 7
Making Installation Decisions Automatic. 7
Designed for User Success 8
Keeping Things Simple. 8

Chapter 3 Easy Setup, Management, and Use 9
Automatic Setup and Configuration 9
    Input is Minimized During Installation 10
    Simple User Information Requests. 11
    Inherent Flexibility 11
    To Do List. 12
    Set Up Computer Wizard 12
        Components of Client Setup 13
Small Business Server Console: A Simplified User Interface. 14
    Ease of Management 14
    Integrated Management. 15
    Task-Based Administration. 15
        Increase User Success 16
        Wizards Streamline Tasks 16
Online Guide 17
    Comprehensive Guidance 17
    Flexible Searching. 17
    Easy Navigation. 18
Client User Guide 18
    User Tutorials, Troubleshooting Tips, and Help. 19
Extending the Intranet. 19

Easy to Support 19
    Support for Growth of the Small Business........................ 19

Chapter 4 Communication in New and More Efficient Ways 21

Small Business Server Internet Connection Wizard....................... 22
    Selecting a New Internet Service Provider 23
    Send E-mail to Customers Immediately............................ 23
Microsoft Fax Server.. 24
    Send Faxes Easily... 24
    Easily Receive and Distribute Faxes 24
    Monitor and Control Fax Use 24
Remote Access Service 25
    Automatic Installation and Configuration 26
    Easily Control User Access..................................... 26
Modem Sharing Server 26
Microsoft Proxy Server 2.0.. 28
    Leveraging Integrated Server Functionalities 28
    Cost-Effective Connectivity 28
    Control User Access.. 28
    Seamless Web Browsing 29
Exchange Server 5.5 29

Chapter 5 Small Business Server Component Feature Summary.............. 31

Components Providing File, Print, and Application Services 31
Components Providing Powerful Communications 32
Components Supporting Access to the Internet 33
Features Providing Easy Setup, Management, and Use.................... 33
Features Facilitating Solution Development and Administration 34

Chapter 6 Benefits of Small Business Server to the Technology Consultant 37

Easy to Replicate an Integrated and Optimized Solution................. 37
Provide Better Customer Service with Reduced Support Cost 38
    Remote Management... 38
    Server Status Tool 38
Excellent Potential for Add-on Sales.................................. 39
    Set Up Computer Wizard Supports Add-on Installation 39
    Extensible Console Facilitates Add-on Management 39
    Exposure to the Internet....................................... 39
Leverage One Set of BackOffice Skills and Solutions................... 39

Chapter 7 Introduction to Small Business Server Solution Development 41
Extensible Console 41
    Customizing Small Business Server Console 41
    Adding Task Pages 42
Application Integration 42
    Extension of Set Up Computer Wizard 42
Remote Server Administration 42

Chapter 8 Training 43

Chapter 9 Other Resources 45

Part 2 Planning

Chapter 10 Planning a Small Business Server Network 49
Small Business Office Network Characteristics 49
    Network Configuration 49
Small Business Server Requirements and Recommendations 51
    Server Computer Hardware Requirements 51
        Internet Connection Hardware 51
        Other Hardware Recommendations 52
        Hardware Compatibility 52
    Client Computer Requirements and Recommendations 52
        PC Hardware Requirements 52
        Dial-Up Networking Server Access 53
        Recommended Operating System Software 53
        Other Operating System Compatibilities 53
Backup System Planning 54
    Controller Device Compatibility with Windows NT Server 4.0 54
    Controller Device Capacity 54
    Installing Controller Drivers 55
    Scheduling and Performing Backups 55
Planning a Fault-Tolerant Disk Configuration 55
    Disk Mirroring 56
        I/O Requests in a Disk Mirroring Configuration 57
        Mirrored Partition Size 57
        Boot and System Partitions 57
        Advantages of Mirrored Disk Sets 58
        Disadvantages of Mirrored Disk Sets 58
    Disk Duplexing 59

Disk Stripe Sets 60
Disk Stripe Set with Parity 60
    Disks and Partition Space in a Stripe Set with Parity 61
    Disk Failure in a Stripe Set with Parity 61
    Advantages of Stripe Sets with Parity 62
    Disadvantages of Stripe Sets with Parity 62
    Guidelines for Choosing Mirrored Sets and Stripe Sets with Parity 63
        Hardware Compatibility 63
        Advantages of Using Identical Disks 64
        Backup Hardware 64
    More Information 64
Disaster Recovery Planning 65
    Windows NT Server 4.0 65
    Exchange Server 5.5 65
    SQL Server 7.0 65
    Backing Up Server Applications Using NT Backup 66
    Restoring Server Applications Using NT Backup 66

Chapter 11 Planning for an Internet Presence 67
Internet Access Proposal to the Small Business 68
Internet Connection Specifications 69
    ISP Capabilities 69
    ISP Locations 70
    Accessing the Internet Directly 70
    Internet Connection Types 70
        Dial-up Modem Connections 71
        Line Protocols 71
        Integrated Services Digital Network 71
    Web Site Development 73
        ISP Web Site Hosting Requirements 73
        Small Business Web Site Hosting with IIS 4.0 73
        IIS 4.0 Services 74
        Internet Access Protocols and Services Available 74
        Web Site Development Resources for the Small Business 74
    Estimating Bandwidth 75
        Calculating Bandwidth Using Bytes Transferred 75
        Calculating Bandwidth Using Connections and Document Size 76

Advantages of an Intranet	76
Extending the Default Intranet Page	77
Intranet Site	77
Intranet Security Precautions	77
Impact of Internet Connectivity on Server Computer Hardware	78
CPU Architecture	78
RAM Requirements May Vary	78
Web Site Testing	79
Internet Connection Process	79
ISP Referral Program	79
The ISP Sign-up Script	80
Automated Server Configuring for ISP Connectivity	80
Offline Sign-up and Configuration	81
Connectivity Issues with Existing ISPs	81
Small Business Server 4.5 and Existing ISP Services	81
Dedicated Internet Connections	83
Existing Small Business POP Accounts	83
Information Required from an Existing ISP	84
Domain Naming Service Configuration Issues	85
Registering a Second-Level Domain Name	85
Configuring Small Business Server to Use an Existing Second-Level Domain Name	85
ISP DNS Tasks	85

Chapter 12 Planning for Remote Access Users 87

Introduction to Windows NT Remote Access Service	87
Remote Access Service Key Features	87
Authentication	87
Secure Encryption	88
Scalability	88
Multi-link	88
Compression	88
Superior Connectivity Options	88
Broad Protocol Support	88
Broad Client Support	88
Open, Extensible Platform	89
Low Cost Hardware and Systems	89
Remote Access Service Management Features	89
Requirements for Implementing Remote Access Service	90
Remote Access to Small Business Server	91

PPTP for Secure Remote Access 91
   Advantages of PPTP.. 91
   Uses of PPTP.. 92
   VPN Key Features 92
PPTP and Virtual Private Networks................................. 93
   When PPTP Is Used 93
   Network Protocols on the Small Business Network 94
Hardware Requirements for a PPTP Client........................... 94
   Additional Connection Hardware 95
Summary of PPTP Deployment Considerations 95
Other Resources 96

Chapter 13   Planning for Microsoft Fax and Modem Sharing Services 97
Pre-Deployment Considerations..................................... 97
   Modem Planning Considerations 98
      Multiple Usage Scenarios 98
      Remote Access Service Modem Requirements 99
      Fax Service Modem Requirements........................... 99
      Recommended Modems for Small Business Server 4.5 100
      Modem Communication Standards........................... 100
   Fax Service Planning Considerations............................ 100

Chapter 14   Planning for Proxy Server 2.0 101
Small Business Network Security 101
Security and Internet Connectivity Modes 101
   Proxy Server Configuration for Dial-up Internet Connectivity 102
      Web Caching Minimizes Demand Dialing......................... 102
Other Planning Resources for Proxy Server 102

Chapter 15   Planning for Exchange Server 5.5............................. 103
Naming Strategy... 103
Naming Standards and Concepts 103
Technical Details 104
   Distinguished Name Example.................................... 104
   Organization Name 104
   Site Name 104
   Server Name 105

Mailbox Names	105
Foreign E-mail Addresses	106
X.400 Addresses	106
SMTP Restrictions	108

Chapter 16 Small Business Server Capacity Planning．．．．．．．．．．．．．．．．．．．．．109

Small Business Server Performance Evaluation	109
Evaluation Summary	110
Evaluation Tests	110
SQL Response Time Under Heavy Load	110
Test Characteristics	110
Exchange Response Time Under Heavy Load	111
Test Characteristics	111
Response Time Calculation	111
File I/O Throughput	112
Test Characteristics	112
Server and Client Test Configurations	112
Server Hardware	112
Server Software	113
Client Configuration	113
Performance Monitoring and Test Results	113
Performance Bottlenecks	113
Memory	115
Processor	115
Disk Subsystem	115
Response Time Test Results	116
Performance Analysis	116
Memory	117
Processor	117
Disk	117
Effect of RAM Changes on Performance	117
Network Capacity Guidelines	118
Disk Space Consumption	118
Hardware Recommendations	118

Part 3 Deployment

Chapter 17 Installing on New Machines 123
Server Requirements and Hardware Compatibility 123
   Computer Requirements 123
   Hardware Compatibility 124
      Network Adapter Cards 124
      Fax Modems 124
      Multiport Serial Adapter Boards.............................. 125
Materials Required for Installation of Small Business Server 4.5 on a New Machine 125
Performing the Small Business Server Installation...................... 125
   Setup Boot Diskettes 125
      Creating Setup Boot Diskettes................................ 126
   Installing Small Business Server.................................. 126
      Stage One: Windows NT Server Text Mode 126
      Stage Two: Windows NT Server GUI Mode....................... 127
      Stage Three: Installing Small Business Server Applications 129
   Completing Setup Using the To Do List 131

Chapter 18 Installing Small Business Server in Existing Environments......... 135
Installing Small Business Server on an Existing NT 4.0 Server 135
   Replacing Existing Windows NT 4.0 and Migrating Users............... 135
      Migrate User Wizard 136
      Migrate User Wizard Modes 136
      Migrating Data 136
Installing Small Business Server on a Windows 95 Machine 137
Installing Small Business Server on a Windows 98 Machine 137
Installing Small Business Server over a 16-Bit Operating System 137
Integrating Small Business Server with a NetWare Network 137
   NWLink Protocol... 138
   Gateway Service for NetWare (GSNW) 138
      A Gateway to NetWare Resources 139
      Providing a Preferred NetWare Server........................... 139
      GSNW Installation Issues 139
   File and Print Services for NetWare................................ 143
      Client Capabilities With FPNW 144

Chapter 19 Small Business Server Setup Issues 147
Hardware Detection Problems 147
    Network Adapter Card Not Detected................................ 148
        Removing the MS Loopback Adapter 149
        Installing Two Identical Network Adapters.................. 150
    Modem Not Detected.. 150
        Undetected Modem 151
        Setup Unable to Verify Modem Installed Correctly 152
        Checking Detected Modem Information 153
        Avoiding Modem Detection Issues............................. 153

Chapter 20 Small Business Server Set Up Computer Wizard 155
Running the Set Up Computer Wizard 155
Configuring the Server for the Client 156
    Logon Script... 156
    Response Folder and Client Application Configuration Files............ 156
        Scw.ini.. 156
        .Inf Files 156
    Machine Account... 157
Configuring the Client's Networking 157
Installing Applications on the Client....................................... 158

Chapter 21 ISP Connectivity Tasks 159
Internet Connection Issues 159
    Registering a Second-Level Domain Name 160
    Configuring Small Business Server to Use an Existing Second-Level
    Domain 160
    Exchange Server and Domain Name Changes 160
    Configuring the ISP Domain Name Server........................... 161
        ISP DNS Entries For E-mail 161
    Dynamic IP Addressing and Internet Mail Issues...................... 161
        NT-Based Solution...................................... 162
    E-mail Information... 162
    Web Hosting Information (Optional)................................ 162
        Web Publishing Resources 163
    Other Information Required from the ISP............................ 163
Configuring Small Business Server to Work with Non-Dialup Connections .. 163
    ISDN Connections... 163
    ISDN Terminal Adapters 163
    ISDN Routers 164

Leased Line Connections. 164
Configuring Windows NT Server 4.0. 164
Configuring Proxy Server 2.0 165
Configuring the Web Publishing Wizard. 165
Configuring Exchange Server 5.5. 165
    Scenario 1: Dial-On-Demand or Dial-Up Networking 165
    Scenario 2: Leased Line or Dedicated Connection 166
Additional Resources for ISP Connectivity. 168
Internet Connection Wizard Walkthrough. 168
  Internet Connection Topologies 168
  Internet Connection Types. 169
  Information Required for the Internet Connection Wizard 170
    Dial-Up Connection 170
    Router Connection 170
    Full-Time Connection/Broadband Device 171
  Starting the Internet Connection Wizard 172
  Running the Internet Connection Wizard 173
    Set Up Connection to Your ISP. 174
    Configure Hardware. 175
    Prepare to Sign Up Online 176
    Set Up Modem Connection to ISP 177
    Set Up Router Connection to ISP 179
    Network Interface Card Configuration. 180
    Set Up Second Network Adapter 181
    Configure Internet Mail Settings. 182
    Configure SMTP Mail Delivery 183
    Receive Exchange Mail. 184
    Set Up Authentication 186
    Send and Receive POP3 Mail 187
    Configure Internet Domain Name. 188
    Configure Web Site Information. 189
    Configure Firewall Settings. 190
    Finishing the Internet Connection Wizard. 192
Manual Configuration of Server Applications for Internet Connectivity. 193
  ISP Dial-Up Networking Phonebook Entry. 193
  Domain Name. 194
  Configuring Proxy Server Internet Connectivity. 195
  Configuring Proxy Server Packet Filtering 199
  Configuring the Proxy Server LAT 199

Configuring Web Publishing Wizard................................ 199
Configuring Exchange.. 200
    Configuring Exchange Server and Outlook Express Clients for POP3
    Mail Exchange 208

Chapter 22   Setting up Remote Client Computers......................... 213
Preliminary Setup Steps 213
Configuring the Remote Client Computer 214
    Create the User Account for the Remote User 214
    Manually Installing Client Applications on the Client Computer......... 215
    Configuring the Client Computer to Use Dial-Up Networking.......... 217
        Windows 95/98 Client Computers 217
        Windows NT Workstation Client Computers 218
Connecting to Small Business Server Using Dial-Up Networking.......... 220
    Connecting with a Windows 95/98 Client Computer.................. 220
        Alternate Connection Procedure for Windows 95/98 Remote Clients .. 221
    Connecting With a Windows NT Workstation Client Computer 221

Chapter 23   Installing PPTP in the Small Business Network 223
Requirements 223
Configuring PPTP on Small Business Server.......................... 224
    Installing PPTP... 224
    Adding VPN Devices as RAS Ports on Small Business Server 225
    Configuring PPTP Server Encryption and Authentication Options 226
        Configuring for Data Encryption on VPN Devices.................. 226
PPTP Client Connections to Small Business Server 227
    Installing and Configuring PPTP on Windows NT-Based Remote Clients . 228
        Installation of the PPTP Client................................. 228
        Adding a VPN Device as a RAS Port on the PPTP Client............. 229
        Configuring Dial-Up Networking on the PPTP Client................ 230
        Creating a Phonebook Entry to Dial a PPTP Server.................. 232
    Installing and Configuring PPTP on Windows 95-based Remote Clients .. 234
        Installation of the PPTP Client................................. 235
        Configuring Dial-Up Networking on the Windows 95 PPTP Client.... 235
        Creating a Connection to the PPTP Server 239
    Using PPTP to Connect to Small Business Server by Dialing an ISP 242
    Dialing up to an ISP PPTP Service to Connect to a PPTP Server......... 242

Chapter 24 Customizing Office 2000 Deployment 243
Customizing Office 2000 Installations 243
    Office Profile Wizard 243
        Creating Office Profiles 244
    Custom Installation Wizard 244
        Office 2000 Transforms 244
        Typical Custom Installation Wizard Scenario 245
    System Policy Editor 245
        System Policy Templates 245

Part 4 Administering and Maintaining

Chapter 25 Small Business Server Wizard Processes 249
Migrate User Wizard 249
    Export Mode 250
        Exporting Existing User Accounts 251
        Exporting Existing User Groups 251
        Information Not Exported 252
        The User Account File 253
        Editing User Account Files 254
        User Account File Default Location 255
    Import Mode 255
    Modifying User Parameters with Other Wizards 256
Console Wizards 256
    User Account Wizard 256
        Add a User Mode 257
        Review or Change User Information Mode 260
        Remove a User Mode 261
    Change Password Wizard 262
    User Access Wizard 264
        User Permissions 265
        Permissions and Resource Access 265
    Access Wizards 266
    Share a Folder Wizard 268
    Move Folder Wizard 270
    E-mail Distribution List Wizard 271
        Create a Distribution List Mode 271
        Review or Change Distribution List Mode 272
        Remove a Distribution List Mode 273

Set Up Computer Wizard		273
Add a New Computer to your Network		274
Configuring the Server for the Client		274
Configuring the Client's Networking		276
Startcli.exe		277
Installing Applications on the Client		277
Add a User to an Existing Client		278
Add Software to an Existing Client		278
Remove a Computer from your Network		278
Small Business Server Internet Connection Wizard		279
Chapter 26 Administrative Tools		**281**
Remote Administration with NetMeeting		281
Remote Connection Considerations		282
Client and Server Interaction with NetMeeting		282
System Policy Administration		282
System Policy and Controlling the User Environment		283
Small Business Server and System Policy		283
How System Policy Works		284
Customizing System Policy for Users, Groups, and Computers		285
System Policy Templates		286
Using System Policy Editor to Create System Policy		286
Using System Policy Editor to Edit the Registry		291
Installing the System Policy Editor on the Client		295
Installing System Policy Editor on a Windows NT Workstation		295
Installing the System Policy Editor on a Windows 95 Computer		296
Creating a Default System Policy		297
Changing the Default User Policy		298
Setting Folder Paths Back to Defaults		298
Creating Alternate Folder Paths		299
User Profiles		300
User Profile Content		300
Types of User Profiles		300
Creating and Administering User Profiles		301
User Profile Structure		301
Configuration Preferences Stored in the Registry Hive		301
Configuration Preferences Stored in Profile Directories		302
Windows 95 and Windows NT Profile Differences		302

User Profile Planning and Implementation 304
    Setting Permissions for User Profiles 304
    Selecting a Location to Save User Profiles 305
Creating a New Roaming User Profile for Windows NT 4.0
Workstations 306
Creating a New Mandatory User Profile for Windows NT 4.0
Workstations 309
Creating a New Roaming User Profile for Windows 95 Clients 311
Creating a New Mandatory User Profile for Windows 95 Clients 312
More Information on User Profiles and System Policies 313
Server Status Tool 314
    How the Server Status Tool Can be Used 314
    How the Server Status Tool Works 314
    Sending Reports 314
        Report Contents 315
        Setting the Server Status Tool Password 316
    Extending the Server Status Tool 317
Internet and Fax Reports 317
    Generating the Reports 318
    Proxy Reports 319
        Proxy Report Content 319
    Fax Reports 320
    Fax Report Content 320
    File Format in the CSV Database 321
Performance Monitor Tool 323
    Configuring Performance Monitor Alerts 323
        The Performance Monitor Utility 323
        Creating an Alert 324
        Testing the Counter 325
        Modifying Existing Alerts 326
        Monitoring the Processor Queue Length 327
        Monitoring Interrupts/Second 328
        Creating an Alert for a Network NT Workstation 329
Task Scheduling Tool 330
    The Scheduled Task Utility 330
    Scheduled Task Wizard 331
    Mobility and Accessibility of Task Files 331

Contents   xvii

Set Up Computer Wizard 273
   Add a New Computer to your Network 274
      Configuring the Server for the Client 274
      Configuring the Client's Networking 276
      Startcli.exe 277
      Installing Applications on the Client 277
   Add a User to an Existing Client 278
   Add Software to an Existing Client 278
   Remove a Computer from your Network 278
Small Business Server Internet Connection Wizard 279

Chapter 26   Administrative Tools 281

Remote Administration with NetMeeting 281
   Remote Connection Considerations 282
   Client and Server Interaction with NetMeeting 282
System Policy Administration 282
   System Policy and Controlling the User Environment 283
      Small Business Server and System Policy 283
      How System Policy Works 284
      Customizing System Policy for Users, Groups, and Computers 285
      System Policy Templates 286
      Using System Policy Editor to Create System Policy 286
      Using System Policy Editor to Edit the Registry 291
   Installing the System Policy Editor on the Client 295
      Installing System Policy Editor on a Windows NT Workstation ... 295
      Installing the System Policy Editor on a Windows 95 Computer .. 296
   Creating a Default System Policy 297
      Changing the Default User Policy 298
      Setting Folder Paths Back to Defaults 298
      Creating Alternate Folder Paths 299
User Profiles 300
   User Profile Content 300
   Types of User Profiles 300
   Creating and Administering User Profiles 301
   User Profile Structure 301
      Configuration Preferences Stored in the Registry Hive 301
      Configuration Preferences Stored in Profile Directories 302
   Windows 95 and Windows NT Profile Differences 302

User Profile Planning and Implementation 304
    Setting Permissions for User Profiles 304
    Selecting a Location to Save User Profiles 305
Creating a New Roaming User Profile for Windows NT 4.0 Workstations 306
Creating a New Mandatory User Profile for Windows NT 4.0 Workstations 309
Creating a New Roaming User Profile for Windows 95 Clients 311
Creating a New Mandatory User Profile for Windows 95 Clients 312
More Information on User Profiles and System Policies 313
Server Status Tool 314
    How the Server Status Tool Can be Used 314
    How the Server Status Tool Works 314
    Sending Reports 314
        Report Contents 315
        Setting the Server Status Tool Password 316
    Extending the Server Status Tool 317
Internet and Fax Reports 317
    Generating the Reports 318
    Proxy Reports 319
        Proxy Report Content 319
    Fax Reports 320
    Fax Report Content 320
    File Format in the CSV Database 321
Performance Monitor Tool 323
    Configuring Performance Monitor Alerts 323
        The Performance Monitor Utility 323
        Creating an Alert 324
        Testing the Counter 325
        Modifying Existing Alerts 326
        Monitoring the Processor Queue Length 327
        Monitoring Interrupts/Second 328
        Creating an Alert for a Network NT Workstation 329
Task Scheduling Tool 330
    The Scheduled Task Utility 330
    Scheduled Task Wizard 331
    Mobility and Accessibility of Task Files 331

Contents   xix

  Security and Scheduled Tasks 331
   Security Features 332
   User Credentials 332
   User Name and Password 333
  Running Tasks 333
  Editing Tasks 334
  Configuring a Task with the Scheduled Tasks Utility 334
  Other Features of the Utility 335
  NT Backup Tool and the Scheduled Task Utility 335
  Application Programming Interfaces (APIs) 335

Chapter 27 Administering Small Business Server Components 337
Microsoft Fax Service 337
  Faxing Model 337
  Managing Microsoft Fax Service 338
   Accessing Fax Service Properties 338
   Adding a Fax Device 339
   Adding and Configuring Fax Printers 340
   User Access to the Fax Printer 340
   Creating Cover Pages for Your Fax Printers 340
   Assigning Cover Pages for Your Fax Printers 341
   Receiving and Routing Incoming Faxes 341
   Checking Received Faxes 342
   Sending and Resending Faxes 342
   Fax Send Notification 342
   Fax Job Management 342
   Status Monitoring 343
  Microsoft Fax Server Fax and E-mail Integration 343
   Inbound Fax Routing 343
   Utilizing Microsoft Exchange Server Features 344
  Faxing Documents 344
   Faxing a Document with the Print Command 344
   Faxing a Message from Outlook or Exchange 345
   Creating a Fax Address 346
   Faxing a Document From Office 2000 Applications 347
  Upgrading to BackOffice Server 347
Microsoft Modem Sharing Service 347
  Administering the Modem Sharing Service 347
   Accessing Modem Sharing Service Properties 348
  Viewing the Modem Pool 349

Configuring Modem Pools 349
Configuring Clients for Modem Pool Connection 350
    Connecting Windows 95-Based Clients to the Modem Pool 350
    Connecting Windows NT Workstation-Based Clients to the Modem Pool 351
Status Monitoring 352
Microsoft Exchange Server 5.5 352
Administrator Program Interface 352
Mailboxes 353
Distribution Lists 353
    End-User Management of Distribution Lists 354
    Distribution List Options 354
Custom Recipients 354
    Address Formats 354
    Migration of New Users 354
    Address Book Views 355
Public Folders 356
    Off-Line Folder Synchronization 356
Managing End-User Objects 357
Protecting Exchange Data 358
Exchange Administration Tips 358
    Automating E-mail Forwarding 359
    Web Access to Exchange 359
Monitoring the Performance of Exchange 359
    Performance Monitor Tool Features 360
    Exchange Performance Monitoring Processes 360
    Performance Monitoring Scenarios 361
    Performance Baseline Definition Phase 361
    Exchange Usage Characteristics 362
    Defining Service Levels 362
    Counter Thresholds 363
    Data Collection and Analysis Phase 364
    Full Utilization of NT Performance Monitor 369
    Accessing Predefined Exchange Performance Monitors 370
    Exchange Performance Monitor Configuration Phase 370
    Queue Monitoring 370
    Server Health Monitoring 372
    Server History 373
    Server Load 374

Server Users	375
Creating Other Performance Monitors	376
Configuring Log Files for the Data Collection Phase	381
Proxy Server 2.0	**389**
User Access Control	390
NT Server Directory and User Access Control	390
Manually Configuring User Outbound Internet Access	391
Other Proxy Features	394
Security	395
Proxy Local Address Table	400
Viewing Active Internet Sessions	412
Caching	413
Using FTP	415
Configuring Performance Monitor Alerts for Proxy Services	415
Web Proxy Service Performance Monitor Alerts	416
Winsock Proxy Service Performance Monitor Alerts	417
Other Winsock Proxy Performance Monitors	418
Creating Proxy Performance Monitors	418
Viewing Proxy Performance Monitors	420
Proxy Performance Logs	421
SQL Server 7.0	**421**
Upsizing Access to SQL Server 7.0	422
Small Business Database Scenarios	422
SQL Server 7.0 Administration	423
NTFS and FAT Volume Security	**424**
NTFS File and Directory Permissions	424
FAT Share Permissions	424
File and Directory Compression on NTFS Partitions	425
Microsoft Outlook	**426**
Team Interaction	426
Configuring Outlook With Public Folders	426
Publishing to a Public Folder	429
Creating a Discussion Group	430
Testing the Discussion Group	433
Allowing Anonymous Access to Public Folders	435
Setting Up Group Task Lists and Contact Databases	438
More Information	442

Chapter 28 Background Information for Administrators 443

Windows NT Server Internet Connection Services for RAS 443
    Benefits of ICS 444
    ICS Components 444
    ICS Component Descriptions 444
        Microsoft Connection Manager 444
        Connection Manager Administration Kit 445
        Internet Authentication Services 449
        Connection Point Services 450

Chapter 29 Administrative Tips and Other Information 453

Simplifying Client Disk Defragmentation 453
    Creating a Context Menu Option 454
    Using the Quick Defrag Option 456

Part 5 Performance Optimization and Tuning

Chapter 30 Small Business Server 4.5 Optimization 459

Overview 459
What Small Business Server Does to Maximize Performance 460
    Windows NT Server 4.0 Default Installation Optimizations 460
        Network Setup Optimizations 461
    Server Application Installation Optimizations 464
    Server Application Capabilities 465
        Exchange Server 5.5 465
        SQL Server 7.0 466
        Proxy Server 2.0 467
        Internet Information Server 4.0 467
        Other Server Application Optimizations 467
    Fault Tolerance 468
    Client Application Optimizations 468
        Small Business Server Version 468
        Fax Client 468
        Internet Explorer 5.0 469
        Microsoft Outlook 2000 470
        Office 2000 471
        Outlook Client Profile Updates with Modprof Utility 471

Contents xxiii

> Server Installation Defaults.. 473
> > Shared Folders 473
> > Default Permissions 474
> > Favorites 476
> > Default Internet... 476
> > Default Intranet and Content................................. 476
> Implementation of Performance Optimizations 477
> > Server Applications Optimized on a Single Platform............ 477
> > > Code Optimizations 477
> > > User Limitations on Applications......................... 478
> > > Viable Integrated Application Performance 479
> > Management Optimizations...................................... 479

Chapter 31 Performance and Scalability Enhancements..................... 481
Overview 481
Performance Tuning 481
> Baseline Hardware Recommendations 482
> > Configuring the Disks 482
> Tuning Server Applications 483
> > Windows NT Server 4.0 with Service Pack 4 483
> > Exchange Server 5.5 with Service Pack 2 485
> > SQL Server 7.0.. 485
> Internet Connectivity and Upsizing 485
> > Router Connectivity....................................... 485
> > Full-Time/Broadband Connections 488
> > LAN Router Configuration 489

Part 6 Integration and Interaction

Chapter 32 E-mail and Internet Connectivity Alternatives.................. 493
Overview 493
Web Browsing Support.. 493
> Single ISP Account Configured Using Microsoft Proxy Server 2.0....... 494
> Multiple ISP Accounts Configured Using Microsoft Modem Sharing Service... 499
> Exchange Server Automatically Set up for Internal E-mail............. 501

Web Browsing and POP3 Support....................................... 501
> Single POP3 Account 502
> Multiple POP3 Accounts... 503
> Using Exchange for Internal and POP3 E-mail.................... 503

SMTP and Web Hosting Support 507
  SMTP Support 507
  Web Hosting Support 507

Chapter 33 Office 2000 Integration Issues 509
Overview 509
  Integrating Office 2000 in a Non-Office Small Business Server
  Installation 509
  Integrating Office 2000 Applications in Custom Deployments 514

Chapter 34 Client Interaction with the Server 515
Overview 515
Client Interactions 515
  MS-DOS Clients 516
  Windows 95/98 Clients 516
  Windows 3.1 and OS/2 Clients Running LAN Manager 516
  Macintosh Clients 517
Client Authentication 517
  MS-DOS Client Authentication 517
  Windows 3.1 Client Authentication 518
  Windows 95 Client Authentication 518
  Macintosh Client Authentication 519
    More Information 519

Chapter 35 Cross-Platform Interoperability 521
Overview 521
Interoperability Layers 522
Operating System Environments Supported by Windows NT Server 4.0 522
NetWare Interoperability 523
  Gateway Service for NetWare 524
  Client Services for NetWare 525
  NWLink 525
  Migration Tool for NetWare 525
  Add-On Utilities for NetWare 526
    File and Print Services for NetWare 526
    Directory Service Manager for NetWare 526
  More Information 527

UNIX Interoperability	528
Network Layer Interoperability	528
TCP/IP	528
File Transfer and Hypertext Transfer Protocols	528
Domain Name Service	529
Dynamic Host Configuration and Boot Protocols	529
Network File System	529
Advanced Server for UNIX	529
Data Layer Interoperability	530
Oracle Database Access	530
Open Database Connectivity and Object Linking and Embedding Database	530
Application Layer Interoperability	530
Microsoft Outlook Express for UNIX	530
Microsoft Internet Explorer for UNIX	531
Transaction Internet Protocol	531
Microsoft Transaction Server 2.0 and Oracle 7.3 Support	531
Distributed Component Object Model and UNIX	532
Management Layer Interoperability	532
Simple Network Management Protocol	532
Administrative Tools	533
More Information	533
Macintosh Interoperability	533
Graphics Performance	534
File Sharing	534
Printer Sharing	535
Administration	535
Connecting Macintosh Computers to the Internet	535
Security	535
Interoperability Benefit Summary of Windows NT Server 4.0 Services for Macintosh	536
More Information	537

Part 7 Security

Chapter 36 Firewall Security and Web Caching with Proxy Server 2.0 541
Overview of Proxy Server 2.0 541
    Managed Network Access Background 542
    Proxy Server 2.0 Integrated Services on a Single Platform 543
        Open Standards Platform 543
    Proxy Server 2.0 as a Secure Gateway 543
    Web Content Caching 544
    Proxy Server 2.0 Services 544
    Security Overview 545
        Firewall Definition 545
        Proxy Definition 545
        LAN and Internet Isolation 546
        Protection of Internal IP Addresses from the Internet 546
        IP Packet Layer Filtering 546
    Web Publishing Support 546
    Proxy Server 2.0 Default Configuration 546
    Advantages of Proxy Server 2.0 Connectivity 547
        Disadvantages of Alternate Connection Methods 547
Key Features of Proxy Server 2.0 548
    Extensible Security 548
    Management 549
        Windows NT Directory Services and User Manager 549
        Windows NT 4.0 Performance Monitor and Event Log Tools 549
        Proxy Server 2.0 Management from IIS Console 550
        Windows NT Security 552
    Security Architecture 552
        Capabilities of Dynamic Packet Filtering 553
        The Inner Processes of Dynamic Packet Filtering 554
        Enabling Dynamic Packet Filtering 556
        Customizing Packet Filters for Proxy Services 558
        Default Configuration of Inbound Access Security 561
    Access Control 561
        Control of Client Outbound Access to Internet Services 562
        Access Control by Domain, IP Address, or Subnet Filtering 563
        Access Control for Winsock Clients 564
        Access Control for Remote Users 565
        Encryption 566
    Web Publishing Support 566

Contents xxvii

    Reverse Proxy... 567
    Server Proxying 567
    Configuring Reverse Proxy for Web Publishing................. 568
Caching... 569
    Passive Caching Process 569
    Active Caching... 570
Characteristics of Other Proxy Server 2.0 Features 571
    Proxy Auto Dial 571
    Local Address Table 572
Proxy Service Architecture...................................... 572
    Web Proxy Service.. 573
    Winsock Proxy Service 579
    SOCKS Proxy Service..................................... 584
    TCP/IP on the Small Business LAN.......................... 585
    Using Web Proxy and Winsock Proxy Services Together............ 585

Chapter 37 Computer Security and Windows NT Server 4.0 587
Overview of Security Levels 587
Physical Security Considerations................................. 587
    Standard Security... 588
    High-Level Security....................................... 588
        Networks and Security................................. 588
        Controlling Access to the Computer 589
        Controlling Access to the Power Switch 589
Standard Software Security Considerations 589
    User Accounts 589
    Administrative Accounts and User Accounts 590
    The Guest Account 590
    Logging On.. 590
    Logging Off or Locking the Workstation 591
    Passwords... 591
    Enforcing Strong User Passwords 591
    Protecting Files and Directories 592
    Protecting the Registry from Network Access 593
    Backups... 593
    Auditing 594
    Secure File Sharing 595
    Controlling Access to Removable Media 597

Chapter 38 Internet Information Server 4.0 Security Model 599
Overview of IIS Integrated Security Model 599
    Central Management 600
    Comprehensive Security Solution. 600
Importance of Web Server Security 600
    Application and Database Security. 601
    Electronic Commerce. 601
    Business Relationships and Extranets 601
    Communicating with Customers. 602
Framework For Using Security. 602
Access Control 603
    User Authentication and Authorization 603
        Anonymous Access 603
        User Name and Password. 604
        Secure Windows Challenge/Response 604
        Digital Certificates 604
        Access Control Using Custom Authentication Filters. 605
    Access Controls 605
        IP Addresses 605
        NTFS File System Permissions 605
        Impersonation 606
        Permissions on IIS Services. 606
    Auditing Access 606
Confidentiality and Data Integrity 607
    Confidentiality 607
    Data Integrity 607
    Digital Signatures. 607
    Secure Sockets Layer. 608
    Secure Electronic Transport 609
    Point-to-Point Tunneling Protocol (PPTP) 609
Security Functionality for Developers 610
    Issuing Digital Certificates with Microsoft Certificate Server 1.0 610
    CryptoAPI. 611
    Programmatically Interacting with Client Certificates 611

Part 8 Migration and Upgrade

Chapter 39 Migrating from a NetWare Environment 615

Integration and Migration Planning. 616
   Deployment Plan 616
      General Agenda 616
      Details of the Plan 617
      Pre-Installation Planning Checklist 617
Integration Overview. 618
   Implementation of Rollout 618
      Test Phase 619
      Integration Phase 620
      Post-Integration Phase Considerations. 620
The Test Phase 621
   Preparation Tasks. 621
      Physical Location 621
      Verify Hardware Components 622
      Determining Tests to be Conducted 624
      Secure the Installation Software 625
      Network Hardware Setup 625
      Documentation 626
   Installation of Small Business Server 4.5 626
      Client Setup. 626
      Client Software Installation. 629
      Client Machine Functionality Testing 629
      Third-Party Application Testing. 631
      NetWare Functionality Testing. 632
The Integration Phase 632
   Integration of Small Business Server 4.5 in the NetWare Network 632
      Installation of NWLink Protocol 633
      Installation of Gateway Service for NetWare 634
      Testing GSNW Functionality 638
      Installing File and Print Services for NetWare 639
      Installing Directory Service Manager for NetWare 641
      Create Login Scripts. 646
      Client Configuration Assumption. 647

NetWare Migration Phase 647
    Creating New User Accounts 648
    Migrating the Data 648
        Starting the Migration Utility 648
        Moving Directories and Files 650
    Configuring the Clients 651
        Configure Windows for Workgroups NetWare Clients 651
        Configure Windows NT Workstation Clients 652
        Configure Windows 95 NetWare Clients 652
    Testing Basic Connectivity 652
    Documenting Migration Results 653
Project Review Phase 654
    Executive Summary 654
    Project Objective 654
    Schedule Analysis 655

Chapter 40 Small Business Server 4.5 Licensing and Upgrade 657

Licensing Issues 657
    Client Access Licenses 657
        Adding Client Access Licenses 658
Upgrading Small Business Server 4.5 659
    Upgrading Integrated Applications 659
        Windows NT Server 4.0 Upgrade 659
        Windows NT 4.0 and Exchange Server 5.5 Upgrades 660
        SQL Server 7.0 Upgrade 660
        Proxy Server 2.0 Upgrade 660
    Upgrade to BackOffice Server 4.5 661

Chapter 41 Migrating from an Existing Windows NT Server 663

Migrating Users to Small Business Server 4.5 663
    Migrate User Wizard Export Mode Processes 663
    Migrate User Wizard Import Mode Processes 664
    Migrate User Wizard Information File 664
        Modifying the Information File 665
    Import Users Task 666
    Additional Tasks 666
    More Information 666

Chapter 42 Migrating an Access Database to SQL Server 7.0 667
SQL Server 7.0 Tools Used in Migration 667
    SQL Server Enterprise Manager. 667
    Data Transformation Services. 668
    SQL Server Query Analyzer. 668
    SQL Server Profiler 668
Migration Phase. 669
    Access Database Backup. 669
    Moving Tables and Data. 669
    Migrating Access Queries. 670
        Transact-SQL Scripts. 670
        Stored Procedures. 670
        Views. 671
    Migrating Access Queries into Stored Procedures and Views 672
    Migrating Access Queries into Transact-SQL Scripts 672
Other Migration Considerations. 674
    Using Parameters. 674
        Access and SQL Server Syntax. 675
    Nested Queries 676
    Verifying SQL Server 7.0–Compliant Syntax. 676
    Connecting the Applications. 677
    Optimizing the Application. 678
        Monitoring Transact SQL-Statements 678
        Implementing Efficient Indexes 678

Part 9 Developing Small Business Server Solutions

Chapter 43 Customizing and Extending the Small Business Server Console... 681
Console Extension Philosophy. 681
    Extension Organization. 682
    User Success. 682
Console Organization 682
    High-Level Pages. 682
    Sub-Level Pages. 683
        Secondary Sub Pages. 683
Page Layout and Design. 684
    Home Page 684
    Tasks and More Tasks Pages 684
    Sub Pages 686

- Watermarks and Symbols ... 686
- Tool Tips ... 686
- Sub Page Content ... 687
- Typical Layout ... 687
- Default Layouts ... 688
- Sub Page Action Capacity ... 691
- Consistency ... 691
  - Text in Lower Case ... 692
  - Similar Tasks on Various Sub Pages Should Be Placed in the Same Location ... 692
  - Sub Page Left Column Content ... 693
  - Similar Tasks Should Have the Same Background Watermarks ... 693
  - All Actions with the Same Associated Verb Should Have the Same Symbol ... 693
  - Background, Content, and Links Should be Consistent ... 693
- Extension Mechanism for Console Pages ... 694
  - Adding Favorite Links to the Home Page ... 694
  - Adding Tasks to the Tasks and More Tasks Pages ... 697
  - Adding Tasks with the Small Business Server Customization Tool ... 699
  - Adding Sub Pages and Secondary Sub Pages ... 700
    - Sub Page Requirements ... 700
    - Sub Page Components ... 700
    - Symbols ... 702
  - Installation Mechanism ... 702
  - Console Page Extension Changes From SBS 4.0a ... 703
  - Upgrading From Small Business Server 4.0(a) ... 704
- Extension Mechanism for the Online Guide ... 704
  - Topic Files ... 704
    - Overview Topics ... 704
    - Manage Topics ... 705
    - Procedure Topics ... 705
    - Troubleshooting Topics ... 705
  - Adding Topic Files ... 706
  - Elements Inside Topic Files ... 706
    - Console Page Links ... 706
    - Topic Links ... 706
  - Extending the Table of Contents ... 707
    - OEM.hhc ... 707
    - Table of Contents File ... 707

Integrating with Console Sub Pages.	709
About Links	709
Overview Links	709
Procedure Links	710
Troubleshooting Links.	710
Installation	710
Online Guide Integration Changes From SBS 4.0a	711

Chapter 44 Extension Mechanism for the Set Up Computer Wizard ... 713

Extension of the Application List in the Set Up Computer Wizard	713
Integration Requirement	714
Creating Your Application INF File	714
Example of INF File	715
Response File Requirements	717
Adding Your Application to Scw.ini	717
Increment the Number of Applications	717
Add Application Information	718
Example of Scw.ini Modification	719
Adding Your Application to Clioc.inf	720
Installation	721
Removing Your Application from the Set Up Computer Wizard	722
Set Up Computer Wizard Extension Changes from SBS 4.0a	723
Upgrading from Small Business Server 4.0(a)	723

Chapter 45 Using the MSDE Solution with Microsoft Access 2000 ... 725

Microsoft Access Features	726
Access Components	726
Overview of Jet Database Engine 4.0 and MSDE	727
Jet Database Engine	727
Microsoft Data Engine	727
Comparing the Jet Database Engine and MSDE	728
Organizational Requirements	728
Jet Database Engine and MSDE Usage Analysis	729
Simplicity of the Jet Database Engine 4.0	729
Data Integrity Advantage of MSDE	730
Performance Advantages of MSDE	730
Amount of Data Handling	731
Jet Database Engine and MSDE Feature Analysis	731

Microsoft Access Upsizing Wizard 732
    Functions of the Upsizing Wizard 732
Summary 733

Chapter 46 Other Extensions and Solutions 735

Extending the Server Status Tool 735
    Registry Configuration by the Customization Tool 738
    Locating and Sending New Application Log Files 740
Creating a Team Intranet Site 740
    Microsoft Office 60 Minute Intranet Kit Features 740
        FrontPage 60 Minute Intranet Site Wizard 740
        Team Web Home Page 741
        Document Library 741
        Auto Updating News Engine 741
        Event Calendar 741
        Online Applications 741
        Search Feature 741
        Help 742
        More Information 742

Chapter 47 Enhancing Office 2000 Functionality 743

Enhancements of Office 2000 743
    File Format Compatibilities 743
    File Error Detection and Fix 744
    Reduced Cost of Ownership 744
    Operating System Shell Update 744
        Install on Demand 745
        Single Document Interface 745
        Web Folders 745
    Increased Integration with the Web 746
    Office 2000 Enhanced by Browser and Web Server Functionalities 746
        Creating and Managing Intranets 746
        Features Enabled by Browsers 747
        Microsoft Internet Explorer 5.0 747
        Web Features Enabled through Server Software 748
        Windows NT Server 4.0 748
        HTTP 1.1 Servers with PUT Protocol 748
        HTTP-DAV Servers 749

Office 2000 Enhanced Web Functionality with Microsoft Internet
  Information Services 749
  IIS with FrontPage Extensions 750
  IIS with Office Server Extensions 750
  NetMeeting Conferencing Software 751
Enterprise Integration and Support with Office 2000 752
  Data Access 753
    OLE DB 753
    Microsoft SQL Server OLAP Services Support 753
    Access 2000 Client Server Tools 753
    Client/Server Design Tools 754
    Microsoft SQL Server-Based Administration Tools. 754
  Corporate Reporting 754
    Enhanced Web Queries 754
    Office Web Components 755
Conclusion 756
More Information 756

Chapter 48 Office 2000 Customer Manager. 757
Information and Resources. 757

Chapter 49 Application Communication with MSMQ 759
Information Sources 759

Chapter 50 TAPI Solutions for Small Business Server 761
Information Sources 761

Part 10   Tools and Utilities

Chapter 51 Small Business Server 4.5 Tool Installation and Access 765
Overview 765
  Installing the Small Business Server Resource Kit. 766
  Accessing Small Business Server Tools 767
    Tools Management Console 767
    Running Tools 768
    Accessing the Tools 769

Chapter 52 Small Business Server 4.5 Tool Descriptions 771
Introduction 771
  Small Business Server Start Menu Tool 772
    Accessing Tasks on the Start Menu 772

Batch User Add Tool 773
Modem Status Tools 773
   TAPI.Exe Tool 774
   Timon Tool 774
   TAPIstate Tool 774
Small Business Server Customization Tool. 775
   Customize SBS Console 776
   Configure Server Status Tool 780
Small Business Server Client Setup Integration Wizard 782
   Information Fields 783
   Customization Process 784
   Running the Small Business Server Client Setup Integration Wizard . . . 785
   Checking the Set Up Computer Wizard Application List. 786
Fax Monitoring and Performance Tools 786
   FaxMon 787
   FaxPerf. 787

Part 11 Troubleshooting

Chapter 53 Small Business Server Setup Troubleshooting. 791
Overview. 791
Troubleshooting during Setup 791
Related Troubleshooting Knowledge Base Articles. 797

Chapter 54 Client Setup Troubleshooting 799
Overview. 799
Troubleshooting during Client Setup. 799
Related Troubleshooting Knowledge Base Articles. 807

Chapter 55 Fax Service Troubleshooting. 809
Overview. 809
Troubleshooting Fax Service 809
Related Troubleshooting Knowledge Base Articles. 825

Chapter 56 Modem Sharing Service Troubleshooting 827
Overview. 827
Troubleshooting Modem Sharing Service. 827
Troubleshoot the Modem with HyperTerminal. 831
Related Troubleshooting Knowledge Base Articles. 832

Chapter 57 E-mail and Internet Troubleshooting **833**
Overview 833
Troubleshooting E-mail and Internet................................ 833
Related Troubleshooting Knowledge Base Articles..................... 838

Glossary **839**

Index **853**

Figures and Tables

Figures

Figure 10.1 Typical Small Business Server Network Configuration   50
Figure 10.2 Disk Mirror Configuration   56
Figure 10.3 Duplexed disk mirror configuration   59
Figure 10.4 Data write to a stripe set with parity   61
Figure 11.1 ISDN scenario   72
Figure 11.2 Intranet and Internet relationship   77
Figure 12.1 Remote access scenarios   91
Figure 12.2 Remote access with PPTP tunneling   94
Figure 13.1 Typical Small Business Server modem configuration   99
Figure 16.1 Performance monitor statistics for memory, processor, and disk counters   114
Figure 26.1 Proxy and Fax report generation   318
Figure 27.1 Receiving a fax with Small Business Server   342
Figure 27.2 Exchange performance monitoring process overview   360
Figure 27.3 Exchange logging processes   383
Figure 31.1 Network topology with a router   486
Figure 31.2 Router IP addressing scheme example   487
Figure 31.3 Network topology with ADSL or cable modem   488
Figure 31.4 LAN router configuration   489
Figure 32.1 Single ISP account configured using Proxy Server   494
Figure 32.2 Multiple ISP accounts configured using Microsoft Modem Sharing Service   500
Figure 32.3 Single POP3 account   502
Figure 32.4 Multiple POP3 accounts   503
Figure 35.1 Gateway Service for NetWare configuration   524
Figure 36.1 Proxy Server 2.0 and LAN configuration   545
Figure 36.2 Component stack for Proxy dynamic filtering processes   555
Figure 36.3 Packet filtering functional equivalent   556
Figure 36.4 Running Internet applications behind secure network connection with server proxying   567
Figure 36.5 Passive caching process   570
Figure 36.6 Proxy Auto Dial configuration   571
Figure 36.7 Web Proxy architecture   575
Figure 36.8 Web Proxy ISAPI filter   576
Figure 36.9 ISAPI application functions   577

Figure 36.10 Windows socket communication channel 580
Figure 36.11 Winsock Proxy call to Internet host 581
Figure 36.12 Windows Sockets control channel 583
Figure 43.1 Task link arrangement on the console 685
Figure 43.2 Add symbol 693
Figure 43.3 Online Guide topic icons 694

Tables

Table 10.1 Stripe Set Configuration 60
Table 10.2 Stripe set with parity configuration 60
Table 11.1 Internet Proposal Factors for the Small Business 68
Table 11.2 Internet Connection Types, Bandwidth, and User Capacity 70
Table 11.3 IIS Service Features 74
Table 12.1 Remote Access Service Required Components 90
Table 15.1 Restricted Characters for Exchange Server Name 105
Table 15.2 Fields in the Mailbox Name 105
Table 15.3 X.400 Address Allowable Characters 107
Table 15.4 Exchange Server Naming Strategy 108
Table 16.1 Exchange Load Simulation 111
Table 16.2 Server Test Configuration 112
Table 16.3 Performance monitor counter average values 115
Table 16.4 Response Times and Throughput 116
Table 16.5 Disk Space Consumption and Usage Scenarios 118
Table 16.6 Minimum Hardware Recommendations (10 Users) 118
Table 16.7 Mid-Range Hardware Recommendations (25 Users) 119
Table 16.8 Maximum Hardware Recommendations (50 Users) 119
Table 21.1 Dequeuing Configurations for Mail Retrieval 185
Table 25.1 Default User Permissions 265
Table 26.1 Windows NT 4.0 Workstation and Windows 95 Registry Files 303
Table 27.1 Performance Monitor Counters for the Initial Exchange Profile 364
Table 27.2 Memory performance counters 366
Table 27.3 Disk I/O Counters 367
Table 27.4 CPU Utilization Counters 368
Table 27.5 Information Store Counters 369
Table 27.6 Suggested Additional Performance Monitors 377
Table 27.7 Event Viewer Components 381
Table 30.1 Small Business Server Favorites Setup 469
Table 30.2 Default Shared Folders 473
Table 30.3 Default Permissions Applied to Recipients 474

Table 30.4 Default Permissions Applied to Folders   474
Table 30.5 Default Favorites   476
Table 35.1 Services for Macintosh Interoperability Benefits   536
Table 37.1 Password Characters for Passfilt.dll   591
Table 37.2 Security Threats and Auditing   594
Table 39.1 Small Business Server Machine Hardware Requirements   622
Table 42.1 Access Queries   670
Table 42.2 Differences Between SQL Server 7.0 and Access Syntax   674
Table 45.1 Organizational Needs for MSDE and the Jet Database Engine   729
Table 45.2 Jet Database Engine and MSDE Feature Comparison   731
Table 53.1 Known Errors   794

Procedures

Part 3 — *Deployment*

Chapter 17

To create setup boot diskettes   126
To begin Small Business Server installation in the Windows NT Server Text Mode   126
To continue Small Business Server installation in the Windows NT Server GUI Mode   128
To continue installation with the Small Business Server Setup Wizard   129
To add a network printer to the server   131
To add a new user to the server   133
To import users to the server   133
To sign up with an ISP   133
To add client licenses   133
To configure Fax Service to receive faxes   133

Chapter 18

To Install the NWLink Protocol   138
To Install GSNW   140
To Verify that Gateway Service for NetWare has been installed   141
To create a NetWare Gateway User Account   141
To configure the Small Business Server portion of GSNW   142
To test the functionality of the GSNW installation   143
To check access to NetWare resources from the Small Busines Server client   143
To Install FPNW   144

Chapter 19

To add a Network Card and remove the Microsoft Loopback Adapter   149
To remove the configuration for the second network adapter   150
To remove the undetected modem and install the modem manually   151
To configure Remote Access Service to use the correct COM port and modem   152

Chapter 21
To create a new dial-up networking phonebook entry 178
To configure an ISP dial-up networking Phonebook entry 193
To configure the DNS domain name 194
To configure a full-time Proxy connection 195
To configure a dial-up Proxy connection 197
To launch the registry editor and create the FTP address entry 199
To launch the Exchange Administrator program and configure the IMS 201
To configure the IMS Address Space page 202
To configure the IMS Dial-up Connections page 203
To configure the IMS Connections page 205
To configure the IMS Routing page 206
To configure the IMS Site, Configuration, Site Addressing properties 206
To set the IMS to automatic startup 208
To configure the Exchange Server for POP3 mail 209
To configure Outlook Express clients to use Exchange Server for POP3 mail 210

Chapter 22
To create the user account for the remote user 214
To install Outlook 215
To install Internet Explorer 215
To configure Internet Explorer for use with Proxy 216
To install the Fax client software 216
To install the Proxy client software 217
To configure the client computer to use dial-up networking 217
To create a machine account 219
To configure a Windows NT Workstation for dial-up networking 219
To create a phonebook entry for a Windows 95/98 client 220
To connect to Small Business Server with a Windows 95/98 client 220
To connect to Small Business Server with a Windows 95/98 client — remotely 221
To create a phonebook entry for a Windows NT client 221
To connect to Small Business Server with a Windows NT Workstation client 222

Chapter 23
To install the PPTP protocol on Small Business Server 224
To configure VPN devices on the PPTP server 225
To enable encryption of a VPN device on Small Business Server 226
To install PPTP protocol on a Windows NT-based remote client computer 228

To configure a VPN device on the PPTP client 229
To create a new ISP entry using the Phonebook Wizard 230
To verify or edit your ISP phonebook entry 231
To create a phonebook entry to dial-up a PPTP server using a VPN device 232
To verify or edit your phonebook entry for the PPTP server 233
To install PPTP protocol on a client running Windows 95 235
To create a connection to the Internet through an ISP 236
To verify or edit the ISP connection 237
To create a connection to dial up to a PPTP server using a VPN device 239
To verify or change the connection to your PPTP server 240
To connect to a PPTP server using a PPTP client to dial up an ISP 242

Part 4 — *Administering And Maintaining*

Chapter 25

Steps performed by the Migrate User Wizard for each user in the user account file 255

Steps performed by the Migrate User Wizard for each group in the user account file 255

Steps performed by the User Account Wizard, Add a User mode, to create the NT User Account 257

Steps performed by the User Account Wizard, Add a User mode, to set up the Exchange Mailbox 258

Steps performed by the User Account Wizard, Add A User mode, to create the Users Shared Folder 259

Steps performed by the User Account Wizard to review or change user information 260

Steps performed by the User Account Wizard to remove a user 261

Steps performed by the Change Password Wizard to change a user's password 263

Steps performed by the User Access Wizard to set system resource permissions, per user 264

Steps performed by the Printer Access Wizard to set printer access permissions 266

Steps performed by the Fax Access Wizard to set fax access permissions 266

Steps performed by the Share Folder Access Wizard to set shared folder access permissions 267

Steps performed by the Internet Access Wizard to grant Internet access permissions 267

Steps performed by the Share a Folder Wizard to share a folder 269

Steps performed by the Move Folder Wizard to move a shared folder 270

Steps performed by the E-Mail Distribution List Wizard, Create a Distribution List mode, to create a distribution list 271

Steps performed by the E-Mail Distribution List Wizard, Review or Change Distribution List mode, to edit a distribution list 272

Steps performed by the E-Mail Distribution List Wizard, Remove a Distribution List mode, to delete a distribution list 273

Chapter 26

To install the System Policy Editor from the Windows 95 CD 296

To install the System Policy Editor from the Windows NT Server 4.0 296

To create a default system policy 297

To change the default user policy 298

To save and implement the new default user policy 298

To restore folder paths back to the default 299

To create shared folders and alternate folder paths 299

To create a new roaming user profile 307

To copy an existing user's profile to another user 308

To copy the template profile to the Default User folder on the domain controller 308

To copy a template profile manually to a number of users 309

To create a new mandatory user profile 309

To create a roaming user profile for a Windows 95 client 311

To create a mandatory user profile for a Windows 95 user 312

To set the Server Status Tool administrator password 316

To create a Performance Monitor alert 324

To modify an existing alert 326

To configure a Processor Queue Length alert 327

To configure an Interrupts/second alert 328

To configure an alert for a network NT workstation 329

To configure a scheduled task for Small Business Server 334

Chapter 27

To open the Fax Server Properties dialog box from Programs 339

To create a shared contacts list in Exchange 344

To fax a document using the Print command 345

To fax a message from Outlook or Exchange 346

To create a fax address in Microsoft Exchange 346

To manage Microsoft Modem Sharing Server 347

To open the Modem Sharing Administration dialog box 348

To view the modem pools configured on the server 349

To configure the modem pools on the server 349

To install a modem — Windows 95-based clients   350

To connect Windows 95-based client computers to the modem pool on the server   350

To install a modem — Windows NT workstation-based clients   351

To connect Windows NT Workstation-based computers to the modem pool on the server   351

To create a new Exchange performance monitor   376

To create an Exchange performance monitor alert   378

To create and view a log for the data collection phase   383

To view Alert logs   387

To manually configure Winsock Proxy access permissions for a user   391

To create a site filter   397

To warn users of the Small Business Server shutdown   401

To disconnect all users   402

To update the DHCP Server with a new base IP address   402

To disable the DHCP server   404

To change the TCP/IP property settings   405

To verify whether the client machine is using DHCP   406

To update client machines using DHCP   407

To update the Winsock Proxy Client   407

To verify that the client machine goes to the new IP address   408

To update the LAT using Construct Table   409

To update the Proxy LAT manually   411

To view active Internet sessions   412

To create a Proxy performance monitor   419

To view a Proxy performance monitor   420

To create a public folder in Outlook 2000   427

To publish to a public folder by dragging and dropping   429

To publish to a public folder by sending an e-mail   429

To create a discussion group in Outlook   431

To configure the discussion group on Exchange Server   431

To test the discussion group   433

To configure anonymous user access to public folders   435

To configure public folder shortcuts on the Exchange Server   436

To verify anonymous user access to the discussion group folder   436

To configure Outlook for a group task list   438

To create a group task in Outlook   439

To configure Outlook for a group contact database   440

To create a group contact in Outlook   441

Chapter 29
To add the Quick Defrag option to your context menu   454

Part 5 — *Performance Optimization and Tuning*

Chapter 30
To configure client IP addresses manually   463

Chapter 31
To configure the page file size   483
To disable unused services   483
To set up server optimization for maximize throughput   484

Part 6 — *Integration and Interaction*

Chapter 32
To configure Small Business Server to use Proxy Server for web browsing support   495
To manually install the Proxy Client   498
To manually configure the Microsoft Internet Explorer client to use Proxy Server   499
To configure a RAS phonebook entry for client web browsing support   500
To configure the Microsoft Outlook client to receive POP3 mail   504

Chapter 33
To integrate Office 2000 in a non-Office Small Business Server installation   509
To remove Outlook 2000 from the client computer   512

Part 7 — *Security*

Chapter 36
To set up a dynamic packet filtering for basic Winsock Proxy service   557
To remove a packet filter from a Proxy service   559
To modify the properties of a packet filter   559
To create a new packet filter using predefined protocol definitions   559
To create a new packet filter using custom protocol definitions   560
To restore the default packet filter parameters   560
To disable IP forwarding on Small Business Server   561
To configure publishing parameters   568

Part 8 — *Migration and Upgrade*

Chapter 39

To add a new user   627
To create a client setup disk   628
To test share access and permissions on the client machine   629
To test use of the network printer from the client   630
To send a test e-mail with the Outlook client to Exchange Server   631
To install the NWLink protocol   633
To install GSNW   635
To check the frame type   636
To install the gateway feature of GSNW   637
To configure the Small Business Server portion of GSNW   637
To test functionality of the GSNW installation   638
To install FPNW   640
To install Directory Service Manager for NetWare   641
To create Exchange mailboxes for propagated user accounts   643
To find which subdirectory is associated with a user   646
To start up and configure the Migration Tool for NetWare   648
To move NetWare data   650
To change the preferred server   652
Tests for basic connectivity   653

Chapter 40

To add client access licenses   658

Chapter 42

To transfer Access data to SQL Server 7.0   669
To migrate Access queries into stored procedures and views   672
To move a statement from Access to a Transact-SQL file   673

Part 9 — *Developing Small Business Server Solutions*

Chapter 43

To create additional links on the Home page   695
To create additional tasks on the Tasks or More Tasks pages   697
To replace an existing page   699
To extend the console with an installation application   702
To remove the installation application   703
To extend the Online Guide with an installation application   710

Chapter 44
To create the INF file for your setup application 715
To add your application to the Setup Computer Wizard application list 722
To remove your application from the Set Up Computer Wizard 722

Chapter 46
To install the Small Business Server Resource Kit 735
To extend the Server Status Tool 736
To verify the application log is included in server status reporting 738

Part 10 — *Tools and Utilities*

Chapter 51
To install the Small Business Server 4.5 Resource Kit 766
To access the Small Business Server 4.5 tools and utilities 769

Chapter 52
To add a custom console link with the Small Business Server Customization Tool 779
To add an application to the Set Up Computer Wizard application list 785
To remove an application from the Set Up Computer Wizard application list 786
To check the Set Up Computer Wizard application list 786

Part 11 — *Troubleshooting*

Chapter 53
To set the default home page to the Client User Guide 792
To manually install the 8255x Intel network interface cards 793
To back up the Windows NT registry to a tape drive 796
To check the Windows registry 796

Chapter 54
To reinstall the Floppy directory for the Set Up Computer Wizard 799
To grant full access permission to the user account performing the copy operation 800
To reinstall the Set Up Computer Wizard files 801
To copy login scripts to the BDC's 801
To run the login script manually 801
To rename the "Installed" file 802

To reinstall the client response directory   802
To install client applications manually and observe error messages   803
To install the Modem Sharing Client on Windows NT Workstation   804
To change NDIS modes   804
To install the correct network interface card on a client computer   805

Chapter 55
To check for Small Business Server modem support and reinstall services   810
To verify the Fax Server sends a test fax   810
To correct the registry key for fax devices   811
To verify the fax client permissions are properly configured   812
To ensure that the Fax Service was correctly installed   814
To clear the print queue   816
To delete the Receive values from the registry   820
To grant domain users the ability to view the Administrator mailbox   820
To configure a route-to account other than Administrator   821
To route faxes to a public mailbox   821
To shorten the share name of a fax printer   822
To identify other files types that use DDE to print   823
To add Fax Address Book and Personal Address Book to Outlook   824
To create a fax address in Outlook   824

Chapter 56
To use the Modem Sharing software on the Small Business Server to make a direct connection to the Internet via the ISP   829
To verify that Windows NT recognizes your modem and can dial out   831
To determine if your modem is a Class 1 modem   831

Chapter 57
To grant a user Internet access permission   833
To disable SSL   834
To give the Everyone group permission to log on locally   834
To modify Telnet settings   835
To modify the Proxy Server's LAT   836
To access the Small Business Server Internet Connection Wizard   837
To open the ports used by FTP   837

About the Resource Kit

Welcome to the Microsoft® BackOffice® Small Business Server Resource Kit, version 4.5. This resource kit contains one copy of the Microsoft BackOffice Small Business Server Resource Guide, and a single compact disc (CD) with Small Business Server software tools, online Help, various utilities, and online (HTML) versions of books for various server applications.

The resource guide provides detailed information for Small Business Server 4.5 and its associated BackOffice applications. The in-depth information is a technical supplement to the Small Business Server 4.5 core documentation, which includes the Getting Started guide and the Online Guide. The resource guide is not intended to replace the core documentation as a source for learning how to use the product features and programs.

About the Small Business Server Resource Guide

This resource guide is organized by Parts containing the following information:

About The Resource Kit

- Outlines the contents of the resource guide.
- Describes the Microsoft BackOffice Small Business Server Resource Kit CD.
- Describes the support policy for the Microsoft BackOffice Small Business Server Resource Kit.

Part 1, *Introductory Information for the Technology Consultant* — Introduces Small Business Server 4.5 to the technology consultant, and also may be used as customer presentation material. The following information is provided:

- Customer profile.
- Design philosophy.
- Ease-of-setup, management, and use.
- Communication in new and more efficient ways.

- Everything needed to run a small business.
- Benefits of using Small Business Server for the technology consultant.
- Solution development.
- Training.
- Other resources.

Part 2, *Planning* — Addresses the issues that arise when planning for the deployment of Small Business Server 4.5 in a small business organization. The following topics are covered:

- Small Business Server network characteristics.
- Client and server computer requirements.
- Backup system and fault-tolerant disk configuration planning.
- Disaster recovery planning.
- Planning for an Internet presence.
- Planning for remote access users.
- Planning for Microsoft Fax and Modem Sharing services.
- Planning for Proxy Server.
- Planning for Exchange Server.
- Network Capacity Planning.

Part 3, *Deployment* — Outlines factors and conditions that should be considered when customizing the deployment of Small Business Server 4.5 in a small business organization. The following topics are covered:

- Installing Small Business Server on new machines.
- Installing Small Business Server in existing environments.
- Setup issues.
- Using the Set Up Computer Wizard.
- Internet service provider (ISP) connectivity tasks.
- Setting up remote client computers.
- Installing Point-to-Point Tunneling Protocol (PPTP) in the small business network.
- Customizing Office 2000 deployment.

Part 4, *Administering and Maintaining* — Describes administration of Small Business Server tools, applications, and components. The following topics are covered:

- Small Business Server wizard processes, including background configuration of applications performed by the console wizards.
- Administrative tools such as remote administration with NetMeeting®, Policy Editor, Server Status, Fax/Internet Reporting, Performance Monitor, and the Task Scheduler.
- Administering Small Business Server components including Fax Service 4.5, Modem Sharing Service 4.5, Exchange Server 5.5, Proxy Server 2.0, SQL Server™ 7.0, and Windows NT® File System/File Allocation Table (NTFS/FAT) volume security.
- Management features of Internet Connection Services (ICS) for Remote Access Service (RAS).
- Administrative tips.

Part 5, *Performance Optimization and Tuning* — Describes how Small Business Server 4.5 is optimized for the small business, including:

- How the overall performance of Small Business Server is maximized.
- How server applications are performance-optimized on a single server platform.
- Why the default configuration of Small Business Server is optimal for the small business.
- The impact of upsizing on Small Business Server components.
- Hardware and tuning recommendations to sustain optimum performance as the small business expands up to the 50-user limit.

Part 6, *Integration and Interaction* — Covers the following:

- E-mail and Internet connectivity alternatives, including web browsing, Post Office Protocol 3 (POP3), Simple Mail Transport Protocol (SMTP), and web hosting support.
- Office 2000 integration issues.
- Client interaction with the server, including MS-DOS, Windows® 95/98, Windows 3.1, and Macintosh® client interactions with Small Business Server.
- Cross platform interoperability, including NetWare, UNIX®, and Macintosh client compatibilities with Small Business Server.

Part 7, *Security* — Discusses the Small Business Server 4.5 features that provide network security, as follows:

- Proxy Server 2.0 overview, managed network access, and key security features, including Proxy Server 2.0 security architecture.
- Windows NT Server 4.0 and computer security.
- Internet Information Server (IIS) 4.0 security model.

Part 8, *Migration and Upgrade* — Outlines the following:

- How to migrate from NetWare to the Small Business Server 4.5 environment.
- Licensing requirements for expanding the Small Business Server user base.
- Client access licenses and the installation of client add packs.
- Upgrade scenarios for integrated server applications.
- Upgrading to Microsoft BackOffice Server 4.5.
- Migrating from an existing Windows NT Server.
- Migrating an Access database to SQL Server 7.0.

Part 9, *Developing Small Business Server Solutions* — Describes how Small Business Server functionalities can be extended or enhanced, using any of the following:

- Architectural background, mechanisms, and procedural information for extending the Small Business Server console.
- The Set Up Computer Wizard extension mechanism.
- Server Status Tool extension.
- Using the Microsoft Data Engine (MSDE) solution with Microsoft Access 2000.
- Team Intranet Starter Kit.
- Enhancing Office 2000 functionality.
- Office 2000 Customer Manager.
- Application communication with Microsoft Message Queue Server (MSMQ).
- Telephony Applications Programming Interface (TAPI) solutions for Small Business Server.

Part 10, *Tools and Utilities* — Covers how to install the *Microsoft BackOffice Small Business Server Resource Kit* on your server and access the Small Business Server tools. Descriptions of the following tools, specifically developed for Small Business Server 4.5, are provided:

- Small Business Server Start Menu tool.
- Batch User Add tool.
- Modem Status tool.
- Small Business Server Customization tool.
- Small Business Server Client Setup Integration Wizard.
- Fax Monitoring and Performance tools.

Part 11, *Troubleshooting* — Provides troubleshooting information for the following:

- Small Business Server setup and upgrade.
- Client setup and the Set Up Computer Wizard.
- Fax Service.
- Modem Sharing Service.
- Internet.

Glossary — Contains definitions of terms used in the Microsoft BackOffice Small Business Server Resource Guide.

Index — Provides a topic index to the resource guide.

Resource Kit Compact Disc

The CD that accompanies the Microsoft BackOffice Small Business Server Resource Guide contains the following:

- Software tools and utilities for Windows NT Server 4.0 and BackOffice-integrated server applications, as well as software tools specifically developed for Small Business Server 4.5.

  The tools are used to simplify the installation, setup, administration, networking, and maintenance tasks for Small Business Server 4.5. The tools may be accessed from the **Start** menu, **Resource Kit**, **Tools Management Console**, once the *Small Business Server Resource Kit* is installed on the server.

- Small Business Server client tools.
- Online (HTML) Help for Small Business Server tool use.

  Updates to these files will be provided on the Microsoft BackOffice Small Business Server web site:
  http://www.microsoft.com/smallbusinessserver
- Online books, which include HTML versions of resource guides for BackOffice Server, Internet Explorer, Internet Information Server, Small Business Server, Systems Network Architecture (SNA), and Windows 98.
- Various utilities including Crystal Reports, Imagination Engineer LE, Internet Explorer 5.0 upgrade, RAS Manager, Web Server Capacity Analysis Tool, Windows Management Instrumentation, and Windows Scripting Host.

Note The tools and utilities on this CD are designed and tested for the U.S. version of Small Business Server 4.5. Use of these tools and utilities on any other version of Small Business Server may cause unpredictable results.

After installing the *Microsoft BackOffice Small Business Server Resource Kit*, please refer immediately to the Release Notes.

Resource Kit Tools

The *Microsoft BackOffice Small Business Server Resource Kit* contains a wide variety of tools and utilities to help you work more efficiently with Small Business Server 4.5 and the other BackOffice applications integrated on the Small Business Server platform. The following tools are included:

- Computer management.
- Deployment.
- Desktop.
- Documentation.
- Diagnostics and troubleshooting.
- File and disk.
- Microsoft Exchange Server 5.5.
- Microsoft SQL Server 7.0.
- Network management.
- Scripting.

The resource kit Help files for the tools listed above provide tool function and usage descriptions. For descriptions of the tools specifically developed for Small Business Server 4.5 and how to access them from the resource kit Tools Management Console, refer to *Part 10, Tools and Utilities*, of this resource guide.

Resource Kit Support Policy

The SOFTWARE supplied in the *Microsoft BackOffice Small Business Server* Resource Kit is not officially supported. Microsoft does not guarantee the performance of the resource kit tools, response times for answering questions, or bug fixes for the tools. However, we do provide a way for customers who purchase the Microsoft BackOffice Small Business Server Resource Kit to report bugs and possibly receive fixes for their issues. You can do this by sending e-mail to RKInput@microsoft.com.

The SOFTWARE (including instructions for its use, all printed documentation, and online Help) is provided "AS IS" without warranty of any kind. Microsoft further disclaims all implied warranties, including, without limitation, any implied warranties of merchantability or of fitness for a particular purpose. The entire risk arising out of the use or performance of the SOFTWARE and documentation remains with you.

In no event shall Microsoft, its authors, or anyone else involved in the creation, production, or delivery of the SOFTWARE be liable for any damages whatsoever (including, without limitations, damages for loss of business information, or other monetary loss) arising out of the use of, or inability to use, the SOFTWARE or documentation, even if Microsoft has been advised of the possibility of such damages.

PART 1

Introductory Information for the Technology Consultant

The information in Part 1 is primarily intended to introduce Microsoft® BackOffice® Small Business Server 4.5 to the technology consultant, although the material could also be used for Small Business Server presentations by the technology consultant to potential small business customers. The information is covered in the following chapters:

Chapter 1 Small Business Server Customer Profile 3

Chapter 2 Small Business Server Design Philosophy 7

Chapter 3 Easy Setup, Management, and Use 9

Chapter 4 Communication in New and More Efficient Ways 21

Chapter 5 Small Business Server Component Feature Summary 31

Chapter 6 Benefits of Small Business Server to the Technology Consultant 37

Chapter 7 Introduction to Small Business Server Solution Development 41

Chapter 8 Training 43

Chapter 9 Other Resources 45

CHAPTER 1

Small Business Server Customer Profile

While small business owners look for easier ways to run their business, Microsoft® BackOffice® Small Business Server 4.5 offers them an easy and attractive way to do so. Small Business Server provides a complete business solution for the small business owner at a reasonable price, based on a single server platform. Using Small Business Server, small business owners can share files and printers, secure their company information, communicate with business partners and customers, connect to the Internet, and run business applications.

Small Business Server is designed for companies that operate from a single location with a maximum of 50 client computers. Because most businesses of this size have a limited number of employees and resources, they typically do not have a full-time information system (IS) professional on staff. Instead, they routinely rely on their accountant or office administrator to set up and manage their networks. This presents a unique challenge, because although these individuals have some experience with computers, they usually have little or no experience dealing with networks. This makes network setup and management a difficult and overwhelming task.

The Need for a Complete Business Solution

In spite of limited resources that often leads to the lack of an onsite IS professional, small businesses need a complete business solution to manage their company. They are looking for programs and products designed to help them take advantage of the business benefits of current information technology. They also want to stay on the leading edge by keeping in touch with their customers and peers through e-mail and the web.

Because of limited resources, the focus of most small businesses is on job completion. While they may want to move toward a technical business solution, rarely is there the time or personnel available to implement and maintain a complex network.

The idea of buying a network—or upgrading poorly performing peer-to-peer networks—intimidates many small business customers. However, the idea of reducing overall costs by investing in technology is often very compelling.

The Importance of Small Business Server to the Customer

Today, small businesses looking for computer solutions face a world of many separate and complicated pieces. They must either purchase separate components from multiple vendors and then contract with a reseller to install and configure them, or teach themselves the technology to implement their own system. Small Business Server addresses these issues for the small business customer, thus making it easier for small business owners to concentrate on growing and managing their company.

Small Business Server contains a suite of server products that allow companies to share information and resources, access the Internet, communicate with customers and partners, and run business-critical applications. Essentially, Small Business Server provides all the services that small business customers want in a single integrated package. It is simple and intuitive, and easy to set up, manage, and use.

Advantages of the Client/Server Model Network

Many growing businesses find that the limits of peer-to-peer networking inhibits the expansion of their business. Peer-to-peer network users would benefit by upgrading to a robust and reliable business solution using a client/server model network for the following reasons:

- To experience better network performance.
- To run line-of-business applications.
- To accommodate remote users (since peer-to-peer will not support them).
- To have secure and controlled access to the Internet.
- To use an integrated Internet and internal e-mail system.

Peer-to-peer networks are adequate for basic file and printer sharing. However, when it comes to getting the most out of a network, issues like performance, security, group e-mail, and scheduling are all better handled by a network based on the client/server model. Small Business Server provides this and also offers many additional features that are not standard in peer-to-peer networks.

Upgrading from an Existing NetWare Network

Small Business Server is a complete and integrated business solution. Small business customers using NetWare 3.x, 4.x or IntranetWare will find this quite significant because it means they will not have to acquire pieces and parts to create an application-rich solution. In order to get the same high level of functionality as Small Business Server, current NetWare users must incur the additional expense of purchasing and installing separate servers for their database, web, and firewall capabilities, and possibly for e-mail and fax as well. Small Business Server provides all this functionality in one box.

CHAPTER 2

Small Business Server Design Philosophy

In developing Microsoft® BackOffice® Small Business Server 4.5, several key design concepts were adopted to allow a satisfying and productive computing experience for the small business customer.

Making Everything Easy to Use

The most important idea behind Small Business Server is that it is easy to use. What administrators or users need to do is clearly defined for them. Most questions a user is asked have an obvious answer. The confusion a small business administrator may experience in identifying the next task is avoided. For example, the Small Business Server console guides administrative users in identifying and addressing tasks they want to perform. Each page in the console, or screen in a wizard, provides them with the necessary information to walk through the required steps to complete each task simply. Each choice is supported with enough information to make an informed decision.

These features also benefit the technology consultant because it is easy for them to teach their Small Business Server customers how to perform various tasks.

Making Installation Decisions Automatic

The small business customer is generally inexperienced in dealing with network, setup, and application problems. Time constraints do not permit them the luxury of researching all the issues and alternatives in enough detail to make informed choices or decisions. As a result, they usually rely upon a technology consultant to install and configure their network setup. For this reason, Small Business Server was designed so the technology consultant can easily provide the appropriate configuration automatically—this avoids confronting the small business customer with complex network decisions. Using information based on typical small business scenarios, the most appropriate decisions are made automatically for the technology consultant, to eliminate confusion and work for the customer and reduce the likelihood of making mistakes.

By making decisions automatically and auto-configuring the network, the result is a network configuration that efficiently addresses small business customer needs and is easy to maintain. For example, during the Windows NT® Server operating system portion of Small Business Server setup, the server is configured automatically as the Primary Domain Controller (PDC), Transmission Control Protocol/Internet Protocol (TCP/IP) is installed, and Dynamic Host Configuration Protocol (DHCP) is set up by default. By making decisions automatically, difficulties are eliminated and unnecessary or less-than-ideal configurations are also avoided. This feature further benefits the technology consultant by producing consistent Small Business Server configurations supporting ease of management.

Designed for User Success

User success is very important. Frequently, users set out to perform a task and they become frustrated by the complexity and time it takes to get it done. Sometimes they even wonder if they actually completed the task. It is important that the small business customer find out how to do things quickly, easily, and completely. Small Business Server is designed to make it easy for users to succeed in the tasks they wish to perform.

Throughout the Small Business Server console, multiple paths for performing tasks are provided. Although there are many paths to choose from, each path provides administrative users with a consistent, concise, and familiar interface. This consistency reduces time and improves the success the user experiences in completing their tasks.

These features also benefit the technology consultant because it enables them to easily train small business customers to perform simple tasks, thus reducing excessive support calls.

Keeping Things Simple

Small Business Server achieves both ease-of-use and user success by keeping things simple. Since most decisions are made automatically for the customer in regard to network setup and management, tasks are inherently simple. There are times, however, when the user needs to make decisions. In these instances, a clear and concise Small Business Server interface asks the user to perform one task at a time—and only the information necessary for completing the task is presented.

The simplicity of this approach makes it easy for users to comprehend the scope of each task, which ultimately enhances the user's confidence level and success rate. This reduces the user's intimidation level and thus contributes to the technology consultant's ability to engage the small business customer in task performance.

CHAPTER 3

Easy Setup, Management, and Use

Microsoft® BackOffice® Small Business Server and its suite of integrated applications were designed specifically to meet the unique needs of the small business owner. The components of Small Business Server are optimized for integration, ease of use, and centralized management. It is exceptionally easy to set up, so the small business owner can get up and running with it right away.

Automatic Setup and Configuration

To make network configuration more viable for the small business, server and client setup are simplified. To achieve this, Small Business Server's setup routine asks only a few questions—the use of excessive technical jargon is eliminated. The entire server-setup process is designed to be simple. Wizards guide the technology consultant through the entire setup process, including creating users, attaching printers, and connecting to the Internet. This simplicity also benefits the technology consultant because it minimizes the time required to install a server and therefore allows them to service more customers. The setup process is launched from a screen similar to the following.

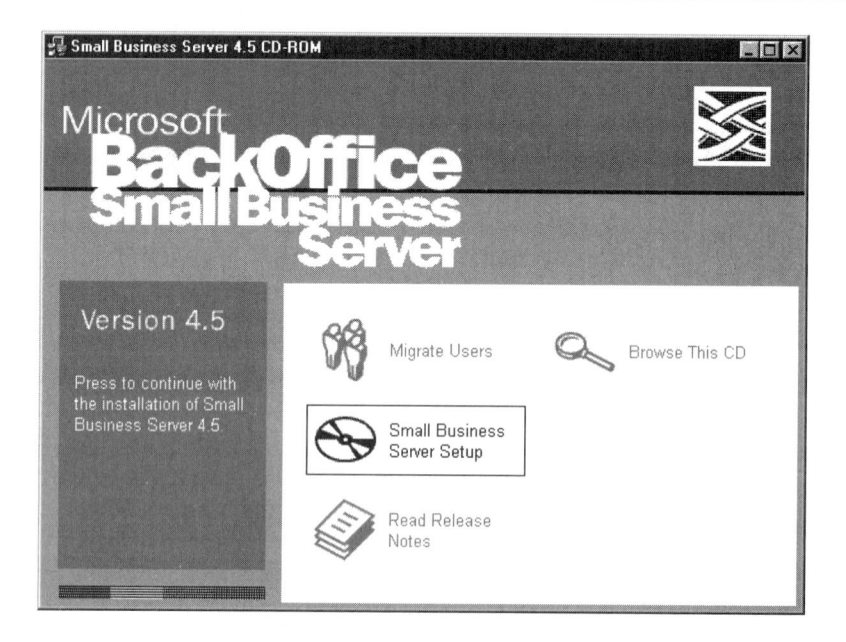

Input is Minimized During Installation

The complexity of installing Windows NT Server 4.0 has been removed through the use of an Unattend.txt file that silently configures the server. Although prompts are presented for initial configuration of hardware devices, complex setups, such as the network configuration, are decided for the technology consultant.

For example, since small businesses typically run on a single server, Windows NT Server 4.0 is installed as the primary domain controller (PDC), which centralizes security so each user has a single password. The routine also installs a Dynamic Host Configuration Protocol (DHCP) server to make the configuration of IP addresses a non-issue. This sets up and optimizes the small business networking without requiring the technology consultant to make these decisions.

Simple User Information Requests

When user input is required, information is requested that the small business can readily supply, such as the company name and address, the time zone, or a CD key. The user is also asked to accept a user license agreement. Default responses are always supplied in order to facilitate a quick installation.

Inherent Flexibility

Setup flexibility allows hardware components and modem configurations to be confirmed, or replaced, if necessary.

Note In order to work with Small Business Server, these devices must appear on the Small Business Server Recommended Hardware List:
http://www.microsoft.com/smallbusinessserver/deployadmin/recommended.htm

Also, the technology consultant can modify other installation configuration options, as follows:

- The server domain name can be changed during setup.
- The hard disk can be partitioned as required.
- Installation components can be offloaded.
- Protocols such as Network Basic Input/Output System Enhanced User Interface (NetBEUI) and Internetwork Packet Exchange (IPX) (included on the *BackOffice Small Business Server Resource Kit CD*) may be installed, if needed.

Note IPX is part of the Internetwork Packet Exchange/Sequenced Packet Exchange (IPX/SPX) protocol.

To Do List

The **To Do List** is presented automatically once BackOffice Small Business Server 4.5 is set up. The **To Do List** guides the technology consultant through the most common tasks that need to be completed for the small business to have a fully functional network. For example, the **To Do List** provides options to install a printer, create user accounts, import users, connect to the Internet, add client licenses, or install client applications. The **To Do List** is shown below.

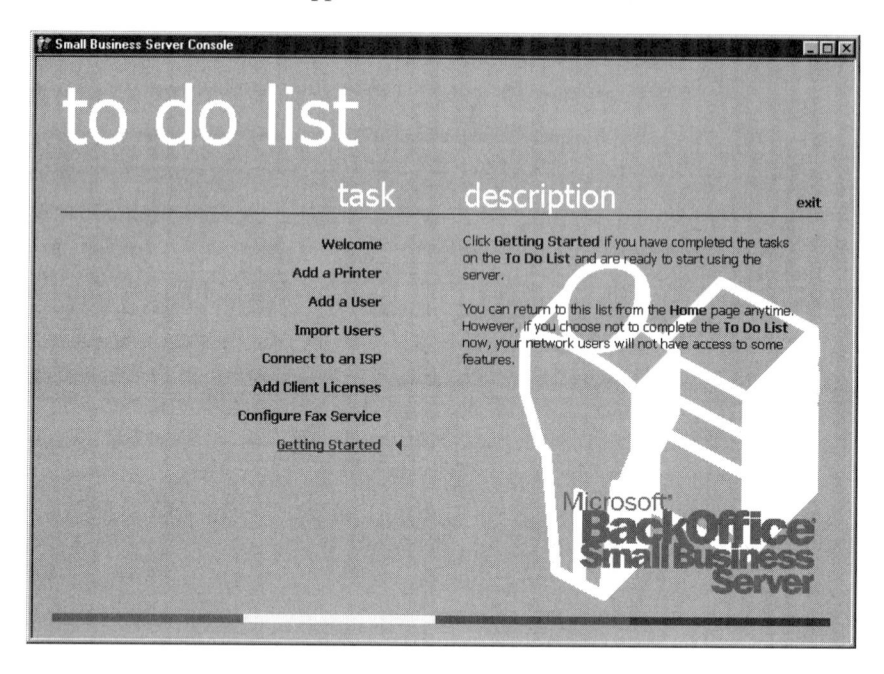

Set Up Computer Wizard

The Set Up Computer Wizard makes it easy to connect a client computer running Windows 95/98 or Windows NT Workstation 4.0 to Small Business Server. The goal of the Set Up Computer Wizard is to allow a user to insert a disk into the computer and within a short time be able to work. Essentially, the installer will not have to reconfigure the client for e-mail to function correctly, figure out where the server is, join a domain, set up TCP/IP, and so on.

Components of Client Setup

Client setup uses the following three components to configure client networking and application installations:

- Set Up Computer Wizard—runs on the server.
- Client networking setup—runs on the client.
- Client Installation Wizard—runs on the client.

When a new workstation is being added to the network, the Set Up Computer Wizard runs on the server and handles the following functions:

- Automatic suggestion of a computer name.
- Automatic completion of company information.
- Specification of which client applications should be installed.

Once these questions are completed, the Set Up Computer Wizard creates a client-specific disk containing the client's configuration information. The disk then runs on the client workstation and performs client networking setup, which includes the following:

- Configuring client network settings.
- Installing the proper network communication protocol (TCP/IP).

The user then logs on to the client computer and the Client Installation Wizard does the following:

- Installs and configures Small Business Server client applications for the user — Microsoft Outlook, Modem Sharing, Fax, Proxy, and Internet Explorer. Office 2000 (including Outlook) is installed if selected in the Set Up Computer Wizard application list.
- Creates shortcuts to shared folders from the user's desktop.
- Configures a default Intranet page on each desktop.

The Set Up Computer Wizard also allows the technology consultant to configure a single machine for multiple users, since many small businesses share computers among their staff. In addition, administrators can easily add applications to a computer already on the network or install application updates using the Set Up Computer Wizard. The Set Up Computer Wizard can also be modified to support third-party applications so that these applications can be installed easily as well. The following screen shows the Set Up Computer Wizard opening page.

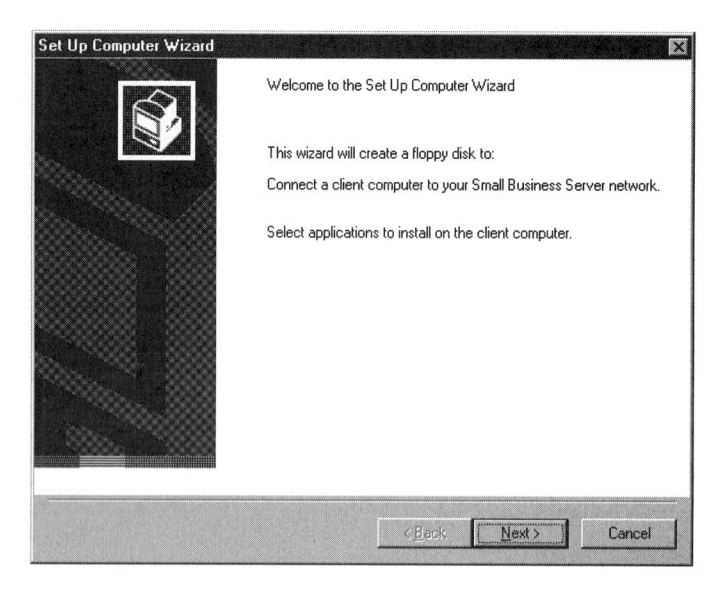

Small Business Server Console: A Simplified User Interface

The Small Business Server console was designed for the needs of the technology consultant and the user. The goal of the console is to make it quick and easy for the technology consultant to handle the tasks of managing the server and supporting users. In addition, the use of console wizards simplifies management to help the user accomplish their tasks. This enables the technology consultant to reduce support time and handle a greater number of small business customer support calls.

Ease of Management

Wizards are employed throughout the product and use simple language to guide the technology consultant through all management tasks. Wizard-based administration from a central console benefits the technology consultant because it makes it easy to do such things as add users or configure e-mail distribution lists. Advanced management features allow control over sensitive company information and expensive resources.

Integrated Management

The console unifies administration procedures and provides one central point from which all Small Business Server 4.5 tasks can be performed. This makes it easy to manage the server. Wizards accessed from the console perform multiple steps behind the scenes to configure the appropriate server applications for any task a technology consultant may be required to perform.

Most small businesses have a person who becomes the administrator by default and provides daily on-site support. The Small Business Server console is designed to save this support person time since the most commonly performed server tasks are located in a unified, task-based console.

Task-Based Administration

Since technology consultants are task-oriented, Small Business Server management is organized around common administration tasks rather than around applications. For example, when the technology consultant wants to add a new user, they launch the **Manage Users** page in the console rather than using the Microsoft User Manager for Domains. The most frequently used management tasks are on the **Tasks** page, while all other tasks are on the **More Tasks** page. The following screen shows the items on the **Tasks** page.

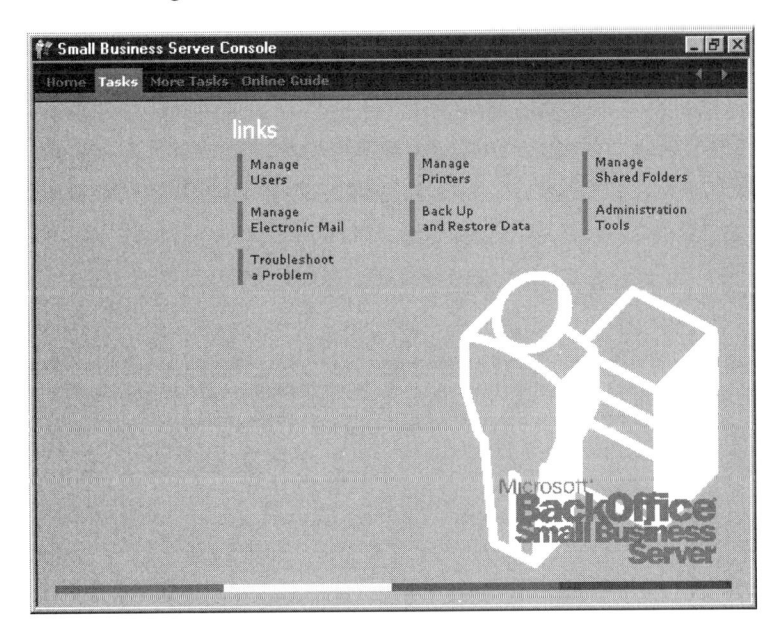

Microsoft wants technology consultants to have a familiar interface for working with the server. Links accessed from the **Tasks** or **More Tasks** pages open screens that always show all the available tasks on the right side. Terminology is consistent in all task pages and taskpads are in similar screen locations. This makes it easy to discover tasks. In addition, visual cues are consistent for the tasks. For instance, a plus sign always indicates "add," a minus sign indicates "remove," and a question mark indicates "troubleshooting," as shown below.

Add   Remove   Troubleshoot

Increase User Success

Once users are trained by the technology consultant, their feeling of accomplishment is enhanced through the use of console features designed to improve their success rate. Tasks are accessible from multiple locations in the console. Links are provided between associated tasks so that backtracking is unnecessary. For example, the user can select the **manage e-mail distribution lists** taskpad from the **Manage Users** page if they didn't know to find it on the **More Tasks** page of the console.

In addition, Microsoft has minimized the number of concepts that users need to learn to complete a task. For example, security groups are not exposed to the user. The technology consultant sees exactly what each user can do with a given resource, rather than the user themselves needing to understand such things as group membership or permission combination rules.

Wizards Streamline Tasks

Wizards are employed throughout the console to guide the technology consultant through the completion of a task. For example, when the technology consultant chooses to add a new user, a wizard is activated that specifies each step required to create a new user account. By using the wizard defaults, the technology consultant can successfully create a user/e-mail account with access to shared resources such as company folders, printers, faxes, the Internet, and dial-up networking—all without having to use separate system tools.

Online Guide

The Online Guide for Small Business Server is designed so the technology consultant may train the small business administrator very quickly and comprehensively. The following shows the opening screen of the Online Guide.

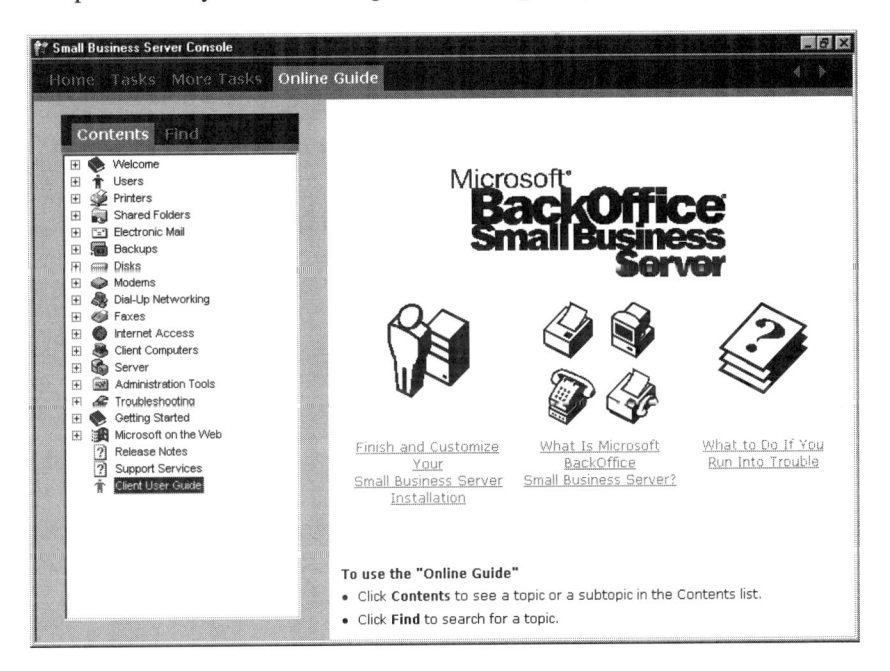

Comprehensive Guidance

The Online Guide is integrated into the Small Business Server Console. It includes tutorials, comprehensive help, and troubleshooting tips along with fast, flexible searching capability. This makes it easy to find the right information when needed.

Flexible Searching

Users can search the Online Guide by task or a full-text search may be conducted. Full-text search is available because Index Server 2.0 serves as the search engine.

Easy Navigation

Because the Online Guide was built using Hyper Text Markup Language (HTML) pages, users can easily navigate the Online Guide using hyperlinks to go directly to the information needed. The Online Guide provides assistance of various kinds, all designed to make managing Small Business Server a straightforward and easy experience.

Client User Guide

The Client User Guide helps educate end users on the capabilities of their system so they can get up and running quickly. This helps reduce support requests since users have the information right on their desktops.

During client setup, Internet Explorer is automatically configured to open the Small Business Server Client User Guide. When users need help, they simply launch Internet Explorer from the desktop, and Internet Explorer takes them right to the following support page.

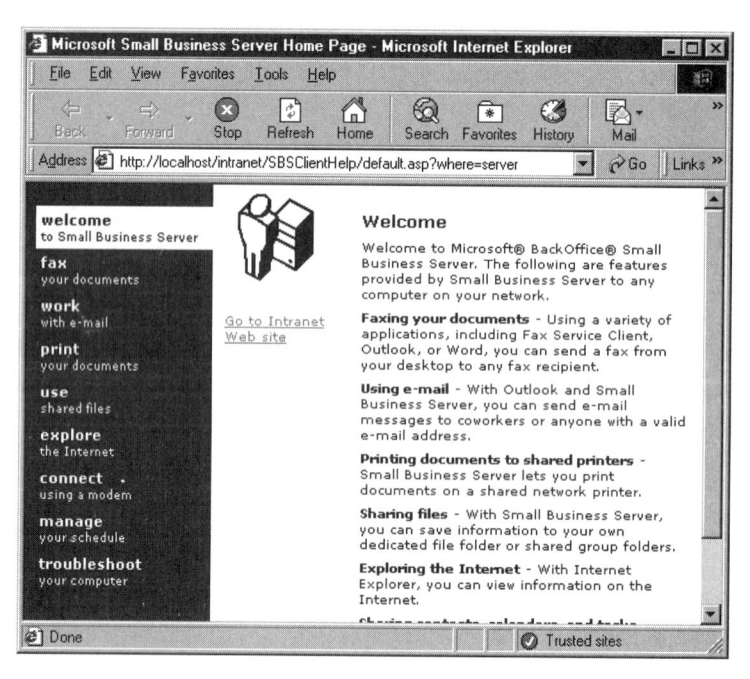

User Tutorials, Troubleshooting Tips, and Help

The Client User Guide provides tutorials to help the user get started immediately with the Internet, faxing, printing, using shared modems, sharing files, reading e-mail, and managing schedules and calendars electronically. The Client User Guide also provides troubleshooting tips and comprehensive Help right from the user desktop, any time of the day.

Extending the Intranet

The basics of an intranet are included with Small Business Server. Even if the small business has no plans for a web site on the Internet, applying web technology to develop an intranet can be very useful to the small business. When a user on a client machine launches Internet Explorer, the Small Business Server Client User Guide appears. This guide provides basic information on the services available on the server. It also contains the **Go to Intranet Web Site** link, which opens the default intranet page with instructions on creating an intranet web site. Using any authoring tool, you can expand the default site to include company policies, services, handbooks, and other private company information. The Intranet site you create is then placed in the following path:
http://Servername/Intranet/Default.htm

Easy to Support

Since the Client User Guide provides extensive online Help, tutorials, troubleshooting tips, and displays the company services available, the user becomes more self-sufficient. This makes it easier for the technology consultant to support Small Business Server.

Support for Growth of the Small Business

Technology represents a significant investment for the small business. Trade-offs are often made between purchasing computer technology or other capital equipment. Small companies want to ensure that their investments will maintain their usefulness over time as the company grows. Small Business Server is designed to grow with the small business:

- Microsoft SQL Server™ 7.0 is included in Small Business Server. Thus, when small businesses acquire applications that demand a more powerful relational database, they already have the capability with SQL Server 7.0.
- When the company grows beyond 50 users, Microsoft provides a path to easily expand to Microsoft BackOffice Server 4.5.

CHAPTER 4

Communication in New and More Efficient Ways

Small businesses want to use current, state-of-the-art technology to communicate with their customers the way big companies do. Having e-mail and an Internet presence are increasingly important for small businesses to enhance their image. To help realize this goal, Microsoft® BackOffice® Small Business Server 4.5 enables small businesses to do the following:

- **Automate Internet Service Provider (ISP) connectivity tasks.**

   Small Business Server's Internet Connection Wizard automates Internet Service Provider (ISP) connectivity tasks, using manual configuration with the wizard instead of online signups. If the small business customer wants to use their existing ISP, the wizard automatically creates the appropriate Small Business Server configuration.

- **Have safe access to the Internet while protecting sensitive company information.**

   Small Business Server enables companies to easily control and manage which employees can access the Internet. Microsoft Proxy Server 2.0 creates a single, secure gateway to the Internet and eliminates the need to share a dedicated machine among multiple users. It also allows companies to determine which web sites their employees can access.

- **Get information to customers and partners when they need it.**

   Microsoft Exchange 5.5 and Microsoft Outlook® 2000 let users send, receive, store, and route e-mail to their employees, customers, and suppliers. The small business can create an intranet and/or Internet site to share and exchange information and ideas within their company and with their customers. All the tools needed — Microsoft FrontPage® 2000, Microsoft Internet Information Server 4.0, and Microsoft Index Server 2.0 — are included with Small Business Server 4.5. Also, Remote Access Services allows small business network users to work away from the office and still be connected so they can respond to customer requests anytime, anywhere.

- **Create and manage large mailings in less time.**

    With Outlook 2000, Exchange Server 5.5, and Fax Server 4.5, companies can automate mass mailings for constant and consistent customer communication. In addition, with Outlook 2000 and Exchange Server 5.5 public folders, users can easily combine individual contact lists to create up-to-date, shared lists of the company's customers.

- **Perform faxing more efficiently.**

    With Small Business Server, companies can send, receive, and schedule faxes from the desktop. The administrator is able to control who can view and send faxes and even determine how faxes are routed.

- **Simplify group scheduling.**

    Outlook 2000 enables companies to view the free and busy times of people and resources (rooms, equipment, etc.), helping to minimize scheduling conflicts.

Small Business Server Internet Connection Wizard

One of the major obstacles preventing small businesses from leveraging the Internet is that they do not understand the requirements nor how to connect to the Internet. The Small Business Server Internet Connection Wizard facilitates connection of the small business to the Internet by gathering data and automating the configuration process. Once the data is input, the Small Business Server Internet Connection Wizard automatically configures Microsoft Exchange and Microsoft Proxy Server to send and receive e-mail on the Internet.

If the small business wants to maintain an existing relationship with an ISP, the Small Business Server Internet Connection Wizard is used to create the correct configuration so Small Business Server works with that ISP. If the small business wants to use a new ISP for their Internet account, the Internet Connection Wizard provides a list of local ISPs that support Small Business Server. Options that address these requirements appear on the following **Set Up Connection to Your ISP** screen of the Small Business Server Internet Connection Wizard.

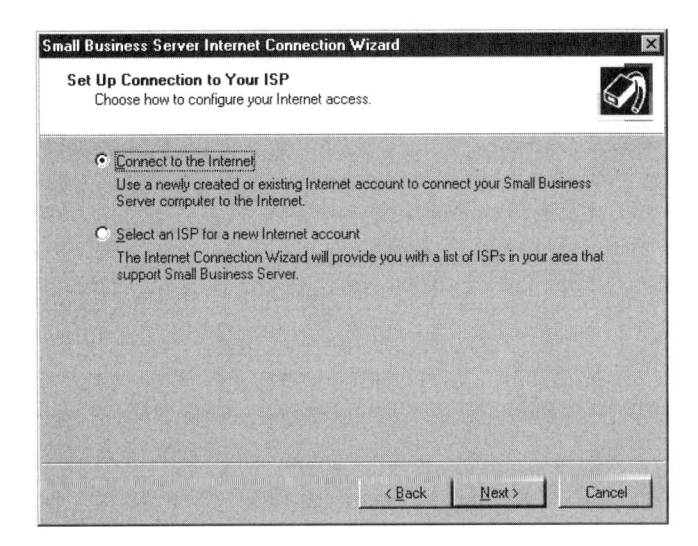

Selecting a New Internet Service Provider

If the small business does not have an ISP, the Small Business Server Internet Connection Wizard simplifies the tasks of locating and choosing an ISP. The wizard retrieves a current list of ISPs serving the local area from the Microsoft Internet Referral Server. The referral service is similar to a Yellow Pages directory. It provides the small business with enough information to choose the ISP that will best serve its needs. The wizard guides the technology consultant to the information forms required and also initiates online signup of the small business with the ISP. Microsoft has tested the online signup process extensively for each ISP listed to help ensure that the Small Business Server customer is able to connect to the Internet easily.

Send E-mail to Customers Immediately

The Small Business Server Internet Connection Wizard automatically configures Small Business Server to send and receive e-mail over the Internet once the small business has chosen an ISP. The wizard automatically configures Proxy Server and the Microsoft Exchange Internet Mail Connector to support inbound and outbound transfers, forwards e-mail to the ISP, inserts the ISP's phone number in the dial options, and sets up Small Business Server to automatically dial the ISP as specified in the wizard. Thus, the small business can send and receive e-mail to and from customers and partners immediately.

Microsoft Fax Server

Microsoft Fax Server allows companies to communicate by fax more efficiently. Today, faxing can be a time-consuming task because users have to print a document, then fill in or create a cover letter, and stand waiting at the fax machine for the fax to be sent. When faxes arrive, they can be misplaced or become lost on someone's desk. With fax services built into Small Business Server, small businesses are enabled with the features described in the following paragraphs.

Send Faxes Easily

Small Business Server makes it simple to send faxes using convenient features:

- Fax messages, notes, and documents right from the desktop using the Fax Send Utility or Outlook 2000 by printing the document to a fax printer.
- Insert a standard cover page, or create a customized company fax cover with the Fax Cover Page Editor.
- Archive outgoing faxes in a common directory.

Easily Receive and Distribute Faxes

When faxes arrive, businesses can print them immediately, save them to a folder on the server, or send them to a local Inbox. Businesses can distribute faxes in the way that is most convenient for them: by hand, by e-mail, by distributing the saved files, or by routing them to the final recipients. These functions are simple Small Business Server tasks that are managed from the **Manage Faxes** page of the console.

Monitor and Control Fax Use

Small Business Server includes fax reports that log details for both sent and received faxes. This gives the small business complete records of fax usage for accounting or other business purposes. By using the **generate fax reports** taskpad on the **Manage Faxes** console page shown below, the technology consultant can display the following fax reports in Internet Explorer:

- Received faxes
- Sent faxes
- Received faxes—top numbers
- Sent faxes—top numbers

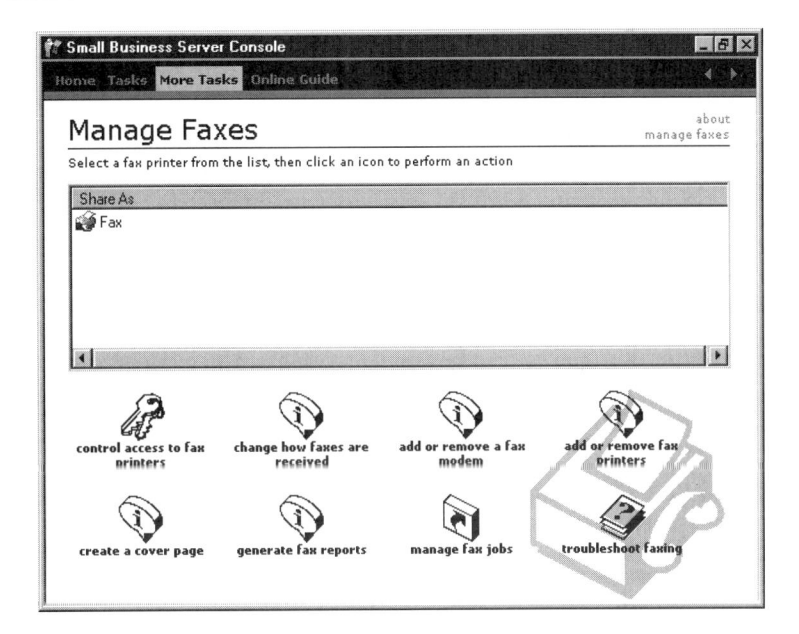

Remote Access Service

Dial-Up Networking, which utilizes Microsoft Windows NT® Server 4.0 Remote Access Service, is of growing interest to small businesses because it allows home and mobile users to work as if they were in the office. These services enable remote users to send and receive e-mail, fax documents, retrieve files, and print documents on an office printer. Small Business Server makes it easy to take advantage of the remote-access capabilities of Windows NT Server.

With Remote Access Service (RAS), small businesses can enable all data to be encrypted so the information cannot be read during transfer. Remote Access Service also securely authenticates users using industry-accepted protocols so that Small Business Server is safe from intruders.

Remote Access Service supports dial-in over regular telephone lines and Integrated Services Digital Network (ISDN), so that businesses can choose the most cost-effective solution for their companies.

Automatic Installation and Configuration

Microsoft Windows NT Server 4.0 Remote Access Service is automatically installed and configured during Small Business Server setup, if a modem is detected. This saves time for the small business and technology consultant during installation and helps the business gain the benefits of dial-up networking immediately.

Easily Control User Access

Small Business Server allows the small business a one-button control over who can dial in to the server. When the technology consultant creates an account using the User Account Wizard, they can grant remote-access privileges by selecting the **Use a modem to access the server** option. The technology consultant can grant or revoke a user's privileges at any time from the **Manage Users** console page.

Modem Sharing Server

Modem Sharing Server allows small businesses to share modems installed on their server eliminating the need for each workstation to have their own modem. In addition, Modem Sharing Server is designed to reduce the possibility of a busy signal as the server automatically uses the next available modem in the pool to handle dial-in or dial-out requests.

If the setup routine detects a modem during installation, it automatically installs and configures the modem-sharing service on the server. This saves time for the technology consultant and small business, which allows the business to begin receiving the benefits of shared modems right away.

Modem sharing is a Small Business Server task that can be managed from the **Manage Modems** page shown below. By sharing modems in Small Business Server, the small business has several benefits, as described in the list that follows.

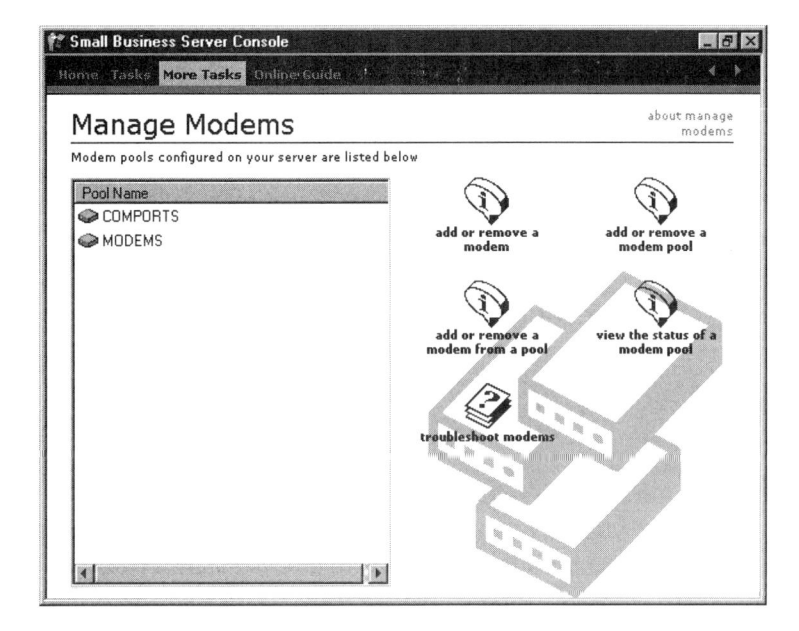

- **Reduction of Hardware Costs.**

    Users no longer need separate modems for their individual computers since they can share modems on the Small Business Server. This means that a business can get the most from its modems and phone lines by sharing access to them.

- **Reduction of Wait Times.**

    If there is more than one modem in a modem pool, Small Business Server automatically uses the next available modem in the pool. In a modem pool, each modem must be the same modem type.

- **Easy Management of Modems.**

    With the Small Business console, modems can be easily managed. Modem pools and their status can be viewed and modems can be added or removed from the modem pool.

Microsoft Proxy Server 2.0

Many small businesses connecting to the Internet today access their ISP or online service from a modem installed in each workstation. However, it is not cost-effective or secure to set up each workstation with its own modem and phone line for Internet access. It is also not cost-effective for each user to have his or her own ISP account. Microsoft BackOffice Small Business Server 4.5 tightly integrates Microsoft Proxy Server 2.0 to provide a single, secure gateway to the Internet, allowing users to seamlessly browse the web.

Leveraging Integrated Server Functionalities

Microsoft Proxy Server 2.0 leverages the Modem Sharing Server integrated into Small Business Server, eliminating the need to install modems for individual workstations. Proxy Server also leverages the security built into Windows NT Server 4.0, allowing small businesses to control access to or from the Internet. The technology consultant can also grant or deny inbound and outbound connections to users, services, ports, or IP domains for access control purposes.

Cost-Effective Connectivity

With Dial-Up Networking, Small Business Server will maintain a connection to an ISP only while traffic is moving across that connection. Shortly after traffic across the dial-up connection stops, Microsoft Proxy Server and Dial-Up Networking terminate the connection, so the ISP "meter" does not run unnecessarily.

Since many users frequent the same web sites, Microsoft Proxy Server first checks the Microsoft Proxy Server cache to see if the user request can be fulfilled. Microsoft Proxy Server will initiate a dial-up connection to the ISP only after checking the cache.

The above two features reduce the cost of Internet access for the small business.

Control User Access

Small businesses want to ensure that their employees are using the Internet for productive purposes. With Microsoft Proxy Server, small businesses can either block access to specific sites or limit access to only specified sites. This ensures that company resources are being used effectively. In addition, Microsoft Proxy Server enables small businesses to restrict the hours during which Internet access is made available to users. For example, a business can make Internet access available to employees at their workstations during business hours, but disable Internet access after business hours.

Seamless Web Browsing

Small Business Server automatically enables the Auto-Dial function in Microsoft Proxy Server with the Internet Connection Wizard configuration. Customers can easily dial in and connect to the Internet as needed. This provides employees with seamless web browsing so they can remain informed of their customers and competitors activities.

Exchange Server 5.5

Microsoft Exchange Server is the client/server messaging system in Small Business Server that integrates e-mail, group scheduling, electronic forms, message routing, groupware, and Internet connectivity. Exchange Server is optimized for small business applications and is automatically configured when the Internet Connection Wizard is run. Once set up, Exchange is managed using console wizards which perform behind-the-scenes steps to create the appropriate operating configurations.

CHAPTER 5

Small Business Server Component Feature Summary

Microsoft® BackOffice® Small Business Server has everything needed to run a small business. It integrates server applications of the BackOffice family to provide a solution for sharing files, databases, printers, e-mail, fax services, applications, Internet connection services, and other resources. Small Business Server provides a complete array of services to allow communication with anyone, anywhere, at any time—all from one server.

Small Business Server combines members of the BackOffice family—Microsoft Windows NT® Server 4.0 operating system, Microsoft Proxy Server 2.0, Microsoft Exchange Server 5.5, Microsoft Internet Information Server 4.0, and Microsoft SQL Server™ 7.0—with Fax Server, Modem Sharing Server, and Internet connectivity, and manages them in an easy-to-use graphical interface. Thus the small business customer is provided with advanced communication services and fast, flexible access to the Internet.

A list of BackOffice products, components, and features contained in Small Business Server 4.5 follows.

Components Providing File, Print, and Application Services

Microsoft Windows NT Server 4.0, the world's leading network operating system, is a secure, reliable operating system on which small businesses can easily share files, back up critical company information, share equipment (such as printers and modems), and run business applications reliably.

Microsoft Internet Information Server 4.0, a tightly integrated web server, is designed to deliver a wide range of Internet and intranet server capabilities so that small businesses have all the tools they need to create powerful and professional web sites. Internet Information Server also provides the most comprehensive platform for building a new generation of web applications.

Microsoft SQL Server 7.0, provides a powerful, secure relational database for running business applications.

Components Providing Powerful Communications

Microsoft Exchange Server 5.5, an Internet mail and collaboration server, includes business solutions to help get customers connected and coordinated; it provides a solid foundation built on Internet and other open standards.

Microsoft Outlook® 2000, desktop information manager helps users manage their messages, appointments, contacts, and tasks, as well as track activities, open and view documents, and share information.

With the **Exchange Server** and **Outlook** combination, the small business can build community through rich electronic messaging, discussion groups, list services, and other groupware capabilities. The small business can communicate with customers and suppliers right from the desktop.

Microsoft Fax Service 4.5, allows companies to communicate by fax more efficiently. Users can fax any document from any program right from their desktops, automatically route faxes via e-mail, and manage fax devices. Companies can control who can view and send faxes and even determine how faxes are distributed within their company.

Microsoft Modem Sharing Service 4.5, allows small businesses to share modems installed on their server, eliminating the need for each workstation to have its own modem. In addition, Modem Sharing Server reduces wait times because the server automatically uses the next available modem in the pool to handle dial-in or dial-out requests.

Components Supporting Access to the Internet

Small Business Server Internet Connection Wizard, allows configuration of Small Business Server to work with an existing ISP or automates location, selection, and connection to a new ISP. It automatically sets up Microsoft Proxy Server and configures Exchange Server to send and receive e-mail across the Internet. The Small Business Server Internet Connection Wizard makes it easy for small businesses to connect to the Internet.

Microsoft FrontPage® 2000, a web site creation and management tool, makes it easy to create and manage professional-looking web sites without programming.

Note Microsoft FrontPage 2000 is only supplied with Small Business Server 4.5 in the Microsoft Office 2000 SKU version.

Microsoft Proxy Server 2.0, creates a single, secure gateway to the Internet, eliminating the need for each workstation to have a modem. Auto-dial is automatically enabled during installation, providing seamless web browsing for all clients.

Microsoft Internet Explorer 5.0, provides the best Internet browser for Windows clients, allowing for a rich user experience in navigating intranets or the Internet.

Remote Access Service, allows home and mobile users to work as if they were in the office. These users can send and receive e-mail, fax documents, and print files to an office printer just as they would in the office. Microsoft Remote Access Service allows the small business to respond to customer requests from anywhere at any time.

Features Providing Easy Setup, Management, and Use

Integrated Server Setup, silently installs all server applications, which eliminates the need to install each application separately. The server setup automatically configures the applications, thus minimizing user input and helping to ensure a successful server installation.

To Do List, takes the technology consultant through the steps of connecting printers and workstations, creating user accounts, and connecting them to the Internet, ensuring that the small business has a complete network.

Small Business Server Console, offers a centralized, easy-to-use interface that places all of the common management tasks in one location.

Wizards, use plain language to guide the technology consultant through the key tasks in managing users, peripherals, and devices on the server.

Set Up Computer Wizard, provides the simplest way to add new machines to a network. The Set Up Computer Wizard makes it easy to connect the Windows® 95 or Windows NT Workstation operating system to Small Business Server. The wizard configures the network settings, installs the appropriate protocol, adds the appropriate client applications for the user, and creates shortcuts to shared folders on the server from the user's desktop, increasing the success rate of getting the client up and running.

Online Guide, provides training to the technology consultant or the small business administrator. It includes tutorials, comprehensive help, and troubleshooting tips, along with a fast search engine to ensure that help is available when needed.

Client User Guide, provides just-in-time training to the users connected to Small Business Server. Users can obtain comprehensive tutorials and troubleshooting tips on topics such as printing, e-mail, and the Internet, so they can become productive more quickly. The Client User Guide is automatically set up as the Microsoft Internet Explorer default page on Small Business Server and each client computer.

Upgrading Small Business Server 4.5 to accommodate growth in the small business is supported. When the small business expands beyond 50 client computers, Microsoft recommends upgrading to BackOffice Server 4.5.

Note Since Small Business Server 4.5 is optimized for small business customers, functionality specific to large enterprises such as Systems Management Server (SMS) and Systems Network Architecture (SNA) Server are not included.

Features Facilitating Solution Development and Administration

Small Business Server Console, is designed to be easily extensible so that technology consultants or third-parties can deliver solutions developed and tailored for the small business application.

Client Application Integration, allows third-party applications to be integrated into the Set Up Computer Wizard so they can be installed at the same time that workstations are being configured for the network. This feature allows the small business to get up and running much faster since client software only has to be installed once.

Consistent Solution Feature, provides the technology consultant and Independent Software Vendor (ISV) with a consistent solution that is easily replicated, since Small Business Server provides a platform where everything has been integrated, tested, and optimized to work together.

Remote Server Administration, allows the technology consultant to administer and manage Small Business Server remotely using the Small Business Server console from Windows 9x or NT Workstation computers running Microsoft NetMeeting. This eliminates the need for a technology consultant to be on-site and thus facilitates the ability to resolve problems more quickly.

Server Status Tool, allows the technology consultant to upload logs and system data in order to monitor the health of the server. The log files allow tracking of specific system activities which the technology consultant may then use for diagnostic purposes. This allows the technology consultant to determine in advance whether the small business customer will encounter any problems with their server. The Server Status Tool is also extensible, which allows the technology consultant to add other application logs to the server reporting list, including those created by a third-party.

CHAPTER 6

Benefits of Small Business Server to the Technology Consultant

Small businesses represents the fastest-growing customer segment today. According to IDC/Link, 74.6 percent of small businesses today have one PC or more, and yet only 29.9 percent are networked. This networking number is expected to rise to 40.9 percent by the year 2001. This will dramatically increase the need for computer professionals who focus on setting up networking systems for small business customers.

Microsoft® BackOffice® Small Business Server 4.5 is a network operating system/integrated platform designed to meet the needs of the small business. The benefits that Small Business Server provides to the technology consultant are discussed in the paragraphs that follow.

Easy to Replicate an Integrated and Optimized Solution

Small Business Server 4.5 provides a solution in which all the essential services, including file, print and applications services, e-mail and fax, and Internet connection services, have been integrated, tested, and optimized to work together. The integration and deployment of third-party applications on Small Business Server, is made easy by the extensibility of the management console and the ability to add applications to the client installation. This allows technology consultants to have a consistent solution that is easily replicated for multiple customers.

Since the complexity of piecing together applications has been removed, it is easier for the technology consultant to install and support more customers in a more cost-effective manner. The technology consultant can focus on customization, configuration, and application integration rather than the chore of making pieces fit together. Since Small Business Server inherently contains everything needed to run a small business, the technology consultant can focus on selling customer-specific solutions to their small business customers rather than just doing network installs.

Provide Better Customer Service with Reduced Support Cost

Technology consultants can provide customers with a complete small business solution that is easy to manage and use. With Small Business Server, technology consultants can offer users an integrated platform that has all of the core services needed from an application development perspective—a robust and reliable database, a complete messaging system, and web services. The technology consultant can also present and address the need for an integrated solution to manage small businesses and accommodate for their expansion.

Remote Management

Small Business Server has taken steps to simplify common administrative tasks. Once the customer is trained, they will be able to handle basic tasks like adding a user, so the technology consultant can then focus on other value-added services. Should a problem arise that the customer can't resolve, the technology consultant can easily manage Small Business Server by accessing the console from a remote location.

Remote management can be performed from any computer with Microsoft NetMeeting® installed and running either the Microsoft Windows NT® Workstation or Windows 95/98 operating system. The technology consultant uses these platforms to access the small business customer's server console with a Microsoft NetMeeting connection. Thus, customers are serviced more cost-effectively, avoiding expensive on-site visits to resolve basic issues. Access to the server from a remote location also allows the technology consultant quick access to the server in order to diagnose and resolve any problems.

Server Status Tool

The technology consultant can monitor the health of the server from a remote location using the Server Status Tool. The technology consultant can upload logs and system data to provide a historical record of system activities which can then be used to troubleshoot a problem. This information can be used by the technology consultant to determine whether the Small Business Server customer may encounter future problems, before workflow is impeded.

The Server Status Tool is preconfigured to send five Small Business Server application logs/reports to the technology consultant by e-mail or fax. In addition, the Server Status Tool may be extended to include reports for other Small Business Server applications, including those created by an Independent Software Vendor (ISV).

Excellent Potential for Add-on Sales

Small Business Server provides excellent value-added service opportunities, including customizing the small business server network, web site design and management, and the integration and management of third-party applications.

Set Up Computer Wizard Supports Add-on Installation

The Set Up Computer Wizard easily facilitates the installation of additional third-party applications. The applications can then be installed at the same time client workstations are being configured for the network.

Extensible Console Facilitates Add-on Management

The Small Business Server extensible console feature easily facilitates management of additional third-party applications, thus the technology consultant can integrate the management of applications tailored for the small business. All management issues will appear seamless to the user. Help for third-party applications can also be integrated into the Online Guide to complete the experience.

Exposure to the Internet

The Small Business Server Internet Connection Wizard enables small business customers to set up and use Internet access services, to learn about Internet services, and use e-mail with unprecedented ease. Once small businesses see how the Internet can help them enhance their customer service and expand their business, we anticipate they will seek connectivity, web design/hosting, and other services.

Leverage One Set of BackOffice Skills and Solutions

Small Business Server is built using the products of the Microsoft BackOffice family, including Windows NT Server, Internet Information Server, Exchange Server, Proxy Server, and SQL Server™. This allows the technology consultant to make a single training investment in learning these products, which can then be applied across a broad spectrum of small to large businesses. The technology consultant can develop solutions that rely on the BackOffice family with the knowledge that all businesses will be able to use their solutions. Also, as small businesses grow, they can upgrade to BackOffice and the technology consultant's solutions still remain viable.

CHAPTER 7

Introduction to Small Business Server Solution Development

Although Microsoft® BackOffice® Small Business Server 4.5 provides an easy way to set up and manage the server/network environment, many technology consultants want to be able to extend the product in order to enhance their customer service. Small Business Server accommodates this requirement since it is designed to allow:

- Customization of the Small Business Server console.
- Integration of third-party applications with the Set Up Computer Wizard and the server setup.
- Remote management of the server using the Small Business Server console.
- Extension of the Server Status Tool.

This flexibility benefits both small businesses and third parties because the small business is able to get the solutions they want and third parties are still able to make use of a consistent platform.

Extensible Console

The Small Business Server console is designed for extensibility in order to allow technology consultants to deliver solutions tailored to their customers. It also allows ISVs the ability to provide seamless application integration into the Small Business Server console.

Customizing Small Business Server Console

Technology consultants can make simple modifications such as adding new taskpads or links. For instance, a technology consultant could add a taskpad to the console that would allow the small business administrator to send e-mail to a paging service that would then page the technology consultant.

Adding Task Pages

Third parties (ISVs) can make more extensive modifications, such as creating, adding, or replacing task pages. These task pages can even be linked to the Online Guide so the information can be searched within the Online Guide. This provides seamless integration with the server and the application.

Application Integration

Small Business Server makes it easy for third-party applications to easily integrate into the client setup. As a result, ISVs can deliver applications that seamlessly install on a customer's network and technology consultants can create solutions targeted to their customers' needs.

Extension of Set Up Computer Wizard

The Set Up Computer Wizard can be extended to allow third-party applications to be a part of the default client installation setup. This allows a small business to perform an automated installation of all its applications. As a result, when workstations are being connected to the network, only a one-time installation of client software is required. In addition, this facilitates application upgrade because applications are managed centrally from the server.

Adding applications for installation is a simple and straightforward process. In order for an application to be incorporated into the Set Up Computer Wizard, the software program must have an unattended or automated installation mode. The application also needs the option to eliminate a restart prompt since the Set Up Computer Wizard has a single restart at the end of client installation. Lastly, there must be no restrictions on the order in which the application installs.

Remote Server Administration

The technology consultant can manage and administer Small Business Server 4.5 by accessing the Small Business Server Console from a remote workstation running Microsoft NetMeeting®. This eliminates the need for the technology consultant to be on-site and thus allows them the ability to respond to their customers more quickly.

CHAPTER 8

Training

Training resources for installing and configuring Microsoft® BackOffice® Small Business Server 4.5 may be found at the Microsoft web site. Pointers to instructor-led training or self-paced training downloads are included on this site: **http://www.microsoft.com/smallbusinessserver/support.htm**

CHAPTER 9

Other Resources

The following additional resources may be accessed to support the planning, deployment, and administration of Microsoft® BackOffice® Small Business Server in your organization.

- Microsoft has a web site dedicated to Small Business Server located at:
  http://www.microsoft.com/smallbusinessserver
- The technology consultant can find the tools and support needed for building and growing small businesses with Small Business Server at the Microsoft Direct Access web site. Included are such things as product guides, sales tools for the technology consultant, training, and a Small Business Server newsgroup. The site is located at:
  http://www.microsoft.com/directaccess

  To register and access resources on the Microsoft Direct Access web site, use the following address:
  http://premium.microsoft.com/directaccess
- You can subscribe to Microsoft TechNet. It includes over 200,000 pages of technical content of Microsoft Knowledge Base, evaluation and deployment guides, white papers, third party integration information, case studies, training materials, and Microsoft Resource Kits.
- The Technical Information CD is one of 15+ CDs included with a subscription to TechNet. You can receive a TechNet trial CD, which is a fully functional version of the monthly Technical Information CD at:
  http://www.microsoft.com/technet/trial/default.htm

PART 2

Planning

When planning for the deployment of Microsoft® BackOffice® Small Business Server 4.5 into the small business environment, consider the issues discussed in this part. They are provided to assist the technology consultant and the small business owner in making decisions about the deployment of Small Business Server 4.5 in the small business environment. Material discussed in Part 2 includes:

Chapter 10   Planning a Small Business Server Network   49

Chapter 11   Planning for an Internet Presence   67

Chapter 12   Planning for Remote Access Users   87

Chapter 13   Planning for Microsoft Fax and Modem Sharing Services   97

Chapter 14   Planning for Proxy Server 2.0   101

Chapter 15   Planning for Exchange Server 5.5   103

Chapter 16   Small Business Network Capacity Planning   109

CHAPTER 10

Planning a Small Business Server Network

When planning for the deployment of Microsoft® BackOffice® Small Business Server 4.5, the technology consultant must first understand the characteristics of the small business network and the general requirements of the server computer. This chapter provides this baseline information in order to help the technology consultant effectively plan for the small business server network environment. Included are minimum hardware requirements for the Small Business Server network. Guidelines defining hardware requirements for varying network capacities are provided in the "Network Capacity Guidelines" section of *Chapter 16, Small Business Server Capacity Planning*, later in *Part 2*.

Small Business Office Network Characteristics

The typical small business office network may be generally characterized by the following features:

- Consists of a single local area network (LAN).
- Uses IP network protocol.
- Has a connection to an Internet service provider (ISP).
- Has no more than 50 client computers.

Network Configuration

For the small business network, ethernet connections are required consisting of network interface cards, cabling, and hubs between your computers. The appropriate configurations and equipment quantities depends on the size of the small business office.

The following illustration shows a typical configuration for a small business network using Small Business Server 4.5. The main server applications of Small Business Server are shown in relation to the LAN and Internet connectivity. This gives the technology consultant a conceptual view of the network along with the components used in a typical small business implementation. Components may vary slightly, as in the case where Access 2000 is used for the small business database instead of SQL Server™ 7.0, or when a dedicated connection to the Internet is used instead of a modem, but the general configuration is still valid.

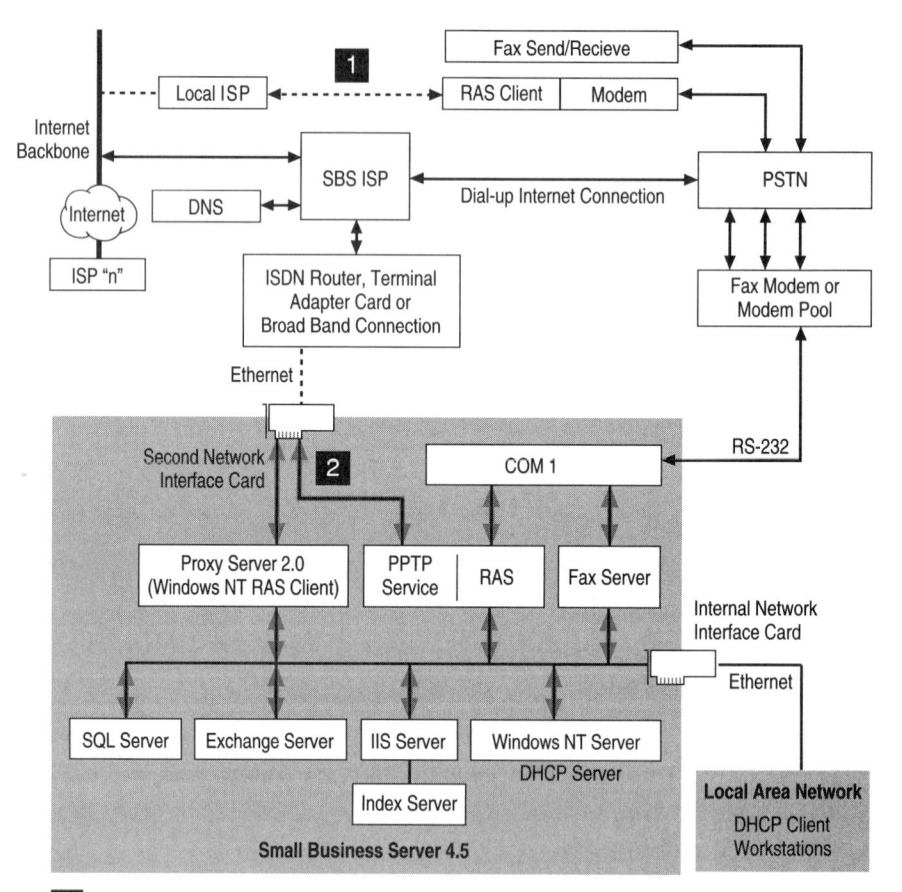

Figure 10.1 Typical Small Business Server Network Configuration

After Small Business Server 4.5 is installed, plan to use the Small Business Server Internet Connection Wizard to configure Internet connectivity for all network scenarios.

Small Business Server Requirements and Recommendations

Small Business Server 4.5 requires the minimum computer configuration described in the paragraphs that follow.

Server Computer Hardware Requirements

The following is the minimum equipment required. As the user base and server use expands, the processor, memory, and disk configurations should be modified in accordance with the recommendations in *Chapter 16, Small Business Server Capacity Planning*.

- An Intel Pentium 120 microprocessor (Pentium 200 or higher is desirable).
- 64 MB or more of random access memory (RAM). The minimum RAM requirement specified here may increase depending on Internet activity involving CPU-intensive sessions.
- 2 GB of hard disk space. If Office 2000 is installed, a total of 3 GB of hard disk space is required.
- One 3.5-inch high-density disk drive. Drive must be configured as drive A.
- SVGA monitor and video adapter; 800 by 600 or higher resolution; 16 colors.
- CD-ROM drive.
- One or more supported modems for using Modem Sharing Service, Fax Service, Dial-Up Networking, and Internet access. All modems must be the same brand and model to take advantage of Modem Sharing Service. If only one modem is used, it must be a business class fax modem with adaptive answering to support high volume fax reception and Dial-Up Networking calls.
- A network adapter card from the Recommended Hardware List referenced in "Hardware Compatibility" later in this chapter.

Internet Connection Hardware

For a Small Business Server connection to the Internet, one of the following hardware solutions is needed:

- A 28.8 kilobits per second (Kbps) or faster modem for a dial-up connection to an Internet service provider (ISP). This is an inexpensive solution that provides satisfactory performance for up to three users.
- An Integrated Services Digital Network (ISDN) modem or terminal adapter if you have an ISDN line and are signed up for ISDN service with an ISP. ISDN is more expensive but provides better performance.

- An additional network adapter card, ISDN demand-dial router, cable modem, or other hardware solution that provides a high-bandwidth Internet connection.

Other Hardware Recommendations

The following hardware is recommended for use with Small Business Server 4.5:

- A tape or other backup system.
- Two phone lines—one dedicated to Fax Service and the other to Dial-Up Networking.
- An uninterruptable power supply (UPS).
- Additional hard disks for file storage or disk mirroring (a dynamically updated duplicate of your computer's information). Disk striping may also be used.

Hardware Compatibility

Since Small Business Server consists of several components that interact closely with each other, there are specific hardware requirements beyond those of Windows NT® Server operating system. In general, most hardware that is compatible with Windows NT Server is compatible with Small Business Server 4.5.

In order to make sure the hardware you are planning to use is compatible with Small Business Server 4.5, refer to the Recommended Hardware List, found on the Small Business Server web site:
http://www.microsoft.com/smallbusinessserver

If your hardware is supported, Small Business Server setup will automatically load the necessary drivers and configure the system.

Client Computer Requirements and Recommendations

Client computers attached to a Small Business Server network must meet the minimum hardware and software requirements described below.

PC Hardware Requirements

For a client PC on the Small Business Server network, the following hardware requirements apply:

- Pentium 90 MHz processor or higher recommended.
- 32 MB of RAM.
- One 3.5-inch high-density disk drive.
- 250 MB free hard disk space. If Office 2000 will be installed, then a total of 550 MB free hard disk space is required.
- An ethernet network adapter supported by the operating system.

- VGA or higher resolution monitor and video adapter.
- Microsoft mouse or compatible pointing device.

Dial-Up Networking Server Access

If remote clients are to access Small Business Server using Dial-Up Networking, at least the following are required:

- A modem, 28.8 Kbps minimum.
- Microsoft Dial-Up Networking (comes with client operating system). The latest version of Microsoft Dial-Up Networking can be downloaded from the following web site:
  http://www.microsoft.com
- TCP/IP and Point-to-Point Protocol (PPP) installed.

Note Remote clients may connect to Small Business Server over the Internet backbone. To accomplish this, Point-to-Point Tunneling Protocol (PPTP) is configured on the server and installed/configured on client computers to facilitate secure virtual private networking (VPN). Also, PPTP must be enabled when the Internet Connection Wizard is run.

Recommended Operating System Software

Users can access all the features of Small Business Server 4.5 from computers running the following operating systems:

- Microsoft Windows 95
- Microsoft Windows 98
- Microsoft Windows NT Workstation 4.0

Other Operating System Compatibilities

With manual configuration of the client computer, the following operating systems can use the Small Business Server file and print services:

- Microsoft Windows NT Workstations 3.x
- Microsoft Windows for Workgroups
- MS-DOS®
- Apple Macintosh®
- Various versions of UNIX®

Backup System Planning

Protecting company data on Small Business Server 4.5 is a critical consideration. The small business may have a fault tolerant disk configuration which provides some immunity from hardware failure, however, this method alone will not protect crucial company data from fire or other natural disasters. The Windows NT portion of Small Business Server has a comprehensive backup utility that permits the technology consultant to back up critical company data to tape media. It allows for backup of data on the server itself and for workstations in the small business network. This includes security information, file and share permissions, and registry data. For data security, only a user from the administrator or backup operator group should backup data to tape. Individual files and directories or the entire server may be restored using the Windows NT Backup utility.

Controller Device Compatibility with Windows NT Server 4.0

In order to implement a tape backup system, a suitable third-party hardware solution supported by Small Business Server is needed. The Windows NT Backup utility supports many different Small Computer System Interface (SCSI) tape devices as well as a few IDE devices. Parallel devices and removable devices, such as a Jaz drive, floppy drive, or magneto-optical devices, are not supported. However, you may find some third-party applications that will support these devices for operation with Windows NT Server 4.0.

Devices that are compatible with the Windows NT Backup utility may be located in the Recommended Hardware List found on the Small Business Server Web site at:
http://www.microsoft.com/smallbusinessserver

Also, the correct drivers for the backup controller device must be installed on Small Business Server in order to support communication with the device. Some devices in the Recommended Hardware List also contain links to the required drivers.

Controller Device Capacity

Before installing a backup tape controller device, consideration should be given to the backup speed and storage capacity of the device. The latter is determined somewhat by the size of the small business network and the amount of data to be backed up. With a full installation of Small Business Server, including Office 2000, the directories alone without any data on the server or network requires approximately 1.2 GB for backup.

Installing Controller Drivers

Drivers for tape controller devices are installed using the Tape Devices utility in Control Panel. Any drivers that are installed appear there when the utility is launched. If there are no drivers installed for the controller device, Windows NT attempts to detect the tape controller device connected to the server. If the drive is successfully queried, you will be prompted to install the driver. If the driver is incorrect or Windows NT could not detect the controller device, a driver must be added using the **Drivers** tab of the Tape Devices utility. Click the **Add** button to see a list of supported tape controller devices and manufacturers from which you can choose. If your tape controller device is not supported, install the drivers using software supplied by the manufacturer.

Scheduling and Performing Backups

For information on backup planning and scheduling, refer to the Online Guide. The Scheduled Tasks utility may be used to automate backups performed at specified intervals. For information on using the Scheduled Tasks utility, refer to the "Task Scheduling Tool" section of *Chapter 26, Administrative Tools,* in *Part 4, Administering and Maintaining*, of this resource guide.

Planning a Fault-Tolerant Disk Configuration

A technology called Redundant Array of Independent Disks (RAID) may be used to minimize loss of data if hard disk access problems occur on Small Business Server. RAID is a fault-tolerant disk configuration in which part of the physical disk-storage capacity of a server contains a redundant data set. The redundant information enables the automatic regeneration of the data if either of the following occur:

- A disk or its access path fails.
- A sector on the disk cannot be read.

Standard fault-tolerant disk systems are categorized in six levels, known as RAID levels 0 through 5. Each level offers various combinations of performance, reliability, and cost. RAID combines multiple disks with lower individual reliability ratings to reduce the total cost of storage. The lower reliability of each disk in a RAID array is offset by the redundancy feature. Windows NT Server 4.0 supports disk striping (RAID level 0), disk mirroring (RAID level 1), and disk striping with parity (RAID level 5). For more information about RAID arrays compatible with Windows NT Server, refer to the Windows NT Hardware Compatibility List at:
http://www.microsoft.com/isapi/hwtcst/hcl.idc

To create a fault-tolerant disk configuration for Small Business Server 4.5, use RAID level 1 disk mirroring or duplexing, or RAID level 5 disk striping with parity, as described in the sections that follow. The Windows NT Server Disk Administrator in the **Administrative Tools** program group on the **Start** menu, is used to configure mirrored or duplexed sets, disk striping with parity, and also to reconstruct the volume if a failure has occurred. Refer to Chapter 5 "Preparing for and Performing Recovery" in the *Windows NT Server Resource Guide* to create a mirror set or stripe set with parity.

Disk Mirroring

Disk mirroring is when an identical redundant disk is created and maintained for duplication of data on a selected primary disk. Disk mirroring uses two partitions on different drives connected to the same disk controller, as shown in the following illustration. All data on the primary disk partition is mirrored automatically onto the secondary (redundant) disk partition—sometimes referred to as a shadow partition. If the primary disk fails, no data is lost since the secondary partition can be used.

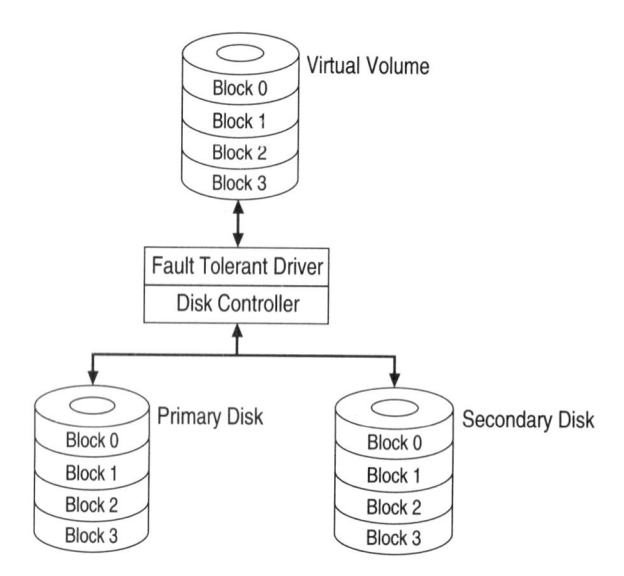

Figure 10.2 Disk Mirror Configuration

I/O Requests in a Disk Mirroring Configuration

In a disk mirroring configuration, all data is written to both partitions, resulting in only 50 percent disk space utilization. From the perspective of the user, only a single read or write occurs to satisfy data requests, although FtDisk, the Windows NT Server fault-tolerant disk driver, creates separate I/O requests for each disk in the mirrored set. If a read failure occurs on one disk, FtDisk reads the data from the other disk in the mirrored set. If a write failure occurs on one disk, FtDisk uses the remaining disk in the mirrored set for all data accesses. Since dual-write operations can degrade system performance, many mirrored set implementations use duplexing, where each disk in the mirrored set has its own disk controller. Refer to "Disk Duplexing," later in this chapter.

Mirrored Partition Size

The secondary mirrored partition is not limited to the size, number of tracks, or the number of cylinders on the primary partition. This eliminates the requirement to replace the primary drive with an identical model, should it fail. In practice, however, mirrored partitions are usually created with identical disks, the same size as the primary partition. Note that the unpartitioned area you use for the shadow partition must not be *smaller* than the primary partition. If it is *larger*, the unused space can be configured as another partition if there are less than four existing partitions on the disk.

Boot and System Partitions

Any partition can be mirrored, including boot and system partitions. The boot partition contains the operating system and support files. Mirroring the boot partition significantly reduces the amount of time needed to get Windows NT Server up and running if the disk containing your operating system has problems. If you configure your system partition as a mirrored set, use identical disks with the same disk geometry. The system partition contains hardware-specific files needed to start Windows NT Server, such as the x86-based files NTLDR and Boot.ini, or the Reduced Instruction Set Computing (RISC)-based files Osloader and Hal.dll. Refer to Chapter 5 "Preparing for and Performing Recovery" in the *Windows NT Server Resource Guide* for details on configuring mirrored sets for system partitions.

Note The boot and system partition can be the same.

Advantages of Mirrored Disk Sets

Some of the advantages of using mirrored disk sets include:

- Disk read operations on a mirrored set are more efficient than on a single partition.

    FtDisk, the fault-tolerant disk driver, has the ability to load-balance read operations across the physical disks. With current SCSI technology, two disk read operations can occur simultaneously. In some cases, a disk read can be done in half the time it takes on a single partition.

- Recovery from a disk failure is very rapid.

    Mirrored sets offer the fastest data recovery since the shadow partition contains all the data and rebuilding is not required for data restoration. If you configure your boot partition on a mirrored set, Windows NT Server reinstallation is not required to restart the computer in the event of disk failure.

- Disk failure does not impact performance.

    A disk mirroring configuration does not impact performance when a member of a mirrored set fails, as stripe sets do.

- Disk mirroring has better overall read and write performance than stripe sets with parity.

Disadvantages of Mirrored Disk Sets

Some disadvantages of mirrored disk sets include:

- Disk write operations are less efficient.

    Because data must be written to both disks, performance is slightly affected. However, since disk writes are done asynchronously, the impact is offset. In most situations, a user application is not affected by the extra disk update.

- Space utilization inefficiencies.

    Mirrored disk sets are the least efficient in terms of space utilization. Since data is entirely duplicated, the disk space requirement for mirroring is higher than a stripe set with parity.

- Boot selection must be created.

    When creating a mirrored set for boot and system partitions, you should create and test a Windows NT startup floppy to facilitate computer startup. For RISC-based computers, you must create an alternate boot selection to use the Windows NT startup floppy. Otherwise, computer restart time increases after a failure, since you have to create the boot selection.

- Incomplete duplication of sectors.

  Creating a mirrored set of a boot or system partition does not implement a sector-by-sector duplication of the primary disk. FtDisk does not copy either the Master Boot Record on track 0 or the Partition Boot Sector, which is the first sector of the partition. Some systems may save information in other parts of track 0 and this will not be duplicated either. Data corruption in these areas can make it much more difficult to recover from primary disk failure. If both disks are affected, it can be extremely difficult or impossible to recover the data.

- More expensive than a disk striping configuration.

Disk Duplexing

Disk duplexing is a mirrored pair with an additional adapter on the secondary disk drive. Duplexing provides fault tolerance for both disk and controller failure, and increases performance. Like mirroring, duplexing is performed at the partition level, therefore Windows NT Server sees no difference between them, with exception of partition locations. A duplexed mirror set has very high data reliability since the entire I/O subsystem is duplicated, as shown in the following illustration.

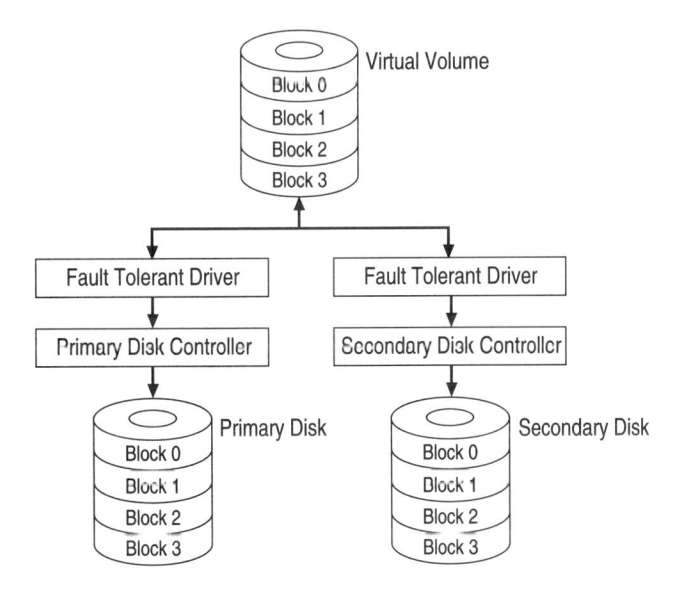

Figure 10.3 Duplexed disk mirror configuration

Disk Stripe Sets

Stripe sets are composed of strips of equal size on each disk in a volume, with 2 to 32 disks in the configuration. For Windows NT Server, strip size is 64 K. When data is written to a stripe set, it is written across the strips of the volume—as in the gray area across disks 1 through 4 in the example below. The following table shows the order in which data is written to a stripe set and how a stripe set is similar to a table.

Table 10.1 Stripe Set Configuration

	Disk 1	Disk 2	Disk 3	Disk 4
Stripe 1	1	2	3	4
Stripe 2	5	6	7	8
Stripe 3	9	10	11	12
Stripe 4	13	14	15	16
Stripe 5	17	18	19	20

If a file 325 K long was written to the above configuration, it would occupy the following areas:

- 64 K in strip 1.
- 64 K in strip 2.
- 64 K in strip 3.
- 64 K in strip 4.
- 64 K in strip 5.
- 5 K in strip 6.

Disk Stripe Set with Parity

A stripe set with parity adds parity information to a stripe set configuration. A stripe set with parity dedicates the equivalent of a strip of disk space for the parity information and distributes this across all the disks in the group. The data and parity information is arranged on the volume so they are always on different disks, as shown in the following table.

Table 10.2 Stripe set with parity configuration

	Disk 1	Disk 2	Disk 3	Disk 4	Disk 5
Stripe 1	Parity 1	1	2	3	4
Stripe 2	5	Parity 2	6	7	8
Stripe 3	9	10	Parity 3	11	12

(continued)

Table 10.2 Stripe set with parity configuration *(continued)*

	Disk 1	Disk 2	Disk 3	Disk 4	Disk 5
Stripe 4	13	14	15	Parity 4	16
Stripe 5	17	18	19	20	Parity 5

The first strip on disk 1 is the parity strip for the four data strips included in stripe 1. The second strip on disk 2 is the parity strip for the four data strips included in stripe 2, and so on. The parity strip is the exclusive OR (XOR) of all the data values for the data strips in the stripe. If no disks in the stripe set with parity have failed, the new parity for a write can be calculated without having to read the corresponding strips from the other data disks. Thus, only two disks are involved in a write operation, the target data disk and the disk containing the parity strip. The following figure illustrates the steps in writing data to a stripe set with parity.

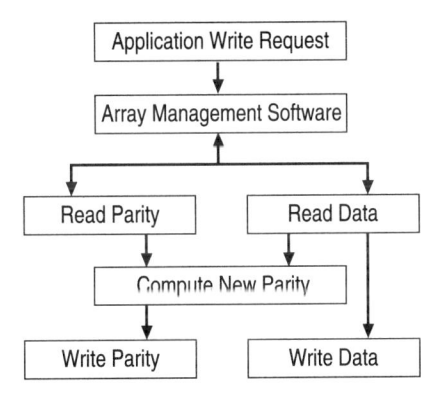

Figure 10.4 Data write to a stripe set with parity

Disks and Partition Space in a Stripe Set with Parity

When implementing a stripe set with parity, there must be at least 3 disks, but no more than 32 in the set. The physical disks do not need to be identical, but they must have equal size blocks of unpartitioned space available. They can also be on the same or different controllers. After the initial configuration, you cannot add disks to a stripe set with parity to increase the size of the volume.

Disk Failure in a Stripe Set with Parity

If one of the disks in a stripe set with parity fails, no data is lost. When a read operation requires data from the failed disk, the system reads all of the remaining good data strips in the stripe as well as the parity strip. Each data strip is subtracted (with XOR) from the parity strip and the result is the missing data strip.

When the system needs to write data to a failed disk, it reads the other data strips and the parity strip and then backs them out of the parity strip, thus leaving the missing data strip. Calculations to modify the parity strip can now be made. Since the data strip has failed, it is not written to—only the parity strip is written to.

Read operations are unaffected if the failed disk contains a parity strip. The parity strip is not needed for a read, but only when there is a failure in a data strip. When the failed disk contains a parity strip, the system does not compute or write the parity strip when there is a change in a data strip.

Advantages of Stripe Sets with Parity

Some of the advantages of using a stripe set with parity include:

- Read operations.

    Disk read operations can occur simultaneously. All disks in the array can be in use at the same time.

- Fault tolerance.

    Provides a high degree of fault-tolerance at a lower cost than a mirrored set.

- Utilization.

    Utilization increases as the number of disks in the array increases.

- Database applications.

    Works well in large database applications where reads occur more often than writes. With the built-in load balancing of a stripe set with parity, database applications that do random reads are also well suited to this configuration.

- Storage space.

    A stripe set is several times more efficient with storage than a mirror set when large numbers of disks are used. The space required for storing the parity information is equivalent to 1/number of disks, therefore a 10-disk array uses 1/10 of its capacity for parity information.

Disadvantages of Stripe Sets with Parity

Some of the disadvantages of using a stripe set with parity include:

- Partition limitations.

    Neither the boot or system partition can be on a stripe set with parity.

- Write operation speed.

    Write operations are substantially slower than for a single disk because the software has to read the old data strip, the old parity strip, and then compute the new parity strip before writing it.

Applications that require high-speed data collection from a process are not well suited for use with a stripe set with parity. This type of application requires continuous high-speed disk writes, and does not work well with the asymmetrical I/O balance inherent to stripe sets with parity.

- Read operation speed.

  If a disk which is part of a stripe set with parity fails, read operations for data strips on that disk are substantially slower than for a single disk—the software has to read all of the other disks in the set to calculate the data.

- Memory requirement.

  A stripe set with parity requires more system memory than a mirrored set.

- Data transfers.

  Applications that require large sequential data transfers are not well suited for a stripe set with parity. This type of data transfer can prevent effective I/O load balancing.

Guidelines for Choosing Mirrored Sets and Stripe Sets with Parity

When choosing mirrored sets or stripe sets with parity, address the following:

- Software and hardware constraints
- Cost
- Reliability

Each vendor you contact should have design guidelines for their system, whether you need a RAID array or want to use the fault-tolerant features of Windows NT Server.

Hardware Compatibility

There are configurations in which fault-tolerance may not work as expected. To avoid problematic situations, make sure all your disk hardware is on the Windows NT Hardware Compatibility List, found at:
http://www.microsoft.com/isapi/hwtest/hcl.idc

If any equipment you are using does not appear on the list, it may not work well.

Advantages of Using Identical Disks

Although not a requirement, if you use identical hardware for your fault-tolerant disk configuration, you have the following advantages:

- Disk performance is the same.

   Faster disks do not have to wait for slower disks.

- The capacity is the same.

   If you want to configure the entire disk for a mirror set or stripe set with parity, identical disks have identical capacity.

- Compatibility.

   Fewer problems with the configuration.

Backup Hardware

When purchasing disks, acquire an extra disk for backup so its available when needed. In the event of a hardware failure, an identical backup disk guarantees compatibility without system performance degradation. All you need is to install the new disk to become operational again, but if you are using SCSI disks, you will have to configure the SCSI ID as well.

If you are not using a duplexed disk controller scheme, obtain a backup disk controller identical to your existing one. A system can continue to operate when a disk fails, but not when a controller fails. There is no way to avoid system downtime if a controller fails, but you can minimize it by having a preconfigured disk controller available. If a non-identical disk controller is used for the replacement, you will have to install a new driver which makes the configuration more complex.

Note If you have configured your system partition on a mirrored set, use the same model controller for a backup. Also be sure to use the same translation for both the original and shadow partitions.

More Information

For more information on planning and setting up a fault-tolerant disk configuration, refer to Chapters 4 and 5 in the *Windows NT Server 4.0 Resource Guide*.

Disaster Recovery Planning

The general strategy of disaster recovery planning for Small Business Server 4.5 encompasses the following two-fold purpose:

- Reduce the potential for problems to occur.
- Develop the necessary plans and procedures to handle failure recovery.

The resources needed to plan specific disaster recovery strategies for Windows NT Server 4.0, Exchange Server 5.5, and SQL Server 7.0 are discussed in this section.

Windows NT Server 4.0

Computers running Windows NT Server cannot be made failure proof, but there are certain things you can do to make failure recovery easier. For information on reliability, recoverability, and disaster recovery preparation, refer to Chapter 4 "Planning a Reliable Configuration" and Chapter 5, "Preparing for and Performing Recovery" in the *Microsoft Windows NT Server 4.0 Resource Guide*.

Exchange Server 5.5

Planning for Exchange Server disaster recovery will minimize downtime and data loss on your mail server. Refer to the resources below for planning information:

- Part 9, "Disaster Recovery" in the *Microsoft Exchange Server Resource Guide*.
- *Microsoft Exchange 5.5 Disaster and Recovery Planning* white paper located at:
  http://www.microsoft.com/exchange/55/whpprs/Disaster.htm

Since Exchange Server uses Windows NT Server security for authentication, Exchange backup and restoration procedures should be considered with respect to Windows NT Server disaster recovery planning. The Online Help launched from the **Backup and Restore Data** page on the Small Business Server console, describes how to use the NT Backup utility for Exchange Server backup and restoration.

SQL Server 7.0

If SQL Server 7.0 is used as a platform for database development in Small Business Server 4.5, you should plan for disaster recovery to preserve the database. Refer to Chapter 11, "Backup and Recovery" in the *Microsoft SQL Server 7.0 Resource Guide*.

Backing Up Server Applications Using NT Backup

You can do an online backup of Exchange data (with Exchange running) using NT Backup, if you use the Exchange window in NT Backup. An offline backup with Exchange stopped is best, but an online backup is adequate when backing up and restoring Exchange.

NT Backup is not SQL-aware since SQL Server 7.0 has its own backup utility. However, NT Backup can be used to backup SQL if you first stop all SQL services and then backup the files. You can also do an online backup of SQL to a file on the hard drive using the SQL backup utility, and then use NT Backup to backup that file to tape.

The NT Backup utility is in the **Administrative Tools** program group on the **Start** menu of Small Business Server 4.5.

Restoring Server Applications Using NT Backup

When using NT Backup to restore, you must restore under the same conditions set up during backup. For example, if the Exchange Server was stopped and you used NT Backup for file backup, then Exchange must be stopped when you restore. If the Exchange Server was running when you did an online backup using the Exchange window of NT Backup, then Exchange must be running when you restore.

Since NT Backup is not SQL-aware, it can only restore the SQL database files when the files are not in use. SQL services must therefore be stopped to restore files with the NT Backup utility.

CHAPTER 11

Planning for an Internet Presence

Businesses today require a presence on the Internet to be competitive and to effectively reach their customers. Microsoft® BackOffice® Small Business Server 4.5 takes full advantage of the Internet with specific focus on benefits for a small business. With an Internet connection in place, a small business can realize the full potential of Small Business Server through Exchange Server, Proxy Server, Internet Information Server, and other capabilities.

Connecting to the Internet means opening an account with an Internet service provider (ISP). An ISP provides a wide range of services to the small business, including browsing access to the World Wide Web, e-mail, and web site hosting. Establishing these services helps the small business create a stronger profile and greater visibility in the marketplace. It is a simple matter to establish an Internet connection using the Small Business Server Internet Connection Wizard. However, before implementing the Internet connection, the technology consultant should consider several issues that will help them create a comprehensive Internet proposal for a small business customer. These issues, which are discussed in this chapter, are as follows:

- ISP capabilities and services
- Internet connection types
- Web site development and hosting
- Bandwidth requirements
- Intranet considerations
- The impact of Internet access on server hardware
- Web site testing
- Location of an ISP
- Sign-up process
- Types of ISP services
- Required ISP connection information
- Domain naming issues

Internet Access Proposal to the Small Business

When the technology consultant is given approval to plan for small business Internet access, a proposal should be made to the small business owner. This proposal should help the small business owner understand the requirements they must meet and the services they must have in order to implement a cost effective Internet solution. Information related to web site hosting and World Wide Web access should be specified, as appropriate. The proposal should include specifications on ISPs, site capacity, and required computer hardware. More specifically, a comprehensive proposal prepared by the technology consultant will do the following:

- Recommend an ISP and their services.
- Ascertain the performance of various connectivity options on the basis of number of users, speed of data transmission, and other performance-related parameters.
- Identify the necessary connection hardware, estimate maximum bandwidth, and specify the appropriate connectivity methods.
- Determine the best approach to web site development, site hosting options, and the advantages of having an intranet.
- Recommend the minimum hardware requirements for the server computer including RAM, hard disk space, and CPU architecture, with respect to the operating parameters for the small business web site.
- Identify the Internet connection process and related connectivity issues.
- Recommend any applicable security features the small business may require. Refer to Proxy Server administration in *Part 4, Administering and Maintaining,* of this resource guide, for security features that may be used for the web site.

The following table may be useful when making decisions about connection types and relative cost. When making calculations and recommendations, the technology consultant should keep in mind the peak hours and the intended purpose of the small business site. The sections that follow this table discuss Internet connection specifications in detail.

Table 11.1 Internet Proposal Factors for the Small Business

Type connection	Bandwidth	Cost relative to other connection types
Leased line (analog)	28 Kbps	1
Leased line (digital)	56–64 Kbps	2.5
ISDN	128 Kbps	4

(continued)

Table 11.1 Internet Proposal Factors for the Small Business *(continued)*

Type connection	Bandwidth	Cost relative to other connection types
ADSL	32 Kbps–50 Mbps	7
Cable modem	3–10 Mbps	10
T1 (DS1)	1.5 Mbps	10
T3 (DS3)	36–45 Mbps	100
ATM OC3	140–161 Mbps	200

Internet Connection Specifications

This section contains descriptions of the following items:

- ISP capabilities, locations, connection types, and services offered.
- Bandwidth calculations that will have to be made before a web site may be implemented for the small business.
- Intranet considerations.
- Web site testing.
- Internet connectivity properties that affect server computer hardware requirements.

ISP Capabilities

The small business organization connects to the Internet by opening an account with an ISP. It is therefore important to determine the capabilities of the ISP, since they are not all alike. Some questions that should be asked of an ISP include:

- How are they connected to the Internet backbone?
- Do they offer dial-up access?
- Do they offer integrated services digital network (ISDN) access?
- What type of security do they offer?
- What are their installation costs for various connection types?
- What are their monthly costs for the various connections?
- What type of e-mail support do they provide?

ISP Locations

ISPs are either local, regional, or national Internet providers. Local ISPs are connected to the Internet through larger ISPs or through a regional net. Local ISPs usually have only one location. The larger regional and national ISPs have multiple locations.

Accessing the Internet Directly

Nets are sites selected by the National Science Foundation (NSF) to provide a common connection point to the Internet. Nets connect through a backbone carrier such as US Sprint®, MCI®, or AT&T® at 155 megabytes per second (Mbps). This facilitates connection to other nets.

If the small business requires a large bandwidth for their Internet site, they can connect directly to a net. The requirements may vary by net provider, but usually a high-speed 45-Mbps line is the minimum connection. The technology consultant should contact the local vendor who operates the net nearest to them for details.

Internet Connection Types

The connection types described in the following table represent typical levels of service for full Internet connections in the United States. The services offered by ISPs varies by area. The speeds shown are approximate and can vary due to the load on the server. The number of simultaneous users supported may vary because of other factors, such as the size of web pages or the number of downloads.

Table 11.2 Internet Connection Types, Bandwidth, and User Capacity

Connection	Kbps	Simultaneous site users supported
Modem	28.8 min	5-10
Dedicated digital line	56	10-20
ISDN	56-1,500	10-500
ADSL	32-50,000	10-500
Cable modem	3,000-10,000	10-500
T1 and fractional T1	128-1,500	50-500
T3	45,000	4500+
ATM OC3	155,000	15,000+

A dial-up modem connection may be used if the small business server is to handle only light traffic. However, a server handling medium traffic should probably use ISDN, a T1 line, or some fraction of a T1 line installed. When growth of the small business requires the server to support heavy Internet traffic, fractional or multiple T1 lines or even T3 service may be needed to handle thousands of users.

Other technologies besides the Public Switched Telephone Network (PSTN) are emerging as methods of connecting to the Internet. These technologies include cable, satellite, wireless, and digital subscriber line.

Dial-up Modem Connections

Modem connections to the Internet are available, but are typically only used for individual client browsing. Modem connections are usually not recommended for servers. Nevertheless, a connection to the Internet using a telephone line and modem can serve up to 10 simultaneous users. Modem connections are often considered slow links because data is transmitted at the speed of the modem, typically from 14,400 through 56,000 kilobytes per second (KBps).

Line Protocols

There are several variations to dial-up accounts that provide different capabilities, depending on the protocols used. All of these connections require the Internet Protocol (IP) and are therefore called IP accounts. The three types of IP accounts are Point-to-Point Protocol (PPP), serial line Internet protocol (SLIP), and CSLIP, which is a compressed version of SLIP.

PPP is the emerging connection of choice because it is faster and more reliable than other protocols. PPP is also more complex, so many computer platforms still only have built-in support for SLIP. Supplemental programs are being developed to enable most platforms to support PPP accounts.

Integrated Services Digital Network

ISDN is a telecommunications service that integrates data, voice, and video onto a digital telephone line. It is available in two different bandwidths: basic rate interface (BRI) and primary rate interface (PRI). The following illustration shows how Small Business Server connects to the ISP through an ISDN interface.

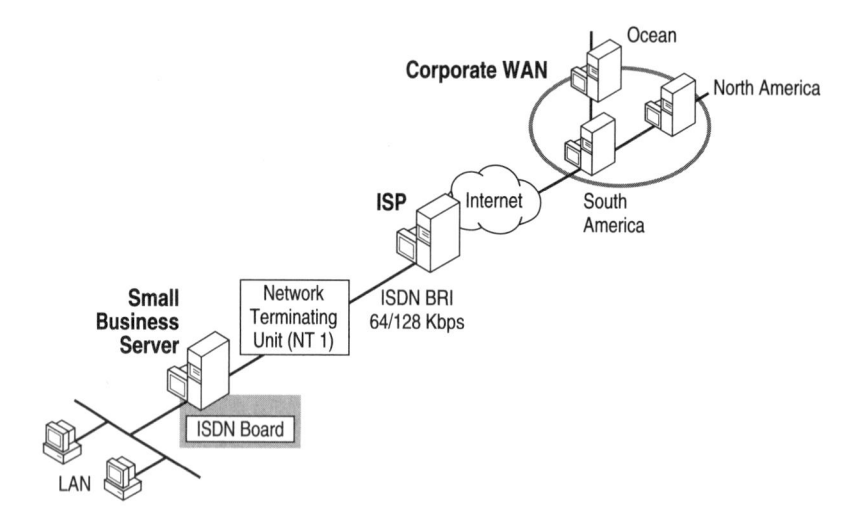

Figure 11.1 ISDN scenario

Basic Rate Interface

The BRI is the most common ISDN bandwidth available. It uses the telephone company's twisted-pair local loop and divides it into three channels. The first two channels, running at 64 Kbps, are the B channels carrying voice and data. The third channel, or the D channel, runs at 16 Kbps and carries signaling and low-speed packet data. BRI is sometimes called 2B+D.

Primary Rate Interface

The PRI is functionally similar to BRI except that 23 data B channels are provided and the D channel is upgraded to 64 Kbps (this varies by country). This is the functional equivalent of moving data at T1 speeds. In Europe, PRI has 30 B channels and one 64 Kbps D channel. These are also known as 23B+D and 30B+D, respectively.

ISDN Connections

ISDN BRI can connect Small Business Server using an NT1 (network terminating) unit. The NT1 box conditions the signal and is attached with an ISDN card inside your computer. ISDN BRI connects the small business LAN using an ISDN bridge. The ISDN bridge allows the computers that plug into it to use standard Ethernet cards.

ISDN PRI uses the same CSU/DSU equipment that a T1 dedicated digital line uses. Special PRI bridges and adapters are also available from a variety of manufacturers.

Web Site Development

Small Business Server 4.5 provides a web site staging area accessible from the **Publish on the Internet** page of the Small Business Server console. Here, a web site can be developed or edited using Microsoft FrontPage®, prior to posting it to the ISP. If the small business is planning for an ISP to host their web site, then the Small Business Server Web Publishing Wizard can be used to post the web pages to the ISP's web server.

When the web site is hosted by the ISP, an alternate means of notification to the small business is needed for responding to inquiry traffic on the site. In this scenario, the simplest solution may be to have the ISP (or an ISV) develop a script to automatically send an e-mail to the small business in response to web site inquiries. This solution is a minimum configuration that may work well for lower volume sites.

ISP Web Site Hosting Requirements

In order to take advantage of the features of Microsoft FrontPage and to use web posting, the ISP needs to support FrontPage extensions and File Transfer Protocol (FTP). The Small Business Server Web Publishing Wizard uses FTP when publishing web content for the small business. Therefore, an FTP address must be obtained from the ISP that corresponds to the location of the small business web content and a UserID/Password for that FTP location.

Small Business Web Site Hosting with IIS 4.0

The small business may host their own web site using the IIS 4.0 application in Small Business Server 4.5. Microsoft FrontPage may be used to develop and maintain the web site. When IIS is used to host the web site, access speed for customers browsing the web becomes an important consideration. The section that follows discusses several methods for estimating the bandwidth needed for quick access to the small business web site. This estimate will have an impact on the modem configuration required to support the determined bandwidth. Generally, a higher volume site requires more bandwidth and as a result, needs more modems (or a faster connection type like ISDN or T1) to handle the traffic.

IIS 4.0 Services

When designing an Internet site, a careful analysis should be made of the services planned. For example, if you plan to offer only Hypertext Transport Protocol (HTTP), then FTP services should not be installed on Small Business Server.

Note Gopher services, which uses FTP, should be shut off completely in order to minimize potential security breaches with an unused Internet service and to prevent wasting resources. An unused service uses CPU cycles, RAM, and other resources that could be better allocated to other processes running on the computer.

When hosting a web site, the use of inbound FTP may be necessary for the small business. FTP services are supplied with Small Business Server 4.5, but not installed by default. Proxy Server will also need to be configured to handle this protocol.

Internet Access Protocols and Services Available

The table below describes the features available with several basic Internet access protocols. Use this information to determine the type of site access that most benefits the small business organization with which you are working.

Table 11.3 IIS Service Features

Feature	HTTP	GOPHER	FTP
Download files	yes	yes	yes
Upload files	no	no	yes
Command line user interface	no	yes	yes
Menu user interface	yes	yes	no
Graphical user interface	yes	no	no
WAIS interface	yes	yes	no
Security available	yes	no	no
Unlimited possibilities for page design	yes	no	no
SQL or Microsoft Access database interface	yes	no	no
CGI interface	yes	no	no
Active Server Pages interface	yes	no	no

Web Site Development Resources for the Small Business

For more in-depth technical information and tools that assist in creating, testing, and deploying web pages, see the *Microsoft Internet Information Server Resource Kit,* available from Microsoft Press.

Estimating Bandwidth

When determining the type of connection for a web site hosted by the small business, make sure to estimate the current *and* future bandwidth of the site correctly. Bandwidth is determined by the number of bits transferred per second (bps). Bandwidth is commonly annotated in kilobytes per second (KBps) or megabytes per second (MBps). Sufficient bandwidth is required for quick access to resources on the small business web site.

One of the best sources for determining current and future bandwidth needs is to discuss the site with the ISP. Their experience is invaluable when estimating initial and future needs. Historical data from other web sites may also be used to estimate bandwidth. The number of bytes transferred is a commonly recorded statistic on web sites. Once the web site is up and running, the technology consultant can gather actual statistics on bytes transferred using the performance counters of Proxy Server. Refer to Proxy Server administration in *Part 4, Administering and Maintaining,* for setting up Proxy performance monitors.

Calculating Bandwidth Using Bytes Transferred

To estimate bandwidth needs, convert bytes to bits by multiplying the number of bytes by 12 (there are 8 bits per byte, plus 4 bits of overhead data). In order to have the proper specification, express the results in terms of seconds. So, if the data transfer statistic you obtained is specified as bytes per hour, multiply the number of hours by 3,600 (60 minutes per hour x 60 seconds per minute).

If a hypothetical web site transfers approximately 250,000,000 bytes in an average 12-hour period, the following formula may be used to calculate the type of connection required for a small business web site with a similar profile:

(Bytes x 12) / (Hours x 3,600 s/hr) = bits/sec

250,000,000 x (8 bits data + 4 bits overhead) / (12 hours x 60 minutes x 60 seconds)

–which is equivalent to–

3,000,000,000 bits / (43,200 seconds x 1,024 bits) = 67.8 Kbps

To accommodate the foregoing estimated use level, a web site would require at least two 56 Kbps leased lines or one ISDN connection.

Calculating Bandwidth Using Connections and Document Size

Another bandwidth calculation method allows you to use the estimated number of connections and the average size of documents transferred. Use the following formula to estimate bandwidth with this data:

(Average connections per day / Number of seconds per day) x (Average document size in kilobytes x (8 bits data + 4 bits overhead)

Substituting the following criteria –

86,400 seconds in one day

8 bits in a byte

4 bits overhead per byte of data

– yields –

(Avg. Daily Connections / 86,400) x (Avg. Document Size in KB x 12)

For example, if you predict that you will have 3,000 connections per day, and that your average file size is 85 KB, the equation would look like:

(3,000 / 86,400) x (85 x 1,024 x (8+4)) = 36.3 KBps

To maintain performance at or above an average bandwidth of 36.3 KBps, you would need to install at least one 56 KBps leased line. Note that bandwidth requirements can change monthly, weekly, daily, and even hourly. Use the above formula as a starting point and make adjustments according to the load on your server.

Advantages of an Intranet

The technology consultant proposal to the small business owner should discuss the advantages of having an intranet. Intranets are a convenient way to share information and data within an organization. An intranet is a network within an organization that uses Internet protocols and technologies for transfer of data. An intranet site requires the same software and hardware as an Internet site, with exception of connections to an ISP.

Extending the Default Intranet Page

From the Small Business Server console **Publish on the Internet** page, the default intranet page can be launched. This is the Small Business Server default intranet site, which may be extended to include any type of company information that may be useful to the small business organization. The default intranet site can also be launched from the Client User Guide, which appears whenever a Small Business Server client launches Microsoft Internet Explorer.

Extensions to the default intranet page may be rendered with FrontPage technology or by using an HTML editor. You can find an overview of intranet site development on the default intranet page.

Intranet Site

The relationship between a small business IIS-hosted intranet site and an ISP-hosted Internet site is shown in the following illustration.

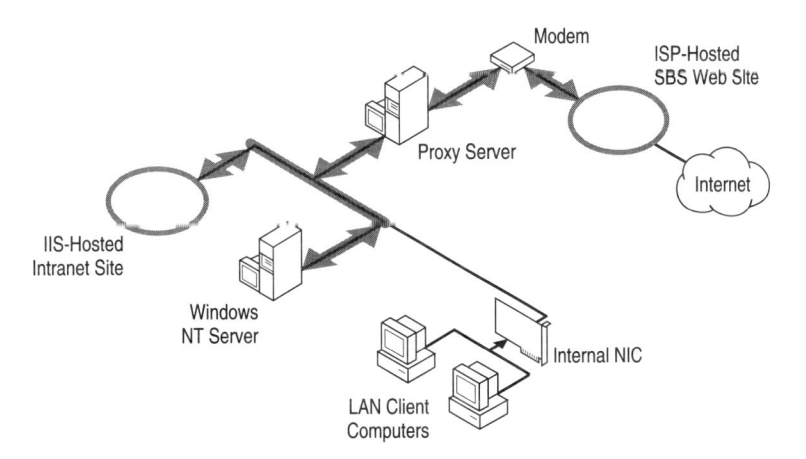

Figure 11.2 Intranet and Internet relationship

Intranet Security Precautions

The small business should always take security precautions when establishing an intranet site. The information that goes on the Internet server and what goes on the intranet server must be separated. Certain documents that may be legal to distribute on the intranet site may violate copyright, trademark, and export laws if they are placed on the Internet server. Care should also be exercised to protect the proprietary information of the organization. An organization should never place sensitive or proprietary research material on the Internet site instead of their intranet site.

Impact of Internet Connectivity on Server Computer Hardware

When using a personal computer as the Small Business Server, the type of CPU chosen and amount of RAM available can affect performance. For example, to facilitate CPU-intensive sessions involving HTML files, select a faster processor. The amount of RAM needed is affected by several factors, including the number of services run.

CPU Architecture

In laboratory conditions, an 80486DX/50 computer with 52 MB of RAM running Microsoft Windows NT® Server and IIS can handle over 100 simultaneous user sessions. The number of simultaneous users that may be accommodated varies according to the type of sessions that are open.

Small Business Server should be able to accommodate more site users when running sessions that are not CPU-intensive, such as e-mail, Telnet, and FTP. Sessions that are CPU-intensive include those running common gateway interface (CGI) scripts, making database queries, and downloading HTML files.

RAM Requirements May Vary

The requirements for small business server discussed in the "Server Computer Hardware Requirements" section of *Chapter 10, Planning a Small Business Server Network*, should suffice for the general small business application. However, the variables described in the list below affect the amount of RAM required, and depends on the level of Internet activity to be supported.

- Number of simultaneous users.
- Number of HTTP users versus Gopher and FTP users.
- Amount of RAM used for cache.
- Size of swap file.
- Free disk space.
- Amount of system RAM used for video.
- Networked IIS versus stand-alone IIS.
- Number of services running.
- CPU type.
- SQL database searches.

With respect to the above variables, a general guideline is to have about 256 KB of RAM for each simultaneous user.

Web Site Testing

Whether the web site is hosted by the small business or the ISP, the design should be tested before the site is published on the Internet. Check for the following:

- Security breaches.
- Proper permissions set on downloadable files.
- Functional links on all pages.
- Proper display of graphics and text at different resolutions and color depth.
- Proper operation of scripts.
- Correct function of gopher menus.

Also make sure that:

- FTP files can be downloaded and function properly.
- Different web browsers can access the web site and activate the site links.
- Simultaneous connections to the server are supported.

Internet Connection Process

Small Business Server 4.5 helps the technology consultant simplify the process of connecting the small business customer to the Internet by providing online referrals to ISPs, facilitating automatic sign-up scripts, and ISP configuration of the server. As soon as some basic information is supplied through the Small Business Server Internet Connection Wizard, the small business has e-mail and World Wide Web capabilities.

ISP Referral Program

Microsoft has set up a network of referral servers to make it easy for a small business customer to find an ISP. If a customer wants to open a new ISP account, the Small Business Server Internet Connection Wizard gathers the appropriate information. The country and area code information supplied by the customer is then used by Small Business Server to dial the nearest Microsoft referral server and download an .isp file. When the .isp file is downloaded, information about local ISPs that support Small Business Server is displayed in HTML format.

The small business customer can then browse the referral information and compare offers from the various ISPs. When **Sign Up** is selected, a connection to the ISP sign-up server is initiated and the automatic sign-up process begins.

Note Some ISPs on the referral server provide only service advertisements and do not support online signup.

The ISP Sign-up Script

The ISP's sign-up server runs a script that asks the small business customer for billing and connection information as well as their desired third-level domain name (a subdomain of the ISP). Once the user completes this information, the sign-up script automatically configures the ISP to set up everything the Small Business Server customer needs for their Internet connection. This includes an Internet access account and a virtual web server to host the customer's web site at the ISP—since the small business customer will probably use a dial-up connection.

The sign-up script also configures the ISP Domain Name Service (DNS) with the appropriate A and MX records so that DNS name resolution and mail routing work correctly for the customer. It also configures the ISP mail server to queue e-mail for the customer while the customer's Small Business Server is not online. Additionally, a password can be configured and shared between the ISP and the small business customer to ensure security during mail dequeing.

Automated Server Configuring for ISP Connectivity

All of the preceding configurations are done at the ISP. On the customer side, Small Business Server eliminates the need for the customer to undertake the complex process of manually configuring their server to communicate properly with the ISP. When the configuration at the ISP is complete, all the necessary information is downloaded to the customer in an .ins file.

The .ins file configures a RAS connection to access the ISP and configures the Exchange Server application in Small Business Server to request its mail from the mail server at the ISP. Everything is done automatically and the customer only has to wait for the sign-up process to complete. After the Internet connection is set up, the customer can browse the web and send mail over the Internet. However, it takes approximately 24 hours for the customer's new domain name to register, so mail should not be sent to the customer's new address during that time.

Offline Sign-up and Configuration

If an ISP does not wish to create an online sign-up process, they can still sign up a Small Business Server customer. In this case, the ISP must provide the small business customer with an .ins file on a diskette containing the configuration settings for the Small Business Server. When the customer double-clicks on the .ins file, the configuration program sets up the customer's Small Business Server to use that ISP. ISPs that do not provide online sign-up must have some method of generating the .ins file. The ISP also must ensure that the corresponding configuration has been done at its hosting site.

Connectivity Issues with Existing ISPs

Small Business Server includes the Internet Connection Wizard to assist the process of creating a Small Business Server account with an existing ISP. Although the Small Business Server Internet Connection Wizard automates most tasks and the setup procedures necessary to configure an Internet connection, the wizard cannot complete its tasks if any information from the existing ISP is incorrect or not available. This section addresses the resolution of connection issues and describes the information needed from the existing ISP, in order to help the technology consultant when planning against these diversities.

Small Business Server 4.5 and Existing ISP Services

If the new small business customer already has service with an ISP and wants to maintain it, the technology consultant must use the Internet Connection Wizard to setup Small Business Server to work with this account, as described in *Chapter 21, ISP Connectivity Tasks,* in *Part 3, Deployment,* of this resource guide.

The functions provided by the existing ISP and the types of accounts that can be serviced should be considered with respect to the needs of the small business organization and the configuration of Small Business Server. Critical requirements that must be addressed with the existing ISP are discussed in the next few paragraphs.

ISP Functions Required for Small Business Server Compliance

The primary functions an ISP should supply in order to support Small Business Server are listed below. These are required at a minimum to support current and future needs of the small business using Small Business Server 4.5.

- Electronic mail routing and queuing
- Internet access
- Web hosting

Types of Existing ISP Services

There are several types of ISP accounts and relationships that a small business may have. The existing ISP handling the Small Business Server customer may provide some or all of the functions indicated above. The information that follows describes the various types of ISP accounts available and the appropriate recommendations for Small Business Server connectivity in each case.

Full-time Internet Connection

The small business may have an existing full-time connection to the Internet through a modem or leased line. Most small businesses do not need a full-time connection to the Internet, although Small Business Server does make it possible for the small business to have a full-time Internet presence while maintaining a demand-dial Internet account only. This may be implemented if the ISP is able to host the customer's web site and receive and store their mail during offline periods. Small Business Server and ISPs work together to provide these services securely and reliably.

If the small business wishes to retain the full-time connection to their existing ISP, the technology consultant must make sure that the ISP fully supports the services planned for Small Business Server. Also, the technology consultant must be sure to configure Exchange Server, Proxy Server, and the web site information using the Internet Connection Wizard, as described in *Chapter 21, ISP Connectivity Tasks*, in *Part 3, Deployment*, of this resource guide.

Dial-up E-mail Accounts

Dial-up accounts from companies like America Online (AOL), Microsoft Network (MSN), and CompuServe are used in small businesses primarily to send and receive e-mail on an individual desktop basis. This does provide a way for a small business to use Internet e-mail, however, such accounts require everyone who wants an e-mail account to have a separate one. In contrast, Small Business Server provides a much richer and cost-effective solution. By using Exchange Server, the small business customer has a full mail solution for the entire company using a single ISP account and a single phone line.

For a small business that already uses dial-up accounts, an ISP that supports mail queuing, web hosting, and dial-up connectivity for Proxy Server should be enlisted. Then, the small business customer can set up their account with an eligible ISP through the Small Business Server Internet Connection Wizard or through another supported configuration process.

Note You can retain a small business's individual accounts if necessary (if already printed on business cards, etc), or you can slowly migrate e-mail being sent to those accounts over to the Small Business Server account.

Web Hosting Services

The small business customer may have an existing ISP who hosts their Internet web pages. While a small business does gain an Internet presence through this relationship, it may not achieve an integrated web posting solution nor receive Internet e-mail.

If a small business customer wishes to keep the existing ISP for web hosting and the ISP also supports web posting using FTP, then the Web Publishing service of Small Business Server can be configured to use the existing ISP, as described in the "Configure Website Information" section of *Chapter 21, ISP Connectivity Tasks*, in *Part 3, Deployment*, of this resource guide.

SMTP Dial-up Mail

Some ISPs support the dial-up connection of a Simple Mail Transfer Protocol (SMTP) server such as Exchange Server. If this is the case for the existing ISP, then the technology consultant must configure Exchange Server accordingly using the Internet Connection Wizard, as described in *Chapter 21, ISP Connectivity Tasks*, in *Part 3, Deployment*, of this resource guide. The technology consultant should be aware that the ISP must support ETRN in order for the small business to have a suitable mail dequeing method.

Dedicated Internet Connections

A dedicated Internet connection may use the following device types:

- ISDN router
- ISDN terminal adapter
- ADSL
- Cable Modem

If the small business customer has any of the above devices, or other dedicated WAN connection devices, the Small Business Server Internet Connection Wizard will be able to complete its tasks only if the routing device has been properly configured. Refer to the device manufacturer's documentation for configuration procedures.

Existing Small Business POP Accounts

If the small business has existing POP mail accounts and wants to retain them, the Exchange Server and Outlook clients can be manually configured to send and receive POP3 mail. Refer to the "Manual Configuration of Server Applications for Internet Connectivity" section of *Chapter 21, ISP Connectivity Tasks,* in *Part 3, Deployment,* of this resource guide.

Information Required from an Existing ISP

This section covers the information required from the small business customer's existing ISP for configuring a new Small Business Server Internet connection.

Connection Information

The following connection requirements are based on the assumption that a modem is being used to connect to the ISP. The configuration requirements of dedicated or high-bandwidth connections are described in "Internet Connection Types" earlier in this chapter. The following is needed from the ISP:

- A dial-in phone number for the modem connection.
- A User-ID and password to authenticate the small business connection.
- The Internet domain name (or IP address) for Small Business Server.
- Dial-up networking configuration information (optional).

DNS Configuration

To communicate on the Internet, the small business must obtain an Internet domain name from the ISP for Small Business Server. This name identifies the location of the small business network server and will also be part of the company's Internet e-mail address. The formats for these are as follows:

- user@InternetDomainName.xxx (e-mail)
- www.InternetDomainName.xxx (URL for a web site)

Internet Domain Name Levels

There are two levels of Internet domain names from which a company may choose:

- **Second-level**. A second-level Internet domain name contains the name by which the small business chooses to be known: @YourCompanyName.xxx
- **Third-level**. A third-level Internet domain name contains the ISP name in addition to the name by which the small business chooses to be known: @YourCompanyName.ISPcompany.xxx

E-mail Information

In addition to the DNS issues described next, the technology consultant will need to know the DNS name and IP address of the ISP's mail host. In some cases, the ISP may have separate hosts for inbound and outbound mail. To configure Exchange Server, the DNS name of both hosts is needed.

Domain Naming Service Configuration Issues

During the Internet connection process, some minor issues may arise regarding the registration of domain names for the small business organization. These particular issues are discussed in the paragraphs that follow so the technology consultant will be aware of them in advance of Small Business Server deployment.

Registering a Second-Level Domain Name

In order for the small business to register a second-level domain name, information for the ISP DNS must be gathered by the Small Business Server Internet Connection Wizard. This wizard executes all of the necessary commands to ensure that e-mail is delivered to the correct accounts and that web posting and hosting works correctly. The technology consultant should be aware that the small business ISP must support the creation and use of second-level domain names in order for the Small Business Server Internet Connection Wizard to complete these tasks.

Configuring Small Business Server to Use an Existing Second-Level Domain Name

A small business may already have the rights to a second-level domain name and may want to configure Small Business Server 4.5 to work with this domain name. To do this, the technology consultant must contact the ISP to change any third-level domain name entries to the second-level domain name. For more information, see *Chapter 21, ISP Connectivity Tasks*, in *Part 3, Deployment*, of this resource guide.

ISP DNS Tasks

For the ISP tasks required for configuring the ISP DNS, see *Part 3, Deployment*.

CHAPTER 12

Planning for Remote Access Users

There is a growing need for small businesses to provide remote users with access to their network. Providing employee access to small business network resources from distant locations is becoming a competitive necessity. A suitable remote access solution enables people to work as productively from home or while traveling, as they do while in the office.

Introduction to Windows NT Remote Access Service

Windows NT® Server 4.0, integrated in Microsoft® BackOffice® Small Business Server 4.5, includes a powerful set of services that deliver the easiest, most cost-effective way to implement remote network access. With Small Business Server, a small business can extend the reach of their office network to remote users through secure, high-performance access, either by dialing directly into the small business network server or by connecting across the Internet backbone with virtual private networking (VPN). Since Windows NT is an open, extensible platform based on industry standards, the Small Business Server customer has not only superior remote access flexibility but also a cost savings.

Remote Access Service Key Features

Access to the small business network from a remote location is enabled by using the Remote Access Service (RAS) feature of Windows NT 4.0 Server. This robust solution from client to server provides several key features as described in the paragraphs that follow.

Authentication

Windows NT Server provides a choice of secure authentication mechanisms for direct-dial and VPN connections based on industry standard CHAP, MS-CHAP—including the new MS-CHAP v 2—and PAP protocols. Authentication services include mutual client/server authentication to ensure that intruders cannot intercept passwords and information.

Secure Encryption

Windows NT Server also provides secure encryption for both direct-dial and VPN access via either 128-bit and 40-bit encryption keys. These services include random and changing encryption keys to protect sensitive data. Other important security enhancements are also available for remote access and VPN, such as digital certificates.

Scalability

Windows NT Server 4.0 remote access technologies provide high performance with room to grow. Windows NT Server provides up to 256 concurrent connections for direct-dial and VPN connections.

Multi-link

Windows NT Server 4.0 supports multi-link PPP. This is an industry-standard that allows the combination of multiple physical remote access links into a single logical link to accelerate data transfers and reduce communications and connect-time costs.

Compression

Windows NT Server 4.0 supports Microsoft Point-to-Point Compression for an accelerated remote user connectivity experience. This can double or quadruple data transfer throughput across a remote connection. Other enhancements available for VPN dramatically improve performance over difficult, high-loss network connections.

Superior Connectivity Options

Windows NT Server 4.0 enables remote access via any type of WAN connectivity —including dial-up PSTN, ISDN, wireless, leased line, frame relay, ISDN, ADSL, XDSL— and enables any type of LAN connectivity, including: Ethernet, FDDI, ATM, and Token Ring.

Broad Protocol Support

Windows NT Server 4.0 supports a wide variety of networking protocols including PPP, multi-link PPP, TCP/IP, IPX/SPX, NetBEUI, and PPTP. This enables the technology consultant to choose the options that provide their organizations the most flexibility and investment preservation.

Broad Client Support

Remote Access Service with Windows NT Server supports a broad variety of client operating systems, including Windows 98, Windows 95, Windows NT Workstation, Macintosh, and UNIX.

Open, Extensible Platform

Microsoft publishes a rich set of Application Programming Interfaces (APIs) for remote access and other operating system services. These APIs enable third-party organizations to build commercial or customized remote access and communications solutions in a variety of forms—all based on Windows NT Server.

Low Cost Hardware and Systems

By applying a PC-industry business model to communications and networking, small business customers are offered unparalleled choice and innovation. Open platforms drive volume, competition, and innovation, yielding lower prices for applications, hardware, and services while reducing risk of obsolescence.

Remote Access Service Management Features

Management features of RAS include:

- **Direct Dial and VPN—with the same client**. Windows NT Server 4.0 provides a consistent client experience for both VPN and direct-dial access to minimize user-training requirements and costs. The Dial-Up Networking client interface also provides a straightforward, end-user managed method of defining connections and phonebook entries on the client PC for direct dial and VPN connections. Microsoft Connection Manager allows the technology consultant to create customized or branded client dialers for remote end user ease-of-use.

- **Integrated management and administration**. Windows NT Server 4.0 allows the technology consultant to manage remote client connections as well as other network-to-network connections from a unified management environment. The technology consultant can use either an easy, intuitive graphical interface, or a scriptable command-line interface—both options enable local or remote management. The standard administrator interface reduces training and the expense required to manage networks.

- **Wizard-based setup**. Wizards for both client and server features make the process of setting up a remote access system fast and easy for the technology consultant and end users.

- **Connection Manager Administration Kit**. This feature enables a business or an ISP to preconfigure a customized Connection Manager client dialer to improve the user experience and reduce support expense.

    - **Central phonebook services**. Connection Point Services allows the technology consultant to manage one of the most expensive and troublesome aspects of supporting a group of remote access users: keeping users up-to-date with remote access dial-up phone numbers. With Windows NT Server, these centralized phonebooks store remote access dial-up numbers and update remote client PCs automatically.

- **Support for third-party tools**. NT Server 4.0 allows numerous third-party vendors to provide management, reporting, and accounting applications that integrate with the server's communications features. This is enabled by the server's APIs, support of Simple Network Management Protocol (SNMP), and other extensibility features.

Requirements for Implementing Remote Access Service

Basic remote dial-up and VPN server support is part of Windows NT Server 4.0; it can be set up and turned on immediately. Basic Dial-Up Networking also ships with each of the client Windows operating systems—Windows NT Workstation 4.0, Windows 98, and Windows 95. When planning RAS for the small business, the following table may be used as a reference for components needed for RAS:

Table 12.1 Remote Access Service Required Components

What you need	Where to get it
Remote Access Service (on the server computer)	Ships with Windows NT Server 4.0.
Windows NT Option Pack for Windows NT Server 4.0	Ships with Windows NT Server 4.0.
Dial-Up Networking (on the client computer)	Ships with Windows 98, Windows 95, and Windows NT 4.0.
Internet Connection Services for RAS including: Connection Manager, Connection Manager Administration Kit, and Connection Point Service	Part of the Windows NT 4.0 Option Pack included with Small Business Server 4.5 (but not installed by default). Also available via Web download for customers who have Small Business Server 4.0a.
Performance and Security Enhancements for remote access and VPN	Performance and Security Enhancements for Remote Access and VPN - available as a web download.

Remote Access to Small Business Server

Small Business Server may be accessed through a direct point-to-point connection with a standard dial-up modem link connecting to RAS across the Public Switched Telephone Network (PSTN), or by establishing a VPN on the Internet backbone using RAS and Point-to-Point Tunneling Protocol (PPTP). These two scenarios are shown in the following illustration.

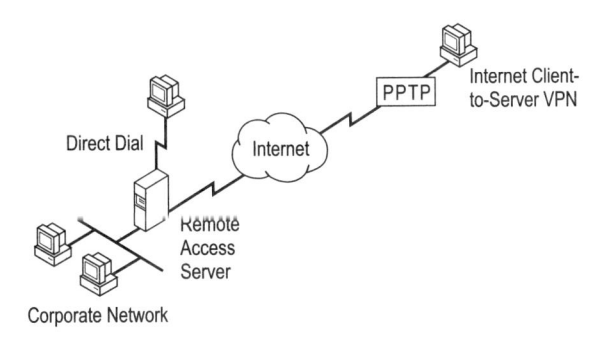

Figure 12.1 Remote access scenarios

PPTP for Secure Remote Access

When a remote client accesses Small Business Server across the Internet, protecting organizational information is an issue that must be addressed. When this is the case, PPTP should be used for the secure transfer of data between Small Business Server and the remote user. The paragraphs that follow provide some planning issues that should be considered before implementing PPTP. A brief description of PPTP and its features are included. For further information on installing and configuring PPTP, see *Chapter 23, Installing PPTP in the Small Business Network,* in *Part 3, Deployment,* of this resource guide.

Advantages of PPTP

One of the primary advantages of PPTP is that it eliminates the need for dedicated telecommunications equipment to support remote and mobile users who need to connect to the small business network. PPTP enables the secure use of public telecommunication networks while also reducing the costs of supporting remote access. By using PPTP, the necessity of owning and maintaining dedicated telecommunication equipment is eliminated.

Uses of PPTP

PPTP is a network protocol that enables the secure transfer of data from a remote client to a private server, by creating a VPN within a TCP/IP-based data network. PPTP supports multiple network protocols (IP, IPX, and NetBEUI) and can be used for virtual private networking over public and private networks.

PPTP can be used to provide secure, on-demand, virtual networks by using dial-up lines, LANs, WANs, or the Internet and other public, TCP/IP-based networks.

VPN Key Features

The key features of VPN provided with Small Business Server include:

- User authentication integrated with Windows NT security. This enables ease-of-use and simple management while also providing for security.
- Information and privacy secured through robust data encryption and key management.
- Productivity of the small business client ensured by easy-to-use features.
- Management across all services made easy through integrated administration.
- Economical and manageable network connectivity enabled by dynamic address assignment.

Small Business Server has secure 128-bit encryption, DHCP support, simple and customizable clients, directory integration, and remote administration. These features allow the small business organization to do the following:

- Leverage existing public infrastructure to reduce communication transmission costs.
- Outsource remote access to reduce capital expenditures for hardware and software.
- Reduce administrative and support costs through a familiar user interface and common management tools.
- Minimize investment risk via open systems and a programmable networking infrastructure.
- Take quick advantage of rich network applications advancements.

Note 128-bit encryption is available only in North America; all other locations use 40-bit encryption.

PPTP and Virtual Private Networks

A VPN can be defined as an on-demand connection between two computers in different locations. It consists of the two computers (one computer at each end of the connection) and a route, or *tunnel*, over a public or private network. To ensure privacy and secure communication, data transmitted between the two computers is encrypted by the remote access protocol known as Point-to Point Protocol (PPP). The data is then routed over a dial-up or LAN connection by a PPTP device. In Windows NT Server terminology, this device is referred to as a *virtual private network* or VPN.

PPTP uses the VPN device to establish and maintain private, secure communication between computers. PPTP utilizes RAS and Dial-Up Networking to communicate over dial-up lines or public and private networks.

When PPTP Is Used

For Small Business Server, the technology consultant can use PPTP to provide secure and encrypted communication when remote users are connecting to the small business network using Dial-Up Networking and an ISP connection to the Internet. Remote access through Dial-Up Networking connects the remote client to the ISP's PPTP-enabled network access server, sometimes referred to as a front end processor (FEP).

The illustration that follows shows a remote client with PPTP installed. The remote client dials up an ISP server configured as a *PPTP client* and establishes a PPP session. The remote client dials a second time, concurrent with the PPP session. The ISP server then accesses a PPTP tunnel that goes from the ISP, and over the Internet, to RAS on Small Business Server (configured as a *PPTP server*). PPP packets are then tunneled through the virtual connection and the client becomes a virtual node on the small business LAN, from across the Internet. Small Business Server handles all validation and can require that data be encrypted in both directions.

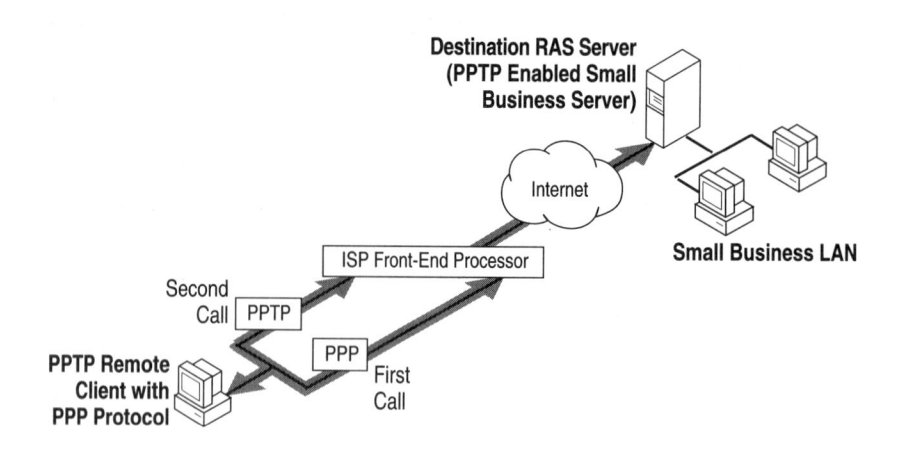

Figure 12.2 Remote access with PPTP tunneling

Network Protocols on the Small Business Network

PPTP enables the use of virtual private networking over public TCP/IP networks while retaining existing network protocols, network node addresses, and naming schemes on the small business network. No changes to existing network configurations and to network-based applications are required when using PPTP to tunnel across the Internet or other TCP/IP-based public networks. For example, IPX or NetBEUI clients can continue to run applications that require these protocols.

Also, name resolution methods—such as Windows Internet Naming Service (WINS) for NetBIOS computers, Domain Name System (DNS) for TCP/IP host names, and Service Advertisement Protocol (SAP) for IPX networking—do not need to be changed. In addition, IP addresses that are not valid on the Internet can be used on the private network.

Note that the address and name resolution schemes on the small business network must be correctly configured. If not, the PPTP remote client will not be able to communicate with computers on the small business network.

Hardware Requirements for a PPTP Client

The minimum hardware configuration for a PPTP client is dependent on the operating system. A PPTP client can be a computer configured with either of the following operating systems:

- Windows NT Workstation 4.0.
- Windows NT Server 4.0.

- Windows 98.
- Windows 95 with Dial-Up Networking, version 1.3.

The hardware requirements for computers running the above operating systems may be found in *Chapter 10, Planning a Small Business Server Network,* earlier in *Part 2.*

Note that an ISP network access server (NAS) can also be a PPTP client. In this case, the NAS hardware can be a PPTP-enabled server or router manufactured by a variety of companies, including the following members of the PPTP Forum:

- Ascend Communications.
- 3/Com/Primary Access.
- ECI Telematics.

Additional Connection Hardware

If the PPTP client is a remote or mobile user that connects to the small business PPTP server by using dial-up lines over the Internet, additional hardware is required. This includes an analog modem or ISDN device and a wall jack for telephone access.

Summary of PPTP Deployment Considerations

When planning the implementation of PPTP in the small business network, consider the following:

- PPTP uses the Microsoft implementation of RAS and PPP to establish connections with remote computers by using dial-up lines, Ethernet networks, or token ring networks. PPP provides remote-user authentication and data encryption between the PPTP client and the PPTP server. In order to use PPTP, RAS with Dial-Up Networking on both PPTP clients and PPTP servers must be installed and configured.
- Since PPTP requires RAS and PPP protocol, a PPP account with an ISP must be established in order to use PPTP over an ISP connection to the Internet.
- PPTP uses virtual devices called VPNs. When configuring PPTP, the technology consultant must install and configure VPNs in RAS, just as if they were physical devices like modems.
- PPTP is installed and configured on PPTP clients and PPTP servers only. Computers on the route between the PPTP client and PPTP server do not require PPTP installation.
- A PPTP server is placed behind a firewall on the small business network which ensure that traffic in and out of the private network is secured by the firewall (Proxy Server).

- To ensure network security, PPTP clients must be authenticated (just like any other remote user using RAS and Dial-Up Networking) in order to connect to the small business network.

- Using the Internet to establish a connection between a PPTP client and a PPTP server means that the PPTP server must have a valid, Internet-sanctioned IP address. However, the encapsulated IPX, NetBEUI, or TCP/IP packets sent between the PPTP client and the PPTP server can be addressed to computers on the small business network using private network addressing or naming schemes. The PPTP server disassembles the PPTP packet from the PPTP client and forwards the packet to the correct computer on the small business network.

Other Resources

For further information on PPTP, you can download several white papers from the Windows NT Server web site located at:
http://www.microsoft.com/ntserver/sitemap/default.asp

CHAPTER 13

Planning for Microsoft Fax and Modem Sharing Services

The information provided in this section on Microsoft® Fax Service and Modem Sharing Service is intended to help the technology consultant and small business owner decide how these services are best implemented in the small business network.

Pre-Deployment Considerations

Fax Service and Modem Sharing Service are installed automatically during Small Business Server setup. Before Small Business Server is installed, the technology consultant should determine the number and type of modems required based on the following small business needs:

- If users will need to dial out frequently, one or more modems using phone lines dedicated to dialing out can be used to ensure that outgoing calls do not block incoming data or fax calls.
- If users will be dialing in from home or the road and you will be receiving faxes, one or more modems dedicated to faxing and one or more modems dedicated to inbound RAS is suggested.
- If modem use is essential to productivity, the cost of extra modems and phone lines should be weighed against the following:
  1. With five to ten users using Fax Service, Remote Access Service (RAS), Exchange Server, and Proxy Server, installing more than one modem is strongly suggested.
  2. Microsoft Modem Sharing Service and Fax Service can each handle a maximum of four modems.
- When purchasing more than one modem for the modem pool, obtain modems of the same brand and model so they can be shared using Modem Sharing Service.

Also, we recommend purchasing external modems. External modems enable viewing modem status lights when troubleshooting a problem. In addition, external modems can be reset by external means, instead of having to shut down the entire Small Business Server network to reset an internal modem.

Modem Planning Considerations

Small Business Server installations require at least one modem detected during setup before modem-dependent server applications such as the following can be installed and/or configured. Also, Fax Service requires a Class 1 modem in order to install properly.

- RAS
- Modem Sharing Service
- Fax Service

A one or two modem configuration for Small Business Server can easily be overloaded by more than 10 users on a moderately busy day. If the small business will be using Fax Service, Dial-Up Networking (DUN), Exchange Server, and Proxy Server with 5 to 10 users on the network, installing more than one modem is strongly suggested.

Separate modems are needed if multiple services are to be facilitated efficiently. Otherwise, services may be disrupted if only one modem is available on the server and it is occupied with other tasks.

Multiple Usage Scenarios

By default, the three services above will share the use of all modems connected to the server. Fax Service can handle a maximum of four modems, Modem Sharing Service can handle up to four modems per modem pool with a maximum of 256 modems, and RAS can handle up to 256 modems. However, in order to support multiple usage scenarios with improved network access, we recommend that modems be dedicated to the specific services.

For example, if you have 4 modems/modem lines and the small business receives and sends a moderate number of faxes, has RAS needs, and is frequently connected to the Internet, a possible configuration is as follows:

- Modem Sharing Service is set up to use two non-fax modems for outbound DUN and ISP connections.
- A Class 1 fax modem is dedicated to faxing.
- One non-fax modem dedicated to inbound RAS.

The following diagram illustrates the configuration:

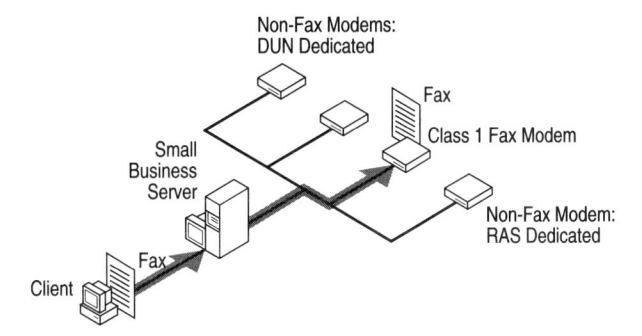

Figure 13.1 Typical Small Business Server modem configuration

Another option is to install a dedicated or leased line for outbound services and leave the dial-up modem(s) for inbound RAS.

Remote Access Service Modem Requirements

Remote users can gain access to Small Business Server using RAS. Remote access users can either dial directly into Small Business Server using DUN, or connect across the Internet with Virtual Private Networking (VPN). If the small business plans to support multiple dial-up connections for remote access users, the technology consultant should consider using a multiport serial device with Small Business Server.

Also, since most microcomputers have only two physical serial ports for supporting modems, and at least one of these ports is used for a mouse or UPS monitoring cable, this leaves only one port for an external modem. Adding a multiport serial card resolves this problem and provides an effective solution for remote access users. Microsoft Windows NT 4.0 currently supports only Digiboard multiport serial cards. For more information on Digiboard, consult their web site at:
http://www.digiboard.com

Fax Service Modem Requirements

If you are planning for intensive faxing, a dedicated business class fax modem is recommended. If you want to do inbound fax and inbound RAS on the same modem, the fax modem and driver must support adaptive answering. If adaptive answering is supported, the modem will be able to distinguish between fax and data calls.

Note The fax modem dedicated to faxing should not be assigned to the modem pool. That way, it will not be used for outbound dial-up networking.

Recommended Modems for Small Business Server 4.5

The Recommended Hardware List should be consulted for modems that work with Small Business Server 4.5. The list may be found on the web at: **http://www.microsoft.com/smallbusinessserver**

The list includes links to a manufacturer support page where you can download the latest drivers for the recommended modems. Modems that do not appear on the Recommended Hardware List may not be compatible with Small Business Server 4.5. Modems that appear on the list may need updated drivers in order to work correctly with Small Business Server.

Modem Communication Standards

Two standards for high-speed modem technology (rates of 33 Kbps or higher) exist today—x2 from companies like US Robotics/3Com Corporation, and K56Flex products from Motorola. The ISP must support the small business' modem technology in order to attain maximum access speed to the Internet. Modem technology used for RAS clients should also match this criteria.

Fax Service Planning Considerations

Small Business Server Fax services have been optimized and tested for up to 50 users. Fax Service is not available on a stand-alone basis and will not be incorporated into other Microsoft products. As with all Small Business Server products, it must be run on a single machine. The following should be considered when planning for Fax service:

- Fax Service allows network users to send and receive fax documents with any fax device capable of handling Group 3 fax calls.
- Network clients do not need a separate fax modem attached to their desktop, thereby reducing small business hardware costs and phone line usage.
- When a Small Business Server client setup disk is created for Windows 95/98 or NT Workstation client computers, Microsoft Fax client software can be conveniently included on the disk using the Set Up Computer Wizard.

CHAPTER 14

Planning for Proxy Server 2.0

Microsoft® BackOffice® Small Business Server 4.5 uses Proxy Server 2.0 to provide Internet connectivity and network security for the entire small business network. Also, Windows® 95/98 or Windows NT® Workstation remote users are protected by Proxy Server security features when they access the Internet through the Small Business Server network.

Small Business Network Security

For an office network with less than 50 clients, a single security policy that applies to all clients may be used. Proxy Server 2.0 provides maximum network security using the following features. With these features, the small business network is secure but also retains an appropriate amount of flexibility for Internet access.

- Password authentication.
- User permissions.
- Protocol definitions.
- Domain filtering.
- Cache filtering.
- Packet filtering.

Security and Internet Connectivity Modes

A full-time ISP connection or a direct connection to the Internet backbone may be used for Small Business Server 4.5, but this type of connectivity may increase security risks. Unless the small business plans to host its own web site with Internet Information Server 4.0, or requires instant access to Internet mail, a dial-on-demand connection is the best method for Internet access.

Proxy Server Configuration for Dial-up Internet Connectivity

With a dial-on demand connection to the Internet, the Auto Dial feature of Proxy Server must be used in order for dial-up connectivity to work. Auto Dial uses a RAS phonebook entry to provide demand-dialing to the Internet. Proxy Server must be configured as a Microsoft Windows NT operating system RAS client in order to implement Proxy Server Auto Dial.

Web Caching Minimizes Demand Dialing

In a typical small business office network configuration, caching should be enabled and configured to minimize the occurrence of demand-dialing to the Internet. This saves money for the small business, improves performance of the network, and also contributes to minimizing security risks. Caching can be used to store a local copy of the most frequented URLs in dedicated disk drive volumes.

A feature known as Active Caching may be used to automatically retrieve the most popular URLs without client initiation. This feature may cause Proxy Server to dial out randomly to update URLs. If continuous URL updating with Proxy dial-outs is too excessive for the small business, Active Caching can be disabled in the **Web Proxy Properties** dialog box, accessed from Internet Information Server portion of the Microsoft Management Console.

Other Planning Resources for Proxy Server

The online documentation supplied with Proxy Server 2.0 may be useful when planning Small Business Server deployment. It is accessible from the **Start** menu of Small Business Server 4.5. It may be used in conjunction with the configuration of Proxy Server described in *Part 4, Administering and Maintaining,* and in *Part 7, Security,* to assist in the development of a security presentation for the small business customer. In *Part 4*, several scenarios are presented to configure client Internet access permissions using Proxy Server features. *Part 7* describes the services and architecture of Proxy Server 2.0 in detail.

Note A default configuration for Proxy Server Internet connectivity is set up by the Internet Connection Wizard, as described in *Chapter 21, ISP Connectivity Tasks,* in *Part 3, Deployment,* of this resource guide.

Technical Details

All directory objects are uniquely identified by a distinguished name that has a series of components identifying the full name, organizational unit, organization, and country. Directory objects are arranged in a hierarchical structure known as the directory information tree (DIT). The distinguished names and the DIT are based upon conventions used in the X.500 specification.

Exchange Server directory naming scheme has three levels. The first two, organization [O] and organizational unit [OU], correspond to the organization and site names and have special meaning to the X.500 naming hierarchy. They also map to the PRMD and organization (O) X.400 address elements. All other directory objects, considered X.500 common named, are at the third level.

Distinguished Name Example

The Distinguished Name for admin mailbox in the organization "MyOrg" and site "MySite" is the following:

o=MyOrg/ou=MySite/cn=Recipients/cn=Admin

The distinguished name can be abbreviated by removing the labels from the naming components:

MyOrg/MySite/Recipients/Admin

Organization Name

All objects in an organization are required to have the same organization name. This name is unique and cannot be changed. In Small Business Server, the organizational name defaults to the domain name. The organization name is used to generate foreign e-mail addresses and the distinguished names of all directory objects such as mailboxes, public folders, and distribution lists. Since the domain name is visible outside the small business network, it should be chosen carefully.

The domain name is usually less than ten characters for practical reasons, but an organization name can contain up to 64 characters. Shorter names also better accommodate connectivity to legacy systems.

Site Name

The site name is based on the company name and may relate to geographical location (countries, regions, cities), physical location (buildings), or business units. Like the organization name, the site name must be unique, cannot be changed, and are used to generate foreign e-mail addresses and directory names. The site name should also follow the standard for domain names and contain less than 10 characters, although up to 64 characters are allowed.

CHAPTER 15

Planning for Exchange Server 5.5

Planning naming conventions for Microsoft® Exchange Server 5.5 before installing and configuring Small Business Server is important. Selection of meaningful and logical names make it easy to use and administer Exchange Server. Planning ahead for naming conventions usually minimizes rework due to changes that may be made later by the small business owner.

Naming Strategy

Each object in the Exchange Directory is uniquely identified by a name—the Distinguished Name. A good naming strategy is one that makes it easy to identify a site, server, gateway, connectors, users, and all of the other objects involved. The naming convention can be based on geography, company structure, building numbers, and so on.

Naming Standards and Concepts

A naming standard is created to provide consistency across the small business network. Once established, it provides a standard way for the technology consultant to name Exchange objects. A major requirement of naming standards is to provide useful information in the object names.

In some organizations, there may be existing naming standards. In that case, the Exchange naming standard needs to be developed in conjunction with existing standards. Also, interoperability with existing systems should be considered when developing naming standards.

Server Name

Exchange Server uses the Small Business Server computer name for the Exchange Server name. It is therefore important to plan Exchange Server names before installing Small Business Server. Server names are unique and cannot be changed without reinstalling Small Business Server. Spaces should be avoided. The server name should reflect the server's location and functionality. The name can contain up to 15 characters but cannot include any of the characters in the following table.

Table 15.1 Restricted Characters for Exchange Server Name

Restricted characters	Name
.	Bullet
¤	Currency sign
¦	Broken vertical bar
§	Section sign
¶	Paragraph sign

Mailbox Names

Mailbox names should be easy to identify. They could be based on existing standards for phone and address books. This also may be a good time to re-engineer the naming standards if the existing standards are too cryptic. Mailbox naming standards could be coordinated with the naming scheme used for Small Business Server or other types of existing user accounts. The fields described in the table that follows can be specified in a mailbox name.

Table 15.2 Fields in the Mailbox Name

Field	Guideline	Restrictions
First Name	The user's first name.	Up to 64 characters. Can be changed.
Last Name	The user's last name.	Up to 64 characters. Can be changed.
Alias Name	A short name to identify the user. The technology consultant can customize how the directory name is created through the Tools Option menu.	Up to 64 characters. Can be changed.

(continued)

Table 15.2 Fields in the Mailbox Name *(continued)*

Field	Guideline	Restrictions
Display Name	The mailbox name as you want it displayed in the Administrator window and in the Address Book.	Up to 256 characters. Can be changed.
Directory Name	The name Exchange Server uses to permanently identify an object in the directory. It is automatically created from the alias name.	Up to 64 characters. Must be unique. Cannot be changed.

Foreign E-mail Addresses

To communicate with foreign mail systems, Microsoft Exchange users must have an address in a format the foreign system can understand. Similarly, users in a foreign system must be represented in Exchange. A custom recipient is a user whose address is on a foreign mail system.

A foreign e-mail address or a proxy address is the address by which Microsoft Exchange Server recipients (mailboxes, distribution lists, public folders) are known to foreign mail systems. Based on the organization, site, and recipient names, Exchange automatically generates an MS Mail (PC), X.400, and SMTP address for each recipient. The E-mail Addresses property page can be used to create, modify, or remove foreign e-mail addresses. Gateways use the Alias Name field to generate foreign e-mail addresses. Different gateways will have different limits for the generated addresses.

X.400 Addresses

Exchange Server supports X.400 addressing which allows other X.400 messaging systems to communicate directly with it. The X.400 address identifies Exchange Server recipients in the global X.400 address space. When a user sends a message to an Exchange Server recipient, the users will typically select the recipient's name from the Address Book. This inherently supplies the directory distinguished name.

Alternatively, the originator can supply the X.400 address of the recipient by typing it directly. A valid X.400 address can contain any of the following hierarchically ordered attributes (the first three are required):

- Country (c).
- Administrative management domain or ADMD (a).
- Private management domain or PRMD (p).
- Organization (o).

- Organizational units (ou1, ou2, ou3, and ou4).
- Common name (cn).
- Generation qualifier (q).
- Initials (i).
- Surname (s).
- Given Name (g).

The following is an example of a valid X.400 address:

X.400:g=nitin;s=bhatia;o=MySite;p=MyOrg;a=mci;c=us

The characters in the following table are allowed in an X.400 address (X.400 O/R names). These characters are called "printable string type" according to X.208 recommendations.

Table 15.3 X.400 Address Allowable Characters

Character	Designation
A, B, ... , Z	Capital letters
a, b, ... , z	Small letters
0, 1, ... , 9	Digits
(space)	Space
'	Apostrophe
(	Left parenthesis
)	Right parenthesis
+	Plus sign
,	Comma
-	Hyphen
.	Full stop
/	Solidus
:	Colon
=	Equals sign
?	Question mark

SMTP Restrictions

When Exchange Server is connected to the Internet or other SMTP systems, the technology consultant should consider the character restrictions that SMTP imposes on its addressing scheme. You can use the following table as a template for planning the standards for your small business Exchange Server naming strategy.

Table 15.4 Exchange Server Naming Strategy

Object	Standard
Organization name	
Site name	
Server name	
Mailbox alias name	
Mailbox first name	
Mailbox last name	
Mailbox display name	
X.400 address	
SMTP address	
MS Mail address	
Connector names	
Monitor names	
Container names	
Distribution List names	
Public Folder names	
Custom Recipient name	

CHAPTER 16

Small Business Server Capacity Planning

This chapter provides a set of guidelines that may be used for capacity planning in the small business network. These guidelines impose different server hardware requirements relative to the number of users in the network, in order to assure optimum performance levels for Microsoft® BackOffice® Small Business Server 4.5. The guidelines were determined by comprehensive tests of Small Business Server 4.5.

The better part of this chapter discusses how performance of Small Business Server 4.5 was evaluated in order to provide background for the technology consultant on how the capacity guidelines were determined. An understanding of the tests and performance analysis will help the technology consultant make the correct hardware recommendations to the small business owner in support of the proposed network size.

This chapter concludes with hardware recommendations that optimize Small Business Server 4.5 performance with user-base sizes ranging from 10 to 50 users in the small business network. Tuning recommendations for server applications that resulted from the evaluation are provided in *Part 5, Performance Tuning and Optimization*. Information in this chapter is presented as follows:

- Small Business Server performance evaluation.
- Evaluation tests.
- Server and client test configurations.
- Performance monitoring, test results, and analysis.
- Network capacity guidelines and recommendations.

Small Business Server Performance Evaluation

A complete installation of Small Business Server 4.5 was tested running load simulation tools for Microsoft Exchange Server, Microsoft SQL Server™ 7.0, and file traffic on a Dell PowerEdge 1300 server. Small Business Server 4.5 was configured with a complete installation of Beta 2 software.

Performance was evaluated by measuring the response time to Exchange Server and SQL Server transactions and also by monitoring potential performance bottlenecks in the processor, memory, and disk. The load on the server simulated the following:

- 50 users constantly accessing a 300,000 customer SQL Server database.
- 50 heavy Exchange Server users.
- 3.5 MBps of constant file traffic.

Evaluation Summary

The results of the tests indicate that Small Business Server 4.5 is able to provide excellent performance to 50 users under simultaneous heavy SQL Server, Exchange Server, and file traffic loads. Using the minimum requirement of 64 MB of RAM, Small Business Server was still able to deliver sub-second response time for Exchange Server transactions while maintaining a heavy file traffic load. With a single Pentium II processor and 128 MB of RAM, SQL Server and Exchange Server both delivered sub-second response time without causing any significant bottlenecks in processor, memory, or disk utilization.

Evaluation Tests

The tests that were run to evaluate the performance of Small Business Server 4.5 are described in the sections that follow.

SQL Response Time Under Heavy Load

SQL Server 7.0 tests were generated using the TPC-C Benchmark. This benchmark replicates a full end-to-end system designed to simulate the transactional requirements of a wholesale supplier who is processing orders. The benchmark simulated company consisted of a number of geographically distributed sales districts that were serviced by associated warehouses. Each regional warehouse serviced 10 districts. Each district served 3000 customers. Each warehouse maintained stock for 100,000 items sold by the company.

Test Characteristics

A 10 warehouse database of approximately 2 GB was used for all tests in the SQL Server evaluation. The 10 warehouse database consisted of 300,000 customers and 1,000,000 stock items. The number of SQL users was restricted to 50 in accordance with the license requirements of Small Business Server 4.5.

The TPC-C benchmark is composed of five transactions, including New-Order, Payment, Order-Status, Delivery, and Stock-Level. A mix of these transactions was maintained during the test and the response time was measured for each type of transaction. Good test performance was considered to be subsecond response time for 90 percent of each transaction type.

Exchange Response Time Under Heavy Load

Exchange Server response times were tested using the LoadSim tool, a publicly available Microsoft load simulation tool. This tool is a multi-client emulator program that mimics the calls of Exchange Server MAPI clients. The load can be controlled to exercise particular elements of an Exchange Server information store such as mailboxes or public folders.

Test Characteristics

For the test, LoadSim was configured for 50 heavy Exchange users. Each user was configured to browse and post to public folders, and to log off Exchange Server once per day. Each user account was configured for the transactions specified in the following table.

Table 16.1 Exchange Load Simulation

Task or condition	Number of heavy user transactions
Send mail	6
Process Inbox	12
Browse mail	20
Schedule +	10

Also, each user mailbox was configured with 60 custom folders that contained 80 messages. This configuration generated a mailbox size of approximately 4,800 messages with a size of approximately 40 MB per mailbox. This yielded a total Exchange private message store size of 2 GB.

Response Time Calculation

LoadSim was run from a single workstation when generating loads for 50 users. LoadSim performance was recorded in a client workstation log file. The response time was calculated from the results in this file. As with the SQL evaluation, a subsecond response time for 90 percent of messages was considered good performance.

File I/O Throughput

File sharing activity was generated with a Ziff-Davis NetBench tool. NetBench measures the throughput rate for file I/O requests from a simulated Dos, Mac, Win16, or Win32 client. In the test, throughput was measured as the number of bytes per second that the server processed. NetBench was used as a load generation tool as well as the response evaluation tool.

Test Characteristics

NetBench was configured to use a 50 MB workspace of files while performing a mix of disk activities. The disk activities were random disk reads and writes, including sequential disk reads and writes. The Disk Mix suite was chosen because it simulates the actual file activity generated by Win32 applications, such as Microsoft Office. A constant file I/O load was generated while the server also performed SQL and Exchange transactions. Evaluation of disk activity was based on the total I/O throughput of the server and the percentage use of the disk subsystem.

Server and Client Test Configurations

The server hardware and software configurations employed for the tests are described in the sections that follow.

Server Hardware

The server hardware consisted of a Dell PowerEdge 1300 server configured according to the specifications in the following table.

Table 16.2 Server Test Configuration

Component	Configuration
Processor	Dual Intel Pentium II 450 MHz processors, restricted to single processor configuration.
Drives	Three 9 GB SCSI-3 disks, arranged into two software RAID arrays:
	OS partition: Disk 1 and 2 in 2GB RAID1 partition (disk mirroring)
	Data partition: Disk 0, 1, and 2 in 14 GB RAID5 partition (stripe set with parity)
Network	3com 3C509B-TX Fast EtherLink
Memory	512 MB 100 MHz SDRAM, restricted to 64, 128, or 256 MB.

The load simulation tests were run on the server using three different configurations: 64, 128, and 256 MB of RAM. Since processor utilization never approached a bottleneck in the single-processor configuration, a two-processor test was not run.

Server Software

A complete installation of Small Business Server 4.5 was installed on the server using the default configuration. Small Business Server applications were not tuned with exception of the following:

- The log file of the TPC-C database was configured to truncate log on checkpoint. This prevented the log file from overloading during the SQL test.
- The pagefile was expanded to 550 MB and left unchanged for all of the different memory configurations used in the tests.

The Small Business Server system files (including NT Server and the pagefile) were installed into the 2 GB mirrored C:\ partition. The 14 GB striped partition, D:\, was used for Exchange Server data and the SQL Server databases. Both RAID arrays were configured by using Windows NT Disk Administrator.

Client Configuration

The clients used in the test were Cyrix 233 MHz PCs with 3 GB hard disks and 128 MB of RAM. Each client was configured with Windows NT Workstation, Microsoft Service Pack 4, and Microsoft Office 2000. The network topology for this test was a shared 10 MB network, running TCP/IP. Although better network performance would have been realized by using a switched 100 MB network, a shared 10 MB hub is more representative of the typical small business environment. The test used three clients: one to generate the SQL requests, one to generate the Exchange requests, and one to generate the file traffic.

Performance Monitoring and Test Results

The first part of this section describes the tests run to monitor performance bottlenecks in critical hardware resources. The results follow.

Performance Bottlenecks

A bottleneck is the part of a system restricting workflow. Generally, it is over-consumption of a specific resource. Some causes of bottlenecks include:

- A slow disk controller or drive when accessing data.
- A processor running at a high percentage utilization.

- Too many active processes needing access to RAM.

In the evaluation tests, NT Server Performance Monitor was used to monitor several important performance counters. This was done to determine if the load placed on Small Business Server 4.5 was causing bottlenecks in any of the following critical hardware resources:.

- Memory.
- Processor.
- Disk Subsystem.

The sections that follow elaborate on performance monitoring of the above resources. A performance monitor chart displaying the counter statistics collected when monitoring these resources on Small Business Server 4.5 is provided immediately below along with calculations of the average performance values.

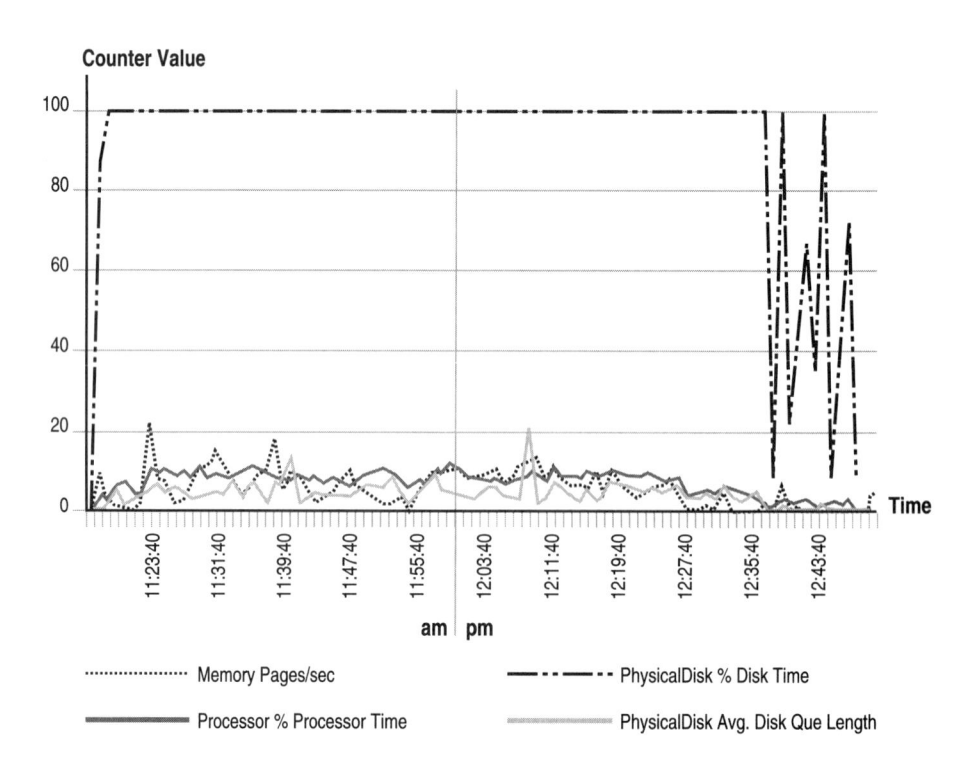

Figure 16.1 Performance monitor statistics for memory, processor, and disk counters.

Average values for the performance monitor counters in the illustration above are given in the table below.

Table 16.3 Performance monitor counter average values

Object:	Memory	Processor	Physical Disk	Physical Disk
Counter:	Pages/sec	% Processor Time	% Disk Time	Avg. Disk Queue Length
Average Values:	5.775	7.237	91.358	4.387

Memory

The best indicator of a memory bottleneck is a sustained, high rate of hard page faults. Hard page faults occur when the data a program needs is not found in its working set (the physical memory visible to the program) or elsewhere in physical memory and must therefore be retrieved from the disk. An acceptable range of pages per second is 0-20. The average pages per second during the test were 5.775, with a lower excursion value of 0.000 and 21.750 at the high end. Although this indicates fairly heavy use of the pagefile, memory usage was not a bottleneck.

Processor

Processor activity is especially important for server-based applications such as SQL and Exchange Server. Two of the most common causes of CPU bottlenecks are CPU-bound applications and excessive interrupts that are generated by inadequate disk or network subsystem components. Processor use in excess of 75 percent is considered a bottleneck. Processor time in this test averaged 7.237 percent.

Disk Subsystem

Just as processor usage is the primary bottleneck for server applications, the disk subsystem is often the primary bottleneck for file I/O performance. Disk performance counters include the percent of disk time and the disk queue length. In this test, the average percentage of disk time was high—about 100 percent when all load simulators were active—while the current disk queue length was also high at an average of 7.66 percent (higher than 2 percent is considered a bottleneck.).

Disk activity was dramatically reduced when the SQL Server and Exchange Server load simulators were turned off at the end of the test. Disk Bytes/Transfer and Disk Bytes/second counters were also recorded at high average values of 8,237 and 431,111 bytes respectively. These values indicate efficient use of the disk subsystem, despite the heavy load.

Although the heavy use of the disk subsystem did not cause unacceptable performance in either SQL Server, Exchange Server, or I/O performance, an upgrade to the disk subsystem should be considered for organizations with load needs approaching those used in this test. Recommended improvements include using a hardware RAID controller rather than software RAID, and moving the pagefile off of the system partition.

Response Time Test Results

Response times for both Exchange Server and SQL Server were under a second, per transaction, for 90 to 95 percent of users under heavy load. The data for a 128 MB RAM server with a single processor is provided in the following table. Test results for file I/O throughput is also included.

Table 16.4 Response Times and Throughput

SQL Server tests	Results
Average response time:	0.37 seconds per new order transaction
Transactions/min:	58.46 new order transactions per minute
Memory usage:	57 MB of RAM
90th percentile response time:	0.63 seconds per new order transaction
Exchange Server tests	
95th percentile response time:	0.936 seconds
Transactions/min:	122 transactions per minute
Database size:	2 GB
Memory usage (Store.exe):	13.5 MB (Store.exe only)
File I/O throughput (NetBench) test	
Average data throughput:	3.419 MBps
	448,074 bytes/second

Performance Analysis

The processes that used the most critical hardware resources is described in the sections that follow.

Memory

The most memory-intensive process by far is SQL Server 7.0. SQL Server consumes most all the available free memory since it is self tuning for optimum memory performance and consumption. In the 128 MB test, SQL Server used 57 MB of RAM, while in the 256 MB test, SQL Server used 112 MB. For this reason, the minimum memory configuration of 64 MB should only be used if there is little or no SQL activity. Otherwise, the recommended memory configuration of 128 MB should be used. In the 64 MB test, SQL Server was started but it was not receiving queries. In this test, SQL Server used 7.5 MB.

Processor

The two most processor intensive applications in Small Business Server 4.5 are Exchange Server and SQL Server. The test server used a single Pentium II 450 MHz processor and rarely spiked over 30 percent, even under extreme loads with 50 users. Therefore, the technology consultant should direct the small business owner's capital outlay for server hardware to more memory and a better disk subsystem (in that order), rather than to faster processors.

Disk

The disk subsystem was the heaviest hit server component in all three server performance tests. At 64, 128, and even 256 MB, the software RAID arrays were running at or near their maximum capacity. Despite this, the server continued to deliver good performance levels for SQL Server, Exchange Server, and file I/O. Several ways to improve the performance of the disk subsystem (if disk performance becomes an issue) are provided in the following recommendations.

Effect of RAM Changes on Performance

The evaluation tests involved the following three RAM configurations:

- 64 MB (minimum). Heavy Exchange Server load for 50 users and 3.5 MBps of file I/O.

- 128 MB (recommended). Heavy SQL Server load for 50 users; heavy Exchange Server load for 50 users and 3.5 MBps of file I/O.

- 256 MB. Heavy SQL Server load for 50 users; heavy Exchange Server load for 50 users and 3.5 Mb/sec of file I/O.

Since SQL Server consumes the most available RAM and was not being load tested in the 64 MB test, Small Business Server 4.5 delivered similar Exchange Server and file I/O performance in all three tests. SQL performance was better in the 256 MB test than the 128 MB test, but in both tests the SQL server delivered excellent response times per transaction.

Although the added memory had only a small impact on application performance, extra memory did have a notable effect on the disk subsystem. Increasing the system RAM to 128 MB and then to 256 MB greatly improved cache and pagefile performance, resulting in less physical disk use.

Network Capacity Guidelines

The sections that follow provide recommendations for disk space and server hardware that facilitates specific Small Business Server 4.5 network usage capacities.

Disk Space Consumption

The table that follows provides general capacity planning guidelines for disk space consumption under light and heavy usage scenarios. These numbers are a conservative estimate based on real-world usage of Small Business Server 4.5. They are not inflexible. When planning a Small Business Server installation, care should be given to address the specific needs of each small business organization in order to accurately determine the amount of storage required.

Table 16.5 Disk Space Consumption and Usage Scenarios

Resource	Light use	Heavy use
System files	1.5 GB	1.5 GB
Exchange mailboxes	30 MB/user	70 MB/user
SQL Server	300 MB	3 GB
File storage	250 MB + 25 MB/user	750 MB + 100 MB/user

Hardware Recommendations

The recommendations in the following tables specify the hardware needed to sustain optimum performance levels of Small Business Server 4.5 with user bases of 10, 25, and 50 users. The tables may be used as a basis of comparison and interpretation. For example, if the number of users in the network is between 25 and 50 but closer to 50 than 25, then the recommendations for 50 users should be followed.

Chapter 16 Small Business Server Capacity Planning

Table 16.6 Minimum Hardware Recommendations (10 Users)

Resource	Recommendations
Processor	Single Pentium II Processor, 350 MHz min.
Memory	64 MB minimum—128 MB if SQL Server is to be used.
Disk	Dual 9 GB SCSI hard drives in a RAID 1 (disk mirroring) software array—configured as a 2 GB OS partition and a 7 GB data partition.

Table 16.7 Mid-Range Hardware Recommendations (25 Users)

Resource	Recommendations
Processor	Single Pentium II Processor, 350 MHz min.
Memory	64 MB minimum—128 MB if SQL Server is to be used.
Disk	Three 9 GB SCSI hard drives in a RAID 5 (stripe set with parity) software array—configured as a 2 GB OS partition and a 16 GB data partition.

Table 16.8 Maximum Hardware Recommendations (50 Users)

Resource	Recommendations
Processor	Single Pentium II Processor, 450 MHz.
Memory	128 MB RAM Minimum—256 MB recommended.
Disk	Three minimum (four recommended) 9 GB SCSI hard drives in a RAID 5 (stripe set with parity) hardware array—configured as a 2 GB OS partition and a 16-25 GB data partition.
Array Controller	Single channel RAID controller in addition to SCSI controller for tape drive. Verify that the RAID controller is on the Small Business Server 4.5 Recommended Hardware List.

PART 3

Deployment

Installation of Microsoft® BackOffice® Small Business Server 4.5 is implemented through a fully integrated setup that silently installs all server applications, eliminating the need to install each application separately. The setup also automatically configures the applications, which minimizes user input and helps to ensure a successful installation. Part 3 contains installation procedures and supplemental information for customizing the deployment of Small Business Server within the small business organization. The following material is covered:

Chapter 17   Installing on New Machines   123
Chapter 18   Installing Small Business Server in Existing Environments   135
Chapter 19   Small Business Server Setup Issues   147
Chapter 20   Small Business Server Set Up Computer Wizard   155
Chapter 21   ISP Connectivity Tasks   159
Chapter 22   Setting up Remote Client Computers   213
Chapter 23   Installing PPTP in the Small Business Network   223
Chapter 24   Customizing Office 2000 Deployment   243

CHAPTER 17

Installing on New Machines

This chapter describes installation and deployment of Microsoft® BackOffice® Small Business Server 4.5 on a new server machine. The installation process consists of the following steps:

- Ensuring minimum server requirements are met and checking hardware against the Small Business Server Recommended Hardware List.
- Gathering floppies, CD's, and other required materials for installing Small Business Server 4.5 on a new machine.
- Performing the Small Business Server installation.

Server Requirements and Hardware Compatibility

Before deploying Small Business Server, verify computer requirements and hardware compatibility. Devices such as a network adapter, serial adapter, disk controller, and fax modems will only be detected by Small Business Server during setup if they appear on the Small Business Server Recommended Hardware List. Otherwise, you will need the drivers provided by your hardware manufacturer.

Computer Requirements

Requirements for Small Business Server and client computers are provided in *Chapter 10, Planning a Small Business Server Network* in *Part 2, Planning*, of this resource guide.

Hardware Compatibility

As a general guide, most hardware compatible with Windows NT® Server 4.0 will be compatible with Small Business Server 4.5. Hardware specifically tested for and integrated into Small Business Server is identified in the Recommended Hardware List. You will find this list in the support section of the Small Business Server Web site at:

http://www.microsoft.com/smallbusinessserver

The Recommended Hardware List may also be referenced for compatible SCSI controllers and multiport serial adapter cards that work with Small Business Server. For some devices identified in the Recommended Hardware List, drivers are available for downloading.

Network Adapter Cards

Small Business Server requires a network adapter card to configure the network. Cards that can be used with Small Business Server are identified on the Small Business Server Recommended Hardware List. Cards that are used with client computers must be identified as compatible with specific operating systems (such as the Windows® 95 or Windows NT Workstation Hardware Compatibility lists). Network adapter cards from the Recommended Hardware List are automatically detected during Small Business Server setup.

If your network adapter is not detected or not on the Recommended Hardware List, refer to *Chapter 19, Small Business Server Setup Issues,* of this resource guide.

Fax Modems

- To complete Small Business Server installation, you need at least one modem recognized during setup. For Fax Service to work properly, this modem should be a Class 1 fax modem. If you want to configure faxing and inbound RAS to use the same modem, the modem must support adaptive answering. Adaptive answering allows the modem to distinguish between data calls and faxes.

- For high-volume fax use (more than 100 faxes per day), a business class fax modem is strongly recommended. Business class modems are identified in the Recommended Hardware List on the Small Business Server web site.

- If your modem is not on the Recommended Hardware List, Small Business Server will prompt you to insert your modem driver.

Multiport Serial Adapter Boards

Multiport boards tested with the Small Business Server Modem Sharing Service are identified in the Recommended Hardware List on the Small Business Server web site.

Materials Required for Installation of Small Business Server 4.5 on a New Machine

Before beginning the installation process, obtain a pen and paper to record your settings for future reference. Items you will need to install Small Business Server 4.5 on a new machine are:

- Small Business Server 4.5 startup boot diskettes 1, 2, and 3.
- Small Business Server Discs 1, 2, and 3.
- Office 2000 Discs 1 and 2, or Outlook 2000 Disc 1.
- Blank diskettes (for emergency repair and client setup diskettes).
- Drivers for network adapters, mass storage devices, modems, and video adapters.

Performing the Small Business Server Installation

There are several steps to installing Small Business Server software on a new machine. The steps are performed in the following order:

- Creating setup boot diskettes.
- Windows NT Server 4.0 Text Mode—run in unattended mode.
- Windows NT Server 4.0 Graphical User Interface (GUI) mode—run in unattended mode.
- Small Business Server Setup Wizard installs server applications.
- The remaining items of setup are completed with the **To Do List**.

Setup Boot Diskettes

In order to install Small Business Server, you must use the setup boot diskettes provided. Using the diskettes avoids problems with Microsoft device detection during the Windows NT Server 4.0 portion of setup. If you do not have the setup boot diskettes, you can create them using Small Business Server Disc 1.

Creating Setup Boot Diskettes

The three setup boot diskettes may be created according to the following procedure:

▶ **To create setup boot diskettes**

1. Insert Disc 1 into the CD-ROM drive. Insert the first diskette into the floppy disk drive on the server.
2. Open a command window or prompt.
3. From here, you may need to change the drive letter for your CD-ROM drive.
4. Type **cd i386** next to the prompt and press the **ENTER** key.
5. Type **winnt32/ox** (or **winnt/ox**). Follow the prompts to insert floppy diskettes as files are copied. Number and label the disks.

Installing Small Business Server

After the setup boot diskettes are prepared, install Small Business Server beginning with the Windows NT Text Mode portion of setup, described in the next section.

Note If your modem is external, make sure that it is connected to the proper serial port on the back of the computer and turned on. This will allow the Setup program to detect the modem.

Stage One: Windows NT Server Text Mode

During the Windows NT Server Text Mode portion of setup, drivers are loaded and storage devices are detected in order to initialize and prepare the computer. Follow the steps below to complete the first stage of Windows NT Server installation.

▶ **To begin Small Business Server installation in the Windows NT Server Text Mode**

1. Insert setup boot diskette 1 into your floppy disk drive and start the machine.

   Setup starts a minimal version of Windows NT which runs an initial Windows NT setup program.

2. Insert boot diskettes 2 and 3 when prompted.

   Setup loads drivers and detects the mass storage devices, such as Small Computer System Interface (SCSI) controllers.

3. When prompted, enter the appropriate installation information for the license agreement, hard disk controller, and partitioning.

   Note If an International English version is being installed, you will be prompted to confirm the hardware that Setup has detected. At this time, the keyboard layout to use from this point forward can be changed. If the keyboard is a Cyrillic keyboard, do not change the layout now—this will prevent entering any information that must be in ASCII characters.

   The U.S. English version of Small Business Server will not display this screen and will assume the use of a U.S. keyboard layout.

4. Setup continues automatically and completes the following:
   - The necessary files are copied.
   - The computer is restarted.
   - The disk partition is configured with NTFS.
   - The computer is restarted.

   Note Setup will allow you to create a FAT partition instead of NTFS, but you will be prompted later by Small Business Server to convert the partition to NTFS. For more information on setting up your partitions, refer to the *Small Business Server Getting Started* Guide.

Stage Two: Windows NT Server GUI Mode

After the Windows NT Server Text Mode portion of setup is complete, the Windows NT Server GUI mode installs the Windows NT Server component. Most of the configuration settings required by the setup program reside in a setup information file named Winnt.sif, and are retrieved by Setup, as needed. After computer restart in stage one, follow the steps below to complete the second stage of Windows NT Server installation.

▶ **To continue Small Business Server installation in the Windows NT Server GUI Mode**

1. When prompted, enter the following information:

   Name. The licensee name is required to define the name of the person to whom Small Business Server is licensed.

   Organization. Setup uses the first 13 characters in the company name to generate the computer and domain names. If you want to change the company or domain name, change this required information at this point of the installation.

   Caution Do not change the computer or domain name after Small Business Server is installed. Changing the name causes problems because the server applications will not recognize the new names.

   ---

2. Setup automatically performs the following tasks. Enter any required information when prompted.

   - Detects the network adapter card.

   Depending on which network adapter you use, Setup does one of the following:

   - Automatically detects and configures network adapters listed in the Small Business Server Hardware Compatibility List (HCL), and many of the adapters listed on the Windows NT HCL.
   - Detects but does not always configure network adapters listed in the Windows NT HCL, depending on the model of the network adapter. If Setup cannot configure the adapter, Setup prompts you to confirm the hardware settings for the network adapter. Small Business Server includes the drivers for these network adapters.
   - Detects and configures the modem(s).

   Setup must detect a modem before it can install the modem-dependent server applications, which include RAS, Fax Service, Modem Sharing Service, and the Small Business Server Internet Connection Wizard. If a modem is not detected, Setup will install the "Undetected Modem" driver.

   Note The "Undetected Modem" driver used by Small Business Server Setup is the same as the "Standard Modem" driver used by Windows NT.

   - Installs the Windows NT networking components.

To install RAS, Setup must detect a network adapter. If Setup did not detect a network adapter, Setup installs the MS Loopback Adapter so that installation can continue. The MS Loopback Adapter is a software component that simulates a network adapter driver.

If the MS Loopback Adapter is installed, you must add a network adapter, remove the MS Loopback Adapter, and then configure Transmission Control Protocol/Internet Protocol (TCP/IP) after the installation is complete so the server can communicate on the network.

- Completes the Windows NT Server installation.

Setup restarts the computer after the installation is complete.

Stage Three: Installing Small Business Server Applications

After the Windows NT Server GUI Mode portion of Setup is complete, the Small Business Server Setup Wizard starts automatically to gather organizational information and to install server applications, additional Small Business Server files, and installation files for the client applications. Follow the steps below to complete Setup with the Small Business Server Setup Wizard.

▶ **To continue installation with the Small Business Server Setup Wizard**

1. The Small Business Server Setup Wizard automatically performs the following:
   - Validates computer hardware, including modems and network adapters.
   - Prompts you to verify the hardware settings.

   If the Setup Wizard has not detected the hardware correctly, you can re-configure the modems, network adapter, or other hardware at this time. After you verify your hardware settings, the Setup Wizard applies Service Pack 4 and restarts the computer, and the installation continues.

   Important To ensure a successful installation, verify that all hardware has been detected and configured correctly by the Small Business Server Setup Wizard. If the hardware is not configured correctly and you continue the installation, the Small Business Server components may not install correctly or may not function properly after the installation.

2. Enter the following when prompted:
   - Registration information
   - Address information
   - CD-Key for Microsoft Outlook 2000 or Microsoft Office 2000
   - Administrator account password

3. When prompted, choose a complete or custom installation.

   Click **Complete Installation** and the wizard installs all the Small Business Server applications. Click **Custom Installation** and the wizard prompts you to select which applications to install. You can customize your Small Business Server network to suit your business needs by installing the following optional components:
   - Microsoft SQL Server™ 7.0
   - Fax Service
   - Modem Sharing Service
   - Client Applications 4.5
   - Microsoft Exchange Server 5.5 with Service Pack 2.0

4. Enter the following information when prompted:
   - Dialing properties for the Fax Service
   - Your telephone area code—required to define dialing properties
   - Your business fax number—required to configure the Fax Service application, when installed (If a fax number is not supplied, you can install the Fax Service after you install Small Business Server.)
   - SQL Server configuration settings

   Note For information on the SQL Server configuration settings, see the *Small Business Server Getting Started* guide.

5. Change the default location of components and data folders, if necessary:
   - Change the default directory for specific components using the **Change Folder** button.
   - Change the default location of the server applications' data folders by typing the appropriate path.

6. The Setup Wizard automatically installs the server applications.
   - After installing Microsoft Internet Explorer 5.0, Setup restarts the server computer and then continues installing the administration files and the installation files for client applications.
   - Setup re-applies Service Pack 4. Windows NT requires the service pack to be re-applied after you install any new components.
   - After the Small Business Server Setup Wizard completes the installation, it prompts for computer restart.

7. The computer restarts and automatically logs on to the server using the Administrator account.

   The computer then displays the Small Business Server console's **To Do List**.

Completing Setup Using the To Do List

Small Business Server installation and configuration is automatic with exception of a few items that require user input in the **To Do List**. This screen provides a clear, concise list of tasks the user can perform before using the server. All these items may be accessed later via the Small Business Server console. You can also return to the **To Do List** from the console at any time.

▶ **To add a network printer to the server**

1. Connect the printer to the server computer's parallel port.

   Note If the parallel cable is missing, pick one up from a computer store. The end with the pins fits into a port on the back of the server computer and the end with the oddly formed centerpiece fits into a slot on the printer. Make sure that the printer is plugged in and the power is turned on before proceeding.

2. From the **To Do List**, click **Add A Printer**.

3. The **Add Printer Wizard** screen appears. Select **My Computer** and then click **Next** to continue.

4. A list of available ports appears. Select **LPT1** unless it is being used by another device. If it is, select another port.

   If you want to use printer pooling, click **Enable Printer Pooling**. This configuration maximizes the use of print devices while minimizing the time users must wait for documents to print.

   Click **Next** to continue.

5. A list of manufacturers and printer models appears. Select the manufacturer and model that corresponds with your printer, and then click **Next**.

6. A message appears asking for your printer name and whether it will be used as the default printer. Enter the printer name using up to 31 characters. Choose the **Yes** button, unless there is a reason to pick otherwise. Click **Next** to proceed.

7. The next screen that appears is for printer sharing on the network. Select the **Shared** button to indicate that the printer will be used by others on the network and give it a share name.

   The share name should be short and precise. For example, if you have an HP Laser Jet IV, you may want to call it HPJ I4, or simply LJ4. If Windows 3.x clients or MS-DOS based clients will be accessing the printer, you must use a share name of eight characters or fewer.

8. Select the operating systems to be used by the printer from the list of available operating systems. Click **Next** to continue.

   Note Windows NT Workstation 4.0 does not appear on the list because it makes use of the driver automatically installed on the Small Business Server computer.

9. After the printer is installed, a message appears asking you to print a test page. Click **Yes**.

   Note A prompt may appear to insert the Windows NT Server CD-ROM. If this occurs, place Small Business Server Disc 1 in the drive and click **OK**.

   If the auto-run feature brings up a splash screen, click the **X** button in the upper right hand-corner. If you are prompted for the Windows 95 compact disc, insert the Small Business Server Disc 2.

10. If prompted for the Windows 95 compact disc, the paths to several file types may have to be entered manually since the installation process may not locate these files on the CD automatically. If the system specifies that it cannot find a file of type INF, specify the path **D:\MS\WIN95\INF**; for file type DRV, specify **D:\MS\WIN95\SYSTEM**; for file type ICM, specify **D:\MS\WIN95\SYSTEM\COLOR**. The actual drive letter of your CD-ROM may substitute for **D:**. If any other file types are not found, perform the following steps:

    - Cancel Setup and exit the **To Do List**. Click **Start**, point to **Find**, and then click **Files or Folders**.
    - Enter the three-letter file extension in the **Named** text box. For example, if the file type needed is ICM, search for "*.ICM".
    - Enter the drive letter of your CD-ROM followed by a colon and backslash (for example, D:\) in the **Look in** text box or click **Browse** to search for the desired drive.
    - Click **Find Now**. Scroll down the list of found files. If you see the file you need, record the file path.
    - To retry the printer setup, click **Start** and then **Manage Server**. The Manage Small Business Server window appears. Click **Manage Printers** and then **Add a New Printer** to restart the installation procedure. Proceed according to instructions and enter the new file information from the **Find** window when you are prompted for the file path.

11. If all required files are found by the installation procedure, the test page should print successfully. A message appears asking for confirmation that the test page printed successfully. Click **Yes** or **No**. If the test page didn't print, follow the troubleshooting instructions in the screens that follow.

Chapter 17 Installing on New Machines

▶ **To add a new user to the server**

Small Business Server automatically creates an Administrator's account from the information entered during setup. However, a personal user account must be created from the **To Do List**.

- From the **To Do List**, click **Add a New User** and follow the instructions of the wizard.

▶ **To import users to the server**

This feature allows you to transfer user accounts to the Small Business Server installation. Before running **Import Users**, however, you must first run the **Migrate User Wizard** from the Small Business Server installation CD auto-run screen.

- After running the **Migrate User Wizard**, from the **To Do List**, click **Import Users** and follow the instructions of the wizard.

▶ **To sign up with an ISP**

Many of the services offered by Small Business Server rely on a connection to the Internet. As a result, it is important to set up an account with an Internet service provider (ISP).

- From the **To Do List**, click **Connect to an ISP** and follow the Internet Connection Wizard instructions. Additional information on ISP connectivity is provided in *Chapter 21, ISP Connectivity Tasks* later in *Part 3*.

▶ **To add client licenses**

This feature allows you to increase the number of Small Business Server client licenses. In the basic configuration you just installed, you have 5 client licenses. This means you can have 5 client computers connected to Small Business Server. To increase the number of client licenses, follow the step below.

- From the **To Do List**, click **Add Client Licenses** and follow the instructions of the wizard.

▶ **To configure Fax Service to receive faxes**

By default during installation, Fax Service is configured to send faxes on each installed fax device. The **Configure Fax Service** feature allows you to configure the Fax Service to receive faxes.

- From the **To Do List**, click **Configure Fax Service** and follow the instructions of the wizard.

CHAPTER 18

Installing Small Business Server in Existing Environments

Microsoft® BackOffice® Small Business Server 4.5 is installed on a new machine according to the procedures in *Chapter 17, Installing on New Machines*. However, it may also be deployed in other environments, as described in the following material of this chapter:

- Existing Windows NT® 4.0 environments.
- A Windows® 95/98 machine.
- Installation over a 16-bit operating system.
- Integration with a NetWare environment.

Installing Small Business Server on an Existing NT 4.0 Server

Small Business Server will not recognize and upgrade an existing installation of Microsoft Windows NT Server 4.0. If installation of Small Business Server is attempted onto a drive where Windows NT Server 4.0 is already present, it results in two separate Windows NT server installations.

Replacing Existing Windows NT 4.0 and Migrating Users

Small Business Server can be installed on a computer with an existing Windows NT 4.0 Server present, however, it is recommended that Small Business Server be installed on a different partition. Microsoft recommends you back up all existing Windows NT Server files and then install Small Business Server.

Since it is not possible to share system information between the two installations, it is necessary to migrate user accounts and/or mailboxes over from Windows NT, install Small Business Server on a separate partition, then perform migration using the Migrate User Wizard—before the existing Windows NT environment is abandoned.

Migrate User Wizard

Small Business Server 4.0 was created based on the assumption it would be installed in a new environment, without an existing network. Later it was found that a large number of small businesses already had Windows NT Servers, and in some cases, were even using Exchange Servers.

Thus for Small Business Server 4.5, a migration tool was developed to help migrate user accounts and mailboxes from an existing NT/Exchange installation to a Small Business Server installation. This tool is the Migrate User Wizard.

Migrate User Wizard Modes

The Migrate User Wizard has two modes—Export and Import. From the Small Business Server Autorun (installation) screen, the wizard is launched in the Export mode. The technology consultant may use this mode to export existing NT user accounts and Exchange mailboxes. A text file for user accounts is created for use in the Import phase.

The Migrate User Wizard is launched in the Import mode from the **To Do List** on the Small Business Server console. In this mode, the user account file created earlier during the Export mode is used to create the NT user accounts and Exchange mailboxes for Small Business Server.

For more information on using the Migrate User Wizard, refer to *Part 8, Migration And Upgrade*, and *Part 4, Administering and Maintaining*, of this resource guide. Also, users will be able to run the Migrate User Wizard in either mode from the associated Help topics in the Online Guide.

Migrating Data

When installing Small Business Server on a computer with a Windows NT Server 4.0 acting as Primary Domain Controller, you should migrate the data, then delete the NT 4.0 installation. Only if the Windows NT Server 4.0 is a member server, can it coexist with Small Business Server 4.5.

Installing Small Business Server on a Windows 95 Machine

Windows 95 and Small Business Server can coexist on the same computer, but they must be on different disk partitions. If Small Business Server is installed to the same partition that contains Windows 95, the partition will be reformatted as an NTFS partition and Windows 95 will not be accessible.

Installing Small Business Server on a Windows 98 Machine

Windows 98 and Small Business Server can coexist on the same computer, but they must be on different disk partitions. Small Business Server does not recognize disk partitions formatted by Windows 98. During installation, these partitions will be displayed as an "Unrecognized Partition". If Small Business Server is to be installed on a FAT32 partition, the partition must be deleted and re-created. Deleting the partition will also delete Windows 98.

Installing Small Business Server over a 16-Bit Operating System

Similar to Windows 95/98, DOS and Windows 3.x operating systems will only run using the FAT file system. Consequently, they are inoperable after Small Business Server is installed. If you want to preserve these installations, install Small Business Server on a different partition.

Important Microsoft recommends you always back up important files or information and then install Small Business Server.

Integrating Small Business Server with a NetWare Network

The following key components allow Small Business Server to perform seamlessly with Novell NetWare operating system.

NWLink Protocol

The first component providing NetWare interoperability with Small Business Server is NWLink protocol. NWLink is the default protocol supported by Novell NetWare. It is required by Windows NT for compatibility with NetWare IPX/SPX protocol. Although NWLink by itself does not provide a high degree of connectivity to NetWare servers, it is the core component that allows a Windows NT-based computer to communicate with a NetWare client or server. NWLink protocol must be installed in Small Business Server in order to create a means of communicating with the tools that enable interoperation with NetWare.

▶ **To install the NWLink Protocol**

1. On the Small Business Server computer, press **CTRL+ALT+DEL** (hold down all three keys) and examine the string "You are logged on as DOMAINNAME\username". Make sure the user name is the same as the name of the individual who installed Small Business Server. If it is, click **Cancel**. If is not, log off the machine and log on with the installer's user name (with administrative privileges).

2. Click **Start**, point to **Settings**, and then click **Control Panel**. Double-click **Network**. Select the **Protocols** tab, and then click **Add**.

3. From the list that appears, select **NWLink IPX/SPX Compatible Transport**. Click **OK**.

4. Click **Have Disk**.

5. If a prompt appears to insert the NWLink installation files, insert Small Business Server Disc 1 into the CD-ROM drive and click **OK**.

6. After the system is finished copying files, click **OK** then click **Yes** to restart the computer.

Gateway Service for NetWare (GSNW)

Gateway Service for NetWare (GSNW) allows the Windows NT Server to function as a NetWare client. Once GSNW is installed using the **Network** applet of **Control Panel**—in addition to the Microsoft servers which appear in the Windows Explorer's Network Neighborhood browse list—any NetWare Servers configured for the same frame type as the Windows NT Servers appear in their list. GSNW is required in order for the NetWare-to-Windows NT Server Conversion Utility to function.

A Gateway to NetWare Resources

A second feature of GSNW is the Windows NT Server to NetWare gateway, which provides Small Business Server network clients with access to NetWare resources. The connection to NetWare resources is transparent to the client. It appears that they are seamlessly connected to a standard Microsoft server resource.

One of the practical uses of GSNW for the small business organization is the ability to allow Small Business Server and connected client computers to access file and print resources on a NetWare server.

For example, a Small Business Server can connect to a NetWare file server's directory using GSNW, just as if the directory were on the Small Business Server itself. Small Business Server network clients can then access the directory on the NetWare server by connecting to the share created on the Small Business Server.

Note GSNW is not intended to function as a full-service router for NetWare services. It is designed more specifically for occasional access to NetWare servers, or to serve as a migration path. Network performance will degrade if it is used for unlimited server access, since all clients are receiving services through the one connection.

Providing a Preferred NetWare Server

During installation, you will be asked to identify a preferred NetWare Server. This is the default NetWare Server a user will logon to from the Windows NT Server. If Windows NT Server is unable to find the selected "preferred" server, two things should be checked:

- Verify that the Novell server is physically on the network and that it is currently running. This server must be version 2.x, 3.x, or 4.x, and must be running in bindery emulation mode.
- Verify that there is not an unmatched frame type between the Windows NT Server and the Novell Server. Information is provided in Step 8 of the next procedure on how to check this.

GSNW Installation Issues

GSNW is a powerful utility for accessing NetWare file and print resources from any Small Business Server client. If you plan on converting all the desktops in the office to Windows 95-based Small Business Server clients, GSNW should be installed so these clients can access the NetWare resources without having to install anything on their machines.

Before installing GSNW, create duplicate administrator names on both the Windows NT Server domain and the NetWare server. You may either:

- Add an "Administrator" account to the NetWare server and give it the same rights as the NetWare "Supervisor" account.
- Add a "Supervisor" account to the Windows NT Server domain and make it a member of the Administrators group and the Domain Admins group.

To do this, use the **add a user** taskpad on the Small Business Server **Manage Users** page, but do not use the Set Up Computer Wizard when the option to proceed with it is presented.

▶ **To install GSNW**

1. Click **Start**, point to **Settings**, and then click **Control Panel**.
2. Double-click **Network**.
3. Select the **Services** tab, and then click **Add**.
4. From the list that appears, select **Gateway (and Client) Services for NetWare**, and then click **OK**.
5. If a prompt appears for a new location of the distribution files, check the path shown and make sure it is correct. If it is not, and you are prompted to insert a disc containing the installation files, insert Small Business Server Disc 1 into the CD-ROM drive, and then click **OK**.
6. Once the system is finished copying files, click **OK** on the Network panel, and then click **Yes** to restart the computer.
7. Log on again with the account that set up Small Business Server. You will be asked to select a **Preferred Server for NetWare** from a list that appears of all known Novell network servers.

Note As a NetWare client, when you log on to this system your account will be validated automatically by the Windows NT Server domain and will also be authenticated by the preferred NetWare server you select.

8. If the preferred server name was not found, check the frame type on the Small Business Server by the following:

   - From the **Control Panel**, click **Network**, select the **Protocols** tab, and then double-click **NWLink IPX/SPX Compatible Transport**.

   Note If the frame type is set to manual, examine it and compare it to the frame type on the NetWare server. To do this, on the NetWare server, type "load monitor" from the system prompt and check the "LAN Information" (or similar option on a version other than 3.x). The frame types should be listed here as 802.2 or 802.3.

   - If the settings between the NetWare server and Small Business Server do not match, select **Auto Frame Type Detection,** click **Apply**, and then click **OK**.
   - Restart the computer. If the NetWare sever name is still not found, go back into the NWLink properties and set the frame type to match exactly what appears on the NetWare Server. Click **Apply**, click **OK**, and then restart the computer.
   - At this point, if the connection is still not found, check the network cables on both machines and make sure the hub indicator lights are showing active connections to the cables from each of the machines.

▶ **To verify that Gateway Service for NetWare has been installed**

1. Click **Start**, point to **Settings**, and then click **Control Panel**. A new **GSNW** icon appears.
2. Start **GSNW** and make sure a dialog box appears to change the preferred server and print options.

Note If you do not need to install the gateway feature of GSNW, skip the steps below and continue with installation of file and print services for NetWare (FPNW) discussed later in this chapter. Be sure the account with which you are logged on to Windows NT Server has administrative rights and is also a NetWare account. Make any necessary changes using the taskpads on the Small Business Server console's **Manage Users** page.

▶ **To create a NetWare Gateway User Account**

The FSNW Services uses the NetWare Gateway User Account to connect to the NetWare server. To create one of these accounts, use one of the existing NetWare clients on the network and run the **NWAdmin** utility from the public directory on the **sys** volume as follows:

1. Go to **User Information** on the NetWare server and press ENTER.
2. Press **Insert** to create a new user.
3. Enter a user name for the gateway account and press ENTER (a good name choice might be "gatewayuser"). Press ENTER again to accept the default home directory path.
4. Click **Yes** to verify creation of new directory and press ENTER. ESC returns you to the main menu.
5. Create a group called "NTGATEWAY". From **NWAdmin**, select **Group Information** and then press ENTER. Type the group name and then press ENTER.
6. Make the user name of the new Gateway User Account a member of the NTGATEWAY group.
7. From **NWAdmin**, to Select User Information and choose the user name you created. Press ENTER.
8. In the new menu that appears, select **Groups Belonged To** and then press ENTER.
9. Press INSERT, highlight the **NTGATEWAY** group in the **Groups Not Belonged To** menu, and then press ENTER. Exit **NWAdmin**.

▶ **To configure the Small Business Server portion of GSNW**

1. Click **GSNW** in **Control Panel**, and then click **Gateway**.
2. Select **Enable Gateway** and type the Gateway User Account and password in the appropriate text boxes. Retype the password in the **Confirm Password** box.
3. Click **Add** to add a Small Business Server shared folder to the NetWare volume. To do this, specify a name for the share, the network path to the NetWare volume to be mapped, and a drive letter.

> **Note** The network path must be specified in a syntax known as the Uniform Naming Convention (UNC). For this syntax, the computer name and the directory name are specified in the format *computername**directoryname*. For example, to map a drive letter to the sys volume of a NetWare server called "netware", type *netware**sys* for the UNC name.

4. Click **OK** on all the open windows when finished to save your changes and exit **GSNW**.

▶ **To test the functionality of the GSNW installation**

1. On the Small Business Server desktop, double-click **Network Neighborhood**, then the Small Business Server computer name.
2. Select the share just created and then click **Map Network Drive** on the **File** menu.
3. Select a drive letter from the drop-down box and then click **OK**.
4. Click **Start**, point to **Programs**, and then click **Command Prompt**. At the prompt, type the following (press ENTER after each line and for N, substitute the selected drive letter):

   ```
   N:
   cd\public
   NWAdmin
   ```

5. Make sure NWAdmin is open on the NetWare server. This verifies successful installation of GSNW.
6. Press ESC to quit NWAdmin.

▶ **To check access to NetWare resources from the Small Business Server client**

1. From the client desktop, open **Network Neighborhood** and select the name of the Small Business Server computer.
2. Inside the new window, double-click the name of the share you created in **GSNW**. Open one of the folders until a list of files appears.
3. Try copying a file to the desktop by clicking it and dragging it to the desktop. If this is successful, the gateway feature of GSNW is functioning.

File and Print Services for NetWare

File and Print Services for NetWare (FPNW) is a separate, add-on product for Windows NT Server. It is provided on the Services for NetWare (add-on) CD for Microsoft Windows NT Server 4.0.

The FPNW component allows the Windows NT Server to act as a NetWare server for all NetWare clients currently in the small business office. With FPNW in place, the same Windows NT Server running Small Business Server appears in the client's File Manager or Explorer list of NetWare or NetWare-compatible servers.

FPNW is a very valuable component of Small Business Server deployment. It offers a high degree of interoperability with an existing NetWare network and allows full utilization of Small Business Server features, both with a minimum amount of changes to existing networked computers.

Client Capabilities With FPNW

A NetWare client can do the following with FPNW installed:

- Map to a shared volume and directory on an FPNW-enabled Windows NT Server as if it were a NetWare server.
- Connect to a printer on the Windows NT Server.
- Logon to the Windows NT Server and have configured system and personal logon scripts execute.
- Use Small Business Server applications services.

▶ **To Install FPNW**

1. Click **Start**, point to **Settings**, and then click **Control Panel**.
2. Double-click **Network**, select **Have Disk**, select the **Services** tab, and then click **Add**. A new dialog box appears.
3. In the **Insert Disk** dialog box, type the path to the FPNW installation files and then click **OK**.

   Note The path to the FPNW files (for Intel processors) should be D:\FPNW\NT40\i386 (substitute the drive letter of your CD-ROM for D:). If the files are not here, browse the CD manually. Select **File and Print Services for NetWare** and click **OK**.

4. Once the files are copied, specify the Windows NT Server directory to be used as the **SYS** volume. The default is C:\SYSVOL.

   Note The server may be given a new name to identify it on the NetWare network. The default name is the Small Business Server computer name followed by an underscore and FPNW. This name can be changed.

   Important In many cases, the NetWare server should be renamed—for example, (OLD_NW312)—and the previous NetWare server name assigned to your Windows NT Server configured with FPNW. This allows existing clients to run untouched.

5. Supply and confirm the password for the new Windows NT Server Supervisor account.

6. In the Tuning section, select one of the following:
   - **Minimize Memory Usage** if the system is primarily used for applications.
   - **Balance Between Memory Usage and Performance** if the server is both an applications server and a file and print server.
   - **Maximize Performance** to provide the best file and print sharing performance. This option will use additional system memory.

   Click **OK**.

7. A special Windows NT Server account called FPNW Service Account is created for running the FPNW services. Supply and confirm a password for the account. Click **OK**. Click **OK** on the **Network Settings** dialog box and restart the computer.

8. Log on to the system as the user name that created the Small Business Server. Click **Start**, point to **Settings**, and then click **Control Panel**, and observe a new **FPNW** icon.

> **Note** A successful installation of FPNW will also create an FPNW menu in the File Manager (run "winfile" from **Run** under the **Start** menu). This allows the management of NetWare partitions. By browsing C:\winnt.sbs\system32 with Windows NT Explorer, you can locate a help icon with the file name "fpnw". This icon is a book with a question mark. When opened, it provides Help for using FPNW.

9. The set up for Windows NT Server in a NetWare environment is complete.

> **Note** If you wish to proceed on with a complete migration from NetWare, refer to *Part 8, Migration and Upgrade*, in this resource guide, to replace the functionality of the NetWare servers.

CHAPTER 19

Small Business Server Setup Issues

Microsoft® BackOffice® Small Business Server 4.5 was designed to be easy to install. However, this ease disguises the complexity of Small Business Server setup. In order to provide a full range of services while also providing simplicity to the small business customer, the different applications and components that comprise Small Business Server must work together in ways that are transparent to the user. As a result, during setup, several issues may arise concerning hardware compatibility, detection, or reconfiguration. These issues, which are listed below, are discussed in this chapter.

- Network adapter detection.
- Modem detection issues.
- Compatible modem installation and RAS reconfiguration.

Hardware Detection Problems

Because Small Business Server supports many common hardware components, setup issues can arise concerning hardware compatibility, detection, and configuration of these components. The most common setup issues occur during the detection and configuration of network adapters and modems.

Before installing Small Business Server, consult the Recommended Hardware List (RHL) on the Small Business Server web site and verify that the hardware components you are using appear there. For further information on hardware detection issues, see the Small Business Server 4.5 Release Notes located on Small Business Server Disc 1. If hardware problems arise during setup, consult the information that follows.

Note A history of Small Business Server Setup events can be viewed in your Small Business Server log file in the ProgramFiles\Microsoft BackOffice directory—a log file is only generated if an error occurs. Log files can be sent to the technology consultant or referenced for further information during a product support call. You can also check the Systemdrive:\Temp directory for error logs.

Network Adapter Card Not Detected

Depending on the model of the network adapter, Windows NT Server Setup may not detect the network adapter correctly. During the hardware detection process, Setup does one of the following:

- Detects the network adapter correctly and continues installing Small Business Server.

- Does not detect the network adapter.

    If Setup does not detect a network adapter, but detects a modem, Setup will install the MS Loopback Adapter, which will enable the remaining network components to install correctly.

    Setup adds the MS Loopback Adapter during the Remote Access Service (RAS) installation. A modem must be installed or the RAS installation will not allow the MS Loopback Adapter to be installed.

    You can remove the MS Loopback Adapter and install and configure the correct network adapter by clicking **Change** on the Small Business Server Setup Wizard **Hardware Confirmation** page.

    If Windows NT Server Setup does not detect a network adapter and a modem, you must configure your network adapter, TCP/IP, and RAS settings before continuing to install the Small Business Server applications. You can configure these settings from the Small Business Server Setup Wizard's **Installed Modems** and **Hardware Confirmation** pages.

- Detects the network adapter incorrectly.

    If Setup detects the network adapter incorrectly, you must remove the incorrect network adapter and install and configure the correct network adapter. You can configure these settings from the Small Business Server Setup Wizard's **Hardware Confirmation** page.

Removing the MS Loopback Adapter

Small Business Server cannot communicate on the network until you install a compatible network adapter and remove the MS Loopback Adapter. To add the correct network adapter and remove the MS Loopback Adapter, follow the steps below.

Note Add the correct adapter *before* removing the MS Loopback Adapter. If you mistakenly close the **Network** utility before adding the correct network adapter, you will lose the configuration settings for the TCP/IP protocol and for all network services.

▶ **To add a Network Card and remove the Microsoft Loopback Adapter**

1. From the Small Business Server Setup Wizard's **Hardware Confirmation** screen, click **Change**, and then double-click **Network** to display the **Network** utility.

2. Select the **Adapters** tab, click **MS Loopback Adapter**, and then click **Remove**.

   A message appears asking you to confirm your actions. Click **OK**.

3. Click **Add**, and then click **Have Disk**.

4. Insert the disk containing the network adapter driver into the Small Business Server floppy drive.

5. Click **OK** and then select the adapter type from the drop-down list. Acknowledge any vendor-specific messages that appear.

6. Select the **Bindings** tab, and then open the tree view so you can see the network adapter listed under each binding type. Move your network adapter to the top of each list.

7. Click **Close** and the **TCP/IP Properties** page is displayed.

8. Select the **IP Address** tab, and then select **Specify an IP address** and type the following:

   10.0.0.2 - for IP address
   255.255.255.0 - for Subnet Mask

9. On the **WINS Address** tab, type *10.0.0.2* for both the **Primary WINS Server** and **Secondary WINS Server**.

10. Click **OK** and then click **Yes** to restart your computer.

After the Small Business Server computer restarts, Setup automatically continues with installation.

Installing Two Identical Network Adapters

If your server has two identical network adapters that were automatically detected and configured during Windows NT Server Setup, only one should be configured to use the IP address of 10.0.0.2. The second network adapter must use a different IP address. If the second network adapter is to be used as a full-time Internet connection, the ISP will provide you with the IP address to assign to it.

It is advised to delete the configuration for the second network adapter using the steps that follow, complete the installation, and then configure the second network adapter.

▶ **To remove the configuration for the second network adapter**

1. From the Small Business Server Setup Wizard's **Hardware Confirmation** screen, click **Change** and then double-click **Network** to display the **Network** utility.
2. Select the **Adapters** tab, and then select the network adapter you want to remove.
3. Click **Remove**.

    A message appears asking to confirm your action. Click **OK**.
4. Click **Yes** to restart your computer.

    Your Small Business Server computer will restart and you can continue installation.

Modem Not Detected

If an external modem is connected to the Small Business Server computer, make sure it is plugged in, turned on, and connected to the correct COM port before you run Small Business Server setup. If you do not have a modem installed, the following services will not be installed:

- RAS
- Microsoft Modem Sharing Service
- Microsoft Fax Service

If your modem is not correctly detected and installed during the NT portion of Setup, Setup will display an error on the **Installed Modems** screen. The following sections outline the error conditions and how to resolve them.

Undetected Modem

During the Windows NT portion of Small Business Server 4.5 setup, Small Business Server queries the modem to retrieve the Unimodem ID that is generated based upon the modem firmware. Small Business Server then attempts to match the Unimodem ID returned from the modem to the Unimodem ID in the modem driver files (.inf) included with Windows NT. If a matching Unimodem ID is not found, the modem is flagged as an **Undetected Modem**.

Once the Windows NT portion of Small Business Server 4.5 setup is complete, the **Installed Modems** screen is displayed. This screen lists the modems that were detected and installed during the Windows NT portion of setup—it also allows the technology consultant to change any of the modems. This ensures the modem is installed correctly before proceeding to install the modem-dependent server applications.

If setup was unable to detect the modem type and model during the Windows NT portion of Setup, the modem is identified as an undetected modem and a red **X** is displayed beside the modem in the list.

It is highly likely that you will receive the undetected modem error indication when running setup. If you receive the above error, it is important that you remove the undetected modem and install the modem manually, using the steps that follow.

Note Failure to install the correct driver for the modem will result in the Fax Service not installing. In addition, you may not be able to utilize all the features your modem supports.

▶ **To remove the undetected modem and install the modem manually**

1. From Setup's **Installed Modems** screen, click **Change**. A screen appears reminding you to reconfigure RAS.
2. Click **OK** to display the **Modem Properties** dialog box.
3. From the **Modem** list, select **Undetected Modem**, click **Remove**, and then click **Yes**.
4. Click **Add** to display the **Install a New Modem** dialog box.
5. Select **Don't detect my modem; I will select it from a list**. Click **Next** to display the list of modem models and manufacturers.
6. In the **Install a New Modem** dialog box, select **Have Disk** and enter the path to the modem driver for your selected modem type. Click **OK**.
7. Select your modem type from the displayed list, then click **Next**.
8. Select the COM port on which you want to install the modem, then click **Next**.

9. A message appears stating that you will need to restart the system before you can use the modem. Click **OK**.

10. Click **Finish** and then click **Close** to exit the **Modems Properties** page.

   A message appears stating that the Dial-Up Networking needs to be configured. In the RAS configuration, you must remove the communications port (COM port) used by the undetected or incorrect modem, and add the newly installed modem to the service. Click **Yes** to display the **Remote Access Setup** dialog box and follow the steps below.

▶ **To configure Remote Access Service to use the correct COM port and modem**

1. In the **Remote Access Setup** dialog box, select **Undetected Modem**, and then click **Remove**.

2. The **Remove Port COM1?** confirmation message appears. Click **Yes** and then click **Add** to display the **Modem** list.

3. Select the correct modem from the list, click **OK**, and then click **Continue**.

4. The following message appears: **You must shut down and restart your computer before the new settings will take effect. Do you want to restart your computer now?** Click **Yes**.

5. When the computer restarts, continue Small Business Server installation.

Setup Unable to Verify Modem Installed Correctly

If the technology consultant removes the undetected modem and installs the driver that came with the modem, it is still possible the driver's Unimodem ID and the one returned by the modem do not match. If this is the case, then after the technology consultant updates the modem and restarts the computer, the **Installed Modems** screen is displayed again, and the modem is flagged with a yellow warning icon indicating that Setup was unable to verify the modem. If the technology consultant continues with the installation at this point, it is highly likely there will be no problems with the Fax Service or other modem-dependent services.

Even if the Unimodem ID does not match and verification of the modem fails, the modem may still work properly since the modem vendor has most likely tested and verified the old driver with the new firmware. Many modem vendors change their firmware every few months, however, they may not update drivers to reflect the new Unimodem ID, thus causing Small Business Server modem verification to fail. This situation is further complicated when the driver name and modem name remain the same. For example, you could have a Courier V.Everything driver installed for a Courier V.Everything modem, and still not have a match between the updated driver's Unimodem ID and the one on the modem.

Installing the Modem Driver From the Manufacturer

There is the possibility you will receive the yellow warning icon after installing the modem manually. If you selected your modem from the list of available modems in the **Modem Properties** dialog box during manual modem installation where you did not use the **Have Disk** option, the wrong modem driver could have been installed. To correct this, reinstall the modem by following the steps outlined in the previous "Undetected Modem" section and use the modem driver provided by the modem manufacturer.

If you installed the modem using the modem driver provided by the manufacturer, you probably have the correct driver. To verify, visit the modem manufacturer's web site to see if an updated driver is available.

Checking Detected Modem Information

To check the modem information detected by Setup, on the **Installed Modems** screen, select the modem and click **Properties**. The **Modem Properties** screen appears listing the modem information.

Avoiding Modem Detection Issues

To avoid modem problems with Small Business Server, you should ensure that you are installing a modem with a modem information (.inf) file that:

- Matches the modem type and model.
- Is compatible with the modem firmware.
- Is listed on the Small Business Server Recommended Hardware List.

CHAPTER 20

Small Business Server Set Up Computer Wizard

Small Business Server includes the Set Up Computer Wizard to enable the technology consultant to easily accomplish the following tasks.

- Configure the server for the client.
- Configure the client's networking.
- Install applications on the client.

This chapter discusses the background processes of the Set Up Computer Wizard in accomplishing these tasks. For details on extending the Set Up Computer Wizard, refer to *Chapter 44, Extension Mechanism for the Set Up Computer Wizard*, in *Part 9, Developing Small Business Server Solutions*, of this resource guide. Also, *Part 10, Tools and Utilities* includes a description of the Small Business Server Client Setup Integration Wizard—this is a tool that automates the extension of the Set Up Computer Wizard's application list.

Running the Set Up Computer Wizard

To set up client computers and the necessary server configuration for the client, the technology consultant uses the **set up a computer** task on the Small Business Server console's **Manage Computers** page to launch the Set Up Computer Wizard. The wizard walks you through the steps of gathering all the necessary user information to accomplish its tasks, in one set of dialogs. Small Business Server automatically configures everything from here, except for the selection of a network card on Windows 95/98 clients.

Configuring the Server for the Client

The Set Up Computer Wizard creates and configures all the necessary files and settings to process client logons and install client applications.

Logon Script

Each time this wizard runs, it creates a logon script for the specified user. If a logon script already exists for that user, the wizard overwrites it with a new one. Any modifications made to an existing Set Up Computer Wizard logon script are not preserved when the wizard recreates the logon script.

The template file used to create a user logon script is called Template.bat and is located in %SystemDrive%\SmallBusiness\Template.

Every time the Set Up Computer Wizard runs, it also attempts to create the following folder: %SystemRoot%\System32\Repl\Import\Scripts\SmallBusiness. If the folder already exists, the wizard simply continues.

Response Folder and Client Application Configuration Files

Each time the Set Up Computer Wizard runs, it creates a set of client application configuration files and places them in a folder under %SystemDrive%\SmallBusiness\Clients\Response. The new folder is named according to the client computer name. The Set Up Computer Wizard always tries to create the Response folder under %SystemDrive%\SmallBusiness\Clients. If the client application configuration files already exist, the Set Up Computer Wizard overwrites them without preserving any modifications made to the existing set.

Scw.ini

The Set Up Computer Wizard uses scw.ini to determine which applications to display in the applications list for each operating system type.

.Inf Files

The Set Up Computer Wizard copies the files from the Template directory to the Response directory for each new computer. The files are modified to reflect the applications and user specified for that computer. The .inf files indicate whether applications should be installed and include the command lines to install them.

Machine Account

Every time the Set Up Computer Wizard runs, it creates a Windows NT® Server machine account for the client if one does not already exist. Setup does not distinguish between Window 95/98 clients and NT Workstation clients, even though Windows 95/98 clients do not require a machine account to access an NT domain. All of the machine accounts that are created are of the Windows NT Workstation or Server type accounts. However, when Window 95/98 clients access the domain, their type will be listed as Windows 95 Workstation.

Configuring the Client's Networking

The Set Up Computer Wizard creates a configuration floppy disk for use on the client PC, when invoked with the **set up a computer** taskpad on the console's **Manage Computers** page or by launching Scw.exe. This floppy disk contains the following four files:

- Setup.exe
- Ipdetect.exe
- Ipdx86.exe
- Netparam.ini

These file names are specified in Scwfiles.inf, which resides in the same location as Scw.exe. Setup.exe launches either Ipdetect.exe or Ipdx86.exe, depending on the client operating system (as determined in real-time), either Windows 95/98 or NT Workstation.

Setup.exe also forces Service Pack 4 (SP4) to run on NT Workstation clients after network configuration is complete. In addition, Internet Explorer 5.0 is installed if it was selected with the Set Up Computer Wizard.

Ipdetect.exe and Ipdx86.exe provide similar functions but on different client operating systems. One major difference is that Ipdetect.exe does not detect network cards; it merely invokes Windows 95/98's native network card selection screen. Ipdx86.exe includes calls to join the client to the domain, which is not necessary for Windows 95/98 clients. Also, NT Workstation clients may require an intermediate reboot in order to fully configure their network, so Ipdx86.exe sometimes creates **RunOnce** entries to handle the continuation of Setup.

The networking configuration that takes place includes:

- Installing a network card with NDIS drivers (only one network card can be installed).
- Installing TCP/IP.
- Setting TCP/IP to access a DHCP server.

- Binding TCP/IP to the NIC.
- Changing the computer name.
- Changing the workgroup name for Win95/98 clients.
- Changing the domain name.
- Setting Windows 95/98 clients to logon to an NT domain.
- Installing Client for Microsoft Networks.
- Joining the domain (NT Workstation only).
- Setting user-level desktop and start menu preferences (Windows 95 only).

In addition to these configuration changes, Ipdetect.exe does additional checks for Dial-up Networking, suitability of existing NIC drivers, and other similar checks.

Windows 95/98 client networking configuration does not require an active network connection to the server, however, the NT Workstation requires this in order to join the domain before the client can log on to the server.

Installing Applications on the Client

When logging on to the server, the client's logon script executes. If a file named *Installed* is in the client computer's Response directory, nothing more happens. If it is not present in the Response directory, then application installation begins. The file Clioc.inf is used to determine which application .inf files to use in the installation.

Upon completion of the installation, the Client component creates the Installed file in the Response folder. This blocks application installs on subsequent logons. Once this process is complete, the logon script will not perform any actions as long as the Installed file exists. If a new push installation of client applications is desired, then the Installed file must be deleted. The Set Up Computer Wizard does this automatically when you select **Add Software to an Existing Client** from the console.

CHAPTER 21

ISP Connectivity Tasks

In its first two sections, this chapter discusses specific tasks that configure Microsoft® BackOffice® Small Business Server 4.5 for Internet service provider (ISP) connectivity. These tasks are applicable whether the small business is using either a new or existing ISP. In the next section, an Internet Connection Wizard walkthrough is provided, describing the Small Business Server Internet connection process. Manual configuration of server applications for Internet connectivity is also provided as background information for the technology consultant. This chapter's information is presented as follows:

- Internet Connection Issues.
- Configuring Small Business Server to Work with Non-Dialup Connections.
- Internet Connection Wizard Walkthrough.
- Manual Configuration of Server Applications for Internet Connectivity.

Internet Connection Issues

This section describes several configuration issues and information the technology consultant will need when connecting Small Business Server to the Internet, as follows.

- Registering a Second-Level Domain Name.
- Configuring Small Business Server to Use an Existing Second-Level Domain Name.
- Exchange and Domain Name Changes.
- Configuring the ISP Domain Name Server.
- Dynamic IP Addressing and Internet Mail Issues.
- E-mail Information.
- Web Hosting Information (Optional).
- Other Information Required from the ISP.

Registering a Second-Level Domain Name

To register a second-level domain name, the technology consultant must contact the ISP. The name to be registered must be checked against an InterNIC database to see if it is presently being used. The InterNIC database is at the following web site:

http:\\www.networksolutions.com

Note The ISP may complete registration for you.

Configuring Small Business Server to Use an Existing Second-Level Domain

If the small business customer already has a second-level domain name, configure Small Business Server to work with it using the Internet Connection Wizard. Contact the ISP and have them change any existing small business third-level domain name entries to the second-level domain name, as follows:

- Create an appropriate Domain Name Service (DNS) record to map the second-level domain name to the existing third-level domain name.
- Change the third-level domain name to the new second-level name in all records.

Exchange Server and Domain Name Changes

Exchange must have the proper domain name configured for each e-mail address in order to send and receive messages properly. If the small business customer asks their ISP to change their domain name from "yourcompany.isp.com" to "yourcompany.com", Exchange may be configured to recognize the new name using the Small Business Server Internet Connection Wizard. The configuration can also be performed manually—refer to "Configuring Exchange" later in this chapter and perform the procedure "To configure the IMS Site, Configuration, Site Addressing Properties."

Configuring the ISP Domain Name Server

For dial-up connectivity, the ISP must configure several entries in their DNS for the small business customer. For e-mail, there should be two DNS MX (Mail eXchange) records for the small business domain and a DNS A (Address) record for your host. One MX record points to Small Business Server and the other points to the ISP's mail host.

Note The technology consultant needs the Internet Protocol (IP) address of the ISP's DNS server to configure Small Business Server.

ISP DNS Entries For E-mail

DNS excerpts look like the following:

"yourdomain.com IN MX 10 yourserver.yourdomain.com"

"yourdomain.com IN MX 20 ISPserver.isp.com"

"yourdomain.yourserver.com IN A x.x.x.x"

The ISP should also configure a reverse lookup entry for yourserver.yourcorp.com (a PTR record):

"x.x.x.x IN PTR yourdomain.yourserver.com"

Dynamic IP Addressing and Internet Mail Issues

Small Business Server is configured by default as a Dynamic Host Configuration Protocol (DHCP) server. This means that IP addresses are dynamically assigned to Small Business Server clients. On the other hand, Simple Mail Transfer Protocol (SMTP) mail delivery typically requires a static or dedicated IP address —the result of the mechanisms used to route and deliver mail on the Internet.

SMTP mail relies on DNS MX records to direct mail for a domain (the part of the address to the right of the "@" sign) to a client destination. The Internet standards for mail require that the MX record point to a host name that has a DNS A (Address) record. The A record maps the host name to an IP address. This configuration relies on the ISP allocating a fixed IP address to the small business Dial-Up Networking session. With a fixed or static IP address, the same IP address is used for the Small Business Server every time the ISP is dialed.

NT-Based Solution

Your ISP might devise a solution to the dynamic IP addressing issue, but it is unlikely. The NT-based solution recommended by Microsoft to Small Business Server referral ISPs takes advantage of some unique features of NT to allow dynamically addressed systems to receive SMTP mail delivery.

Note Some ISPs have developed alternative solutions to the dynamic IP addressing issue. Check with the ISP for more information.

E-mail Information

In addition to coordinating the DNS entries performed by the ISP, the technology consultant must obtain the DNS name or IP address of the ISP's mail host. In some cases, the ISP may have separate hosts for inbound and outbound mail. To configure the Exchange Server, the DNS name or IP address of both hosts is required.

Web Hosting Information (Optional)

Small Business Server 4.5 includes Microsoft FrontPage® for creating web pages. FrontPage is not installed by default, but you can use Online Guide instructions to install it. After your web pages are created with FrontPage and tested, use Microsoft's Web Publishing Wizard to publish them to the ISP hosting the small business web site. To facilitate publishing your web site, the ISP must support FrontPage extensions and the Web Publishing Wizard.

The Web Publishing Wizard, accessed from the **update your web site** taskpad on the Small Business Server console, uses File Transfer Protocol (FTP) to publish web content. In order to use the Web Publishing Wizard, the Internet Connection Wizard requires the following information from the ISP:

- Web posting Uniform Resource Locator (URL). The FTP address where the initial data and updates for the small business web site are located. If the small business web site URL is http://www.yourcompany.internetserviceprovider.tld the web posting URL may look like this: ftp://ftp.yourcompany. internetserviceprovider.tld, where .tld refers to a top level domain such as .com, .edu, .net, and so on.
- Web posting account name and password. The account name and password required for making changes to the web site at the FTP address.
- Web site URL. The web page URL publicly available on the Internet.

Web Publishing Resources

More information on the Microsoft Web Publishing Wizard can be found at: **http://www.microsoft.com/windows/software/webpost**

Other Information Required from the ISP

Other information required from the ISP for various hardware connectivity options is provided in the "Internet Connection Wizard Walkthrough" section, later in this chapter.

Configuring Small Business Server to Work with Non-Dialup Connections

The Small Business Server Internet Connection Wizard is designed to assist first-time users to find an ISP, sign up for an account, and configure Small Business Server. For higher levels of service such as dial-on demand router, frame-relay, and T-1 connections, Small Business Server has some advantageous optimization features. But this requires some manual configuration tasks, as described in "Internet Connectivity and Upsizing" of *Chapter 31, Performance and Scalability Enhancements,* in *Part 5, Performance Optimization and Tuning,* of this resource guide. In the paragraphs that follow, several types of non dialup connections are discussed along with some application issues.

ISDN Connections

How you install an Integrated Services Digital Network (ISDN) device depends upon the type of hardware purchased. ISDN devices are available as ISA or PCI cards that may be installed inside the computer just like an internal modem. These are typically called ISDN Terminal Adapters or ISDN modems. ISDN devices are also available as external devices, sometimes called dial-on-demand routers.

Both internal and external ISDN devices can be operated in two modes—dial-up or dedicated. The dial-up mode is the most common because of the cost advantage. In the dedicated configuration, the line is up all the time and has the same characteristics as the Leased Line solutions discussed below, with bandwidths of either 64 KB or 128 KB.

ISDN Terminal Adapters

Internal ISDN terminal adapter cards are available from several vendors with a variety of features. Some are installed as network cards through the Control Panel and Network icon, and others are installed as modems.

ISDN Routers

ISDN routers are often used in a dial-on-demand configuration. This is possible since the call setup times for ISDN are extremely fast compared to standard analog modems (2-3 seconds vs. 20-30 seconds). In this configuration, Small Business Server is configured with two network interface cards (NIC's)—one for the internal network and one for the external network that connects to the ISDN router. Whenever there is outbound traffic from Small Business Server, the router automatically raises the connection to the ISP. To the clients on the Small Business Server network (and to the Small Business Server itself), it appears as if there is a full-time connection.

This configuration is unique. From the perspective of the ISP host, it appears like a normal dial-up connection.

Leased Line Connections

Leased line connections typically range from 56 KB to 1.544 MB (T-1) lines. The feature they all share in common is they are dedicated connections and available all the time. Like dedicated modems or ISDN lines, there are also some special configuration issues with leased line connections–primarily with Exchange Server. Leased line connections require a router for operation. For security purposes, Small Business Server should be configured with two NIC's for these connections—one for the internal Local Area Network (LAN) and one for the external connection with the leased line router.

Configuring Windows NT Server 4.0

If an external ISDN or leased line solution is chosen, consider the following when setting up Small Business Server for Internet connectivity:

- The ISP will need to provide fixed IP addresses for both the router and the second NIC in Small Business Server.

Configuring Proxy Server 2.0

In the dial-on demand and dedicated connection configurations, dial-up networking is not used, therefore Proxy Server 2.0 is not configured for Auto Dial. All other Proxy Server configuration is done by the Internet Connection Wizard.

Note The Proxy Server Local Address Table (LAT) must be configured to differentiate the internal and external networks, whenever the base IP address is changed on Small Business Server. See *Chapter 27, Administering Small Business Server Components,* in *Part 4, Administering and Maintaining*, of this resource guide for LAT configuration procedures.

Configuring the Web Publishing Wizard

The Web Publishing Wizard configuration set up with the Internet Connection Wizard is sufficient for non-dialup connectivity to the Internet. You can also manually configure the Web Publishing Wizard by following the procedures outlined in the "Manual Configuration of Server Applications for Internet Connectivity" section, later in this chapter.

Configuring Exchange Server 5.5

The range of high-speed Internet connections available present the following two scenarios when configuring the Exchange Server.

Scenario 1: Dial-On-Demand or Dial-Up Networking

In this scenario, the basic configuration for Exchange is identical to the set up in the "Manual Configuration of Server Applications for Internet Connectivity" section, later in this chapter.

In this scenario, the Exchange Server can send outbound mail immediately, but the Internet connection must be established to receive mail. While the Internet connection is down, mail will be queued on the ISP's mail host. Exchange and most ISP's now support the SMTP extension, defined in RFC1985 (called ETRN).

In previous Exchange versions, the only way to send an ETRN to the ISP's mail host when dial-up connections were not in use was using an external program. With Exchange 5.5, a new registry key has been added to force the Internet Mail Service (IMS) to send an ETRN whenever it connects, to deliver outbound mail. However, it is a requirement to use the **Forward all mail to:** option for the outbound mail.

The following registry key is a DWORD with possible values of 0 (off - do not send) and 1 (on - send):

HKLM\SYSTEM\CurrentControlSet\Services\MSExchangeIMC\Parameters\AlwaysUseETRN

The registry entry forces mail to dequeue from the ISP every time outbound mail is sent from Small Business Server. This delivery rate may not be acceptable for small business inbound mail delivery requirements. To address this, schedule the delivery of a dummy mail message at required delivery intervals using either a Link Monitor or an AT, WINAT, CROND (shareware), or another scheduling package running a command line utility to generate and send the mail message.

If the small business ISP does not support ETRN, the technology consultant and the ISP need to select a suitable dequeuing method. Visit the following Web site to select a mutually agreeable dequeuing method:
http://www.swinc.com/resource/exch_dq.htm

Scenario 2: Leased Line or Dedicated Connection

In this scenario, the basic configuration for Exchange is identical to the set up in the "Manual Configuration of Server Applications for Internet Connectivity" section, later in this chapter, except that a dial-up connection is not created. Using the components described in this scenario, the Exchange Server can always send outbound mail immediately and receive inbound mail immediately.

POP Mail

Post Office Protocol (POP) is a commonly used messaging protocol. The most widely used implementation of this protocol is POP3. POP3 is a retrieval protocol, used to retrieve mail messages from a POP server. E-mail messages received by the POP server are delivered to a server mailbox and messages reside there until an individual with a POP mail client retrieves them. Depending on the POP mail client used, a user can choose to:

- Download all of the messages that are queued on the POP server and then remove the messages from the server.
- Download all messages or all new messages and then leave a copy on the POP server.
- Download just the message headers and then mark the messages they want to download. (This feature is not found in all POP mail clients).

Since POP3 is a messaging protocol designed for retrieval only, it must work in conjunction with a protocol capable of sending messages, such as SMTP.

SMTP

SMTP is the standard protocol for mail transfer over the Internet. It defines how a message is formatted for delivery and also provides the delivery mechanism over connection-based protocols, such as Transmission Control Protocol/Internet Protocol (TCP/IP).

The Exchange Server IMS uses SMTP to send and receive mail. In addition, POP clients use SMTP to send messages to SMTP hosts to route and deliver over the Internet.

Differences Between POP and SMTP

POP3 protocol is only capable of retrieving mail from a POP3 host, and is therefore dependent on the SMTP protocol to deliver outbound messages. The SMTP protocol is a more robust transport protocol, capable of two-way communication with other SMTP hosts.

The Benefits of Using an SMTP Server

Microsoft Exchange Server is a server application that provides not only messaging capabilities between users on a local network, but messaging capabilities over the Internet as well. The version of Microsoft Exchange included with Small Business Server comes with IMS and uses the SMTP protocol to send and receive messages over the Internet, therefore making it an SMTP server. The advantages of using an SMTP server over a POP mail client are many.

Limitations of the POP mail client include:

- Messages not received in real time.
- Messages cannot be viewed from multiple clients after download.
- Storage increase because multiple message copies are stored by multiple recipients.
- Online backups are difficult to perform.
- No transactional integrity of the message store (client-side files).
- ISP POP accounts require additional UserID and Password maintenance.

Advantages of the Exchange Server include:

- Single-instance storage of messages addressed to multiple recipients.
- On-line backups and transactional integrity of message flow.
- Message size limits can be imposed.
- Access to Exchange Public Folders.

- Robust offline capabilities.
- Server-based rules, which dictate how a message is handled when the server receives it.
- Security is integrated with Small Business Server security.

Advantages of the Exchange Client include:

- Messages received in real time.

Additional Resources for ISP Connectivity

There are several good sources of additional information for the technology consultant, ISP, and small business customer that may be useful in relation to ISP connectivity issues. These sources include:

- The Microsoft Small Business Server web site:
  http://www.microsoft.com/smallbusinessserver
- The Microsoft Exchange Internet connectivity white papers:
  http://www.microsoft.com/exchange/DeployAdmin.htm
- Simpler-Webb, Inc.'s Exchange and SMTP web site:
  http://www.swinc.com/resource/exch_smtp.htm

Internet Connection Wizard Walkthrough

This section contains an Internet Connection Wizard walkthrough to assist the technology consultant in gathering the necessary information for configuring Small Business Server Internet connectivity settings. The walkthrough also serves as a guide to explain the configurations made by the wizard, thus ensuring that settings are correctly made for the network environment.

Internet Connection Topologies

Before starting the Internet Connection Wizard, it might be useful to review how Small Business Server connects to the Internet. See *Chapter 10, Planning a Small Business Office Network,* in *Part 2, Planning,* for an overall network topology diagram. *Chapter 31, Performance and Scalability Enhancements,* in *Part 5, Performance Optimization and Tuning,* describes several hardware connectivity configurations supporting fast Internet connections for heavy traffic scenarios.

Internet Connection Types

Small Business Server supports many types of connectivity hardware which can be grouped into the three categories described below.

- Dial-up.

  Characterized by any Internet connection established using Dial-Up Networking or Remote Access Service (RAS). Connection hardware includes analog modems and ISDN terminal adapters. Devices are connected to Small Business Server through either a serial port, multiport serial board, or an internal card, and configured with the **Modem Properties** utility in **Control Panel**.

- Router.

  Characterized by any dial-on demand or full-time Internet connection established using a routing device. A router can be connected on the LAN where it acts as a default gateway for all client computers, handling requests outside the address space of the Proxy Server LAT. This configuration requires each client computer to have a static IP address, unless the router is capable of Network Address Translation (NAT).

  Another router configuration supported by Small Business Server requires two network adapters—an internal adapter for the LAN and a second network adapter attached to a router connected to the Internet. The default gateway is configured on the second network adapter causing all Internet connections to be filtered by Proxy Server.

  Refer to *Chapter 31, Performance and Scalability Enhancements,* in *Part 5, Performance Optimization and Tuning,* for further information about router configurations.

- Full-Time Connection/Broadband Devices.

  Characterized by any Internet connection established using an Asynchronous Digital Subscriber Line (ADSL) modem, cable modem, or Multichannel Multipoint Distributed System (MMDS) device. This is similar to the router configuration, requiring both an internal and second network adapter. The default gateway is configured on the second network adapter, causing all Internet connections to be filtered by Proxy Server. In this configuration, a static IP address obtained from the ISP is required for the device's external network adapter.

  Refer to *Chapter 31, Performance and Scalability Enhancements,* in *Part 5, Performance Optimization and Tuning,* for further information about full-time connection/broadband device configurations.

Information Required for the Internet Connection Wizard

Before using the Internet Connection Wizard, obtain the information outlined below from the ISP for the type of Internet connection you are using. Print out and use "Small Business Server ISP Information Forms" from the Online Guide to record the information.

Dial-Up Connection

For a modem connection or any dial-up connection that uses a phonebook entry to dial, the following information is required:

- Account name. The UserID required to dial into the ISP.
- Account password. The password associated with the account name.
- Mail type used. Either Exchange (SMTP) Server or POP3.

    For Exchange (SMTP) mail, you need the host name or IP address of the ISP's SMTP Server. If the ISP is queuing mail for your dial-up connection, obtain the appropriate signaling (dequeuing) command.

    For POP3 mail, obtain the host name or IP address of the ISP's POP3 and SMTP servers.

- Internet domain name. The Small Business Server Internet domain name.

Router Connection

For a router connection, the following information is required:

- Information listed in the previous "Dial-Up Connection" section.
- ISP DNS server name(s). The name or IP address of the ISP's DNS host(s).
- IP address of the router. Use a static IP address if your router connection is full-time.

- Subnet mask and default gateway addresses. When using a second network adapter with the router, these are the IP addresses identifying the small business LAN on the Internet and the default gateway address of the adapter.

Note The Internet Connection Wizard requires you to determine if your router is a dial-on demand configuration or not.

Note If you want to utilize the security features of Proxy Server with a router connection, you must use a second network adapter on Small Business Server to interconnect Proxy Server and the router. Use the **Network** utility in **Control Panel** to configure the second network adapter with the correct IP address and protocol information. See *Chapter 31, Performance and Scalability Enhancements,* in *Part 5, Performance Optimization and Tuning,* for more information on router connectivity.

Full-Time Connection/Broadband Device

For a full-time connection/broadband device, the following information is required:

- The information listed in the "Dial-Up Connection" section, earlier in this chapter.
- ISP DNS server name(s). The name or IP address of the ISP's DNS host(s).
- Static IP address for the device's external network adapter. The Internet-routable IP address to be binded to the device external network adapter connected to the Internet.
- Subnet mask address. An IP address assigned to the second network adapter, identifying the address space of the small business LAN on the Internet.
- Default gateway address. The IP address that identifies the default gateway to the Internet.

Note For a full time connection/broadband device, a second network adapter is needed to interconnect Proxy Server and the device. See *Chapter 31, Performance and Scalability Enhancements,* in *Part 5, Performance Optimization and Tuning,* for more information on broadband device connectivity.

Starting the Internet Connection Wizard

Start the Internet Connection Wizard for the first time from the Small Business Server Console using either of the following:

- **Connect to an ISP** link from the **To Do List**.
- **Connect to the Internet** taskpad from the **Manage Internet Access** page.

When the Internet Connection Wizard is first started, the following Welcome screen is displayed:

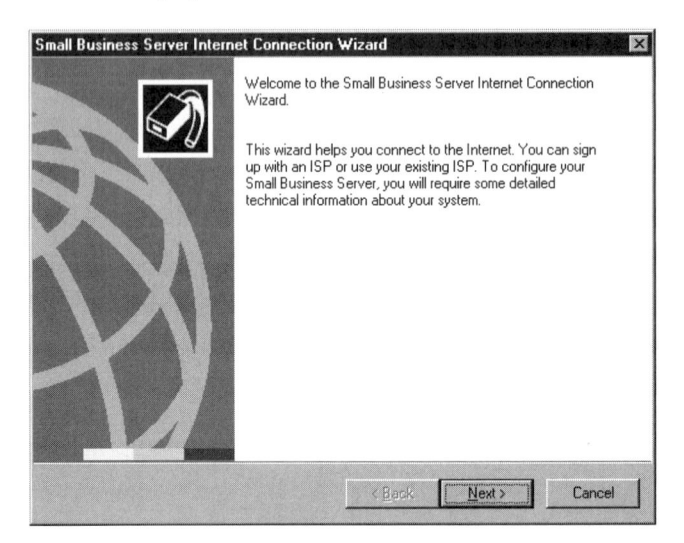

If Internet connectivity changes need to be made after initially running the Internet Connection Wizard, start it again using either of the following taskpads from the **Manage Internet Access** page:

- **Configure Internet hardware**.
- **Change Internet settings**.

Note Each taskpad above opens the Internet Connection Wizard at the respective task being performed.

Running the Internet Connection Wizard

To begin running the Internet Connection Wizard, click **Next** on the Welcome screen. When the wizard is run, the following tasks may be performed:

- Set Up Connection to your ISP.
- Configure Hardware.
- Prepare to Sign Up Online.
- Set Up Modem Connection to ISP.
- Set Up Router Connection to ISP.
- Network Interface Card Configuration.
- Set Up Second Network Adapter.
- Configure Internet Mail Settings.
- Configure SMTP Mail Delivery.
- Receive Exchange Mail.
- Set Up Authentication.
- Send and Receive POP3 Mail.
- Configure Internet Domain Name.
- Configure Web Site Information.
- Configure Firewall Settings.

Each of the above tasks is described in detail in the sections that follow.

Set Up Connection to Your ISP

When performing this task of the Internet Connection Wizard, the following **Set Up Connection to Your ISP** screen is displayed.

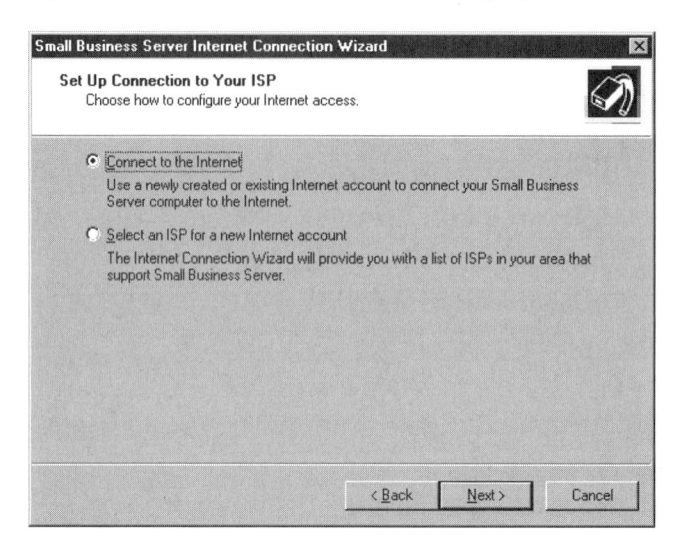

Choose the appropriate option for setting up your ISP connection as follows.

- **Connect to the Internet**. Causes the Internet Connection Wizard to run through the appropriate tasks listed in the "Running the Internet Connection Wizard" section, earlier in this chapter, thus configuring Small Business Server for Internet connectivity.
- **Select an ISP for a new Internet account**. The Internet Connection Wizard connects you to a Microsoft Referral Server and downloads a list of ISPs in your area that support Small Business Server 4.5. ISPs with online signup programs and special Small Business Server 4.5 customer offerings are also provided. You must have a configured modem on Small Business Server to utilize the referral service.

  ISPs that support Small Business Server 4.5 online signup automatically configure Small Business Server applications and services. In this scenario, the Internet Connection Wizard is not required. After the ISP has received the small business customer's system, user, and billing information, an .ins file is generated by the signup server and then downloaded to configure the following on Small Business Server:
  - Dial-Up Networking.
  - Proxy Server.

- Exchange Server.
- Web Publishing Wizard.

Note Some ISPs with online signup programs distribute signup diskettes. If your ISP does this specifically for Small Business Server 4.5 customers, use the signup diskette instructions to configure Internet connectivity.

Configure Hardware

If you selected **Connect to the Internet**, the following **Configure Hardware** screen is displayed.

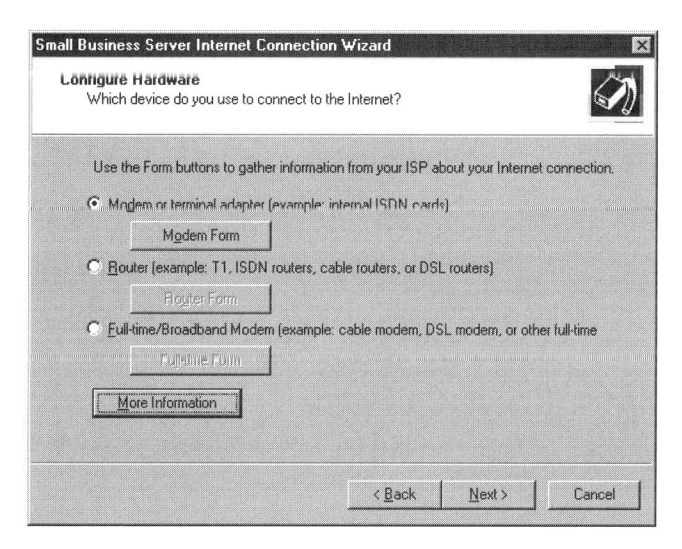

Choose Internet communications hardware options for the ISP connection, as follows:

- **Modem or terminal adapter**. Use when you have an analog modem or ISDN terminal adapter accessed through Dial-Up Networking or RAS. Selecting this option causes the wizard to display the **Set Up Modem Connection to ISP** screen, described later in this section.

  Install these devices using the **Modem Properties** utility in **Control Panel** prior to using the Internet Connection Wizard. Also, configure them as RAS ports with dial-out access—refer to the Online Guide for procedures.

- **Router**. Use when an ISDN, frame relay, cable, or Digital Subscriber Line (DSL) router is being used to connect to the Internet. Selecting this option causes the wizard to display the **Set Up Router Connection to ISP** screen, described later in this section.

If a second network adapter is attached to the router, configure it with a valid IP address prior to using the Internet Connection Wizard—in **Control Panel**, use the **Network** utility, **Protocols** tab. Refer to the manufacturer's documentation for router configuration procedures.

Note If you use a router to connect to the Internet, it must do network address translation to ensure delivery of SMTP mail.

- **Full-time connection/Broadband Modem**. Use for a full-time, high-speed connection to the ISP, for example, when using ADSL or cable modems, and MMDS devices. Requires a second network adapter. Selecting this option causes the wizard to display the **Network Interface Card Configuration** screen, described later in this section.

  You must configure a static IP address on the second network adapter connected to the broadband device, prior to using the Internet Connection Wizard in **Control Panel**, use the **Network** utility, **Protocols** tab. Also configure a static IP address obtained from the ISP on the device's external network adapter. Refer to the manufacturer's documentation for device configuration procedures.

Note Click **More Information** to display Help on configuring hardware.

Prepare to Sign Up Online

If you selected **Select an ISP for a new Internet account**, the following **Prepare to Sign Up Online** screen is displayed:

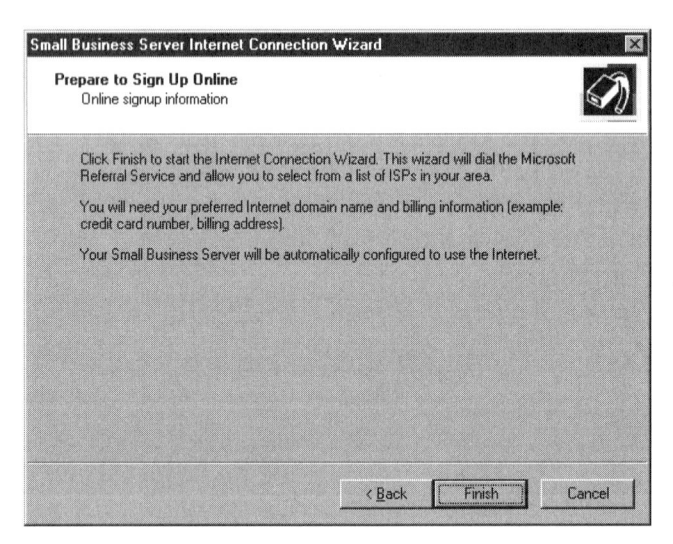

This screen is a reminder to select an ISP. Click **Finish** to launch the Internet Connection Wizard in the automatic setup mode. A Microsoft Internet Referral Server will be automatically dialed using a configured modem. The Internet Referral Server displays the ISPs in your area to which you may connect. If the ISP supports online signup and configuration of Small Business Server 4.5, Internet connectivity is configured automatically.

Set Up Modem Connection to ISP

If you selected **Modem or terminal adapter** in the **Configure Hardware** screen, the following **Set Up Modem Connection to ISP** screen is displayed:

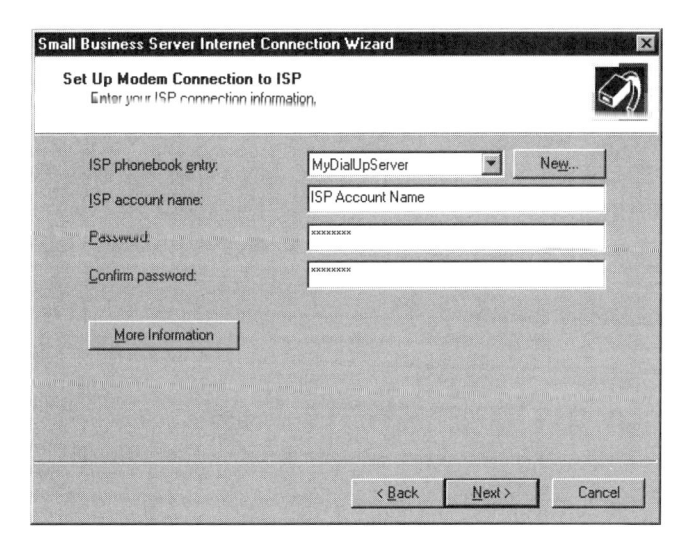

Enter your ISP credential information as follows:

- **ISP phonebook entry**. The dial-up phonebook entry used to connect to the ISP. If an entry was previously created, select it. If not, use the procedure below to create a new phonebook entry.
- **ISP account name**. The name of the account assigned by the ISP to Small Business Server.
- **Password**. The password for your account, obtained from your ISP.
- **Confirm password**. Confirmation of the account password.

Note Click **More Information** to display Help on setting up a modem connection to the ISP.

The credentials used in the **Set Up Modem Connection to ISP** screen are automatically configured by the wizard on the Proxy and Exchange servers, for use when connecting with the ISP. They are entered in both of the following two places: 1) on the **Credentials** tab of the **Microsoft Proxy Auto Dial** dialog box within the Internet Information Server (IIS) Console, and 2) on the **Dial-up Networking** tab of the Exchange Administrator **Internet Mail Service Properties** dialog box.

▶ **To create a new dial-up networking phonebook entry**

1. From the **Set Up Modem Connection to ISP** screen, click **New** to display the following **New Phonebook Entry Wizard**.

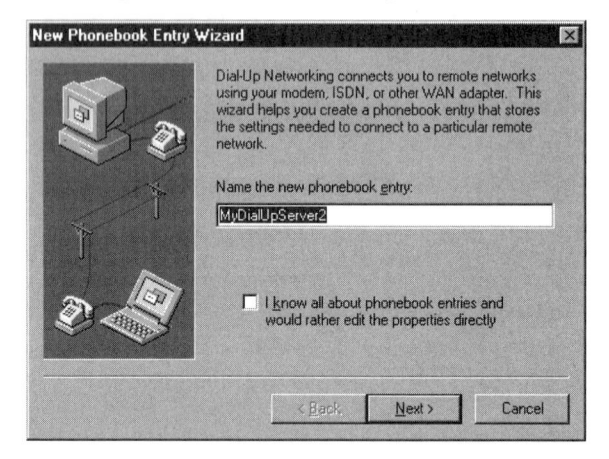

2. Follow the steps of the wizard to create a new phonebook entry, using the configuration information received from the ISP.

3. Click **Finish** when complete.

Set Up Router Connection to ISP

If you selected **Router** in the **Configure Hardware** screen, the following **Set Up Router Connection to ISP** screen is displayed:

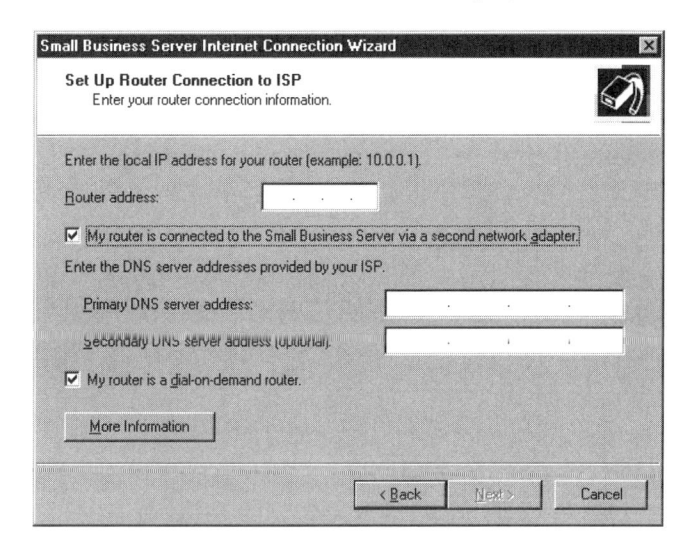

Provide the information used to configure the Small Business Server Internet connection with a router, as follows:

- **Router address**. Enables TCP/IP connectivity from the Small Business Server network to the Internet. In the LAN router configuration (see *Part 5*), use a local IP address such as 10.0.0.1. In the default gateway configuration, use an IP address on the same subnet as the second network adapter.

- **My router is connected to the Small Business Server via a second network adapter**. Select this option if you are using Small Business Server as the default gateway to the Internet and you want to utilize the security features of Proxy Server. This causes the **Network Interface Card Configuration** screen to display for configuring network adapter use.

- **Primary DNS server address**. Use the primary DNS server IP address provided by the ISP.

- **Secondary DNS server address**. Use the secondary DNS server IP address, if available from the ISP.
- **My router is a dial-on-demand router**. Select this option if your router is not a full-time connection, for example, when using a demand-dial ISDN router. When selected, the Exchange IMS is configured to forward outgoing mail to the ISP SMTP relay host specified in the **Configure SMTP Mail Delivery** screen, described later in this section.

Note Click **More Information** to display Help on setting up a router connection to the ISP.

Network Interface Card Configuration

The **Network Interface Card Configuration** screen is displayed next if you selected either of the following:

- My router is connected to the Small Business Server via a second network adapter in the Set Up Router Connection to ISP screen.
- **Full-time/Broadband Modem** in the **Configure Hardware** screen.

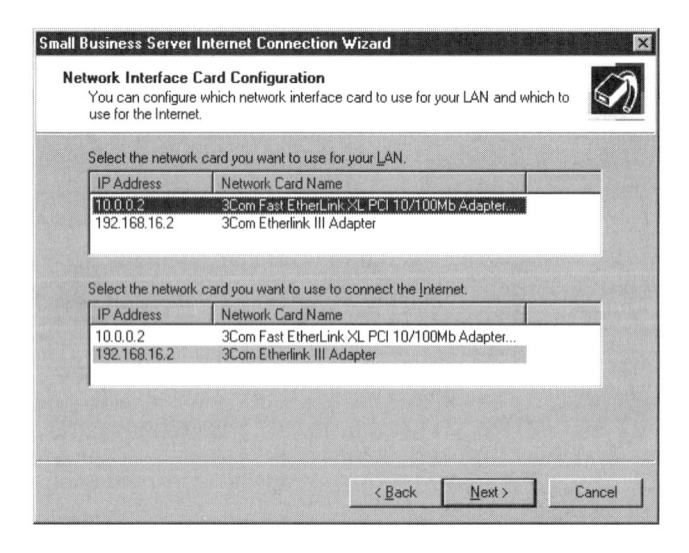

This screen is displayed when Small Business Server is configured as the default gateway to the Internet. In this configuration, a second network adapter is used to interconnect Small Business Server and the Internet communications device (router, ADSL modem, etc.). The screen identifies all configured network adapters, as follows:

- **Select the network card you want to use for your LAN.** Select which network adapter to use for the LAN. Make sure the internal network adapter is configured with the base IP address of Small Business Server and that the Proxy LAT configuration includes it.

- **Select the network card you want to use to connect to the Internet.** Select the second network adapter used for Internet communications. Make sure the second network adapter IP address is not within the internal address space of the Proxy Server LAT configuration.

Set Up Second Network Adapter

After the second network adapter is selected in the **Network Interface Card Configuration** screen, the following **Set Up Second Network Adapter** screen is displayed.

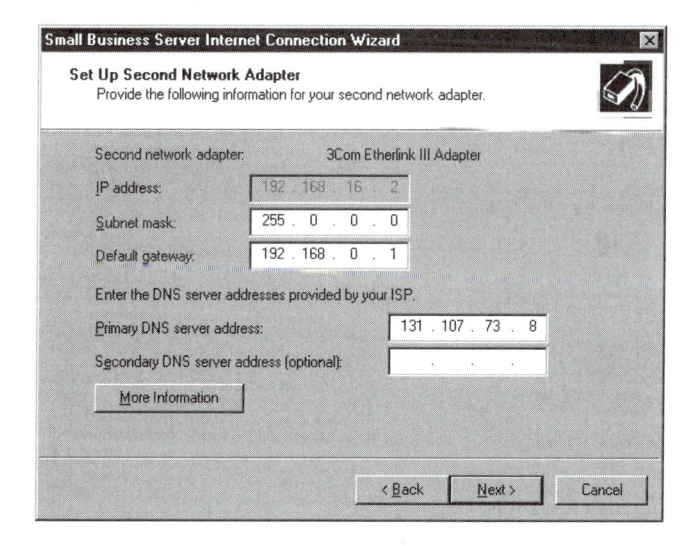

![Set Up Second Network Adapter dialog box showing Second network adapter: 3Com Etherlink III Adapter; IP address: 192.168.16.2; Subnet mask: 255.0.0.0; Default gateway: 192.168.0.1; Primary DNS server address: 131.107.73.8; Secondary DNS server address (optional): blank]

Provide the information used to configure the second network adapter to work with a broadband device or router, as follows.

- **IP address**. Identifies the static IP address assigned to the second network adapter. This cannot be modified from this dialog box once the second network adapter is configured with a valid IP address using the **Network** utility's **Protocols** tab. To change the IP address, use the **Network** utility in **Control Panel**. The second network adapter cannot be configured to obtain a dynamic IP address since the DHCP Server on Windows NT Server does not support a DHCP client and server on the same computer

- **Subnet mask**. Identifies the address space of the LAN on the Internet. An entry appears in the **Subnet mask** text field after a static IP address for the second network adapter is configured using the **Network** utility's **Protocols** tab.

- **Default gateway**. Identifies the default gateway address of the second network adapter so that client Internet requests may be routed through this network gateway. Type the address, unless already configured using the **Network** utility's **Protocol** tab.
- **Primary DNS server address**. Identifies the address of the ISP's primary DNS. Type the address, unless already configured using the **Network** utility.
- **Secondary DNS server address (optional)**. Identifies the address of the ISP's secondary DNS. Type the address if available, unless already configured.

Note Click **More Information** to display Help on configuring the external network adapter.

Configure Internet Mail Settings

When performing this task of the Internet Connection Wizard, the following **Configure Internet Mail Settings** screen is displayed.

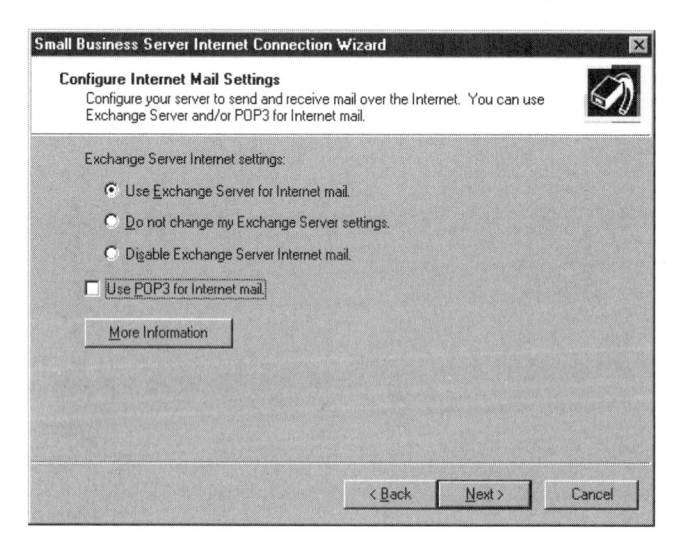

Provide the information used to configure Small Business Server for Internet e-mail exchange, as follows:

- **Use Exchange Server for Internet mail**. Enables Microsoft Exchange IMS on Small Business Server. Select this option to use SMTP mail through the Exchange Server if you have either of the following:

- A full-time Internet connection that uses SMTP mail.
- A dial-up connection to the ISP where e-mail is queued until connecting for delivery.

Selecting this option causes the **Configure SMTP Mail Delivery** screen to display next.

- **Do not change my Exchange Server settings**. Prevents Exchange Server settings from being overwritten by the wizard configuration. Select this option if Exchange Server settings are already configured and you want to retain them.
- **Disable Exchange Server Internet mail**. Disables Exchange Server IMS. Select this option when you want to disable Internet mail through Exchange Server. Retains e-mail exchange between LAN recipients.
- **Use POP3 for Internet mail**. Enables retrieval of e-mail from an ISP POP3 mail server instead of an SMTP server.

Note Click **More Information** to display Help on configuring Internet mail settings.

Configure SMTP Mail Delivery

If you selected **Use Exchange Server for Internet mail** in the **Configure Internet Mail Settings** screen, the following **Configure SMTP Mail Delivery** screen is displayed.

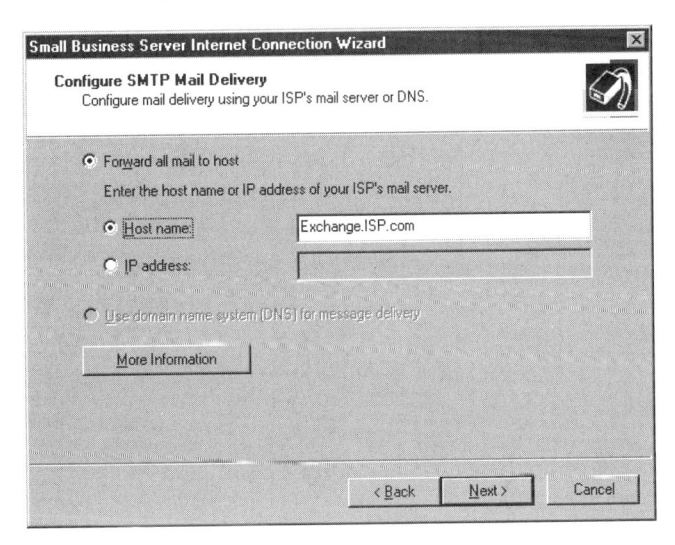

Provide the information used to configure Exchange Server Internet Mail Service sending properties, as follows:

- **Forward all mail to host**. Sets the Exchange Server IMS to forward all messages to an ISP SMTP relay host. Select this option if you have an Internet connection which is not full-time, such as a dial-up modem or dial-on demand router connection.
- **Host name**. Identifies the domain name of the SMTP relay host, for example, *Exchange.ISP.com*.
- **IP address**. Identifies the IP address of the SMTP relay host, for example, *161.123.17.1*.
- **Use domain name system (DNS) for message delivery**. Enables DNS resolution of Internet e-mail addresses. Select this option if you have a full-time Internet connection, for example, with a router or broadband device. If a dial-up connection is set with the wizard, the DNS option is unavailable.

Note Click **More Information** to display Help on configuring SMTP mail delivery.

Receive Exchange Mail

If Exchange Server is used for SMTP mail, the following **Receive Exchange Mail** screen is displayed next.

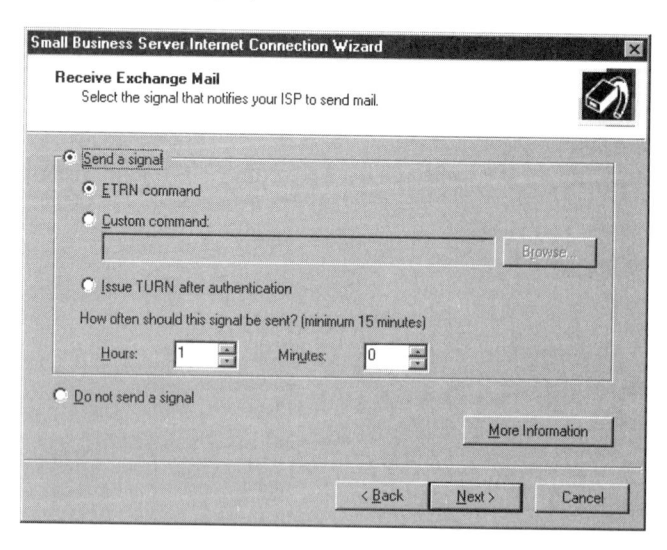

Provide the information used to configure mail retrieval options. To do this, obtain the appropriate configuration information from the ISP for the mail dequeuing method in use. The following table describes some of the common mail dequeuing configurations compatible with Small Business Server.

Table 21.1 Dequeuing Configurations for Mail Retrieval

IP address type	Full-time connection	Dial-up connection	Demand-dial router connection
Fixed	Do not send a signal	ETRN or a custom command	ETRN or a custom command
Dynamic	Not supported	Custom command	Custom command

For more information on mail dequeuing methods, refer to the following web site: **http://www.swinc.com/resource/exch_dq.htm**

Mail retrieval options are configured in the **Receive Exchange Mail** screen as follows:

- **Send a signal**. Configures the Exchange Server IMS to send a signal or command to the ISP's SMTP server to dequeue messages destined for the Small Business Server domain. Select this option to retrieve mail queued at the ISP only if you have a dial-up or dial-on demand Internet connection.

- **ETRN command**. The most common command in use for dequeuing mail from an ISP, supported by sendmail, version 8.8.x or higher.

  If chosen for a dial-up connection, the ISP must configure an "MX" and "A" record to point directly to Small Business Server. Also, the ISP must add another "MX" record with a preference number pointing to the ISP SMTP server—the lower the preference number, the higher the priority. This allows the ISP to queue mail until the time Small Business Server connects with the ISP and sends the dequeuing command. Mail then flows directly to the Small Business Server domain with minimum delay.

  Note ETRN is the most likely scenario for Internet connections using demand-dial routers with static IP addresses. If a static IP address is not used, ETRN will not work, and a custom dequeuing command must be supplied by the ISP.

- **Custom command**. Permits the use of a custom mail dequeuing command supplied by the ISP.

  SBSETRN is an example of a custom dequeuing command which allows dial-up connections to receive a dynamic IP address when connecting to the ISP. This special form of ETRN designed and implemented by Microsoft, is located on Small Business Server at: %systemdrive%\SmallBusiness When in use, the parameters for SBSETRN are read by default from the registry.

- **Browse**. Click this button to locate the custom dequeuing command application, downloaded from the ISP.

- **Issue TURN after authentication**. A mail dequeuing command that may be used if the ISP specifically supports Small Business Server and TURN.

- **How often should this signal be sent?** Sets the frequency at which the dequeuing signal is sent to the ISP. The frequency is the time interval that elapses between connection attempts. The signal is sent each time a connection is established with the ISP or whenever you click the **send and receive now** taskpad on the **Manage E-Mail** page of the Small Business Server console. The default value is 1 hour and the minimum allowable interval is 15 minutes.
- **Do not send a signal.** Prevents the Exchange Server IMS from sending a dequeuing signal to the ISP. Select this option if you are using a full-time Internet connection and hosting SMTP mail for the Small Business Server domain. Note that some ISPs have their own solution for detecting when Small Business Server is connected.

  A full-time Internet connection does not require ISP mail queuing. This type of connection does require that the "MX" and "A" records for the Small Business Server domain point directly to the Exchange Server. Since static "A" records are needed, a full-time connection also requires a static IP address.

Note Click **More Information** to display Help on configuring Exchange mail retrieval.

Set Up Authentication

If you selected **Issue TURN after Authentication** in the **Receive Exchange Mail** screen, the following **Set Up Authentication** screen is displayed.

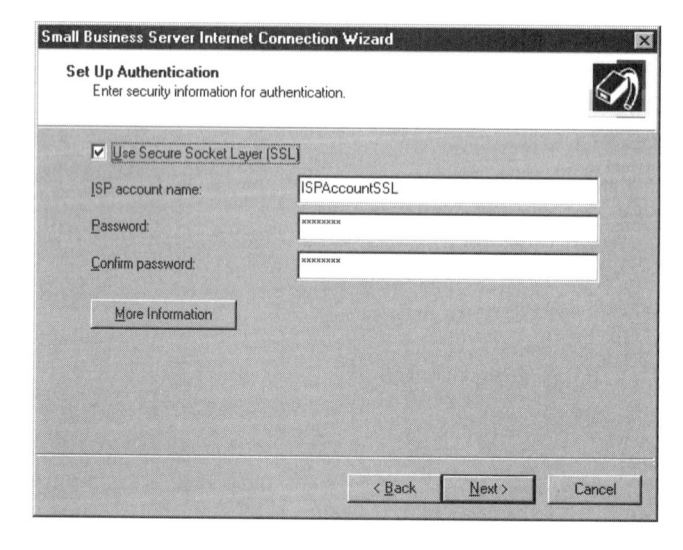

This screen is used to set up a very secure dequeuing signal configuration for dial-up SMTP or demand-dial router Internet connections, as follows:

- **Use Secure Sockets Layer (SSL).** Configures SSL encryption protocol for the dequeueing password. Authentication is performed by the SMTP command AUTH. When the dequeueing password is sent, it is safe because SSL is encrypting the pipe. This method must be supported by the ISP.
- **ISP account name.** The name of the SSL account assigned by the ISP.
- **Password.** The password for the SSL account, obtained from the ISP.
- **Confirm password.** Confirmation of the SSL account password.

Note The account name and password used in this screen may differ from the ones used to log on to the ISP.

Note Click **More Information** to display Help on configuring SSL.

Send and Receive POP3 Mail

If you selected **Use POP3 for Internet mail** and **Disable Exchange Server Internet mail** in the **Configure Internet Mail Settings** screen, the following **Send and Receive POP3 Mail** screen is displayed.

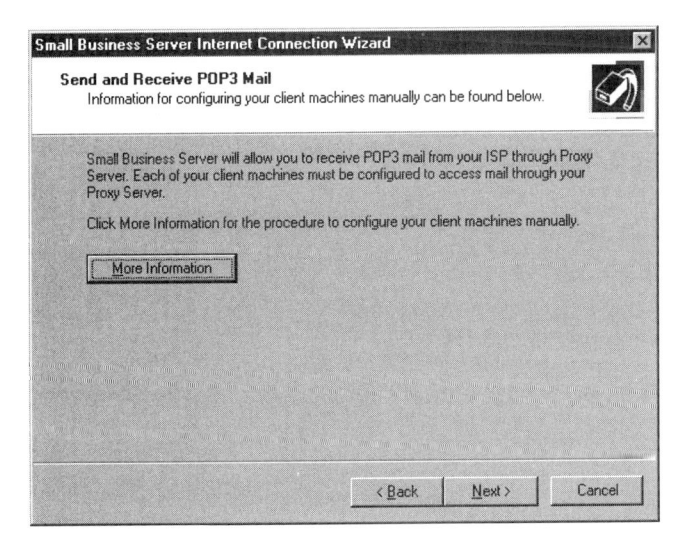

This screen provides the means for configuring Outlook 2000 clients to send and receive POP3 mail, as follows:

- **More Information**. Click this button to display the Online Guide procedure for manually configuring Outlook clients to send and receive POP3 mail through Proxy Server. In the procedure, the **Internet E-Mail** service is added to the client's Outlook profile for POP3 account access. Configuring is manual since each user must specify their unique POP3 account name and password.

> **Note** To facilitate the use of POP3 mail through Proxy Server, configure users with the Small Business Server console **add a user** taskpad, so they appear on the Proxy Server Access Control List (ACL). Also, the Winsock Proxy client must be included on the Set Up Computer Wizard application list when applications are deployed to client machines requiring POP3 mail access.

Configure Internet Domain Name

When performing this task of the Internet Connection Wizard, the following **Configure Internet Domain Name** screen is displayed. If you have an Internet domain name or the Exchange Server is used for SMTP mail, you must enter the domain name information here.

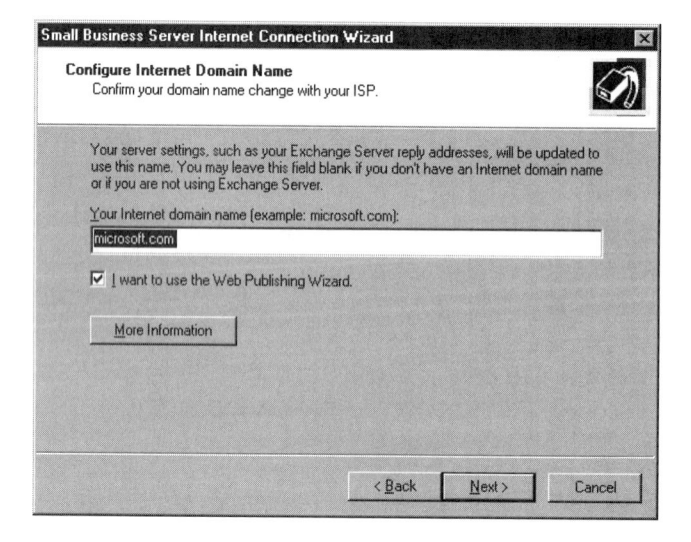

Update the Exchange Server reply address setting with the domain name and select use of the Web Publishing Wizard, as follows:

- **Your Internet domain name**. Configures the reply address for all recipients appearing under Site Addressing Properties in the Exchange Server Administrator. The domain name must be registered with a Domain Name Registry service on the Internet, or provided to you by the ISP. If you have a dial-up Internet connection, the entered domain name is configured automatically on the **Dial-up Connections** tab of the Exchange Server IMS and thus used for mail retrieval.
- **I want to use the Web Publishing Wizard**. Select this option to display the **Configure Web Site Information** screen next, so the Web Publishing Wizard can be used.

Note Click **More Information** to display Help on configuring the Internet domain name.

Configure Web Site Information

If you selected **I want to use the Web Publishing Wizard** in the **Configure Internet Domain Name** screen, the following **Configure Web Site Information** screen is displayed.

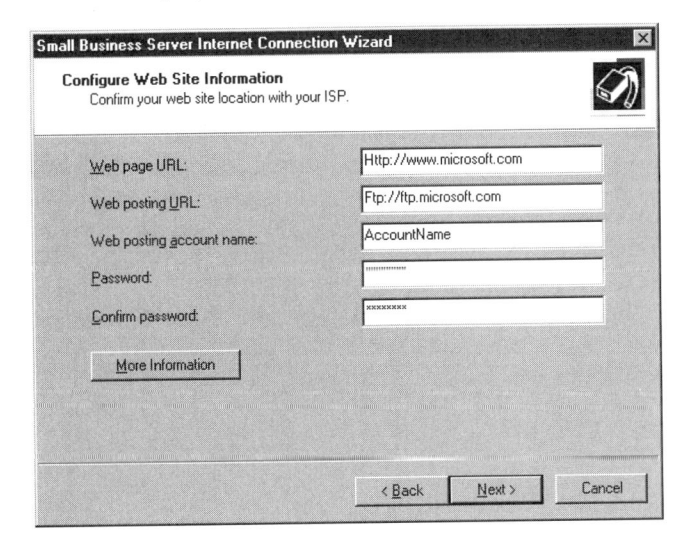

Provide the information required for accessing your web site and web posting site, as follows:

- **Web page URL**. The address of your web site on the Internet.
- **Web posting URL**. The address of the ISP site where the data composing your web site and all subsequent site updates are placed for publishing on the Internet.
- **Web posting account name**. The name of the web posting account provided by the ISP or a web publishing company.
- **Password**. The password for the web posting account provided by the ISP or web publishing company.
- **Confirm password**. Confirmation of the web posting account password.

Note The web posting account name and password may be different than the ones used to log onto the ISP.

Note Click **More Information** to display Help on configuring the web site information.

Configure Firewall Settings

When performing this task of the Internet Connection Wizard, the following **Configure Firewall Settings** screen is displayed.

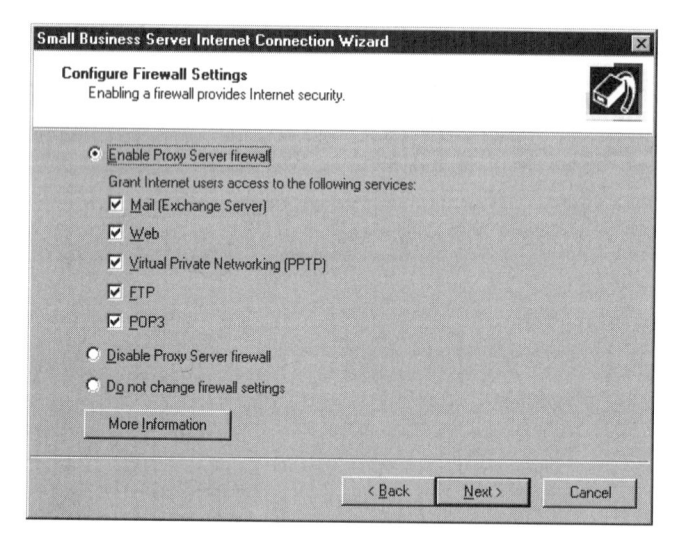

Here you can provide security for the LAN through a Proxy Server firewall, as follows:

- **Enable Proxy Server firewall**. Enables packet filtering so that LAN users have Internet access through the Web Proxy or Winsock Proxy service. The following packet filters are installed by default:
  - ICMP Ping Echo.
  - ICMP Ping Response.
  - ICMP Source Quench.
  - ICMP Timeout.
  - ICMP Unreachable.
  - ICMP Outbound.
  - UDP DNS.

  If you select only **Enable Proxy Server firewall** without also selecting any of the Small Business Server services described below, LAN users will be able to utilize the services outbound to the Internet, but inbound requests for these services will be denied. Enable specific services for inbound Internet requests by selecting from the following:

- **Mail (Exchange Server)**. Enables Transmission Control Protocol (TCP) port 25 (SMTP) on Small Business Server for mail exchange with the ISP's SMTP server.
- **Web**. Permits your Small Business Server-hosted web site to be accessible on the Internet. Allows Small Business Server to listen for Internet requests on TCP ports 80 (HTTP) and 443 (HTTPS), to serve web pages from Internet Information Server (IIS).
- **Virtual Private Networking (PPTP)**. Enables remote clients to connect to Small Business Server over the Internet through Point-to-Point Tunneling Protocol (PPTP). Opens the PPTP call and receive filters (TCP port 1723) so that remote clients can connect to the LAN through a secure tunnel.
- **FTP**. Permits Internet users to access the Small Business Server's File Transfer Protocol (FTP) service by allowing the server to listen on TCP ports 20 and 21 for FTP and FTP-data, respectively.

- **POP3**. Allows Small Business Server to listen to POP3 requests from the Internet on TCP port 110.
- **Disable Proxy Server firewall**. Disables Proxy Server protection of LAN security.
- **Do not change firewall settings**. Select if you have previously configured Proxy Server settings you do not want changed by the wizard configuration.

Note Click **More Information** to display Help on configuring the firewall settings.

Finishing the Internet Connection Wizard

When Internet Connection Wizard configuring is complete, the following screen is displayed.

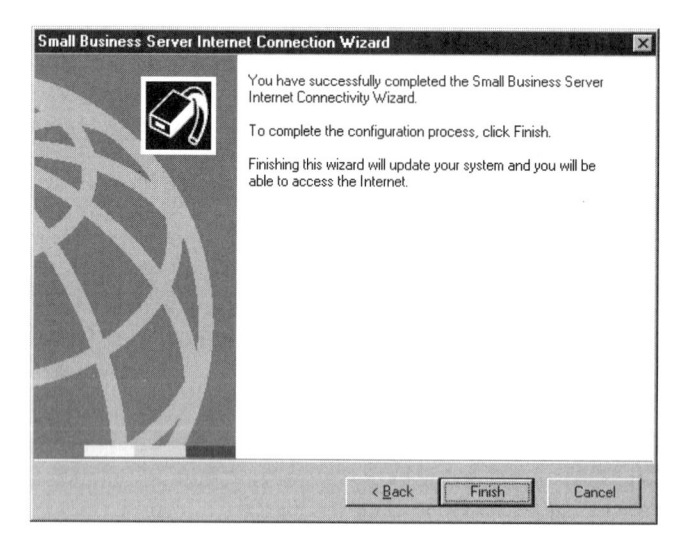

Click **Finish** to start the Internet Connection Wizard's automatic configuration process of Small Business Server applications.

4. Click **Auto Dial** to display the following **Microsoft Proxy Auto Dial** dialog box.

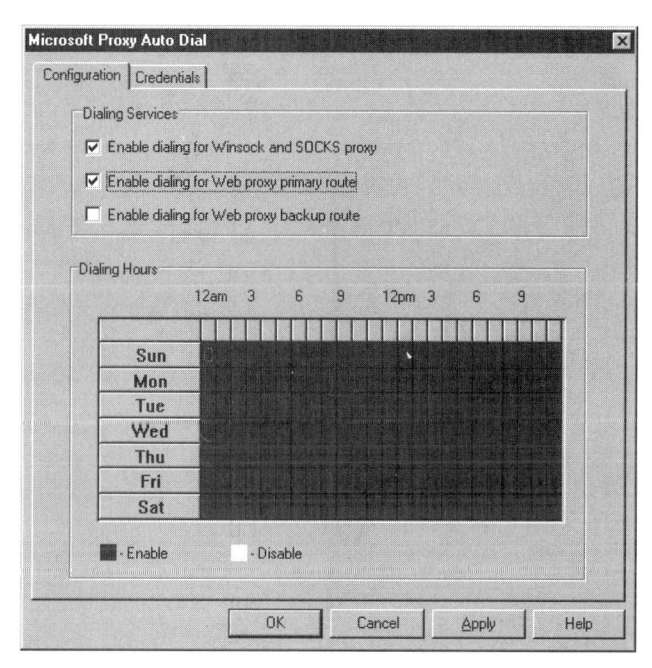

5. Select the **Configuration** tab, and then select **Enable dialing for Web proxy primary route** and **Enable for Winsock and SOCKS Proxy**.
6. By clicking on the **Dialing Hours** grid, set the days and hours during which auto-dial will be allowed.
7. Click **Apply**, and then click **OK**.
8. Click **OK** to exit the **Properties** box.

A dial-up connection for Proxy Server is accomplished by creating a RAS phonebook entry for the ISP account.

Configuring Proxy Server Internet Connectivity

Proxy Server must be configured to connect to the right ISP account for web browsing. Perform the steps below to establish either a full-time or dial-up connection.

▶ **To configure a full-time Proxy connection**

1. Click **Start**, point to **Programs**, point to **Microsoft Proxy Server**, and then click **Microsoft Management Console** to display the following **IIS Console**.

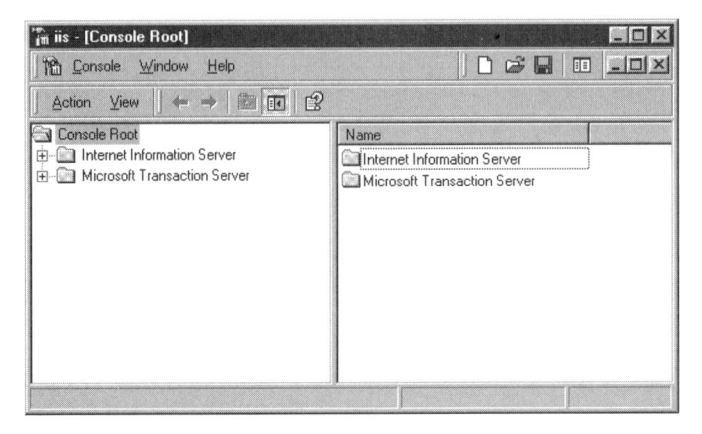

2. Double-click **Internet Information Server**, and then double-click the server.

3. Right-click **Web Proxy**, and then click **Properties** to display the following **Web Proxy Service Properties** dialog box.

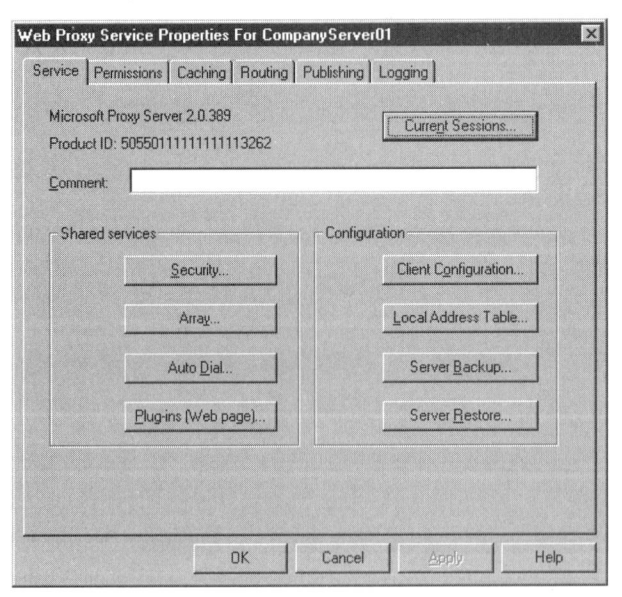

Domain Name

The DNS domain name for Small Business Server must be configured to enable Internet communications. Follow the steps below.

▶ **To configure the DNS domain name**
  1. Click **Start**, point to **Settings**, and then click **Control Panel**.
  2. Double-click the **Network** icon, and then select the **Protocols** tab.
  3. Select **TCP/IP**, and then click **Properties**.
  4. Click the **DNS** tab to display the following **TCP/IP Properties** dialog box.

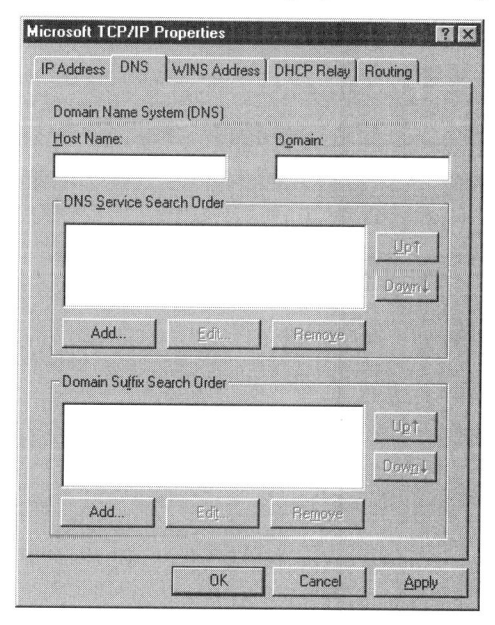

  5. Type your domain name (e.g., yourcompany.com) in **Domain**.
  6. Click **OK** to exit.

Manual Configuration of Server Applications for Internet Connectivity

The Internet Connection Wizard automatically configures Small Business Server for Internet connectivity by creating the appropriate configurations across the necessary server applications. If you want a more comprehensive understanding of the Internet Connection Wizard process, you can manually duplicate the server application configuration by using the procedures in the following sections.

ISP Dial-Up Networking Phonebook Entry

Small Business Server must have a dial-up networking phonebook entry for dialing out to the ISP. Follow the steps below to set up the entry.

▶ **To configure an ISP dial-up networking Phonebook entry**

1. Click **Start**, point to **Programs**, point to **Accessories**, and then click **Dial-Up Networking** to display the following **Dial-Up Networking** dialog box.

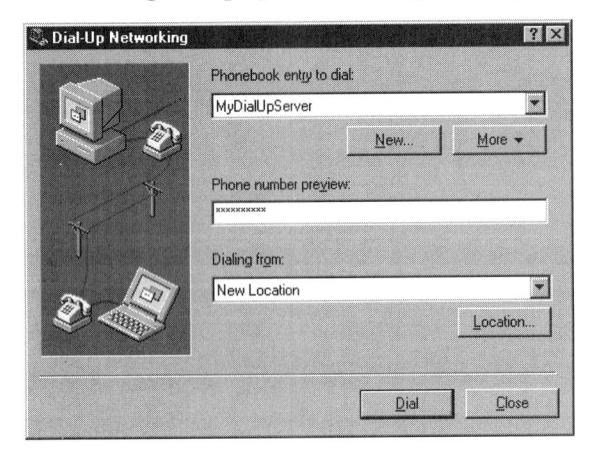

2. Click **New**.
3. Follow the instructions in the wizard to create the Phonebook entry.
4. Click **Close** when finished.

▶ **To configure a dial-up Proxy connection**

1. Click **Start**, point to **Programs**, point to **Accessories**, and then click **Dial-Up Networking** to display the following **Dial-Up Networking** dialog box.

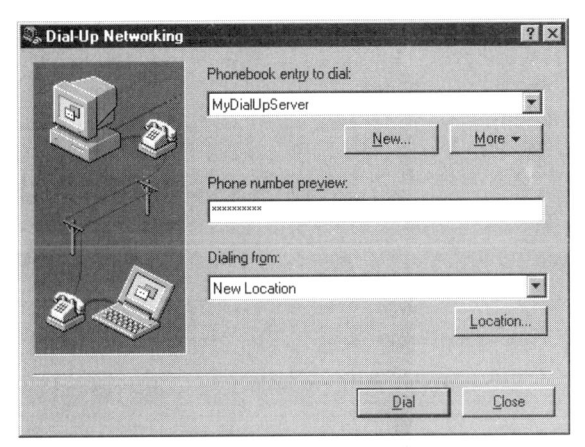

2. Click **New** and follow the steps of the wizard to create a dial-up connection. Click **Close** when finished.

3. Click **Start**, point to **Programs**, point to **Microsoft Proxy Server**, and then click **Microsoft Management Console** to display the following **IIS Console**.

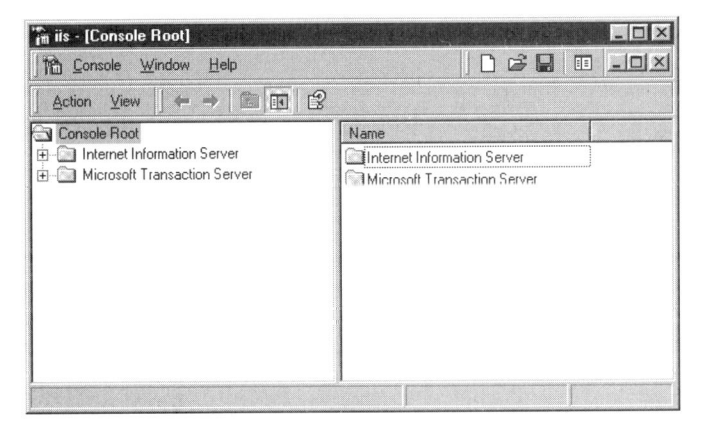

4. Double-click **Internet Information Server**, and then double-click the server.

5. Right-click on **Web Proxy**, and then click **Properties** to display the following **Web Proxy Service Properties** dialog box.

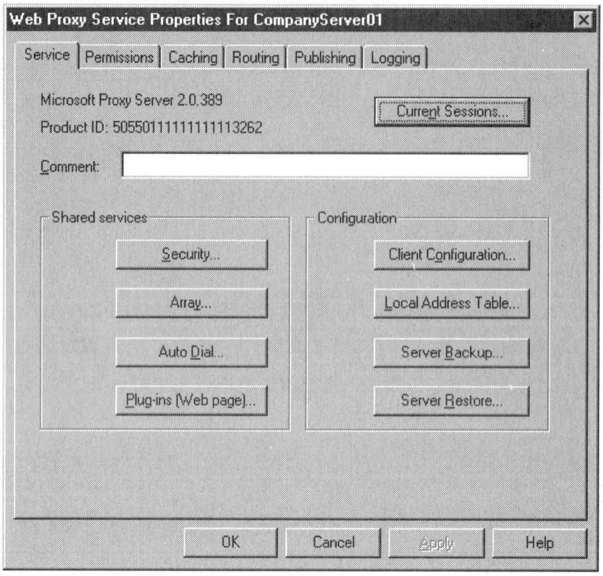

6. Click **Auto Dial**, then select the **Credentials** tab to display the following **Microsoft Proxy Auto Dial** dialog box.

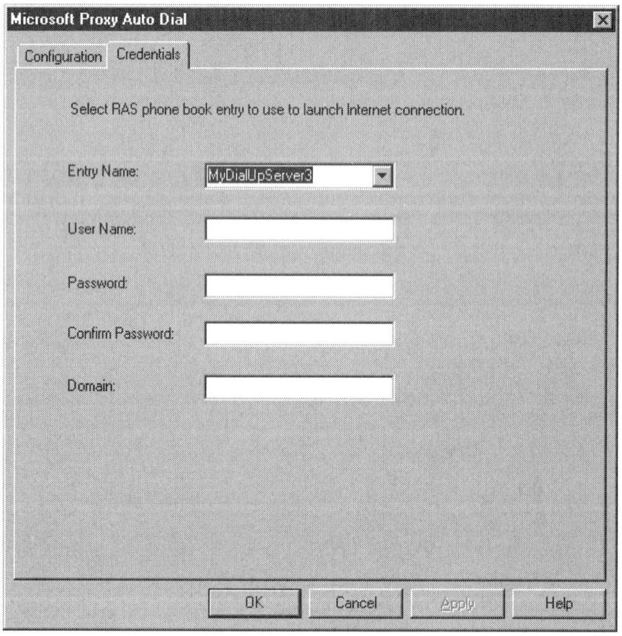

7. Select the phone book entry you created in step 2, and fill in the **User Name** and **Password** provided by the ISP.

   Note Depending on your ISP's configuration, there may not be a value for **Domain**.

8. Click **OK**.

Configuring Proxy Server Packet Filtering

To configure Proxy Server's predefined or custom packet filters manually, refer to the "Security Architecture" section in *Chapter 36, Firewall Security and Web Caching with Proxy Server 2.0* in *Part 7, Security*, of this resource guide.

Configuring the Proxy Server LAT

To manually configure or update the LAT, refer to the "Proxy Local Address Table" section in *Chapter 27, Administering Small Business Server Components* in *Part 4, Administering and Maintaining*, of this resource guide.

Configuring Web Publishing Wizard

The Web Publishing Wizard on the Small Business Server console uses FTP to publish web content. If the ISP supports this method of web publishing, manually configure Small Business Server with the appropriate information. A registry entry must be created for the FTP address.

▶ **To launch the registry editor and create the FTP address entry**

1. Click **Start**, click **Run**, type *regedt32.exe*, and then click **OK** to launch the following **Registry Editor**.

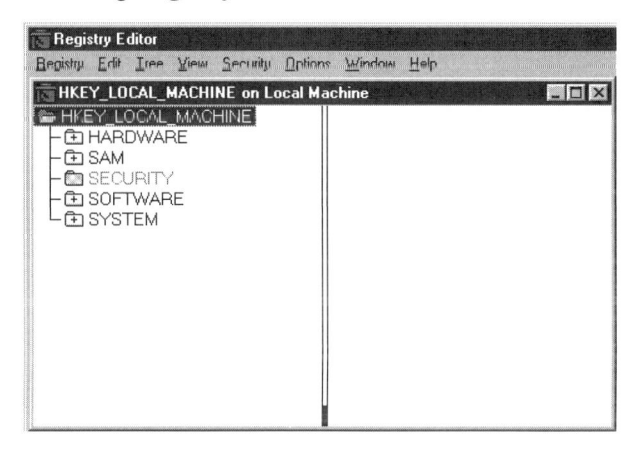

2. Select **HKEY_LOCAL_MACHINE on Local Machine**.
3. On the **Registry** menu, click **Open local**.
4. On the **Edit** menu, click **Add Key** to display the following **Add Key** dialog box.

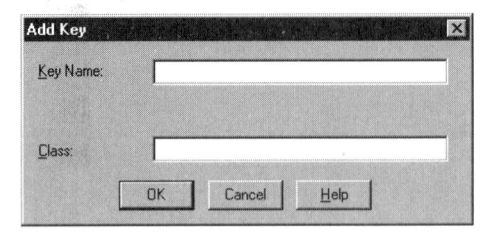

5. Create the following new keys:
   - HKLM\Software\Microsoft\Small Business\Internet\WEB_INFO
6. In the WEB_INFO folder, create the following values:
   - FTP_PATH (REG_SZ)= ftp://webftproot
   - InternetSite (REG_SZ)= http://www.yourcompany.internetserviceprovider.tld, where .tld refers to the top level domain.
   - Name (REG_SZ)= *publishing account ID*
   - Password (REG_SZ)= *publishing account password*
7. On the **Registry** menu, click **Exit** when finished.

Caution Using the **Registry Editor** incorrectly can cause serious problems that may ultimately require a complete reinstall of the operating system. Proceed cautiously.

For more information on editing the registry, see the online Help in the **Registry Editor**. Back up your registry before editing it.

Configuring Exchange

When Small Business Server is installed, Exchange Server is also installed. Exchange Server's IMS connector for receiving and delivering your e-mail is created on first use, however, it must be configured as follows.

Chapter 21 ISP Connectivity Tasks 201

▶ **To launch the Exchange Administrator program and configure the IMS**

1. Click **Start**, point to **Programs**, point to **Microsoft Exchange**, and then click **Microsoft Exchange Administrator** to launch the following **Microsoft Exchange Administrator**.

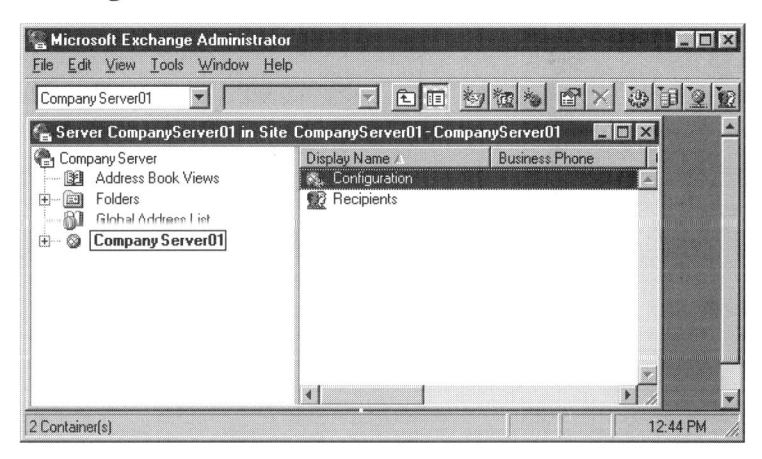

2. In the **Display Name** pane, double-click **Configuration**, **Connections**, and **Internet Mail Service** in succession to display the following **Internet Mail Service Properties** dialog box.

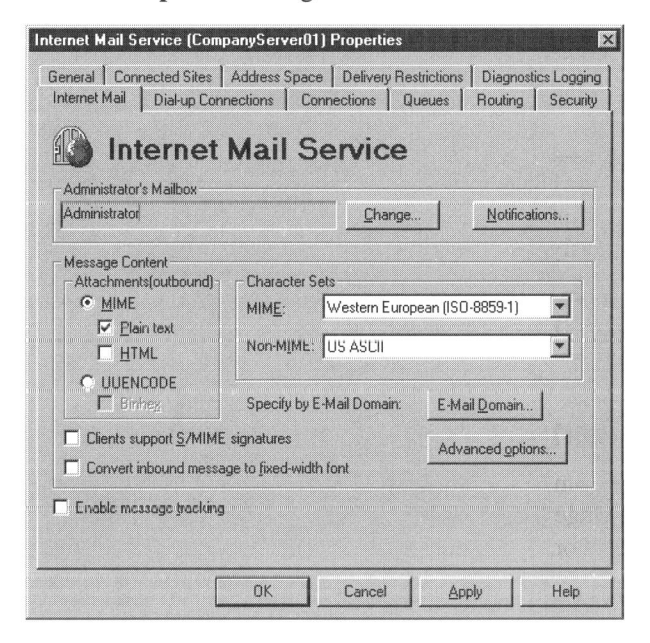

3. Select the **Internet Mail** tab, click **Change** to set the administrator mailbox: select or type the name of the user who will receive administrative messages, alerts, or notifications.

4. Click **Apply**, and then click **OK**.

▶ **To configure the IMS Address Space page**

1. From the **Internet Mail Service Properties** dialog box, select the **Address Space** tab.

2. Click **New** to display the following **New Address Space** dialog box.

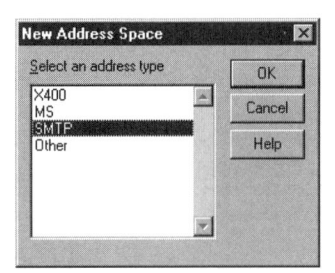

3. Select **SMTP**, and then click **OK** to display the following **SMTP Properties** dialog box.

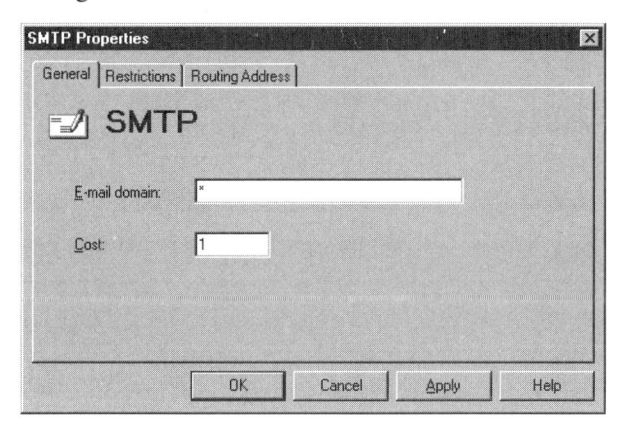

4. Type an **E-mail domain** of "*" and a **Cost** of "1".
5. Click **Apply**, and then click **OK**.

▶ **To configure the IMS Dial-up Connections page**

1. From the **Internet Mail Service Properties** dialog box, select the **Dial-up Connections** tab.

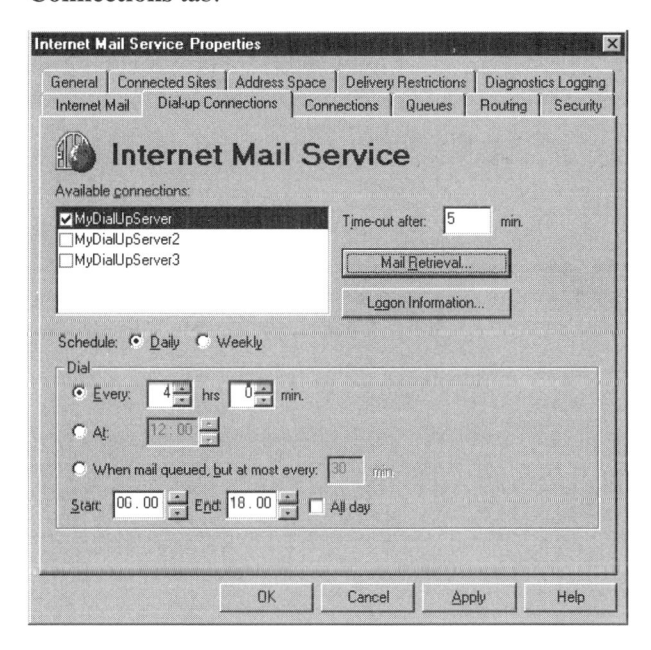

2. Select the schedule you want and then click **Mail Retrieval** to display the following **Mail Retrieval** dialog box.

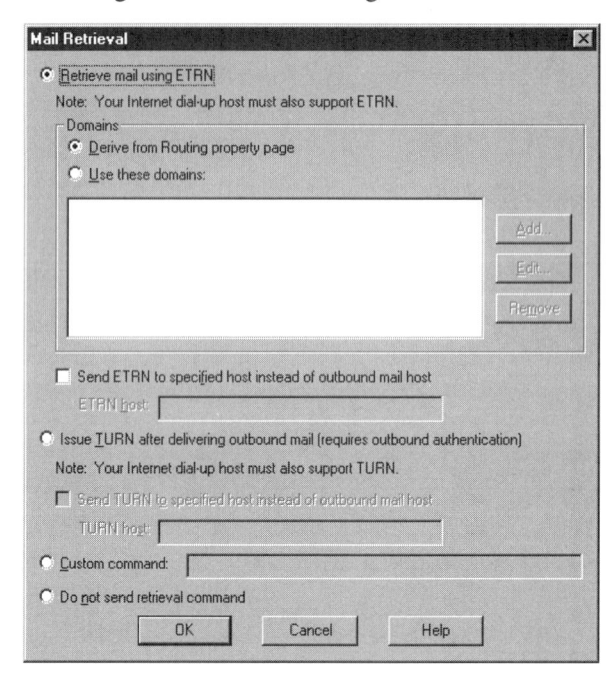

3. Enter the appropriate information. If your ISP supports ETRN, select **Retrieve mail using ETRN**.

4. Click **Apply**, and then click **OK**.

▶ **To configure the IMS Connections page**

1. From the **Internet Mail Service Properties** dialog box, select the **Connections** tab.

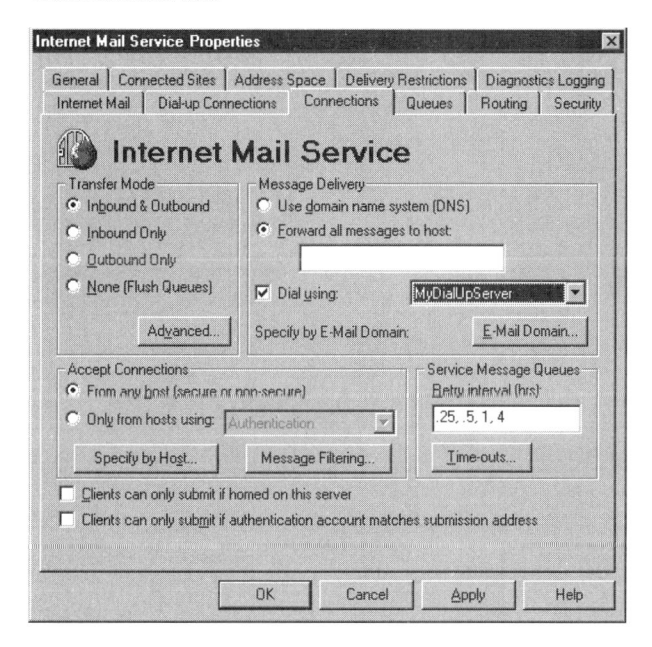

2. Select **Forward all messages to host** and type the IP address or DNS name of the ISP mail host in the text field.

3. Select **Dial Using**, then from the drop-down list, select the Dial-Up Networking phonebook entry for the small business.

4. Click **Apply**, and then click **OK**.

▶ **To configure the IMS Routing page**

1. From the **Internet Mail Service Properties** dialog box, select the **Routing** tab.

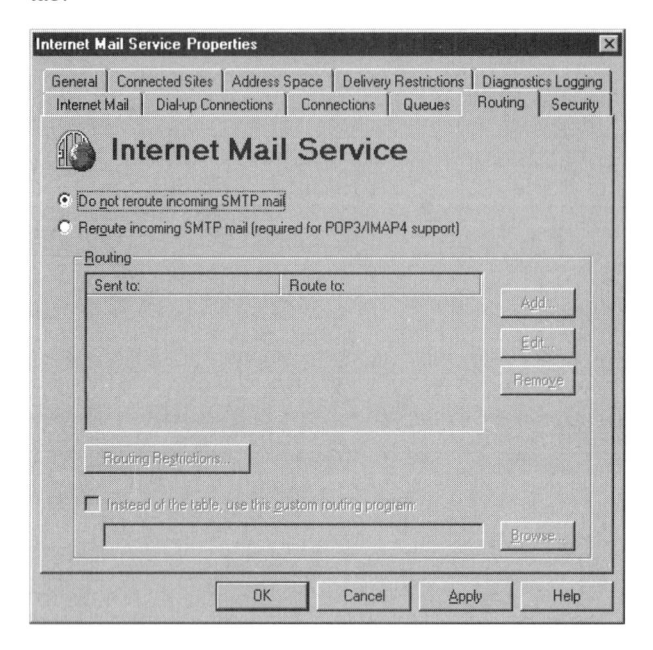

2. To disable message routing, select **Do not reroute incoming SMTP mail**.

3. Click **Apply**, and then click **OK**.

Use the procedure below to configure Small Business Server's Exchange site addressing with the correct domain name.

Note Also use this procedure to reconfigure Exchange site addressing if the Small Business Server domain name is being changed from a third level name (e.g., yourcompany.isp.com) to a second-level name (e.g., yourcompany.com).

▶ **To configure the IMS Site, Configuration, Site Addressing properties**

1. In Exchange Administrator, expand the server, and then select **Configuration**.

2. In the **Display Name** pane, double-click **Site Addressing** to display the following **Site Addressing Properties** dialog box.

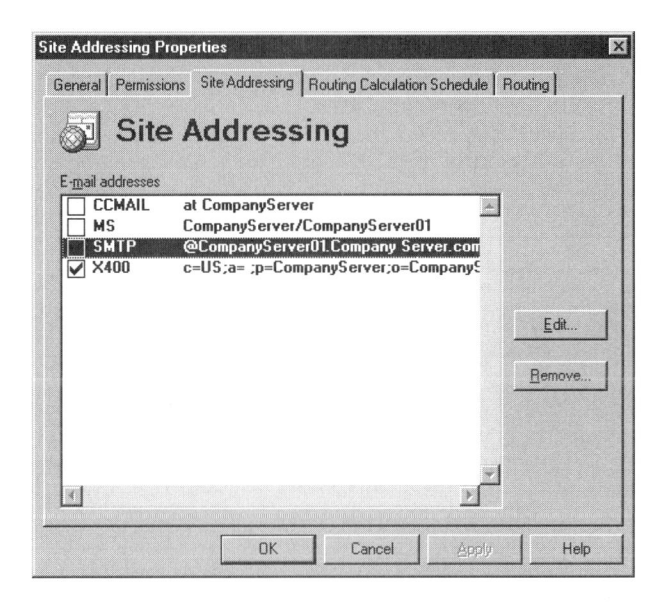

3. On the **Site Addressing** tab, make sure the **SMTP** address setting corresponds with the domain name in use.
4. If you need to modify the SMTP address, click **Edit** to display the following **SMTP Properties** dialog box.

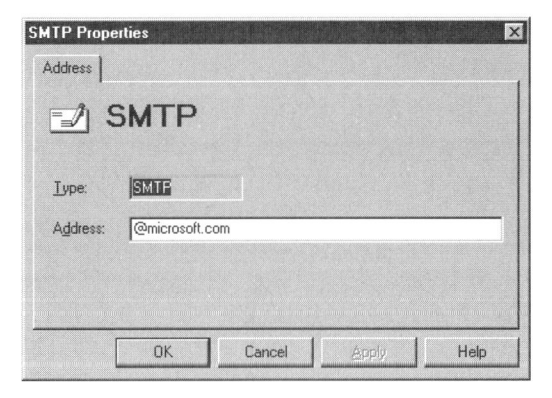

5. Change the **Address** field to the correct domain name. For example, if the domain name is "yourcompany.com", then set the **Address** field to "@yourcompany.com".

   Note If the SMTP Address is changed to match the small business DNS domain name, Exchange will ask if it should start a background job to update all the mail recipients with the new address. Click **Yes**.

6. Click **OK** in the **SMTP Properties** dialog box.
7. Click **OK** in the **Site Addressing Properties** dialog box.

▶ **To set the IMS to automatic startup**
1. Click **Start**, point to **Settings**, and then click **Control Panel**.
2. Double-click the **Services** icon to display the following **Services** dialog box.

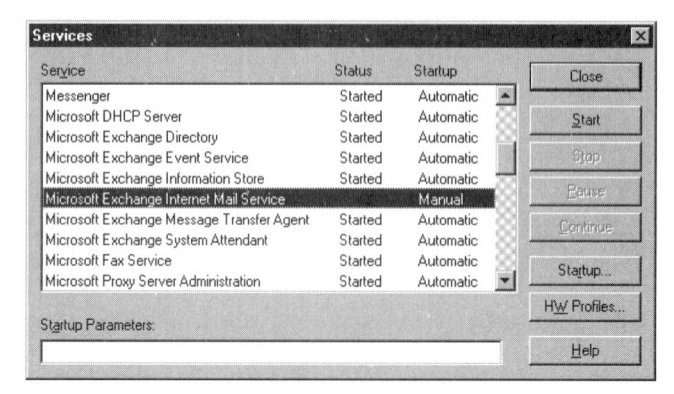

3. Select **Microsoft Exchange Internet Mail Service**, and then click **Startup** to display the following **Service** dialog box.

4. In **Startup Type**, select **Automatic**.
5. Click **OK**, and then click **Close**.

Configuring Exchange Server and Outlook Express Clients for POP3 Mail Exchange

If you want Small Business Server users with the Outlook® Express e-mail client to send and receive POP3 mail using the Exchange Server, configure both the Exchange Server and Outlook Express clients, as follows.

▶ **To configure the Exchange Server for POP3 mail**

1. Click **Start**, point to **Programs**, point to **Microsoft Exchange**, and then click **Microsoft Exchange Administrator** to launch the following **Microsoft Exchange Administrator**.

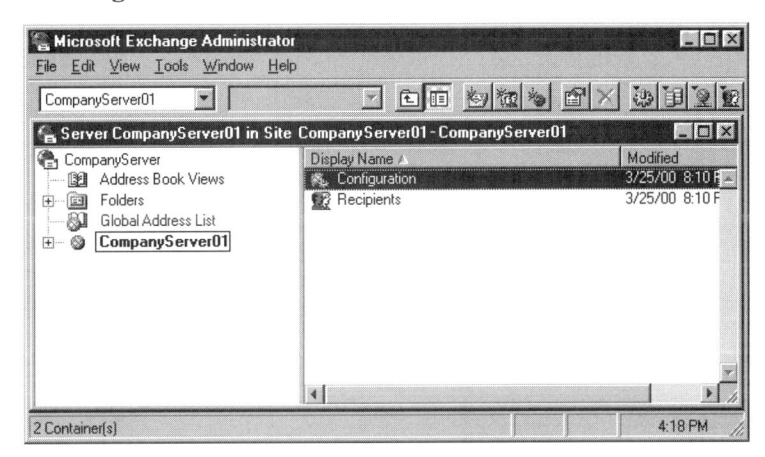

2. In the **Display Name** pane, double-click **Configuration**, **Connections**, and **Internet Mail Service** in succession to display the following **Internet Mail Service Properties** dialog box.

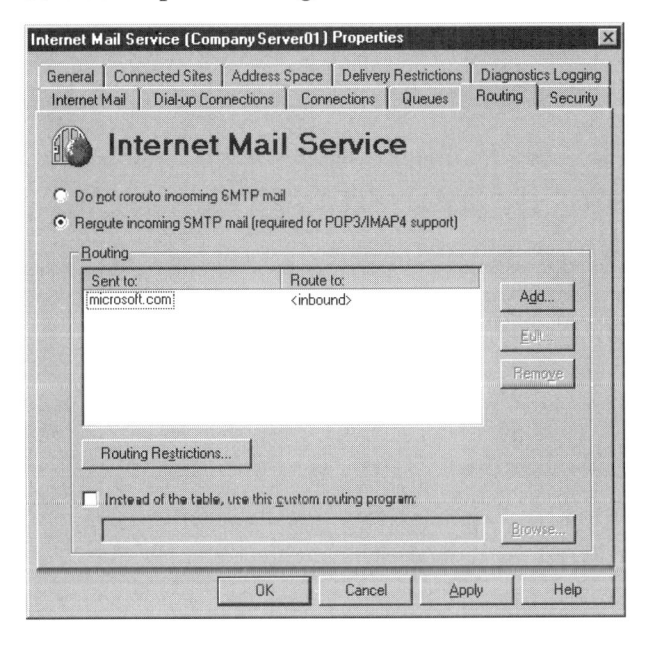

3. Select the **Routing** tab, and then select **Reroute incoming SMTP mail (required for POP3/IMAP4 support)**.

4. Click **Apply**, and then click **OK**.

▶ **To configure Outlook Express clients to use Exchange Server for POP3 mail**

1. Click **Start**, point to **Programs**, and then click **Outlook Express** to launch Outlook Express.

2. On the **Tools** menu, click **Accounts** to display the following **Internet Accounts** dialog box.

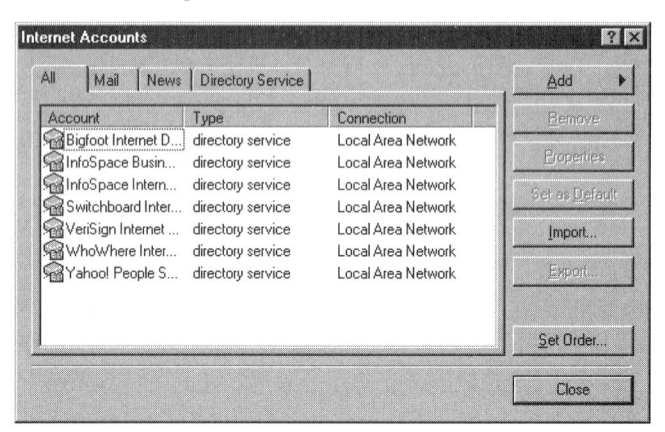

3. Click **Add** and **Mail** to display the following **Your Name** dialog box of the Internet Connection Wizard.

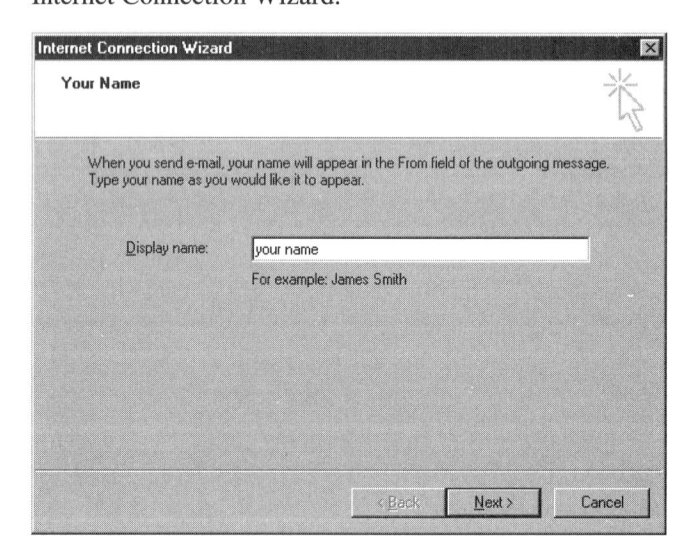

4. Type your name in **Display name** as you want it to appear in the **From** field of outgoing messages. Click **Next** to display the following **Internet E-mail Address** dialog box.

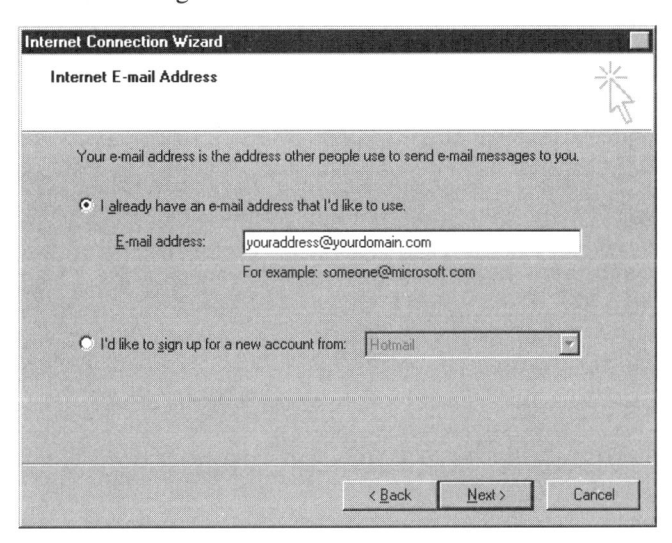

5. Type your existing e-mail address in **E-mail address**. Click **Next** to display the following **E-mail Server Names** dialog box.

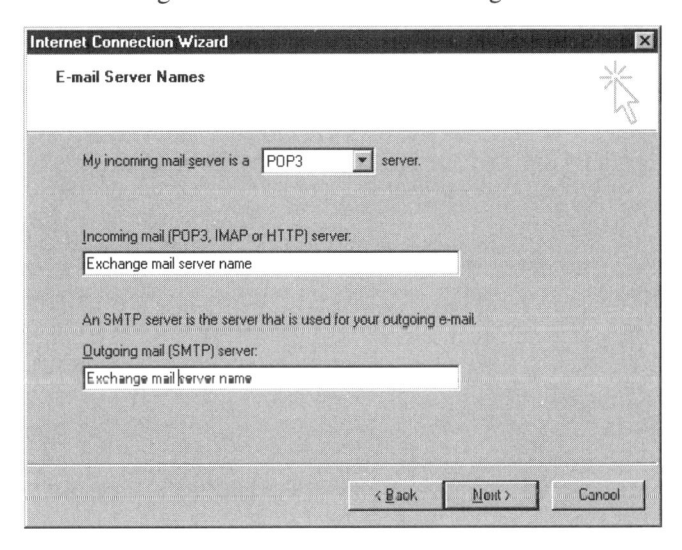

6. From the drop-down list, select **POP3**.
7. Type your Exchange Server mail server name in **Incoming mail (POP3, IMAP, or HTTP) server**.

8. Type your Exchange Server name in **Outgoing mail (SMTP) server**. Click **Next** to display the following **Internet Mail Logon** dialog box.

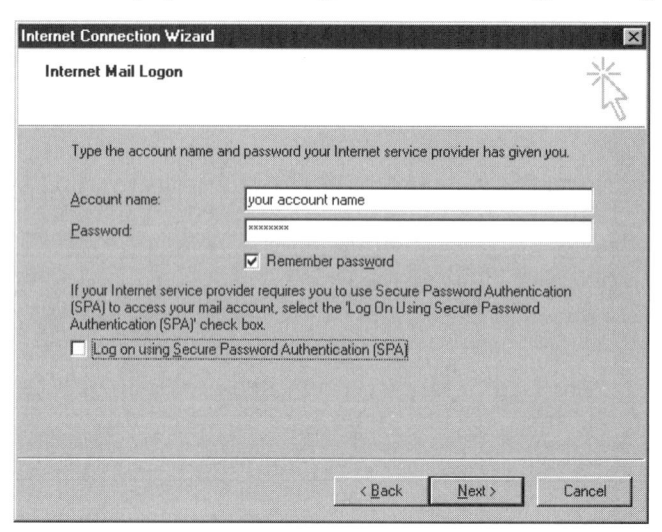

9. Type the NT account name and password.
10. Click **Next** and then **Finish** to exit the wizard.

CHAPTER 22

Setting up Remote Client Computers

This chapter covers procedures for setting up remote client computers to access Microsoft® BackOffice® Small Business Server. Setup includes installation and configuration of the client applications on the remote client computers. It also includes the steps necessary to configure remote clients to access Small Business Server through dial-up networking. Topics covered in this chapter include:

- Preliminary setup steps.
- Configuring the remote client computer.
- Connecting to Small Business Server using dial-up networking.

Preliminary Setup Steps

Before beginning the setup process, make sure that you have met the following pre-setup conditions:

1. On Small Business Server, the Remote Access Service (RAS) is installed and configured.

   Note This is performed by default during Small Business Server setup.

2. On the client computer to be configured, the following exists:
   - Windows® 95/98 or Windows NT® 4.0 Workstation (Service Pack 3 or later) is installed.
   - A modem must be installed—refer to the Recommended Hardware List at the following web site:
     http://www.microsoft.com/smallbusinessserver
   - The Microsoft Back Office Small Business Server CD's is available if the remote client computer cannot be directly connected to the local network via a network adapter.

Configuring the Remote Client Computer

This section describes the procedures necessary to configure remote client computers to work with Small Business Server. Configuration of remote client computers requires the following:

- A user account must be created for the remote user.
- Applications must be installed on the remote client computer.
- The remote client computer must be configured to use dial-up networking.

Create the User Account for the Remote User

Set up remote clients through the Manage Server.

▶ **To create the user account for the remote user**

1. Under **Tasks** on the Small Business Server console, click on **Manage Users**.
2. Click **Add a User**.
3. Fill in the appropriate information for the user account, password, user information, and resources.
4. When the **Select Additional Access Rights** screen displays, select **Use a modem to access the server computer**. This grants dial-in permissions to the remote user.
5. Once the user is created, you will be asked to run the Set Up Computer Wizard.
   - If you do not have access to the local network, click **Cancel** and skip to the section "Manually Installing the Small Business Server Client Applications."
   - If your remote client computer has a network card installed with access to the local network and Small Business Server, continue with the Set Up Computer Wizard. Be sure to follow the entire wizard process on the client computer to configure appropriate networking and install client applications on the remote client computer. To finish the configuration, proceed to the section entitled "Configuring the Client Computers to Use Dial-Up Networking."

Manually Installing Client Applications on the Client Computer

For remote client computers without access to the small business network, complete the steps below to manually install client applications on the client computer.

▶ **To install Outlook**

1. Insert the following Small Business Server compact discs into the client CD-ROM drive.
   - For an Office SKU, use Office disk 1.
   - For a non-Office SKU, use the Office with Outlook disk.
2. Click **Start**, and then click **Run** to display the **Run** screen.
3. Type the following: *<CD Drive>:\setup.exe*

   where *<CD Drive>* is the drive letter of the CD-ROM drive.
4. Follow the installation instructions to set up as a remote client, as required.
5. Click **Start**, point to **Settings**, and then click **Control Panel**.
6. Double-click **Mail and Fax** (or **Mail**).
7. Click **Add** to add a mail profile.
8. Select **Microsoft Exchange Server**.
9. Enter the Small Business Server name and the mailbox created when the remote user account was configured.
10. Follow the instructions off-screen to complete the Outlook setup and then restart the client computer.

▶ **To install Internet Explorer**

1. Click **Start**, and then click **Run**.
2. Type the following: *<CD Drive>:\ie5\EN\ie5setup.exe*

   where *<CD Drive>* is the drive letter of the CD ROM drive.
3. Follow the installation instructions for the components desired and restart the client computer.

Note Only perform this step if you intend to use Dial-Up Networking for your Small Business Server's sole Internet connection. If you use a separate ISP for Internet access, you do not need to configure Internet Explorer for use with Proxy.

▶ **To configure Internet Explorer for use with Proxy**

1. Click **Start**, point to **Programs**, and then click **Internet Explorer** to launch Microsoft Internet Explorer.
2. On the **Tools** menu, click **Internet Options**.
3. Select the **Connections** tab, and then click **LAN Settings** to display the **Local Area Network (LAN) Settings** dialog box.
4. Select **Use a proxy server** and **Bypass proxy server for local addresses**.
5. Type *http://servername* in the **Address** field, where *servername* is the name of the small business company server.
6. Type *80* in the **Port** field.
7. Click **Advanced**, and then select **Use the same proxy server for all protocols**.
8. Make sure the servername and port number specified in steps 5 and 6, respectively, appear in the **HTTP** protocol fields.
9. Click **OK** and exit all dialog boxes.

▶ **To install the Fax client software**

> **Note** If the Fax client is required on the remote client computer, it must be installed while connected to the Small Business Server. To configure DUN while connected to Small Business Server, refer to the sections ahead entitled "Configuring the Client Computers to Use Dial-Up Networking" and "Connecting to the Small Business Server using Dial-Up Networking."

1. Click **Start**, and then click **Run**.
2. For Windows 95/98, type the following:

   \\<*servername*>*clientapps**ms**fax**win95**setup -s -fsetup.ins -f1c:\setup.iss -f2c:\fax.log*

   where <*servername*> refers to the name of the Small Business Server.
3. For Windows NT, type the following:

   \\<*servername*>\ *clientapps**ms**fax**i386**faxsetup -tc -usetup**setup**i386**ntfax.txt*

   where <*servername*> refers to the name of the Small Business Server.

▶ **To install the Proxy client software**

> **Note** If the Proxy client is required on the remote client computer, it must be installed while connected to the Small Business Server. To configure DUN while connected to Small Business Server, refer to the sections ahead entitled "Configuring the Client Computers to Use Dial-Up Networking" and "Connecting to the Small Business Server Using Dial-Up Networking."

> **Note** Only perform the following steps if you intend to use the dial-up networking connection to Small Business Server as your sole Internet connection. If you use a separate ISP for Internet access, you do not need the Proxy client. If you install the Proxy client on a client computer that has a separate dial-up connection to an ISP, the Proxy client must be disabled when the ISP connection is used.

1. Click **Start**, and then click **Run**.
2. Type the following:

   \\<*servername*>*mspclnt**setup.exe*

   where <*servername*> refers to the name of the Small Business Server computer.
3. Follow the instructions on-screen to install the Proxy client.

> **Note** The Modem Sharing client should not be required for remote clients that already access the network through a modem.

Configuring the Client Computer to Use Dial-Up Networking

The following sections outline the necessary steps to configure a client computer for logon to the Small Business Server using Dial-Up Networking.

Windows 95/98 Client Computers

Complete the following steps to configure a Windows 95/98 client computer with dial-up networking to connect to the Small Business Server.

▶ **To configure the client computer to use dial-up networking**

1. Click **Start**, click **Settings**, and then click **Control Panel**.
2. Double-click **Network**.
3. Select the **Identification** tab.
4. In **Computer Name**, type a unique computer name that does not presently exist on the network.

5. In **Workgroup**, type the domain name configured on the Small Business Server.
6. Select the **Configuration** tab.
7. If Client for Microsoft Networks is not listed, do the following:
   - Click **Add**.
   - Double-click **Client**.
   - Under Manufacturers, select **Microsoft** and **Client for Microsoft Networks**.
   - Double-click **Client for Microsoft Networks**.
   - Place a check in the **Log on to Windows NT domain box**.
   - Enter the Small Business Server domain name under **Windows NT domain**.
8. If **Dial-Up Adapter** is not listed:
   - Click **Add**.
   - Double-click **Adapter**.
   - Under manufacturers, select **Microsoft** and then **Dial-Up Adapter**.
9. If **TCP/IP** is not listed:
   - Click **Add**.
   - Double-click **Protocol**.
   - Under manufacturers, select **Microsoft** and **TCP/IP**.
10. If **File and printer sharing for Microsoft Network** is not listed:
    - Click **Add**.
    - Double-click **Service**.
    - Under manufacturers, select **Microsoft** and **File and printer sharing for Microsoft Network**.

Windows NT Workstation Client Computers

To properly configure a Windows NT Workstation client to connect to the Small Business Server, you must first create a machine account. Then, configure the Windows NT Workstation client dial-up networking to connect to Small Business Server. Complete the following steps to create the machine account.

Connecting to Small Business Networking

The following sections outline th[e procedure for connecting to] Small Business Server using dial[-up networking.]

Connecting with a Windows 95/98 [client]

Before the remote Windows 95/9[8 client can connect,] you must create a phonebook ent[ry...]

> **Note** Two phonebook entries wi[ll be needed for] a secure virtual private network ([VPN]), one for the ISP and the other for [the phonebook entry]. configured on remote clients in th[e...see] *Chapter 23, Installing PPTP in t[he...]* Otherwise, follow the steps belo[w.]

▶ **To create a phonebook entry fo[r Windows 95/98]**
   1. Double-click **My Computer** [on the desktop.]
   2. Double-click **Dial-Up Networ[king.]**
   3. Double-click **Make New Con[nection.]**
   4. From the **Make New Connec[tion...]** telephone number for the Sma[ll Business Server.]
   5. Once the phonebook entry is c[reated,] point to **Properties**.
   6. Select the **Server Types** tab a[nd ensure] selected for the **Dial-Up Serve[r.]**
   7. Under **Advanced Options**, Lo[g on...]
   8. **TCP/IP** should be the only pro[tocol...] be changed when additional pr[otocols...]

▶ **To connect to Small Business Se[rver]**
   1. Double-click the phonebook e[ntry.]
   2. Type the user name and passw[ord...]
   3. The client computer will now b[e connected to the] domain.

Procedure for Windows 95/98

[In the prev]ious procedure, the client computer can be connected using the following steps (after the phonebook entry...

...acc]ess Server with a Windows 95/98 client

[When as]ked for a user name and password—click **Cancel** or hit [to d]elay authentication until the computer is connected to [the serv]er.

...[comp]uter on the desktop.
...[N]etworking.
...[phonebo]ok entry.
...[user name and] password, and then click **OK**.
[Once the connection is es]tablished, you will be asked for your user name and [password], and then click **OK**.

[Connecting with a Windows NT] Workstation Client Computer

[Before a Windows N]T client can connect to Small Business Server, a [...follow the] steps below.

▶ **[To create a phonebook en]try for a Windows NT client**
   1. [Double-click **My Comp**]**uter** on the desktop.
   2. [Double-click **Dial-Up N**]**etworking**.
   3. [Double-click **New Phonebook**] **Entry**.
   4. [Enter the] name and telephone number for the RAS connection.
   5. ...Edit Entry and Modem Properties.
   6. ...and make sure **PPP: Windows NT Server** is selected
   7. ...[the o]nly protocol listed under network protocols. This may ...[additi]onal protocols are required.
   8. [Once the phonebook entry h]as been created and the Windows NT Workstation ...[Windo]ws NT domain, follow the steps below to connect to

▶ **To connect to Small Business Server with a Windows NT Workstation client**
　1. Double-click the phonebook entry.
　2. Type the user name and password, and then click **OK**.
　3. The client computer will now be connected to the Small Business Server domain.

CHAPTER 23

Installing PPTP in the Small Business Network

Remote users can access Microsoft® BackOffice® Small Business Server 4.5 securely across the Internet backbone by establishing a virtual private network (VPN) using Remote Access Service (RAS) and Point-to-Point Tunneling Protocol (PPTP). PPTP is installed on Small Business Server as a network protocol via the **Protocols** tab in the **Network** option of Control Panel. PPTP can be added, configured, or removed using the **Protocols** tab. The following information is provided in this chapter to install and configure PPTP:

- System requirements.
- Configuration of PPTP on Small Business Server.
- PPTP client connections to Small Business Server.

Requirements

Before installing and configuring PPTP on Small Business Server, review the requirements below to assure successful deployment.

- Small Business Server has Windows NT® Server, version 4.0.
- One or more network adapters are installed. In most cases, two or more network adapters are required: one to connect to the Internet and the other to connect to the small business network.
- TCP/IP is installed and bound to the small business internal network adapter and the adapter is connected to the Internet.
- The PPTP server is configured with a static IP address.
- RAS with dial-up networking is installed and configured.
- You have identified the number of simultaneous connections with remote PPTP clients you want Small Business Server (PPTP-configured) to support, so the correct number of virtual private network (VPN) devices can be configured.

Configuring PPTP on Small Business Server

Configuring Small Business Server (running Windows NT 4.0) as a PPTP server involves these steps:

- Installing PPTP and selecting the number of VPN devices.
- Adding the VPN devices as RAS ports.
- Configuring encryption and authentication options.

Installing PPTP

Install PPTP per the following steps.

▶ **To install the PPTP protocol on Small Business Server**

1. Click **Start**, point to **Settings**, and then click **Control Panel**.
2. Double-click **Network**.
3. Select the **Protocols** tab, and then click **Add** to display the **Select Network Protocol** dialog box.

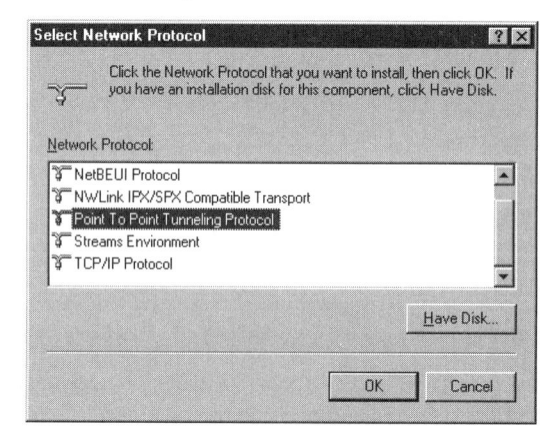

4. Select **Point To Point Tunneling Protocol**, and then click **OK**.
5. Type the drive and directory location of the Windows NT Server 4.0 installation files in the **Windows NT Setup** dialog box and then click **Continue**. The PPTP files are copied from the installation directory and the **PPTP Configuration** dialog box below appears.

6. Select the **Number of Virtual Private Networks** the server will support. A maximum of 256 clients may be enabled with simultaneous VPN connections.
7. Click **OK** twice.
8. Continue installation of PPTP by clicking **Add** to add the VPN devices installed with PPTP to RAS.

Note You must complete the steps in the following procedure to complete the configuration of PPTP.

Adding VPN Devices as RAS Ports on Small Business Server

After the initial installation of PPTP, VPN devices must be added to RAS on Small Business Server per the following steps.

▶ **To configure VPN devices on the PPTP server**

1. Click **Start**, point to **Settings**, and then click **Control Panel**.
2. Double-click **Network**.
3. Select the **Services** tab, and then click **Remote Access Service**.
4. Click **Properties** to display the **Remote Access Setup** properties page.
5. Click **Add**. The **Add RAS Device** properties page below appears.

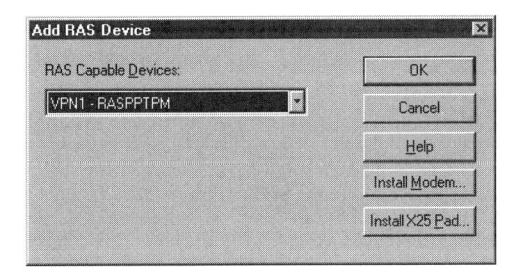

6. Select the VPN devices you want to use in the **RAS Capable Devices** drop-down list.
7. Click **OK**. Repeat steps 5, 6, and 7 until all desired VPNs are added.
8. In the **Remote Access Setup** dialog box, select a VPN port and click **Configure**. Verify that the **Receive calls only** option in the **Port Usage** dialog box is selected and then click **OK** to return to the **Remote Access Setup** properties page. (If this server is ever used as a PPTP client and you want to use this VPN device to dial out as a PPTP device, select **Dial-out**.)
9. Repeat the last step for each VPN device displayed on the **Remote Access Setup** properties tab. On Small Business Server, VPN devices are configured automatically with the **Receive calls only** option by default, but this configuration should be verified.

10. Click **Network** to display the **Network Configuration** dialog box. Verify that only **TCP/IP** is selected in the **Server Settings**. Click **OK** to return to the **Remote Access Setup** properties page.
11. Click **Continue**.
12. Click **Close** to exit **Network**, and then restart the computer.

Configuring PPTP Server Encryption and Authentication Options

This section provides information for configuring the Small Business Server with PPTP in three steps.

- Configuring for the encryption of data sent over the Internet.
- Configuring for the acceptance of PPTP packets from the Internet.
- Configuring LAN routing in the small business network.

Configuring for Data Encryption on VPN Devices

Encryption of data is performed by the remote access protocol known as Point-to-Point Protocol (PPP). Encryption is enabled by configuring each VPN device added and configured in RAS properties. This is identical to configuring encryption for other RAS devices, such as a modem.

▶ **To enable encryption of a VPN device on Small Business Server**

1. Click **Start**, point to **Settings**, and then click **Control Panel**.
2. Double-click **Network**.
3. Select the **Services** tab, and then click **Remote Access Service**.
4. Click **Properties** to display the **Remote Access Setup** properties page.

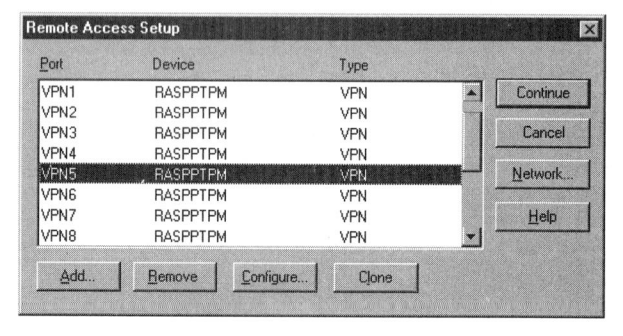

5. Select a VPN device for which you want to enable encryption, and then click **Network**. The **Network Configuration** dialog box appears.

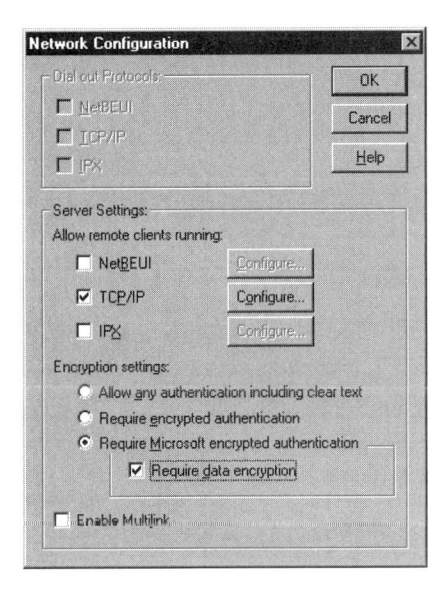

6. Select **Require Microsoft encrypted authentication** and **Require data encryption**. RAS and PPP will now enforce Windows NT-based authentication of all remote clients connecting to Small Business Server set up as a PPTP server.

7. Click **OK** to return to the **Remote Access Setup** properties page.

8. Click **Continue**.

9. Click **Close** to exit the **Network** utility, and then restart the computer.

PPTP Client Connections to Small Business Server

A PPTP client can connect to Small Business Server (PPTP-configured) in the following three ways:

- Using dial-up lines to the Internet.
- Using a LAN connection, such as an Ethernet connection and adapter.
- Using an Internet-connected network tap, found in mobile office work areas such as a conference room.

Before the remote client can connect to Small Business Server, PPTP must be installed on the client side. In the sections that follow, PPTP is installed and configured on Windows NT Workstation and Windows 95/98 client computers.

Installing and Configuring PPTP on Windows NT-Based Remote Clients

The following are required before performing the procedures in this section:

- Windows NT Workstation version 4.0 or Windows NT Server version 4.0 installed on the remote client computer.
- TCP/IP installed.
- RAS with Dial-Up Networking installed.
- An analog modem, ISDN device, or other modem device installed and configured in RAS to enable the remote client for dial-out connection.
- If the Internet is used to connect to Small Business Server (PPTP-configured), a PPP account is established with an ISP.

Installation of the PPTP Client

Use the following steps to install PPTP on a Windows NT-based remote client.

▶ **To install PPTP protocol on a Windows NT-based remote client computer**

1. Click **Start**, point to **Settings**, and then click **Control Panel**.
2. Double-click **Network**.
3. Select the **Protocols** tab, and then click **Add** to display the **Select Network Protocol** dialog box.

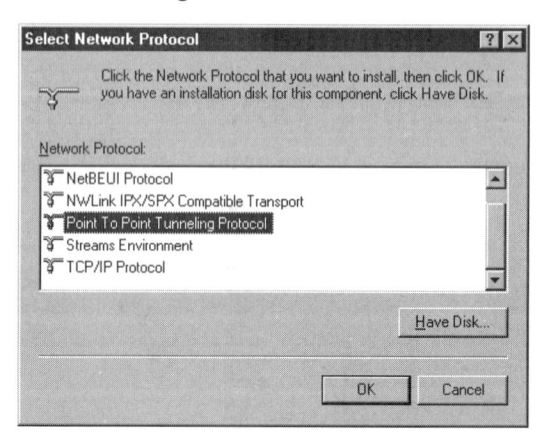

4. Select **Point-To-Point Tunneling Protocol**, and then click **OK**.

5. Type the drive and directory location of your installation files in the **Windows NT Setup** dialog box, and then click **Continue**. The PPTP files are copied from the installation directory and the **PPTP Configuration** dialog box appears.

6. Select the **Number of Virtual Private Networks** the client will support. You can select a maximum number of 256. Typically, however, only one VPN is installed on a PPTP client.

7. Click **OK**, and then click **OK** again.

8. Continue installation by clicking **Add** to add the VPN device installed with PPTP.

Adding a VPN Device as a RAS Port on the PPTP Client

After installing PPTP, a VPN device must be added to RAS on the PPTP client computer per the following steps.

▶ **To configure a VPN device on the PPTP client**

1. Click **Start**, point to **Settings**, and then click **Control Panel**.
2. Double-click **Network**.
3. Select the **Services** tab, and then click **Remote Access Service**.
4. Click **Properties** to display the **Remote Access Setup** properties page.
5. Click **Add**. The **Add RAS Device** properties page appears.

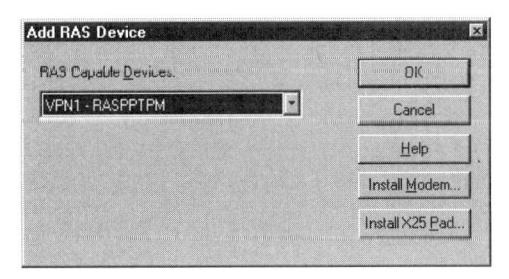

6. Select in the drop-down list, the VPN devices you want to use in the **RAS Capable Devices**.

7. Click **OK**. If you installed PPTP with more than one VPN device, repeat steps 5, 6, and 7 until all the VPNs are added.

8. By default, the VPN device on a Windows NT Workstation computer is configured to dial out only. Select the VPN port and click **Configure**. Verify that the **Dial out only** option in the **Port Usage** dialog box is the only option selected. Click **OK** to return to the **Remote Access Setup** properties dialog box.

9. Click **Network** to display the **Network Configuration** dialog box.

10. Verify that only **TCP/IP** is selected in **Dial out Protocols**. Click **OK**.

11. Click **Continue**.

12. Click **Close** to exit the Network, and then restart the computer.

Configuring Dial-Up Networking on the PPTP Client

When PPTP is configured for remote client access to the small business network, the PPTP client must have two phonebook entries: one to connect to the ISP and one to connect to the small business (PPTP) server. The following procedures describe how to use dial-up networking to create both phonebook entries. Before performing the following steps, however, ensure that:

- All network protocols used on the small business network (to which the remote connection is being made) are installed.

- RAS is configured to dial out using those network protocols.

▶ **To create a new ISP entry using the Phonebook Wizard**

1. Click **Start**, point to **Programs**, **Accessories**, and then click **Dial-Up Networking**. If this is the first phonebook entry created, the **Dial-Up Networking** dialog box appears. Click **OK**.

2. Click **New**. The New Phonebook Entry Wizard appears.

3. Type the name of the ISP in **Name the new phonebook entry** and then click **Next**. An ISP name can be no longer than 20 characters and with no spaces in it.

4. Click **I am calling the Internet**, and then click **Next**. This configures the phonebook entry to use TCP/IP and PPP as the dial-up networking protocols.

5. Select your modem device in **Select the modem or adapter this entry will use** in the **Modem or Adapter** dialog box, and then click **Next**.

6. Type the ISP phone number in **Phone number** in the **Phone Number** dialog box. Click **Use Telephony dialing properties** if you need to add an area code or other prefix. Click **Alternatives** if you have an alternative phone number for your ISP.

7. Click **Next**, and then click **Finish**.

8. Verify the phonebook entry in the steps that follow.

▶ **To verify or edit your ISP phonebook entry**

1. In **Dial-Up Networking**, click **More**, and then click **Edit entry and modem properties** to verify the entry in the **Edit Phonebook Entry** dialog box.

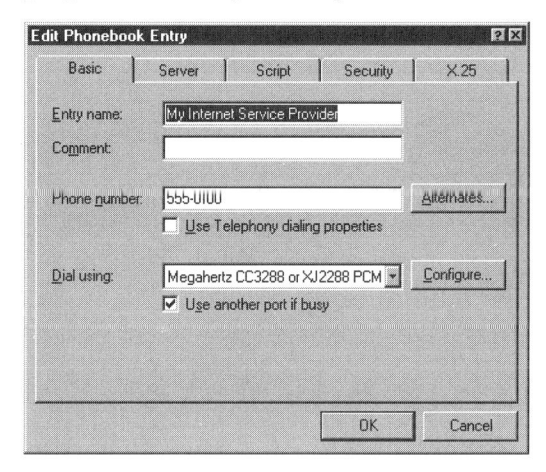

2. Select the **Basic** tab and verify the phone number is correct and the correct modem or ISDN device is selected. Make any necessary changes.

3. Select the **Server** tab and verify that the **Dial-up server type** displays "PPP: Windows NT, Windows 95 Plus, Internet."

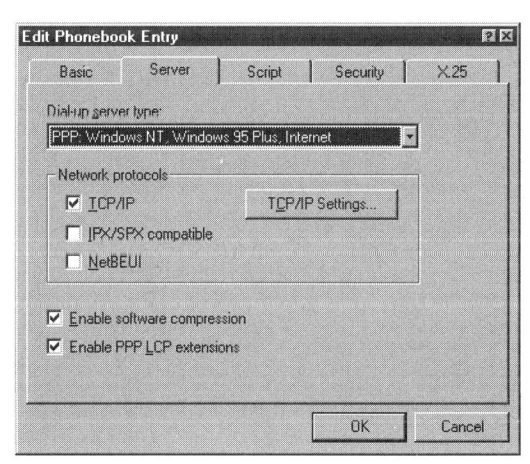

4. In the **Network protocols** box, ensure that **TCP/IP** is selected.

5. Click **TCP/IP Settings** to display the **PPP TCP/IP Settings** dialog box. Ensure that the TCP/IP settings conform to the IP address and server name specified by the ISP. Click **OK** to close the dialog box.

6. By default, the options **Enable Software Compression** and **Enable PPP LCP extensions** are selected. These settings are compatible with most ISP services; check with the ISP, however, before changing the settings.

7. Select the **Script** tab, and then select **None**. The PPP protocol provided in RAS is designed to automate remote logon. If the ISP requires a manual logon, obtain the correct configuration.

8. Select the **Security** tab and select an encryption and authentication scheme supported by your ISP.

9. Click **OK**, and then click **Close** to complete the ISP phonebook entry.

Creating a Phonebook Entry to Dial a PPTP Server

A phonebook entry must also be created to connect to Small Business Server (PPTP-configured) when using a VPN device.

Note You do not need to create a Phonebook entry for your PPTP server if your computer is not PPTP-enabled and you are using a PPTP service provided by your ISP.

Before performing the following steps ensure that:

- TCP/IP and PPTP network protocols are installed on the small business network to which the remote connection is being made.
- RAS is configured to dial out using the TCP/IP network protocol.

▶ **To create a phonebook entry to dial-up a PPTP server using a VPN device**

1. Click **Start**, point to **Programs**, **Accessories**, and then click **Dial-Up Networking**. If this is the first phonebook entry, a **Dial-Up Networking** dialog box appears. Click **OK**.

2. Click **New**. The New Phonebook Entry Wizard appears.

3. Type the name of your PPTP server in **Name the new phonebook entry** and click **Next**. A PPTP server name can be no longer than 20 characters, with no spaces in it.

4. Click **I am calling the Internet**, and then click **Next**. This configures the phonebook entry to use TCP/IP and PPP as the dial-up networking protocols.

5. Select **RASPPTPM(VPN1)** in the **Select the modem or adapter this entry will use** list in the **Modem or Adapter** dialog box, and then click **Next**.

Chapter 23 Installing PPTP in the Small Business Network 233

6. Type the IP address of the adapter on the PPTP server that is connected to the Internet in the **Phone Number** dialog box.

> **Note** If your PPTP server has an Internet registered DNS name, you could alternatively enter its DNS name in this field.

7. Click **Next**, and then click **Finish**. Verify the phonebook entry in the steps below.

▶ **To verify or edit your phonebook entry for the PPTP server**

1. In **Dial-Up Networking**, click **More**, and then click **Edit entry and modem properties** to verify the entry in the **Edit Phonebook Entry** dialog box.

2. Select the **Basic** tab and check that the phone number is correct and the **RASPPTPM (VPN1)** device is selected. Make any necessary changes.

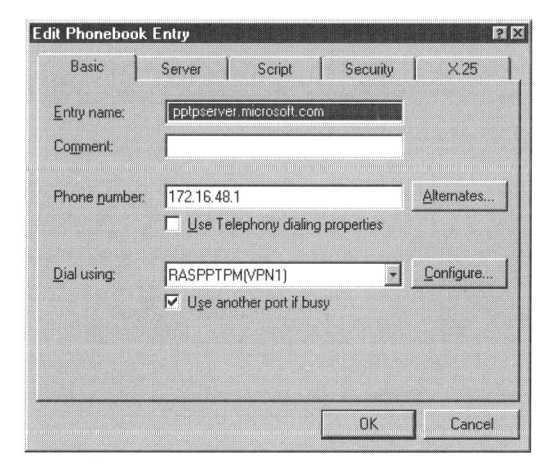

3. Select the **Server** tab and ensure that the **Dial-up server type** displays "PPP: Windows NT, Windows 95 Plus, Internet."

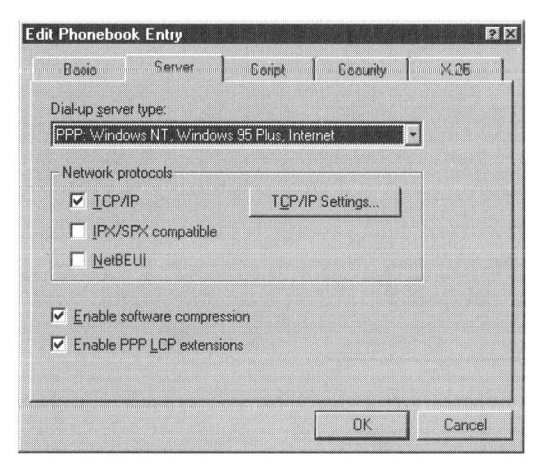

4. In the **Network protocols** box, ensure that the TCP/IP network protocol used on the small business network is selected. This protocol must already be installed and RAS must be configured to use this protocol to dial out.

5. Since TCP/IP is used on the small business network, click **TCP/IP Settings** to display the **PPP TCP/IP Settings** dialog box. Ensure that the TCP/IP settings conform to the settings required by the RAS configuration on the PPTP server. This includes the **Enable Software Compression** and **Enable PPP LCP extensions** settings. Click **Close**.

6. Select the **Script** tab, and then select **None**. The PPP protocol used in RAS is designed to automate remote logon. If the ISP requires a manual logon, consult them for the correct configuration.

7. Select the **Security** tab. Click **Accept only Microsoft encrypted authentication**. The PPP protocol encrypts the user name and password for remote logon. The user name and password used to log on for all current sessions can be used by selecting **Use current username and password**. The client is prompted by the PPTP server if this box is not selected. Both methods are encrypted and are therefore secure.

8. Close all open dialog boxes.

Installing and Configuring PPTP on Windows 95-based Remote Clients

This section explains how to install and configure PPTP on a Windows 95-based client.

Note VPN, which includes PPTP, is provided as a stand-alone upgrade to Windows 95 under the software title "Dial-Up Networking 1.2 Upgrade." Locate the upgrade at the following web site:
http://www.microsoft.com

The following are required before performing the steps in this section:

- Windows 95 must be installed on the remote client computer.
- An analog modem, ISDN device, or other modem device must be installed and configured in Dial-Up Networking to enable a dial-out connection from the remote client computer.
- Must have an established ISP PPP account, if the Internet is being used to connect to the PPTP server.
- All ISP and private network protocols must be installed.

- The Dial-Up Networking upgrade must be installed, including the most recent version of the executable file **Msdun.exe**. Refer to the following web site for the latest version of Dial-Up Networking:
  http://www.microsoft.com

Installation of the PPTP Client

Use the following steps that follows to install PPTP on a Windows 95-based remote client.

▶ **To install PPTP protocol on a client running Windows 95**

1. Insert the Windows 95 DUN upgrade disk in the CD-ROM drive and double-click **Msdun12.exe**.
2. Click **Yes** when you are asked if you want to install Microsoft Dial-Up Networking.
3. Setup displays a license agreement. After reading it, click **Yes** if you accept the terms.
4. Setup copies several files and asks you to restart the computer. Click **Yes**. Depending on your configuration, a logon may be required after computer restart.
5. Setup copies more files, including some files from your original Windows 95 installation source. If Setup cannot locate your installation source, it will ask you for your original Windows 95 compact disc or setup disks.

   Note If a version conflict is identified, Setup asks you if you want to keep your original file. Click **Yes**.

6. If you are running Setup for the first time, a dialog box appears explaining that the DHCP client was unable to obtain an IP address. You will be asked if you want to see this message again later on. Click **Yes**.
7. Setup restarts the computer. Depending on your configuration, another log on may be required after computer restart. Dial-Up Networking is now ready to be configured.

Configuring Dial-Up Networking on the Windows 95 PPTP Client

PPTP enables secure and encrypted communications to the small business network through either a serial modem or ISDN connection to the Internet. When setting up dial-up networking on a Windows 95 client, both of the following connections must be configured:

- A connection to the Internet through an ISP.
- A tunnel connection to the PPTP-configured server on the target network.

The exception is when using a dial-up modem link through the Public Switched Telephone Network (PSTN) to access Small Business Server (PPTP-configured). In this case, only the connection to the PPTP server must be configured. The following steps describe how to configure dial-up networking to configure ISP and PPTP connections for the remote Windows 95 client.

▶ **To create a connection to the Internet through an ISP**

1. Click **Start**, point to **Programs**, point to **Accessories**, and then click **Dial-Up Networking**. **The Dial-Up Networking** dialog box appears.
2. Click **Make New Connection**. The **Make New Connection Wizard** appears.
3. Click **Next**. The following screen appears.

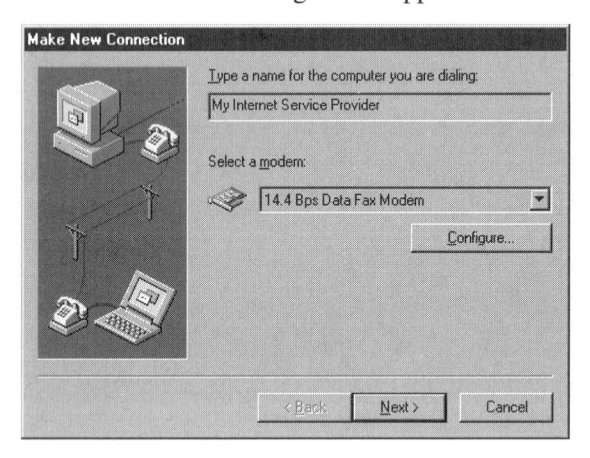

4. Type a name for the connection, for example, an ISP name, in the **Type a name for the computer you are dialing** box.
5. Select your modem device in **Select a modem**, and then click **Next**. The following screen appears.

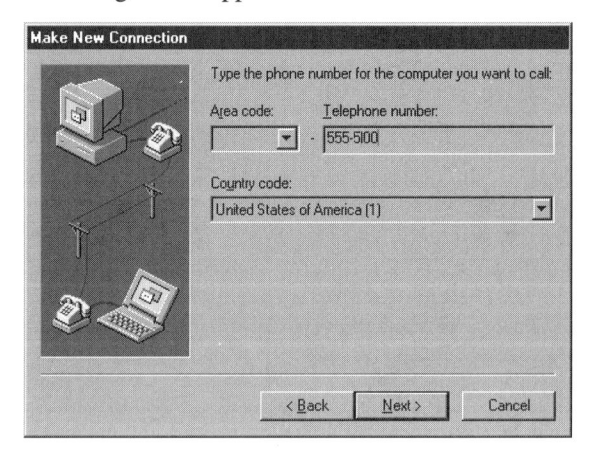

6. Type the ISP phone number in the **Telephone number** box.

7. Click **Next**, and then click **Finish**. A connection icon is created in the **Dial-Up Networking** folder.

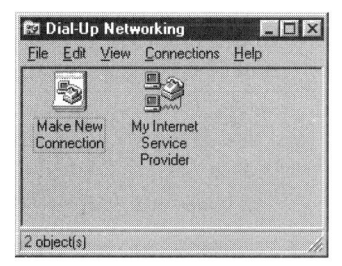

8. Verify your connection by using the steps that follow.

▶ **To verify or edit the ISP connection**

1. In **My Computer**, right-click the ISP connection icon in the **Dial-Up Networking** folder. Next, click **Properties** to verify that your ISP connection is correctly configured. The following dialog box appears.

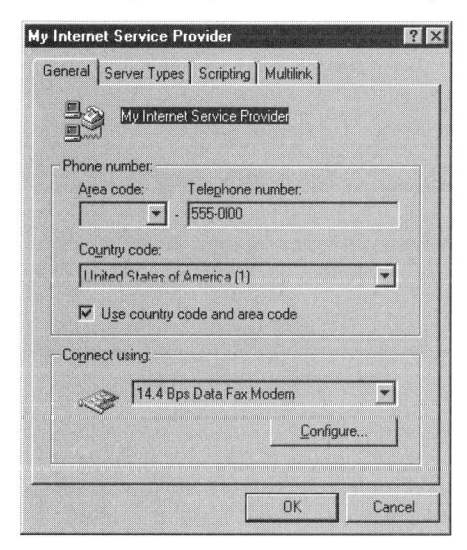

2. Select the **General** tab and verify the phone number is correct and the correct modem or ISDN device is selected. Make any necessary changes.

3. Select the **Server Types** tab and verify the **Type of Dial-Up Server** box displays "PPP: Windows 95, Windows NT, Internet."

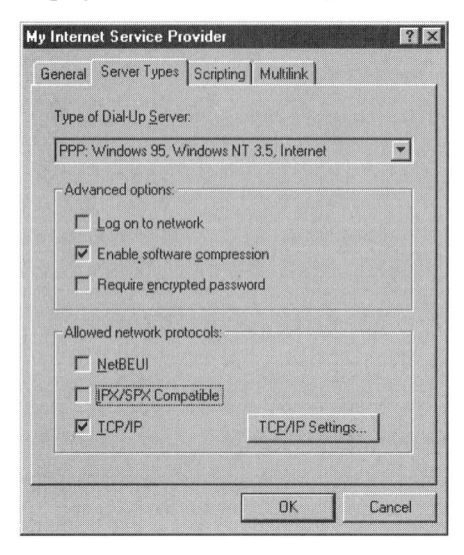

4. In the **Advanced options** box, clear **Log on to the network**. This option is not necessary for ISP connections. However, clearing it will enable a quicker connection to the ISP.

Note Generally, it is not necessary to change the **Enable software compression** or **Require encrypted password** options.

5. Make sure that **TCP/IP** is selected in the **Allowed network protocols** box and that other network protocols are not selected. Canceling the selection of other network protocols will enable a quicker connection to the ISP.

6. Click **TCP/IP Settings** to display the **PPP TCP/IP Settings** dialog box. Make sure that TCP/IP settings conform to the settings required by your ISP.

Note Generally, do not change the values on the **Scripting** tab. If your ISP requires a manual logon, however, you can use a script to automate the process. If you wish to use a script, consult your ISP for the correct configuration.

Also, the values on the **Multilink** tab usually will not have to be changed. Multilink enables you to use two devices (such as modems or ISDN devices) of the same type and speed for a single dial-up link. If you have two such devices and your ISP supports the multilink feature, consult your ISP for the correct configuration.

7. Click **OK**.

Creating a Connection to the PPTP Server

The connection to Small Business Server (PPTP-configured) for remote Windows 95 clients is created using a VPN device. Perform the following steps to set up a PPTP connection to Small Business Server.

▶ **To create a connection to dial up to a PPTP server using a VPN device**

1. Click **Start**, point to **Programs**, point to **Accessories**, and then click **Dial-Up Networking**. The **Dial-Up Networking** window appears.

2. Click **Make New Connection**. The **Make New Connection Wizard** shown below appears.

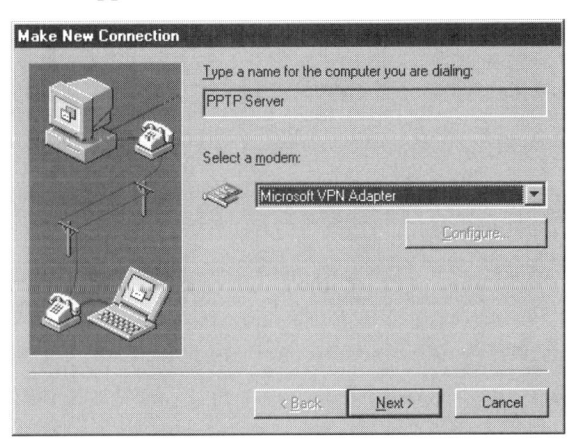

3. Type a connection name, for example, the Small Business Server name, in the **Type a name for the computer you are dialing** box.

4. Select **Microsoft VPN Adapter** from the **Select a modem** box and then click **Next**. The following dialog box appears.

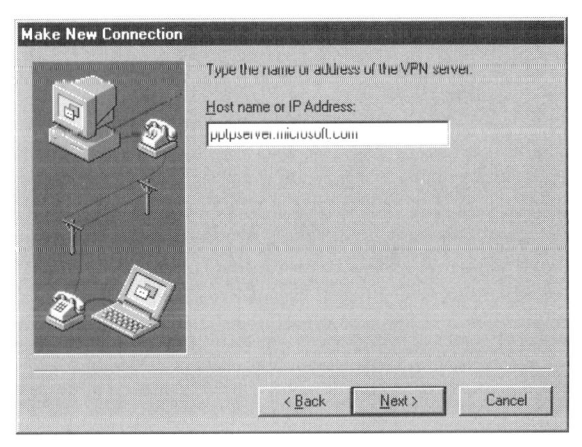

5. In the **Host name or IP address** box, type the name or IP address of Small Business Server (PPTP-configured).

6. Click **Next**, and then click **Finish**. A connection icon is created in the **Dial-Up Networking** folder, as shown below.

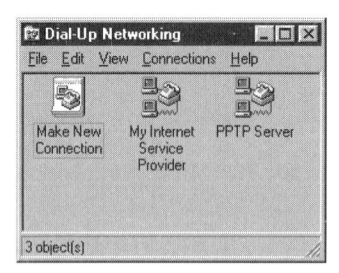

7. Verify the PPTP server connection by using the steps that follow.

   Note Be sure that your remote workstation and its applications support the protocols native to the Small Business Server network. After connecting, your remote Windows 95 workstation will be integrated into the small business network just as if it were physically connected to it.

▶ **To verify or change the connection to your PPTP server**

1. In **My Computer**, right-click the **PPTP Server Connection** icon in the **Dial-Up Networking** folder. Next, click **Properties** to verify that your PPTP server connection is correctly configured. The **PPTP Server** dialog box shown below appears.

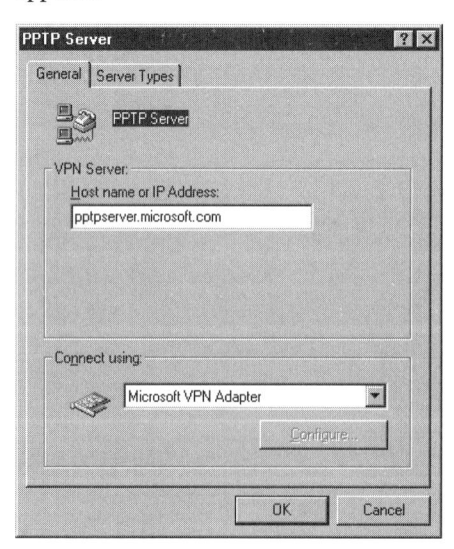

2. Select the **General** tab and verify the host name or IP address is correct and that **Microsoft VPN Adapter** is selected. Make any necessary changes.
3. Select the **Server Types** tab, in the **Advanced options** box, and select **Log on to network** only if the target small business network requires workstation logons.

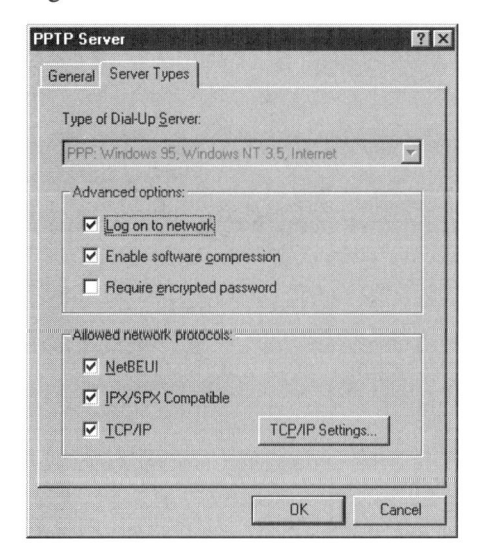

![PPTP Server dialog box showing Server Types tab with Type of Dial-Up Server set to PPP: Windows 95, Windows NT 3.5, Internet; Advanced options with Log on to network and Enable software compression checked, Require encrypted password unchecked; Allowed network protocols with NetBEUI, IPX/SPX Compatible, and TCP/IP checked.]

Note Network operating systems such as Microsoft Windows for Workgroups, Microsoft Windows NT, and Novell NetWare require you to log on to the network. UNIX-based networks generally do not have this requirement.

4. In the **Allowed network protocols** box, make sure **TCP/IP** is selected since it is the default protocol used on Small Business Server.

Note TCP/IP must already be installed on the remote client Windows 95 workstation.

5. Click **TCP/IP Settings** to display the **TCP/IP Settings** dialog box. Make sure that TCP/IP settings conform to the settings required for a client on the small business network. (The default settings are appropriate for most networks.)
6. Click **OK** and exit all open windows.

Using PPTP to Connect to Small Business Server by Dialing an ISP

A PPTP-enabled client must have two phonebook entries to connect to Small Business Server (PPTP-configured), as described earlier. The following explains how to actually make the connection. After successful connection, all traffic through the remote client modem is routed by the ISP over the Internet to Small Business Server. Traffic is then routed to the correct computer.

▶ **To connect to a PPTP server using a PPTP client to dial up an ISP**

1. If the client is a Windows NT Workstation, access Dial-Up Networking from **Accessories** on the **Start** menu. If the client is Windows 95, access Dial-Up Networking from **My Computer** on the desktop.
2. When the **Dial-Up Networking** screen appears, click **More**.
3. Select **User Preferences**, and then select the **Appearance** tab. Clear the **Close on dial** checkbox, and then click **OK**.
4. In the **Dial-Up Networking** dialog box, click the drop-down arrow in the **Phonebook entry to dial** list to select the entry for your ISP phonebook entry, and then click **Dial**.
5. After connecting to your ISP, click the drop-down arrow in the **Phonebook entry to dial** list once more to select the entry for your PPTP server. Click **Dial**.

Dialing up to an ISP PPTP Service to Connect to a PPTP Server

A PPP client can be used to make a connection to Small Business Server (PPTP-configured) across the Internet if the ISP provides a PPTP service. This can be done by using Dial-Up Networking and a modem or an ISDN device to connect to the ISP server. A second dial-up call is not required since the ISP server configured as a PPTP client makes the connections to the Small Business Server for the PPP client.

Contact your ISP for information about whether they provide a PPTP service and if so, how to connect to their server that provides the PPTP service.

CHAPTER 24

Customizing Office 2000 Deployment

This section describes customizing the installation configuration of Office 2000. Included is a discussion of the wizards and tools used in the process and the installation customizations that can be implemented with them.

Customizing Office 2000 Installations

By default in Small Business Server 4.5, Office 2000 is rolled out in a standard configuration to the server during set up. When client computers are set up with Small Business Server's Set Up Computer Wizard, a standard configuration is applied to each Office 2000 application the technology consultant chooses to install. If the technology consultant wants to modify the standard configuration and do custom installs of Office 2000 applications, the two Office 2000 tools described below are used.

- Office Profile Wizard.
- Custom Installation Wizard.

Note For custom Office 2000 installations, do not use the Set Up Computer Wizard. When setting up client computers on Small Business Server, Office 2000 applications listed in the Set Up Computer Wizard screens must be deselected. The technology consultant should consult the *Office 2000 Resource Kit* for the procedures on how to use the custom install tools.

Office Profile Wizard

The Office Profile Wizard is a tool for saving or restoring customizations of Office 2000 applications, which includes settings for the following features:

- Toolbars.
- Tool/Options (most settings).
- User profile templates.

- Custom dictionaries.
- Exchange profiles.
- Auto correction list.
- Other personal settings.

Creating Office Profiles

The Office Profile Wizard allows you to save all the current Office 2000 settings in a single .ops file or to restore settings from a previously saved .ops file. The Office Profile Wizard can be run using command-line options to perform all the functions of the wizard with no other user interaction required. The wizard can also restore default application settings before restoring the settings saved in the .ops file. Refer to the *Microsoft Office 2000 Resource Kit* for more information on how to use this wizard and customize the settings it stores.

Custom Installation Wizard

The Custom Installation Wizard replaces the Network Installation Wizard of previous Office releases. It is designed to provide the technology consultant with an easy method of modifying and managing the Office 2000 client setup environment. Types of Office 2000 setup customizations that may be implemented with the Custom Installation Wizard include the following:

- Specifying default installation location.
- Removing or retaining previous versions of Office.
- Setting feature installation states (for example, Run from Server, or Never Install).
- Setting default application settings through the use of an Office profile.
- Adding custom files, registry settings, and shortcuts.
- Configuring Outlook settings.
- Configuring Internet Explorer 5.0 settings.

Office 2000 Transforms

The Custom Installation Wizard reads the original windows installation database setup files (.msi) and creates a customized setup transform file (.mst). Office 2000 setup uses the .mst file to customize the way the software is installed on the client computer. The transform file makes changes to some elements of the installation database, which allows for control of the installation process.

Typical Custom Installation Wizard Scenario

There are numerous ways a technology consultant can employ the Custom Installation Wizard to roll out a customized Office 2000 setup package to Small Business Server clients. In a typical scenario, the technology consultant may do one or all of the following with the wizard:

- Deploy Office 2000 to several groups of users with a different configuration to each group.
- Add files, registry entries, and shortcuts.
- Set properties and change the default install state of Office 2000 applications.

System Policy Editor

After the Office 2000 custom installation is performed, the System Policy Editor may be used to further customize Office 2000 applications to enforce, modify, or disable application capabilities. System policies use settings in the registry to determine how applications should look and feel in addition to what the user can and cannot do in the applications. System policies can be used in the following general ways:

- Prevent users from damaging the corporation.
- Prevent users from making unnecessary changes that require assistance to resolve.
- Limit access to features not needed for the user's job function.
- Provide a consistent application look and feel that helps control the total cost of ownership of the small business organization.

More specifically, policies set up with System Policy Editor can be used to limit the user's ability to do such things as:

- Password-protect corporate files.
- Turn off the status bar.
- Modify toolbars.
- Set default backup options.

System Policy Templates

Several system policy templates are included on the Office 2000 installation compact discs provided with Small Business Server 4.5. Refer to the *Microsoft Office 2000 Resource Kit* for further information how to set up policy templates.

PART 4

Administering and Maintaining

Part 4 contains supplementary techniques and procedures for the administration and maintenance of Microsoft® BackOffice® Small Business Server 4.5. This includes administration of various server applications and components. The inner workings of Small Business Server wizards are provided to describe the processes behind administrative wizard tasks regularly performed on Small Business Server 4.5. In addition, Administrative tools, tips, and unique processes are also provided. Part 4 contains the following chapters:

Chapter 25	Small Business Server Wizard Processes 249
Chapter 26	Administrative Tools 281
Chapter 27	Administering Small Business Server Components 337
Chapter 28	Background Information for Administrators 443
Chapter 29	Administrative Tips and Other Information 453

CHAPTER 25

Small Business Server Wizard Processes

Microsoft® BackOffice® Small Business Server 4.5 is designed for a single server, single location small business. Small Business Server utilizes a suite of server applications and components configured during setup and administration. During integrated administration processes, Small Business Server uses wizards to streamline and automate administrative tasks. The wizards combine multiple administrative tasks into a few steps within a single interface. They operate across the server applications of the Small Business Server platform and automatically configure them.

The processes of Small Business Server 4.5 wizards are normally transparent to the technology consultant or user. The sections that follow present the background processes of the wizards and how you can replicate these processes manually. This information is primarily intended to provide the technology consultant with an overview of the automated processes occurring during wizard-based administration of Small Business Server.

Migrate User Wizard

It is not possible to perform an in-place upgrade of an existing Windows NT® Server 4.0 and Exchange Server installation to Small Business Server 4.5. However, user accounts and mailboxes may be migrated from the existing server installation to Small Business Server using the Migrate User Wizard.

Note The Migrate User Wizard will not migrate existing mail messages. These messages should be moved to a local .pst file prior to the migration.

The Migrate User Wizard shown in following screen is launched from the AutoRun screen of the Small Business Server installation CD 1. The wizard has two modes — export and import. A description of the processes for each mode is provided in the sections that follow.

Export Mode

This mode is accessed from the AutoRun screen of Small Business Server during installation. The Migrate User Wizard performs the following in export mode:

- Reads the existing user account information from an NT 4.0 Server computer.
- Reads the existing mailbox and the group Global Address List (GAL) information from an Exchange Server on the same computer as the Windows NT 4.0 installation.
- Creates the user account file containing the gathered information.

Note The Migrate User Wizard can <u>only</u> be used to migrate user data from a Windows NT Server 4.0 computer. The option to Migrate Users is not displayed on the AutoRun screen if the machine is not running Windows NT Server 4.0. Also, Exchange Server must be on the same computer as Windows NT Server 4.0 to enable migration of Exchange data.

Exporting Existing User Accounts

For each user, the Migrate User Wizard reads the following information from the existing Windows NT Server 4.0:

- **Username**. The NT User Manager username associated with the user account.
- **Full Name**. The NT User Manager user full name.
- **Description**. The NT User Manager description.
- **Remote Access Services (RAS) permissions**. If RAS is not installed, this value is left blank.

If Microsoft Exchange is installed on the computer, the following information will also be read for the Exchange mailbox associated with the NT username.

- **Global Address List Information**. This includes address, communication information, and so on.

Exporting Existing User Groups

The following information is collected from the existing Windows NT 4.0 Server installation and used by the wizard to create group accounts.

- **Groupname**. The NT User Manager group name.
- **Description**. The NT User Manager description of the group.
- **Members**. The NT User Manager username for each user in the group.

The collected group information is then added to the user account file. The group information in the user account file is broken out into sections identified by brackets. The first section [Group] contains a list of *all* groups to be created on the Small Business Server installation, in the following format.

[Groups]

Group0=Managers

Group1=Payroll

Group2=Sales

...

The next section contains each group identified in the [Groups] section and all the information used to create the group and its members. The format for these sections follows with items in bold indicating required fields:

[Group0]

Groupname=Management

Description=All Managers in the company.

Members=JohnD%username%username

[Group1]

Groupname=Payroll

Description=Payroll employees

Members=username%username%username%

....

Note Although the Migrate User Wizard exports NT group information, groups are not used in Small Business Server 4.5 to manage users.

Information Not Exported

The Migrate User Wizard will not export the following information—this information must be entered once on Small Business Server 4.5 using Small Business Server wizards.

- **User passwords**. The Migrate User Wizard can not migrate user password information. As a result, when the user account is created, the password is initially set to be blank, and the user is forced to change it during the first logon. As an alternative, the Change Password wizard can be used to reset user passwords after user accounts are imported to Small Business Server.

- **Internet Access Permissions**. The Migrate User Wizard does not set Internet Access permissions. By default, all created users do not have Internet access (this behavior is the same as the default behavior of the Add User Wizard). To give the user Internet access, use the Internet Access Wizard or User Resource Wizard.

- **Exchange Distribution Lists**. The Migrate User Wizard does not migrate Exchange Distribution Lists. To create them on Small Business Server, use the Create Distribution List Wizard.

- **Existing mail messages**. The Migrate User Wizard will not migrate existing mail messages. These messages should be moved to a local .pst file prior to the migration.

The User Account File

The information collected from the existing Windows NT 4.0 and Exchange servers is used by the wizard to create the user account file. The user information in the user account file is broken out in sections identified by brackets. The first section [Users] contains a list of *all* the users to be created on the Small Business Server installation, in the following format:

[Users]

User0=username

User1=username

....

The next section contains each user identified in the [Users] section and all the information used to create individual user accounts and mailboxes, and to set the GAL information. The format for these sections follows, with bold indicating the required fields.

[User0]

Username=JohnD

Fullname=John Doe

Description=Company Employee

UserCanChangePW=1

CompanyTitle=President

CompanyName=John's Company

CompanyDepartment=Management

CompanyOffice=1

AssistantPhone=(123)456-7890

CompanyPhone=(123)456-7890

Home1Phone=(123)456-7890

Business2Phone=(123)456-7890

Home2Phone=(123)456-7890

FaxPhone=(123)456-7890

MobilePhone=(123)456-7890

PagerPhone=(123)456-7890

Address=1 John Way

City=Johnville

State=WA

ZipCode=12345

Country=United States of America

CheckRasAccess=1

[User1]

Username=Jane Doe

....

In the above section, the **UserCanChangePW** field can have one of two values, as follows.

- UserCanChangePW=1 → the user can change their password.
- UserCanChangePW=0 → the user cannot change their password.

In the above section, the **CheckRasAccess** field can have one of two values as follows:

- CheckRasAccess =0 → the user cannot access the server via RAS.
- CheckRasAccess =1 → the user can access the server via RAS.

Editing User Account Files

In the user account files, entries left blank (fields not required with no associated value to enter) will not be set to any value during the import. Also, you cannot selectively export users and groups using the wizard since all existing user accounts, groups, and GAL information on the Windows NT Server 4.0 and Exchange Server are exported.

Once the user account file has been created, however, you can manually edit this ASCII text file using Notepad. Here you can add new user accounts and groups or remove those that should be deleted. You can also selectively remove user accounts using the **Remove a User** taskpad on the Small Business Server console's **Manage Users** page, once all of the users have been imported.

User Account File Default Location

The default location for the user account file is a:\users.txt, which ensures it is available for the import mode. If you change the location of this file, make sure it is saved in a location that will be accessible after Small Business Server is installed.

Import Mode

The Migrate Users Wizard uses the information from the user account file created during the export mode to create all of the user accounts, groups, and mailboxes in the import mode.

▶ **Steps performed by the Migrate User Wizard for each user in the user account file**

1. The user account with the specified username is created. If the Wizard encounters a user account with the same username it is attempting to create, it does not overwrite the current account information. Instead, it moves to the next user in the user account file.

2. The Exchange mailbox is created with the same name as the username. If the Wizard encounters a mailbox with the same mailbox name, it does not create a duplicate. This step is performed regardless of whether there was an Exchange Server on the export machine.

3. The data is imported, including global address list information and RAS permissions.

4. A shared folder is created for the user.

   Note The name of this folder is the user's username; its location is in the Users shared folder; and its owner is the Administrator. The user is given full access to this folder. Domain Admins also have full control and Domain users have read only permissions.

5. The user is added to the default company distribution list.

6. The user account Logon Script name in NT User Manager is set to:

   SmallBusiness\username.bat

▶ **Steps performed by the Migrate User Wizard for each group in the user account file**

1. The group is created. If the group already exists, it will not be recreated.
2. Specified members are added to the group.

Modifying User Parameters with Other Wizards

Although the import mode of the Migrate User Wizard performs the functions of the Add User Wizard, certain tasks can be performed for each user by other wizards as follows:

- User information can be changed using the User Account Wizard.
- User passwords can be changed using the Change Password Wizard.
- User permissions can be set using the User Access Wizard.
- User computers can be set up using the Setup Computer Wizard.

Console Wizards

There are several console wizards used during Small Business Server administration as follows:

- User Account Wizard
- Change Password Wizard
- User Access Wizard
- Access Wizards
- Share a Folder Wizard
- Move Folder Wizard
- E-mail Distribution List Wizard

The steps each console wizard follows to perform its task are described in the following sections.

Note In the steps, bulleted lists are procedures the technology consultant may follow if they wish to perform the configuration process manually.

User Account Wizard

The User Account Wizard shown below may be evoked in any of the following three modes:

- Add a User mode.
- Review or Change User Information (Edit) mode.
- Remove a User mode.

![User Account Wizard welcome screen]

Add a User Mode

The Add a User mode does the following:

- Creates the NT user account.
- Sets up the Exchange mailbox.
- Creates the user's shared folder.

The steps performed for each of these tasks are described in the sections that follow.

▶ **Steps performed by the User Account Wizard, Add a User mode, to create the NT User Account**

1. The NT user account is created on the server.
   - Click **Start**, point to **Programs**, point to **Administrative Tools**, and then click **User Manager for Domains** to open the NT User Manager.
   - Select **New User** on the **User** menu to display the **New User** screen.
   - Type the **Username**, **Full Name**, and **Description**.

2. User account password and password options are set.

> **Note** If **Username can change the password at any time** is selected in the wizard, **User Must Change Password at Next Logon** is enabled in the NT User Manager. If **Username is not allowed to change the password** is selected in the wizard, **User Cannot Change Password** and **Password Never Expires** are enabled in the NT User Manager.

- Type the **Password** and **Confirm Password**.
- Select the appropriate password option checkboxes.

3. The user account is added to the Domain Users group. This is the default behavior of the NT User Manager.

4. The user account Logon Script name is set to:

SmallBusiness\username.bat

- From the **New User** screen, click on **Profile** to display the **User Environment Profile** screen.
- In the **Logon Script Name**, type SmallBusiness/username.bat, where the username is specified in Step 1.
- Click **OK**.

> **Note** All other values typically set by the NT User Manager when creating a user account, are left as the default values.

▶ **Steps performed by the User Account Wizard, Add a User mode, to set up the Exchange mailbox**

1. The Exchange mailbox is created with the mailbox name=username.
   - From the **New User** screen, click on **Add** to display the **Connect to server** dialog box.
   - In the dialog box, type a period and click **OK**.
   - The properties for the user's mailbox appears.

2. The address book information is set.
   - Fill in the appropriate address information.
   - Click **OK** to return to the NT User Manager where you can enter another user.

3. The following restrictions are set on message sizes:

Outgoing: 1000 KBytes

Incoming: none

4. The user is added to the default company distribution list created during Small Business Server setup and to any other distribution lists specified.
   - Click **Start**, point to **Programs**, point to **Microsoft Exchange**, and then click **Microsoft Exchange Administrator** to display the **Connect to server** dialog box.
   - In the dialog box, type a period and then click **OK**.
   - Double-click **Recipients**.
   - Double-click on the company distributions list (it will be defaulted to the name of the organization as entered during setup).
   - Click **Modify** under the **Members** list.
   - Select the new user, click **Add**, and then **OK**.
   - Click **OK**.
   - Repeat the above steps for each additional distribution list the user should be added to.

   Note All other values typically set by the Exchange Administrator when creating a mailbox, are left as the default values.

▶ **Steps performed by the User Account Wizard, Add A User mode, to create the Users Shared Folder**

1. A shared folder for the user is created in Users Shared Folders.
   - From **Windows NT Explorer**, double-click **Users Shared Folders**.
   - On the **File** menu point to **New** and click **Folder**.
2. The username is used for the folder and share name.
   - In the folder namespace, type the user's **username** for the folder name.
   - Right-click on the new folder and left click on **Properties** to display the **Username Properties** screen.
   - Select the **Sharing** tab, and then select **Shared As**.
3. The owner of the folder is set to Administrator.
4. The user is given full access to the folder, Domain Admins are granted full control, and Domain users have read-only permissions.
   - From **Username Properties**, select the **Security** tab, and then click **Permissions** to display the **Directory Permissions** screen.
   - Click **Add** to display the **Add Users and Groups** dialog box.
   - Click **Show Users**.
   - Select the new user and then click **Add**.

- Set the type of access to **Full Control**.
- Click **OK** to return to the **Directory Permissions** screen.
- Click **OK**.
- Click **OK** to close the **Property** sheet.

> **Note** All other values typically set when creating a shared folder through Windows NT Explorer are left as the default values.

When you click **Finish** in the User Account Wizard, the above tasks are performed automatically. Also, the Add a User mode launches the User Access Wizard followed by the Set Up Computer Wizard. For the steps performed by each of these wizards, refer to their sections later in this chapter.

Review or Change User Information Mode

The Review or Change User Information mode of the User Account Wizard performs the steps below to change user information as follows.

▶ **Steps performed by the User Account Wizard to review or change user information**

1. The user's full name and description are updated.
   - Click **Start**, point to **Programs**, point to **Administrative Tools**, and then click **User Manager for Domains** to display the NT User Manager.
   - Double-click the user from the **Username** list to display the **User Properties** screen.
   - Type new information to update the **Full Name** and **Description**. Click **OK**.

2. The mailbox is re-created if necessary (for example, if it was accidentally deleted).
   - Click **Start**, point to **Programs**, point to **Microsoft Exchange**, and then click **Microsoft Exchange Administrator** to display the **Connect to server** dialog box.
   - In the dialog box, type a period and click **OK** to display the **Exchange Administrator**.
   - Double-click **Recipients** to show the **Display Names** list.
   - On the **File** menu, click **New Mailbox** to display the mailbox **Properties** page.
   - Type the appropriate alias, display, and address book information in the **Properties** dialog box.
   - Click **OK**.

- A message box appears asking if you want to link the mailbox with a Windows NT account, or create a new Windows NT account. Accept the default and click **OK**.
- Select the user's Windows NT account from the list presented, then click **OK**.

3. The user's address book information is updated.
   - Click **Start**, point to **Programs**, point to **Microsoft Exchange**, and then click **Microsoft Exchange Administrator** to display the **Connect to server** dialog box.
   - In the dialog box, type a period and click **OK**.
   - Double-click **Recipients** to show the **Display Names** list.
   - Double-click on the user's mailbox in the **Display Name** pane on the right.
   - On the mailbox **Properties** page, update the appropriate information, and then click **OK**.

4. The user is added to specified distribution lists.
   - Select the **Distribution List** tab, and then double-click the distributions list where the user is being added to display the server **Properties** page.
   - Click **Modify** under the **Members** list.
   - To add the user, select them from the list on the left, and then click **Add**.
   - To remove the user, select them from the list on the right, and then delete the name.
   - Click **OK**.
   - Repeat the above steps for each additional distribution list to be modified.

Remove a User Mode

The Remove a User mode performs the steps listed below.

▶ **Steps performed by the User Account Wizard to remove a user**

1. The NT User Account is removed.
   - Click **Start**, point to **Programs**, point to **Administrative Tools**, and then click **User Manager for Domains** to display the NT User Manager.
   - Highlight the user in the **Username** pane.
   - From the **User** menu, select **Delete**.
   - Click **OK** and **Yes** in the **User Manager For Domains** pop-up message boxes.

- Type the server name or click **Browse** when the **Connect to Server** dialog box appears. Click **OK**.
- Click **Yes** in the **Microsoft Exchange User Manager Extension** pop-up message and the user is removed.

Note The Remove a User mode does not remove the Users Shared Folder. This prevents the loss of information that other members of the company might need to access.

Change Password Wizard

The Change Password Wizard shown below is used to change user passwords and set password options. The steps of the wizard process follows.

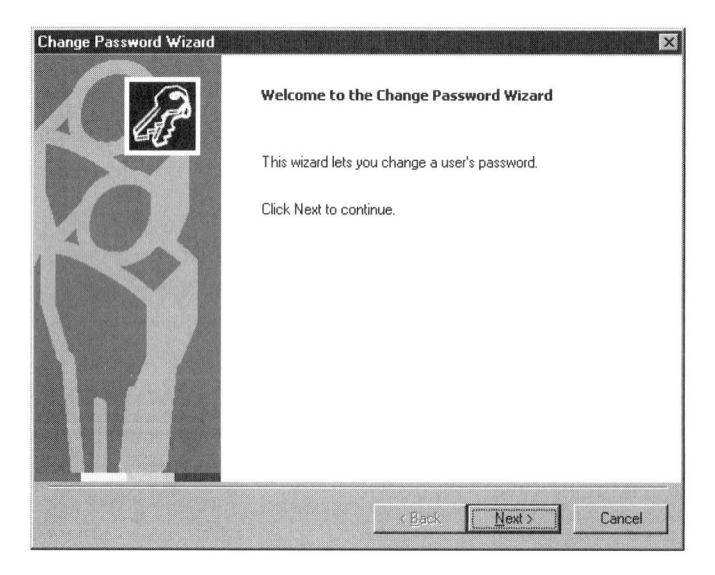

▶ **Steps performed by the Change Password Wizard to change a user's password**

1. The user account password and password options are reset.

   Note If **Username can change the password at any time** is selected in the wizard, **User Must Change Password at Next Logon** is enabled in the NT User Manager. If **Username is not allowed to change the password** is selected in the wizard, **User Cannot Change Password and Password Never Expires** are enabled in the NT User Manager.

2. Click **Start**, point to **Programs**, point to **Administrative Tools**, and then click **User Manager for Domains** to display the NT User Manager.
3. Double-click the user from the **Username** list.
4. Type the new password in **Password** and **Confirm Password**.
5. Select the appropriate password options.
6. Click **OK**. The steps that follow only apply if you change the Administrator password.
7. Click **Start**, point to **Settings**, and then click **Control Panel**.
8. Double-click **Services** to open the **Services** dialog box.
9. Select **Microsoft Exchange Directory** and click **Startup** to display the **Service** dialog box.
10. Type the new password for the Administrator account in **Password** and **Confirm Password**.
11. Click **OK**.
12. In the **Services** dialog box, click **Start**.
13. Repeat the last four steps for the following dependent services:
    - Exchange Information Store
    - Exchange Internet Mail Service
    - Exchange Message Transfer
    - Exchange System Attendant
    - Microsoft Fax Service
14. Restart the computer.

Note If you set the password using the Change Password Wizard or the Windows NT User Manager for Domains, you must manually reset the Server Status Tool administrator password. Refer to the "Setting the Server Status Tool Password" section in *Chapter 26, Administrative Tools*, later in *Part 4*.

User Access Wizard

The User Access Wizard shown below sets the permissions for system resources on a per-user basis. For each specified user, the wizard process contains the steps that follow.

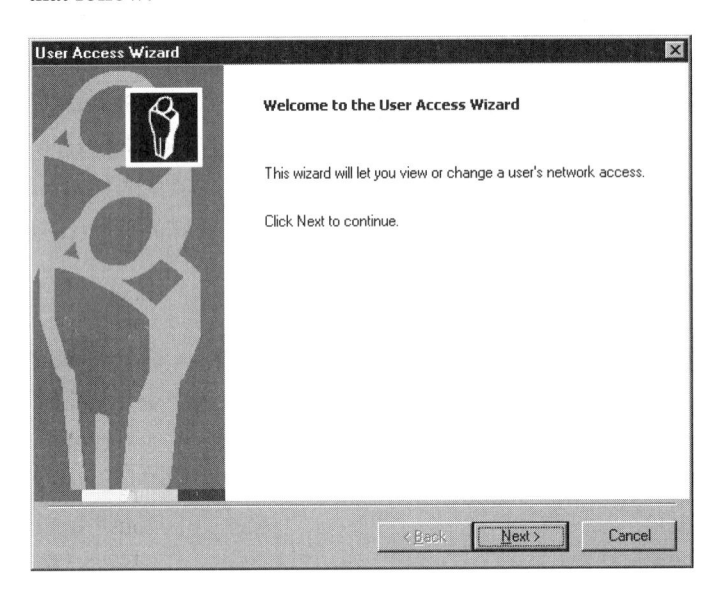

▶ **Steps performed by the User Access Wizard to set system resource permissions, per user**

1. Security permissions on shared folders are set.
2. Security permissions on shared printers are set.
3. Security permissions on shared fax printers are set.
4. Internet access permissions are set.
5. RAS access is set, granting dial-up access if specified in the wizard. **Grant dial in permission to user** is also set in the NT User Manager. Call Back is set to **No Call Back**.
6. Administrative privileges are set. The user is added to Domain Admins group if specified in the wizard.

Note For details on how permissions are set manually, see the Access Wizards later in this chapter.

User Permissions

All users are in the **Domain Users** group and therefore have the default permissions defined in the following Table:

Table 25.1 Default User Permissions

Read Access	Full Access
User Shared folders	Company Shared Folders
Folders of other users	Shared folder with their username
ClientApps	Fax store - Change permissions
	Shared printers - Everyone has print permissions
	Shared fax printers - Everyone has print permissions

Additionally, the **Domain Admins** group has full access to all resources.

Permissions and Resource Access

In the Small Business Server console, permissions are set on a per-user basis regardless of the groups created. As a result, in various User Access Wizard processes, the group **Domain Users** (or any group created) does not appear. The wizard processes enumerate the users in the particular group that has access to the resource and displays each user individually.

Because resource permissions are set with the User Access Wizard on per user basis, when the permissions for a resource are changed in any way (a user is revoked permissions), the permissions are also set on an individual basis. Users added after this point will not have the same default permissions since the groups initially given access to a resource may no longer be on that resource's permission list.

For example, Mary and Joe are given access to the Company Shared Folders through the User Access Wizard. The Company Shared Folders permissions (Properties, Security tab, Permissions) for that folder show Domain Users group as having full control. Then Bob is added as a user, but <u>not</u> given access to the folder. The permissions now show Mary and Joe listed as individuals with full access and the Domain Users group is removed.

Note For printers, Everyone has **Print** control is the default. After a user is not given permission, each account has **Full** control.

Also, the Domain Admins group has full access to all system resource folders. If the user is given administrative privileges in the wizard, they are added to Domain Admins group and therefore have full access to all shared folders, regardless of what other settings were made in the wizard.

Access Wizards

The Access Wizards are a suite of wizards that set permissions on a per-resource basis, in contrast to the User Access Wizard which sets permissions on a per-user basis. The Access Wizards are the following:

- Printer Access Wizard
- Fax Access Wizard
- Shared Folder Access Wizard
- Internet Access Wizard
- The steps of the Access Wizards processes follow.

▶ **Steps performed by the Printer Access Wizard to set printer access permissions**

1. Sets the access permissions to the printer.
    - From **My Computer**, double-click **Control Panel**.
    - Double-click **Printers** to display the **Printers** screen.
    - Right-click on the printer and click **Properties**.
    - Select the **Security** tab, and then select **Permissions**.
    - Click **Add**.
    - On a **Type of Access** basis, select the user with the required level of access and click **Add**. (Click **Show Users** to view all user accounts.)
    - Click **OK**.

▶ **Steps performed by the Fax Access Wizard to set fax access permissions**

1. Sets the access permissions to the fax printer.
    - Follow the steps outlined above for the Printer Access Wizard.

▶ **Steps performed by the Share Folder Access Wizard to set shared folder access permissions**

1. Sets access permissions to the folder.
   - From Windows NT Explorer, right-click on the shared folder and then click on **Properties** to display the **Shared Folders Properties** screen.
   - Select the **Security** tab, and then click **Permissions** to display the **Directory Permissions** screen.
   - Click **Add** to display the **Add Users and Groups** dialog box.
   - Select the users and groups to receive permissions to the folder. Click **Show Users**, if necessary.
   - Set the **Type of Access** for each user or group.
   - Click **OK** and exit all screens.

▶ **Steps performed by the Internet Access Wizard to grant Internet access permissions**

1. Grants access to Winsock Proxy services with Unlimited Access to all protocols.
   - Click **Start**, point to **Programs**, point to **Microsoft Proxy Server**, and then click **Microsoft Management Console** to display the **IIS Console** root.
   - Double-click **Internet Information Server** to show the server.
   - Double-click on the server to display the Proxy services.
   - Right-click on **WinSock Proxy** and click **Properties** to display the **Winsock Proxy Service Properties** screen.
   - Select the **Permissions** tab and select **Unlimited Access** from the **Protocol** drop down list.
   - Click **Edit** to display the **Unlimited Access Permissions** screen.
   - Click **Add** to display the **Add Users and Groups** screen.
   - Select the group and users to receive Internet access. Click **Show Users** if necessary.
   - Click **OK** to save the permissions and exit all screens.

2. Grants access to Web Proxy services with FTP Read, Gopher, WWW, and Secure Sockets Layer (SSL) protocols.
   - Click **Start**, point to **Programs**, point to **Microsoft Proxy Server**, and then click **Microsoft Management Console** to display the **IIS Console** root.
   - Double-click **Internet Information Server** to show the server.
   - Double-click on the server to display the Proxy services.

- Right-click on **Web Proxy**, and then click **Properties** to display the **Web Proxy Service Properties** screen.
- Select the **Permissions** tab.
- For each of the above protocols, perform the following. You may switch protocols via the drop-down **Protocol** list.

1. Click **Edit** to display the **Permissions** screen for the selected protocol.
2. Click **Add** to display the **Add Users and Groups** screen.
3. Select the users you want to give access to. Click **Show Users** to view all user accounts if necessary.
4. Click **OK** to save the permissions and exit all screens.

Share a Folder Wizard

The Share a Folder Wizard shown below can be used to share an existing folder or to create a new folder, and then share it. The steps of the wizard process follows.

▶ **Steps performed by the Share a Folder Wizard to share a folder**

1. Creates a folder when a new one is specified.
   - Open Windows NT Explorer.
   - On the **File** menu, select **New**, then click **Folder**.
   - Type the folder name in the folder's namespace.
2. The folder with a specified name is shared.
   - Right-click on the folder, and then click **Properties** to display the folder **Properties** page.
   - Select the **Sharing** tab, and then select **Shared As**.
   - Enter the appropriate share name. Click **Apply** and **OK**.
3. Permissions on the share is set to Everyone = Full Access.
   - From the folder **Properties** page, select the **Sharing** tab and then **Permissions** to display the **Access Through Share Permissions** screen.
   - Click **Add** to display the **Add Users and Groups** screen.
   - Highlight **Everyone** in the **Names** list, and then click **Add**.
   - Set the **Type of Access** to **Full Control**.
   - Click **OK** and then exit all screens.
4. Access permissions on the folder are set.
   - From the folder **Properties** page, select the **Security** tab, and then select **Permissions** to display the **Directory Permissions** screen.
   - Click **Add** to display the **Add Users and Groups** screen.
   - On a **Type of Access** basis, select the user with the required level of access and click **Add** to add the user. (Click **Show Users** to view all user accounts.)
   - Click **OK** and exit all screens.

Note Security on shared folders is enforced through the file system. Share permission is set to Everyone = Full access, so that everyone can see the share. Permissions are set on the file system itself (folders and files) so that if the share is removed, the permissions still exist.

Move Folder Wizard

The Move Folder Wizard shown below can be used to move shared folders while preserving user access. The steps of the wizard process follows.

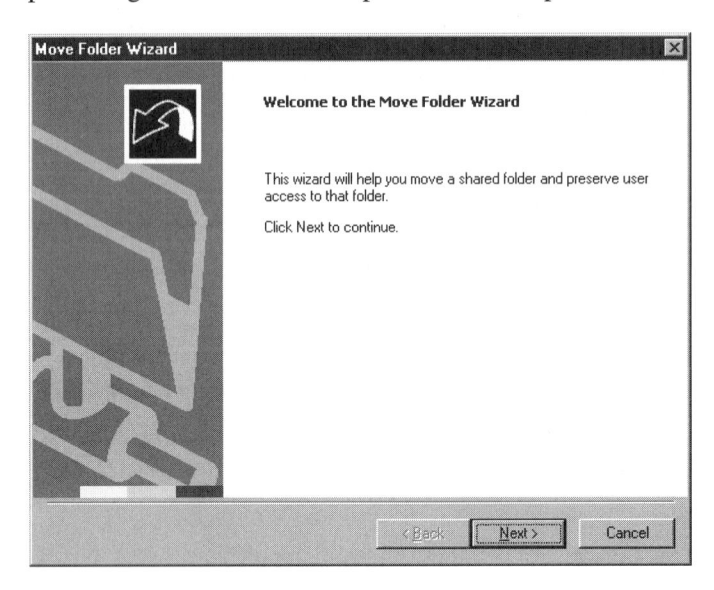

▶ **Steps performed by the Move Folder Wizard to move a shared folder**

1. The folder is moved to the new location.
   - In Windows NT Explorer, move the folder to the new location.
   - When the **Sharing** message box is displayed, click **Yes**.
2. The folder is re-shared.
   - Right-click on the folder in its new location and click **Properties**.
   - Select the **Sharing** tab, and then select **Shared As**.
   - Enter the appropriate share name. Click **Apply** and then click **OK**.

Note If a folder has multiple share names, only the first share name will be preserved (according to alphabetic order) in the move. You may have to recreate the appropriate share manually.

In addition, the Move Folder Wizard only permits moving folders between NTFS drives. This means you do not have to reset permissions on the **Security** tab in the **Properties** page since the permissions are preserved in the move.

E-mail Distribution List Wizard

The E-mail Distribution List Wizard shown below may be evoked in the three modes listed below.

- Create a Distribution List mode.
- Review or Change (Edit) a Distribution List mode.
- Remove a Distribution List mode.

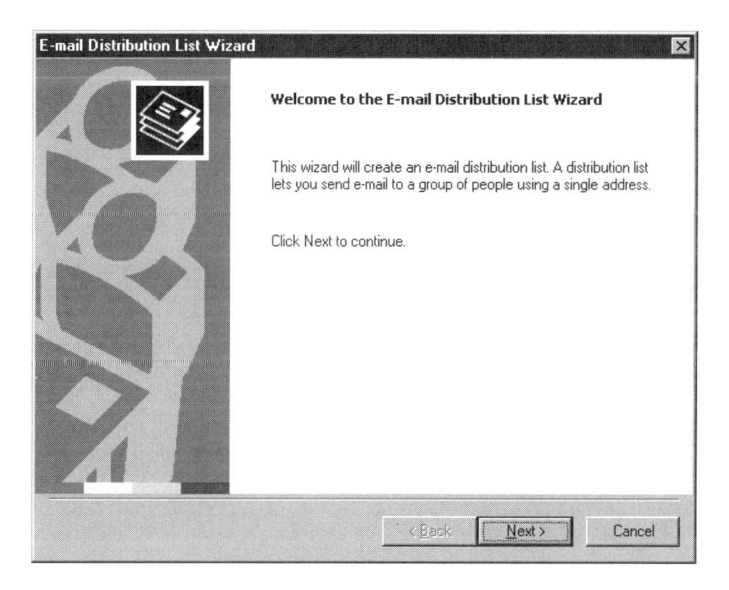

Create a Distribution List Mode

In this mode, the E-mail Distribution List Wizard creates an Exchange distribution list, names it, adds members, and sets the ownership to Administrator. The steps of the wizard process for this mode follows.

▶ **Steps performed by the E-mail Distribution List Wizard, Create a Distribution List mode, to create a distribution list**

1. The Exchange Distribution List is created with the specified alias (mailbox) name.
    - Click **Start**, point to **Programs**, point to **Microsoft Exchange**, and then click **Microsoft Exchange Adminstrator** to display the **Connect to Server** dialog box.
    - In the dialog box, type a period then click **OK**.
    - Double-click **Recipients** to display the **Display Names** list.

- From the **File** menu, select **New Distribution List** to display the distribution list **Properties** page.
- Enter the **Alias Name**.

2. The display name is set.
   - In the distribution list **Properties** page, enter the **Display Name**.

3. The notes are set.
   - In the distribution list **Properties** page, enter the **Notes**.

4. The specified members are added.
   - In the distribution list **Properties** page, click **Modify** under the **Members** list to display the **Distribution List** screen.
   - To add users, select them from the list on the left, and then click **Add**.
   - Once all users have been added, click **OK**.

5. The owner of the distribution list is set to Administrator.
   - In the distribution list **Properties** page, click **Modify** under the **Owner** box to display the **Distribution List**.
   - Highlight **Administrator**, and then click **OK**.
   - Click **OK** to create the distribution list.

Review or Change Distribution List Mode

This mode is use to modify attributes of a distribution list. The steps of the wizard process in this mode follows.

▶ **Steps performed by the E-mail Distribution List Wizard, Review or Change Distribution List mode, to edit a distribution list**

1. The display name is revised.
   - Click **Start**, point to **Programs**, point to **Microsoft Exchange**, and then click **Microsoft Exchange Adminstrator** to display the **Connect to server** dialog box.
   - In the dialog box, type a period and click **OK**.
   - Double-click on **Recipients** to display the **Display Names** list.
   - Double-click on the distribution list you want to edit.
   - In the distribution list **Properties** screen, revise the **Display Name**.

2. Notes are revised.
   - In the distribution list **Properties** page, revise the **Notes**.

3. Members are revised.
   - In the distribution list **Properties** page, click **Modify** under the **Members** list to display the **Distribution List** screen.

- To add users, select them from the list on the left, and then click **Add**.
- To remove users, select them from the list on the right, and then press **Clear**.
- Click **OK**.

4. The owner is reset to Administrator.
   - In the distribution list **Properties** page, click **Modify** under the **Owner** section to display the **Distribution List** screen.
   - Highlight **Administrator** and then click **OK**.
   - Click **OK** to save changes to the distribution list.

Note The distribution list alias can not be changed once the list is created.

Remove a Distribution List Mode

This mode is used to delete a distribution list. The steps of the wizard process in this mode follows.

▶ **Steps performed by the E-mail Distribution List Wizard, Remove a Distribution List mode, to delete a distribution list**

1. The Exchange Distribution List is deleted.
   - Click **Start**, point to **Programs**, point to **Microsoft Exchange**, and then click **Microsoft Exchange Administrator** to display the **Connect to server** dialog box.
   - In the dialog box, type a period and then click **OK**.
   - Double-click on **Recipients** to display the **Display Names** list.
   - Highlight the distribution list you want to delete.
   - On the **Edit** menu, select **Delete**.
   - Click **Yes** in the **Microsoft Exchange Administrator** message box to confirm the deletion.

Set Up Computer Wizard

The Set Up Computer Wizard shown below may be evoked in the four modes listed below.

- Add a New Computer to your Network.
- Add a User to an Existing Client.
- Add Software to an Existing Client.
- Remove a Computer From your Network.

Add a New Computer to your Network

The Set Up Computer Wizard does the following in this mode:

- Configures the server for the client.
- Configures client networking.
- Installs applications on the client.

The Set Up Computer Wizard gathers all necessary information to accomplish these actions in one set of dialogs. All further configuration occurs without additional user input, with the exception of selecting a network card on Windows 95/98 clients. The steps performed in each of these actions are described in the sections that follow.

Configuring the Server for the Client

The Set Up Computer Wizard creates and configures all the necessary files and settings for the server to process client logons and install client applications, as discussed in the following sections.

Logon Script

A logon script is necessary to start installation of client applications on the client machine. The template file used to create a user logon script is called Template.bat and is located in the following directory:

%systemdrive%\SmallBusiness\Template

The template file contains several replaceable parameters. For example, %SBSUser% corresponds to the username for the user specified in the Set Up Computer Wizard and %SBSServer% corresponds to the machine name of Small Business Server.

Each time the Set Up Computer Wizard runs, it creates a logon script for the specified user. It does this in the Template.bat file by dynamically replacing the variables with their correct values. The Set Up Computer Wizard will replace every instance of these variables, regardless of their location in the Template file. The file is then renamed to %SBSUser%.bat and placed in the following folder:

%systemroot%\System32\Repl\Import\Scripts\SmallBusiness

The Set Up Computer Wizard attempts to create the above folder every time it runs. If the folder already exists, the Set Up Computer Wizard simply continues. If a logon script already exists for that user, the Set Up Computer Wizard overwrites it with a new one. Any modifications made to an existing Set Up Computer Wizard logon script are not preserved when it recreates the logon script.

Response Folder and Client Application Configuration Files

The client application configuration files contain the installation information necessary to install the applications specified in the Set Up Computer Wizard. The template configuration files are located in the following directory:

%systemdrive%\SmallBusiness\Template

Variable substitution occurs in the same manner for client application files as it does for the logon script. Each time the Set Up Computer Wizard runs, it creates a set of client application configuration files and places them in a folder in the following directory. The folder is named according to the client computer name chosen when Set Up Computer Wizard runs.

%systemdrive%\SmallBusiness\Clients\Response

The Set Up Computer Wizard tries to create the above folder every time it runs. If the folder already exists, the Set Up Computer Wizard simply continues. If the client application configuration files already exist, the Set Up Computer Wizard overwrites them without preserving modifications made to the existing set.

Machine Account

Every time the Set Up Computer Wizard runs, it creates a Windows NT Server machine account for the client if one does not already exist. The Set Up Computer Wizard does not distinguish between Windows 95/98 clients and NT Workstation clients, even though Windows 95/98 clients do not require a machine account to access an NT domain.

All of the machine accounts created are of the Windows NT Workstation or Server type, but when Windows 95/98 clients access the domain, their type will be listed as "Windows 95."

Configuring the Client's Networking

The Set Up Computer Wizard creates a configuration floppy disk for the client machine, containing the following files:

- Setup.exe
- Ipdetect.exe.
- Ipdx86.exe
- Netparam.ini
- Ipd2000.exe

Setup.exe

Setup.exe launches either Ipdetect.exe or Ipdx86.exe, depending on whether the client operating system (as determined in real-time) is a Windows 95/98 or NT Workstation, respectively.

Ipdetect.exe and Ipdx86.exe

Ipdetect.exe and Ipdx86.exe function similarly on different client operating systems. Ipdetect.exe does not detect network cards; it merely invokes Windows 95/98's native network card selection screen. Ipdx86.exe includes calls to join the client to the domain, which is not necessary for Windows 95/98 clients. Also, Windows NT Workstation clients may require an intermediate reboot in order to fully configure their network, so Ipdx86.exe sometimes creates RunOnce entries to handle the continuation of the setup.

Netparam.ini

This file contains the domain and computer names.

Network Configuring

The networking configuring that takes place is the following:

1. A network card is installed with NDIS drivers (only one network card can be installed).
2. Transmission Control Protocol/Internet Procotol (TCP/IP) is installed.
3. TCP/IP is set up to access a Dynamic Host Configuration Protocol (DHCP) server.
4. TCP/IP is binded to the network interface card (NIC).
5. The computer name is changed.
6. The workgroup name for Windows 95/98 clients is changed.

7. The domain name is changed.
8. Windows 95/98 clients are set to logon to an NT domain.
9. The client for Microsoft Networks is installed.
10. The domain is joined (NT Workstation only).
11. User-level desktop and start menu preferences are set (Windows 95 only).

Note None of the Windows 95/98 client networking configuration requires an active network connection to the server. The NT Workstation networking configuration requires an active network connection in order to join the domain. This must be accomplished before the client can log on to the server.

Startcli.exe

Startcli.exe forces Service Pack 4 (SP4) to run on NT Workstation clients in two steps after network configuration is complete:

1. A link is made to the SP4 executable in the client's RunOnce registry key.
2. The registry key that states a Service Pack has already been installed is removed, in case SP4 already exists on the client.

Installing Applications on the Client

When logging on to the server, the client's logon script executes. The logon script has a single command line:

Startcli.exe + parameters

Startcli.exe searches the client machine's Response directory for a file called Installed. If this file exists, Startcli.exe completes without further actions. If the file does not exist, Startcli.exe invokes the setup engine to install the client applications on the client PC.

The setup engine reads the install command lines from the client application files to determine what components to install. All of these files are in the Response folder corresponding to the client's machine name.

Upon completion of the installation, the client component creates the Installed file in the Response folder. This blocks application installs on subsequent logons. Once this process is complete, the logon script will not perform any actions as long as the Installed file exists.

Add a User to an Existing Client

The Add a User to an Existing Client mode of the Set Up Computer Wizard behaves similarly to the Add a New Computer to your Network mode. In this mode, the logon script for the new user is created and the response files in the Response directory for the client machine being set up are overwritten with the information for the new user. The remainder of the process is the same as in the Add a New Computer to your Network mode, with the exception that a configuration disk is not created since networking should already be set up.

Note Since the Response directory for the client machine is overwritten, if the first user has not logged on to the machine and completed their client installation, their specific information (applications) will be lost. At this point, whichever user logs on first will execute their logon script and have the client installation process complete.

If you have two computers and one user, the logon script always looks for the response folder that matches the computer name.

Add Software to an Existing Client

The Add Software to an Existing Client mode of the Set Up Computer Wizard behaves similarly to the Add a New Computer to your Network mode. In this mode, the response files in the Response directory for the client machine being set up are overwritten with the new information. Then the Installed file is deleted from the Response directory to force an installation of the client applications. The remainder of the process is the same as in the Add a New Computer to your Network mode, with the exception that a configuration disk is not created since networking should already be set up.

Note There is no way to remove applications through the Set Up Computer Wizard. If you wish to remove an application, it must be done from the client machine.

Remove a Computer from your Network

The Remove a Computer from your Network mode of the Set Up Computer Wizard removes the NT Server machine account for the selected computer. Since Windows 95/98 clients do not require an NT Server machine account to connect to the server, this option does nothing to forcibly prevent the client machine from connecting to the server.

Small Business Server Internet Connection Wizard

For a description of the background processes of the Internet Connection Wizard, refer to the "Manual Configuration of Small Business Server for ISP Connectivity" section of *Chapter 21, ISP Connectivity Tasks,* in *Part 3, Deployment*, of this resource guide.

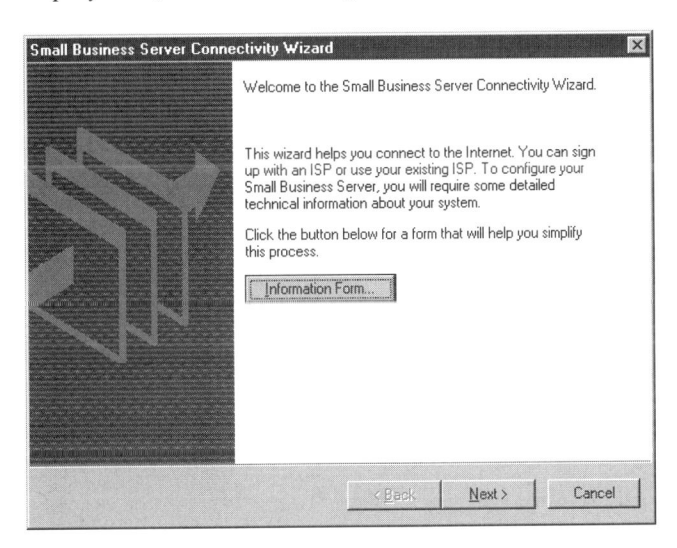

CHAPTER 26

Administrative Tools

Microsoft® BackOffice® Small Business Server 4.5 consists of many applications, components, and features that must be configured correctly to function properly together. Proper administrative techniques can smooth the administration process and give you better control over component configurations and system performance. The administrative techniques in this section are intended to supplement the general administration procedures included in the Online Guide. This chapter presents several tools and techniques to enhance the administration of Small Business Server in the following areas:

- Remote administration with NetMeeting
- System policy administration
- Server Status Monitoring
- Fax and Internet Reports
- Performance Monitoring
- Task Scheduling

Remote Administration with NetMeeting

The technology consultant can administer Small Business Server from a remote location using Microsoft NetMeeting 2.11 configured on a Windows 95/98 or NT workstation. From there, the technology consultant can connect with the Small Business Server console to perform regular administrative tasks. This allows the technology consultant to support the small business network from a convenient remote location when changes or adjustments are required. In order to administer Small Business Server 4.5 using NetMeeting, NetMeeting's desktop sharing features for Windows-based applications and file transfer are utilized. For developing additional NetMeeting functionalities that may be useful to the technology consultant in remote administration scenarios, refer to the *Microsoft NetMeeting Software Development Kit*. Refer to the Online Guide for specific steps on how to share the Small Business Server console remotely.

Remote Connection Considerations

Remote administration can be performed from a location outside the small business local area network (LAN), or from a client station on the LAN. When connecting to Small Business Server from outside the LAN, use a direct dial-up modem link instead of the Internet since the transmitted data is not encrypted—since remote administration may involve setting passwords or creating new user accounts across the Internet, this information should be protected.

Client and Server Interaction with NetMeeting

Sharing the console remotely requires NetMeeting to be installed and configured on both the server and client. Small Business Server setup automatically installs NetMeeting on the server.

In order to initiate a remote administration session, a NetMeeting call must be placed from the remote computer. To facilitate the call, both client and server NetMeeting applications must be up and running. To make a connection to the console, responses from the server side are required. Once the connection is made and the console is shared, the technology consultant can control the Small Business Server console and perform all its functions from the remote location. The call may be ended from the client or server when remote administration is complete.

System Policy Administration

System Policy defines computer resources available to an individual or group of users and the various facets of the desktop environment that the technology consultant needs to control. This includes such things as which applications are available, which applications appear on the user's desktop, which applications and options appear in the **Start** menu, who can change their desktops and who cannot, and so on. This section covers the necessary information for the technology consultant to have a comprehensive control over system policy in Small Business Server. The first part of this section includes the following:

- Controlling user environments with System Policy.
- What can be done with System Policy on Small Business Server 4.5.
- How system policies work, including customization and policy templates.
- How to create system policies with the System Policy Editor.
- Installing the System Policy Editor on client machines.
- Creating a default system policy.

The remainder of this section discusses the following:

- User profiles (including creating and administering them).
- Differences between Windows 95 and Windows NT user profiles.
- User profile planning and implementation.
- Roaming and mandatory user profiles.

System Policy and Controlling the User Environment

A System Policy is defined in a set of registry settings. System policies can be implemented for specific users, groups, computers, or for all users, and are created with the System Policy Editor. When a System Policy is applied, the new policy overwrites existing registry settings, thus giving the technology consultant the ability to set restrictions for the client machine and user, despite the user's preferences and regardless of where the user logs on.

When a user logs on to a Windows NT Server computer, the user profile is uploaded to the server first and then System Policy is downloaded to the user machine. Any reconfigured registry settings (whether machine-specific changes or specific to the user logging on) are changed before the user receives control of the desktop. System policy changes are not dynamic—if changes are made to the policy, affected users must log off and log back on so the new policy can be downloaded and applied.

Small Business Server and System Policy

In Small Business Server, the registry stores the look, feel, and configuration of the user desktop and the logon and network access configurations for each computer. For clients running Windows NT Workstation, the user profile is taken from the user portion of the Windows NT registry. The server portion of the registry contains configuration settings and user profiles, and is managed using the System Policy Editor. With this tool, a comprehensive system policy can be created to control user work environments and actions, and to enforce system configuration for NT Workstations and all other client computers in the small business network.

The technology consultant can manage user profiles by enforcing mandatory profiles or use system policy to manage specific user account configurations. With the latter, the technology consultant can define specifically what users can do from their desktop including restricting certain options in the Control Panel, customizing parts of the desktop, and configuring network settings.

How System Policy Works

Desktop, logon, and network access settings for each user are stored in the Windows NT 4.0 registry database. System policy for users overwrites settings in the current user area of the registry and system policy for computers overwrites the server computer area of the registry. This allows control of user actions (user profiles) and computer actions for users and groups.

Using System Policy Editor, you can manage the user desktop by changing the **Default User** settings; logon and network settings are managed by changing the **Default Computer** settings, as shown in the System Policy Editor screen.

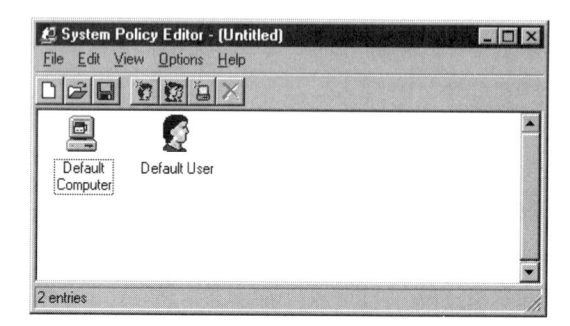

With the System Policy Editor, a file called NTConfig.pol is created containing user settings (profiles) and computer settings (logons and network access). To enable a uniform policy for all networked Windows NT Workstations, this file is saved to the Netlogon share in the system root folder of Small Business Server.

When a Windows NT user logs on to the network, the operating system looks in the Netlogon share in the logon server's system root folder to see if there is an NTConfig.pol file. If found, the contents of the file are copied to the client computer's registry, thus overwriting the current user and client machine portion of the registry.

Changes to the Client Computer Registry

Using the System Policy Editor, you can change the client computer registry settings in the following ways:

- From Default User desktop settings, you can modify the HKEY_CURRENT_USER registry key, which defines the contents of the user profile in effect for the client computer.
- From Default Computer, you can modify the HKEY_LOCAL_MACHINE registry key which defines the Logon and network access settings for the client computer.

When a user logs on to Small Business Server, the contents of the NTConfig.pol file on the server is merged with the NTuser.dat file found in the user profile location of the registry. Settings in NTuser.dat that do not match NTConfig.pol settings are overwritten. Also, settings for Default Computer that are not contained in the user profile (NTuser.dat) are added to the client machine portion of the registry. This allows system policy to control the user profile settings for the entire small business network.

Note The System Policy Editor does not give access to the entire registry. Only those values exposed by policy templates can be modified.

Customizing System Policy for Users, Groups, and Computers

If you have special users or computers needing different policy settings, the default settings can be changed to accommodate special needs applying to users, groups, and computers as necessary. Those you add receive separate entries in the NTConfig.pol file defining the settings different from default policy settings. When a user or group member who has special policy settings in NTConfig.pol logs on, the system finds NTConfig.pol along with the special settings that apply to the specific user or group member. Similarly, if a computer is added and special settings are entered in the System Policy Editor, anyone logging on to that computer receives the special computer settings.

Profile Evaluation for Clients and Computers

When multiple profiles apply to one client, a user profile for a specific client takes precedence over a user profile for a group in which the client is a member. Similarly, if a specific user profile has not been defined for a client, a group profile to which the client belongs is used (if available) before the Default User profile is used. If a profile has not been defined for a specific computer, the Default Computer profile is used. If multiple group profiles apply to a client, they are applied in the order specified in the **Group Priority** dialog box accessed from the **Options** menu of System Policy Editor.

System Policy Templates

System policy templates provide baseline configurations for the technology consultant to set system policy in networks having Windows NT Workstation and Windows 95 clients. User profiles must be enabled on computers running Windows 95. System policy templates provide the necessary framework for overwriting registry keys on the different operating systems. When the System Policy Editor is installed on client machines, the following templates are automatically installed:

- **Winnt.adm**. This template provides System Policy Editor settings that are specific to the Windows NT operating system and registry structure.
- **Windows.adm**. This template provides System Policy Editor settings that are specific to the Windows 95 operating system and registry structure.
- **Common.adm**. This template provides System Policy Editor settings that are common to both Windows NT and Windows 95 registry structures and which do not appear in either the Winnt.adm or Windows.adm files.

Note System policy files created on computers running Windows NT cannot be used on computers running Windows 95, and vice versa.

For more information about enabling and using user profiles and system policy on Windows 95 computers, refer to the *Windows 95 Resource Kit*.

Using System Policy Editor to Create System Policy

The System Policy Editor creates system policy as follows:

- Creates default settings for the computer and user policy for the small business network.
- Creates custom settings that apply to individual users, groups of users, or individual computers.
- Specifies the manner and location from which to download policy for all or some users.

Note The user options described in the following sections are for computers running Windows NT. For information about Windows 95 system policy settings, refer to the *Windows 95 Resource Kit*.

Default System Policy Settings: Default Computer and Default User

When a new system policy file is created, the System Policy Editor displays two icons representing the computer and user portions of the registry. When you click either **Default Computer** or **Default User**, a graphic representation of categories in the associated portion of the registry appears. Within each major category, settings in subcategories provide options for changing the way computers and users operate. For some settings, selecting a check box opens a set of choices or text boxes. For other settings, specific information must be provided.

Some settings available in the System Policy Editor use the terms *disabled, removed*, or *hidden*. These terms explain how the item appears to the user:

- A disabled command appears dimmed on the menu.
- A removed command or item does not appear on the menu.
- A hidden item cannot be seen by the user.

For example, if you select **Hide Screen Saver Tab**, the **Screen Saver** tab in the **Control Panel Display** option does not appear to the user.

Check-Box Selection Levels

In addition to the usual on/off aspects of check boxes, the **System Policy Editor** check boxes have a third setting, which is grayed or dimmed. The purpose of this setting is to indicate that there is no change to the previous setting in the registry.

User Policy: Setting Restrictions on User Profiles

The **Default User** option allows you to control user profile settings. Each selection in the following **Default User Properties** dialog box contains options you can use to control the user desktop work environment.

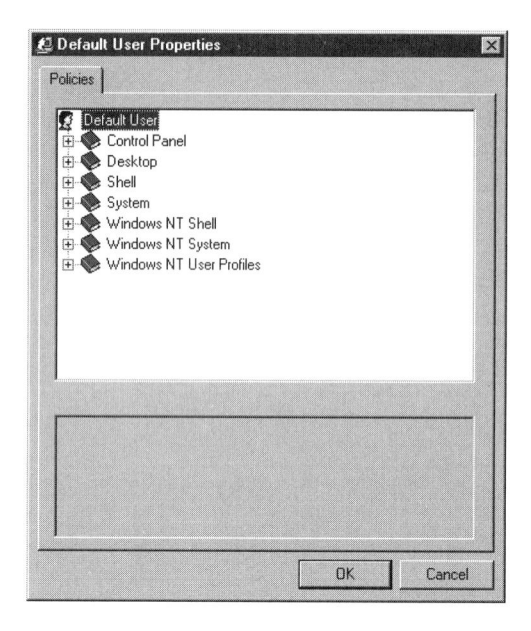

Control Panel

Use the Display option in the Control Panel category to restrict user activity in the desktop Control Panel or to deny access to it.

Desktop

Use this option to specify the background wallpaper or color scheme for the desktop.

Shell

Use this option to restrict the use of the **Run**, **Find**, and **Shut Down** commands in the **Start** menu and what appears in **Settings** menu. You can also restrict what appears in **Network Neighborhood** or hide it completely, hide drives in **My Computer**, or hide all items on the desktop.

System

Use this option to disable Windows NT Registry Editor (Regedt32.exe) and Windows 95 Registry Editor (Regedit.exe) so users cannot edit their registry files. You can also identify a list of Windows-based applications users can use—any application not on the list is unavailable.

Windows NT Shell

Use this option to select the shell or customize desktop folders to restrict what appears on the desktop. You can create custom folders by entering paths to **Network Neighborhood**, **Program**, **Startup**, or **Start** menu items you want to source from a location other than user profile folders—this allows you to specify the applications provided in these folders. You can also provide locations for custom desktop icons or hide **Start** menu subfolders. In addition, you can restrict options that appear on Explorer menus.

Windows NT System

Use this option to disable the task manager, lock workstation, change password and logoff, show welcome tips at logon, or parse the Autoexec.bat file.

Note When **Parse Autoexec.bat** is selected, Windows NT reads the environment variables from this file, merges them with user environment variables, and overrides any different settings there.

Windows NT User Profiles

Use this option to set the user profile storage space and to notify the user when this is exceeded. You can also restrict which directories roam with the user profile.

Computer Policy: Determining Logon and Network Access

The **Default Computer** options allows you to control logon and network access settings for computers. Each selection in the **Default Computer Properties** dialog box contains settings used to prevent users from modifying the hardware and environment settings of the operating system.

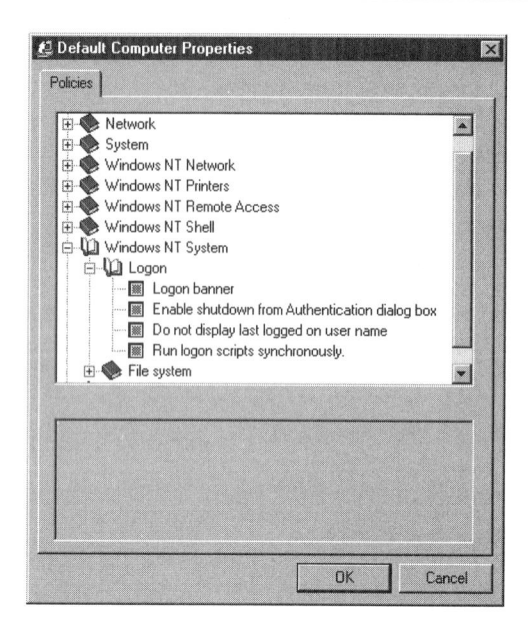

Network

Use this option to provide remote updates of system policies, instead of updating from NTConfig.pol on the NT Server. By typing a path to a different policy file, you can enable manual update of the policy file in a location other than the server. You can also specify to have error messages displayed when a policy cannot be applied.

System

Use this option to specify the contents of the Run and Run Once to specify which applications should run at startup. You can also change SNMP (Simple Network Management Protocol) configuration by adding or removing communities, managers, and public community traps. The default for these settings are established when the SNMP service is configured on the host. The System option provides three selections for changing default SNMP configurations.

Windows NT Printers

Use this option to disable the print spooler browse process that periodically sends information to other print servers about which printers the server shares. This browsing consumes some CPU and network capacity which may not be necessary for some print operations.

You can also change the priority of print job assignments to ports and also set the print spooler to beep every 10 seconds if an error condition occurs for a remote print job.

Windows NT Remote Access

Use this option to set a maximum for the number of unsuccessful authentication retries and a time limit for authentication when using remote access service. You can also set the time interval between call back attempts or a time limit for automatic disconnection from Small Business Server.

Windows NT System

Use this option to do the following on the Windows NT System:

System security. Set logon policy for user accounts, including creating a logon banner and enabling or disabling automatic logon. Automatic logon allows the user to bypass the CTRL+ALT+DELETE key combination when the system is started to help prevent intrusive programs from searching for passwords.

Logon security. Enable or disable the **Shut Down** button in the logon screen. Disabling the button on servers ensures that an unauthorized user cannot shut down the system.

Using System Policy Editor to Edit the Registry

The System Policy Editor allows you to easily update the registry settings and implement a revised system policy. You can use the **Open Registry** command on the System Policy Editor **File** menu to make changes to the Windows NT Registry settings on the Small Business Server computer. When using **Open Registry**, the changes you set in the System Policy Editor are made immediately in the registry when you save them.

Connecting to Remote Registries

Use the **Connect** command on the System Policy Editor **File** menu to make adjustments to Windows NT registry settings on a remote client computer. Type in the name of the computer whose registry is to be modified and then select from the list of available user profiles to edit. Once connected to the computer registry you want to modify, changes made affect only the user or machine you are connected to. The check boxes are regular binary check boxes since the values are being directly edited.

Note System policy is designed to manage registry settings for the entire small business network. Direct changes to registry settings therefore are not recommended unless a specific instance of user or computer incompatibility occurs.

System Policy Revision Methods

The System Policy Editor allows you to revise registry settings and generate the correct environment for a particular user or group of users. Use the editor in the following ways:

- To open the registry of a client computer and change settings for the local user and computer.
- To modify an existing policy file or create a new one to contain the settings needed for enforcing the policies required on a per user, per computer, or combined basis.

When opening the System Policy Editor in registry mode, the registry of the client computer can be modified without having to use Regedt32.exe or Regedit.exe (as used on NT Workstations and Windows 95 clients, respectively).

Note The System Policy Editor does not give access to the entire registry. Only those values exposed by policy templates can be modified.

System Policy Editor Template Files

The System Policy Editor uses administrative (.adm) files to determine which registry settings can be modified. An .adm file is a hierarchical template consisting of categories and subcategories that dictate which settings are available through the user interface. An .adm file contains the registry locations that identify the following:

- Where changes should be made for a particular selection.
- Additional options for a particular selection.
- Restrictions.
- The default value for a selection (in some cases).

When the System Policy Editor is run and **Policy Template** is selected from the **Options** menu, the dialog box shown below appears. The names of the .adm files currently in use are shown. If changes are required for custom applications, a template may be added to this list. To ensure that the system uses the latest administrative information, the System Policy Editor reads the custom .adm files each time it starts.

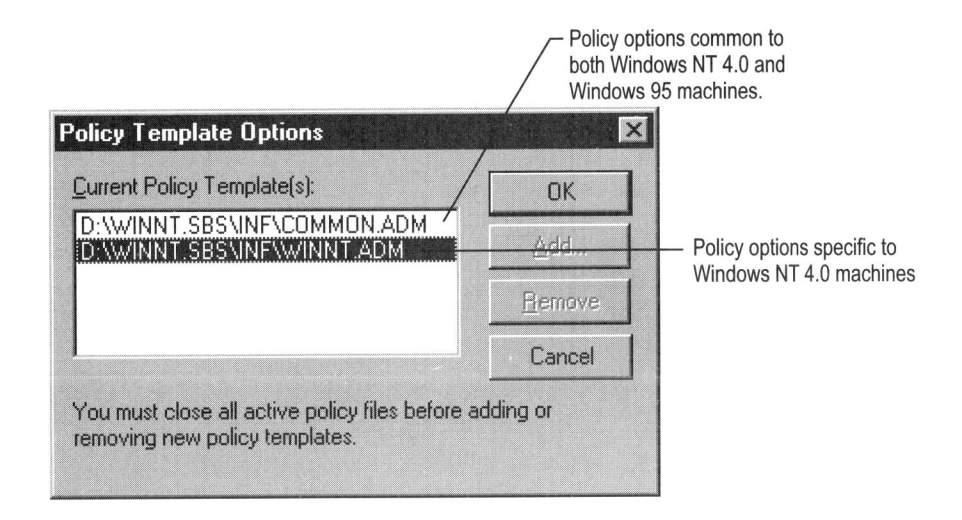

[Figure: Policy Template Options dialog box showing Current Policy Template(s): D:\WINNT.SBS\INF\COMMON.ADM (Policy options common to both Windows NT 4.0 and Windows 95 machines) and D:\WINNT.SBS\INF\WINNT.ADM (Policy options specific to Windows NT 4.0 machines). Buttons: OK, Add, Remove, Cancel. Note text: "You must close all active policy files before adding or removing new policy templates."]

Note The option to Add or Remove will be grayed-out if there is a policy file currently open. Close the file in use and then change the template configuration.

Configuring Policy Settings

The configuration options available fall into a tree structure determined by the layout of the .adm file. By navigating through these options, you can select settings that determine actions taken when the policy file is applied.

Application of Policies

Using System Policy Editor, default user policies are applied as follows. Refer to the Default User Properties screen below.

- If the box is **checked**, it is implemented. When the user next logs on, the user's computer conforms to the policy. If the option was checked the last time the user logged on, Small Business Server makes no changes.
- If the box is **cleared**, the policy is not implemented. If the settings were previously implemented, they are removed from the registry.

- If the box is **grayed**, the setting is ignored and unchanged from the last time the user logged on. Small Business Server does not modify this setting. The grayed state ensures that Small Business Server provides quick processing at system startup, since it does not need to process each entry every time a user logs on.

Note When deciding whether a value should be checked or cleared, be careful you understand the terminology of the setting, or unexpected results may occur. For example, if the **Don't save settings at exit** option is checked, settings cannot be saved. If you clear the check box, the settings can be saved.

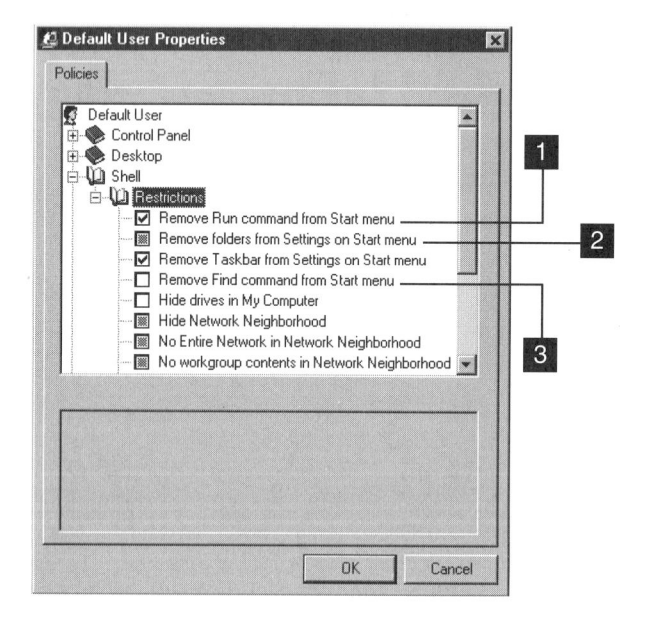

1 Flag this setting to overwrite the target client machine registry with the "enabled" value. Regardless of the current state, when the policy file is applied next, the user will no longer have the Run command.

2 In this state, when the policy file is applied next, the registry setting on the client machine will not be modified. If it was enabled before, the user will still not receive the Settings folders. If it was not enabled, these folders would be available.

3 In this state, this flags the setting to overwrite the target client machine registry with the "disabled" value. Regardless of the current state, when the policy file is applied next, the user will have the Find command on the Start menu.

Policy Options and Consistency

When you select certain options, the lower pane contains information about the option and other related configurable items as well. When administering system policies, if you specify paths for particular options such as wallpaper, ensure that the paths are consistent across all workstations receiving the policy file.

Installing the System Policy Editor on the Client

The System Policy Editor and policy templates must be installed on client computers to modify client registries and allow system policies to function correctly with the client machine. The System Policy Editor is included with the Windows NT® Server 4.0 portion of Small Business Server and can be installed easily on Windows NT Workstation-based and Windows 95-based client machines. After completing the installation, the System Policy Editor appears in the administrative tools group on the client machine.

Note A policy file is valid only for the platform on which it was created. As a result, Windows 95 and Windows NT policy files are not interchangeable.

Installing System Policy Editor on a Windows NT Workstation

Use one of the two installation method options when installing the System Policy Editor on a Windows NT Workstation-based computer, as follows:

- Run Setup.bat file from the Windows NT 4.0 CD ROM \Clients\Svrtools\Winnt directory.
- The System Policy Editor executable—Poledit.exe, located in the Winnt.sbs folder on the server—can be copied to the workstation along with the template files. The template files have an .adm extension and are located in the %systemroot%\Inf directory, which is hidden by default.

Note Hidden files can be shown by selecting **Show all files** in the **Options** dialog accessed from the Windows NT Explorer **View** menu.

Installing the System Policy Editor on a Windows 95 Computer

Use one of the following ways to install the System Policy Editor on a Windows 95-based computer:

- From a Windows 95 Upgrade or retail CD
- From the Windows NT Server 4.0.

Use the procedures that follow to install the System Policy Editor on Windows 95-based client machines.

▶ **To install the System Policy Editor from the Windows 95 CD**

1. Insert the Windows 95 Upgrade or retail CD into your CD-ROM drive.
2. Click **Start**, point to **Settings**, and then click **Control Panel**.
3. Double-click **Add/Remove Programs**.
4. Select the **Windows Setup** tab, and then click **Have Disk**.
5. Browse to locate the directory x:\Admin\Apptools\Poledit\ (where x is the drive letter) on the Windows 95 CD.
6. Select both Group Policies and the System Policy Editor, and then click **OK** to install.

Note It is important to run the setup program as described above. Undesirable results will occur if the System Policy Editor and related files are merely copied to the Windows 95-based computer.

▶ **To install the System Policy Editor from the Windows NT Server 4.0**

1. Copy the Poledit.exe file from the Windows NT Server to the \Windows directory of the Windows 95-based machine.
2. Copy the Common.adm and Windows.adm files from the Windows NT Server to the \Windows directory of the Windows 95-based machine.
3. Create a shortcut to the System Policy Editor executable, Poledit.exe, now located in the \Windows directory.

Creating a Default System Policy

In order to create a new system policy and make it active, you must first create the policy and then move or copy it into the Netlogon directory of Small Business Server. It must then be named NTConfig.pol.

Note Before making changes to an existing system policy, it is recommended to make a copy of the current system policy and store it in a safe location. This will serve as a backup if the original policy must be restored.

A new default system policy may be created according to the procedure that follows.

▶ **To create a default system policy**

1. Click **Start**, point to **Programs**, point to **Administrative Tools**, and then click **System Policy Editor** to launch the System Policy Editor.
2. On the **File** menu, click **New Policy**.
3. Double-click **Default Computer** to display the **Default Computer Properties** page shown below.

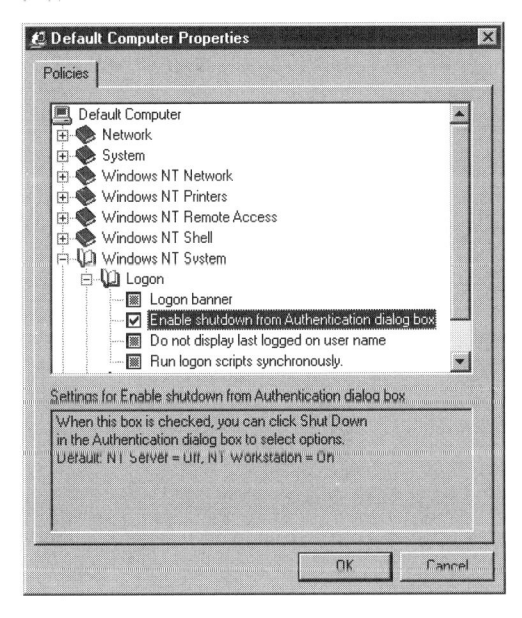

4. Each book (node) in the **Default Computer Properties** page represents an area of the registry that can be modified. Open the book for the policy that you want to modify. For example, to have all computers in the network shut down from the logon dialog box, open the **Windows NT System** and **Logon** books, then select the **Enable shutdown from Authentication dialog box** check box, shown above.

> **Note** Since the check boxes in the System Policy Editor have three different states (cleared, checked, and gray) as discussed earlier, do not click on check boxes you don't want to change.

5. After the changes are made, click **OK** to return to the main System Policy Editor window.

Changing the Default User Policy

To change and implement a new default user policy, use the steps that follow.

▶ **To change the default user policy**

1. From the System Policy Editor, double-click **Default User** to display the **Default User Properties** page. Here, you can change how users configure their desktops and use the Control Panel, or you can apply a variety of restrictions to various aspects of the user interface.
2. Click **OK** to return to the System Policy Editor opening screen.

▶ **To save and implement the new default user policy**

1. On the **File** menu, choose **Save As**.
2. Type the default configuration policy filename and location:
   \\SBS*Name*\Netlogon\NTConfig.pol
3. Click **Save** and the new policy will be in effect for all future logons.

> **Note** We recommend saving policy changes to a separate folder under a descriptive file name before copying the data to the default configuration file. This makes it easier to recover to a known condition if the change made was not well thought out or if a change audit trail is needed.

Setting Folder Paths Back to Defaults

If a policy file is created and then the path is changed to any of the custom shared folders or custom user-specific folders, the change overrides the default setting established in the .adm file. By default, a user's program folder path is %Userprofile%\Start Menu\Programs. If the policy file is not modified from the default, this path is not changed for the client computer.

The path can be changed to point to a server location that contains different shortcuts. To do this, click the appropriate option in the System Policy Editor and specify the path to the folder containing the shortcuts. Once this change is applied, the user will receive the new shortcuts. If you want to restore the user's environment to the state it was in before the change was made, follow the steps below.

▶ **To restore folder paths back to the default**

1. Open the policy file and click folder options until each check box is clear.
2. Save and close the policy file.
3. Reopen the policy file and click the option to re-enable it. The original settings should be displayed pointing to the user's machine.

Creating Alternate Folder Paths

It may be necessary to create shared folders for groups of users who need a common set of tools and shortcuts. Follow the steps to create these shared folders.

▶ **To create shared folders and alternate folder paths**

1. Create a folder on the server that contains shortcuts to network applications or to locally installed programs.
2. Share the folder.
3. From the System Policy Editor, double-click **Default Computer**.
4. From the **Windows NT Shell** option, double-click **Custom Shared Folders**, then enable the **Custom Shared Program Folder**. By default, the local **All Users** folder for the workstation is used, however, you can use the lower pane of the Default Computer Properties screen to define the path to the folder created in Steps 1 and 2.
5. Save the policy file. When the user logs on, the policy file will be parsed for this information which replaces the common groups of the user machine with the shortcuts and applications in the created folder.

Note This can be done per user for personal program groups and/or for other folder settings such as the startup group, Start menu, and desktop icons.

User Profiles

User error often causes a loss of desktop productivity. For example, if the system configuration is accidentally changed, then the computer is rendered unworkable. Other problems arise from having too many desktop distractions and complexities (excessive features or nonessential applications installed). To resolve these problems on Small Business Server, the technology consultant can restrict user access to key configuration files, features, and applications that are not required for a user's job. The technology consultant is able to control the computer configurations for individuals or groups of users, based on user job responsibilities and computer literacy.

User Profile Content

A user profile for Small Business Server describes the Windows NT configuration for a specific user. This includes the user's environment, configuration options, and preference settings—installed applications, desktop icons, color options, and so on. This profile is built in part from system policy information and in part from saved changes users make to customize their desktop.

Types of User Profiles

A user profile can be local, roaming, or mandatory. A local profile is specific to a certain computer. A user who creates a local profile on a particular computer can gain access to that profile only while logged on to that computer. A roaming profile is stored on a network share and can be accessed from any networked computer. A user who has a roaming profile can log on to any networked computer for which the profile is valid and the profile can be accessed. A mandatory profile is a preconfigured roaming profile the user cannot change. Mandatory profiles may be used for a group of users who require a common interface and standard configuration.

One of the primary goals of a user profile is to have a user's system and desktop settings travel with them from computer to computer, without requiring reconfiguration of settings. When a user logs on to any computer that supports their roaming profile, the desktop appears just as the user left it the last time they logged off. With roaming user support, users can share computers while each user retains their personal desktop on any computer in the network. Both roaming and mandatory profiles support this functionality.

Creating and Administering User Profiles

User profiles can be created and administered in several different ways as follows:

- A user profile is created that cannot be modified for a particular user or group. This is a mandatory profile.
- A network default user profile is established that applies to all new users on the small business network. After logging on and downloading the default profile, the user can customize it (unless it is a mandatory profile).
- A new roaming user is permitted to use the default user profile on the computer where the user logs on. After logging on, the user can customize the profile, unless it is a mandatory profile.
- A template user profile is copied and the copy is assigned to a user. The user can then customize the profile, unless it is a mandatory profile.

User Profile Structure

A user profile consists of a Windows NT registry hive and a set of profile directories. The registry is a database used to store machine- and user-specific settings. Portions of the registry can be saved as files called hives which are then reloaded for use as necessary. User profiles take advantage of this feature to provide roaming profile functionality.

The user profile registry hive is the NTuser.dat in file form and is mapped to the HKEY_CURRENT_USER portion of the registry when the user logs on. The NTuser.dat hive maintains the user's environment preferences when the user is logged on. It stores those settings that maintain network connections, Control Panel configurations unique to the user (such as desktop color and mouse), and application-specific settings. A series of profile directories store shortcut links, desktop icons, startup applications, and so on. Together, registry hives and profile directories record all user-configurable settings that can migrate from computer to computer.

Configuration Preferences Stored in the Registry Hive

The NTuser.dat file contains the following configuration settings:

- **Windows NT Explorer settings**. All user-defined settings for Windows NT Explorer and persistent network connections.
- **Taskbar**. All personal program groups and their properties, program items and their properties, and all taskbar settings.
- **Printer settings**. All network printer connections.
- **Control Panel**. All user-defined settings made in the Control Panel.

- **Accessories**. All user-specific application settings affecting the Small Business Server environment, including Calculator, Clock, Notepad, Paint, and HyperTerminal.
- **Help bookmarks**. Any bookmarks placed in the Small Business Server Online Guide.

Configuration Preferences Stored in Profile Directories

The profile directories are designed to have the following configuration settings:

- **Application data**. Application-specific data such as a custom dictionary for a word processing program. Application vendors decide what data is storable in this directory.
- **Desktop**. Desktop items including files and shortcuts.
- **Favorites**. Shortcuts to program items and favorite locations.
- **NetHood**.* Shortcuts to Network Neighborhood items.
- **Personal**. Shortcuts to program items. Also a central store for any documents that the user creates. Applications should be written to save files here by default.
- **PrintHood**.* Shortcuts to printer folder items.
- **Recent**. Shortcuts to the most recently used items.
- **SendTo**. Shortcuts to document storage locations and applications.
- **Start Menu**. Shortcuts to program items.
- **Templates**.* Shortcuts to template items.

> *Note These directories are hidden by default. To see these directories, change the View Options in Windows NT Explorer.

Windows 95 and Windows NT Profile Differences

Windows 95 profiles are very similar in behavior to those of Windows NT 4.0 Workstation, however, there are some differences. Windows 95 downloads and writes user profiles to the user's home directory. When the Windows 95 user first logs on, the Uniform Naming Convention (UNC) path specified in the user account's home directory path is checked for the Windows 95 user profile. This behavior can be modified, however. See the *Windows 95 Resource Kit* for more information.

Windows 95 user profiles also have other functional differences from Windows NT 4.0 Workstation profiles as follows:

- Windows 95 does not support common groups.
- Windows 95 can be configured to copy only the shortcut (.lnk) and Program Information Files (.pif) when the user profile is downloaded, whereas Windows NT downloads all file, shortcut, and directory objects.
- Windows 95 user profiles do not support a centrally stored default user profile.
- Windows 95 uses different files (see the following table) for the registry portion of user profiles. Windows 95 and Windows NT 4.0 Workstation profiles are not interchangeable primarily because the registry hive, a key component of the user profile, is incompatible between the two operating systems.

Table 26.1 Windows NT 4.0 Workstation and Windows 95 Registry Files

NT WORKSTATION FILE	EQUIVALENT WINDOWS 95 FILE
NTuser.dat	User.dat
NTuser.dat.log	User.da0
NTuser.man	User.man

Note The Windows NT 4.0 Ntuser.dat.log and Windows 95 User.da0 files are equivalent, although they provide slightly different functionalities.
Windows NT uses the Ntuser.dat.log file as a transaction log file, which allows for fault tolerance in the event that a user profile must be recovered.
Windows 95 writes a copy of User.dat to User.da0 each time the user logs off.

- Windows 95 and Windows NT 4.0 file structures are identical with the exception of the Application Data directory. Windows 95 does not support this directory.

Note Windows 95 user profiles can be stored on NetWare servers. For more information on configuring a client with a **Primary Network Logon** of **Client for NetWare Networks**, see the chapter "Windows 95 on NetWare Networks" in the *Windows 95 Resource Kit*. For more information on configuring a client that uses Microsoft Service for NetWare Directory Services, see the online Help that accompanies the service.

User Profile Planning and Implementation

A successful implementation of user profiles requires planning and preparation. Before creating user profiles, answer the following questions:

- How much of the user environment do you want to control? Would system policies—either in conjunction with user profiles or by themselves—be a better solution?
- Will users be required to use a specific set of desktop folders and environment settings?
- Will users be able to make modifications to their profiles?
- What features will you be implementing in user profiles? Optional features include persistent network connections, custom icons, backgrounds, and so on.
- For roaming profiles, will users be allowed to use the default profile from the client workstation or will a standardized, server-based default profile be used instead?
- Where will the profiles be stored? Is there enough drive space to store them?
- Where do existing user home directories reside?
- How will shortcuts and links be displayed for the user?
- What are the speeds of the links between the clients and the server storing the profiles?

Setting Permissions for User Profiles

When troubleshooting or preparing for a rollout of user profiles, pay careful attention to permissions at the NTFS File System (NTFS) and share levels. If the profile is mandatory, the user account should have at least Read permissions on the network share where that user's profile is stored. If the user's profile is roaming, the user must have Change permissions (or greater) since the client will need to write changes back to the central profile on the shared network drive when the user logs off.

If roaming profiles are stored on an NTFS partition, you can choose to remove the Delete permission from the default Change permissions at the NTFS level.

Note Directories containing roaming user profiles need at least Add and Read permissions for profiles to be read correctly. If you use Add permissions only, when Windows NT checks for the existence of the profile, it will fail because it looks for the path first. If Read rights are not given, the check will fail.

Permissions are also important on a client machine where the user is logging on. If Windows NT is installed in an NTFS partition on the client computer and the user does not have at least the default permissions, errors can occur. For example, if permissions are incorrect on the root of the system directory, the following message appears: "Can't access this folder—the path is too long." A blank desktop is displayed, and the user's only option is to log off.

If permissions are set incorrectly in the %systemroot%, %systemroot%\System, %systemroot%\System32, or %systemroot%\System32\Config directories, the following message appears: "Unable to log you on because your profile could not be loaded."

Selecting a Location to Save User Profiles

A roaming profile can be placed in any shared directory and then the user account profile path may be configured to point to the profile. The Profiles directory in the system root stores local user profiles, all users profile settings (including any user who uses the computer), the default user profile, and cached user profiles. Avoid using the %systemroot%\Profiles directory as the domain user's profile path to store roaming or mandatory server-based profiles. The path for these profiles should be configured to allow the user's profile to roam with the user and be available on any networked computer the user logs on to. If you specify a path to the %systemroot%\Profiles directory, the client computer always uses the local profile instead.

Storing Windows NT Workstation Profiles on any Shared Network Drive

You can save Windows NT 4.0 Workstation profiles on the Small Business Server because the client computer only needs the path where the profile is stored to download it and to write the modified user profile at log off. Since the process of downloading the profile is controlled by the client computer—all the client needs is the correct path—profiles can be stored on any shared network drive. Note that storing profiles on a Windows NT 4.0 Server makes it easier for the technology consultant to open a user's NTuser.dat file to make any required modifications.

User Profile Paths

If a client is not receiving a user profile at logon, the **Start** menu **Run** command can be used to check the profile path. For example, to see if you can locate the profile, type \\server\share\mydomainuser. If the path to the user's profile contains spaces, put quotation marks around the path when typing in the **Run** command.

Except in the case of mandatory profiles or when a slow network is detected, any changes to a user's profile are saved to the central profile when the user logs off. Because users cannot modify mandatory profiles, changes do not need to be written to the server.

Note In situations where the same user account logs on to multiple machines, the last user to log off dictates the profile settings because that user was the last one to write data to the profile. Similarly, if a group of users all point to the same profile, the final logoff settings are saved and will overwrite previous settings.

If the user profile is flagged as a local profile and is not mandatory, any changes the user makes while logged on are written to the locally cached version of the profile, but not to the server-based version.

Note Do not make the home directory and user profile path the same. If the profile path encompasses the home directory path and the server-based profile is more recent than the local profile on the workstation, all directories and files that exist in the user's home directory will be copied to the user's workstation at each logon. These files are then written back to the server (if modified) when the user logs off. Also, even if the user logs off and the technology consultant deletes all of the unnecessary files from the home directory, the versions of these files that reside on the workstation will not be deleted at logon and will be written back to the server again at log off. This file copy process is avoided if you place the profile in a subdirectory of the home directory \\Server\Share\Domainuser\Profile.

Creating a New Roaming User Profile for Windows NT 4.0 Workstations

There are four major steps to create a new roaming user profile, as follows:

- Determine where the user's profile will be stored.
- Create a user account (if one does not already exist).
- Specify a user profile path.
- Specify whether a given user will use a specific profile or can use a default profile.

▶ To create a new roaming user profile

1. Create a directory on the server and establish a network share. Give the user a minimum of Change permissions to the shared directory. If your implementation stores user profiles within users' home directories, make the profile directory a subdirectory of the user's home directory.

   Note This approach precludes the use of the %Username% variable. Also, to prevent the share from being browsed, append "$" to the share name.

2. If this will be a domain user, use the User Manager for Domains in the Administrative Tools group on the server to create the account. If this will be a Windows NT 4.0 Workstation account, use the version of User Manager included in the Administrative Tools program group on the workstation. Refer to your operating system documentation and online Help for procedures when using these tools.

   Note For the example that follows, the user account is called *mydomainuser*.

3. Enter the user profile path. This is the location where the user profile will be stored, for example:

   \\Myserver\Myshare\Mydomainuser

   If the profile is being stored within the user's home directory, use:

   \\Myserver\Myshare\Myusershomedir\Profile

4. If the user is to receive the default user profile from the workstation where they log on, no further administration is required.

5. If the user's profile will be a copy of an existing user profile, skip to Step 10. Otherwise, use User Manager to create an account for establishing a template profile. Name the account *TemplateUser* so it can be easily identified.

6. Using the template account *TemplateUser*, log on to the domain. A new directory with the same name as the user name created in Step 5 will be created in the %systemroot%\Profiles directory when you first log on. For example, if the user name is TemplateUser, the resulting directory name will be %systemroot%\Profiles\TemplateUser.

7. Modify any items that need to differ from the current default. For example, you may choose to modify the background color or bitmap, shortcuts on the desktop, and View options in My Computer.

8. Log off, and then log back on to the same computer using an account with administrative privileges.

9. Place the template profile in the appropriate location for the type of profile distribution that will be used. The template profile, including customizations, is stored initially in: %systemroot%\Profiles\TemplateUser

10. If the template profile will be distributed manually to multiple users, perform the following steps:
    - Create a directory where the template profile will be stored for distribution to each user account created.
    - From Small Business Server (NT-based machine hosting the template profile to be used), log on as an Administrator.
    - From **Control Panel**, click **System** to display the **System Properties** page.
    - Select the **User Profiles** tab, and then click **Copy To** to enter the path of the directory just created.
    - Modify the permissions to allow the **Everyone** group to use the profile. To do this, click **Change**, select the **Everyone** group, and then click **Add** and **OK**.
11. In the *server**share* from Step 1, create the directory structure you specified as the path in Step 3. For example, create the directory *mydomainuser* under \\Myserver\Myshare. If the profile is to be stored in the user's home directory, use the following directory structure: \\Myserver\Myshare\Mydomainuser\Profile
12. Copy the profile appropriate to your implementation.

    ▶ **To copy an existing user's profile to another user**

    a. From Small Business Server (the NT-based machine hosting the profile to be used), log on as an Administrator.

    b. From **Control Panel**, click **System** to display the **System Properties** page.

    c. Select the **User Profiles** tab, highlight the profile to be copied, and then click **Copy To** to enter the path of the directory you created in Step 11.

    d. Modify the permissions to reflect the proper account. To do this, click **Change**, select the account, and then click **Add** and **OK**. Click **OK** again to copy the profile.

    ▶ **To copy the template profile to the Default User folder on the domain controller**

    a. From Small Business Server (the NT-based machine hosting the profile to be used), log on as an Administrator.

    b. From **Control Panel**, click **System** to display the **System Properties** page.

    c. Select the **User Profiles** tab, highlight the profile to be copied, and then click **Copy To**, to enter the path of the Default User directory on Small Business Server.

    d. Modify the permissions to reflect the **Everyone** group. To do this, click **Change**, select the **Everyone** group, and then click **Add** and **OK**. Click **OK** again to copy the profile.

▶ **To copy a template profile manually to a number of users**

a. Copy the entire contents (files and subdirectories) from the directory containing the template user profile created in Step 10 to the directory created in Step 11.

b. Repeat this for each of the user profile directories to receive the template user profile.

Once these steps are complete, the user receives the appropriate profile, as follows:

- If the user is to receive the default user profile from a Windows NT 4.0-based workstation, the workstation's default profile is used when the user first logs on. When the user logs off, the profile is written automatically to the local cache and to the server-based profile.

- If the user is to receive the default user profile from the domain controller, the default profile from Small Business Server is used when the user first logs on. When the user logs off, this profile is written automatically to the client cache and the server-based profile.

- In all other cases, the profile—including the folder trees and the NTuser.*xxx* file originally included with the profile—is written to the user's profile directory. The permissions are also encoded into the binary NTuser.*xxx* file.

Creating a New Mandatory User Profile for Windows NT 4.0 Workstations

Use the steps below to create a mandatory user profile for Windows NT Workstation clients.

▶ **To create a new mandatory user profile**

1. If a location has not already been prepared, create a directory on the server and establish a network share. Users who will have mandatory profiles need only Read permissions to the shared directory. If your implementation stores user profiles within user's home directories, make the profile directory a subdirectory of the user's home directory.

   Note This approach precludes the use of the %Username% variable. To prevent the share from being browsed, append "$" to the share name.

2. If this will be a domain user, use User Manager for Domains in the Administrative Tools group on the server to create the account. If this will be a Windows NT 4.0 Workstation account, use the version of User Manager in the Administrative Tools group on the workstation. Refer to your operating system documentation and online Help for procedures when using these tools.

   Note For the example that follows, the user account is called *mydomainuser*.

3. Enter the user profile path. This is the location where the user profile will be stored, for example:

   \\Myserver\Myshare\Mydomainuser

   If the profile is being stored within the user's home directory, use:

   \\Myserver\Myshare\MyUsersHomeDir\Profile

4. Determine if an extension needs to be appended to the user profile path. If it is mandatory that the user reads the profile from the server, and if logon will be denied unless this is the case, add the extension ".man" to the user profile path, for example:

   \\Myserver\Myshare\Mydomainuser.man

5. Use User Manager to create an account for establishing the template profile. Name this account *TemplateUser* so it may by easily identified.

6. Using the template account, TemplateUser, log on to the domain. A new directory with the same name as the user name created in Step 2 will be created in the %systemroot%\Profiles directory when you first log on. For example, if the user name is TemplateUser, the resulting directory name will be: %systemroot%\Profiles\TemplateUser

7. Modify any items that need to differ from the current default. For example, you may choose to modify the background color or bitmap, shortcuts on the desktop, or **View** options in **My Computer**.

8. Log off, and then log back on to the same computer using an account with administrative privileges.

9. In the *server**share* from Step 1, create the directory structure you specified as the path in Step 3. For example, create the directory *mydomainuser* under \\Myserver\Myshare—if the profile is stored in the user's home directory, create the following directory structure:
   \\Myserver\Myshare\Mydomainuser\Profile

   Note If you appended the .man extension to the user profile path in Step 4, append the .man suffix to the directory name for the folder where the profile will be stored. The .man extension identifies a Windows NT 4.0 mandatory profile that must be accessible for the user to logon. For example, if the user name is *mydomainuser*, the path to the mandatory profile would be:
   \\Myserver\Myshare*Mydomainuser.man*

10. From Small Business Server (the Windows NT-based machine hosting the template profile to be used), log on as an Administrator.

11. From the **Control Panel**, click **System**. In the **User Profiles** dialog box, select the profile to be copied and use the **Copy To** option to enter the path of the directory you created in Step 9.

12. Modify the permissions to allow the user or group to use the profile. To do this, click **Change**, select the account, then click **OK**. You can select any group or specific user when setting the permissions, however only the user or group specified will be able to use the profile.

13. The profile—including the folder trees and the NTuser.xxx file originally included with the profile—is written to the location you designated. The permissions are also encoded into the binary NTuser.xxx file.

14. In the directory that the profile was copied to in Step 3, check the NTuser.xxx file for the .man extension. If the extension is .dat, the profile can still be modified. Change the extension to .man if necessary, so the profile will be recognized as mandatory.

Creating a New Roaming User Profile for Windows 95 Clients

If you have Windows 95 users in your domain, you can create roaming user profiles for them.

▶ **To create a roaming user profile for a Windows 95 client**

1. On the Windows 95-based client, start **Control Panel** and double-click **Passwords** to display the **Password Properties** page.

2. Select the **User Profiles** tab, and then set the **Primary Network Logon** to **Client for Microsoft Networks** to enable users to have individual profiles.

3. Restart the client machine.

4. Open the User Manager for Domains (Administrative Tools group) on the server to create the user account (if it does not already exist).

5. On the **User** menu, point to **New User** to display the **New User** dialog box.
6. Type in the appropriate information, and then click **Profile** to display the following **User Environment Profile** dialog box.
7. For the user's home directory, specify the location where the user profile will be stored. Click **OK**.

   This automatically creates a folder with the user name. If a dialog box is displayed stating that the operation failed, create the folder manually before continuing.

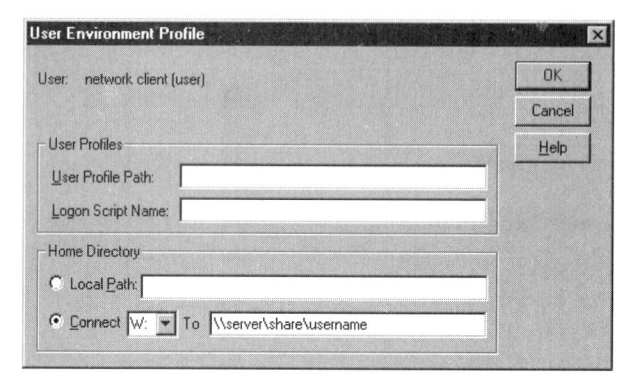

8. Decide whether the user will receive a specific profile or a default profile and proceed as follows:
   - If the user is to receive a specific profile, copy (from the Windows 95-based computer hosting the profile) the complete contents of the local Profile folder to the folder created in Step 7. This writes the profile to the destination, including the folder trees and the User.xxx file originally included with the profile.
   - If a default profile will be used, no action is required. When the user logs on, the default user profile from the Windows 95-based machine will be used. At log off, this profile will be written to the user's home directory with any user customizations.

Creating a New Mandatory User Profile for Windows 95 Clients

If you have Windows 95 users in your domain, you can create new mandatory user profiles.

▶ **To create a mandatory user profile for a Windows 95 user**

1. On the Windows 95-based client, start **Control Panel** and double-click **Passwords** to display the **Password Properties** page.
2. From the **User Profiles** tab, set the **Primary Network Logon** to **Client for Microsoft Networks** to enable users to have individual profiles.

3. Restart the client machine.
4. Open the User Manager for Domains (Administrative Tools group) on the server to create the user account (unless it already exists).
5. On the **User** menu, point to **New User** to display the **New User** dialog box.
6. Type in the appropriate information, then click **Profile** to display the following **User Environment Profile** dialog box.
7. Specify the path where the user profile will be stored. Click **OK**.

    This automatically creates a folder with the user name. If a dialog is displayed stating that the operation failed, create the folder manually before continuing.

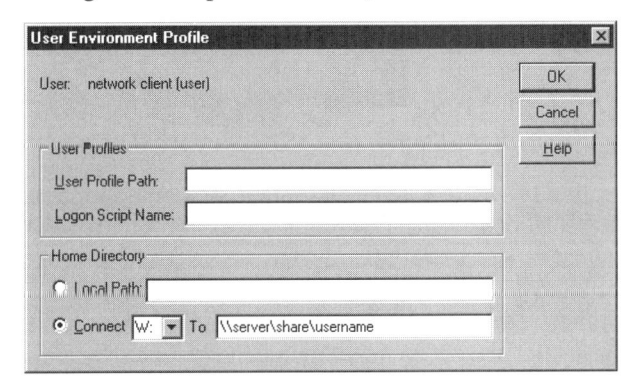

8. Copy the Template Profile that you are using for mandatory profiles to the user's home directory:

    - From the Windows 95-based machine hosting the mandatory profile, copy the complete contents of the local Profile folder to the folder created in step 7. This writes the profile to the destination, including the folder trees and the User.xxx file originally included with the profile.
    - If you have not already done so, rename the User.dat file to User.man so it is recognized as a mandatory profile.

Note At logon, the user will download the mandatory profile, cache it, and no changes will be written back to the server at log off.

More Information on User Profiles and System Policies

For further details on user profiles and system policy, refer to the *Windows NT Server 4.0 Concepts and Planning* guide. For information on administering user profiles and system policies, refer to *Microsoft Windows NT 4.0 Profiles and Policies* at:

http://www.microsoft.com/ntserver/management/deployment

Server Status Tool

The Server Status Tool, running on Small Business Server 4.5, allows the technology consultant to monitor the status of the server. The technology consultant can send an e-mail or fax containing various server status logs to either a local machine on the small business network or an external Internet address for remote monitoring. Server status logs contain system data which provides a record of status and activities the technology consultant can use for troubleshooting or analysis in the detection and prevention of potential server problems. The logs provide the data necessary to evaluate whether the server is experiencing bottlenecks or prone to performance degradation and failure, in advance of these occurrences.

How the Server Status Tool Can be Used

The Server Status Tool allows the technology consultant to proactively monitor and report on the servers of multiple customers. To facilitate this, service accounts could be set up that include monthly fees to customers for support and server monitoring. The Server Status Tool can be configured to send reports to the technology consultant on a daily or weekly basis to provide data for a consolidated report sent to small business customers at the end of each month. The consolidated report could include the preconfigured server status logs described in the section ahead entitled "Report Contents." The Server Status Tool can also be extended to include logs from other applications in the report.

How the Server Status Tool Works

The Status Server Tool locates the status log for a reported service by searching the server for the most up to date service log file, based on a specified file pattern. For example, if the log file is proxy*.log, where * is the current update, the Status Server Tool searches for the most recently created proxy.log file. Once the file is found, it is attached to an e-mail or fax and sent to the address specified by the technology consultant.

Sending Reports

Reports are sent using the **send server status** task on the **Administrative Tools** page of the Small Business Server Console—but first, they must be configured using the **configure server status** task, also on the **Administrative Tools** page. This task displays Online Guide configuration procedures which link to the **Server Status Configuration** dialog box below for configuring server status reports. The following configuration options are provided:

- **Send Options**. Sends reports by e-mail attachment or fax.
- **Reports**. Selects reports to be sent.

- **Schedule**. Configures the intervals at which reports are sent.
- **Settings**. Configures certain events when reports are sent or not sent.

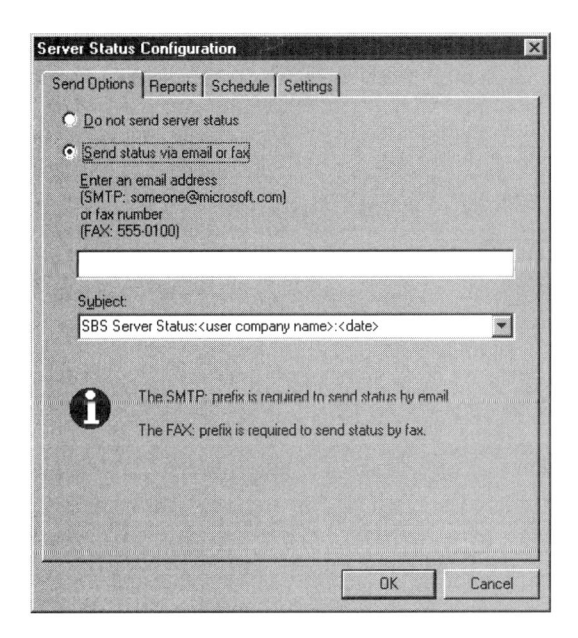

Report Contents

The Server Status Tool is preconfigured to send five key status reports, as follows:

- **Hard Disk Space**. Contains the percentage of drive space available.
- **Server Status**. Contains the status of each NT service. Includes the status (started, stopped, or not installed) and the startup type (automatic, manual, or disabled).
- **Internet Information Server Logs**. Contains records of Internet Information Server (IIS) activities which includes the time stamp, Internet protocol (IP) address of requester, request method, location of activating source, and a status code.
- **Web Proxy Logs**. Parameters include client IP address, client name, Internet Explorer version, date, time, node type, search string, host address, transfer protocol, IP, request method, and search object.
- **Winsock Proxy Logs**. Same format as Web Proxy Logs.

Setting the Server Status Tool Password

When the Server Status Tool is configured to send reports, the Online Guide presents instructions to set the server reporting administrator password. However, you must manually reset the Server Status Tool administrator password using the steps below, if the administrator password is ever changed with either of the following components:

- Change Password Wizard.
- Windows NT User Manager for Domains.

▶ **To set the Server Status Tool administrator password**

1. From the Small Business Server desktop, double-click **My Computer**.
2. Double-click **Scheduled Tasks**.
3. From the list of scheduled tasks, double-click **Server Status Tool** to display the following **Server Status Tool** dialog box.

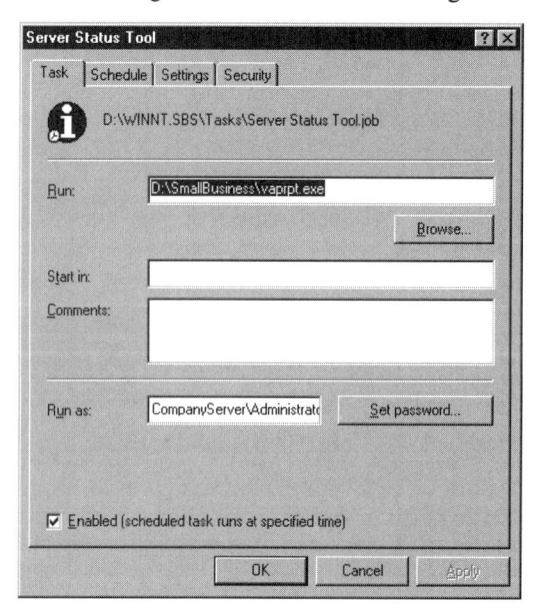

4. Select the **Task** tab, and then click **Set Password** to display the following **Set Password** dialog box.

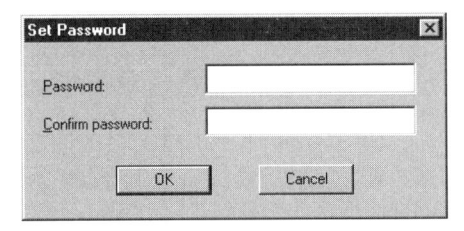

5. Type the administrator password in **Password** and **Confirm Password**.
6. Click **OK**.
7. In the **Server Status Tool** dialog box, click **Apply**, and then click **OK**.

Extending the Server Status Tool

The Server Status Tool report list can be extended to include other application reports. To extend the Server Status Tool, refer to *Chapter 46, Other Extensions and Solutions* in *Part 9, Developing Small Business Server Solutions*, of this resource guide.

Internet and Fax Reports

Internet (Proxy) and Fax reports may be obtained for Small Business Server 4.5 using the **Administrative Tools** link on the Tasks page of the console. When the appropriate taskpad is activated for generating a report, Internet Explorer launches an active server page (ASP) for the Proxy or Fax report to be displayed. The ASP pages are generated from comma separated value (CSV) files. The CSV files are created from Microsoft Proxy Server logs and from Fax application logs stored in the NT Event Viewer.

Note Proxy and Fax reports can be added to the Server Status Tool report list using the Small Business Server Customization Tool.

Generating the Reports

Refer to the illustration below during the discussion that follows for the components and files used to generate the Proxy and Fax reports.

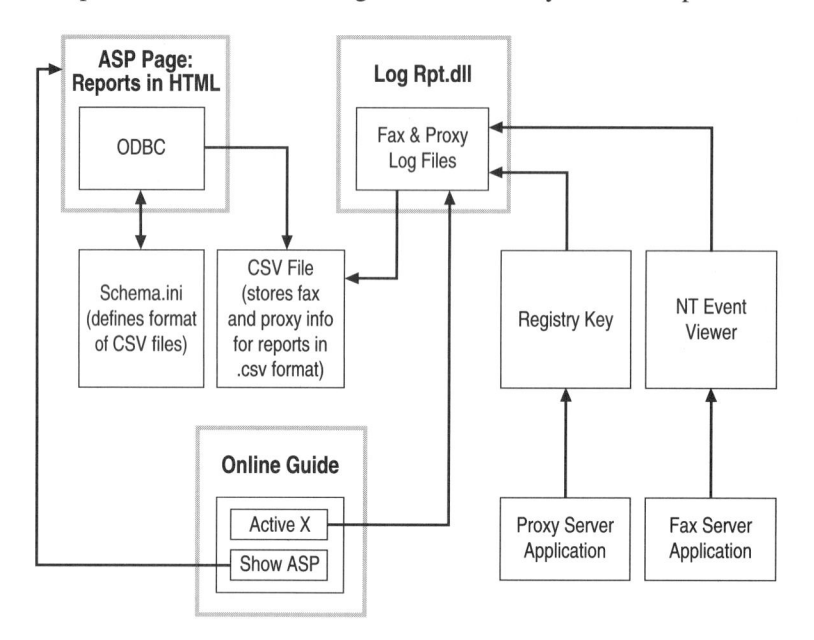

Figure 26.1 Proxy and Fax report generation

When Proxy Server logs information, it uses a registry key to find the pointer to the location where Proxy logs are to be stored. When Microsoft Fax Server is ready to log information, NT Event Viewer is used to store the information in the following location: Winnt\System32\Config\AppEvent.evt.

Proxy and Fax reports are launched from the Online Guide. The Online Guide page launching the specific report contains an active control that accesses the logrpt.dll file in order to generate the relevant .csv file. An Open Database Connectivity (ODBC) text driver is then used to establish a connection to the .csv file database. Then, the Fax or Proxy ASP (rpt.asp) is displayed by Internet Explorer. The Schema.ini file describes the format of the tables in the .csv file database—refer to the section ahead entitled "File Format in the CSV Database."

Note For the Fax logs, the records are read directly from the NT Event Viewer and written to the .csv files.

Proxy Reports

The four Proxy reports below are generated from Proxy log files and displayed on the console using the **generate Internet reports** taskpad on the Administration Tools page.

- Top ten Internet sites.
- Top ten users.
- Activity by hour of the day.
- Cached to non-cached comparisons.

These reports provide the technology consultant with an indication of company wide web usage including the content of Uniform Resource Locator (URL) requests, destination hosts, and traffic patterns on the Internet for Small Business Server. The report information may be used to create an Internet activity profile tracking such things as the top Internet users in the company, peak usage times, and web sites most frequently visited. This information can help the technology consultant implement better small business Internet strategies and fine-tune Internet connectivity for optimum performance with Small Business Server 4.5.

Proxy Report Content

Proxy reports contain the following information. An example of a Proxy Top Ten Users report follows.

- **Top ten Internet sites**. A listing and graph of the top 10 Internet site accesses, ordered from the most active to least active. Total hits for each site, the percentage of overall total hits this represents, and the overall total hits are included.

- **Top ten users**. A listing and graph of the top users ordered from the most active to least active. Includes the number of accesses for each user and the percentage of total hits each user represents, compared to the overall number of site hits. Also includes total bytes received and URL information for each user.

- **Activity by hour of the day**. A listing and graph showing hits on a per-hour basis versus total number of hits. Includes the most active hours/hits, least active hours/hits, and total activity during work and after hours.

- **Cached to non-cached comparison**. A listing and a graph of cached and non-cached access counts, the percentage of total accesses, and total bytes received.

Note Proxy and Fax reports for Small Business Server 4.5 replace the reports previously provided by Crystal Reports on Small Business Server 4.0 and 4.0a.

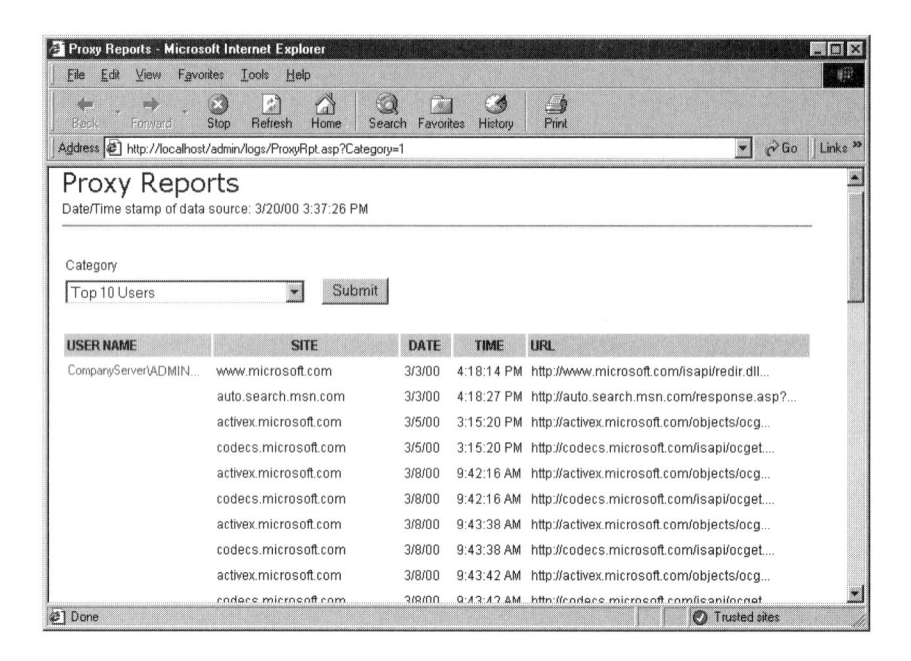

Fax Reports

Relevant information from the Fax logs is retrieved from the NT Event Viewer to generate the Fax reports below. These reports are displayed on the console using the **generate fax reports** taskpad on the Administration Tools page.

- Received faxes.
- Sent faxes.
- Received faxes—Top numbers.
- Sent faxes—Top numbers.

Fax Report Content

Fax reports provide the technology consultant with an indication of fax activity including the total number of sent and received faxes and the top 10 in each category. From this information, a company-wide fax profile can be developed to assist the small business in fine-tuning company fax strategies and resources. Fax reports contain the information below. An example of a Sent Faxes report follows.

- **Received faxes**. Shows the date, time, "from" number, "to" number, number of pages, reception time, total pages, and the total time.

- **Top ten received fax numbers.** Contains the "from" number and the number of faxes from the top 10 users including other details such as the "to" number, date, time, and number of pages.
- **Sent faxes.** Shows the time, "to" number, sender (username), number of pages, transmission time for each fax sent. Also tallies the page and transmission time totals.
- **Top ten sent fax numbers.** Shows the total number of faxes, pages, and transmission times for each of the top 10 fax recipient numbers.

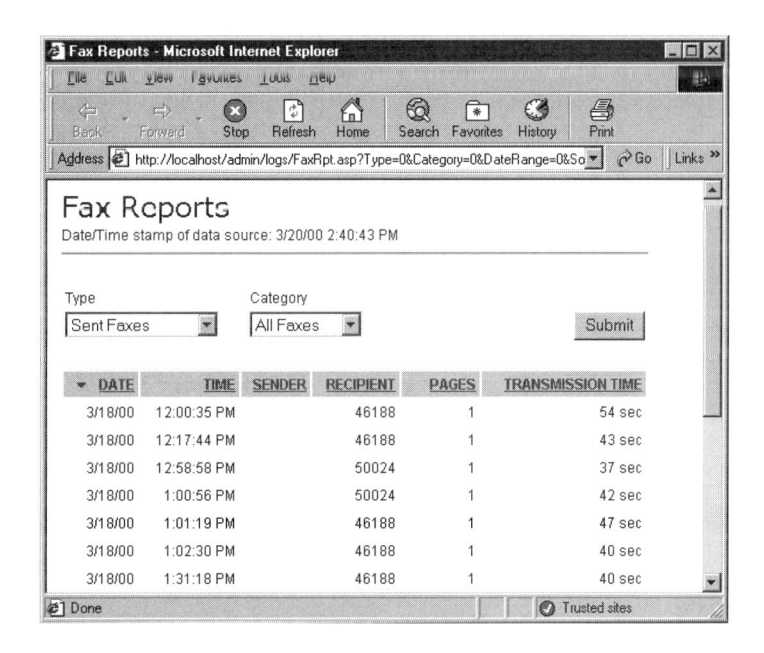

File Format in the CSV Database

The format of the Proxy and Fax files stored in the tab-delimited database file (with a .csv extension) is determined by a Schema.ini file for each report type. Schema.ini creates tab-delimited files defined by parameters such as those in the example below. Essentially, the Schema.ini file is a driver for the .csv files that store the report information. The Schema.ini file for Proxy .csv files contains the following:

ColNameHeader=False

Format=TabDelimited

MaxScanRows=25

CharacterSet=UNICODE

Col1=ClientIP Char

Col2=ClientUserName Char

Col3=ClientAgent Char

Col4=ClientAuthenticate Char

Col5=LogDate Date

Col6=LogTime Date

Col7=Service Char

Col8=ServiceName Char

Col9=ReferredServer Char

Col10=DestHost Char

Col11=DestHostIP Char

Col12=DestHostPort Char

Col13=ProcessingTime Date

Col14=BytesSent Float

Col15=BytesRecvd Float

Col16=Protocol Char

Col17=Transport Char

Col18=Operation Char

Col19=URL Char

Col20=MimeType Char

Col21=ObjectSource Char

Col22=ResultCode Char

Col23=CacheInfo Float

Performance Monitor Tool

With the Performance Monitor tool, you can view the usage of system resources on Windows NT-based machines. Alerts can be set up to monitor Small Business Server performance. Problems and bottlenecks can be identified before network users are affected. Individual system resource usage thresholds can be set so that Performance Monitor provides notification if the system exceeds them. Also, Performance Monitor can be configured to monitor up to 25 network computers and alert you if any of them are showing signs of trouble.

Performance monitors for Exchange Server and Proxy Server are configured in *Chapter 27, Administering Small Business Server Components*.

Configuring Performance Monitor Alerts

In this section, several sample Performance Monitor alerts are created with typical values to provide notification of when critical resource measurement thresholds are exceeded. Also, an example is provided on how to set up a performance monitor alert to monitor Windows NT Workstation system resources.

Important Performance Monitor can not be used to monitor system resources on Windows 95-based computers.

The Performance Monitor Utility

Since each system is unique, there are no set rules on how to monitor system resources. Knowing what to look for takes time and practice. Performance Monitor tracks information about your system through the use of objects and counters. Objects are the components of your system, such as the processor, physical disk, and memory. Counters are the statistics that can be tracked for each object. There are more than 350 counters that can be used. One example is the *% Processor Time* counter, which measures the percentage of time the processor is doing useful work. Each object has its own unique set of counters.

Thresholds of acceptable performance can be set using the counters of Performance Monitor. For example, if you decided that your *% Processor Time* should not regularly exceed 80 percent, an alert can be configured to provide notification when that threshold is exceeded.

Creating an Alert

To create an alert, perform the steps below.

▶ **To create a Performance Monitor alert**

1. Click **Start**, point to **Programs**, point to **Administrative Tools**, and then click **Performance Monitor** to display the **Performance Monitor** utility.

   Note When Performance Monitor first runs, it opens in chart view. This view is used to track system counters in real time (or to display logged data).

2. On the **View** menu, click **Alert** to display the following **Performance Monitor** dialog box.

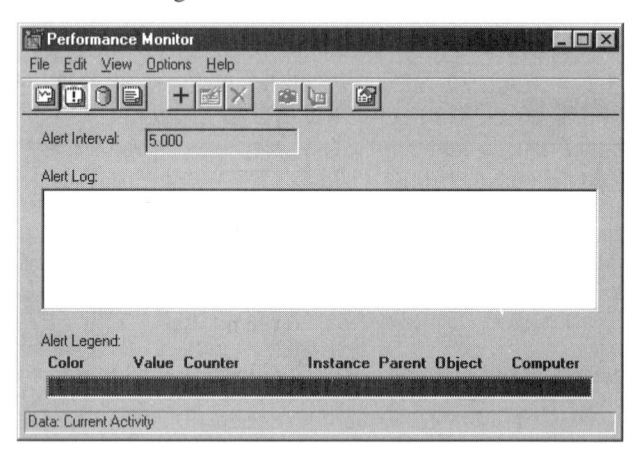

3. To set options for your alerts, click **Alert** in the **Options** menu to display the following **Alert Options** dialog box.

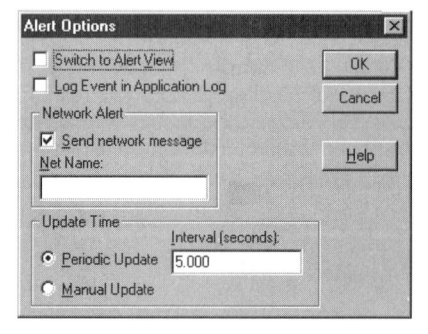

4. Select **Send network message**. This configures Performance Monitor to send a network message when a threshold has been exceeded.

5. Type the name of your computer in **Net Name**, and then click **OK** to close the dialog box.

6. On the **Edit** menu, click **Add to Alert** to display the following **Add To Alert** dialog box.

> **Note** The **Processor Object** and **% Processor Time** counter are selected by default when **Add to Alert** appears.

> **Note** The **Explain** button provides a description of the features of other counters that may be used when configuring performance monitor alerts.

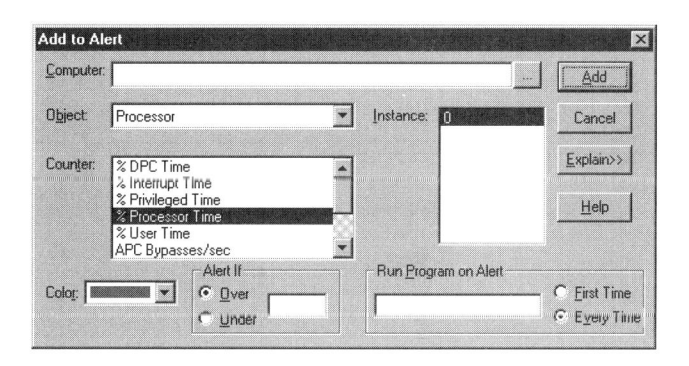

7. In the **Alert If** section, click **Over** and type the threshold variable in the text field. For this example, type in the number 5.
8. Click **Add** to create the alert, then click **Done** to close the dialog box.

> **Important** Performance Monitor is *not* a service. It must be started and left running in order to send out alerts.

Testing the Counter

Start opening programs on your system. Very few programs will need to be running to exceed a 5 percent processor usage threshold. A message box like the following should appear.

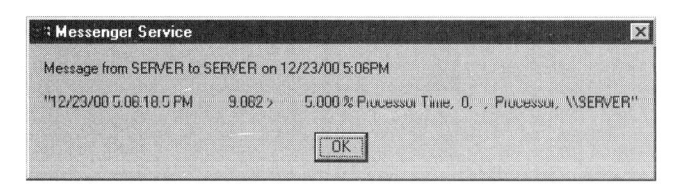

If you look at the **Performance Monitor** dialog box again, you will notice the alerts were also logged there, as follows.

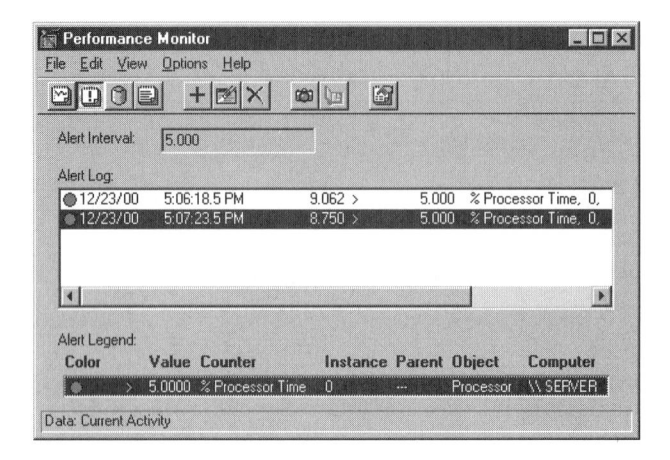

Modifying Existing Alerts

In practice, 5 percent processor time is too low a threshold for normal processor operation. If you want to modify the alert previously created, follow the steps of the procedure below.

▶ **To modify an existing alert**

1. In the alert screen shown above, highlight the alert in the **Alert Legend**. On the **Edit** menu, click **Edit Alert Entry**.

> **Note** The **Edit Alert** dialog will only allow changes to **Color**, the **Alert If** condition, and the **Run Program on Alert settings**. If any other setting needs to change, a new alert must be created.

2. Change the **Alert If** variable for the alert to *80*. This is a common setting for the **% Processor Time** counter.

> **Note** If alert warnings occur consistently stating that percent processor time is exceeding 80 percent, consider moving some of the applications off the server or upgrading the processor.

Monitoring the Processor Queue Length

Another important measure of resource use is the Processor Queue Length, which is the length of the processor queue in units of threads. All processors use a single queue in which threads wait for processor cycles. Monitoring the **Processor Queue Length** counter can provide an alert if threads waiting to be processed are overrunning the processor in Small Business Server.

An alert for the **Processor Queue Length** counter is created in the same manner as the **% Processor Time** counter. Follow the steps below to configure the alert.

▶ **To configure a Processor Queue Length alert**

1. Click **Start**, point to **Programs**, point to **Administrative Tools**, and then click **Performance Monitor** to display the **Performance Monitor** utility.
2. On the **View** menu, click **Alert**.
3. On the **Edit** menu, click **Add To Alert** to display the **Add To Alert** dialog box.
4. On the **Object** drop-down list, select **System** since the **Processor Queue Length** is a counter of the **System** object.
5. From the **Counter** list, locate **Processor Queue Length** and click on it to highlight the counter.

6. Click **Over** in the **Alert If** field section and type 2 in the text field to provide an alert when the counter is over two.

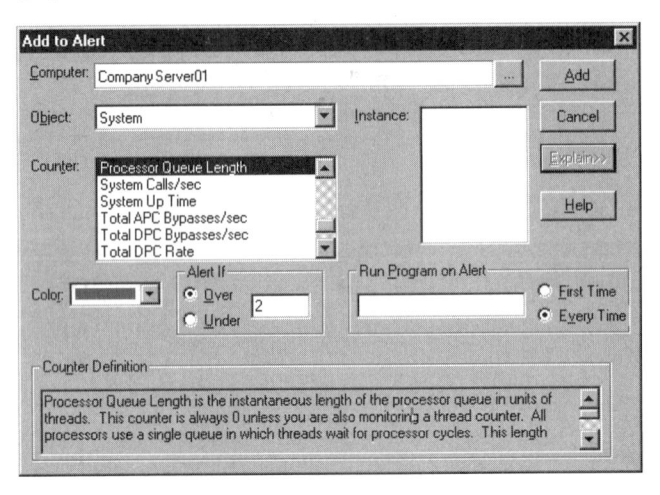

7. Click **Add** and then **Done** to create the alert.

Note The Processor Queue Length threshold for your system may need to be modified, but in general, if this counter consistently exceeds two, too much is being asked of your system with current processor capabilities.

Monitoring Interrupts/Second

In this example, the **Interrupts/second** counter of the **Processor Object** is configured. This counter shows the rate of requests from I/O devices. A sudden increase can indicate a hardware problem. To configure the counter, follow the steps below.

▶ **To configure an Interrupts/second alert**
  1. Click **Start**, point to **Programs**, point to **Administrative Tools**, and then click **Performance Monitor** to display the **Performance Monitor** utility.
  2. On the **View** menu, click **Alert**.
  3. On the **Edit** menu, click **Add To Alert** to display the **Add To Alert** dialog box.
  4. On the **Object** drop-down list, select **Processor** since **Interrupts/second** is a counter of the **Processor** object.

Task Scheduling Tool

Small Business Server 4.5 inclu[de]d Task Wizard, you can schedule any script, rudimentary, recurring tasks by [sta]rt at any time or interval, from every day to once a specified time on a regular basis[.] configured to trigger when certain operating system Scheduled Task Wizard. The wi[zard] boot, user logon, or system idle. The wizard provides application at any time or interv[al t]o be run, configure schedule settings, set permissions, Scheduled Task utility integrate[s ...]ices.
and also provides an API that e[nables ...]
their applications.

The Scheduled Task Utility

The Scheduled Task Wizard — [...]
integrated into the operating sys[tem ...]
executable, found in the **Schedu[led ...]**
drag-and-drop programs right in[to ...]
quickly add a new task or use th[e wizard to]
configure the schedule.

[Scheduled Ta]sk Files

[Because tasks are saved with] a .job extension in the \Winnt\Tasks folder,
[it is easy to copy or move] the tasks from computer to computer. For example, the
[administrator can cr]eate scheduled maintenance task files and add them
[to multiple servers]. The Scheduled Tasks folder can also be shared and
[accessed via Net]work Neighborhood or sent across the network by e-
[mail.]

[Because sc]heduled tasks are created and executed based on
[secur]ity permissions. Tasks are persistent files
[an]d access control lists (ACLs), to set which users or
[mod]ify, or use a task. The items that make up a task
[compon]ents) are also controlled by whatever ACLs are
[set on these i]tems. In Small Business Server, this provides a high
[level of security when task f]iles are accessed.

Security Features

Security features can be set for task files on the **Security** tab of the task's properties window, accessed by double-clicking on the task in the opened Scheduled Tasks folder. You can change permissions for groups and users, audit the use of a file by groups and users, and set file ownership options. See the online Help available from the task's properties for further information on configuring these options.

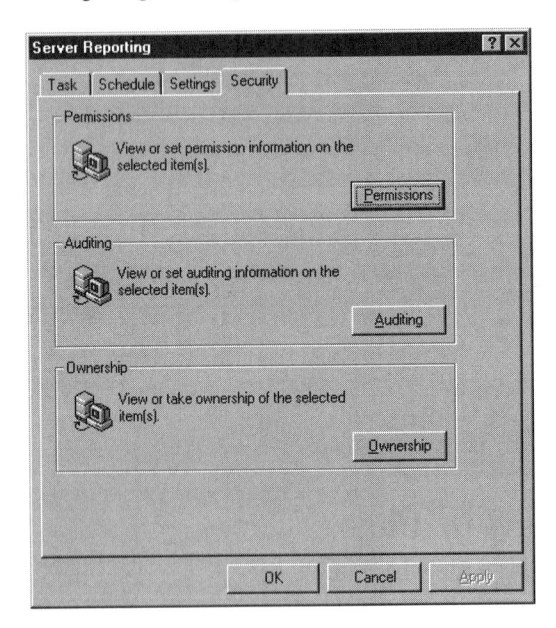

User Credentials

When a .job file is moved on a Windows NT system, user credentials do not transfer with the file because credentials are not stored with the task, but by the security system of Windows NT. Re-enter the user credentials after moving the file.

User Name and Password

Since Small Business Server is a multiuser environment, a user name and password are required when tasks are created in order to set the current security context in which the task will execute. Refer to the following screen. Multiple tasks run on a single computer in the security context that was supplied.

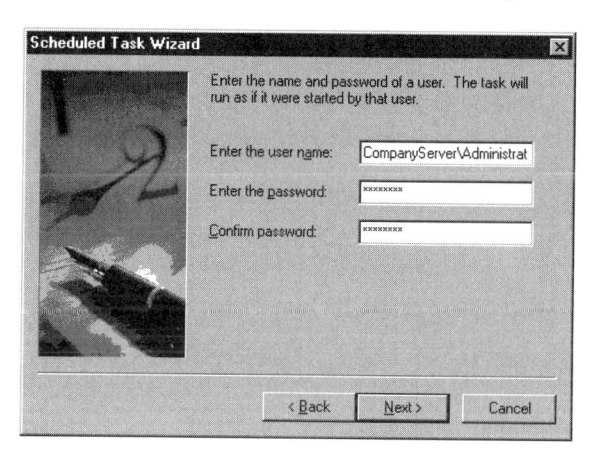

Running Tasks

Some sample tasks that could be scheduled to run on Small Business Server are listed below:

- Scan disk.
- Disk defragmenter and/or other disk utilities.
- Virus checks.
- Phone dialer.
- Maintenance wizard.
- NetMeeting session.
- Any other program, script, or document to open.

Note Internet/Fax reports and the Server Status Tool use the Scheduled Task utility when sending reports to the technology consultant, although the report configuration process runs in the background.

Editing Tasks

With the Scheduled Tasks utility, you can also edit tasks you have created or customize how a task runs at a scheduled time using the task's property tabs. Double-click the task in the opened Scheduled Tasks folder to edit the task. The following dialog box shows the property tabs for a scheduled Phone Dialer task.

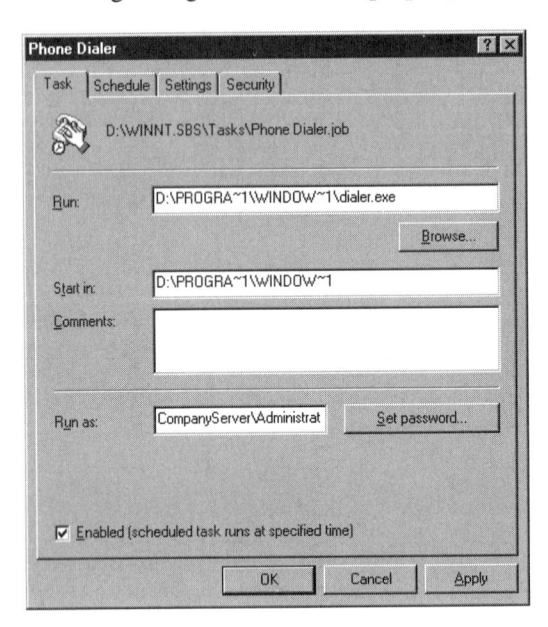

Configuring a Task with the Scheduled Tasks Utility

To configure a task for Small Business Server and add it to the list of scheduled tasks, perform the steps that follow.

▶ **To configure a scheduled task for Small Business Server**

1. From **My Computer**, double-click the **Scheduled Tasks** folder.
2. Double-click **Add Scheduled Task** to start the **Scheduled Task Wizard**.
3. Follow the steps of the wizard to configure the scheduled task.

Note You can also add tasks by dragging scripts, programs, or documents from NT Explorer or the desktop to the Scheduled Tasks window. After dragging the task, double-click on it to bring up the properties tabs for the task and configure the appropriate settings.

Other Features of the Utility

With the Scheduled Task utility, you can also pause, stop, or delete the tasks that have been scheduled, view a log of past scheduled tasks, view tasks scheduled on a remote computer, or be notified of missed tasks. Access these features by selecting **Advanced** on the menu bar of the **Scheduled Tasks** window.

NT Backup Tool and the Scheduled Task Utility

The NT Backup Tool uses the **AT** command with the Scheduled Task utility. Tasks that are scheduled using the **AT** command are stored in the registry. For more information on using the **AT** command, refer to *Windows NT Help*.

Application Programming Interfaces (APIs)

The Scheduled Task utility provides a common and fully programmable set of interfaces. The scheduled task utility is a COM-based object, which adds all the advantages of COM, including language and platform independence (as well as remote capabilities provided by DCOM). If a developer has an application to run under both Windows 95 and Windows NT, the same interfaces can be written to, regardless of the platform.

All of the functionality in the Scheduled Task utility is completely accessible from these APIs. This simplifies things when an ISV wishes to provide scheduling services for a newly developed Small Business Server application. Also, it is unnecessary for the developer to write their own scheduling property pages. The property pages of the Scheduled Task utility can be invoked from the same APIs. Property pages and dialog boxes specific to the application may be created and then the property pages of the Scheduled Task utility can be accessed as needed.

CHAPTER 27

Administering Small Business Server Components

This chapter discusses supplementary concepts and procedures for administering the Microsoft® BackOffice® Small Business Server 4.5 applications and components listed below.

- Fax and Modem Sharing Services.
- Exchange Server.
- Proxy Server.
- Microsoft SQL Server™.
- NTFS/FAT volume security.

Microsoft Fax Service

Microsoft Fax Service provides fax services to clients on the small business network. Once the fax client software is installed, users can send and receive faxes using fax devices installed on the server. At least one Class 1 fax modem must be installed during Small Business Server setup in order to enable Fax Service installation.

Faxing Model

Fax Service uses the concept of a fax printer to send faxes. During installation, the Fax Service creates a default shared fax printer that enables sending and receiving faxes. Users can fax documents by printing them to the shared fax printer, just as if they were sending a document to a shared printer. The fax printer then communicates with the fax device to send the fax.

Managing Microsoft Fax Service

The **Manage Faxes** page of the Small Business Server console shows the most common tasks for managing the Fax Service. To manage the Fax Service using the console, select **Manage Faxes** on the **More Tasks** page of the console. You can manage the following tasks from **Manage Faxes** page:

- Control access to fax services.
- Change how faxes are received.
- Add or remove a fax modem.
- Add or remove fax printers.
- Create cover pages.
- Generate fax reports.
- Manage fax jobs.
- Troubleshoot faxing.

Accessing Fax Service Properties

Most of the tasks for configuring Fax Service involve setting options in the **Fax Server Properties** page. Although this page is easily launched from **Manage Faxes** tasks on the Small Business Server console, it can also be opened in the following ways:

- From the **Start** menu using **Programs** and **Fax (Common)**.
- From the **Start** menu using **Settings** and **Control Panel**.

▶ **To open the Fax Server Properties dialog box from Programs**
- Click **Start**, point to **Programs**, point to **Fax (Common)**, and then click **Fax Configuration** to display the **Fax Server Properties** dialog box shown below.

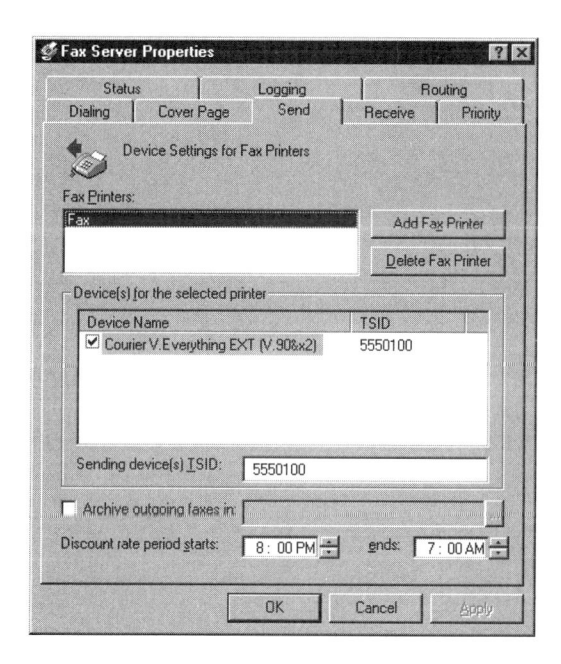

Adding a Fax Device

When Small Business Server installs Fax Service, it configures any fax modems installed during setup to send and receive faxes. If your fax modem was not automatically installed, refer to *Chapter 19, Small Business Server Setup Issues,* in *Part 3, Deployment,* and *Chapter 56 Modem Sharing Service Troubleshooting* in *Part 11, Troubleshooting* of this resource guide. Make sure your fax modem(s) has the following requirements:

- Must be a Class 1 fax modem. Business class fax modem is recommended.
- If using the same modem for inbound faxes and RAS, it must support adaptive answering.

To install additional modems after setup, use the Small Business Server console **Manage Faxes** page. After installing a fax modem, use the **Manage Faxes** page to enable the modem to send or receive faxes and to configure how Fax Service uses the device. These devices must model their ports as modems. To install such devices, refer to the manufacturer's instructions.

Fax Service can also be configured to work with some specialized fax cards.

Note Fax Service does not support advanced Private Branch Exchange (PBX) routing features such as Direct Inward Dialing (DID).

Adding and Configuring Fax Printers

When Small Business Server installs Microsoft Fax Service, it creates a fax printer. This fax printer can be configured to use a single modem or multiple modems.

Different fax printers can be set up for different people or groups in the small business organization. Each printer can be configured to archive sent faxes to a specific destination directory and to use a different fax modem.

To add a fax printer, refer to the Online Guide.

Windows NT Clients

For Windows NT Workstation clients, after Fax Service setup, additional fax printers may be created to serve different needs in the small business organization. For example, if you have different discount billing rate periods for domestic and international long-distance calling, you can create one fax printer with the discount rate period set for international use and another for domestic.

User Access to the Fax Printer

The technology consultant can control who uses a fax printer in the same way that access to any printer is controlled—by changing the security and sharing settings for the fax printer. On Small Business Server, clients are given access to the fax printer using the console's **Manage Faxes** page.

Creating Cover Pages for Your Fax Printers

Fax Service includes a fax cover page editor for Windows NT Workstation clients. The editor is similar to Microsoft Wordpad and allows you to insert text, shapes, and fax fields on a what-you-see-is-what-you-get (WYSIWYG) window. Custom fax pages can be created for your company, for specific users, or for specific fax printers. Refer to the Online Guide for procedures.

Assigning Cover Pages for Your Fax Printers

When Small Business Server installs Fax Service, it sets up a fax printer and assigns four default cover pages that users can send with faxes. For each fax printer, you can create new cover pages, add existing cover pages, edit the cover pages, or delete them. Refer to the Online Guide for specific procedures.

Receiving and Routing Incoming Faxes

When Small Business Server installs Fax Service, it enables all the fax modems on your computer to only *send* faxes. To *receive* a fax, a fax device must be selected in the **Fax Server Properties** dialog box **Receive** tab. For each fax modem, you can specify several routing options for received faxes, as follows:

- Automatically print faxes as they are received.
- Save faxes in a shared folder anywhere on the network. You can view these faxes in the folder online using a Tagged Image File Format (TIFF) viewer. In a typical installation, all clients have access to the share.

  When Fax Service is installed during setup, the default location for received faxes, %systemroot%\FaxStore, can be changed. The **Receive** tab on the **Fax Server Properties** dialog box can be used to change the default location of the *received* fax store. The destination directory for archiving *sent* faxes can be specified using the **Send** tab. With these tabs, you can also choose to not archive received and sent faxes.

  Note If you archive sent and received faxes, delete them periodically from the saved location to reduce disk space consumption.

- Send faxes to a local profile (such as the administrator's) if Microsoft Exchange Server is installed. Faxes are saved as an attachment to the e-mail message (using TIFF file format). The e-mail may then be sent by the administrator to any supported e-mail client. Once received, the fax can be viewed with a TIFF viewer. Refer to the Online Guide for specific procedures on configuring fax routings.

  After installation, fax modems can be disabled or enabled to receive faxes and the way faxes are routed can be changed. For example, all received faxes could be sent to an office manager's mailbox. The office manager would then open the faxes in the fax viewer and use the **Send** command to forward each one to the cover page addressee.

The following diagram illustrates the various ways a fax can be received and routed.

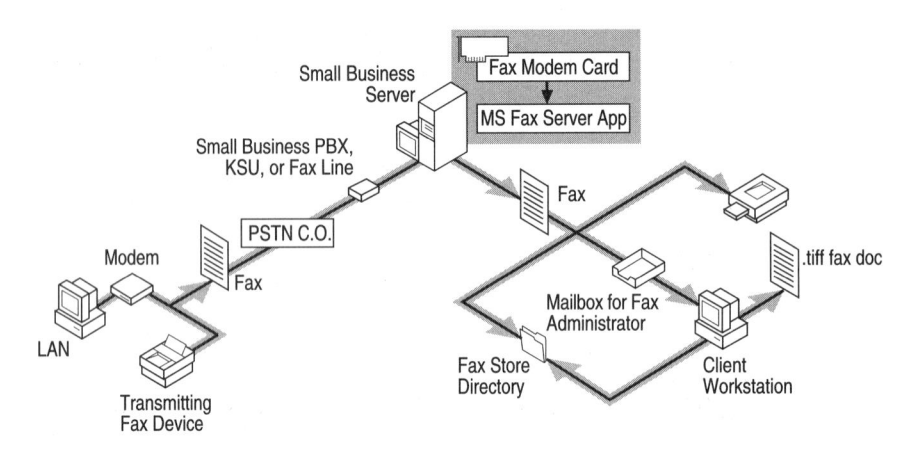

Figure 27.1   Receiving a fax with Small Business Server

Checking Received Faxes

Microsoft Fax Service routes faxes through the fax printer queue. When the Fax Service is unable to route an incoming fax, such as when a shared directory is unavailable, it keeps the fax in the fax jobs list until it successfully delivers the fax. Once the destination is available, the fax jobs list can be opened for any fax printer and the print job for the incoming fax can be restarted.

Sending and Resending Faxes

Fax Service can be configured to solely send and not receive faxes. Fax Service can also be configured to resend messages up to a maximum of 15 times. The amount of time to wait in between redial attempts may also be specified.

Fax Send Notification

Clients receive e-mail notification of fax-send status whether it succeeded or failed. Since Fax Service is set up like a printer driver, the printer queue can be viewed to see the fax printer and obtain the status of the fax.

Fax Job Management

Fax jobs may be paused, restarted, or canceled from the Small Business Server console **Manage Fax Jobs** page. These functions may also be performed from client machines using the Windows Print Manager.

Status Monitoring

Small Business Server has fax monitoring tools that report real-time status of each fax device. The tools also generate a history log of all fax activity. The tools may be accessed from the Small Business Server **Start** menu, once the *Microsoft Small Business Server Resource Kit* is installed. For further information on what the fax monitoring tools can do, refer to *Part 10, Tools and Utilities,* of this resource kit.

Microsoft Fax Server Fax and E-mail Integration

Small Business Server 4.5 integrates fax and e-mail services by routing messages between the Fax Service and Exchange Server. With Small Business Server, the following options are available:

- You can receive and view incoming fax messages in your Outlook 2000 Inbox.
- You can send fax messages to a contact from within Outlook 2000
- You can create distribution lists that contain both e-mail addresses and fax numbers.
- You can send faxes to contacts using the Windows Send-To command.
- You can create shared fax distribution lists using Microsoft Exchange Public Folders.

Inbound Fax Routing

Inbound fax messages can be routed to an Exchange Server mailbox. To do this, you must specify an Exchange profile on the server that points to the mailbox. After inbound faxes are routed to the Exchange mailbox, they can be forwarded to other Exchange users from Outlook. When fax routing is enabled, faxes are routed by default to the Administrator messaging profile. This profile is created on the server during Small Business Server installation and is the messaging profile for the Administrator account. Incoming faxes can be received by users other than administrator if one of the following is done:

- Give the user permission to view the Administrator mail box.
- Change the routing settings at the Fax Server to route faxes to a different messaging profile.

For instructions on how routing settings may be changed, refer to the Online Guide or to *Chapter 55, Fax Service Troubleshooting,* in *Part 11, Troubleshooting,* of this resource guide.

Utilizing Microsoft Exchange Server Features

Microsoft Exchange public folders can be created to contain company-wide shared fax and e-mail contacts. These public contact lists can be configured as address books for use in Microsoft Outlook 2000. This provides individual users the ability to add contacts to this list—in contrast, the global address list can only be configured using the Exchange Administrator. Use the following steps to create a company-wide shared contacts list in Exchange Server.

▶ **To create a shared contacts list in Exchange**

1. Using Outlook 2000, create a new public folder. On the **File** menu, click **New** and then click **Folder** to display the **Create New Folder** dialog box.
2. In the **Name** text field, enter a name for the folder, such as *Company Rolodex*.
3. In the **Folder** contains drop-down list, select **Contacts**. Select **OK** to create the folder, and then close and reopen Outlook.
4. Right-click the newly created public folder and select **Properties**. Select the **Outlook Address Book** tab, and then select **Show this folder as an e-mail address book**. Perform this step on every machine that will use the public folder as an address book.

Note This option only works if Outlook Address Book is installed as a service.

Note The user who creates this public folder becomes the owner of the folder. Additional permissions can be set on the folder by right-clicking the folder, selecting **Properties**, then selecting the **Permissions** tab.

5. After the public folder has been created, make a shortcut to the public folder by dragging it onto the Outlook bar.

Faxing Documents

On the Small Business Server, there are several ways to fax documents, as described in the following sections:

Faxing a Document with the Print Command

Any document may be faxed to a fax recipient using the program's Print command. The fax is addressed by entering a recipient's name and fax number or by selecting a fax address from the Exchange or Microsoft Outlook Address Book if an e-mail client is installed. To send a fax using the Print command, use the following procedure.

▶ **To fax a document using the Print command**

1. Open the document you want to fax. You can also right-click the document and select **Print**.
2. On the **File** menu, click **Print** (or follow the procedure for printing documents in your program).
3. Select a fax printer and then click **OK** in the **Print** dialog box.
4. The **Compose New Fax** dialog box opens. Either click **Address Book** (if an e-mail client is installed) or type a name and fax number. For **Country**, click the location of the recipient.
5. To send a fax to more than one recipient, click **Add**, and then repeat step 4.
6. Click **Next** and follow the instructions to add a cover page and send the fax.

Note Do not use the **File/Send To/Fax Recipient** command to send a fax with Fax Service. This menu item is for Microsoft Fax installed on a stand-alone machine and it does work on Microsoft Small Business Server 4.5 fax.

Note To allow a client to send faxes from Microsoft Access, change the spool settings of the client PC's fax printer to EMF.

Faxing a Message from Outlook or Exchange

A message may be sent from Outlook or Exchange to fax and e-mail addresses either separately or concurrently. Messages are composed and documents may be inserted as in any other message. Faxes may be sent as follows:

- **From within Microsoft Outlook**. Outbound fax sending is set up for Outlook contacts when you enter the business fax number. Messages are routed to these contacts by the Fax Service. Distribution lists created within Outlook can have both e-mail addresses and fax numbers. If both the e-mail address and business fax number are entered for an Outlook contact, then Outlook offers the choice of which method to use whenever a message is sent to that contact.

- **Using the Send-To command**. By right-clicking a document and then clicking **Send-To** and **Mail Recipient**, a user routes a document to the fax server. The **Outlook New Message** dialog box appears with the global address list and personal and shared contact lists available.

Virtually any type of file can be sent through Outlook as an e-mail message, but the file must be rendered properly in order to be sent to a fax contact. Refer to *Chapter 55, Fax Service Troubleshooting,* in *Part 11, Troubleshooting,* of this resource guide for information on rendering fax documents. The procedure below describes how to send a fax from Outlook or Exchange.

▶ **To fax a message from Outlook or Exchange**

1. Compose an e-mail message as you normally would.
2. For **To** or **Cc**, specify one or more fax addresses.
3. Specify e-mail addresses if sending messages to both fax and e-mail addresses.
4. After specifying a fax address, the fax printer and other fax message attributes may be changed, if required, by clicking **Fax Attributes** on the **Tools** menu.
5. Click the **Send** button to send the message.

Creating a Fax Address

A fax address is needed when faxing documents and messages using Microsoft Outlook® 2000 or Exchange. Outlook automatically creates a fax address for each contact's fax number entered in the Outlook Contacts folder. In order to fax with Exchange, you must first create a fax recipient address in the Address Book.

Note If you wish to use fax addresses from the Microsoft Exchange Client Address Book rather than using an Outlook Contact, you must install the Fax Address Book as well.

Use the steps that follow to create a fax address in Exchange.

▶ **To create a fax address in Microsoft Exchange**

1. Open the Microsoft Exchange Administrator.
2. On the **Tools** menu, click **Address Book**.
3. On the **File** menu of the **Address Book**, click **New Entry**.
4. In the **New Entry** dialog box, click **Fax Address**.
5. Click **OK**. The **New Address Properties** dialog box appears.
6. For **Fax Recipient**, type the full name of the fax recipient.
7. For **Country**, click the location of the recipient.
8. For area code and fax number, type the area or city code and telephone number for the fax recipient.
9. On the **Business** tab, enter any additional information you want to appear on the cover pages, then click **OK**.

Note When viewing entries in either the Exchange or Outlook Address Book, the entry type for fax addresses is shown as "FAX."

Faxing a Document From Office 2000 Applications

Faxes can also be sent from Office 2000 applications. See the *Office 2000 Resource Kit* for details.

Upgrading to BackOffice Server

If the small business upgrades to BackOffice Server, new users can still access Fax Service. When upgrading to a full version of Windows NT Server, you can keep the functionality you have. If you want more users to use Fax Service, they must each have a Windows NT Server Client Access License for file and print services.

Microsoft Modem Sharing Service

The Microsoft Modem Sharing Service allows Small Business Server clients to use modems installed on the server, to connect to remote networks, bulletin board systems, and online services such as MSN™ (the Microsoft Network). By sharing modems installed on Small Business Server, hardware costs are reduced since users do not need modems for their individual computers. Users can then connect to and use the modem pool in the same way they use modems connected to the COM ports on their computers. When users need access to a remote network or online service, the modem sharing application is run. This application uses a COM port connected over the network to a modem pool on Small Business Server.

Modem Sharing Server also allows modems on the Small Business Server to be pooled together. When a modem from the modem pool becomes available, it dials the remote network or online service. If there is more than one modem in the modem pool, the server automatically uses the next available (idle) modem in the pool.

Administering the Modem Sharing Service

Small Business Server installs the Modem Sharing Service during setup and automatically shares and configures modem pools based on the installed modems. However, the modem pools should serve the unique needs of the small business organization. The material that follows explains how to administer and configure the Modem Sharing application.

▶ **To manage Microsoft Modem Sharing Server**

1. On the Small Business Server console, click **More Tasks**.
2. Click **Manage Modems** to display the **Manage Modems** page.

From this page, you can perform the following tasks:

- Add, remove, and configure modems and modem pools.
- Add or remove a modem from a pool.
- View the status of a modem pool.
- Troubleshoot modem problems.

Accessing Modem Sharing Service Properties

Most of the tasks for configuring Microsoft Modem Sharing Server involve setting options in the **Modem Sharing Administration** dialog box, accessed using the procedure below.

▶ **To open the Modem Sharing Administration dialog box**

- From **Control Panel**, double-click **Modem Sharing** to display the following **Modem Sharing Administration** dialog box.

Note The **Modem Sharing Administration** dialog box is also accessed within Online Guide procedures launched from various taskpads on the **Manage Modems** page.

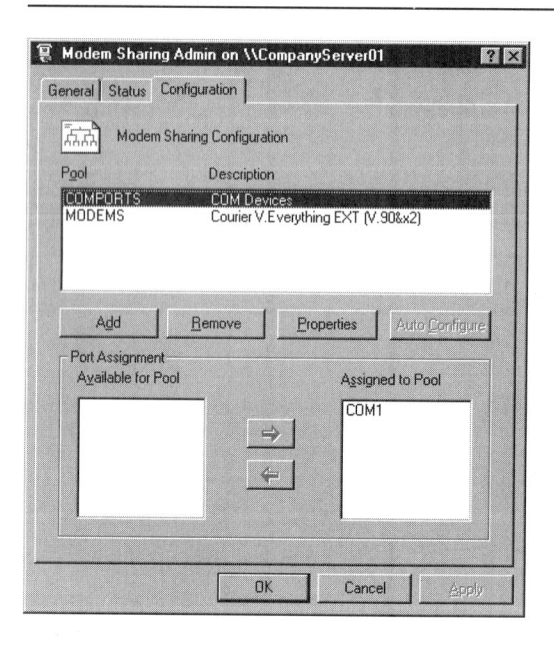

Viewing the Modem Pool

Small Business Server setup configures modem pools using the modems found during installation. To view the modem pool from a client computer, you must specify the modem pool name when connecting to it on the server. To view a modem pool name for connecting with it, refer to the procedure below.

▶ **To view the modem pools configured on the server**
1. On the **More Tasks** page of the console, click **Manage Modems**.
2. Click **View the status of a modem pool** to display the online Help procedure.
3. Click the **Modem Sharing utility** link in Step 1 of the online Help to display the **Modem Sharing Administration** utility.
4. Select the **Configuration** tab to show a list of the modem pools, a short description of each pool, and the COM ports assigned to the pool. Client computers use this pool name to specify the modem pool to which they want to connect.

Configuring Modem Pools

Although Small Business Server automatically configures modem pools on the server for modems found during setup, in some cases you may not want these modems assigned to a modem pool. You may also prefer to organize the modems into different pools. Refer to the steps that follow to configure modem pools.

▶ **To configure the modem pools on the server**
1. On the **More Tasks** page of the console, click **Manage Modems**.
2. Click **View the status of a modem pool** to display the online Help.
3. In the online Help, click the **Modem Sharing utility** link to display the **Modem Sharing Administration** utility.
4. Select the **Configuration** tab.
5. In the **Pool** pane, select the modem pool name.
6. Add or remove COM ports as follows:
    - To add a COM port to the modem pool: Select the COM port in the **Available for Pool** box, and click the right arrow. The COM port appears in the **Assigned to Pool** box along with the other COM ports assigned to the pool.
    - To remove a COM port from the modem pool: Select the COM port in the **Assigned to Pool** box, and click the left arrow. The COM port appears in the **Available for Pool** box.

7. Click **Apply**.
8. Select the **General** tab, click **Stop**, and then **Start** to restart the service and apply the changes to the Modem Sharing Server.

Configuring Clients for Modem Pool Connection

Modem Sharing Server supports client computers running Windows 95 and Windows NT 4.0 Workstation. Both of these modem sharing clients may connect to a modem pool configured on Small Business Server. However, the modem sharing client must be installed by the Set Up Computer Wizard and a modem driver, the same as the one on the server, must be configured before connecting to the modem pool.

Warning Performing these client configuration procedures will disconnect all users from the modem pool. Before proceeding, refer to the Online Guide for procedures that identify which users are connected.

Connecting Windows 95-Based Clients to the Modem Pool

During client setup, a modem sharing port is installed on your computer. To use this shared port, you must first install a modem and then configure it to use the shared port. Perform the following steps.

▶ **To install a modem**

1. Click **Start**, point to **Settings**, and then click **Control Panel**.
2. Double-click **Modems**.
3. Follow the on screen instructions to install a modem. Install the modem that matches the modem attached to the server computer.

▶ **To connect Windows 95-based client computers to the modem pool on the server**

1. Click **Start**, point to **Settings**, and then click **Control Panel**.
2. Click **Add/Remove Programs**.
3. Select the **Modem Sharing Client** and then click **Add/Remove** to display the **Modem Sharing Setup** utility.
4. Follow the instructions for adding a port to your Windows 95-based computer.
5. For the modem pool path, specify \\servername\poolname (for example by typing *smallbiz**modems*), then click **Finish**.
6. Click **OK** to exit **Add/Remove Program**.
7. On the Windows 95-based desktop, right-click **My Computer**, then click Properties.

8. Click the **Device Manager** tab.
9. Click the plus sign (+) next to **Ports**. Ports assigned for modem sharing are shown with a corresponding port number.
10. Select the new port and click **Properties** to verify that Modem Sharing is assigned to a COM port. Change any settings necessary.
11. Click **OK** and exit.

Connecting Windows NT Workstation-Based Clients to the Modem Pool

During client setup, a modem sharing port is installed on your computer. To use this shared port, you must first install a modem and then configure it to use the shared port. Perform the following steps.

▶ **To install a modem**

1. Click **Start**, point to **Settings**, and then click **Control Panel**.
2. Double-click **Modems**.
3. Follow the on screen instructions to install a modem. Install the modem that matches the modem attached to the server computer.

▶ **To connect Windows NT Workstation-based computers to the modem pool on the server**

1. Click **Start**, point to **Settings**, and then click **Control Panel**.
2. In **Control Panel**, double-click **Ports**, and then click **Add**.
3. Click **Modem Sharing Port**, and then click **OK**.
4. For **COM Port Number**, accept the default COM port or any available port from the drop-down box.
5. For **Server**, type the name of your Small Business Server computer that has the shared port resources available.
6. For **Pool**, enter the name of the modem pool to which you are connecting on the server.
7. Click **OK** and exit.

After connecting to the modem pool, the client computer uses the remote serial port as if it were a local serial port. To run client applications that require a shared modem, for example, Remote Access Service (RAS) or CompuServe, the user must first install a modem on the newly connected remote port. Refer to the Online Guide for details.

Status Monitoring

Small Business Server includes Modem Status Tools that allow identification of telephony application programming interface (TAPI) line states and the manipulation of calls, lines, and devices. The Modem Status Tools may be accessed from the Small Business Server **Start** menu, once the *Microsoft Small Business Server Resource Kit* is installed. For further information on what the modem tools can do, refer to *Part 10, Tools and Utilities,* of this resource kit.

Microsoft Exchange Server 5.5

Microsoft Exchange Server 5.5 is a client/server messaging system that integrates e-mail, rules, group scheduling, electronic forms, groupware, and Internet connectivity. As an integrated application of Small Business Server 4.5, the Exchange Server platform is scaled and optimized for the typical small business application. When Small Business Server 4.5 is installed, Exchange Server is set up automatically to support this configuration. Refer to *Part 5, Performance Optimization and Tuning* of this resource kit for the Exchange default set up.

Once Small Business Server is up and running, Exchange is managed with console wizards that perform behind-the-scenes steps to create the appropriate operating configurations for Exchange and other integrated applications. However, Exchange Server is also accessible as a stand-alone application on Small Business Server. This allows the technology consultant to have a more comprehensive control of certain Exchange features and interactions beyond the basic application through manual configuration.

This section discusses several Exchange features and tools available to the technology consultant for fine-tuning the messaging system of the small business network. The material presented here is intended to give the technology consultant a greater knowledge of these features as well as the information necessary to streamline the administration techniques that use them.

Administrator Program Interface

The Administrator program is the window into Exchange Server. All Exchange Server components may be accessed through this window and the entire system may be managed through a single set of commands. The Administrator program displays the small business organization in a hierarchical manner, making it easy to navigate and manage the elements at each level in the hierarchy.

Exchange Server consists of a series of objects. Some of these objects belong to the end user while others facilitate connectivity, communication, and team collaboration. All of these objects are centrally managed through the Administrator program which simultaneously contacts each object's instance.

The end-user objects that may be managed by the Administrator program are mailboxes, end-user distribution lists, custom recipients, and public folder objects. The management techniques and commands for these objects are consistent for all administration procedures.

Mailboxes

End-user mailboxes may be configured manually using the **New Mailbox** command on the **File** menu in the Administrator program. You may associate up to 22 predefined attributes and 10 custom-defined attributes for each end user mailbox. The mailbox's **Properties** window allows for sufficient flexibility to design user and organizational details to suit the needs of the small business network. A sample Administrator Properties dialog box follows. Mailboxes may also be used as a repository for a wide range of data about each employee in the small business.

Distribution Lists

Distribution lists are groups of users that can be addressed as one user. A large mail system may include many distribution lists, often totaling more than the number of single mailboxes. Distribution lists are created with Small Business Server wizards, but may also be generated manually with the Administrator program using the same commands and terminology used for creating mailboxes.

End-User Management of Distribution Lists

The Exchange permissions model can be used to delegate management of certain distribution lists to some users, thus providing an element of decentralized control within a centralized administration model. The model also facilitates departmental distribution lists, allowing members to be added to a team-specific distribution list, controlled at the team level. To create a distribution list or add users to it, use the Small Business Server console **manage e-mail distribution lists** taskpad.

Distribution List Options

The management of distribution lists can account for a significant part of small business information systems overhead (a manually intensive aspect of the system). Microsoft Exchange Server automates distribution list management, making it cost-effective for the small business organization to offer users a wide range of distribution list options.

Custom Recipients

Custom recipients are addresses of users on other mail systems that appear in the Exchange Server address book because they are used frequently by users in the small business network. The technology consultant may use the simple management tools of the Administrator program to configure these addresses manually.

Address Formats

Custom recipient addresses can appear in a format that clearly depicts them as users of another mail system or they can appear indistinguishable from Exchange Server user addresses. This option is particularly useful in a migration/coexistence scenario where users will be migrated to Microsoft Exchange Server gradually. For instance, representing IBM® PROFS® users in the Exchange Server format sets the stage for a seamless migration strategy.

Migration of New Users

When users are migrated to Exchange Server, their display names remain unchanged in the address book, so other users don't need to change the way they communicate with migrating colleagues. Custom recipients appear in the address book the same way as users of Exchange Server. They each can be sent mail or included on distribution lists in the same way as regular Exchange Server users. Custom recipients are created, managed, and deleted with the identical commands used for mailboxes and distribution lists.

Address Book Views

Address Book views are virtual containers that allow the technology consultant to group recipient objects together logically based on common directory attributes. By grouping recipients together in views, the technology consultant can sort recipient lists according to tasks or functions.

For example, the technology consultant needs to scroll to a particular recipient or use the Find feature to modify or obtain information in a directory with a large number of entries. Although there are tools to do this easily, having users grouped specifically by job functions allows the technology consultant to locate the entry in a manner more suitable to the small business context. Views do not provide filtering, only groupings of users.

Address Book views are created in the Administrator program from the **File** menu, **New Other**, and **Address Book View** option as follows.

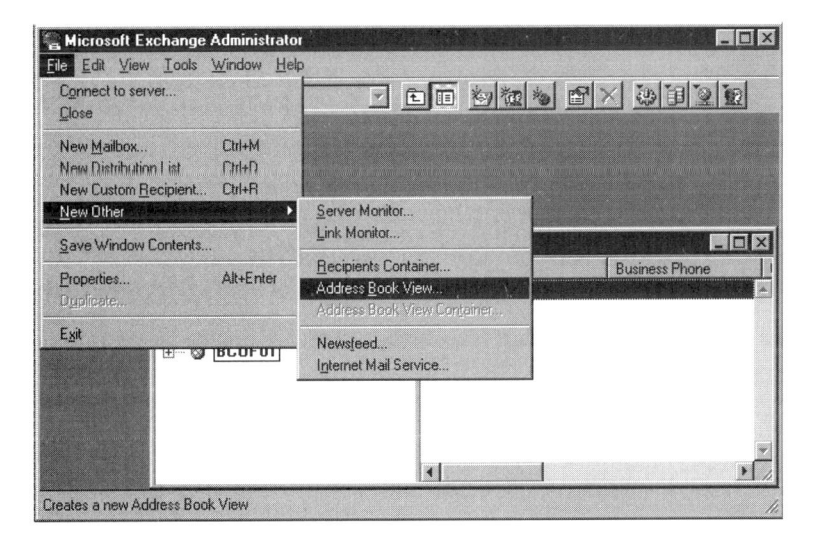

The technology consultant can create a directory and display name for the Address Book view. The technology consultant can also control how the address view is grouped based on attributes assigned to the mailbox user (City, State, Site, custom attributes, and so on). In the dialog box that follows, the **Group By** tab allows the technology consultant to specify the order that recipients are grouped by. These groups are nested if more than one directory attribute is defined.

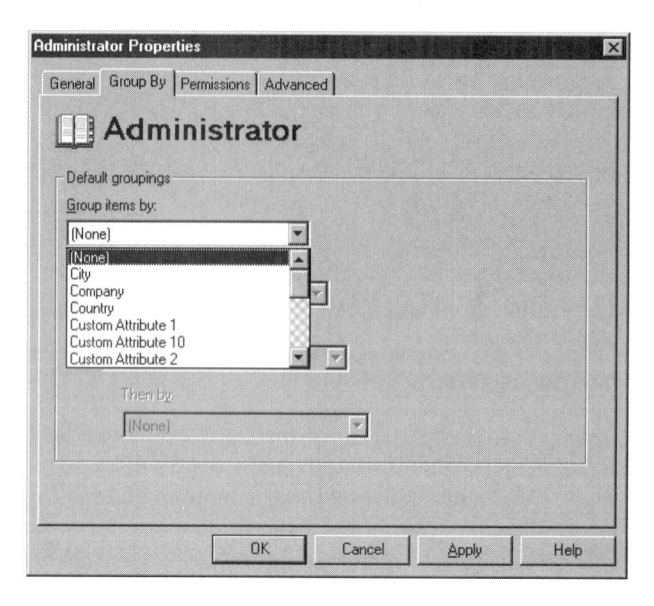

Public Folders

The public folder is the fourth end-user object existing on an Exchange Server that may be configured manually with the Administrator program. Public folders are created from the client but are managed from the Administrator program with the same commands used to manage the other end-user objects.

Off-Line Folder Synchronization

Exchange Server enables users to automatically perform two-way synchronization between a server folder and a copy of that folder on a local PC. Off-line folder synchronization enables users to maintain up-to-date information without having to be continuously connected to the small business network.

For example, a user can create an off-line folder (a snapshot or replica) of a customer-tracking application to take on a business trip and update it based on interactions with customers during the trip. Then by reconnecting to the server—either remotely via modem or by connecting to the small business LAN upon returning to the office—the user can bidirectionally synchronize the off-line and server folders. Changes made on the local PC (including forms and views) are updated to the server and changes to the server-based folders automatically show up on the user's PC.

Creating an off-line folder is different from simply copying a server folder to the hard disk, because an off-line folder remembers its relationship with the server folder and uses that relationship to perform the bidirectional update. Only changes are copied and not the whole folder. This also helps minimize network traffic.

An offline folder is created in Outlook. First the client specifies that they want an offline folder (.ost). Then they set up offline synchronization in the folder properties.

Off-line folder synchronization provides an alternative to continuous network connection. Exchange Server supports off-line folder synchronization sessions from many different locations simultaneously. Built-in conflict resolution for public folders ensures that all changes are added. The owner of the folder is notified of any conflicts and asked which version to keep.

Managing End-User Objects

The four end-user objects can all be managed from the Administrator program. By providing a single user interface for managing these four objects, Exchange Server provides rich layers of functionality for end users. The four end-user objects reside in the Recipients container of the Administrator program. Mailboxes, distribution lists, and public folders exist whether or not Small Business Server is connected to another mail system. Custom-recipient objects exist only if Exchange Server is connected to another mail system or the Internet.

Accessing object management is done with a double-click. For example, double-click **Recipients**, and the technology consultant can view all the mailboxes, distribution lists, public folders, and custom recipients on Small Business Server, as follows.

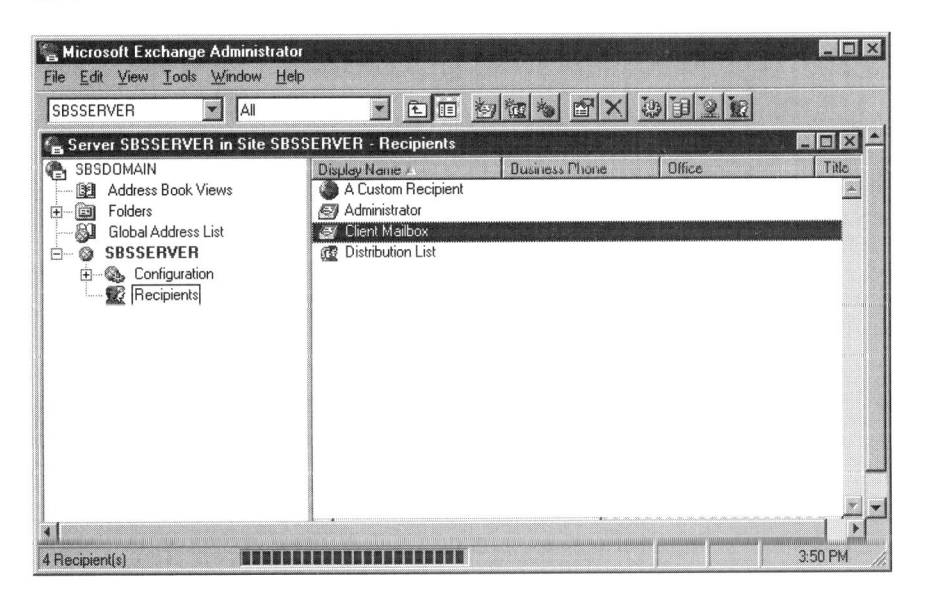

Protecting Exchange Data

Exchange Server includes an enhanced version of the Windows NT Backup utility included with Small Business Server. This utility includes all the standard file and directory backup functions as well as the ability to back up and restore Exchange Server directories and information stores.

Backups are done while Small Business Server is up and running, so downtime is not necessary to secure the data. The new Windows NT Backup program recognizes Exchange Server and backs up the directory and/or information store as an object. It is not necessary to know which files make up the service, only the components that are to be backed up.

Backups can be full, differential, incremental, or copy. Exchange Server backup capabilities are also included in the command-line mode of Windows NT Backup, which allows backup jobs to be batched and scheduled. The following window displays the NT Backup utility configured for backup of Exchange data in the Small Business Server domain. Refer to the Online Guide for further information on using the NT Backup utility.

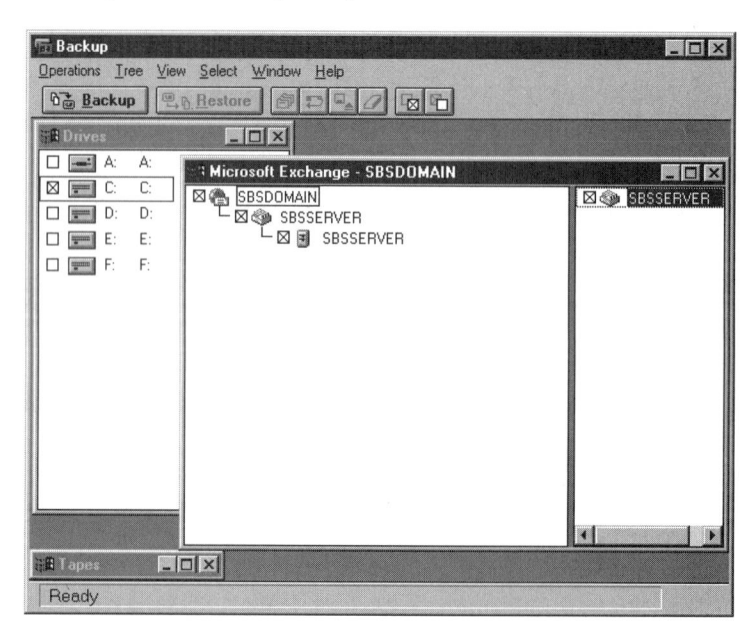

Exchange Administration Tips

This section provides several tips for Exchange Server administration, including the automation of e-mail forwarding and web access to Exchange.

Automating E-mail Forwarding

From the Administrator program, automate e-mail forwarding by changing the user's Simple Mail Transfer Protocol (SMTP) e-mail address to their new one (usually off site).

Web Access to Exchange

Exchange Server can be accessed over the Internet using a web browser. In order to utilize this feature, install Outlook Web Access from Small Business Server installation CD 3 using the following path:

Drive:/ExchSrvr/Server/Setup/i386/Setup, where *Drive*: is your CD ROM partition.

Accessing Exchange from the Internet does not compromise security since Proxy Server blocks all access to client computers on the small business network. When the Outlook Web Access client establishes a connection to Exchange Server, the following functionality is available to the user.

- Send and receive e-mail.
- Review and publish to public folders.
- View the Global Address List (GAL).

When an e-mail message, public folder, GAL, or other Exchange resource is viewed with a browser, the Outlook Web Access client, it is converted to HTML. Also, inbound access to Exchange resources through a browser requires conversion from HTML to a MAPI-based call. This is accomplished using Exchange Active Server Pages (ASPs) and Collaboration Data Objects (CDOs).

Monitoring the Performance of Exchange

Small Business Server 4.5 includes an NT Performance Monitor tool that allows the technology consultant to collect and analyze performance data on the Exchange Server. This tool was used to pre-configure several key performance monitors supplied with Exchange, to reveal its important underlying operating characteristics. These monitors enable the technology consultant to maintain an accurate view of the overall health of the Exchange system in the small business network.

The monitors provide quick system feedback and statistics to help the technology consultant detect and eliminate problems before they occur.

Performance Monitor Tool Features

The Performance Monitor Tool can provide the technology consultant with statistics on more than 300 system characteristics for processor, process, memory, disk, and network objects. The counters in the Performance Monitor may be used to view such things as access bottlenecks and errors, browse operations, reads/writes, and thread use on the Exchange directory, Exchange Information Store, and other Exchange services. Using the features of Performance Monitor, the load and activity of users requesting addresses or updating directory information may be easily determined in the small business network.

Exchange Performance Monitoring Processes

The diagram that follows presents an overview of the processes involved in setting up accurate and meaningful performance monitors for the Exchange Server. The different phases for accomplishing this task are depicted in diagrammatic format in order to present the technology consultant with an up-front view of the scope of material covered in this section.

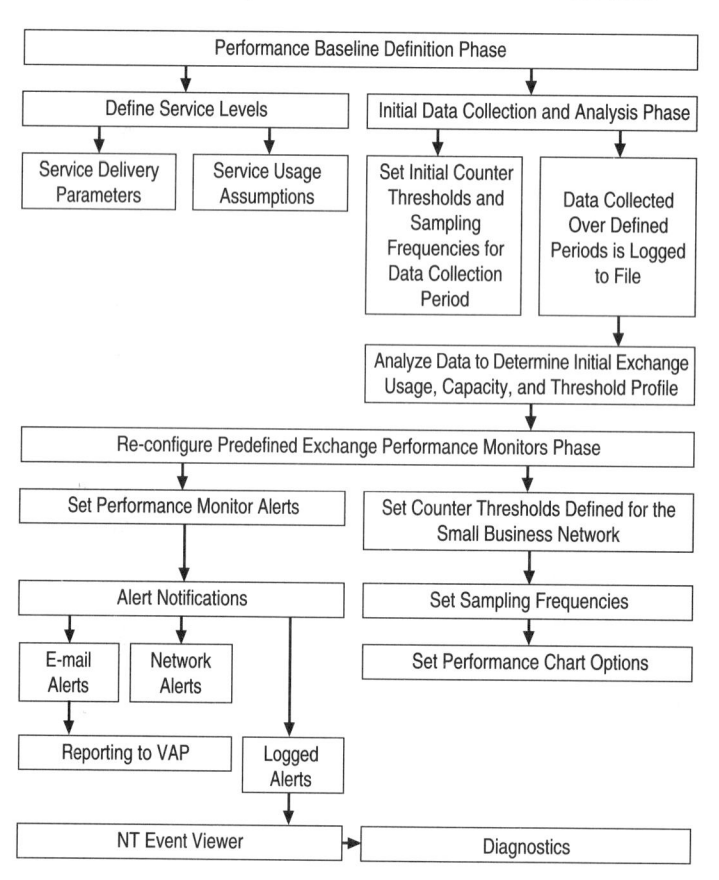

Figure 27.2 Exchange performance monitoring process overview

Performance Monitoring Scenarios

The sections that follow include several scenarios in which the NT Performance Monitor may be utilized to assess Exchange Server performance.

Collecting and Analyzing Data

Exchange Server 5.5 is a complex application with multiple components that place varying performance demands on Small Business Server. For example, the Information Store must manage all communication with the various clients connecting to the server. In order to understand how this demand and others translate to actual system performance in the small business environment, it is exceedingly useful to perform the data collection process.

The data collection process involves running a number of performance monitor tests over defined periods and logging the results to a file for analysis. If the correct set of counters were used in the tests, the technology consultant can easily assess the major performance characteristics of Exchange. We recommend performing this process periodically to identify long term trends in server performance.

This process is invaluable in developing a comprehensive understanding of Exchange performance characteristics. This understanding is essential for the technology consultant to define realistic baselines for the initial Exchange usage and capacity profile.

Problem Detection and Notification

Once thresholds are defined, Performance Monitor can then be configured to alert the appropriate support group when a particular threshold has been exceeded. Methods for configuring Performance Monitor to act in this manner are outlined in the section ahead entitled "Performance Monitor Alerts."

Problem Analysis

Once a performance problem is detected, Performance Monitor can be used to identify a particular system component that may be the cause of the problem. However, the effectiveness of using Performance Monitor in this way is greatly dependent on the technology consultant's level of understanding.

Performance Baseline Definition Phase

The predefined performance monitors included with the Exchange Server are set up with counters, but not with counter thresholds, since counter threshold levels are uniquely dependent upon the usage characteristics of the small business network. Before using the predefined Exchange performance monitors, it is necessary to establish an Exchange usage, capacity, and performance counter threshold profile by collecting initial data on the system.

Using the information gathered in the data collection process, baseline performance thresholds can be defined. The logical values for these thresholds will be based on the load characteristics present during the data collection period. It will be obvious if these thresholds are incorrect—thresholds set too low will generate unnecessary alerts, while those set too high may result in undetected problems.

Exchange Usage Characteristics

Over time, the usage characteristics of Exchange Server may change, resulting in a negative impact on performance. Changes in usage levels can be detected early if they are measured on a regular basis.

For example, a common characteristic of e-mail systems is the gradual increase in the average message size. Continuous monitoring of message size can provide early warning of any trends that invalidate initial key operating assumptions made about Exchange in the small business network. In order to detect changes in usage levels, you must first define basic service expectations so you can establish a substantial basis of comparison.

Defining Service Levels

Performance measurement must have baselines in order to be comprehensive. Defining basic service levels is the most effective way to focus performance measurement activities. Some service levels the technology consultant may want to define include:

- Service Delivery Parameters
    - System availability
    - Average message delivery time
    - Average time to read a message
    - Average time to send a message

- Service Usage Assumptions
    - Maximum user mailbox size
    - Average message size
    - Average number of active users
    - Average number of messages sent per user per day

Once these levels are defined and understood by both the service delivery and user groups, a clear framework to work within can be established. This also forms in part, the basis on which logical thresholds for performance monitor counters is founded.

Counter Thresholds

In order to define meaningful thresholds, the technology consultant collects and analyzes initial data from the network to create the Exchange usage and capacity profile. The table that follows describes the significant counters to be monitored for capturing initial data on Exchange in the small business network. Once this data is evaluated and understood, the appropriate counter thresholds for the network capacity can be calculated for use with the key performance monitors that continuously track Exchange health. To create the performance monitors for the counters that follow, refer to the "Method For Creating A New Performance Monitor" section later in this chapter.

Table 27.1 Performance Monitor Counters for the Initial Exchange Profile

Object	Counter
Memory	Pages/sec
	Page Faults/sec
	Available Bytes
	Committed Bytes
Process	Page Faults/sec
Paging File	% Usage
Logical Disk	Average Disk Queue Length
	Current Disk Queue Length
	Disk Reads/sec
	Disk Writes/sec
	Free Megabytes
Processor	% Processor Time
Process	% Processor Time (individual Exchange processes)
MSExchangeIS	User Count
MSExchangeIS Private (+Public)	Average Local Delivery Time
	Send Queue Size
	Receive Queue Size

Data Collection and Analysis Phase

For the data collection and analysis process, the most significant performance counters are provided in this section for both Windows NT 4.0 and Exchange servers. Background information on each counter and its relationship to other counters is also discussed.

Note Only a small subset of the counters used in the data collection process is used in the key performance monitors that continuously track the health of Exchange.

When using the counters specified for data collection, you create performance monitor charts that write performance data to log files. The duration of the logging process depends on user capacity. In most cases, the data collection period is a minimum of one day and a maximum of one week. It is important to consider counter sampling rate—the sampling frequency must be short enough to get a realistic average, but not so long that you run the risk of missing temporary spikes. In general, sampling ranges between 20 minutes and 120 minutes are suitable for data collection purposes.

Disk space requirements must also be considered since log file growth will vary proportionally with the sample frequency selected. Refer to the section ahead entitled "Configuring Log Files for the Data Collection Phase" for log configuring.

Critical Subsystem Monitors

On a Small Business Server installation, Exchange and Windows NT 4.0 Servers are tightly integrated. As a result, there are several areas of NT and Exchange that should be monitored. The critical subsystems are listed below.

- System Memory
- Disk I/O
- System CPU
- Information Store (IS)

The first three in the list above deal with standard Windows NT counters used to detect degradation in NT performance. The fourth deals with counters that monitor user access to the IS.

System Memory

System memory counters are used in detecting whether memory is a bottleneck in the Exchange system. If Exchange performance has degraded, monitor the system memory. CPU and disk I/O time may appear as a bottleneck, as a result of trying to mask a deficiency in system memory. The key to assessing memory performance is in determining how much the system is paging data in and out of memory. The relevant memory counters to watch are provided in the following table and described in the paragraphs that follow.

Table 27.2 Memory performance counters

Object	Counter
Memory	Pages/sec
	Page Faults/sec
	Available Bytes
	Committed Bytes
Process	Page Faults/sec
	Virtual Bytes
Paging File	% Usage

- **Memory – Pages/sec**. The total in and out paging activity. Paging occurs when an application references data not in its working set (physical memory). If this counter is consistently greater than 5, this is an early indication of a memory bottleneck.

- **Memory – Page faults/sec**. The actual number of times application data was not found in its physical memory working set and had to be paged from the disk. This counter should never display a consistently high single figure amount or a memory bottleneck is indicated.

- **Memory – Available Bytes**. The amount of physical memory still available to the system. For acceptable performance, we recommend a minimum of 4MB available on an Exchange server with less than 256MB of RAM.

- **Memory – Committed Bytes**. Indicates how much virtual memory space has been committed to an application. This counter must not exceed the overall size of the pagefile or it will indicate that too much application data has been committed to virtual memory space.

- **Process – Page Faults/sec**. Monitors individual processes to help identify which one is suffering the most from lack of virtual memory.

- **Process – Virtual Bytes**. Each process running on Small Business Server has 2GB of virtual memory available. If the store's virtual memory is approaching the limit, it may encounter an out-of-memory condition.
- **Paging File – % Usage**. Indicates how much of the page file is in use. Also determines if there is a possible memory bottleneck.

> **Note** It is more reliable to set these counters at 3 to 5 second intervals so a clear average value is reached. If the pagefile has a usage greater than 50 to 60 percent with less than 25 percent memory available to the system, increase the RAM.

The detection of memory bottlenecks is covered in greater detail in Chapter 12 of the *Windows NT Workstation Resource Guide*.

Disk I/O

Exchange Server must be able to move information in and out of the three Exchange databases at the fastest possible speed. All Exchange database write transactions are first written to a transaction log and then committed to the database, once there is a sufficient amount of data ready to be committed.

Exchange cuts down on the necessity of requesting information from its databases by keeping the most recent data in buffer memory. If a piece of information is not in one of these buffers, Exchange must make a disk I/O request.

The relevant counters to monitor for disk I/O in relation to Exchange are provided in the following table. These disk counters should be collected every 5 or 10 seconds during a relatively short period of time (2 to 4 hours) during peak utilization.

Table 27.3 Disk I/O Counters

Object	Counter
LogicalDisk	Average Disk Queue Length
	Current Disk Queue Length
	Average Disk sec/Read
	Average Disk sec/Write
	Average Disk sec/Transfer
	Free Megabytes

- **Average Disk Queue Length**. The average queue length during the monitoring period. This value should not average more than 2 under normal operating conditions.
- **Current Disk Queue Length**. Interpreting this counter depends on the function of the logical disk being monitored. On most Exchange servers, there are two key logical disks—one for the transaction logs and the other for the Information Store. The Current Disk Queue Length is interpreted differently for each:
    1. Transaction logs. The log volume should never have a queue length above 1 since the I/Os are synchronous and single-threaded. It is unsafe to assume there is no disk performance problem if the queue length is below 1. It will *never* be above one in normal operations (not including backup operations). If a performance problem is detected on the log volume, the only real remedy is to employ a write-back cache.
    2. Information Store. The database volume can be subject to a burst of write operations every 30 seconds—up to a maximum of 64 seconds. In between two bursts, the only I/O activity is read operations. So you will get peaks above the acceptable queue length (which is generally the number of spindles divided by 2, every thirty seconds). If you do have a queue length larger that half of the spindles between the peaks, it means that you are short on read I/Os and that you should add more spindles. To shorten the duration of the peak queue length, you should use caching (write-back), and increase the number of spindles—or possibly shift from RAID5 to RAID0+1, if the RAID array controller is not very powerful.
- **Average Disk sec/Read**. Calculates the latency on disk reads. Increases from the calculated baselines are a good indicator there is a disk bottleneck.
- **Average Disk sec/Write**. Calculates the latency on disk writes. Increases from the calculated baselines are a good indicator there is a disk bottleneck.
- **Average Disk sec/Transfer**. Calculates the latency on disk transfers. Increases from the calculated baselines are a good indicator there is a disk bottleneck.
- **Free Megabytes**. This is a very important counter to use. Configure alerts on this counter so disks that contain Exchange databases or log files will issue an alert as soon as they approach capacity. Exchange shuts down if its log files or databases have no more space to grow.

System CPU

Abnormally high CPU utilization is typically a side effect of a problem with a separate system component such as the disk or network subsystems. Continuous high CPU utilization (over 80 percent) may also be attributed to software issues. It is therefore critical that the correct CPU is in use for the projected server load. The relevant counters that should be monitored to detect a CPU utilization problem are provided in the table below.

Table 27.4 CPU Utilization Counters

Object	Counter
Processor	% Processor Time
Process	% Processor Time (individual Exchange processes)
	Elapsed Time

- **Processor – % Processor Time**. The time that the processor is running active threads. If this value is consistently above 75 percent, the server is overloaded; take actions to lower this time, such as adding a second processor or changing the CPU.

- **Process – % Processor Time**. Individual processes can be tracked using this counter. This is key to identifying which particular process is causing high CPU utilization.

- **Process – Elapsed Time**. The total running time, in seconds, a process has been active. This can be used for overall system maintenance purposes. A zero value here indicates a non-active process.

Note When overall processor usage is showing a consistently high value, compare it against how many users are currently connected to the system. Do this by adding the **MSExchangeIS – User Count** counter to the performance monitor chart in question to correlate the information.

Information Store

The Information Store (IS) is the interface between the user and the Exchange Server. It is therefore critical that IS performance is measured continuously. Performance problems normally result in slower response times at the client and a lengthened message delivery time. It is imperative the Information Store is always available and performing at optimum performance levels.

IS performance is regularly impacted by problems with other Exchange core components. The IS uses the Directory service to look up user addresses and to retrieve information about a user, thus problems with the Directory service can have an impact on IS performance. The most relevant counters to monitor in relation to the Private and Public stores are provided in the following table.

Table 27.5 Information Store Counters

Object	Counter
MSExchangeIS	User Count
MSExchangeIS Private + Public	Average Time for local Delivery
	Send Queue Size
	Receive Queue Size
	Message Opens/sec
	Folder Opens/sec

- **MSExchangeIS – User Count**. The actual count of people (not connections) currently using the IS. Performance measurement must always be correlated with current user numbers.

- **MSExchangeIS Private + Public – Average Time for Local Delivery**. The average time it took for the last 10 messages to be submitted for local delivery within the IS. This counter should never remain at a nonzero value for longer than a few seconds.

- **MSExchangeIS Private + Public – Send Queue Size**. The queue of messages outbound from the IS. Under normal operating conditions, this queue rarely stays at a nonzero value for any significant duration.

- **MSExchangeIS Private + Public – Receive Queue Size**. The queue of all messages destined inbound for the IS. As with the Send Queue, this should also stay at a nonzero under normal operating conditions.

- **MSExchangeIS Private + Public – Message Opens/sec**. Shows how often users are opening messages. Peak load may show this coinciding with other system behavior.

- **MSExchangeIS Private + Public – Folder Opens/sec**. Shows how often users are opening public folders. Another good indicator of user activity.

Full Utilization of NT Performance Monitor

To maximize your utilization of the NT Performance Monitor, an in-depth technical knowledge of Windows NT and Exchange is helpful. Detailed information on the Performance Monitor is provided in Chapters 10 and 11 of the *Windows NT Workstation Resource Guide*.

Accessing Predefined Exchange Performance Monitors

The Exchange performance monitors included with Small Business Server 4.5 may be easily adapted to small business applications. Access these predefined monitors from the **Start** menu—point to **Programs**, click **Exchange Server**, and then select the performance monitor. Statistics displayed by these monitors can provide accurate performance data that helps the technology consultant determine where problems occur and when system expansion is required. The latter may be of particular interest to the growing small business. Observing these monitors also serves as training for the technology consultant.

Exchange Performance Monitor Configuration Phase

With profiles obtained from the data collection and analysis phase, you can apply meaningful counter thresholds to predefined Exchange performance monitors. Descriptions of the key Exchange performance monitors useful for Small Business Server and their related counters follows.

- Queue monitoring, including Internet Mail Service (IMS) and Server queue monitors.
- Server monitoring, including Server health, load, history, and user monitoring.

Queue Monitoring

An immediate indication of possible Exchange service interruption is a message queues buildup on the services responsible for routing messages. Queue monitoring involves tracking the IMS queue and the overall Exchange Server queue status.

IMS Queue

The following Performance Monitor chart shows inbound and outbound message queue activity for the IMS. The queue status for messages going out to the Internet may show where bottlenecks exist or if messages are being sent randomly. For the growing small business network, this monitor (along with the IMS Statistics and Traffic monitors) may indicate when a faster Internet connection is needed. The counters in this chart indicate the following:

- **Queued Inbound**. The number of messages from the Internet destined for the Exchange server.
- **Queued Outbound**. The number of messages from Exchange for delivery to the Internet.
- **Queued MTS IN**. The total number of messages awaiting final delivery in the Exchange Message Transaction Server (MTS).
- **Queued MTS OUT**. The total number of messages waiting to be converted to Internet mail format in the Exchange MTS.

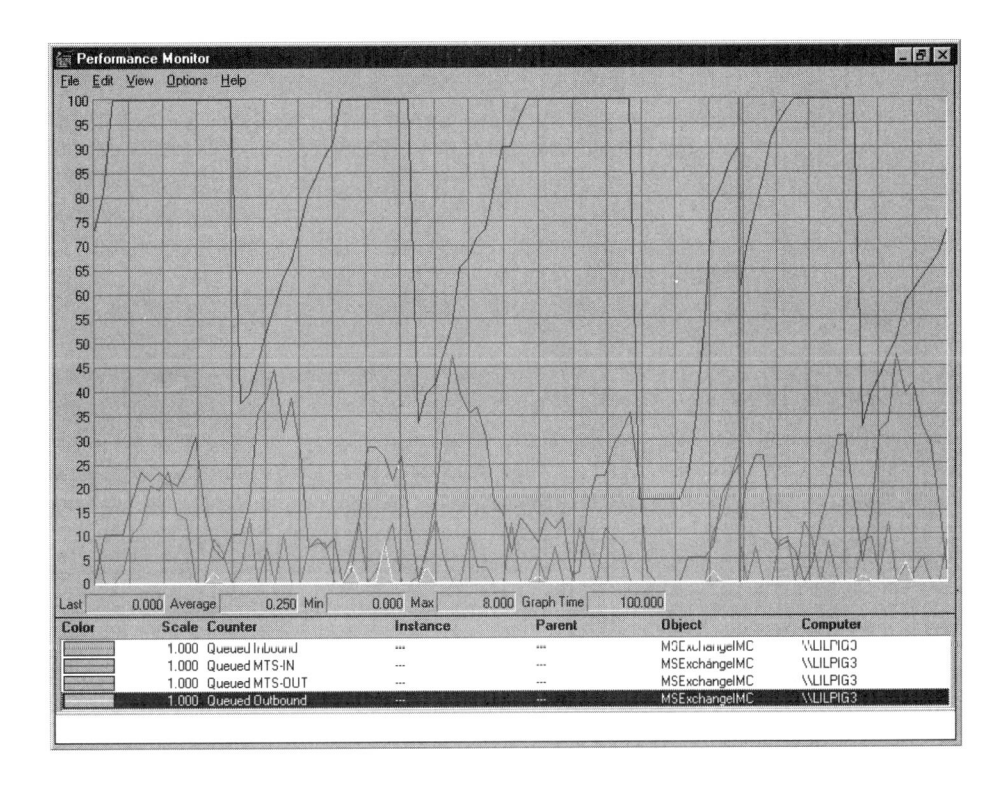

Server Queue

The following Performance Monitor chart shows the send and receive message queue size for the Exchange Server, which may provide the technology consultant with an indication of overall message volume in Exchange. The counters in this chart indicate the following:

- **Send Queue Size**. The number of messages in the private or public information store's Send queue.
- **Receive Queue Size**. The number of messages in the private or public information store's Receive queue.

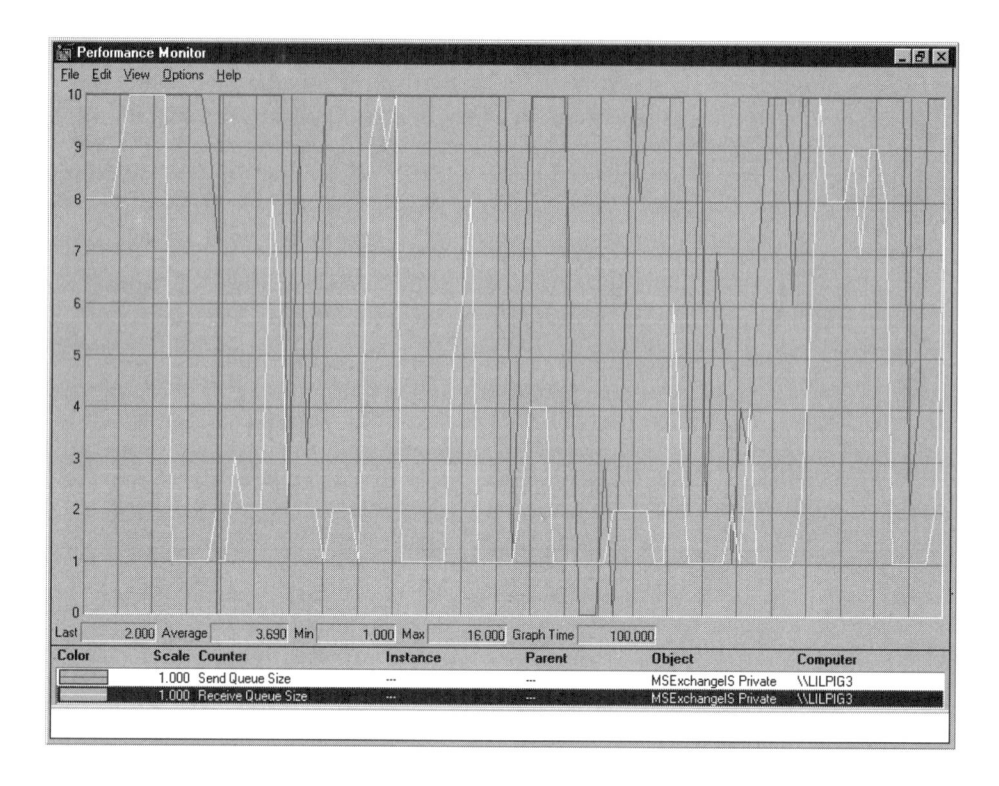

Server Health Monitoring

The server monitoring capabilities in Exchange help maintain system availability by enabling the technology consultant to monitor the general health of the Exchange Server. The Performance Monitor chart that follows is used for this purpose. The counters shown in the chart for the objects monitored indicate the following:

- **System – % Total Processor Time**. This counter is linked to the System object. It charts the total percentage of CPU utilization time of the system.
- **Process – % Processor Time**. This counter is linked to the Process object. Several counters are used in this monitor to chart the percentage CPU time of each Exchange core process. This chart is good for immediately identifying a process utilizing too much CPU time.

- **Memory – Pages/sec**. This counter is linked to the Memory object. This is the number of pages read from the disk, or written to the disk, to resolve memory references to pages that were not in memory at the time of the reference. This is the sum of Pages Input/sec and Pages Output/sec. This counter includes paging traffic on behalf of the system cache, to access file data for applications. This value also includes the pages to/from non-cached mapped memory files. This is the primary counter to observe if there is concern about excessive memory pressure and the excessive paging that may result.

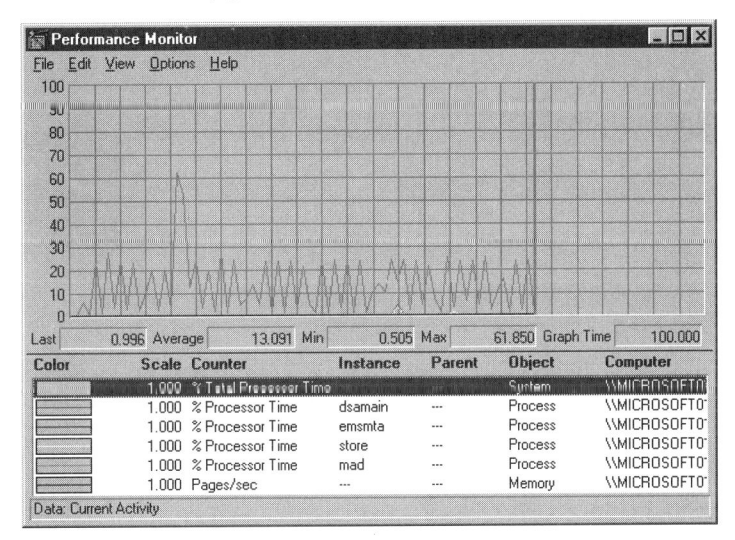

Server History

This Performance Monitor chart provides a general overview of system performance. It displays the number of users currently on the system and it also charts the memory in and out paging rate. The counters shown in the chart for the objects monitored indicate the following:

- **MSExchangeIS – User Count**. The actual count of people (not connections) currently using the IS. Performance measurement must always be correlated with current user numbers.
- **Memory – Pages/sec**. The total in and out paging activity. Paging occurs when an application references data not in its working set (physical memory). If this counter is consistently greater than 5, this is an early indication of a memory bottleneck.

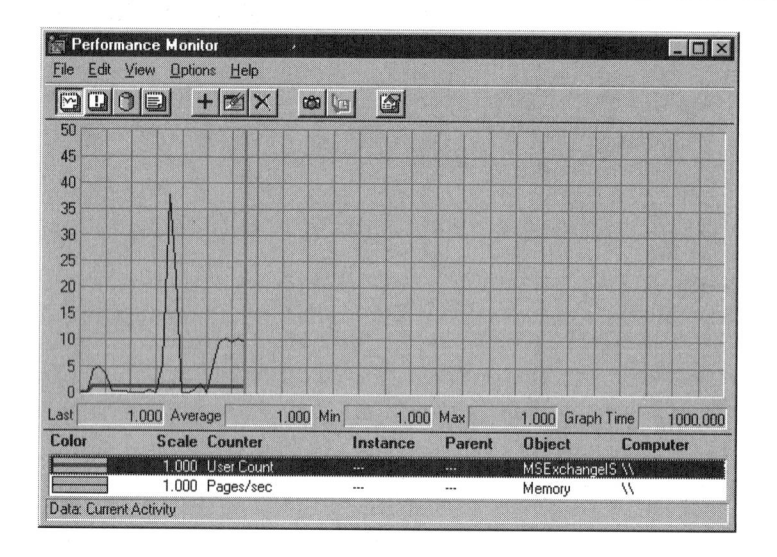

Server Load

This Performance Monitor chart goes deeper into Exchange Server functionality and tracks items such as address book usage and the number of messages being submitted and delivered. The counters shown in the chart for the objects monitored indicate the following:

- **MSExchangeIS – Message Recipients Delivered/min**. This is the rate at which recipients receive messages.
- **MSExchangeIS – Messages Submitted/min**. This is the rate that messages are submitted by clients.
- **MSExchangeIS – RPC Packets/sec**. This is the rate that (Remote Procedure Call) RPC packets are processed.
- **MSExchangeDS – AB Browses/sec**. This counter charts the rate at which Address Book clients perform browse operations.
- **MSExchangeDS – AB Reads/sec**. This counter charts the rate at which Address Book clients perform read operations.
- **MSExchangeDS – ExDS Reads/sec**. This is the rate at which Extended Directory Service clients perform read operations.

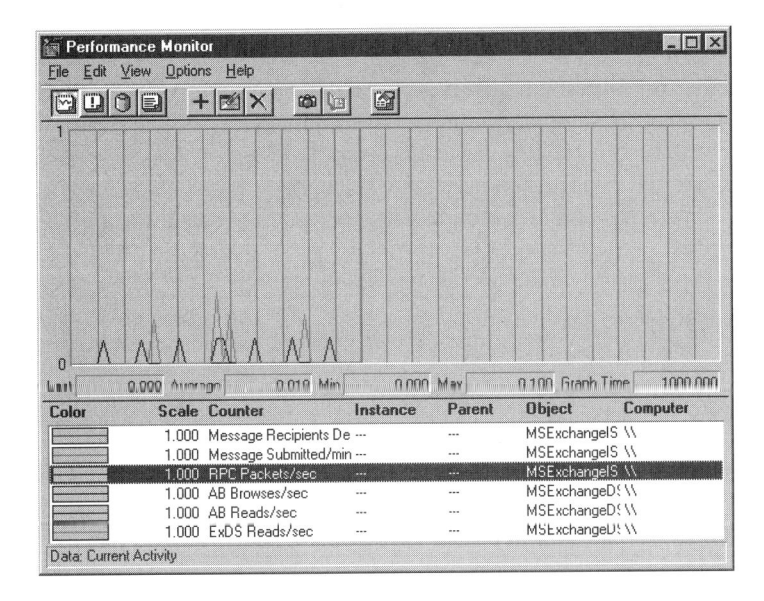

Server Users

This Performance Monitor chart uses the User Count counter to display the current number of users connected to the Exchange IS.

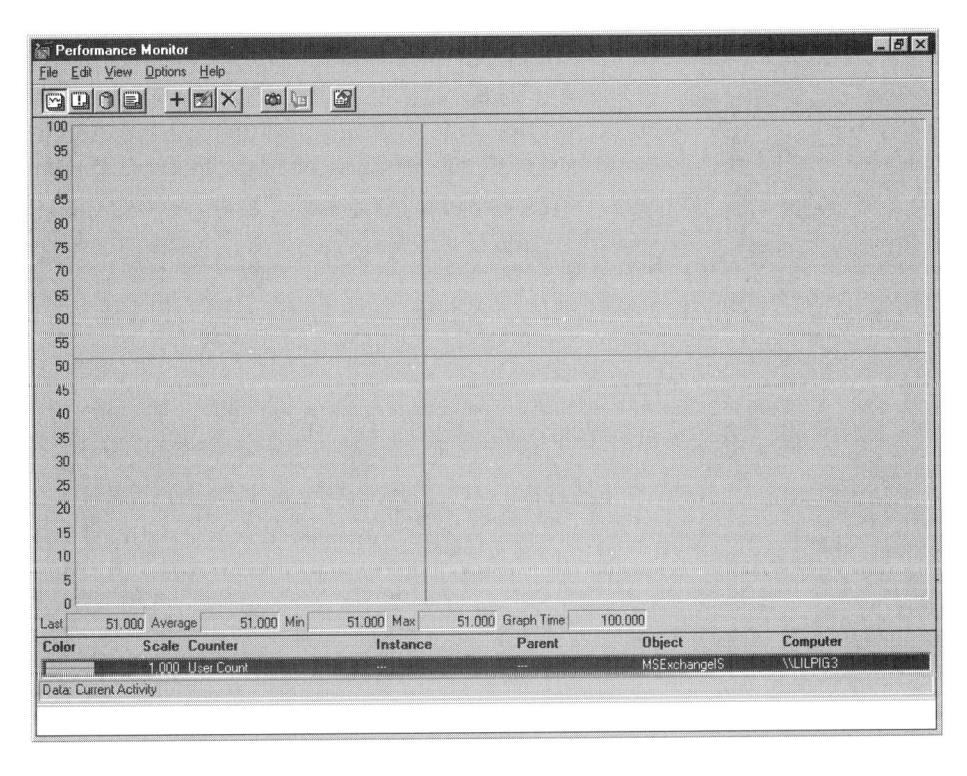

Creating Other Performance Monitors

If you wish to create other performance monitors for Exchange, you can use any of the monitors recommended from the data collection phase. Two important monitors you may want to consider adding are listed in the table below. This section covers creating a new Exchange performance monitor, options that may be set, and setting up an Exchange performance monitor alert.

Table 27.6 Suggested Additional Performance Monitors

Object	Counter
LogicalDisk	Free Megabytes
MSExchangeIS Private (+ Public)	Messages Submitted/min

Method for Creating a New Exchange Performance Monitor

You can create new Exchange performance monitors using selected objects and counters by following the procedure below.

▶ **To create a new Exchange performance monitor**

1. Click **Start**, point to **Programs**, point to **Administrative Tools (Common)**, and then click **Performance Monitor** to display the **Performance Monitor** utility.

2. On the **File** menu, click **New Chart**.

3. On the **Edit** menu, click **Add to Chart** to display the **Add to Chart** dialog box.

   From here, select the desired objects and counters (see "Creating Other Performance Monitors," above and refer to the Performance Monitor Help).

4. On the **Options** menu, select **Chart** to display the **Chart Options** dialog box for chart settings and parameters. See "Performance Monitor Chart Options" below for details.

5. On the **File** menu, click **Save Chart Settings As** to save the performance monitor chart.

For more details on creating performance monitors, refer to the "Performance Monitor Tool" section of *Chapter 26, Administrative Tools*.

Performance Monitor Chart Options

Exchange Performance Monitor chart options allow for several parameter variations when customizing monitoring features. Parameter variations may be introduced in new or existing performance monitors. The variables or options listed below appear in the **Chart Options** dialog box (on Performance Monitor **Options** menu, click **Chart**).

- **Sample rate interval**. Varies the rate at which the counter samples the object.
- **Relative (vertical) amplitude settings**. Sets the Performance Monitor chart vertical axis value.
- **Grid configuration**. Selects vertical and horizontal grid lines.
- **Legend and value bar**. Displays counters in use and statistics.

Note Other counters may be added to any performance monitor with the **Edit** menu, **Add to Chart** option. This option displays a dialog box that allows you to select an object to monitor and the type of counter used. If you need an explanation of counter functions, select the counter and click **Explain**. It may take some time to discover the usefulness and application of the many counters and objects available.

Performance Monitor Alerts

When a system event occurs, an alert can be sent to designated users or the technology consultant. For example, if you want to provide an alert when the Queued Outbound counter for the IMS exceeds a predefined threshold, you can configure the system to send it to the technology consultant or other recipient. Alerts are important for maintaining the availability of the system because the right people can be notified about problems that have occurred or about potential problems that are likely to occur.

Alert Mechanisms

The Performance Monitor tool has a flexible alert mechanism that specifies whether the alert does one of the following:

- Sends a network message. A network alert is sent to a specific computer or user logged on to the network.
- Updates an application log. Alerts are sent to the application log of the NT Event Viewer.
- Displays the alert view. The Alert dialog appears in real time and requires immediate attention.

Configuring a New Exchange Performance Monitor Alert

If you wish to configure an alert for an existing Exchange Server performance monitor, use the procedure below.

▶ **To create an Exchange performance monitor alert**

1. On the **View** menu, click **Alert** to display the **Alert** dialog box.
2. On the **Edit** menu, click **Add to Alert** to display the **Add to Alert** dialog box.

   From here, select the alert threshold value and program to run (refer to the Performance Monitor Alert Help).
3. On the **Options** menu, select **Alert** to display the **Alert Options** dialog box for update time and alert notification settings.
4. On the **File** menu, click **Save Alert Settings As** to save the performance monitor alert.

For further details on setting up performance monitor alerts, refer to the "Configuring Performance Monitor Alerts" section of *Chapter 26, Administrative Tools*.

Windows NT Event Viewer and Alert Logging

The Windows NT part of Small Business Server provides a logging facility in which application, security, and system events can be recorded. The status of Exchange Server may be viewed locally with the Windows NT Event Viewer; Exchange-related events are written to the Application log.

When an alert condition is detected, various configurable actions may be taken. The most basic is to write to the NT Event log. The most complex is to call a program in which more advanced alert notification processes can be utilized (with a third-party extension). An example of an NT Event Viewer log follows.

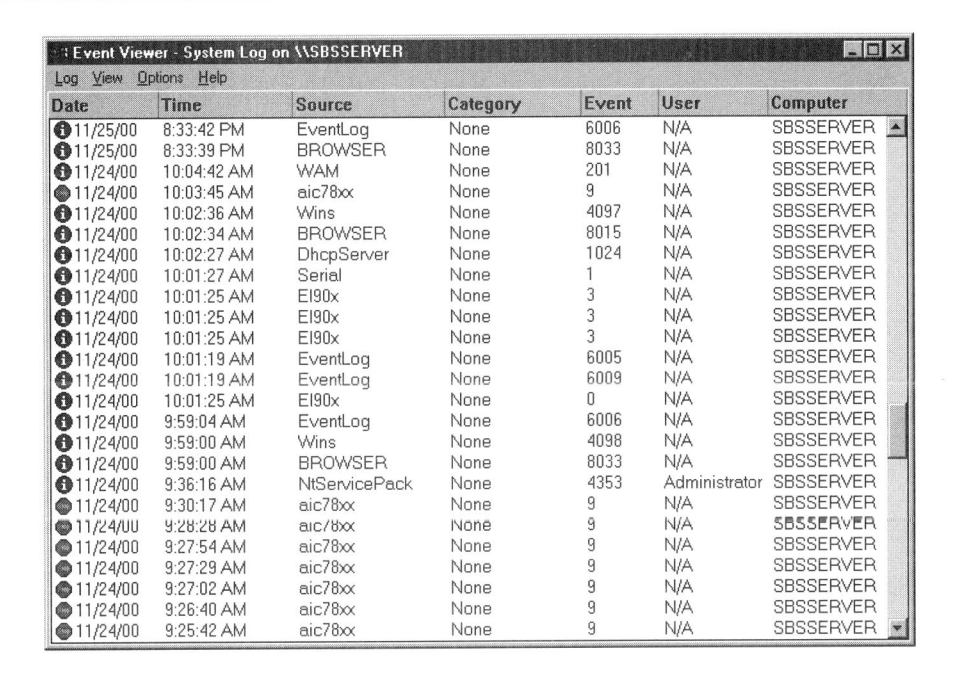

Date	Time	Source	Category	Event	User	Computer
11/25/00	8:33:42 PM	EventLog	None	6006	N/A	SBSSERVER
11/25/00	8:33:39 PM	BROWSER	None	8033	N/A	SBSSERVER
11/24/00	10:04:42 AM	WAM	None	201	N/A	SBSSERVER
11/24/00	10:03:45 AM	aic78xx	None	9	N/A	SBSSERVER
11/24/00	10:02:36 AM	Wins	None	4097	N/A	SBSSERVER
11/24/00	10:02:34 AM	BROWSER	None	8015	N/A	SBSSERVER
11/24/00	10:02:27 AM	DhcpServer	None	1024	N/A	SBSSERVER
11/24/00	10:01:27 AM	Serial	None	1	N/A	SBSSERVER
11/24/00	10:01:25 AM	El90x	None	3	N/A	SBSSERVER
11/24/00	10:01:25 AM	El90x	None	3	N/A	SBSSERVER
11/24/00	10:01:25 AM	El90x	None	3	N/A	SBSSERVER
11/24/00	10:01:19 AM	EventLog	None	6005	N/A	SBSSERVER
11/24/00	10:01:19 AM	EventLog	None	6009	N/A	SBSSERVER
11/24/00	10:01:25 AM	El90x	None	0	N/A	SBSSERVER
11/24/00	9:59:04 AM	EventLog	None	6006	N/A	SBSSERVER
11/24/00	9:59:00 AM	Wins	None	4098	N/A	SBSSERVER
11/24/00	9:59:00 AM	BROWSER	None	8033	N/A	SBSSERVER
11/24/00	9:36:16 AM	NtServicePack	None	4353	Administrator	SBSSERVER
11/24/00	9:30:17 AM	aic78xx	None	9	N/A	SBSSERVER
11/24/00	9:28:28 AM	aic78xx	None	9	N/A	SBSSERVER
11/24/00	9:27:54 AM	aic78xx	None	9	N/A	SBSSERVER
11/24/00	9:27:29 AM	aic78xx	None	9	N/A	SBSSERVER
11/24/00	9:27:02 AM	aic78xx	None	9	N/A	SBSSERVER
11/24/00	9:26:40 AM	aic78xx	None	9	N/A	SBSSERVER
11/24/00	9:25:42 AM	aic78xx	None	9	N/A	SBSSERVER

Event Types

There are four types of Exchange events logged in the Event Viewer, as defined below. The icon on the left side of the Event Viewer screen classifies the event by type. Since each event type is unique, they are not combined.

- **Error**. A red stop sign icon, indicating significant problems, such as a loss of data or loss of functions. For example, an Error event might be logged if a service was not loaded during startup of Small Business Server.

- **Warning**. A red stop sign icon, indicating events that may pose future problems. For example, a Warning event might be logged when disk space is low.

- **Information**. An icon with an "i" encapsulated in a black circle. These are infrequent but significant events describing successful operations of major Small Business Server services. For example, when an information store program loads successfully, it may log an information event (if configured).

- **Failure Audit**. A "//" symbol, indicating audited security access attempts that failed. For example, if a user tried to access a network drive and failed, the attempt can be logged as a Failure Audit event (if configured).

- **Success Audit**. An icon of a key indicates audited security access attempts, such as when a user successfully logs on to the system.

Viewing Event Logs

Before using the Event Viewer to diagnose a problem, it is essential to be able to interpret the event that is logged. Event entries consist of three main parts, the header information, event description, and additional data. For Exchange logs, only the date, time, user, computer, and category are contained in the header. The components of an event log are described in the table below.

Table 27.7 Event Viewer Components

Event Section	Information	Meaning
Header	Date	Date the event occurred.
	Time	Time the event occurred.
	User	In Exchange, the user is commonly the service account ID, since this is the account the service logged in under.
	Computer	The name of the computer the event occurred on.
	Event ID	The numerical identification of the event for diagnostics and logging.
	Category	Signifies specific auditing categories—primarily used by the security log.
Description		Contains the information on the exact event that occurred.
Additional Data		At the bottom of the event, binary data can be displayed—used for advanced troubleshooting by Microsoft Technical Support.

Filtering Events

Filters may be applied to focus on certain types of events in the Event Viewer. For example, you may view only the Error events while excluding warnings, information, and audit events. The Event Viewer also allows you to filter events based on the source of the event. Events generated by Exchange services usually fall into the following groups:

- Internal configuration errors
- Directory access errors

- Internal operating system errors
- Internal processing errors

Searching for Events

The Search option of the Event Viewer is useful for finding specific events by Source or Category. It can perform individual searches with a granularity similar to the Filtering option. The Search feature is most beneficial when viewing events from a very large log file.

Diagnostics Logging

Diagnostics logging is probably the most powerful diagnostic feature built into Exchange. All Exchange components can be configured to varying diagnostic reporting levels. In most cases, once logging is enabled it is immediate and does not require any service restarts.

Diagnostics logging settings can be modified by displaying the properties for the Server object in the Exchange Administration program. Individual diagnostic logging settings can be modified by selecting the properties for each distinct object in the Configuration container.

Default Exchange Logging

By default, Exchange performs basic logging, which includes information events such as backup and restore success or failures, service initialization or shutdown, and background maintenance notifications. More importantly, it also logs events such as low disk space warnings or IS and Directory Services (DS) database errors. Exchange generally logs any errors or warnings that signify an event that may cause degradation or disruption of service.

Configuring Log Files for the Data Collection Phase

To implement the initial data collection phase, set up a log file for the counters specified earlier. The set up process for logs is identical, whether for the data collection phase or any period in which you collect statistical data for performance counters. Also, set up an alert log in the Performance Monitor to facilitate analysis of the data collected in the initial phase.

During normal Exchange operation in the network, alerts should also be reported to the NT Event Log in order to maintain an easily accessed record of alerts in real-time. The diagram that follows provides a functional overview of the processes involved when setting up Exchange logs for the initial data collection phase and thereafter.

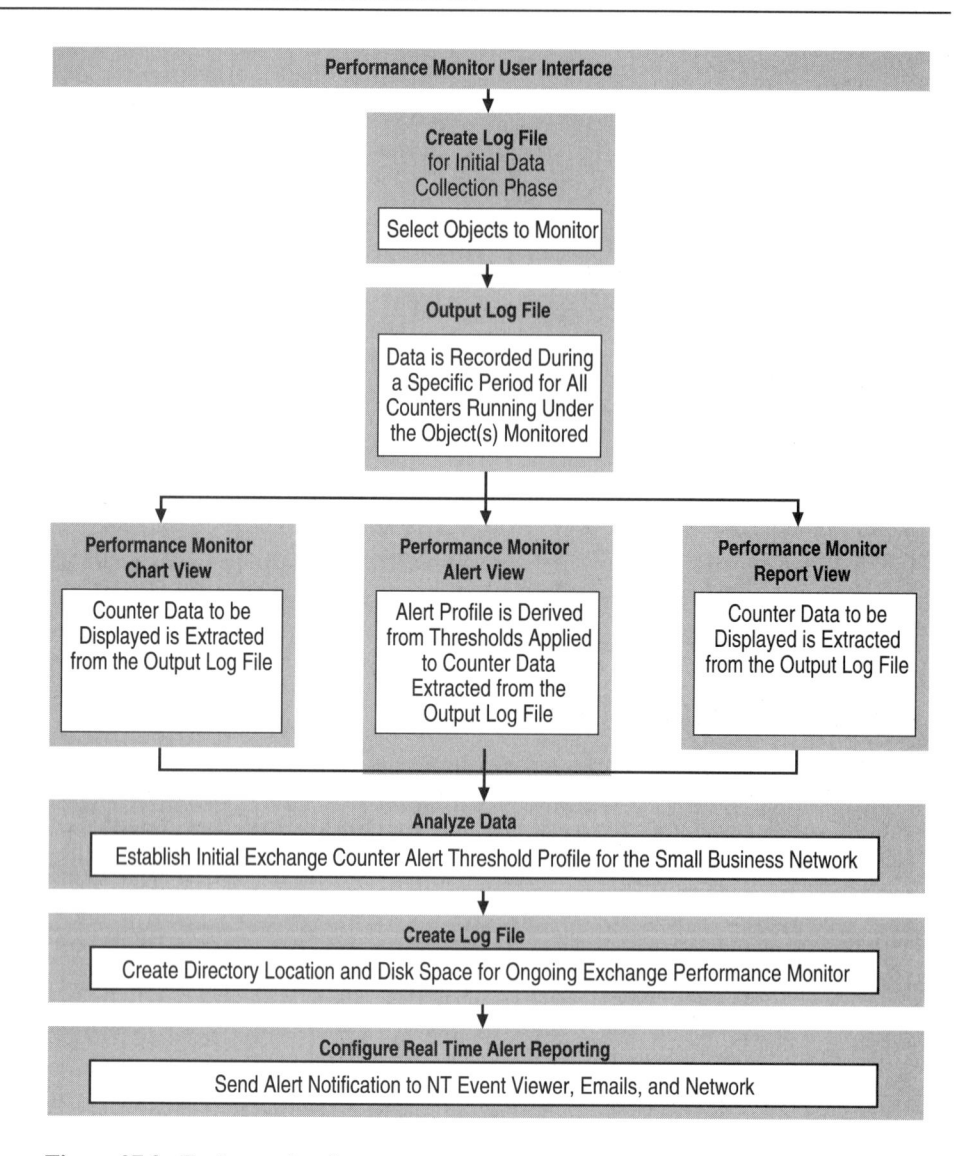

Figure 27.3 Exchange logging processes

Displaying Performance Data in the Chart View

Use the Performance Monitor Chart view to see either current activity in real-time or logged data. When current activity is selected, the chart view begins tracking counter statistics from the point it is configured, for as long as the Performance Monitor chart view is open. When log data is displayed, the chart view shows the data captured from the point the log file was started, up until the current time of viewing (when data is extracted from the log file). Specific windows of time may be set to view counter statistics at points of the data collection period that are of particular importance.

Defining Windows of Data with Bookmarks

When data from a log file is being displayed in Performance Monitor Chart view, you can bookmark the data display within a particular window of time. Bookmarks are added only after the log file starts running. Bookmarks can only be set in real time to mark intervals of particular interest during a data collection period. Bookmarks may be set up to support a granular analysis of the data collected, depending on how narrow the window of time you set.

After the bookmarks are set, implement them from the **Time Window**, accessed from the **Edit** menu of the Performance Monitor in Chart view—the window appears only when log file data is being displayed. When the bookmarks are entered into the Chart view data, markers first appear defining the start and end points of the data window. When you click **OK** in the **Time Window**, the horizontal excursions (time axis) of the chart view expands to display only the time interval you specified with the bookmarks.

Creating and Viewing Exchange Log Files

Use the following steps to set up and view log files for Exchange.

▶ **To create and view a log for the data collection phase**

1. Click **Start**, point to **Programs**, point to **Administrative Tools**, and then click **Performance Monitor** to display the Performance Monitor chart view.

2. On the **View** menu, click **Log** to display the Performance Monitor log view.

3. On the **Edit** menu, select **Add to Log** to display the following **Add to Log** dialog box.

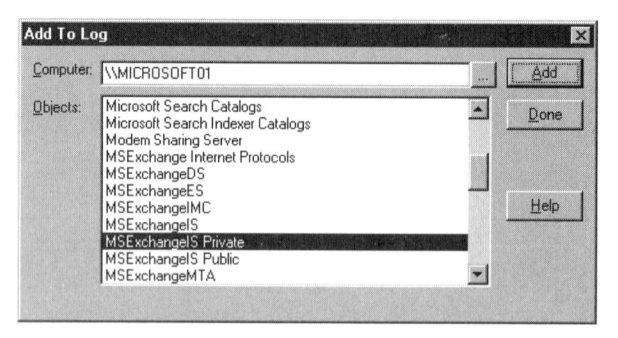

4. Select the object(s) you wish to monitor. Click **Add** and **Done**. The following dialog box appears to show you the objects you selected for monitoring.

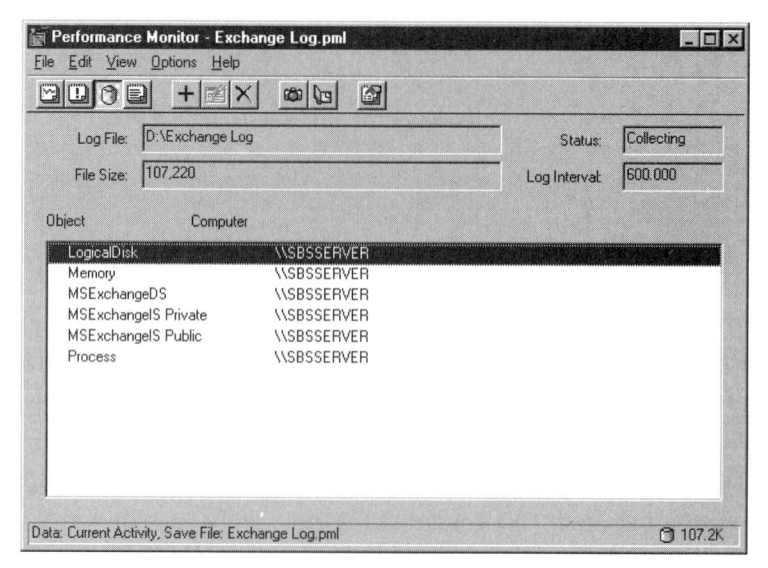

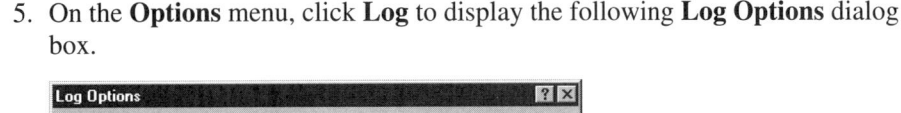

5. On the **Options** menu, click **Log** to display the following **Log Options** dialog box.

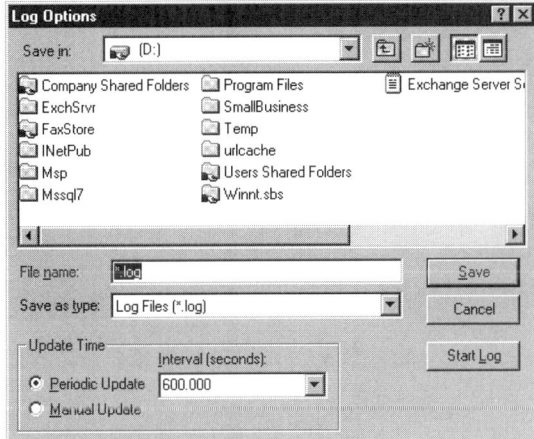

6. To create and save the Log file, follow the steps below.
   - Type the file name in **File name**.
   - Specify the interval for updating the log in **Periodic Update**.
   - Click **Start Log** to save the file and start logging data.

7. On the **Options** menu, click **Bookmark** to display the following **Add Bookmark** dialog box.

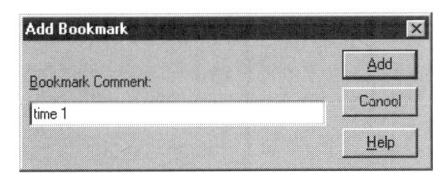

8. Set starting and ending times to define a real-time window in which you want to view data on the object selected—click **Add** for the start and end points at the appropriate moments in real-time. The text entered (**time 1** in the example) is tagged by Performance Monitor with the current time.

Note For example, in the initial data collection phase, you might set your first bookmark at the time logging is initialized. Then, when you want to view the data on the last day of the collection period, you enter a bookmark again at the moment in real time that defines the upper limit of your time window. You can also enter multiple bookmark start and end points to define other windows in which you want to look at performance data during the data collection period.

9. When a log is created, an object is selected and all the counters internally associated with it begin running. When you want to view the statistics of a particular counter, do the following:

  - On the **View** Menu, click **Chart**.
  - On the **Options** menu, click **Data From** to display the following **Data From** dialog box.

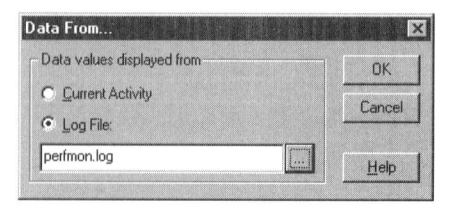

  - Select **Log File** and enter the name of the log file or browse for it. Click **OK**.
  - On the **Edit** menu, click **Add to Chart** to select the specific counter statistics you want to view. Click **Add** and **Done**. The performance of the counter over the entire period is displayed, starting from the point at which the logging was initialized.
  - On the **Options** menu, click **Chart** to configure the display parameters, if necessary.
  - To look at data only from within the time window you specified with the bookmarks, click **Time Window** on the **Edit** menu to display the following dialog box.

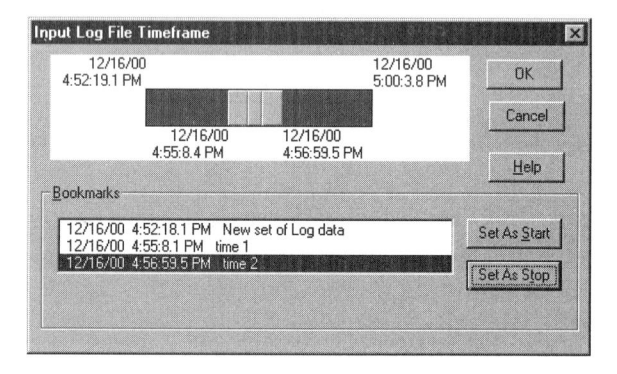

  - Click **Set as Start** and **Set as Stop** to define the window where you want to observe the data. Click **OK**. The Chart view shows the counter statistics only within the window points you bookmarked. Adjust Chart display parameters if necessary.

Viewing Performance Monitor Alert Logs

Performance monitor alerts may be applied to the counter statistics gathered during the data collection period. When you set a threshold and apply it to a log file that has already run for a specific time period, you can view alerts related to specific counters that have recorded data in the log file. This provides an emulation of the alert profile that would have occurred if the counters viewed were actually set to provide real-time alert notification (as you would have when monitoring the normal operation of Exchange in the network).

This feature allows you to experiment and observe the alert log response to different threshold settings. This is helpful when trying to calculate the threshold levels you will need to establish in relation to your baseline Exchange performance profile. Once data is collected, an alert profile may be derived from the logs and viewed using the procedure that follows.

▶ **To view Alert logs**

1. On the Performance Monitor **View** menu, click **Alert**.
2. On the **Options** menu, click **Data From** to display the following dialog box.

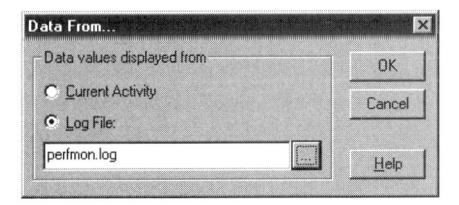

3. Type the name of the log file or browse for it, then click **OK**.
4. On the **Edit** menu, click **Add to Alert** to display the following **Add to Alert** dialog box. Select the counter(s) you want to observe and specify a certain threshold.

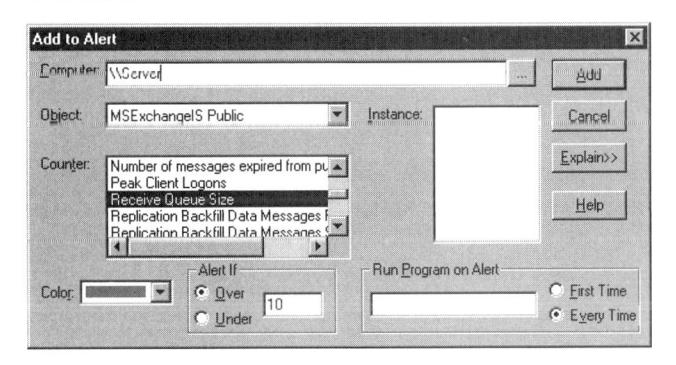

5. Click **Add** and **Done**. A mock alert record appears indicating the alerts occurring for the thresholds applied to the logged data.

> **Note** Change threshold values to generate other mock alert profiles.

Generating Reports

Report view can be used to select the current activity and display statistics for any counter in the system—use **Add to Report** for counter display. By selecting log, the report view displays only the counters for the objects in the log (entered when the log was first created). The report view provides a decimal readout value that dynamically tracks the chart view values, as shown below. Time windows may also be utilized in the report view.

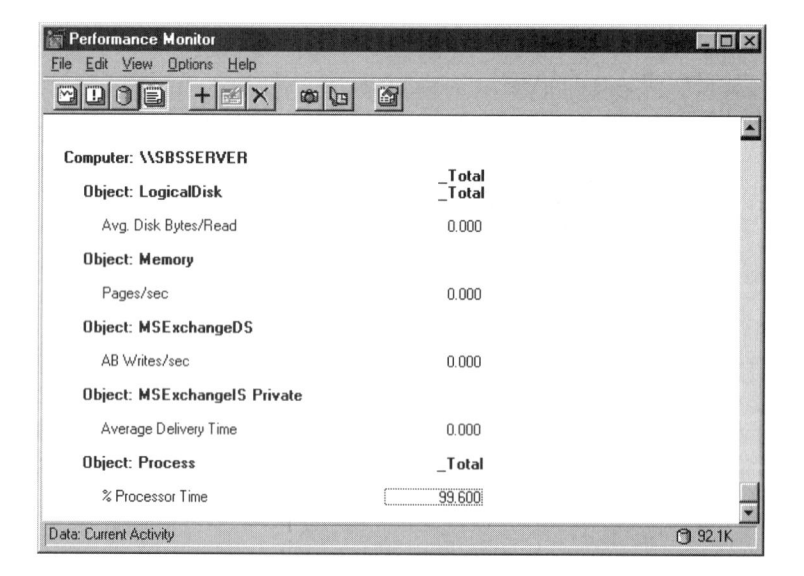

Sending Performance Monitor Alerts to the NT Event Log

For the data collection phase and later on during routine monitoring, the Performance Monitor should be configured to report alerts to the NT Event log, in addition to the regular performance monitor alert log. This may be configured by editing a registry key setting. Refer to the Performance Monitor online Help for the procedure.

Memory Considerations for Logging

Before setting up log files, consider disk space requirements. Disk space for logs is consumed in proportion to the counter collection rate and the log file update interval. The items listed below have an impact on memory requirements; consider them when allocating disk space for log files. When data is being logged, the rate at which memory is used per the update interval is displayed in Performance Monitor log view.

- **Counter sampling rate during the data collection period**. The sampling rate is configurable in seconds from 20 to 120 minutes.
- **Log update interval**. Can be specified using values from 1 to 3600 seconds.
- **Logging period during the data collection period**. This is not a configurable parameter. The logging period ends at the discretion of the technology consultant, at whatever point it is decided to end the data collection period, from one day to a week.

Note The counter sampling rate is the interval at which data is collected on the counter. The logging interval is the rate at which the log file is updated. The logging interval should not be shorter than the counter sampling rate or some counter statistics may not be captured.

Proxy Server 2.0

Microsoft Proxy Server 2.0 is an extensible firewall with high performance content caching that provides secure and managed Internet access for client desktops in the small business organization. As an integrated application of Small Business Server 4.5, the Proxy Server platform is optimized for the typical small business application. When Small Business Server 4.5 is installed, Proxy Server is set up automatically to support this configuration. Refer to *Part 5, Performance Optimization and Tuning* of this resource kit for Proxy Server's default configuration.

Once Small Business Server is up and running, the console's Internet Access Wizard and User Resource Wizard allow management of Internet access permissions on a per-user basis. The wizards perform the steps necessary behind-the-scenes to create the corresponding permissions list configuration for Proxy Server.

To customize user Internet access permissions or to add other enhancements to the basic Proxy Server configuration, Proxy Server must be accessed as a stand-alone application on Small Business Server. By manually configuring Proxy Server, the technology consultant has a more comprehensive control of Proxy features, beyond what is done with console wizards.

This section discusses several Proxy features useful to the small business application, that can be configured manually by the technology consultant. This information is supplementary to the Proxy online documentation (available from the **Start** menu of Small Business Server). The material presented in this section is intended for enhancement of small business Internet access management, to supplement the technology consultant with knowledge of the applicable techniques required for these enhancements. Proxy Server performance monitoring is also discussed.

User Access Control

An issue that may concern small business organization management is how to manage employee Internet access in a highly selective manner. Sometimes management is concerned that too much time might be spent surfing the Internet, thus detracting from employee productivity. If this is the case, you may want to limit employee Internet activity on the small business network or deny unauthorized access altogether.

Microsoft Proxy Server 2.0 is an ideal way to address this situation. With Proxy Server, the technology consultant can exert the appropriate control over Internet and intranet resources. This access control can be applied to the entire small business organization or only to individual users.

For example, the technology consultant may allow Gopher and browser-based World Wide Web (WWW) access for all employees, but permit only certain managers to use the Internet for conferencing or other multimedia services. By configuring the access protocol for users, the technology consultant controls the type of resources they can access on the Internet.

NT Server Directory and User Access Control

Configuring user access permissions manually is identical for both the Web Proxy and Winsock Proxy services included with Small Business Server 4.5. User names and domain information of the Windows NT Server directory serves as the basis for user access control, since Proxy Server 2.0 is tightly integrated with this directory. As a result, the technology consultant does not have to maintain a separate database or directory of Internet users.

Manually Configuring User Outbound Internet Access

When a user goes out to the Internet, the Web Proxy service is used by default. This service has the basic Internet services and protocols available: File Transfer Protocol (FTP), Gopher, Secure Sockets Layer (SSL), and World Wide Web (WWW). The technology consultant can manually configure Internet access permissions using these protocols, as required.

If the technology consultant needs a more diverse selection of protocols to configure Windows client Internet access permissions, use the Winsock Proxy service, as specified in the steps below.

Note If you manually configure Internet access in the Winsock Proxy service using Groups, and then use the console wizards to change Internet access, the group permission will be removed and the group members at the time of the change will be given access.

▶ **To manually configure Winsock Proxy access permissions for a user**

1. Click **Start**, point to **Programs**, point to **Microsoft Proxy Server**, and then click **Microsoft Management Console** to display the following IIS Console.

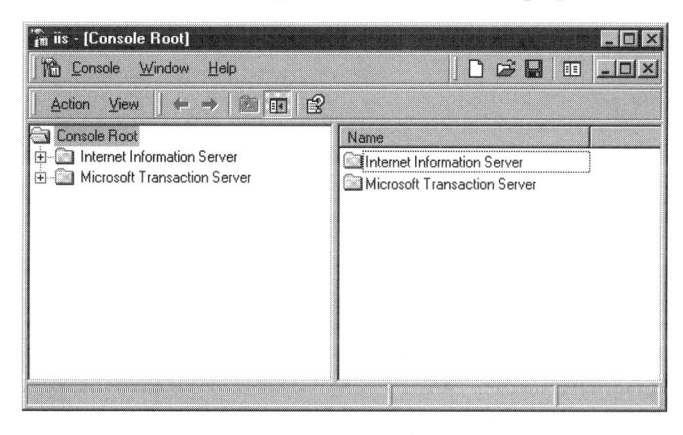

2. In the left pane, double-click the **Internet Information Server** folder.

3. Expand the Server icon, right-click **Winsock Proxy**, and then click **Properties** to display the following **Winsock Proxy Service Properties** page.

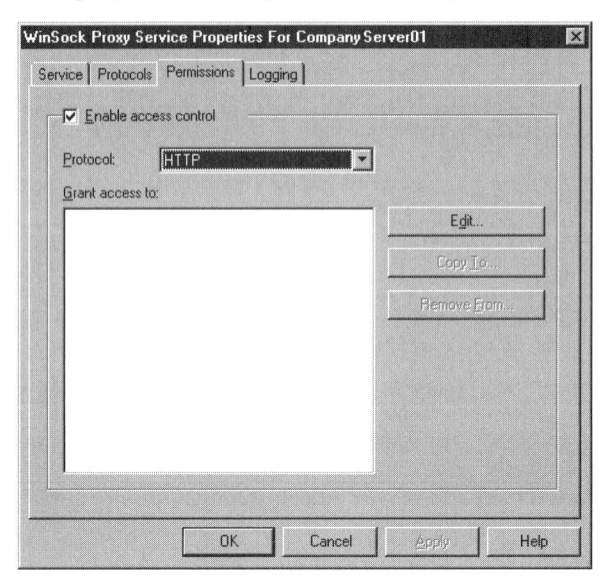

4. Select the **Permissions** tab, and then select **Enable access control**.

   Note **Unlimited Access** appears in the drop-down **Protocol** list by default, indicating the default user Internet access level.

5. From the drop-down **Protocol** list, select **HTTP** to limit the user to HTML-based resources on the Internet.
6. Click **Edit** to display the following **HTTP Permissions** dialog box.

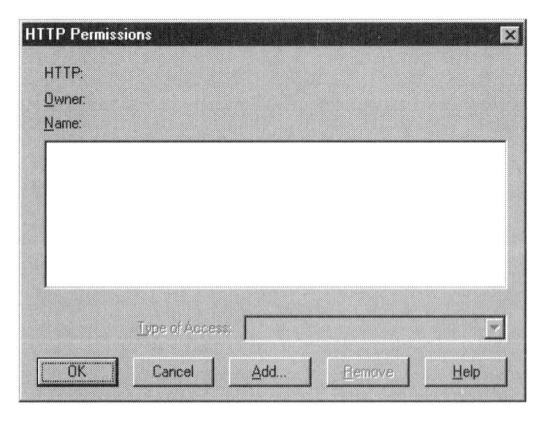

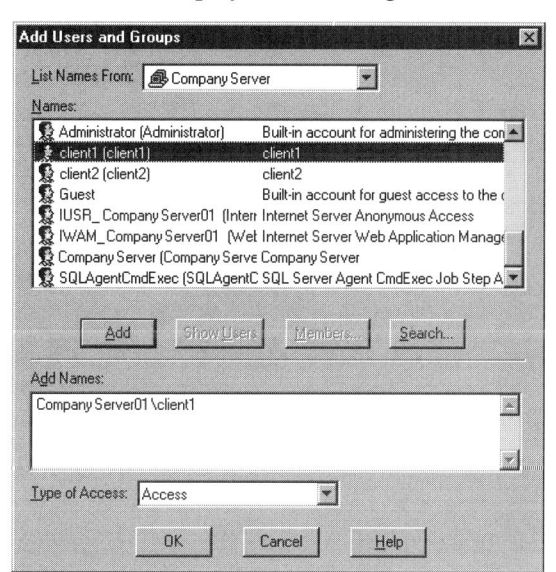

7. Click **Add** to display the following **Add Users and Groups** dialog box.

8. Click **Show Users** to display the network users. Select a user and click **Add**. The name of each user you select appears in the **Add Names** pane at the bottom of the dialog box.
9. Click **OK** in the **Add Users and Groups** dialog box.
10. Click **OK** in the **HTTP Permissions** dialog box. All users configured with HTTP permissions appear in the **Permissions** tab **Grant access to** box.

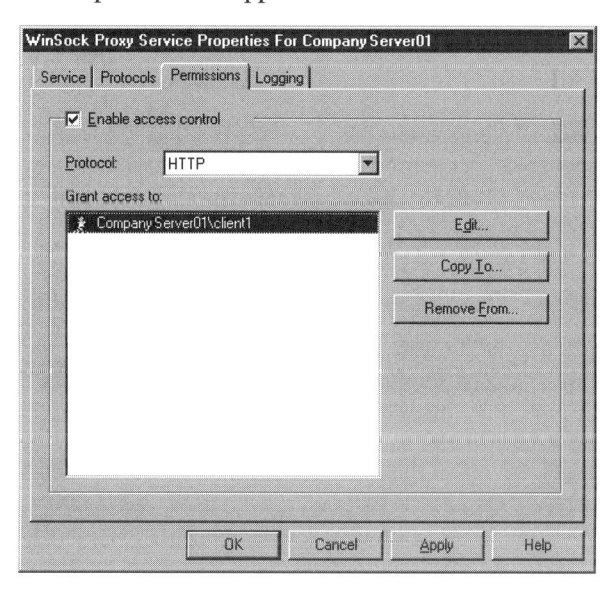

11. Click **Apply**, and then click **OK**.
12. Add other protocols to the newly created user permissions configuration per the following the steps. Each protocol allows the user to access different Internet resources.
    - On the **Winsock Proxy Service Properties** page, click on **Copy To**.
    - Select the protocol you want to add, and then click **OK**.
    - When finished, click **Apply**, and then click **OK**.

    Note Protocols may be removed from the user with the **Remove From** button in the **Winsock Proxy Service Properties** page.

13. Repeat the preceding steps for each user that requires modified permissions in the Winsock Proxy service.

Other Proxy Features

Several other Proxy features that may be of interest to the small business are found on the **Proxy Service Properties** dialog box **Services** tab. These are security, local address table, and current sessions, as shown in the **Winsock Proxy Service Properties** dialog box below. These features are discussed in the sections that follow.

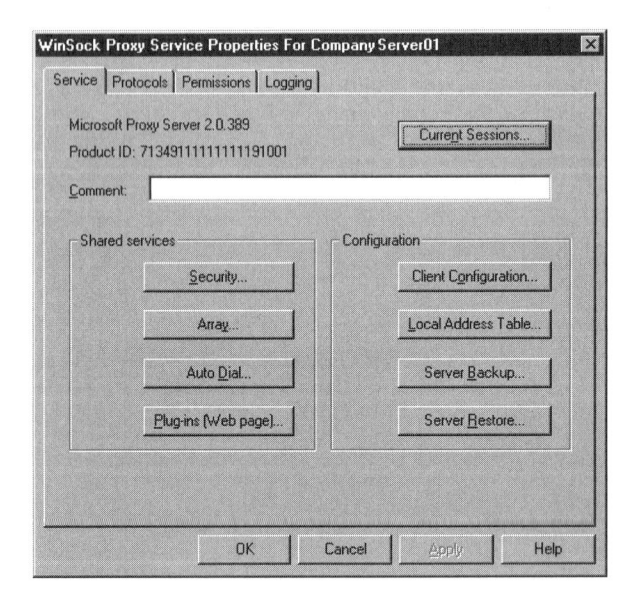

Security

To display the **Security** dialog box with tabs for packet filtering, domain filtering, alerting, and logging, click **Security** in the **Proxy Service Properties** dialog box. The technology consultant may configure these services manually to enhance or customize the Proxy configuration in several different ways.

Dynamic Packet Filtering

Packet filtering is a security feature of Proxy Serve 2.0. When enabled, all ports in the firewall are closed until they are opened by an access request. After the request, the ports are shut again unless a response is required, in which case, the port will stay open—up until the time the request is received. When a request opens a port, only certain types of packets are allowed to be interchanged at the external interface, depending on the protocols specified. If packet filtering is enabled with the Internet Connectivity Wizard, it is selected in the **Packet Filters** tab, as shown below. You may also manually enable or disable packet filtering on the **Packet Filters** tab.

You can edit, remove, or create new packet filters in the **Exceptions** list shown below—refer to the online Help and *Part 7, Security* of this resource kit for more information. Filters appearing in the **Exceptions** list contain the only protocols recognized by Proxy Server 2.0 when an access request to the small business network is received.

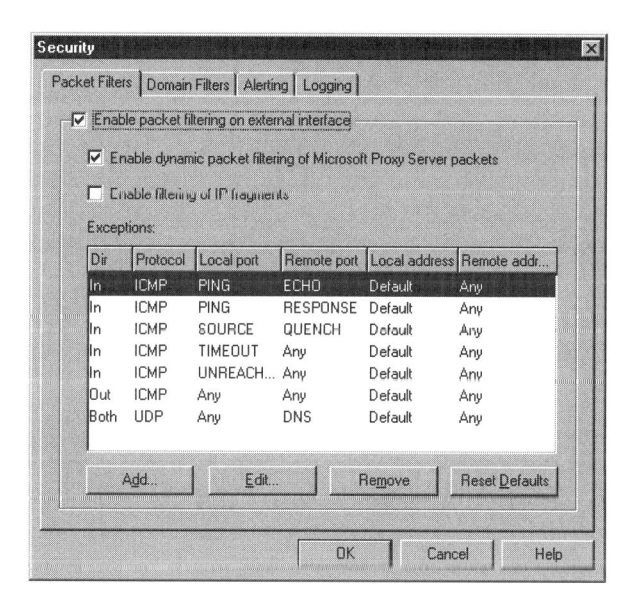

Alerting

When packet filtering is enabled by the Internet Connection Wizard, alerting on rejected packets is also enabled by default. When alerts occur on rejected packets, it is usually a sign that a network intruder is trying to breach the server (even though the ports are closed, they are still monitored). On the following **Alerting** tab, the technology consultant can set the threshold for the number of packet rejection events that occur before a system-level event is reported.

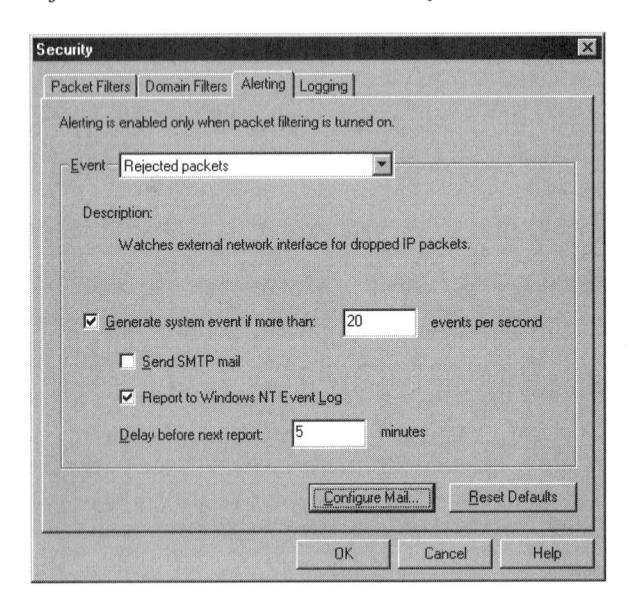

Alerts are reported to the NT Event Viewer, which the technology consultant should monitor regularly—especially for attempted intrusion events. Alert notification may be sent by Simple Mail Transfer Protocol (SMTP) mail to an appropriate recipient. Click **Configure Mail** to display the following **Configure Mail Alerting** dialog box.

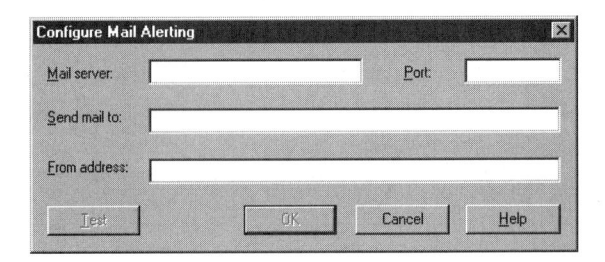

In the **Configure Mail Alerting** dialog box, click **Help** for assistance when configuring the e-mail alert. It is strongly recommended to send e-mail alerts to an internal mail server and not to a mail server on the Internet. Sending an e-mail alert on a path that may be under attack is not advised.

Before configuring the e-mail alert, make sure a new user mail account is created (or an existing mail account is used). Use the Small Business Server Online Guide for help.

Domain Filters

This Proxy feature lets the technology consultant selectively deny or allow small business network access to specific web sites, computers, or groups of computers. This filtering feature applies to web sites on the Internet or on the small business intranet. The technology consultant has the ability to indicate a specific Internet Protocol (IP) address, a range of IP addresses for a group of computers, or a domain name for any Proxy service (Web, Winsock, or SOCKS). Defaults can be set to grant access with exceptions or to deny access with exceptions. Follow the steps below to create a site filter.

▶ **To create a site filter**

1. Click **Start**, point to **Programs**, point to **Proxy Server**, and then click **Microsoft Management Console** to display the IIS Console.
2. In the left pane, double-click the **Internet Information Server** folder.
3. Expand the Server icon, right-click the required Proxy service, and then click **Properties** to display the **Proxy Service Properties** page.
4. Select the **Service** tab, and then click **Security** to display the following **Security** dialog box.

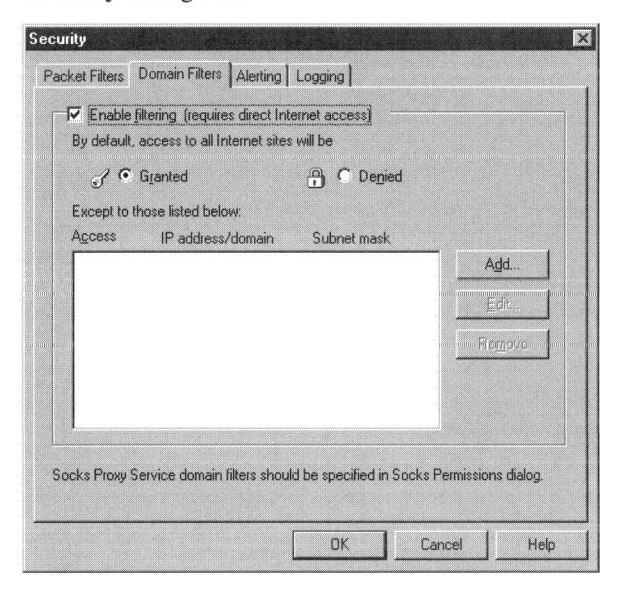

5. Select the Domain **Filters** tab, and then select **Enable filtering**.

6. Select **Granted** to set the default access. If access is to be granted to only a few Internet sites, then select **Denied**.

   Note If **Granted** is selected, use the **Deny Access To** dialog box to specify an Internet site that no users in the small business network are allowed to access. If **Denied** is selected, use the **Grant Access To** dialog box to specify an Internet site that all users are allowed to access.

7. Click **Add** to enter the excluded sites in the exception box. The **Deny Access To** dialog box shown below is displayed.

   This dialog gives you several choices. You can block a group of IP addresses, an entire domain, or a single address. If you select **Single Computer**, the button with three dots to the right of the **IP address** box displays the **DNS Lookup** dialog box. This is useful if you know a site's name, but not its IP address.

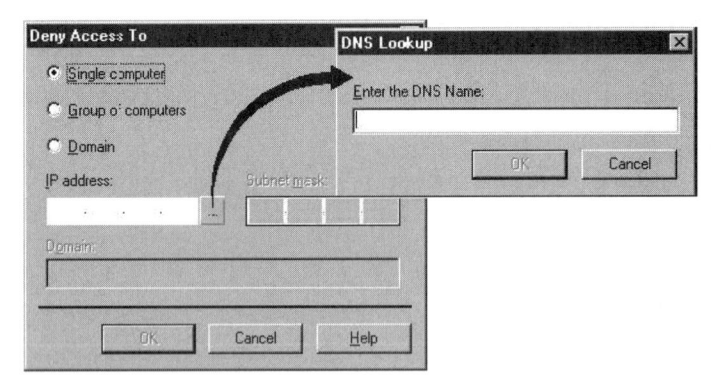

8. Click **OK** and **Apply** to enable the access settings.

Note When you use the Winsock Proxy service, filtering by domain name does not affect Internet requests when the client application accesses a site using an IP address. To effectively filter a site, you may find it useful to create filters both on the domain name and the IP address.

Value-Added Site Filtering Services

With new web sites going live every day, it can be an ongoing challenge for a technology consultant to know the address of each and every Internet site having material that should be filtered for users. This has initiated the development of value-added services that complement the core site-filtering features of Microsoft Proxy Server 2.0.

Third-Party Filtering Services

Third-party solution developers utilizing the extensibility of Proxy Server can offer subscription services that essentially plug in to Proxy Server site filtering. For example, with these services a technology consultant does not need to know the web address for each and every undesirable web site in order to deny user access to those sites. Instead, the technology consultant can use a simple checkbox to select the *categories* of web content to be filtered. The third-party companies offering filtering services keep continuously updated lists of those sites by category, as a value-added service.

Logging

Proxy reports are generated from Proxy log files and displayed on an HTML page using the **generate Internet reports** taskpad on the Small Business Server console, as described in *Chapter 26, Administrative Tools*. On the following **Logging** tab, the technology consultant may configure several Proxy log file parameters useful to the small business.

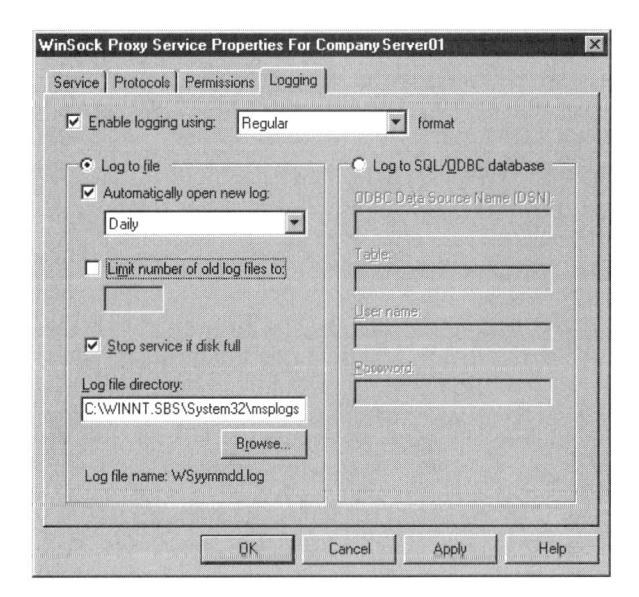

Log Files and Hard Disk Space Usage

Log files generated by Proxy consist not only of those used for displaying Internet reports on the console, but also of packet rejection alerts that are sent to the NT Event Viewer. Proxy logs contribute to the usage of hard disk space, which can fill up quickly depending on the rate at which events are logged.

On the **Logging** tab, the technology consultant can limit the logging rate with the **Automatically open new log** drop-down menu. To curtail disk space consumption, the logging rate should be changed to a longer interval (weekly or monthly). The number of old log files retained may also be limited as another measure to conserve disk space. Select the **Limit the number of old log files to** box and type a number in the data entry box. Adjust these parameters for all applicable Proxy services accessed in the IIS root directory.

Important Do not change the default location of the Proxy log file directory since this is used to find the data for generating Internet reports displayed on the Small Business Server console. The default log directory is also accessed by the Server Status Tool when it generates reports to send to the technology consultant.

Proxy Local Address Table

The Local Address Table (LAT) maintains a record of the IP address range that spans the internal network address space used by the Dynamic Host Configuration Protocol (DHCP) Server. This tells Proxy Server whether client-requested IP addresses are to be found on the intranet or Internet, so appropriate routing may occur. When a client in the small business network makes a Unified Resource Locator (URL) request from the Internet, the LAT tells Proxy Server to route that request outside the local address space and to the Internet. When the resource is retrieved, Proxy Server consults the LAT, which then tells it where to route the request so it reaches the network client who asked for it.

The Transmission Control Protocol/Internet Protocol (TCP/IP) address of Small Business Server is set by default to 10.0.0.2. The IP address range in the Proxy LAT is also configured by default during Small Business Server setup. The only time the LAT may need to be reconfigured is if the base IP address of Small Business Server is changed. If this is required, the IP address *range* in the LAT must be changed for compatibility with the new base IP address of the server. This is also necessary since the LAT enables Proxy Server to distinguish between internal nonroutable network IP addresses and external (Internet-routable) IP addresses. This is a security feature that prevents direct client connection with Internet hosts (having external IP addresses). Before the LAT is modified, the DHCP Server scope must be changed to accommodate the new IP address range. The appropriate changes to the LAT can then be added automatically by the **Local Address Table Configuration** dialog box **Construct Table** button—refer to the section ahead entitled "Updating the Proxy LAT."

The sections that follow describe how to change the TCP/IP address of Small Business Server 4.5 manually and how to reconfigure the LAT.

Before Beginning Update Procedures

Before changing the Small Business Servers default TCP/IP address, make a complete backup of Small Business Server files and create an Emergency Repair Disk. Refer to the Online Guide for backup procedures. Use the Small Business Server Console **Manage Disks** page to create an Emergency Repair Disk. After backup and disk creation, but before the updates to the default TCP/IP address are made, inform users the server will be unavailable during the update process.

Disconnecting All Users

Users need advance notice that the server will not be available for a period of time in order to plan their use of server resources accordingly. Also, all users must be disconnected from the server and all queued mail must be sent before changing the server IP address. Perform the following steps to accomplish this.

▶ **To warn users of the Small Business Server shutdown**

1. On the **Start** menu, point to **Programs**, **Administrative Tools**, then click **Server Manager** to display the **Server Manager** utility.

2. On the **Computer** menu, click **Send Message** to display the following **Send Message** dialog box.

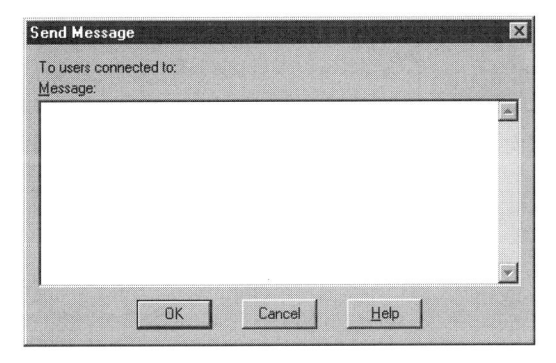

3. Compose and send a message warning users that the server is shutting down. Be sure to give them time to close any open files and save their work to the server.

> **Note** Winpopup must be running on the Windows 95 client computers to receive system messages. If Winpopup is not running, either start the program on the client computers or inform users in another manner that the server will be shutting down.

▶ **To disconnect all users**

1. On the Small Business Server Console **Manage Users** page, click the **manage connected users** taskpad.

2. Click **Disconnect All Users** to disconnect all current user sessions.

Changing the Default TCP/IP Address

There are several components of the Small Business Server that use the default TCP/IP address. In order to change the default TCP/IP address, it is important that the appropriate changes are made to each of the dependent components. The following sections describe the modifications that must be made.

Updating the DHCP Server

A DHCP Server provides the ability to dynamically assign IP addresses to DHCP clients. If a DHCP Server is being used to assign IP addresses to clients in the small business network, then the DHCP Server's scope will need to be changed on the Small Business Server to give out IP addresses valid for the IP subnet. If a static IP address is to be used, then the DHCP Server should be disabled. Perform the steps of the appropriate procedure below.

▶ **To update the DHCP Server with a new base IP address**

1. On the **Start** menu, point to **Programs**, **Administrative Tools**, then click **DCHP Manager** to display the **DHCP Manager** utility.

2. Double-click on **Local Machine** to display **[10.0.0.0]Default Subnet** as shown below.

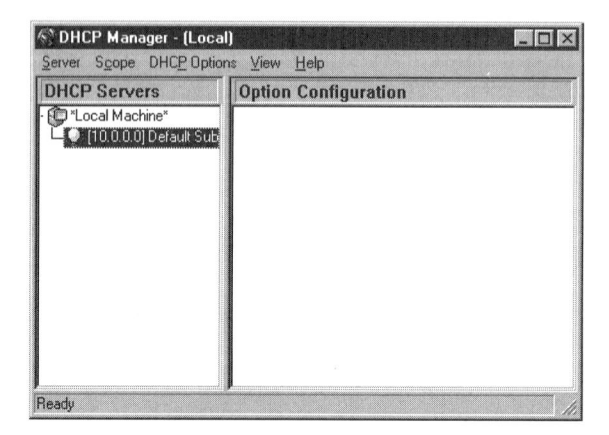

Chapter 27 Administering Small Business Server Components 403

3. From the **Scope** menu, select **Properties** to display the following **Scope Properties** dialog box.

4. Update the **IP Address Pool** details: **Start Address**, **End Address**, **Subnet Mask**, and **Exclusion Range**.
5. Click **OK** and exit the **DHCP Manager**.

> **Note** For further information on configuring DHCP Server scope, see the article "How to Configure Your DHCP Server Scope" at the following web address:
> **http://support.microsoft.com/support/kb/articles/q139/9/04.asp**

▶ **To disable the DHCP server**

1. On the **Start** menu, point to **Settings**, then click **Control Panel**.
2. Double-click **Network** to display the following **Network** utility.

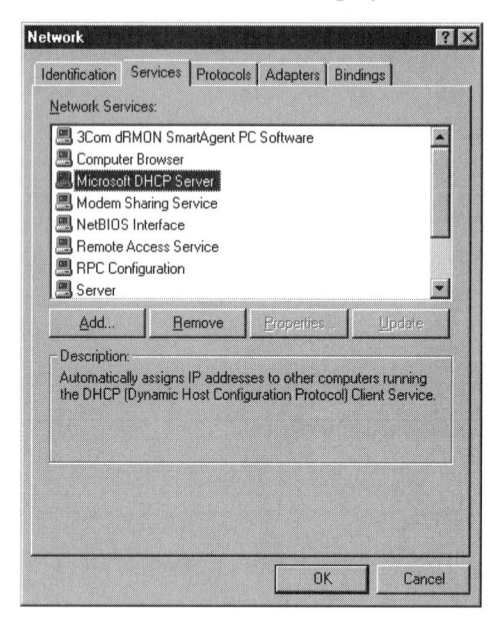

3. On the **Services** tab, select **Microsoft DHCP Server**.
4. Click **Remove** to remove the DCHP Server.

Updating the Remote Access Server

By default, Small Business Server's Remote Access Server (RAS) is setup to give out IP addresses gathered from the DHCP Server. RAS stores the addresses in the registry. To clear out these addresses and to reference more information on this topic, see the following two articles:

- "RAS Server Assigns Cached IP Addresses to RAS Clients" at:
  http://support.microsoft.com/support/kb/articles/q124/3/58.asp
- "Understanding DHCP IP Address Assignment for RAS Clients" at:
  http://support.microsoft.com/support/kb/articles/q160/6/99.asp

Note If you configure RAS to use a static pool, make sure the range you use is in the Proxy Server LAT.

Updating the TCP/IP Property Settings

The server's IP address, subnet mask, default gateway, and WINS server settings must be updated in the TCP/IP property settings. Use the steps that follow to configure these components.

▶ **To change the TCP/IP property settings**

1. On the **Start** menu, point to **Settings**, then click **Control Panel**.
2. From **Control Panel**, double-click **Network** to display the following **Network** utility.

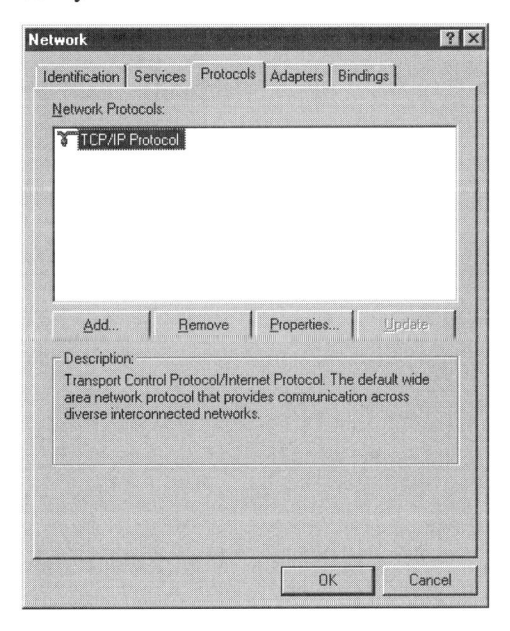

3. Select the **Protocols** tab, **TCP/IP** protocol, then click **Properties**.
4. In **TCP/IP Properties**, select the **WINS Address** tab, then set the **Primary and Secondary WINS Server** addresses to Small Business Server's new IP address.
5. Select the **IP Address** tab, then highlight the internal network adapter to which the new IP address will be binded.
6. In the **IP Address** text field, change the IP address of Small Business Server to the new IP address.
7. In the **Subnet Mask** text field, change the Subnet Mask (if necessary).
8. If Small Business Server dials an ISP for Internet access, clear the **Default Gateway** text field.
9. Click on **OK** and exit.
10. Click **Yes** to restart the server when asked.

Updating Existing Small Business Server Client Machines

After the server has been reconfigured with the new IP address, the client machines must also be updated with a new IP address and Proxy Server settings.

Updating the Small Business Server Client IP Address

The Small Business Server client machine IP addresses only need to be updated if the client machines are using DHCP to obtain an IP address.

▶ **To verify whether the client machine is using DHCP**

1. On the client machine, go to the **Start** menu, point to **Settings**, then click **Control Panel**.
2. Double-click **Network** to display the **Network** utility. Select the **Configuration** tab.
3. For Windows 95/98 machines, select **TCP/IP - network card** (the name of your network card), then click **Properties** to display the following **TCP/IP Properties** dialog box.

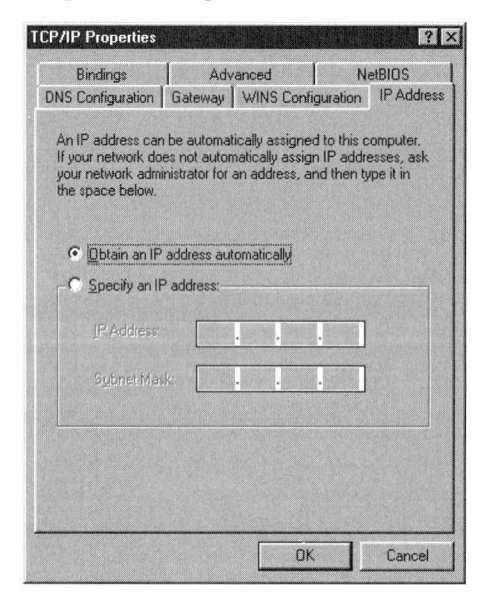

4. For NT Workstation client machines, select the **Protocols** tab, select the **TCP/IP** protocol, then click **Properties** to display the **TCP/IP Properties** dialog box.
5. In **TCP/IP Properties**, select the **IP Address** tab, then verify that **Obtain an IP address automatically** is selected.
6. Click **OK** to exit.

▶ **To update client machines using DHCP**

1. If the client machine is running Windows 95/98, perform the following steps:
   - On the **Start** menu, click **Run**, type *winipcfg* in the **Open** text field, then click **OK**.
   - In the **IP Configuration** dialog box shown below, make sure your network card is selected in the drop-down list. Click **Release All**.
   - Once the IP address is released (displays as 0.0.0.0), click **Renew All**.
   - Verify that an IP address from Small Business Server's DHCP server appears in the **IP Address** field, and that it is on the new IP subnet.

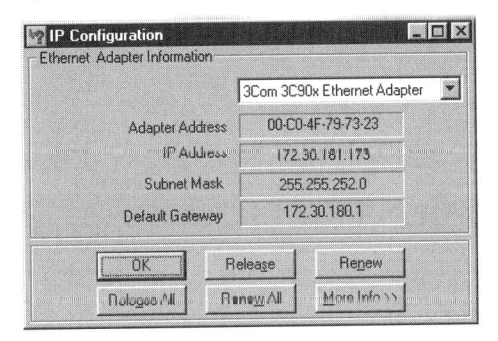

2. If the client machine is running Windows NT Workstation, perform the following steps:
   - On the **Start** menu, click **Run**, type *cmd* in the **Open** text field, then click **OK**.
   - At the command prompt, type the following commands:

     ipconflg /release all, then press ENTER

     ipconfig /renew all, then press ENTER
   - To verify the new IP address, type:

     ipconfig, then press ENTER

Updating the Winsock Proxy Client

The Winsock Proxy client must be updated for compatibility with the new IP address.

▶ **To update the Winsock Proxy Client**

1. Copy the updated Mspclnt.ini file in Small Business Server %systemroot%\Msp\Clients to the client machine's %systemdrive%\Mspclnt directory.

2. Restart the client machine.

Updating Internet Explorer's Proxy Settings

For each user logging on to a Small Business Server client machine, or Small Business Server itself, Internet Explorer must be set to go to Small Business Server's new IP address. Perform the steps below to configure Internet Explorer.

▶ **To verify that the client machine goes to the new IP address**

1. Logon to the Small Business Server client machine as the user.
2. Right-click **Internet Explorer** on the desktop, then click **Properties** to display the following **Internet Properties** dialog box.

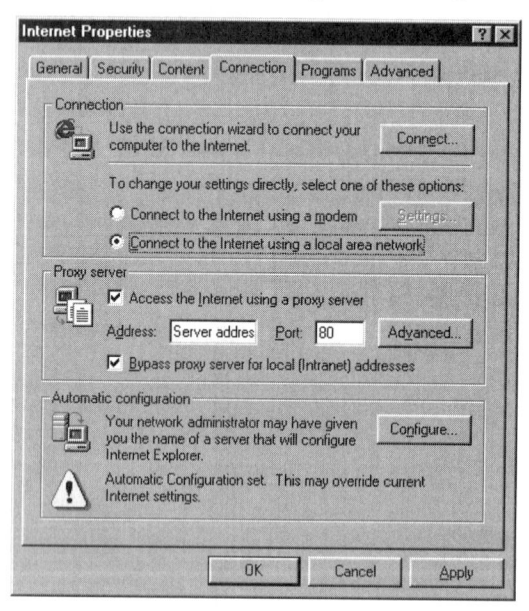

3. On the **Connection** tab under **Proxy server**, make sure **Access the Internet using a proxy server** is selected.
4. Verify that Small Business Server's new IP address appears in the **Address** text field. If not, change it to match the new IP address or server name.

Updating the Proxy LAT: Using Construct Table

In order to ensure that Proxy Server knows which addresses are on the small business LAN, the Proxy Local Address Table must be updated. Use the steps that follow to update the Local Address Table.

Note The LAT is used by all Proxy services. Configuring the LAT for one Proxy service, configures it for all.

▶ **To update the LAT using Construct Table**

1. Click **Start**, point to **Programs**, **Microsoft Proxy Server**, then click **Microsoft Management Console** to display the **IIS Console**.

2. In the left pane, double-click the **Internet Information Server** folder.

3. Expand the Server icon, right-click the **Winsock Proxy** service, then click **Properties** to display the following **Winsock Proxy Service Properties** dialog box.

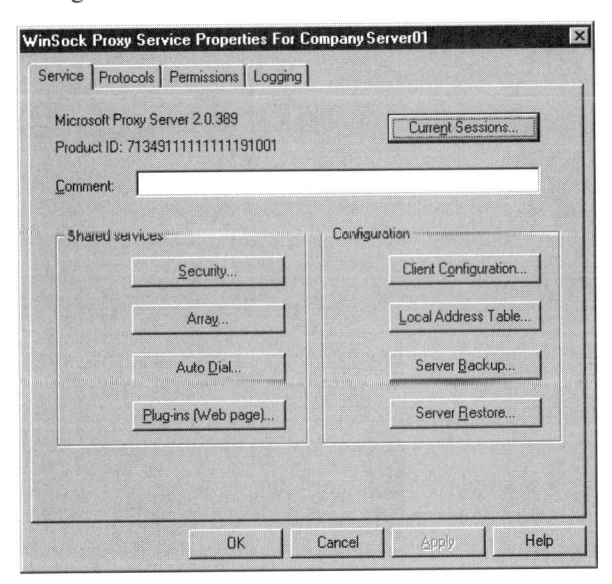

4. On the **Services** tab, click **Local Address Table** to display the following **Local Address Table Configuration** dialog box.

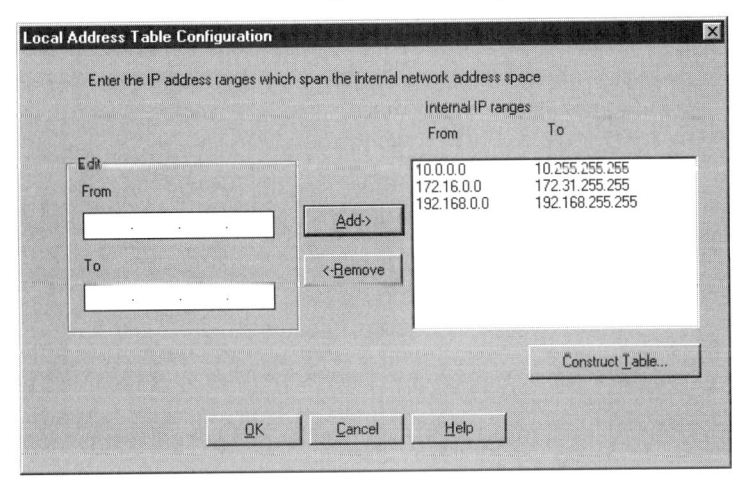

5. To add the new range of internal IP addresses configured in the DHCP Server, click **Construct Table** to display the following **Construct Local Address Table** dialog box.

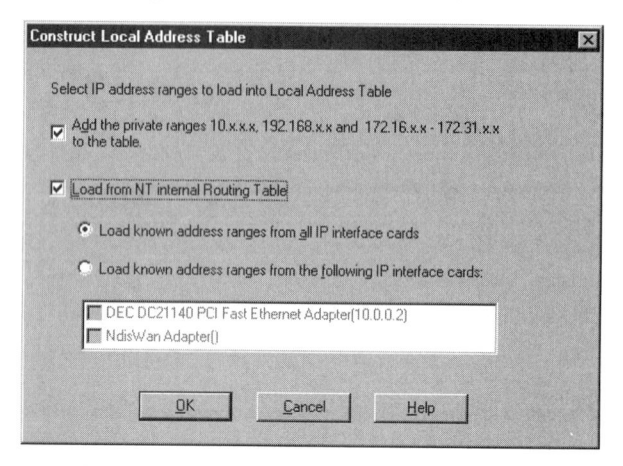

> **Note** When using the Construct Local Address Table dialog box, the DHCP IP address range, private IP address ranges, and those found in the NT Internal Routing Table are all added to the Proxy LAT by default. The routing table includes addresses that are bound to all network adapter cards in the system. The IP addresses that are of interest in the LAT are the ones bound to the *internal* network adapter cards. IP addresses bound to external network adapter cards are routable Internet IP addresses which do not belong in the Proxy LAT.

6. If you can identify the internal network adapter, configure the **Construct Local Address Table** dialog box to take the address range directly from this card by selecting **Load known address ranges from the following IP interface cards**—then place a check mark next to the internal network adapter card in use.
7. If you cannot identify the internal network adapter, select **Load known address ranges from all IP interface cards**.
8. Click **OK** in the **Construct Local Address Table** screen. The newly configured IP address range for the DHCP Server will be consulted and the address values will be automatically added to the Proxy LAT.
9. Click **OK** to the **Setup Message**.

    If you selected **Load known address ranges from all IP interface cards** in this procedure, IP addresses bound to the external network adapter are loaded into the Proxy LAT. In the **Local Address Table Configuration** dialog box, select the external IP addresses and click **Remove** to delete them.
10. Click **OK** and restart Small Business Server for the changes to take effect.

Manually Updating the Proxy LAT: Without Using Construct Table

If you want to add only the range of IP addresses configured in the DHCP **Scope Properties** dialog box, without the private address ranges or those binded to external network adapter cards, you may configure the LAT manually without using the **Construct Table** button. Follow the steps below to configure the Proxy LAT manually.

Note The LAT is used by all Proxy services. Configuring the LAT for one Proxy service, configures it for all.

▶ **To update the Proxy LAT manually**

1. On the **Start** menu, point to **Programs, Proxy Server**, then click **Microsoft Management Console** to display the **IIS Console**.
2. In the left pane, double-click the **Internet Information Server** folder.
3. Expand the Server icon, right-click the **Winsock Proxy** service, then click **Properties** to display the following **Winsock Proxy Service Properties** dialog box.

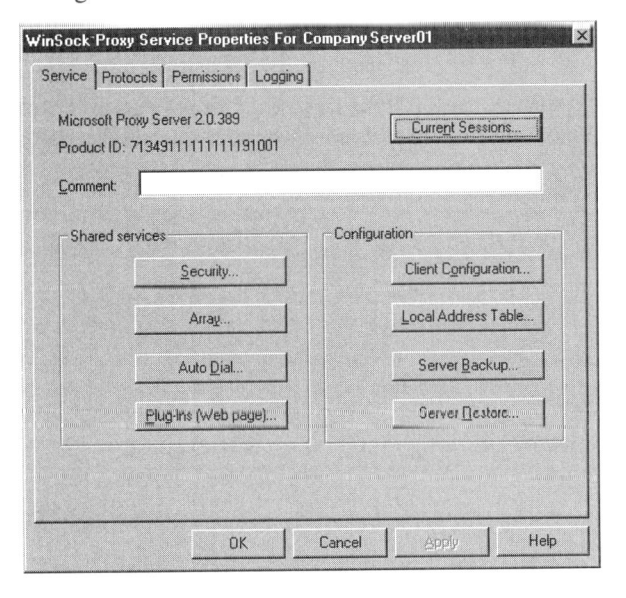

4. On the **Service** tab, click the **Local Address Table** button to display the **Local Address Table Configuration** dialog box.

5. In the **Edit From** and **To** text fields, enter the correct range of IP addresses for the network. Use the values configured in the DHCP **Scope Properties** dialog box (refer to the earlier section entitled "Updating the DHCP Server").

Note For example, if the IP address for the DHCP Server is to be changed to use a 169.254.1.1 IP address, with a subnet mask of 255.255.255.0, then the LAT should include an IP address range of 169.254.1.0 — 169.254.1.255.

6. Click **Add** to enter the new range in the **Internal IP ranges** box.
7. Click **OK** and exit all dialog boxes.

Viewing Active Internet Sessions

The technology consultant can monitor Proxy Server active sessions via the **Proxy Service Properties** dialog box **Services** tab. Use the steps that follow to view the active Internet sessions.

▶ **To view active Internet sessions**

1. On the **Start** menu, point to **Programs**, **Proxy Server**, then click **Microsoft Management Console** to display the **IIS Console**.
2. In the left pane, double-click the **Internet Information Server** folder.
3. Expand the Server icon, right-click the **Winsock Proxy** service, then click **Properties** to display the following **Winsock Proxy Service Properties** dialog box.

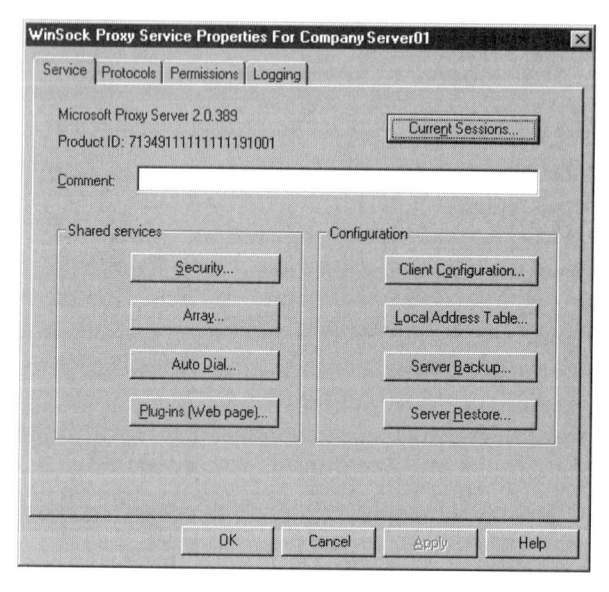

4. On the **Service** tab, click **Current Sessions** to display the following **User Sessions** dialog box.

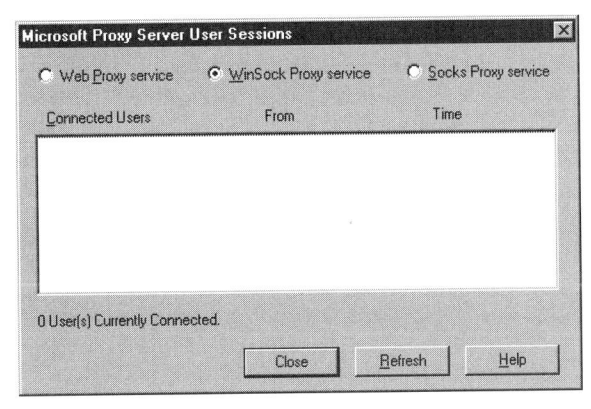

[Microsoft Proxy Server User Sessions dialog box showing options for Web Proxy service, WinSock Proxy service, and Socks Proxy service, with columns for Connected Users, From, and Time. 0 User(s) Currently Connected. Buttons: Close, Refresh, Help.]

5. From here, you can view the users connected to the Internet, their nonroutable IP address, and the time the Internet session started. Select the other radio buttons to view the Internet sessions in progress for each Proxy service. Click **Close** and exit all dialog boxes when finished.

Caching

Caching is enabled by default during Small Business Server setup. It may be manually modified in the **Web Proxy Service Properties** dialog box shown below. Caching helps to minimize the number of Internet accesses on frequently visited sites. However, it is not recommended that small businesses use the **Enable active caching** option, since this results in nonstop dial-ups at regular intervals to the Internet to update the cached sites.

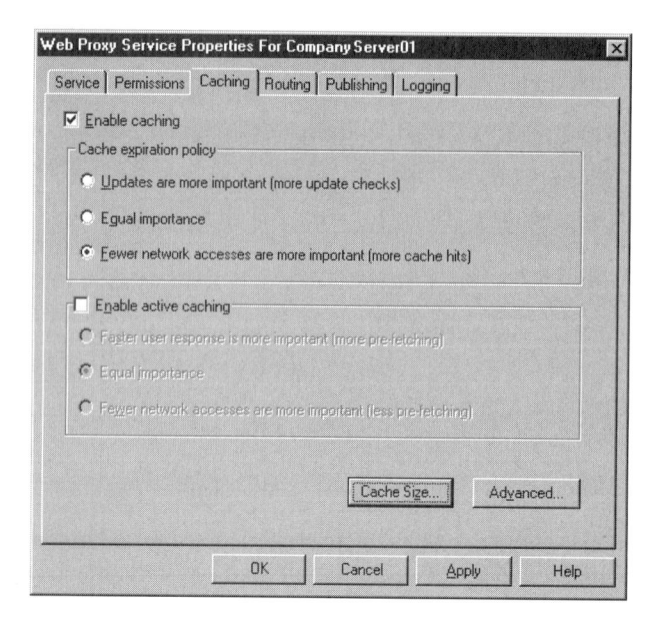

Cache Size

The size of the cache may be limited to conserve disk space. Click **Cache Size** to display the following **Proxy Server Cache Drives** dialog box, then set the cache's maximum size, in megabytes.

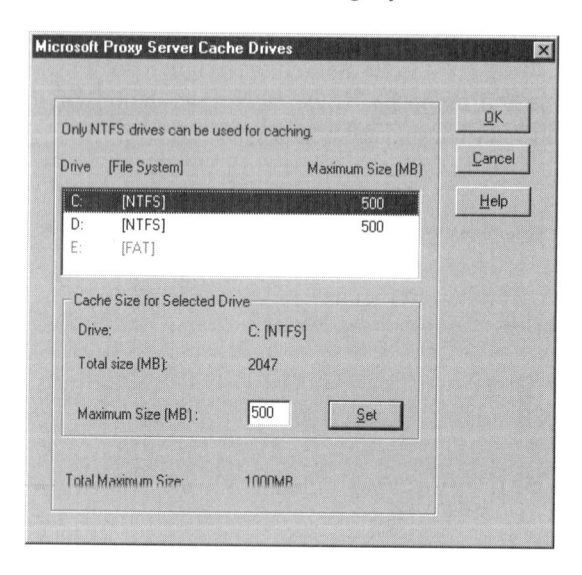

Using FTP

FTP for inbound requests from the Internet is not installed by default in Small Business Server 4.5 setup, although an optional installation procedure is provided in the *Getting Started g*uide. Only FTP Read service is enabled on Small Business Server 4.5 for outbound requests.

In order to use the FTP protocol for inbound requests into the small business network, the FTP service must be installed and the FTP default site properties must be configured. When installed, site properties are accessed in the **IIS Console** by right-clicking on **Default FTP Site** to display the **Properties** dialog box. Refer to the online Help supplied with the service to configure the FTP site. Site properties that must be configured follow.

Note The technology consultant should be aware that using the FTP protocol with a full-time Internet connection to accommodate inbound requests poses a security risk to the small business network. However, this is not an issue for typical Small Business Server installations where the ISP hosts the web site.

- **FTP Site property sheet**. Used for configuring FTP Site identification, maximum connections, and logging.
- **Security Accounts property sheet**. Used for configuring anonymous access and FTP Site operators.
- **Messages property sheet**. Used for configuring welcome, exit, and maximum connection messages.
- **Home Directory property sheet**. Used for configuring home directory and directory listing style.
- **Directory Security property sheet**. Used for configuring access restrictions.

Configuring Performance Monitor Alerts for Proxy Services

Microsoft Proxy Server 2.0 is heavily instrumented for performance counters. Several of these can be set up for Proxy services to monitor Internet-related activities on the server and provide performance data and alerts, meaningful to the small business application. These include performance monitors for the Web Proxy and Winsock Proxy services, which are discussed in this section.

Web Proxy Service Performance Monitor Alerts

Some performance monitor counters for Web Proxy capacity that may be applied to Small Business Server are listed below. Additional performance monitors may be configured using some of the other Web Proxy counters. When choosing other counters in the **Add to Alert** dialog box, click **Explain** for a description of the selected counter. Refer to the "Performance Monitor Tool" section in *Chapter 26, Administrative Tools,* for general information on how to set up a performance monitor alert or refer to the Performance Monitor online Help for more information.

- **Cache Hit Ratio (%)**. The percentage of requests served using cached data, out of the total number of requests to the Web Proxy Server. This statistic can help the technology consultant determine whether caching is being effectively utilized in the small business network. The statistics of this counter indicate the hit rate for objects in the cache. A suggested threshold for this counter is 50 percent. If you have a large number of users and a hit ratio of less than 50 percent, you might consider adding more cache space.

- **DNS Cache Hits (%)**. The percentage of Domain Name Service (DNS) domain names served from the Web Proxy Server cache, from the total of all DNS entries retrieved by the Web Proxy Server. The threshold for this counter should be set close to 90 percent. If the system does not meet this criteria, more DNS cache space may be required.

- **HTTP Requests**. The number of HTTP requests made to the Web Proxy Server. This statistic can give the technology consultant a profile on the number of HTTP requests made by users with permission to access this type of web resource through the Web Proxy service.

- **Current Users**. Number of users currently connected to the Web Proxy Server.

- **Maximum Users**. The maximum number of users connected to the Web Proxy Server simultaneously.

- **Sites Granted**. The total number of Internet sites to which the Web Proxy Server has granted access.

- **Thread Pool Failures**. The number of requests rejected because the thread pool was over committed.

- **Total Cache Fetches**. The total number of requests served by using cached data from the Web Proxy Server cache.

- **Total Requests**. The total number of requests ever made to Web Proxy Server.

Winsock Proxy Service Performance Monitor Alerts

Of all the counters available for the Winsock Proxy service, those described below are the most suitable for setting up performance monitor alerts, while others (discussed in "Other Winsock Proxy Performance Monitors") are better used for informative purposes. Descriptions of how counter thresholds may be applied to the performance monitors are discussed.

- **Active TCP Connections counter**. Registers the total number of active Transmission Control Protocol (TCP) connections currently passing data. Connections that are pending or not yet established are counted elsewhere. This counter provides a more accurate resolution of active connection count than the Active Sessions counter, since with the latter, users are still considered connected for at least 20 minutes after they have actually disconnected from their Internet session. The Active TCP Connections counter registers only users that are actually connected and currently passing data.

   An alert set up for this counter may help the technology consultant detect when there is too much Internet traffic for current modem capacity, thus providing an indication that a faster Internet connection is needed in the small business network. The value for the alert threshold of this counter should be set at a critical point where internet access time starts to become slower than what is tolerable for the network. It may take some experimentation to determine this value, since it is dependent upon variables such as the speed of the modem in use.

- **Active Sessions counter**. Registers the total number of active sessions for WinSock Proxy service. This provides the technology consultant with an indication of the total number of Winsock clients in the network making connections to the Internet, thus helping to develop an overall client Internet usage profile. The value for the threshold of this counter can be set at a level that alerts the technology consultant when a specified number of active connections has been exceeded.

> **Note** The technology consultant can use the Active Sessions counter (or the Active TCP Connections counter) to track extended client Internet sessions or to determine when a client has left their workstation unattended for too long with a live internet connection in progress.

- **DNS Cache Entries counter**. The current number of DNS domain name entries cached by the Web Proxy Server. When DNS names are cached, it allows IP address mapping to be done from the cache (by WINS) without going to a DNS server at the ISP. This saves web site access time for the small business network. The DNS Cache Entries counter registers the number of DNS domain names requested by Small Business Server clients.

  Since the DNS Cache Entries counter contributes to consumption of allocated cache disk space, the technology consultant may want to be notified before too many DNS domain names are cached. To do this configure a performance monitor alert and set the alert threshold for the DNS Cache Entries counter to correspond with the level at which currently allocated cache memory space is near full. Note that cache memory size is allocated using the **Web Proxy Properties** dialog box **Caching** tab.

Other Winsock Proxy Performance Monitors

The counters described below are linked to the Winsock Proxy object. Configuring these counters with an alert is not necessarily meaningful, however, they may be viewed periodically at the discretion of the technology consultant to provide indications of system performance.

- **DNS Cache Hits**. Registers the total number of times a DNS domain name was found in the DNS cache. This identifies the most frequented web sites accessed from the small business network.
- **Pending DNS Resolutions**. Registers the number of gethostbyname and gethostbyaddr API calls pending resolution. These calls are used to resolve host DNS domain names and IP addresses for Winsock Proxy connections. As such, this counter basically indicates how many calls are queued up awaiting to be resolved. This may give the technology consultant an indication when a bottleneck in DNS resolutions is causing an increase in Internet access time for small business network users.
- **Bytes Read/second**. Registers the number of bytes read per second by the data pump. Along with the Bytes Written counter, this gives an overall indication of byte traffic across Winsock Proxy connections.
- **Bytes Written/second**. Registers the number of bytes written per second by the data pump. Along with the Bytes Read counter, this gives an overall indication of byte traffic across Winsock Proxy connections.

Creating Proxy Performance Monitors

Create Proxy performance monitors using the steps that follow. To configure alerts for these performance monitors, follow the procedures generally in "Creating an Alert" in *Chapter 26, Administrative Tools*.

Chapter 27 Administering Small Business Server Components 419

▶ **To create a Proxy performance monitor**

1. On the **Start** menu, point to **Programs**, **Administrative Tools**, then click **Performance Monitor** to display the following **Performance Monitor** utility.

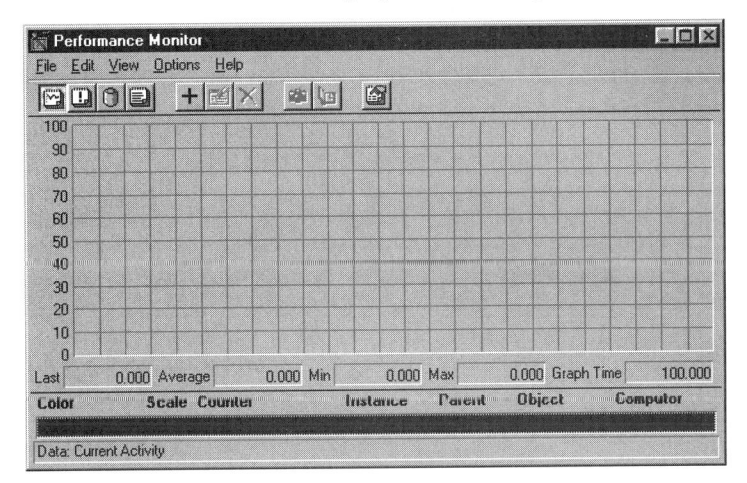

2. On the **Edit** menu, select **Add to Chart** to display the following **Add to Chart** dialog box.

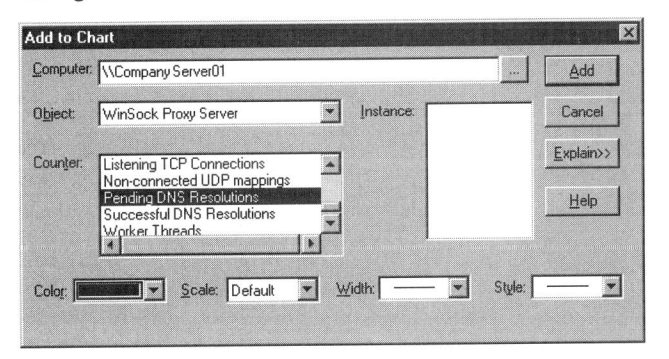

3. Select the Winsock Proxy Server **Object**, then highlight and click **Add** for all counters you want to use. You can add all the counters into one performance monitor since each one is tracked by a different color coding, or you can create separate performance monitors for each counter if desired. When finished, click **Done**.

Note You can configure separate performance monitors for up to 25 network client workstations by browsing for client machines using the **Computer ...** (ellipsis) button. These machines must be running Windows NT Workstation or the Performance Monitor will not work.

4. In **Performance Monitor** chart view, on the **Options** menu, select **Chart** to display the following **Chart Options** dialog box.

5. Customize the chart(s) for the counters you are using, then click **OK**.
6. In the **Add to Chart** dialog box, click **Add** and then **Done** when you are finished. The Performance Monitor will begin registering the counter statistics you configured.
7. On the **File** menu, click **Save Chart Settings** and store the file in a convenient location. Name the file according to its function for ease of identification later. The technology consultant may want to create a desktop folder for easy access to important performance monitors.

Viewing Proxy Performance Monitors

When you want to view an instance of Proxy performance, you can retrieve the performance monitor file you configured using the following steps.

▶ **To view a Proxy performance monitor**

1. On the **Start** menu, point to **Programs**, **Administrative Tools**, then click **Performance Monitor** to display the **Performance Monitor** utility.
2. On the **File** menu, click **Open** to display the following **Performance Monitor - File Open** dialog box.

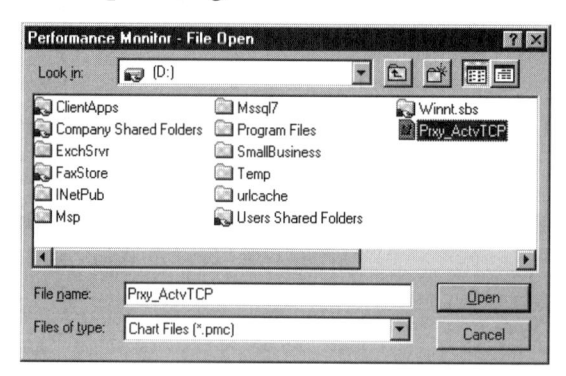

3. Locate the desired Proxy performance monitor in the directory where it was stored, then click **Open**.
4. The Proxy performance monitor will be launched displaying the statistics collected by configured counters.

Proxy Performance Logs

If you want to monitor and assess Proxy performance over a certain period of time, set up a log file using the counters discussed earlier. To do this, the log file must be properly configured. The section "Creating and Viewing Exchange Log Files" earlier in this chapter, contains the general guidelines you need for configuring a Proxy performance monitor log file. When log file creation is complete, leave the Performance Monitor utility up and running to collect the data. When the Performance Monitor is closed, it ceases to collect data on performance counters.

Note Proxy performance monitor logs are not the same as the Proxy logs used to display Proxy reports on the Small Business Server Console (using the **generate Internet reports** taskpad).

SQL Server 7.0

Small Business Server 4.5 is provided with SQL Server™ 7.0. The SQL Server application contains a single database engine that scales to deliver solutions spanning from mobile laptops running Windows 95/98, to small user group applications, all the way up to terabyte symmetric multiprocessor clustering environments. As the small business expands, SQL Server 7.0 easily supports growth in transactions, data handling, and users while maintaining the security and reliability necessary for mission-critical business systems.

Upsizing Access to SQL Server 7.0

The small business may already be using an early version of Microsoft Access as a client database, or may want to create an Access 2000 prototype database using the Microsoft Data Engine (MSDE) before migrating to SQL 7.0. Microsoft Access 2000, included with Office 2000, is a powerful relational database application that targets the desktop category and works best for individuals and workgroups managing data in the order of megabytes. Microsoft Access also allows multiuser access to the same database using file-server architecture (rather than client-server architecture). However, when the small business (using Access 2000 or earlier) encounters one of the following situations, upgrading to SQL Server 7.0 is recommended:

- The database expands to over two GB.
- The database must support a mission-critical application.
- The application's usage grows beyond the individual or small group it was intended to support.
- The data needs to be accessed through the Internet.
- The application requires a more comprehensive security infrastructure.

SQL Server 7.0 resolves these problems for the small business owner. It provides scalability, advanced database management, replication, advanced and easy-to-manage security features, and Web-page building wizards to support the small business application. When migrating data to Microsoft SQL Server 7.0, the small business can continue to use Access as the development environment or the database application can be redeveloped using Visual Studio®.

When expansion to SQL Server 7.0 is imminent, Access 2000 can easily migrate to SQL since MSDE is completely compatible with the SQL Server 7.0 code base. Earlier versions of Access can also migrate to SQL Server 7.0, although an Upsizing Tool is required and some Access functionalities are impaired in the migration.

Small Business Database Scenarios

One of the scenarios below may apply to database planning in the small business network. Depending on the scenario, follow the directives specified below to prepare for implementation of the small business database.

- A new database application will be created using SQL Server 7.0.

    Refer to SQL Server 7.0 online documentation for information on setting up a database and to the SQL Server web site for various white papers at:
    http://www.microsoft.com/sql

- An existing Access database will be migrated over to SQL Server 7.0.

  If an Access database (Office 97 or earlier) exists and you want to migrate to SQL Server 7.0, obtain information about Microsoft's Upsizing Tool at the following web site:
  http://premium.microsoft.com/da_smallbiz/tech/archive/tip_98_0515.htm

  As an alternative to using the Upsizing Tool, you can accomplish a seamless migration of earlier Access applications to SQL Server 7.0, by first upgrading to Access 2000 and then using the Upsizing Wizard included with Microsoft Office 2000. Refer to *Part 8, Migration and Upgrade* of this resource kit for Access 2000 to SQL Server 7.0 migration procedures.

- An existing Btrieve database will be migrated over to SQL Server 7.0.

  Refer to the Microsoft Direct Access web site at the following address to obtain the download for the *Btrieve to SQL Server 7.0 Migration Guide*:
  http://www.microsoft.com/directaccess/prodinfo/sql/btrieve.htm

- Access 2000 will serve as the new database.

  If you are planning to use Access 2000 as your new database in the small business network and future expansion is anticipated, MSDE should be used instead of Jet 4.0. This will better accommodate migration to SQL 7.0 when the small business has expanded to the point where it can utilize the robust features of SQL Server. Refer to *Part 9, Developing Small Business Server Solutions,* of this resource kit, for scalability advantages of using MSDE with Access for application development. Refer to Access 2000 online documentation for setting up a database.

- When you are ready to upsize to SQL Server 7.0, the Access 2000 Upsizing Wizard (available with Microsoft Office 2000) may be used to move Access tables and queries into SQL Server 7.0. Refer to *Part 8, Migration and Upgrade* of this resource kit for Access 2000 migration procedures.

SQL Server 7.0 Administration

Whether you have developed a new database application for SQL Server 7.0 or you have migrated Access to SQL 7.0, all the administrative techniques necessary for a small business implementation are found in the SQL online documentation provided with Small Business Server 4.5.

The online SQL documentation also describes key counter statistics recorded by predefined performance monitors for SQL 7.0. The performance monitors which gather this data are discussed, along with how to set them up for alert notification when critical operating threshold points are exceeded. This enables the technology consultant to oversee the health and status of the server and to be notified of trends in server usage that are problematic.

NTFS and FAT Volume Security

Small Business Server must be installed on a Windows NT File System (NTFS) partition. If you choose to install it on a FAT partition, setup will auto-correct the partition to NTFS. Small Business Server requires NTFS so that permissions can be used to protect individual files. This protection can be applied for access locally (at the workstation or server where the file is stored), or for Internet access. This provides exceptional performance, reliability, networking, and security for file sharing over FAT partitions.

NTFS File and Directory Permissions

On NTFS volumes, you can set access permissions on files and directories that specify the users that are allowed to access the files. NTFS file and directory permissions apply both to users working at the computer where the file is stored and to users accessing the file over the network when the file is in a shared directory.

Share permissions for NTFS volumes work in combination with file and directory permissions. When a directory is shared, the permissions set through the shared directory allows users to connect to the share. Using default permissions (Full Control) for NTFS shared directories, you can manage the security of the files with directory and file permissions.

Note Using "Full Control Permission for Everyone" for all NTFS shared directories is the easiest way to manage NTFS file security. You can apply directory and file permissions and allow share access to Everyone through share permissions. This is also what the Small Business Server Shared Folder Wizard does—it provides added security since, if the share is removed, permissions still exist on the files and directories.

FAT Share Permissions

With volumes that have the FAT file system, you can only protect share directories. Once a directory is shared, you can only protect it by specifying one set of share permissions that applies to the share point and all files underneath, and thus to users who connect to the shared directory over the network. Share permissions are significantly less versatile than the file and directory permissions used for NTFS volumes. File-level protection is not available for FAT volumes.

File and Directory Compression on NTFS Partitions

Files on NTFS volumes (but not FAT volumes) can be compressed and uncompressed using Windows NT Explorer or the Compact command line utility. In Explorer, right-click any directory or file, then click **Properties** to compress or uncompress. The following compression configurations can be set:

- You can compress one file or all files in a directory. Compressing a directory ensures that new files created in the directory are automatically compressed. Uncompressing a directory ensures that new files created in the directory are created uncompressed.

- When you copy a file into a directory or subdirectory within an NTFS volume (or from one NTFS volume to another), the file inherits the compression state of the destination directory.

- When you move a file into a directory or subdirectory within an NTFS volume, the file retains its compression state, regardless of the compression setting of the destination directory.

- When you compress or uncompress a directory, NT Explorer prompts you to indicate whether to compress or uncompress existing subdirectories in the selected directory. Existing subdirectories in compressed or uncompressed directories retain their compression state unless you change it.

- You can highlight compressed files and directories in an alternate color via the Explorer **View** menu **Options**.

Note You can also compress shared folders using the Small Business Server console **manage folder size** taskpad on the **Manage Shared Folders** page.

Microsoft Outlook

Microsoft Outlook 2000, included in the Office 2000 suite of applications, is a messaging and collaboration client for Small Business Server 4.5 users that supports Internet and Microsoft Exchange Server e-mail standards, combining them with integrated calendar, contact, and task-management features. The Exchange Server and Outlook combination is an ideal platform for creating collaborative applications using your existing messaging infrastructure.

Team Interaction

Collaborative applications facilitate team interaction, enabling individuals and teams to do such things as share information, coordinate projects, and conduct online meetings across the network. To help individuals and teams in the Small Business Server network interact, the following information is covered in this section:

- Configuring Outlook with public folders for information sharing.
- Publishing to a public folder.
- Creating discussion groups.
- Testing the discussion group.
- Allowing anonymous access to public folders.
- Setting up group task and contact lists.

Configuring Outlook With Public Folders

Public folders are folders configured for accessibility to small work groups or the entire small business network. They may contain any type of information, including e-mail messages and documents. They are well suited to be accessed by discussion groups in the organization or made public on the Internet. Public folders reside on the Exchange Server, however, they can be synchronized to the local hard drive for offline access. Perform the following steps to create a public folder.

▶ **To create a public folder in Outlook 2000**

1. On the **Start** menu, point to **Programs**, and then click **Microsoft Outlook** to launch the Outlook 2000 application.

2. On the **View** menu, click **Folder List** to display the Outlook **Folder List**, as follows.

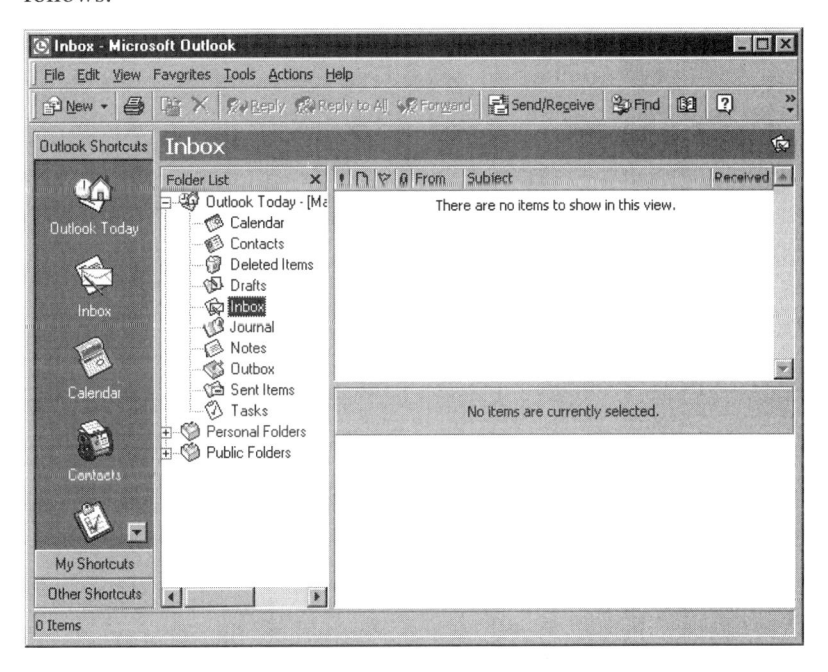

3. Double-click **Public Folders**.

4. Right-click **All Public Folders** and then click **New Folder** to display the following **Create New Folder** dialog box.

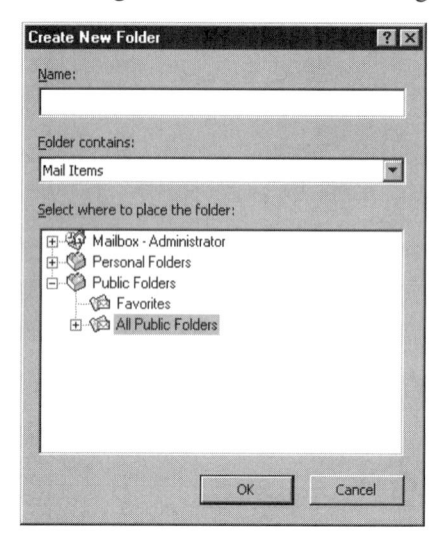

5. In **Name**, type a new folder name.
6. In the **Folder contains** drop-down list, select the type of folder you want.
7. Click **OK**.
8. When asked to add this folder to the Outlook bar, click **Yes**.
9. In the Outlook **Folder List**, right-click the newly created folder and then click **Properties** to display the following **Folder Properties** dialog box.

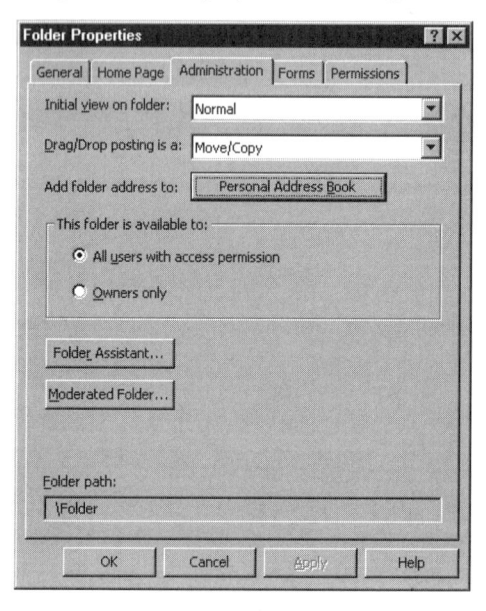

10. On the **Administration** tab, click **Personal Address Book** to add the folder to your personal address book, which is usually your Outlook Contact folder.
11. Click **OK**.

Publishing to a Public Folder

To publish to a public folder, you can either drag and drop to the public folder in the Outlook bar, or send an e-mail to the folder, as described in the following steps.

▶ **To publish to a public folder by dragging and dropping**

1. In Outlook, click **Inbox**.
2. Select a message, then drag and drop it onto the Outlook bar public folder you created in the previous procedure.
3. In the Outlook bar or **Folder List**, click the public folder and verify that the message appears there.

Note You can drag and drop any type of item to the public folder, including Word documents.

▶ **To publish to a public folder by sending an e-mail**

1. On the Outlook **Actions** menu, click **New Mail Message** to display the following **Untitled - Message** dialog box.

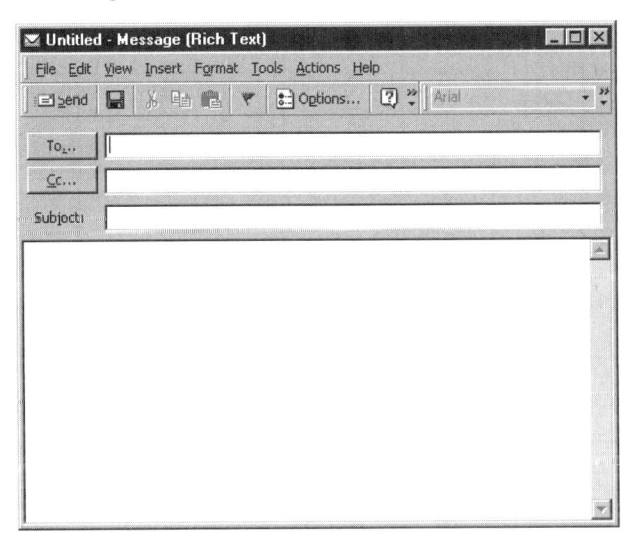

2. Compose a message and fill in the **Subject**.

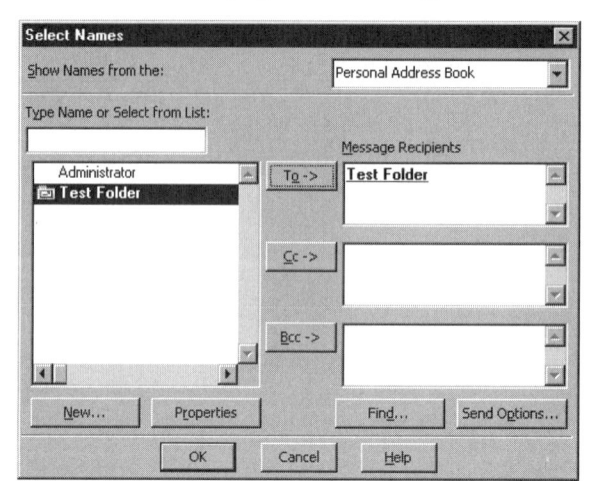

3. Click **To** which displays the following **Select Names** dialog box.

4. In the **Show names from the:** drop-down list, select **Personal Address Book**.
5. From the list, select the public folder to which you are publishing, then click **To**.

> **Note** If the public folder you want to publish to does not appear in the list, make sure the address book is configured to keep personal addresses in the Personal Address Book. You do this from the **Addressing** dialog box—from the Outlook 2000 **Tools** menu, click **Address Book** to display the **Address Book** dialog box. From the **Address Book Tools** menu, click **Options** to display the **Addressing** dialog box.

6. Click **OK**.
7. In the **Message** dialog box, click **Send** to route the message.
8. In the Outlook bar or **Folder List**, click the public folder and verify that the message appears there.

Creating a Discussion Group

Discussion groups allow users to collaborate and share information. They can also be used to host list servers and knowledge bases for use by co-workers, business partners, and customers. Discussion groups are accessed using any Internet newsreader, a Web browser, or with Outlook itself.

> **Note** The Network News Transfer Protocol (NNTP) connector must be configured on Exchange Server to allow anonymous client access for reading and posting Internet news articles in public folders. Refer to the Exchange Administrator online Help for information on configuring the NNTP properties.

Perform the following steps to create a discussion group.

▶ **To create a discussion group in Outlook**

1. On the **Start** menu, point to **Programs**, and then click **Microsoft Outlook** to launch the Outlook 2000 application.
2. On the **View** menu, click **Folder List** to display the Outlook **Folder List**.
3. On the **File** menu, point to **Folder**, then click **New Folder** to display the following **Create New Folder** dialog box.

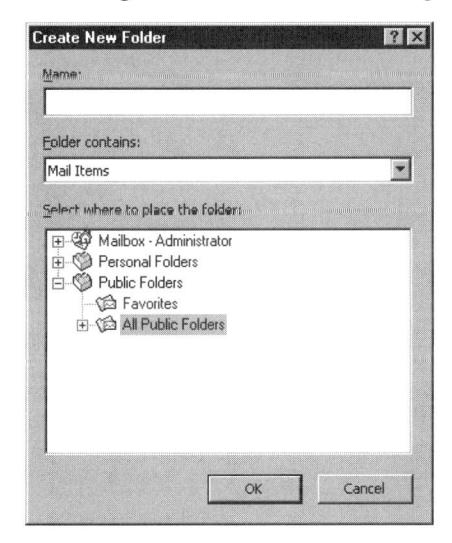

4. In **Name**, type a name for your discussion group.
5. In the **Folder contains** drop-down list, select **Mail Items**.
6. Click **OK**.
7. When asked to add this folder to the Outlook bar, click **Yes**.

▶ **To configure the discussion group on Exchange Server**

1. If you are not logged on as the Administrator, on the **Start** menu, click **Shutdown** and then select **Close all programs and logon as a different user**.
2. Enter the administrator password, then click **OK**.

3. On the **Start** menu, point to **Programs**, **Microsoft Exchange**, and then click **Microsoft Exchange Administrator** to display the following **Microsoft Exchange Administrator** utility.

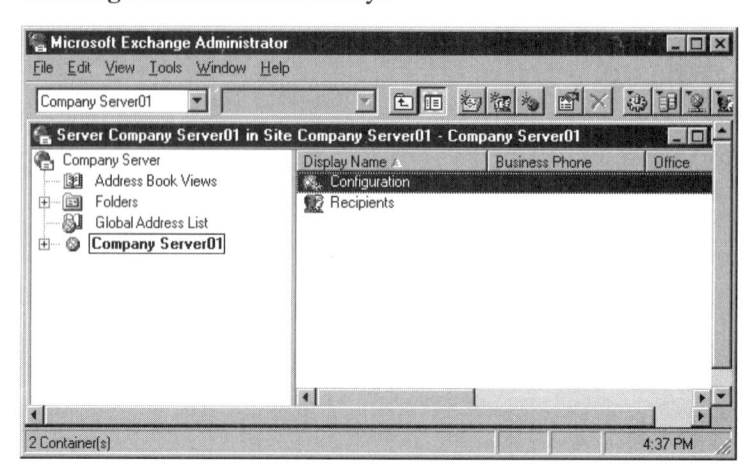

4. On the **Tools** menu, click **Newsgroup Hierarchies** to display the following **Newsgroup Hierarchies** dialog box.

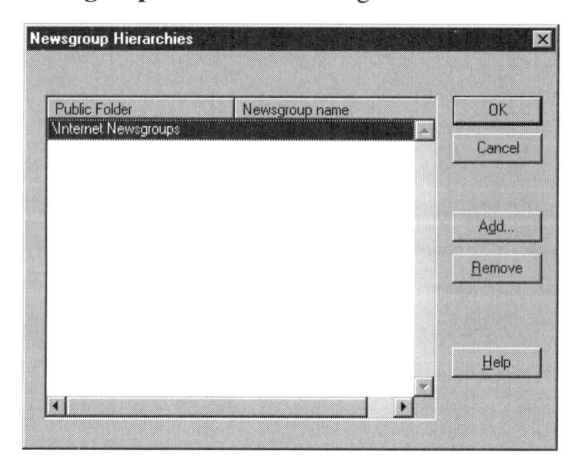

5. Click **Add** to display the following **Add Newsgroup Hierarchy** dialog box.

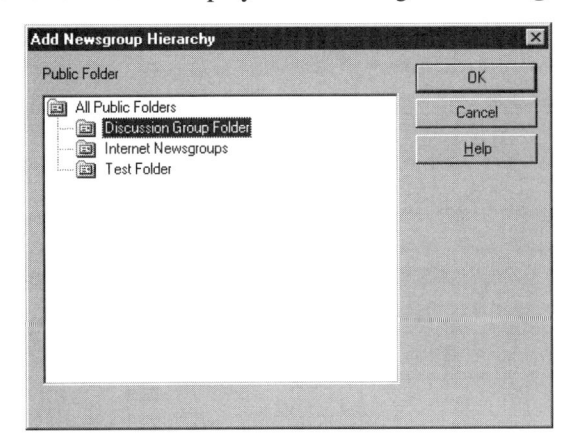

6. Select your discussion group folder, then click **OK**.
7. If necessary, add a newsgroup name in the **Root Newsgroup Name** dialog box. Click **OK**. Your discussion group folder should now appear in the Public Folder list in the **Newsgroup Hierarchies** dialog box.
8. Click **OK**.
9. On the **File** menu of **Exchange Administrator**, click **Exit**.

Testing the Discussion Group

You can test the discussion group you just created by posting messages to the discussion group folder, using the following steps.

▶ **To test the discussion group**

1. On the Outlook **View** menu, click **Folder List**.
2. From the Folder **List**, double-click **Public Folders**, **All Public Folders**, then select the discussion group folder created in the previous procedure.

3. Click **New** above the Outlook bar to display the following **Untitled - Discussion** dialog box.

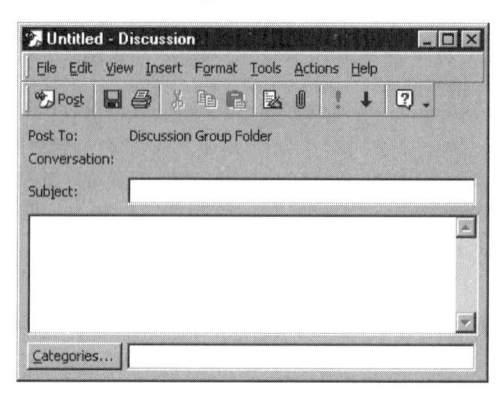

4. Create several messages with different subject fields. To do so, on the **Actions** menu, click **New Post in this Folder** when you want to open more **Untitled - Discussion** dialog boxes.

5. Click **Post** in each open **Discussion** dialog box and observe that postings are automatically filtered by message topic.

6. On the Outlook **View** menu, point to **Current View** and then click **By Conversation Topic** to group the postings according to conversation topic, as shown below.

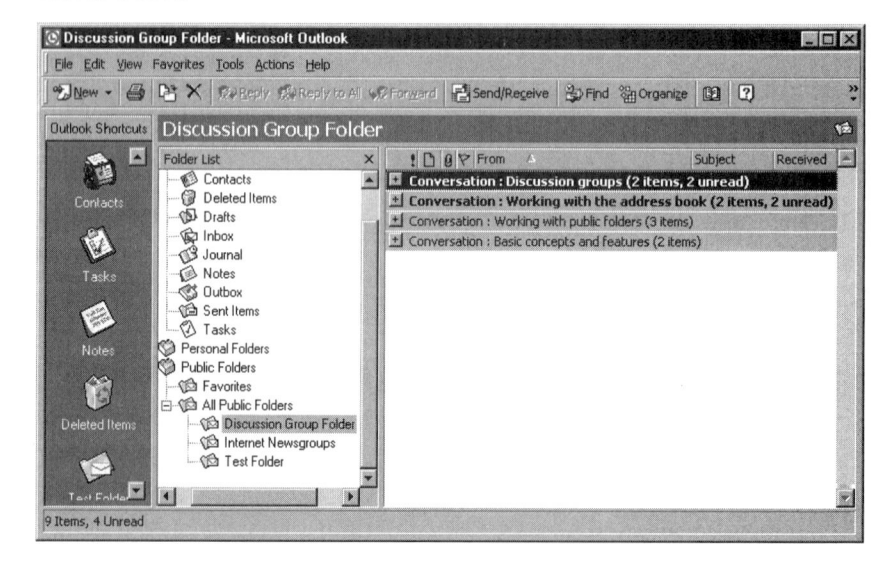

Allowing Anonymous Access to Public Folders

In order to open a discussion group to customers of the small business and other users on the Internet, you must allow anonymous access to the public folder. With anonymous access, users do not need a Windows NT account on Small Business Server to participate in discussions. To allow anonymous user access to Microsoft Exchange Server public folders, perform the following steps.

▶ **To configure anonymous user access to public folders**

1. On the Outlook **View** menu, click **Folder List**.
2. From the **Folder List**, double-click **Public Folders**, **All Public Folders**, then right-click the discussion group folder to display the following **Folder Properties** dialog box.

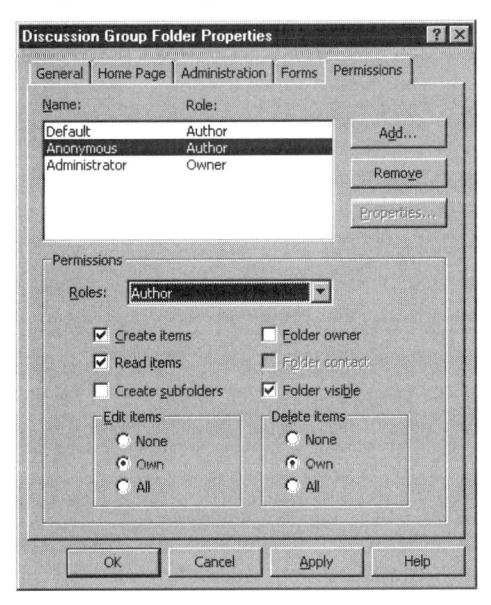

3. On the **Permissions** tab, select **Anonymous**.
4. In the **Roles** drop-down list, select **Author**.
5. Click **Apply** and then **OK**.

Before anonymous users can access a public folder, the Exchange Server's **HTTP Site Settings Properties** must be configured with a shortcut to the public folder, by following the steps below.

▶ **To configure public folder shortcuts on the Exchange Server**

1. On the **Start** menu, point to **Programs**, **Microsoft Exchange**, and then click **Microsoft Exchange Administrator**.
2. Double-click **Configuration** and then in the **Display Name** pane, double-click the **Protocols** object.
3. Double-click **HTTP (Web) Site Settings** to display the **HTTP (Web) Site Settings Properties** dialog box.
4. On the **General** tab, select **Allow anonymous users to access the anonymous public folders**.
5. On the **Folder Shortcuts** tab, click **New** to display the **Public Folders** dialog box.
6. Select the appropriate public folder for anonymous access.
7. Click **OK** and exit all open dialog boxes.

Note Including only the Public Folder tree object will not provide anonymous access to any of the top level public folders.

▶ **To verify anonymous user access to the discussion group folder**

1. On the **Start** menu, point to **Programs**, and then click **Internet Explorer** to launch your Internet Explorer 5.0 web browser.
2. In the Add**ress** field, type *http://CompanyServerName/Exchange* to display the following **Outlook Web Access** page.

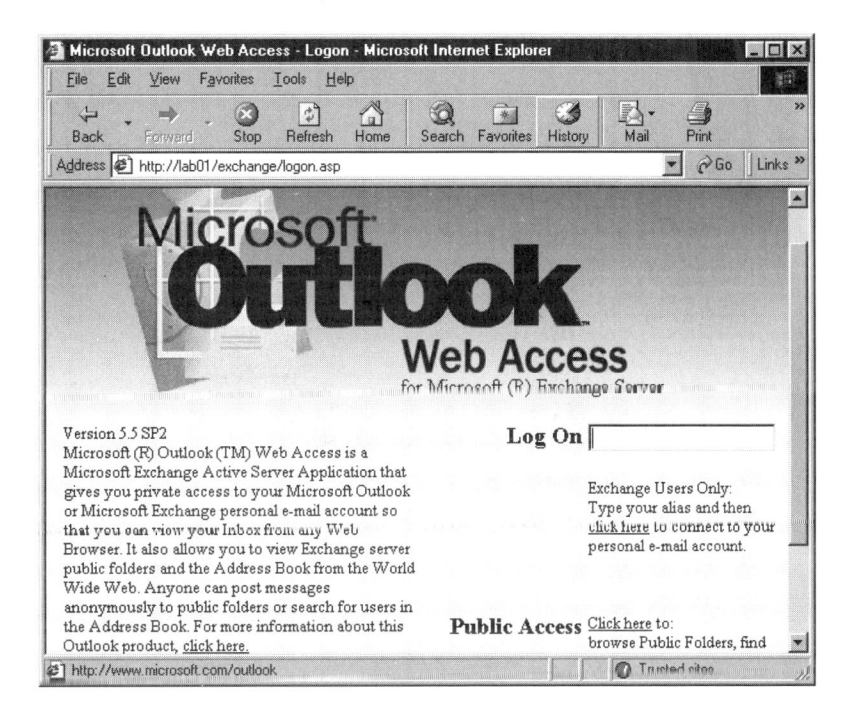

Chapter 27 Administering Small Business Server Components 437

3. Click **click here** to display the following Outlook **All Public Folders** view.

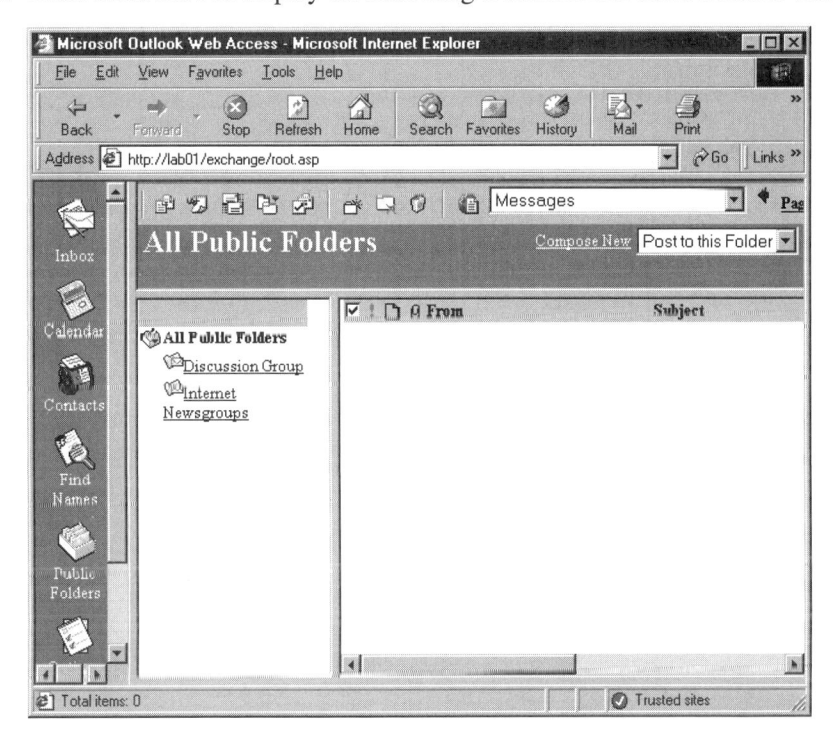

4. Click the public discussion group folder you created with anonymous access.
5. In the **Compose New** drop-down list, select **Posting to this Folder** to post a message to the discussion group folder.
6. Click **Compose New** to display the following **New Post - Microsoft Internet Explorer** dialog box.

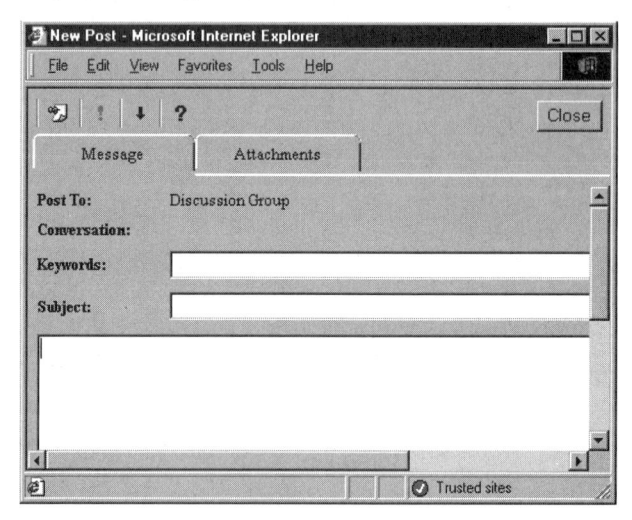

7. Complete the above posting form, then click the **Post** icon under the **File** menu.
8. Verify that the posted message appears in the Outlook discussion group folder.

Note For troubleshooting information on Outlook Web Access, refer to the white paper *Troubleshooting Guide for Outlook Web Access* at the following location: **http://support.microsoft.com/support/exchange/content/whitepapers/owa_tshoot.asp**

Setting Up Group Task Lists and Contact Databases

Public folders can be used to host other shared information such as task and contact lists, thus creating easy ways for users or groups to manage projects or contact databases. Perform the following steps to set up a group task list and a contact database.

▶ **To configure Outlook for a group task list**

1. On the **Start** menu, point to **Programs**, and then click **Microsoft Outlook** to launch the Outlook 2000 application.
2. On the **View** menu, click **Folder List** to display the Outlook **Folder List**.
3. From the **Folder List**, double-click **Public Folders**, then single-click **All Public Folders**.

4. On the **File** menu, point to **New** and then click **Folder** to display the following **Create New Folder** dialog box.

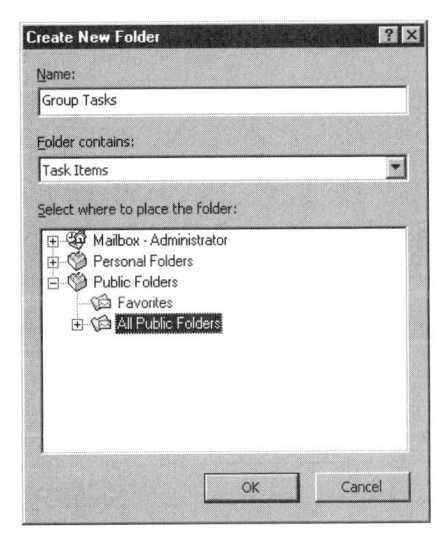

5. In **Name**, type *Group Tasks*.
6. In the **Folder Contains** drop-down list, select **Task Items**.
7. Click **OK**.
8. When asked to add this folder to the Outlook bar, click **Yes**.

▶ **To create a group task in Outlook**

1. On the Outlook bar, click **Group Tasks** to display the Outlook **Group Tasks** list.
2. On the **File** menu, point to **New**, and then click **Task** to display the following **Untitled - Task** dialog box.

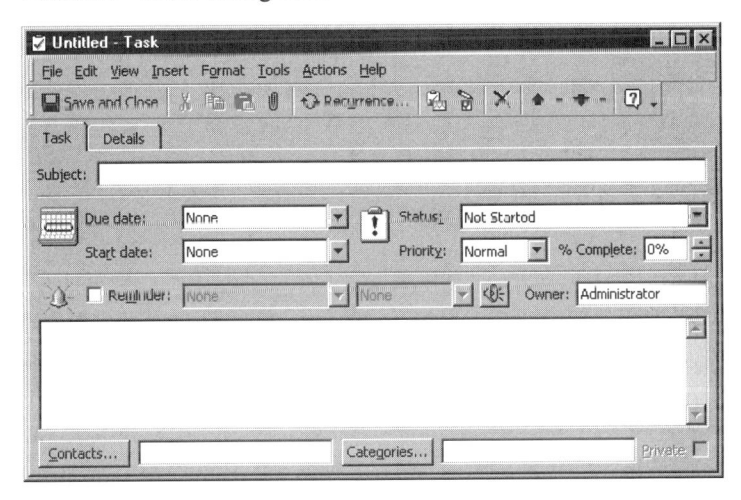

3. Enter all appropriate information and type a task name in **Subject**.
4. Click **Save and Close**.
5. Verify that the task appears in the following Outlook **Group Tasks** folder.

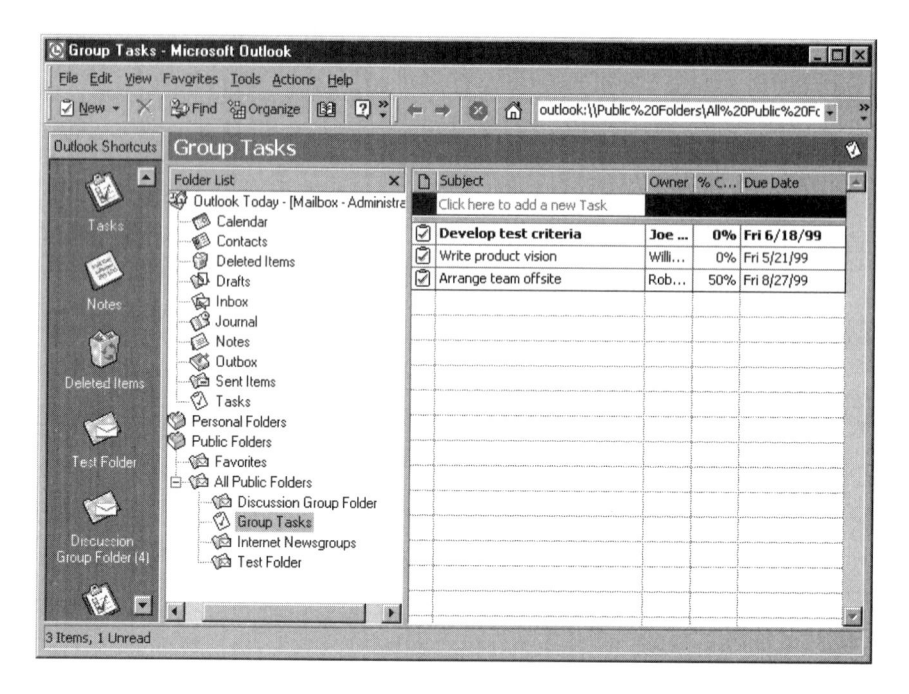

▶ **To configure Outlook for a group contact database**

1. On the **Start** menu, point to **Programs**, and then click **Microsoft Outlook** to launch the Outlook 2000 application.
2. On the **View** menu, click **Folder List** to display the Outlook **Folder List**.
3. From the **Folder List**, double-click **Public Folders**, and then single-click **All Public Folders**.

4. On the **File** menu, point to **New**, and then click **Folder** to display the following **Create New Folder** dialog box.

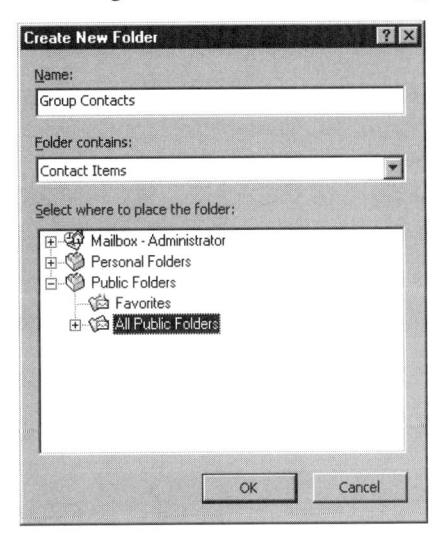

5. In **Name**, type *Group Contacts*.
6. In the **Folder Contains** drop-down list, select **Contact Items**.
7. Click **OK**.
8. When asked to add this folder to the Outlook bar, click **Yes**.

▶ **To create a group contact in Outlook**

1. On the Outlook bar, click **Group Contact** to display the Outlook **Group Contacts** list.
2. On the **File** menu, point to **New**, and then click **Contact** to display the following **Untitled - Contact** dialog box.

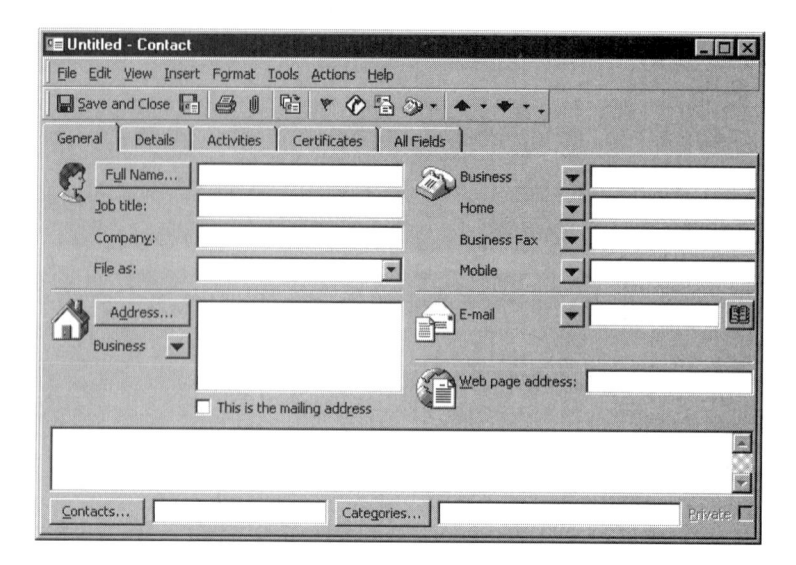

3. Type in all appropriate information, including a contact name.
4. Click **Save and Close**.
5. In the Outlook **Group Contacts** list, verify that the new contact appears.

Note If you want to define permissions for the **Group Contact** list, right-click the **Group Contact** folder, click **Properties**, and then select the **Permissions** tab.

More Information

For additional information on collaborative solutions with Microsoft Exchange and Outlook, refer to the *Introduction to Collaboration* white paper at the following web site:
http://www.microsoft.com/exchange/55/whpprs/collab.htm

CHAPTER 28

Background Information for Administrators

This chapter provides supplemental background information for the technology consultant, on unique components found in Microsoft® BackOffice® Small Business Server 4.5 that can be used to enhance the performance of the small business network.

Windows NT Server Internet Connection Services for RAS

The Microsoft Windows NT® Server operating system provides multiprotocol remote access features for small business networks using traditional dial-up networking over the public telephone network and secure virtual private networking (VPN) on the Internet. To better accommodate a mobile or remote workforce, the small business owner can simplify employee remote access and reduce remote access costs while still maintaining network security with Internet Connection Services (ICS).

The new ICS included in the Windows NT 4.0 Option Pack, contains enhancements to the current Windows NT 4.0 Server Remote Access Service (RAS). These enhancements enable the small business to reduce remote access costs through customizable client software, centrally managed phone book services, integrated authentication services, and simple administrative tools.

If you wish to use ICS, you must install the service since it is not installed by default with Small Business Server setup. You can locate this service in the Windows NT 4.0 Option Pack setup using the following path on Small Business Server installation Disc 2:

    <Diskdrive>\Ntoptpak\En\Winnt.srv\Setup

Benefits of ICS

Windows NT Server 4.0 ICS can be employed to implement an economical communication infrastructure that takes advantage of the Internet and ISP services. These technologies can also be used to lower the total cost of remote access services by outsourcing remote access hardware, administration, and support to an ISP. For a small business, the benefits of implementing ICS include improved client productivity, lower access fees, and centralized management of network access point phone numbers.

ICS Components

ICS for RAS includes the following four components:

- Microsoft Connection Manager
- Connection Manager Administration Kit
- Internet Authentication Services
- Connection Point Services

ICS Component Descriptions

Each of the ICS components listed above have important features that encompass the functionality of ICS. Descriptions of these features are contained in the sections that follow. For implementations of ICS services, go to the **Start** menu, **Programs** group, and consult the Windows NT 4.0 Option Pack online product documentation.

Microsoft Connection Manager

Microsoft Connection Manager (CM) is a new versatile client dialer with an intuitive custom user interface for connecting to network resources on either a public network or securely connecting to private networks over the Internet. This eliminates the need for users to manage their access configuration, including their dial-in and VPN access numbers. CM runs on top of Dial-Up Networking and simplifies the network access experience through use of the following features.

- **Automated wizard assistance**. The CM includes a set of step-by-step wizards which are automatically launched should a novice client inadvertently corrupt their custom Dial-Up Networking (DUN) configuration. These wizards make each client more self-sufficient, which lowers support costs. Integrated wizards include modem setup and DUN, including Point-to-Point Tunneling Protocol (PPTP) Setup and default network protocol installation.

- **Transparent support for PPTP**. In association with the Connection Manager Administration Kit (CMAK), the CM client supports the presentation of standard direct dial phone numbers and Point of Presence (POP) phone numbers (ISP dial-in numbers). The POP phone numbers can be preconfigured with the CMAK to be associated with secure (PPTP) connections to the small business network.

  This transparent dual-dial support for secure connections over the Internet ensures that novice users can make secure connections in a simple manner. This feature enables ISP/Netops and Corporations to provide simple and secure VPN Services.

- **Phone book**. The CM supports the clear presentation of both POP phone books (Internet access numbers) and private dedicated or leased line phone numbers in an integrated or segmented manner by country, state, and region.

  This simple interface ensures that each client will have immediate access to the correct access number. In addition, this dual support allows for hybrid network implementations and allows corporations to choose the most economical remote access method.

- **Password support**. The CM provides support for both an Internet logon password as well as a private network password.

- **Auto redial/disconnect support**. Support for automatic redial enables remote clients to automate the dial-up procedure so that manual launch on each dial attempt is not required. Similarly, automated support for connection termination in response to inactivity prevents over billing and access line tie up.

- **Multiple service profiles support**. The CM is a single host executable on the client that can support multiple custom service profiles. For example, a client can have a custom VPN icon on their desktop and a custom ISP/Netop icon. Each icon could represent different attributes with its own custom configuration. This model has the benefit of streamlining the size of subsequent downloads of Service profiles since the CM code does not have to be included.

Connection Manager Administration Kit

The CMAK is basically a step-by-step wizard that creates connection information tailored for individual employees. This connection information (called a Service profile) supports the appending of an application to create what is called the Installation Package. When installed on the PC, the Service profile merges with the resident CM dialer to enable the employee or subscriber to connect to a public or private network.

The CMAK component allows the technology consultant or ISP to preconfigure connection manager clients. Preconfiguration both improves the user experience (especially for novice users) and reduces support costs. The benefits provided by CMAK are realized by utilizing the following features:

- **Icons (Desktop, Tray)**. CMAK supports the customization of both a desktop icon and a taskbar tray icon. The tray icon can be configured as an interface to additional applications distributed by the ISP. This functionality enables the small business to increase the visibility of branded network access to the desktop and facilitate access to additional applications or higher margin network/ application services.

- **Animated Dialer logon screen**. Support for animation in the dialer interface and keys for integration with connection status allows the ISP (Netop or Corporation) to communicate to the client in a graphic manner using branding or connection status information. This allows the service provider to create advertising or provide notification of new services while the connection process takes place.

- **Create an integrated custom phone book**. CMAK integrates phone books generated with the Phone Book Administrator tool of the Connection Point Services (discussed later in this chapter). This can include POP and RAS (dedicated line) access numbers from multiple service providers. These numbers are accessed through the easily navigated user interface of the CM so remote client employees will always have a local phone number for network access at their fingertips. CMAK also enables the client phone book to be graphically branded for clear communication of the service provider or the partnership alliance that provides the access infrastructure.

- **Interface support for multiple service types**. Specification of multiple service types enables the ISP to clearly communicate to the end user information about the nature of the service to which they are connected. This ability also enables the ISP to segment their access services and the associated POPs that provide those services, so they can offer various access services at different price points.

- **Connect actions**. Connect actions are client events that are preconfigured to occur by the technology consultant. These events are keyed upon the onset or termination of network services.

    Automated phone book updates. The automated updating of the client's resident POP/RAS phone book is a connect action. This update downloads new POP/RAS information (incrementally) upon initiation of logon, if needed. This feature ensures that each client will always have an updated version of a phone book and economical network access via a local POP.

Auto-applications. Auto-applications are connect actions configured to automatically launch or close resident applications upon the start or end of a connection. This allows the technology consultant to facilitate the use of their services by launching a browser or other resident application (e-mail client) upon logon and closing that application upon termination of the connection.

- **License agreement**. An ISP may choose to create special licensing arrangements for VPN services. Also, corporations may want to inform their employees of their responsibilities, duties, and obligations to the corporation regarding confidentiality of information. For this reason (and since the ISP may wish to append their own proprietary application to custom service profiles) the CMAK supports the appending and distribution of custom contracts to the client.

- **Connection status**. The CM interface can be configured to keep the client informed of the connection status with specific terminology. This feature can be coupled with animation support to keep each client informed of the connection status at all times. This relieves any uncertainties that may be experienced during the time that the connection is being established.

- **Support phone number**. Quality of service and support is critical to maintenance of employee productivity and subscriber satisfaction. The CMAK configures the CM interface for the specification of a support phone number at the logon screen. This ensures that the client will always have a support phone number available and also facilitates the outsourcing of support services to reduce total costs of network ownership.

- **Custom Help file**. The CMAK allows for a custom Help file in the Service profile.

- **Language support**. Service profiles can be easily created in multiple languages including English, French, German and Spanish and Japanese.

- **Automatic password**. The technology consultant can use the CMAK to specify if end users passwords can be saved for either Internet access or access to the small business network. This functionality can be enabled or disabled depending on the security policy of the organization or ISP.

- **Realm name prefix/suffix**. Many service providers require the appending of some very specific syntax to logon to their servers. Non-intuitive logon script results in end-user frustration and support calls. The CMAK tool allows the technology consultant to preconfigure the realm name (@bigco.com) and either the prefix or the suffix extensions to facilitate the provision of basic internet access and VPN services. This is implemented by allowing the client to enter in a simple memorable user ID.

- **Transparent web application integration.** The CMAK supports the automated and transparent authentication of a client off the central membership database of Microsoft Site Server or the Microsoft Commercial Internet System upon logon. This functionality enables clients to seamlessly log on to the Internet or to a host of highly integrated and scalable web application servers.
- **Assignment of secure connections.** The CMAK allows a technology consultant to associate a PPTP configuration status with each POP phone number. PPTP is an encapsulation technology provided in Windows NT Server that enables multiprotocol portability, including Internet Packet Exchange/Sequenced Packet Exchange (IPX/SPX), Network Basic Enhanced User Interface (NetBEUI), and Transmission Control Protocol/Internet Protocol (TCP/IP), and IP addressing of packets for transmission across the Internet. Windows NT Server also provides for 128-bit and 40-bit encryption of packet data for additional security of the encapsulated data. Refer to the "Internet Authentication Services" section for data on available authentication protocols.
- **Append an application.** The CMAK allows the technology consultant to append applications to the custom Service profile information in the creation of an Installation Package. This enables the technology consultant to ensure that the client at the receiving end has all the software and information they need to immediately engage in VPN activity. Examples of software that can be included in the Installation Package include the following:

    Connection Manager. The dialer itself can be included.

    Internet Browser. The CMAK and the CM are both browser-independent technologies.

    Note Using the Internet Explorer Administration Kit (IEAK) and the CMAK together, a corporation or ISP can provide a seamlessly integrated branded experience. This end-to-end branding starts from the first click of the desktop icon, continues with the automated launch of resident applications (browser, e-mail), and ends with termination of the network session.

    Additional files. Any application or files can be appended to the Service profile if total file size of a network distribution model should be considered.
- **Edit existing service profiles.** The CMAK allows for the editing of preexisting service profiles so the technology consultant does not need to re-enter data when service profiles change only in a minor fashion.

Internet Authentication Services

The Internet Authentication Services (IAS) is new addition to the core Windows NT Server networking RAS. It uses Remote Authentication Dial-In User Service (RADIUS) protocol to provide remote authentication, authorization, and accounting services. These services can be used to allow remote clients to connect to the small business LAN via an ISP network access server (NAS) from local access points around the world. IAS has the following features:

- **Authentication**. IAS ensures that the person who is seeking Internet access has a valid account by comparing the user's password to a known value in a central database. This database can reside at either the ISP or the small business location (remote management is possible).

- **Authorization**. IAS enables the ISP to tailor the access service for a specific logon policy (for the ISP or small business).

- **Accounting services**. IAS enables the ISP to track network usage. The small business authentication database, also known as the back end, can maintain or forward accounting data to the ISP's server for verification of its billing or tracking systems. By keeping track of network usage statistics, IAS can provide valuable data for more efficient planning of network services.

- **Support for multiple authentication protocols**. IAS supports a variety of authentication protocols offering different degrees of protection against password theft and impersonation. IAS supports RADIUS, Asynchronous NetBEUI for Windows 3.11 client support, MD4-CHAP and MD5-CHAP for Windows 95 and NTW client support, Password Authentication Protocol (PAP), and Shiva's SPAP.

- **Interoperability**. IAS provides network access server vendor independence through the use of the RADIUS standard. IAS is compatible with proposed IETF RADIUS standards and with market leading vendors of network access servers that support RADIUS.

- **RADIUS Attributes Editor**. IAS provides editing tools that allow for adding new attributes within the RADIUS paradigm to accommodate new technologies. This tool provides support for vendor specific attributes and non-standard RADIUS attributes to insure compatibility with network investments.

- **Authentication provider support**. With IAS, RADIUS can seamlessly communicate with Small Business Server 4.5, ensuring compatibility and allowing integration of RADIUS and Windows-based environments.

- **Authentication templates**. IAS provides the ability to create Authentication profiles which specify the sites or gateways a given client is permitted to access. These profiles can be edited as needed to accommodate the changing needs of the small business organization.

Connection Point Services

The Connection Point Services (CPS) component provides phone book services. It automatically aggregates access numbers from multiple disparate sources and provides a single updated list to the CM client in a transparent manner. Access numbers can be dedicated access lines or VPN access points. In addition to facilitating network access and improving end-user satisfaction, the technology consultant can easily expand or contract network access points, accommodate acquisitions, and more easily enter into peering arrangements with other network providers. The phone book server can be centrally managed either by the technology consultant or the ISP.

- **Phone Book Service**. Phone Book Service is a core Windows NT Server-network service running on the Internet Information Server (IIS). IIS compares a client's resident connection configuration with the most recent files available on the server and downloads the appropriate phone book updates. Key features of the Phone Book Service include the following:

    Client integration. Tight integration of the CM client enables the CPS to validate and automatically (incrementally) update each client's access and connect options. This centralized administration and control reduces distribution and support costs, and also improves the flexibility with which a company can expand their network and quickly service new needs.

    Secure remote administration. To ensure secure remote management, the Phone Book administration tool can be placed behind a firewall. In this configuration, update information is posted through the firewall to the server by the administration tool. For more information on Microsoft firewall and caching solutions, refer to the following web site:
    http://www.microsoft.com/proxy

- **Phone Book Administrator**. Phone Book Administrator is an administrative tool that facilitates the creation and integration of multiple phone books. It also updates the phone book database and posts new phone book information to the IIS-based CPS. Key features of the Phone Book Administrator include the following:

    Customized database. This feature enables the ability to create a phone book database containing customized information about your POPs/RAS. This allows the small business or ISP to more explicitly define which service types they provide to the remote subscriber. Segmentation of services can occur along organization or technical lines. For example, competing vendors of 56 K modems require specific assignments of POP/RAS for each vendor's equipment. A corporation or ISP can easily associate the correct POP/RAS with a host of access numbers through this interface. Then, they can provide supplemental information in the dialer interface or custom help file to reduce support calls and improve the end-user experience.

Simple archiving. Since network access can be mission critical, it is necessary that all information be archived on a regular basis. In addition, a small business organization may want highly segmented phone book services. For these reasons the Phone Book Administrator provides for easy archiving of backup copies of phone book data.

Simple administration. Similar to the CMAK, the Phone Book Administrator allows editing of existing phone books. This enables the technology consultant to fine-tune their access policies simply and efficiently.

Data compression. For the best throughput and highest degree of scalability, the Phone Book Administrator enables the compression of phone book data before posting to the server. By minimizing the size of phone book files and supporting incremental updates, the periodic client downloads of phone book data is made transparent to the end-user. Windows NT Server also natively supports compression with Microsoft Point to Point Compression (MPPC). Using MPPC to compress transmitted data improves throughput and performance. To see how you can further improve network responsiveness through caching see the following web site:
http://www.microsoft.com/proxy

CHAPTER 29

Administrative Tips and Other Information

This chapter provides useful tips for Microsoft® BackOffice® Small Business Server administration.

Simplifying Client Disk Defragmentation

Disk defragmentation is a simple process that can be quickly accomplished if done on a regular basis. It is usually more difficult to convince users to take a few minutes at least once a week to run the program, particularly if their workstations have multiple drives. One of the easiest ways to increase the performance of a Windows® 95 workstation is to use the built-in system tool known as Disk Defragmenter. The material in this section allows the technology consultant to set up a disk defragging process that Windows 95 clients in the small business network can perform in one simple step. The information here may be applied to an NT Workstation as well, if Disk Defragmenter is installed and you know the logical path to it.

Note Disk Defragmenter is not included with Windows NT® Workstation.

Creating a Context Menu Option

In order to make the defragging process seamless, a Quick Defrag option can be added to the context menu appearing when right-clicking a disk in **My Computer**. To accomplish this, follow the steps below.

▶ **To add the Quick Defrag option to your context menu**

1. Open Windows Explorer.
2. On the **View** menu, click **Folder Options** to display the following **Folder Options** dialog box.

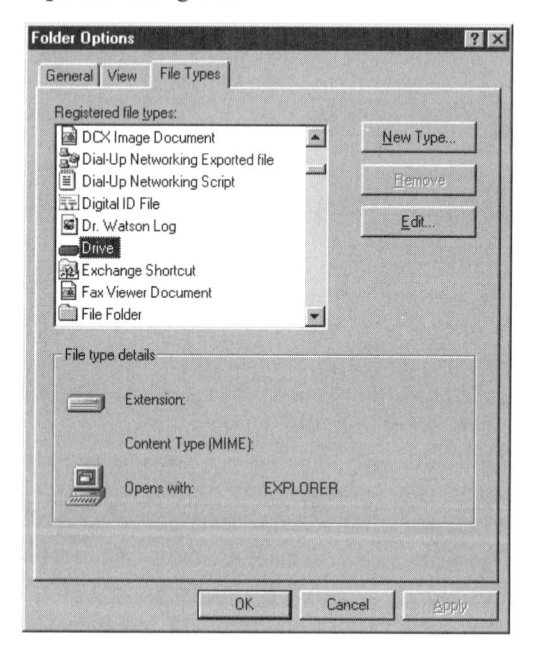

3. Select the File **Types** tab, and then scroll through the **Registered File Types** list and select the **Drive** icon.

4. After the Drive file type is selected, click **Edit** to display the following **Edit File** dialog box. This allows you to add the defrag action to the Drive file type.

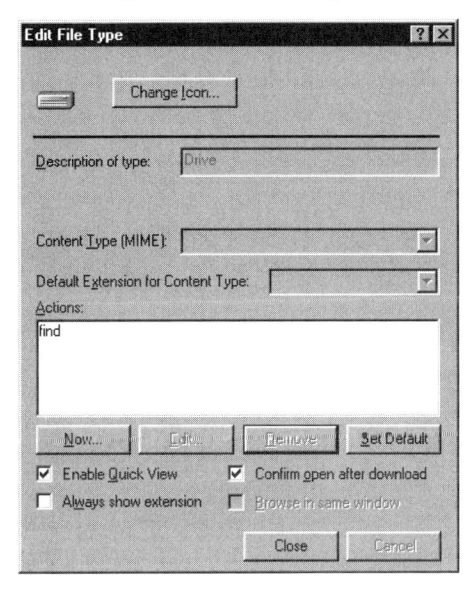

Note In the **Actions** list box, **Find** appears. Also, **Scan for Viruses** will appear only if you have antivirus software installed.

5. Click **New** to display the following **New Action** dialog box.

6. In the **Action** text box, type *Quick Defrag* to name the context menu command.
7. To associate the Quick Defrag process with an application, type *C:\WINDOWS\DEFRAG.EXE "%1" /NOPROMPT* in the **Application Used to Perform Action** text box.
8. Click **OK**.

Note The *NOPROMPT* switch at the end of *DEFRAG.EXE* causes Disk Defragmenter to start immediately on the selected drive and to exit as soon as it has finished. The user will not be prompted for any confirmations.

Using the Quick Defrag Option

To use the Quick Defrag menu option you just created, from **My Computer** or Windows Explorer, right-click on the drive to be defragmented, then click **Quick Defrag**. The Disk Defragmenter begins automatically and no other user interaction is required.

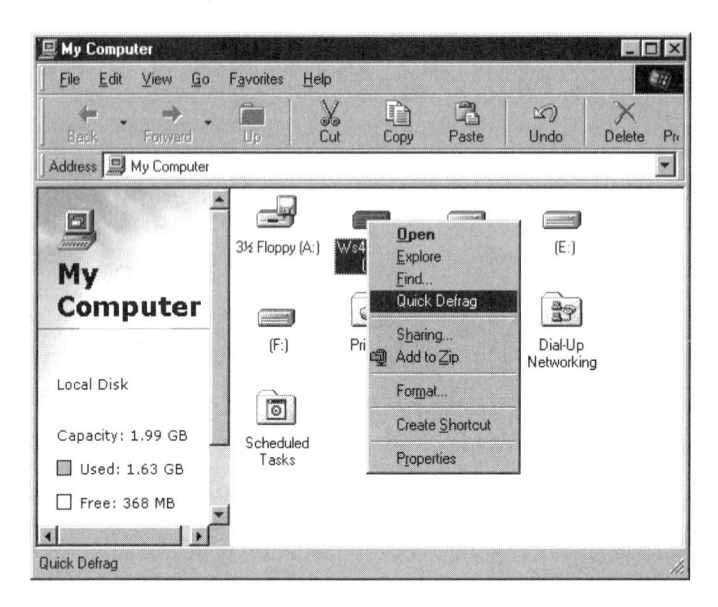

Note The user may continue to work while defragging their hard disk, but it is not recommended. Since the defragging process gets the highest priority, other tasks will run much slower.

PART 5

Performance Optimization and Tuning

Part 5 covers the following material:

- How the overall performance of Microsoft® BackOffice® Small Business Server is optimized.
- How server application performance is optimized on a single server platform.
- Why the default configuration of Small Business Server is the optimum configuration for the small business.
- Hardware and tuning recommendations to sustain optimum performance as the small business expands up to the 50-user limit. Recommendations include both hardware additions and software tuning.
- The impact of upsizing on Small Business Server Internet connectivity.

The information is presented in the following two chapters:

Chapter 30   Small Business Server 4.5 Optimization   459

Chapter 31   Performance and Scalability Enhancements   481

CHAPTER 30

Small Business Server 4.5 Optimization

Overview

Microsoft® BackOffice® Small Business Server 4.5 and its integrated application suite is uniquely optimized for use in small business networks that support up to 50 client PCs. This optimization makes it easy for the small business to share documents, faxes, printers, modems, and other company resources on one server platform, while also facilitating communication with employees, customers, and suppliers. Although the number of client machines supported by Small Business Server is limited to 50, there is no limit to the number of user accounts that can be created.

The stand-alone version of the Windows NT® Server 4.0 operating system and the BackOffice suite of applications were built to scale to the needs of larger organizations. As a result, these products openly provide sophisticated and detailed mechanisms for optimization. Small Business Server 4.5 is not designed for large organizations, yet it still has all the sophistication and performance of the original versions of Windows NT and BackOffice applications.

Since Small Business Server was built specifically for small businesses, it is already optimized for maximum performance. This design provides a simple and efficient install process and management system that lowers the total cost of ownership. Furthermore, since the technology consultant does not need to devote time to optimizing, the Small Business network provides optimum performance immediately.

What Small Business Server Does to Maximize Performance

The optimizations of Small Business Server can be best understood with respect to the installation process, which is divided into the following two parts:

- Operating system—Microsoft Windows NT Server installation and configuration.
- Applications—BackOffice applications Exchange, SQL Server™, Proxy, and so on).

The sections that follow discuss:

- How the optimizations of Small Business Server have a positive impact on the installation process.
- How server application capabilities are optimized for the integrated platform.
- Optimization of Small Business Server management, along with some additional optimization features.

Windows NT Server 4.0 Default Installation Optimizations

The 50 client computer limit on the small business network does not confine the number of user accounts or mailboxes that can be created on Small Business Server. By only allowing a set number of clients, however, specific configurations and settings were enabled in Small Business Server to save time, resources, and money. The resultant simple Windows NT Server installation process produces the following optimizations by default:

- NTFS File System (NTFS) is chosen by default during installation.

  When setting up the stand-alone version of Windows NT Server 4.0, the user must specify either the file allocation table (FAT) file system or NTFS. With Small Business Server, the customer does not have to choose between the two file systems since NTFS is installed by default. Since Small Business Server requires NTFS, removing the option to use the FAT file system with Windows NT Server simplifies setup. Also, when Small Business Server installs Windows NT Server, it automatically converts hard drives with the FAT system to NTFS.

- Server and domain names are created automatically from the administrator account.

  After Setup copies files and goes into the graphical portion of installation (GUI mode), the installer is prompted to enter the administrator and organization names. From the administrator name, Small Business Server creates the administrator account, which is used to manage the addition of users, assign permissions, and so on.

From the administrator account, Small Business Server automatically generates the name of the server and the domain name for the network, thus providing the small business customer a consistent naming scheme.

- Windows NT Server 4.0 is installed automatically as the Primary Domain Controller (PDC), thus it is unnecessary to understand domain security issues to set up Small Business Server.

    During installation of the original version of Windows NT Server 4.0, the technology consultant has to decide whether to configure the machine as a PDC, a Backup Domain Controller (BDC), or a stand-alone server. Small Business Server is automatically installed as a PDC, and can only be installed as a PDC. Additional Windows NT servers can only be installed as BDCs, or as stand-alone servers. Other Small Business Servers cannot be added to the existing domain. All the issues involving domain structures and security between the domains and the server are excluded by designing Small Business Server to install in this fashion.

- Domain trusts are disabled.

    Small Business Server does not support trust relationships with other domains. In an enterprise environment, there are often multiple domains that need to communicate with each other and share resources. This is done through trusts—and much time and money is spent on creating a domain trust design that fits the company. Since small businesses only have a single domain, trusts are not needed. This configuration saves memory and system planning time.

- Security groups are not used.

    The concept of security groups generally applies to enterprise organizations. In Small Business Server 4.5, security groups are removed from the console to simplify things.

- Shared Folder configuration is streamlined.

    To streamline and optimize the shared folder configuration, the company, faxstore, and user files are created with the appropriate permissions during setup. At the end of setup, Small Business Server sets Access Control Lists (ACLs) on the appropriate folders. As a result, the company shared folder can only be accessed by users who have logged into the NT domain.

Network Setup Optimizations

The network setup portion of Small Business Server 4.5 setup has been optimized to provide the small business customer with exactly what they need for an efficient, reliable, and secure network.

Default Network Protocol and Services

While the NetBEUI and Internetwork Packet Exchange (IPX) protocols are included, the Transmission Control Protocol/Internet Protocol (TCP/IP) protocol is installed by default for intranet and Internet connectivity. In addition, the Windows Internet Naming Service (WINS) is installed.

Default IP Addressing

By default, Small Business Server optimizes Internet Protocol (IP) address allocation by doing the following:

- The IP address of Small Business Server is set to 10.0.0.2.

    This address automatically provides security because it is non-routable—this prevents routers on the Internet from routing packets directly to Small Business Server. Inbound packets must first be routed through Proxy Server, which uses network address translation (NAT) to convert its Internet service provider (ISP)-assigned IP address to the Small Business Server base IP address of 10.0.0.2.

- The subnet mask is set to 255.255.255.0.

    The subnet mask is preconfigured to automatically define the range for dynamically assigned client IP addresses on the small business network.

- IP forwarding is turned off on the server.

    This minimizes the possibility of intrusive attacks on client computers due to exposure to the Internet.

Note Because of the complexity of reconfiguring services to use a new IP address, we strongly recommend you do not change the base IP address of Small Business Server.

DHCP Configured Automatically

To further simplify the networking environment, the dynamic host configuration protocol (DHCP) is enabled by default so the technology consultant and small business customer do not have to be concerned with client IP address configuration issues. The DHCP Service assigns IP addresses to clients dynamically when they log on—it is therefore unnecessary to configure clients on an individual basis with static IP addresses.

DHCP is automatically configured to use nonroutable IP addresses—the IP subnet is a reserved, nonroutable address set, so that all network workstations are inaccessible from the Internet.

Enabling DHCP in Small Business Server is an optimum configuration for dealing with the complexities of IP address allocation. We recommend not disabling DHCP since this prevents the Set Up Computer Wizard from correctly performing its tasks. Normally, during client setup with the wizard, the client computer is configured to use DHCP to obtain an IP address. If DHCP is disabled after setup, client IP addresses must be configured manually using the following steps.

▶ **To configure client IP addresses manually**

1. Click **Start** on the client computer, point to **Settings**, and then click **Control Panel**.
2. Double-click **Network**.
3. For Windows 95/98 client machines, select **TCP/IP network card** (where "network card" is the name of the network card in the network component list. Click **Properties** and then perform the following.
   - Select the **IP Address** tab, and then select **Specify an IP address**.
   - Type the **IP address** of the client machine and **Subnet Mask**.
   - Select the **Gateway** tab, and then type in the **Default Gateway** address. Click **Add**, and then click **OK** to exit.
   - Click **Yes** to restart the client machine.
   - Repeat these steps for all Windows 98 client machines on the network.
4. For Windows NT Workstation client machines, select the **Protocols** tab, and then click **TCP/IP Protocol**. Click **Properties** and then perform the following.
   - Select the **IP Address** tab, and then select **Specify an IP address**.
   - Type the **IP Address**, **Subnet Mask**, and **Default Gateway** address.
   - Click **Apply** and then click **OK**.
   - Click **Yes** to restart the client machine.
   - Repeat these steps for all Windows NT Workstation clients on the network.

Note Client IP addresses must match the Proxy Local Address Table (LAT) of Small Business Server, which in turn must be compatible with other services that use the base IP address for packet routing. Refer to the "Proxy Local Address Table" section in *Chapter 27, Administering Small Business Server Components,* in *Part 4, Administering and Maintaining,* of this resource guide to configure other services with a new IP address.

Proxy Server Configuration

When packet filtering is turned on using the Small Business Server Internet Connection Wizard, TCP/IP ports 20 and 21 are disabled to prevent Internet exposure through these connections, which are normally used for Web publishing. In this configuration, the Web Publishing Wizard cannot be run on the server machine. When the small business is ready to publish on the Internet, these Proxy Server ports can be opened by running the Internet Connection Wizard, and the Web Publishing Wizard may then be used.

RAS Configuration

The following Remote Access Service (RAS) configuration is set up by default:

- RAS is not configured as a protocol gateway.

  This provides added security to clients on the network by permitting inbound traffic access to only the server and not to clients on the network.

- RAS auto-dial service is disabled, since Proxy Server is used to initiate auto dial connections.
- RAS and DHCP are configured so that clients dialing in through RAS receive a dynamically allocated IP address.

Client Networking Configuration

The Set Up Computer Wizard of Small Business Server 4.5 automatically configures client machines to take advantage of NT domain networking features as well as DHCP, Windows Internet Naming Service (WINS), and the Proxy Server 2.0 security configuration.

Server Application Installation Optimizations

After Setup completes the installation of Windows NT Server, it begins to install the BackOffice applications. One of the most significant features of Small Business Server setup is that everything is installed at once. Microsoft Exchange, SQL Server, Internet Information Services (IIS), Proxy, and all the services and components needed by a typical small business are installed and configured in one simple process. The integration of server applications optimized for small businesses essentially makes Small Business Server 4.5 a single product serving many business needs.

It is through the integration of applications that the console is enabled as a simple, centralized management tool. After the BackOffice applications have been installed and configured, the To Do list appears as the first introduction to the console. From here, the technology consultant can configure the remaining installation items necessary to get the server up and ready to use.

Server Application Capabilities

Since the individual server applications (Exchange, SQL, Proxy, IIS, and so on) of Small Business Server have been optimized and tested to work together on a single server platform, their capabilities are uniquely tuned for single Small Business Server installations. The sections that follow describe the capabilities of the server applications in this configuration.

Exchange Server 5.5

Small Business Server ships with Exchange 5.5 standard edition, which includes the following connectors and capabilities:

- Internet Mail Service (IMS)—this service is installed by default. To simplify configuration of this service, you can use the Internet Connection Wizard. The IMS can also be configured manually using the Exchange Administrator.
- Network News Transfer Protocol (NNTP) Service—used for News Group implementation.
- MS Mail Connector—for interoperability with MS Mail systems.
- CC:Mail Connector—for interoperability with CC:Mail systems.
- Microsoft Outlook® Web Access—for access to e-mail and public folders using a web browser.

Small Business Server is built for small organizations not needing the features of the X.400 or site connectors, which are normally used to connect to other Exchange Servers or sites. Because these connectors are unnecessary for the small business, they have not been included in Small Business Server 4.5.

Exchange Installed as its Own Organization

Significant efforts have gone into making Exchange perform at an optimum level in a single-server environment. Since this is the case, only a single Exchange organization is needed. As a result, the Exchange configuration in Small Business Server does not support site replication. This optimal configuration saves memory and disk space.

During setup, the technology consultant only needs to enter the company name in order to install Exchange Server. Setup configures the organization name based on the company name and the site name based on the domain name. Also, the service account is set to be the administrator account, including setup of an administrator mailbox and profile. In addition, a default distribution list is created.

Exchange Optimizations for Small Business E-mail

Exchange optimization tools have been used to pretune Exchange for small businesses. Based on research, typical users in a small business environment send 10-15 e-mail messages per day. Based on this usage level, the Exchange working set size is tuned to 8 MB versus the default of 24 MB—and performance is still unaffected. The saving in server memory means Small Business Server can run on a machine with 64 MB of memory that can also be used as a workstation.

Exchange Service Accounts

During the installation process, the service account for each of the following components is set to the administrator account along with the password specified in setup.

- Exchange Directory
- Exchange Information Store
- Exchange Internet Mail Service
- Exchange Message Transfer
- Exchange System Attendant

Important Only change passwords from the Small Business Server console's **Change Password Wizard**, which uses the administrative-context to change service passwords. **Do not** change passwords for any of the above service accounts from either the **Logon** dialog box or Windows NT **User Manager for Domains**. If you do, the service password will not match the administrator account and the service will not start.

SQL Server 7.0

Since Small Business Server 4.5 is designed for 50 clients or less, a huge database that takes up large amounts of hard drive space is not required. The SQL Server 7.0 user database included with Small Business Server is limited to a total of 10 GB of disk space (not including log space). This is the optimum for small business database requirements. Within this memory constraint, SQL Server 7.0 still retains the performance levels of an enterprise application.

Note If more than a 10 GB database is needed, SQL Server 7.0 should be deployed on a separate machine.

Proxy Server 2.0

The Proxy LAT is configured during installation to contain all nonroutable IP addresses. This ensures that all internal site addresses appear here so Proxy Server does not initiate a dial-up connection to find them. Also, Proxy permissions are set and enforced. By default, user Internet access permission is denied by Proxy Server, however, users may be granted access to the Internet by running the User Resource Wizard.

Internet Information Server 4.0

IIS is tightly integrated with Windows NT Server 4.0. One of the services that Windows NT Server supports is the Gopher service which uses File Transfer Protocol (FTP). This service is generally not needed since most small businesses do not have a full-time Internet connection. By removing this service from the installation, memory is saved. However, Small Business Server is configured by default with *outbound* FTP services, to allow client access to Internet resources using this protocol. Also, the following are configured on IIS during the installation process:

- Basic Authentication and NT Challenge Response is set up.
- The virtual roots below are created:

    %systemdrive%:\Winnt.sbs\Help

    %systemdrive%:\SmallBusiness\Html

    %systemdrive%:\InetPub\wwwroot\Intranet

    %systemdrive%:\InetPub\wwwroot\Intranet\SBSClientHelp

These virtual roots must exist in order for the Small Business Server console and client help to function correctly. They are referenced within the HTML pages of the console and client help, and in the console itself.

Other Server Application Optimizations

In keeping with optimization strategies for the small business, the following additional optimizations occur on Small Business Server 4.5:

- Modem Sharing Server supports up to four shared serial ports.
- Fax Server supports up to four Class 1 Fax modems.

> **Note** During the installation process, the service account for Fax Services is set to the administrator account along with the password specified in setup.

Fault Tolerance

Fault tolerance of Small Business Server is optimized to support the same options for software-level fault tolerance (RAID 1 and 5) as the standard version of Windows NT Server. RAID sets allow the server to continue to operate with all production data intact in the event of a hard disk failure. In that event, the server continues to operate and you can replace the hard disk when users are off the system. Hard disk redundancy for Small Business Server can be either of the following:

- RAID 1—disk mirroring
- RAID 5—stripe set with parity configuration

A RAID array requires SCSI hard drives, as well as two hard disks for RAID 1 and a minimum of three hard disks for RAID 5.

Client Application Optimizations

In order to optimize client setup, client applications and components are set to a typical configuration for Small Business Server users. This includes configuration of the following components described in this section.

- Small Business Server version number
- Fax
- Internet Explorer 5.0
- Outlook 2000
- Office 2000
- Outlook client profile updates with Modprof utility

Small Business Server Version

During client setup, the following registry key is set to indicate the version of Small Business Server 4.5:

HKLM\SOFTWARE\Microsoft\SmallBusiness, *Version, 0, 4.5.*

Fax Client

The Fax client is configured to use the fax service on Small Business Server and to receive e-mail notification when faxes arrive.

Internet Explorer 5.0

During client setup, Internet Explorer 5.0 is configured for each user as follows.

Set Favorites

Favorites are set up as described in the following table.

Table 30.1 Small Business Server Favorites Setup

Title	URL
Microsoft Small Business Server web site	http://www.microsoft.com/SmallBusinessserver
My Internet home page	http://SBSServer
My Intranet home page	http://SBSServer/Intranet
Small Business Server 4.5 User Guide	http://SBSServer/Intranet/SBSClientHelp/Default.asp

Internet Explorer Home Page Configuration

The Internet Explorer Home Page is configured as follows.

- Home page points to:
  http://SBSServer/Intranet/SBSClientHelp/Default.asp

- Internet Explorer Welcome page points to:
  http://SBSServer/Intranet/SBSClientHelp/Default.asp

  The Welcome page only appears to the client the first time Internet Explorer 5.0 is launched. Thereafter, the Small Business Server client Help appears whenever Internet Explorer 5.0 is launched.

Proxy Settings

The following proxy settings are implemented:

- The proxy client is configured to access the Internet through Proxy Server.
- The Proxy Server name and port is set for HyperText Transfer Protocol (HTTP), FTP, Gopher, Secure Sockets Layer, and Socks services.
- All protocols are set to use the Proxy Server.
- Internet Explorer 5.0 is set to bypass Proxy Server for local IP addresses.

Install.ins

Internet Explorer 5.0 allows configuration of several settings in the Install.ins file during client application installation. These settings in Install.ins are applied to each new user profile after initial Internet Explorer 5.0 installation computer restart. Before the restart, this file is copied into <ie install dir>\signup on the client computer. The following settings are added into Install.ins:

- Favorites.

    Favorites are added into [FavoritesEx] section.

- Home Page.

    The following is added to the URL section:

    Home_Page=http://SBSServer/Intranet/SBSClientHelp/Default.asp

    FirstHomePage=http://SBSServer/Intranet/SBSClientHelp/Default.asp

- Proxy Settings.

    The following section is added to Install.ins:

    [Proxy]

    HTTP_Proxy_Server=http://SBSServer:80

    FTP_Proxy_Server=http://SBSServer:80

    Gopher_Proxy_Server=http://SBSServer:80

    Secure_Proxy_Server=http://SBSServer:80

    Socks_Proxy_Server=http://SBSServer:80

    Use_Same_Proxy=1

    Proxy_Enable=1

    Proxy_Override= "<local>"

Microsoft Outlook 2000

This section describes the configuration set up for the Outlook 2000 client.

Outlook First Run Wizard

The following registry keys are set to configure Outlook 2000 in the corporate mode instead of the Internet mode so the user does not see the Outlook First Run Wizard:

HKLM, "SOFTWARE\Clients\Mail\MicrosoftOutlook", "MSIComponentID", "{FF1D0740-D227-11D1-A4B0-006008AF820E}"

HKLM, "SOFTWARE\Microsoft\Office\9.0\Outlook\Setup", "MailSupport",0x00010003,1.

E-mail Profile

An e-mail profile is created for each Small Business Server user. The following services are added to the user profile:

- Microsoft Outlook Client
- Microsoft Exchange Server
- Outlook Address Book

If the user has an existing profile, the above services are appended to the profile. For further details on profile creation, refer to the "Modprof Utility" section, later in this chapter.

Welcome Mail

A Welcome to Small Business Server e-mail is sent to all new Outlook 2000 users. So the message appears properly, it is named offer.msg and copied into the following location on the server during client setup:

Program Files\MicrosoftOffice\Office

Office 2000

Office 2000 is installed in the typical configuration, excepting that OfficeTools and Converters is added.

Outlook Client Profile Updates with Modprof Utility

All Outlook 97/98 clients have an existing e-mail profile. The Modprof Utility automatically updates these existing Outlook 97/98 client profiles to include the basic Exchange services a Small Business Server client needs. Modprof does this by appending the following services to existing Outlook profiles:

- Microsoft Outlook Client
- Microsoft Exchange Server
- Outlook Address Book

Scenarios Where the Utility is Used

Modprof is used in the following scenarios:

- Scenario 1.

   Outlook 98 Internet Mode (IMO) user is upgrading to Outlook 2000 corporate.

   Modprof is used to add Exchange Server to the configuration without eliminating the existing Internet configuration.

- Scenario 2.

  Outlook 98 corporate user is connected to MS Mail or cc: Mail.

  Modprof is used to add Exchange Server to the configuration while preserving existing Internet connectivity.

What the Utility Does

New Outlook client profiles are created by the Newprof Utility, which uses the information specified in a Small Business Server .prf file to create the profile. For existing Outlook 97/98 client profiles, Modprof extends the format of this file to include the following new information in Outlook 2000 profiles:

- Identifies the profile to modify and includes an option to modify the default profile.
- Decides whether to abort, replace, or append the existing profile.
- Decides whether to overwrite or leave intact current settings for services that can only have a single instance in the profile, such as Exchange Server.
- Inserts a flag in all service definitions to indicate that each service may have only one instance in the profile.

Launching Modprof

Modprof is called by the first run of Outlook 2000. For this to occur properly, Small Business Server client setup writes the following registry key for each new user.

- Key: HKCU\Software\Microsoft\Office\9.0\Outlook\Setup\Execute
- Value: The path to modprof, including command line parameters.

  \\%sbsserver%\ClientApps\MS\SBSUtil\Modprof.exe

This registry key instructs Outlook 2000 first run to call a custom executable before doing a Mail Application Programming Interface (MAPI) logon. If there is no profile, Modprof is executed after Newprof runs. If there is an existing profile, Newprof will not run and Outlook calls Modprof.

Note Since Outlook first run may also occur when switching mail support modes or after new component installation, Modprof deletes the "execute" registry key after successfully modifying the profile to avoid running multiple Modprof executions.

Compatibilities

Modprof functions the same on Windows® 95/98 and Windows NT Workstation clients. Modprof only runs on Outlook 2000 and operates on profiles created by the following applications:

- Windows Messaging Subsystem (WMS)
- Exchange versions 4.0, 5.0, and 5.5
- Outlook 97, 98, and 2000

Server Installation Defaults

The items described in the sections that follow are created by default during the installation process. The automatic configuration of these components contributes to the optimization of the Small Business Server installation process.

Shared Folders

The following table describes the folders that are setup by default during installation of Small Business Server.

Table 30.2 Default Shared Folders

Folder Name	Share Name	Location
Company Shared Folder	Company	User specified during setup; default: %systemroot%
User Shared Folders	Users	User specified during setup; default: %systemroot%
Clients	Clients	%systemroot%\SmallBusiness
ClientApps	ClientApps	User specified during setup
FaxStore	FaxStore	User specified during setup; default: %systemroot%

Note The Clients share above must exist in the installed locations in order for the Add User Wizard and Set Up Computer Wizard to function correctly. The FaxStore folder must exist in the installed location in order for Microsoft Fax Service to function correctly. These folders should only be moved using the Move a Folder Wizard and its associated Online Guide topic.

Default Permissions

During installation of Small Business Server, default permissions are applied as described in following tables.

Table 30.3 Default Permissions Applied to Recipients

Permission recipient	Permission level
Administrator	Full
Creator/owner	Full
Server operators	Change
System	Full

Note In order for the Small Business Server console and wizards to function correctly, the permissions for Administrator, Creator/owner, Server operators, and System should not be changed.

In addition, the following default permission are applied to folders.

Table 30.4 Default Permissions Applied to Folders

Folder name	Access control lists (ACLs)	Contents
Company Shared Folder	Domain admins: full Domain users: full	For use by end users.
User Shared Folders	Domain admins: full Domain users: read	Contains the shared folders for each user.
FaxStore	Domain admins: full Domain users: change	Contains incoming faxes. End users need to read and delete files.
System drive	Domain admins: full Domain users: read	
%systemdrive%\InetPub\wwwroot\Intranet\SBSClientHelp	Domain admins: full Domain users: change	SBS intranet client help.
%systemdrive%\InetPub\wwwroot\Intranet	Domain admins: full Domain users: change	SBS intranet.
%systemdrive%:\Winnt.sbs\Help\Sbs.srv\Htm	Domain admins: full Domain users: read	Online Guide files.

(continued)

Table 30.4 Default Permissions Applied to Folders *(continued)*

Folder name	Access control lists (ACLs)	Contents
%systemdrive%:\Winnt.sbs\Help\Sbs.srv\Misc	Domain admins: full Domain users: read	Online Guide files.
%systemdrive%\SmallBusiness	Domain admins: full	Contains admin files (wizards, dll's, etc.).
%systemdrive%\SmallBusiness\Clients	Domain admins: full Domain users: read	Contains response and setup directories.
%systemdrive%\SmallBusiness\Clients\Response	Domain admins: full Domain users: full	Folders for each client computer: contains information files used by OCManager during client setup.
%systemdrive%\SmallBusiness\Clients\Setup	Domain admins: full Domain users: read	Contains I386 and Win95 directories.
%systemdrive%\SmallBusiness\Clients\Setup\i386	Domain admins: full Domain users: read	Setup files for NT clients.
%systemdrive%\SmallBusiness\Clients\Setup\Win95	Domain admins: full Domain users: read	Setup files for Win95/98 clients.
%systemdrive%\SmallBusiness\Floppy	Domain admins: full	Networking setup files copied to floppy by the Set Up Computer Wizard.
%systemdrive%\SmallBusiness\Html	Domain admins: full	Console.
%systemdrive%\SmallBusiness\Template	Domain admins: full	Information files copied to response directories by the Set Up Computer Wizard.
%systemdrive%\SmallBusiness\HTML\Logs	Domain Admins: full Domain Users: read	

Favorites

The favorites described in the following table are set up during the installation process.

Table 30.5 Default Favorites

Favorite name	Address
Microsoft Small Business Web site	http://www.Microsoft.com/SmallBusinessServer
My Intranet Home Page	http://Localhost/Intranet
My Internet Home Page	http://LocalHost
SBS User Guide	http://LocalHost/Intranet/SBSClientHelp/Default.asp?where=server

Default Internet

Small Business Server installation sets up a default Internet site. The location of the Internet page is: %systemroot%InetPub/wwwroot/Default.htm.

Default Intranet and Content

Small Business Server installation sets up a default intranet page and default intranet content. The content contains all of the client help for the product. The location of the default intranet page is:

%systemroot%\InetPub\wwwroot\Intranet\Default.htm

The help content for the default intranet page is installed in the following folder:

%systemroot%\InetPub\wwwroot\Intranet\SBSClientHelp

The corresponding Uniform Resource Locator (URL) for the default intranet help content on the server is:
http://Servername/Intranet/SBSClientHelp/Default.asp?where=server

The corresponding URL for the default intranet help content on the client machines is:
http://Servername/Intranet/SBSClientHelp/Default.asp

Implementation of Performance Optimizations

Microsoft BackOffice Small Business Server 4.5 along with its enterprise-class server applications, is designed to run on a single server computer. In the past, Microsoft has specifically recommended that the server applications run on separate, dedicated machines in order to achieve optimum performance and reliability. With Small Business Server, this has changed—although some limitations are inherent to this configuration. This section describes how the server applications were optimized on the Small Business Server platform along with the engineering techniques that enable Small Business Server to run multiple services on a single machine while achieving enterprise-level performance.

Server Applications Optimized on a Single Platform

In order for enterprise server applications to work well together on a single platform, several modifications were made to achieve successful integration, as follows.

- Code was optimized to reduce memory consumption—each server application is tuned to use a limited amount of memory. This enables the entire platform of applications to work well together using only 64 MB of random access memory (RAM).
- Other limitations were placed on user applications (see "User Limitations on Applications."
- All server applications support a silent and scriptable setup.
- All server applications use the client access licenses (CALs) shipped with Small Business Server 4.5.

Code Optimizations

In Small Business Server 4.5, new code optimizations were made to conserve memory usage while still delivering optimal performance. Because of the way Exchange Server 5.5 and SQL Server 7.0 dynamically allocate memory, full-featured versions of these and other applications are now included in Small Business Server 4.5 with the user limitations described in the section ahead entitled "User Limits on Applications."

Reduction of Application Memory Consumption

Most stand-alone BackOffice server applications are specifically designed to scale up, which means the more memory on a machine, the more the application will use. This type of design is important in the enterprise where a separate machine is provided for each application. However, on Small Business Server, a more conservative approach to memory consumption was adopted to optimize the platform for small business applications. As a result, each application is tuned to use only enough memory to accomplish its task. The memory constraints adopted for Small Business Server accomplished the following:

- Memory usage was reduced by limiting the buffers available to the Exchange database engine.
- SQL Server 7.0 still maintains enterprise-level performance with the reduced database size.

User Limitations on Applications

Microsoft imposed user limits on applications in the BackOffice Small Business Server family to ensure that the server can support all services running on a single 64 MB RAM machine. Limitations include:

- **50-user limit**. The technology consultant can create an unlimited number of user accounts, but the actual number of connected computers is limited to 50 PCs, to ensure acceptable performance levels for all users.
- **Disabled trusts**. Trusts which are used to segment the administration of large numbers of users and machines are intended for businesses with more than one physical network location. This is not applicable to most small business network scenarios. By disabling trusts, Small Business Server reduces the administrative overhead associated with managing trust relationships and the amount of memory and processor overhead required by the server domain controller processes.
- **SQL Server Database Size**. Small Business Server limits each SQL Server 7.0 database to 10 GB. If you expect to use SQL Server on a regular basis, a minimum of 128 MB of RAM installed on the server is recommended.
- **Single Exchange site**. Since Small Business Server runs on a single server in one location, the need for Exchange Site Connectors is eliminated. Also, hard disk resources are conserved since Exchange Server as integrated into the Small Business Server platform.

- **Fax limited to four ports**. The maximum number of ports that can be assigned to the Fax Service is four.

- **Modem Sharing limit is four ports**. The maximum number of ports that can be assigned to the Modem Sharing Server is four.

- **RAS limited to 255 ports**. The maximum number of ports that can be assigned to Remote Access Service is 255, as supported by the Windows NT Server operating system.

Viable Integrated Application Performance

Reduction of memory is only part of the formula for successful single-platform integration. The server applications also demonstrate that they can support the tasks of a typical small business without significant delay. Using Exchange as an example, it was demonstrated that it could support 50 users while using only 8 MB of RAM, with 90 percent of all user requests handled in less than one second. User requests included the following:

- Opening a message
- Forwarding a message
- Opening the global address list

Management Optimizations

Management of Small Business Server 4.5 is optimized through the use of the console, which consolidates and automates most server administration tasks. Microsoft improved the usability features of Small Business Server 4.5 in order to create enterprise-level functionality in the small business environment without the need for enterprise-level information technology staff. These features include the following:

- **Small Business Server console**. The console is an HTML-based application that consolidates all of the common administration tasks into a single, wizard-based user interface.

- **Preconfigured shared folders**. The Small Business Server Set Up Computer Wizard creates a company shared folder and user folders automatically. When the Set Up Computer Wizard adds a workstation to the domain, it also creates desktop shortcuts to the company shared folder and to a user's personal folder. The technology consultant can also enable additional shares using the console.

- **Single Setup Process**. Small Business Server 4.5 consolidates the entire setup process into a single wizard. Information entered in the wizard during setup is used to perform behind-the-scenes configuration across all server applications.
- **Configuration Wizards**. Small Business Server 4.5 configuration wizards can be used for most administration tasks. These wizards enable the technology consultant to confidently and accurately configure and deploy BackOffice applications. A few of the key wizards of Small Business Server 4.5 include:

    Internet Connection Wizard. This wizard takes the technology consultant through the process of signing up the small business customer with an ISP and configures Microsoft Windows NT Server, Exchange Server, and Proxy Server.

    Add User Wizard. This wizard creates users, configures Exchange accounts and permissions, configures RAS and Proxy settings, and automatically runs the Set Up Computer Wizard for the user.

    Set Up Computer Wizard. This wizard creates a setup disk for a client computer that configures network settings, installs client applications, and configures user settings.

CHAPTER 31

Performance and Scalability Enhancements

Overview

As the small business network expands up to the 50-user limit, the performance of Microsoft® BackOffice® Small Business Server 4.5 should be optimized. The components the most stressed by increasing performance demands include disk utilization, random access memory (RAM), and several server applications including Windows NT®, Exchange, and SQL Server™. This chapter describes the tuning recommendations for optimizing performance of these components. The impact of network expansion on Internet connectivity is also discussed.

Performance Tuning

Although Small Business Server 4.5 provides a high quality of service with heavy use in a small business with up to 50 users, this performance is sustained only when certain performance tunings and hardware recommendations are applied. Guidelines for different server hardware requirements relative to network size were determined by comprehensive tests to which Small Business Server was subjected. The guidelines and tests are described in detail in *Chapter 16, Small Business Network Capacity Planning,* in *Part 2, Planning,* of this resource guide. This includes how the performance of Small Business Server was evaluated, as well as hardware recommendations for facilitating network expansion up to the 50-user limit. In the sections that follow, we describe the recommendations for a baseline hardware configuration and tuning server applications for optimal performance.

Baseline Hardware Recommendations

Although details on minimum hardware recommendations for network capacities with 10, 25, and 50 users are described in Part 2, a baseline hardware configuration is discussed in this section to highlight what we consider to be the most cost-effective configuration for the small business. Recommendations for the baseline hardware configuration include specifications on processor speed, disk configuration, and RAM requirements. Even though the small business may not initially require this capacity and the up-front cost may be higher, the overall long-term cost will likely be much less. RAM and disk capacity is becoming increasingly cheaper—obtaining the additional capacity up front may minimize consultant fees to upgrade the system later when server downtime is at risk. Recommendations for the baseline configuration include:

- A single Pentium-class processor running at 350 MHz or greater speed.
- 128 MB of RAM. If you expect regular heavy server use in addition to SQL Server use, consider using 256 MB of RAM.
- Small Computer System Interface (SCSI) controller with at least three disks configured with redundant array of independent disks (RAID) software. More disks will increase performance and a hardware RAID controller will provide optimal disk input/output (I/O) performance.

Configuring the Disks

A good, fault-tolerant disk configuration is likely to be the most important configuration setting made when setting up Small Business Server. Always set up a RAID 1 (disk mirror) for the Windows NT Server operating system. For the data partition, set up a RAID 5 partition (stripe set with parity) and place there the data stores for SQL Server and Exchange Server. For even further performance tuning, another RAID 1 or RAID 5 partition for the page and log files may be set up, however this is probably excessive for a small business installation.

These RAID configurations create performance advantages, but more importantly, they minimize the risk of data loss and downtime. If any of the hard disks fail, the chances of data loss are minimal and the server should still run—although you will likely notice performance degradation. Even with disk failure, the small business can continue running during the day and schedule time during the evening to replace the disk, reset the RAID partition, and be up and running the next day.

Tuning Server Applications

This section covers tuning recommendations and procedures for the Windows NT, Exchange, and SQL Servers.

Windows NT Server 4.0 with Service Pack 4

The Windows NT Server 4.0 operating system is mostly self tuning. You can further optimize by doing the following:

- Configure the page file to a size sufficient to prevent Windows NT from having to expand it during operation. Using system RAM plus 125 MB is recommended.
- Disable any unused services and devices—for example, the Scheduler service or SQLAgent service.
- Set up server optimization to maximize throughput.

▶ **To configure the page file size**

1. Click **Start**, point to **Settings**, and then click **Control Panel** to display the **Control Panel** applet.
2. Double-click the **System** icon to display the **System Properties** page.
3. Select the **Performance** tab, and then click **Change** to display the **Virtual Memory** dialog box.
4. Select the drive on which Windows NT Server is installed.
5. Enter the recommended values for the paging file size.
6. Click **Set** and then click **OK**.
7. Click **Close** to exit the **System Properties** page.

▶ **To disable unused services**

1. Click **Start**, point to **Settings**, and then click **Control Panel**.
2. Double-click **Services** to display the following **Services** dialog box.

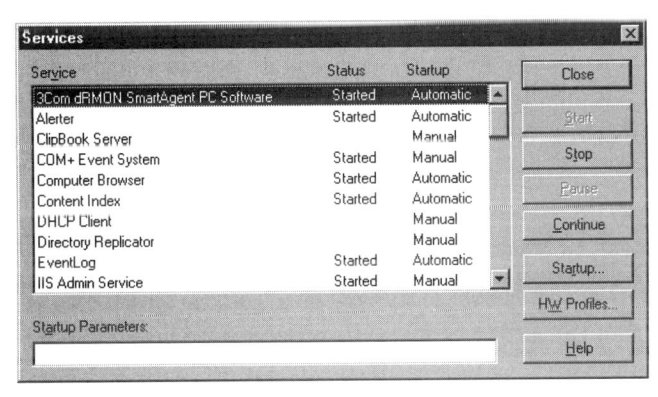

3. From the **Service** list, select the unused service and then click **Stop**. The status of the service in the **Status** column (Stopped) should be indicated.
4. Repeat Step 3 for each service to be disabled.
5. When finished, click **Close**.

▶ **To set up server optimization for maximize throughput**

1. Click **Start**, point to **Settings**, and then click **Control Panel**.
2. Double-click **Network** to display the following **Network** dialog box.

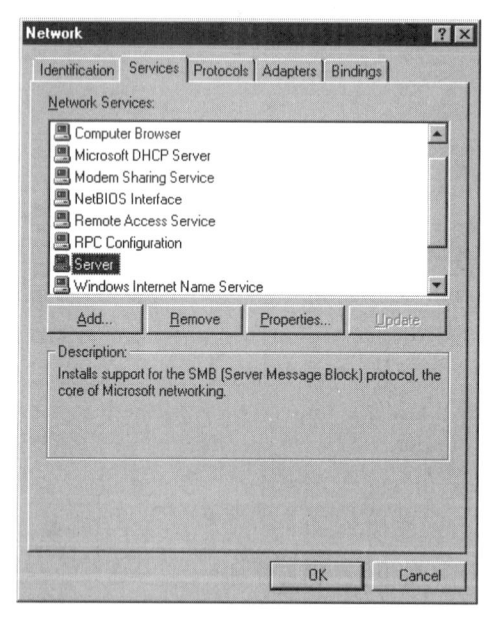

3. Select the **Services** tab, select **Server**, and then click on **Properties** to display the following **Server** dialog box.

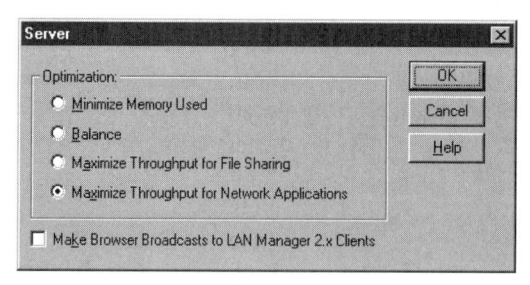

4. If Small Business Server is used primarily for SQL or Exchange, select **Maximize Throughput for Network Applications**.

5. If Small Business Server is used primarily for file and print sharing, select **Maximize Throughput for File Sharing**.
6. Click **OK**.

Exchange Server 5.5 with Service Pack 2

The Exchange Server Performance Optimizer is run automatically during Small Business Server installation. If you add additional drives or partitions after installation, then rerun the Exchange Optimizer again. The Exchange Optimizer should split data and log files onto separate drives and move them for you automatically. Other than this, Exchange Server is self tuning.

SQL Server 7.0

Use Transmission Control Protocol/Internet Protocol (TCP/IP) Sockets for Network Connections to SQL Server, rather than the default Named Pipes. TCP/IP Sockets offer performance gains over Named Pipes. SQL Server 7.0 is dynamically self tuning and will adjust its memory settings for each database dynamically. Small business customers should use the tuning settings generated by SQL Server.

Internet Connectivity and Upsizing

Most small businesses use a dial-up networking connection to the Internet. An analog modem usually facilitates this type of connection using an internal device or a serial port connection. However, when the small business network expands up to the 50-user limit, a faster connection to the Internet may be needed to accommodate heavier usage by internal clients and larger traffic volumes from the web. Several possible scenarios exist to allow the small business to access the Internet more quickly, as described in the following sections.

Router Connectivity

A router may be used as a gateway for quick Small Business Server access to the Internet. The following topology illustration shows the configuration of a Small Business Server connection to the Internet with a router. The router is placed outside the firewall so the small business network still has the security of Proxy Server 2.0. The router is connected to Proxy Server through a second network card on Small Business Server which is configured as the default gateway. Figure 2.1, "Typical Small Business Server Network Configuration" in *Chapter 10, Planning a Small Business Network*, of *Part 2, Planning*, shows this type of connection.

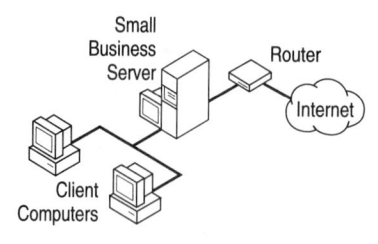

Figure 31.1 Network topology with a router

When using a router for the small business Internet connection, the Small Business Server Internet Connection Wizard must be run to set up the connection properly. Refer to the "Internet Connectivity Wizard Walkthrough" section of *Chapter 21, ISP Connectivity Tasks,* in *Part 3, Deployment,* of this resource kit for procedures. The section entitled "Router Connection Requirements" below describes the information you will need to run the wizard.

IP Addressing Scheme

The figure below illustrates what a router IP addressing scheme might look like when a second network adapter is used as the default gateway to the Internet. Notice the second network adapter is on the same subnet as the router's local network adapter, to enable communication across this interface.

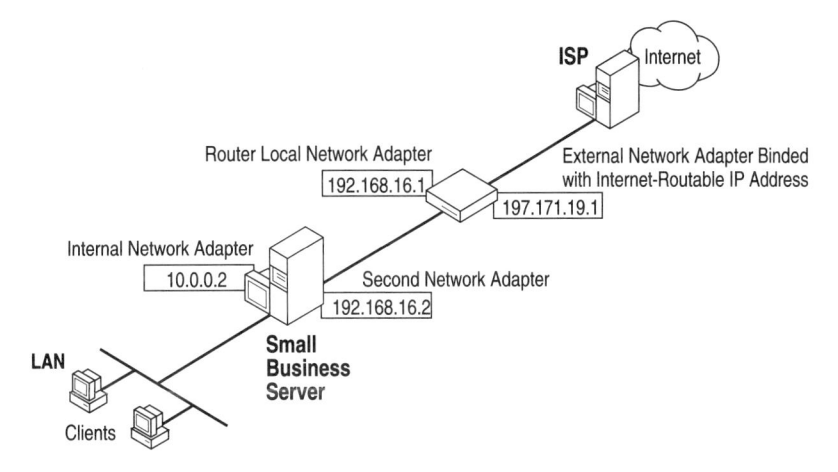

Figure 31.2 Router IP addressing scheme example

Note Many routers are supplied by the manufacturer with a local IP address of 192.168.16.1. If you use this IP address, make sure to remove the 192.168.0.0 - 192.168.255.255 internal address range from the Proxy Server LAT, or Small Business Server will fail to make an Internet connection. Refer to *Chapter 27, Administering Small Business Server Components,* in *Part 4, Administering and Maintaining,* of this resource guide for LAT procedures.

Router Connection Requirements

To correctly configure Small Business Server for Internet connectivity through a router, the information listed below is required.

- Account name (or UserID required to dial into the Internet Service Provider (ISP)).
- Account password.
- Mail type used: Exchange Simple Mail Transfer Protocol Server (SMTP) or POP3.

  For Exchange (SMTP) mail, the host name or Internet Protocol (IP) address of the ISP's SMTP server is needed. If the ISP is queuing mail, you will need to know the appropriate signaling command for dequeuing and a fixed IP address.

  For POP3 mail, the host name or IP address of the POP3 and SMTP server at the ISP is needed.
- Internet domain name.
- Router IP address.
- ISP Domain Name System (DNS) IP address.
- Router type (whether dial-on demand or not).

Disabling the Router's DHCP Server

If your router includes a Dynamic Host Configuration Protocol (DHCP) server, it should be turned off in order to prevent having two DHCP servers on the same network. If it is left on, it will cause Small Business Server's DHCP service to be disabled—the DHCP service installed by default in Small Business Server has a rogue detection feature that shuts down the service if another DHCP server is detected.

If your router's DHCP Server is used, then clients on the small business network will not be able to receive DHCP addresses from Small Business Server. As a result, we recommend disabling the router's DHCP server to avoid the complexities of reconfiguring the network IP addressing scheme of Small Business Server 4.5. An overview of the complexities is discussed in the next paragraph.

Full-Time/Broadband Connections

Full-time/broadband connections to the Internet may use an Asynchronous Digital Subscriber Line (ADSL), cable modem, or a Multichannel Multipoint Distribution System (MMDS) device. Refer to the following network topology illustration. With a full-time/broadband connection to the Internet, a second network adapter is required as in the previous router example. This configuration is also secure since all inbound and outbound Internet requests are first filtered by Proxy Server and then routed to internal clients. When using a full-time/broadband connection to the Internet, a static IP address must be obtained from the ISP for the broadband device's external network adapter, as in full-time router configurations.

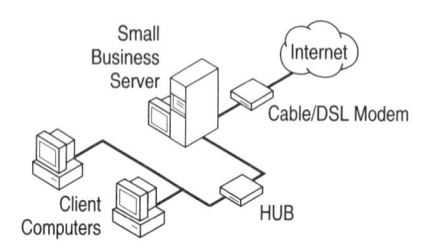

Figure 31.3 Network topology with ADSL or cable modem

Full-Time/Broadband Connection Requirements

For a full-time/broadband connection, you will need all the information listed in the previous section entitled "Router Connection Requirements" plus a static IP address for the second network adapter.

LAN Router Configuration

Another possible scenario supported by the Internet Connection Wizard is connecting a router directly to the small business local area network (LAN) for direct client Internet access. In this configuration, the router is set as the default gateway for each computer on the LAN and handles client requests outside the local address space. This requires every client on the local network to have a static Internet IP address, unless the router is capable of doing network address translation (NAT) and DHCP. In this case, client IP addresses will be assigned by the router's DHCP server. The network topology for this configuration is shown below.

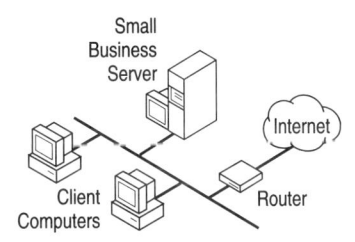

Figure 31.4 LAN router configuration

Using the Router's DHCP Server

If the router's DHCP server is enabled and the router does network address translation (NAT), check with your ISP to see whether you need to bind a fixed IP address to the router. Also, the router's DHCP server routable and non-routable IP addresses must match the Proxy Server LAT. In addition, Small Business Server components such as TCP/IP properties, Proxy client, Internet Explorer, Exchange, and RAS must be configured with the correct base IP address.

Important The LAN router configuration is not recommended because it defeats the security features of Proxy Server 2.0. Also, since most routers contain multiple features, including DHCP server and NAT capabilities, interference with Small Business Server routing functions may result from improper router or network IP address configurations. Since the task of setting up a LAN router in the small business network may cause the technology consultant to be faced with reconfiguring the entire IP addressing scheme of Small Business Server, we advise using the router with a second network adapter instead.

PART 6

Integration and Interaction

The earlier chapters of Part 6 describe several integration issues regarding e-mail and Internet connectivity and a discussion of how Office 2000 is integrated with Microsoft® BackOffice® Small Business Server 4.5. The later chapters describe various client interactions with the server, Small Business Server coexistence with a NetWare server, and interoperability issues for UNIX® and Macintosh® clients. The information is presented as follows.

Chapter 32	E-mail and Internet Connectivity Alternatives 493
Chapter 33	Office 2000 Integration Issues 509
Chapter 34	Client Interaction with the Server 515
Chapter 35	Cross-Platform Interoperability 521

CHAPTER 32

E-mail and Internet Connectivity Alternatives

Overview

When setting up an Internet connection for Microsoft® BackOffice® Small Business Server 4.5, it is not necessary to use an Internet service provider (ISP) on the referral server. The benefit of having an ISP on the referral server is the automated sign-up and configuring process, however, a large of number of ISPs who are not on the referral server support Small Business Server 4.5. This chapter outlines what an ISP not on the referral server can do to provide support for Small Business Server.

Web Browsing Support

Any ISP can support Small Business Server by offering web browsing. This allows users in the small business network to connect to the Internet to browse the web or connect to other mail services to receive Internet e-mail via a web-based account. The sections that follow describe two ways that web browsing support can be configured to work with the Small Business Server to provide web access for clients on the small business network.

Single ISP Account Configured Using Microsoft Proxy Server 2.0

This configuration utilizes Proxy Server 2.0, an application-component of Small Business Server 4.5. In this configuration, Proxy Server is configured so that when any client launches their web browser, a connection to the ISP account is initiated. Once this single connection is established, all clients on the network can share access to the Internet, as shown in the following illustration.

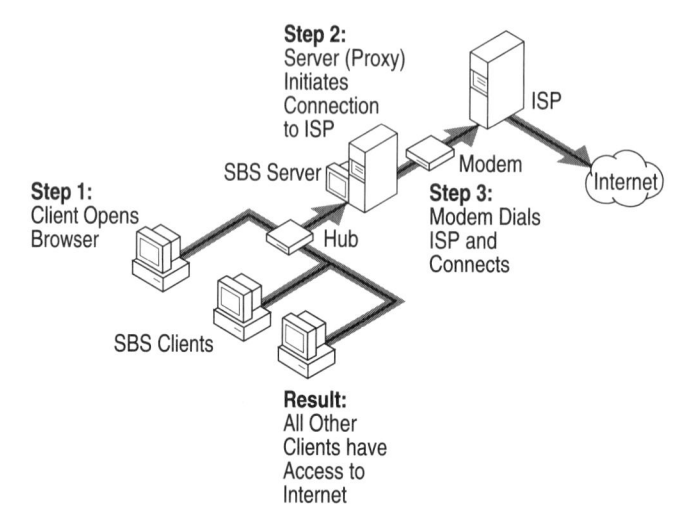

Figure 32.1 Single ISP account configured using Proxy Server

To set up this configuration, you can use the Internet Connection Wizard, or you can perform the following manual configuration steps.

▶ **To configure Small Business Server to use Proxy Server for web browsing support**

1. From **My Computer**, double-click **Dial-Up Networking** to display the following **Dial-Up Networking** dialog box.

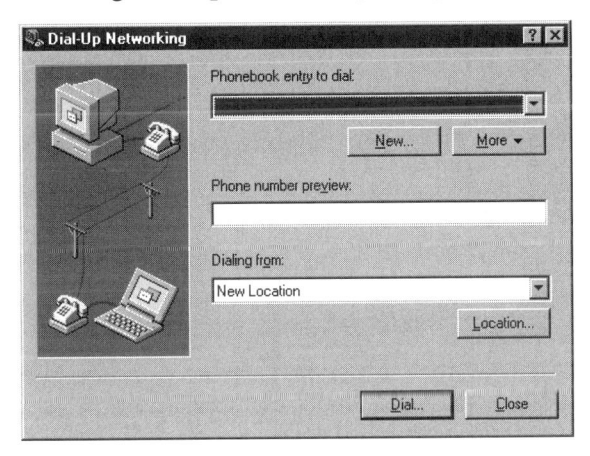

2. Click **New** and follow the instructions to create a Remote Access Service (RAS) phonebook entry for the ISP account.

3. Click **Finish** when the RAS phonebook entry is complete. Click **Close** to exit.

4. Click **Start**, point to **Programs** and **Microsoft Proxy Server**, and then click **Microsoft Management Console** to display the following IIS console.

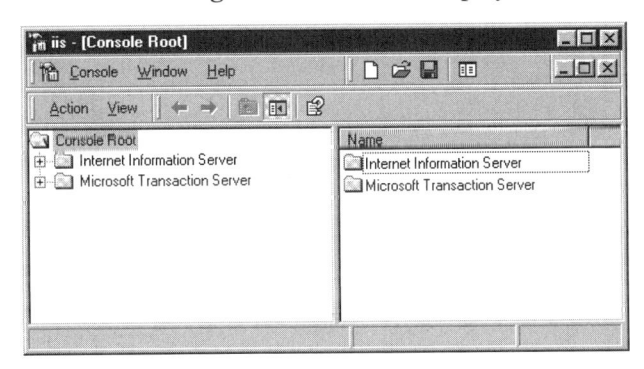

5. Double-click Internet Information Server, then double-click on the server to display the Proxy Services, as follows.

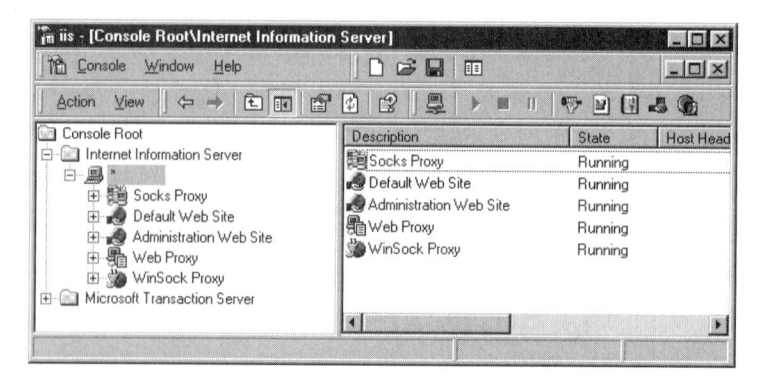

6. Right-click on **Web Proxy** then click **Properties** to display the following **Web Proxy Service Properties** page.

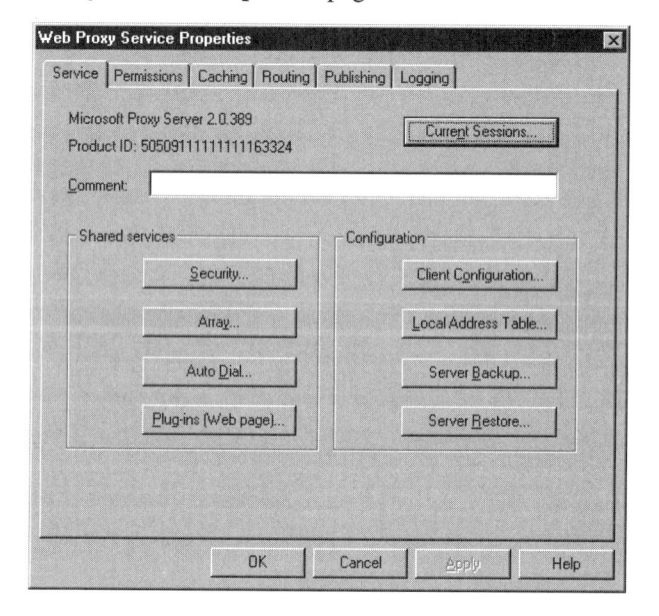

7. Click **Auto Dial** to display the following **Microsoft Proxy Auto Dial** dialog box.

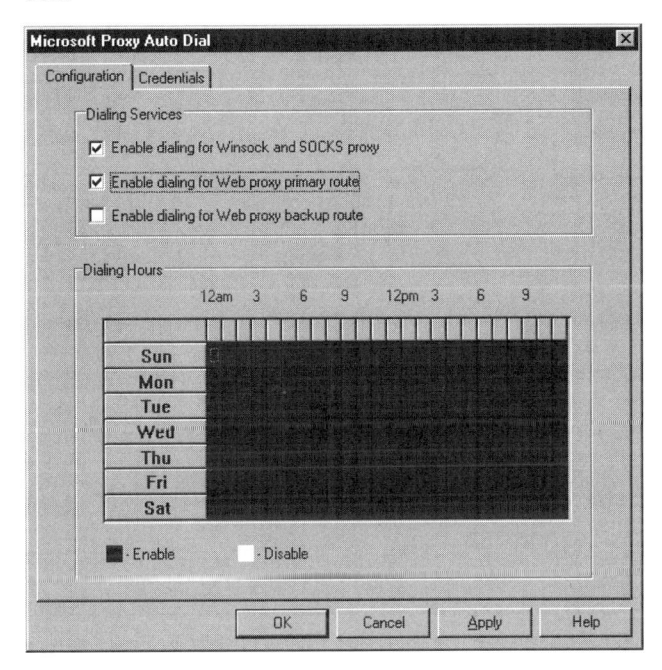

8. Select the **Configuration** tab, and then select **Enable dialing for Web proxy primary route**.

9. Select the **Credentials** tab, and then select the RAS phonebook entry created in step 2 and type in the appropriate **User Name** and **Password**—obtain this from the ISP.

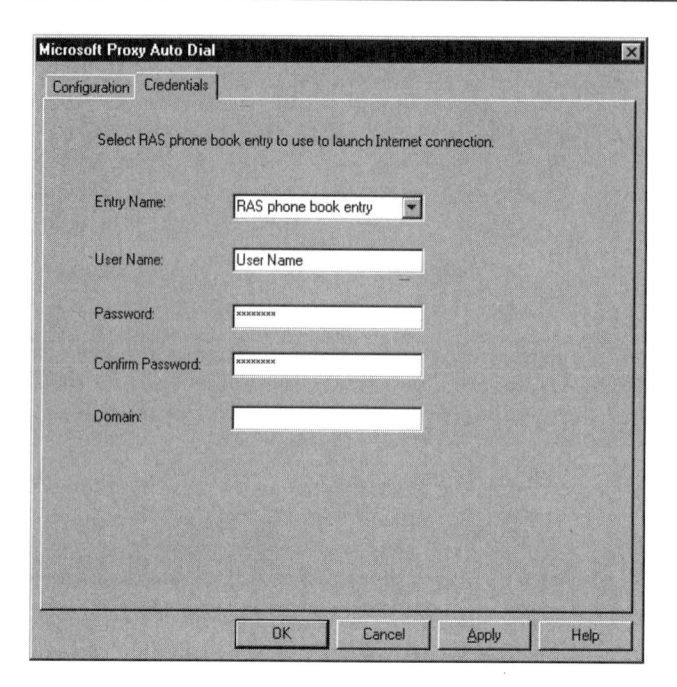

> **Note** Depending on your ISP's configuration, there may not be a value for the **Domain** field.

10. Click **Apply** and then click **OK**.

When the Proxy Client is installed using the Set Up Computer Wizard, then client computers are automatically set up to use Proxy Server to browse the Internet. If the Proxy Client must be installed manually, perform the following steps.

▶ **To manually install the Proxy Client**

1. From the client machine, double-click **Network Neighborhood**.
2. Double-click the server icon to display the Small Business Server directory.
3. Double-click the **mspclnt** folder.
4. Double-click **Setup** to launch the Proxy Client setup program and install the Proxy Client from the server to the client machine.
5. Click **OK** and exit Setup when Proxy Client installation is complete.

To manually configure Microsoft Internet Explorer to use Proxy Server when initiating an Internet connection, perform the following steps.

▶ **To manually configure the Microsoft Internet Explorer client to use Proxy Server**

1. Click **Start**, point to **Programs**, and then click **Internet Explorer** to launch Microsoft Internet Explorer.
2. On the **Tools** menu, click **Internet Options**.
3. On the **Connections** tab, click **LAN Settings** to display the **Local Area Network (LAN) Settings** dialog box.
4. Select **Use a proxy server** and **Bypass proxy server for local addresses**.
5. Type *http://servername* in the **Address** field, where *servername* is the name of the small business company server.
6. Type *80* in the **Port** field.
7. Click **Advanced** and select **Use the same proxy server for all protocols**.
8. Make sure the servername and port number specified in steps 5 and 6, respectively, appear in the **HTTP** protocol fields.
9. Click **OK** and exit all dialog boxes.

Multiple ISP Accounts Configured Using Microsoft Modem Sharing Service

This configuration utilizes the Microsoft Modem Sharing Service, a component of Small Business Server which allows users to share modems. In this configuration, the connection to the ISP is initiated from the client and not the server computer. The client uses the Modem Sharing Service to connect using a modem attached to the server computer—this eliminates the need for an individual modem for each client computer. The resulting connection between the client computer and ISP cannot be shared with other client computers on the network, as shown in the following illustration.

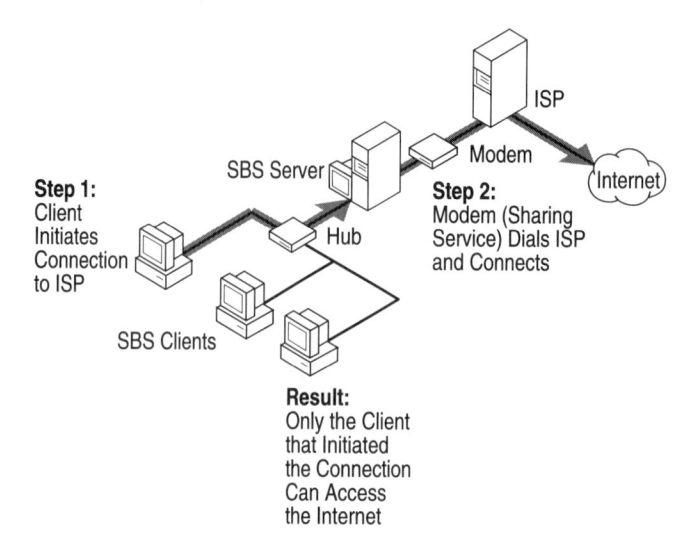

Figure 32.2   Multiple ISP accounts configured using Microsoft Modem Sharing Service

To set up a client to use the Modem Sharing Service for web browsing support, follow the steps of the procedure below.

▶ **To configure a RAS phonebook entry for client web browsing support**

1. From **My Computer**, double-click **Dial-Up Networking** to display the following **Dial-Up Networking** dialog box.

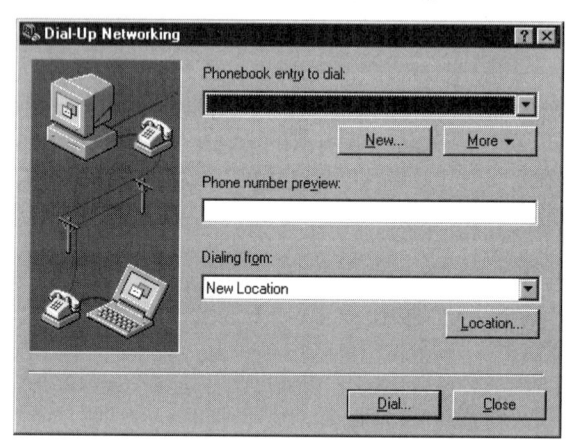

2. Click **New** and follow the instructions to create a Remote Access Service (RAS) phonebook entry for the ISP account.

3. Click **Finish** when the RAS phonebook entry is complete. Click **Close** to exit.

Note We recommend using the Modem Sharing Service for connecting to proprietary systems such as banks. The Modem Sharing Service should not be used to connect to the Internet. If you do use it this way, you must disable the Proxy client before connecting.

Exchange Server Automatically Set up for Internal E-mail

If Microsoft Exchange Server is selected during the Small Business Server installation, it will automatically be set up and configured for internal e-mail. Also, if the Microsoft Outlook client is installed using the Set Up Computer Wizard, the client computer will automatically be set up to use the Microsoft Exchange Server for internal e-mail.

With web browsing support, clients can use Microsoft Exchange Server and Outlook® for internal e-mail and scheduling, in association with an Internet e-mail account, with no additional configuring required.

Note POP3 can be configured to deliver mail into the Exchange Server universal mailbox.

Web Browsing and POP3 Support

Web browsing support from the ISP provides both browsing and Internet e-mail functionality, however, the following client e-mail address format obtained in this configuration may not always be appropriate for purposes of identification in the business community:

- Client@mailservice.com

More appropriate are the formats of e-mail addresses obtained with POP3 support, as follows:

- Client@microsoft.internetserviceprovider.com - or -
  Client@microsoft.com

Also, with POP3 support, a universal mailbox can be configured where the user manages both internal and Internet mail. The sections that follow describe two ways that POP3 support can be configured to work with the Small Business Server, depending on how web browsing support is configured.

Single POP3 Account

In this configuration, one client configures Microsoft Outlook to receive corporate Internet mail using the POP3 account. This single account dials out to the ISP to receive and send *all* Internet e-mail for the small business.

If the single POP 3 account is used in combination with the Microsoft Exchange Server, the account owner can manually forward the received Internet e-mail to other clients on the network. Forwarding is accomplished using the internal mail features of Exchange Server, as depicted in the following illustration.

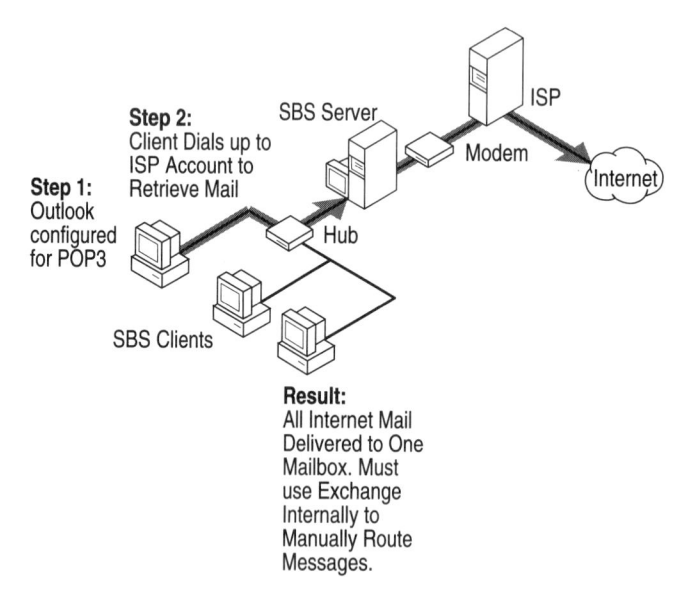

Figure 32.3 Single POP3 account

Multiple POP3 Accounts

In this configuration, all clients configure Microsoft Outlook to receive mail with their own POP3 account. Each client is then able to dial out to the ISP and receive their Internet e-mail, as depicted in the following illustration.

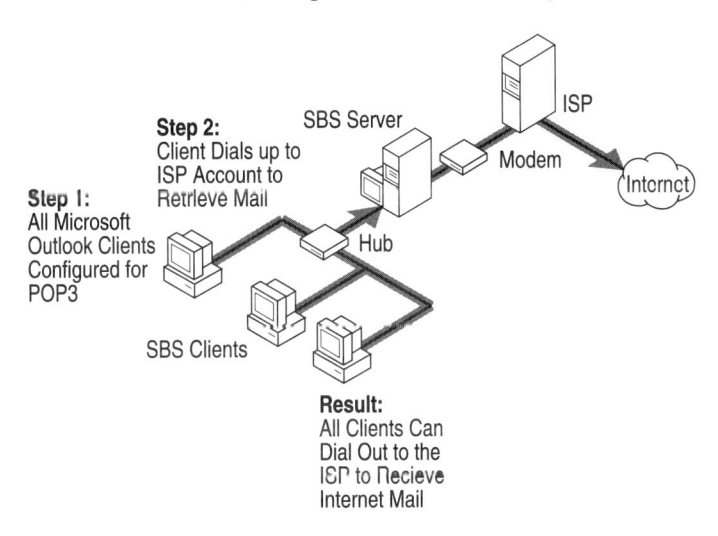

Figure 32.4 Multiple POP3 accounts

Using Exchange for Internal and POP3 E-mail

In this configuration, clients have normal access to Microsoft Exchange Server and Outlook for internal e-mail and scheduling. However, you can use the following procedure to configure Outlook clients to also accept Internet e-mail from a POP3 server, reducing the number of inboxes managed by the client.

▶ **To configure the Microsoft Outlook client to receive POP3 mail**

1. From the client desktop, launch Microsoft Outlook.
2. On the **Tools** menu, click **Services** to display the following **Services** dialog box.

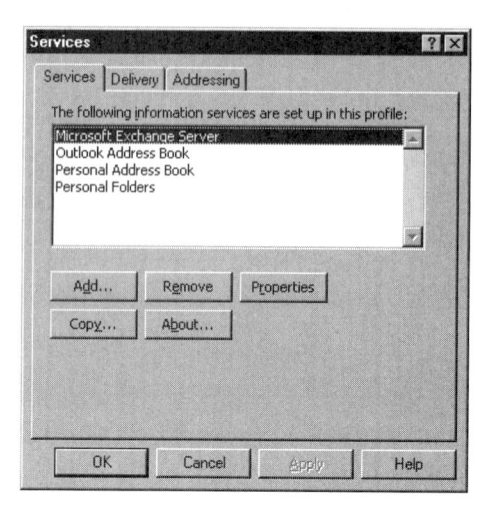

3. Select the **Services** tab, and then click **Add** to display the following **Add Service to Profile** dialog box.

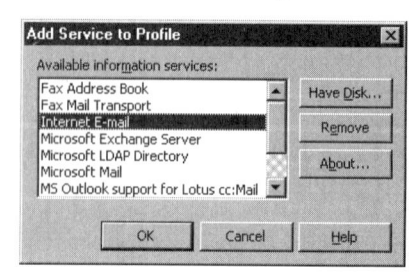

4. Select **Internet E-mail**, and then click **OK** to display the following **Mail Account Properties** page.

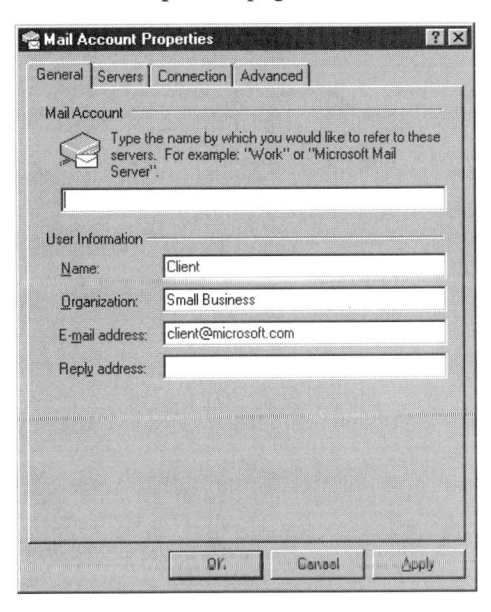

5. Select the **General** tab and type in the appropriate information.
6. Select the **Servers** tab and type in the appropriate information.

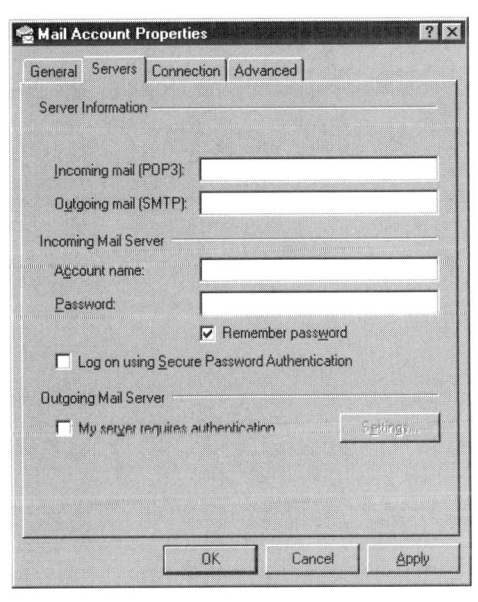

7. Select the **Connection** tab, select **Connect using my local area network (LAN)** and then specify the dial-up networking connection in the **Use the following Dial-Up Networking connection** drop-down list.

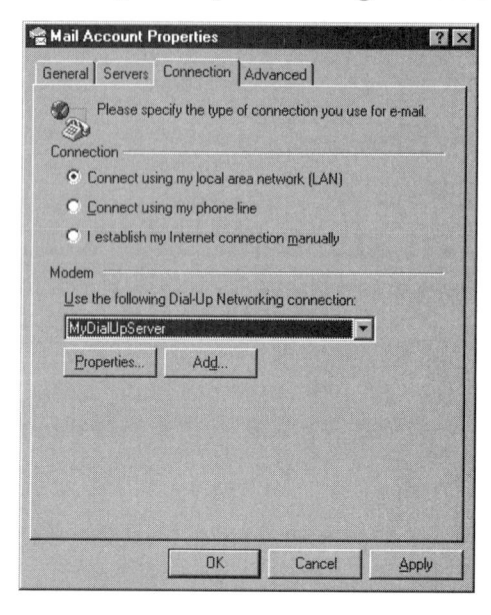

8. Click **Apply**, and then click **OK**.
9. Click **OK** on the **Add Service to Profile** pop-up message when you are asked to restart Outlook.
10. In the **Services** dialog box, select the **Delivery** tab.

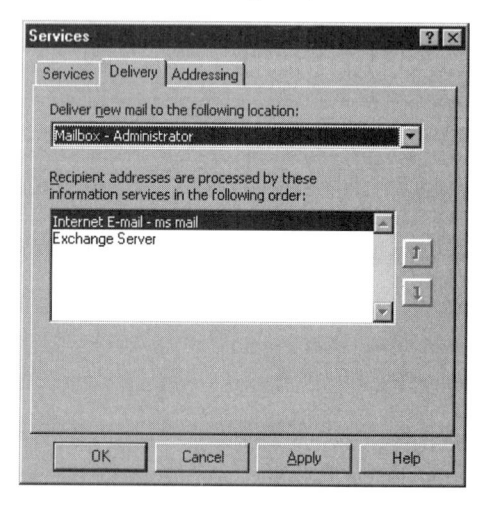

11. Select **Internet E-mail**. If necessary, move this information service to the top of the list using the up-arrow to establish the order in which recipient addresses are processed by the information services listed.
12. Click **Apply** and then **OK**.
13. From the Microsoft Outlook **File** menu, click **Exit** and then log off.

By default, Exchange Server routing is disabled. In order to use the Exchange Server and POP3 mail, perform the steps below.

SMTP and Web Hosting Support

While POP3 support does offer Internet e-mail access and a single inbox for users, in some cases manual mail forwarding is required and the number of e-mail addresses and distribution lists you can have is limited. If POP3 is inadequate for the needs of the small business organization, Simple Mail Transfer Protocol (SMTP) is the next level of e-mail support to acquire.

SMTP Support

SMTP allows the use of Microsoft Exchange Server 5.5 for both internal and Internet e-mail, giving full control over the e-mail accounts you create and use. This improves manageability, and by having a single log-on to retrieve all Internet e-mail, security is improved and the need for multiple POP3 accounts is eliminated. Refer to *Chapter 21, ISP Connectivity Tasks,* in *Part 3, Deployment,* of this resource guide for using the Internet Connection Wizard to configure Exchange Server to dial up and receive e-mail from an ISP.

Web Hosting Support

Although web browsing support allows clients to browse the web, a small business can only host its own website with web hosting support from an ISP. With web hosting support, the ISP hosts the small business web site on their server—you can post any changes to small business web pages there. By using an ISP to host the small business web site, a full-time Internet connection is not needed. Refer to *Chapter 21, ISP Connectivity Tasks,* in *Part 3, Deployment,* of this resource guide for using the Internet Connection Wizard to configure web site information used by the Web Publishing Wizard (which creates and updates the small business web site).

CHAPTER 33

Office 2000 Integration Issues

Overview

This chapter discusses Office 2000 integration with Microsoft® BackOffice® Small Business Server. Instructions are provided to integrate Office 2000 in a non-Office Small Business Server installation. A brief discussion of integrating Office 2000 applications in custom deployments is also provided.

Integrating Office 2000 in a Non-Office Small Business Server Installation

This section describes how you can integrate Office 2000 onto the server in the following Small Business Server installations:

- Small Business Server 4.0a to 4.5 upgrade.
- Non-Office 2000 version of Small Business Server 4.5.

By doing so, you can make Office 2000 applications available for client setup using the Set Up Computer Wizard, in Small Business Server installations that did not originally include Office 2000. To enable deployment of Office 2000 applications during client setup, perform the following steps.

▶ **To integrate Office 2000 in a non-Office Small Business Server installation**

1. Click **Start**, point to **Programs**, and then click **Windows NT Explorer** to launch Windows NT Explorer.

2. Locate the Disc 1 directory in the following path and then delete it: *sbsserver*\Clientapps\Ms\Office\CD1, where *sbsserver* is the name of Small Business Server.

Note In a non-Office Small Business Server installation, the Disc 1 directory contains Outlook bits only. The bits must be removed prior to Office 2000 installation, by deleting the Disc 1 directory.

3. Insert Disc 1 of Office 2000 into the CD-ROM drive.
4. Perform an administrative installation of Office 2000 Disc 1, as follows:
   - Click **Start**, point to **Programs**, and then click **Command Prompt** to display the Command Prompt screen.
   - At the prompt, type the CD-ROM drive letter, for example *E:*.
   - At the drive letter prompt, for example *E:*, type *Setup/A* to display the following **Microsoft Office 2000 Administrative Mode** screen of the Microsoft Office 2000 Professional Installation Wizard.

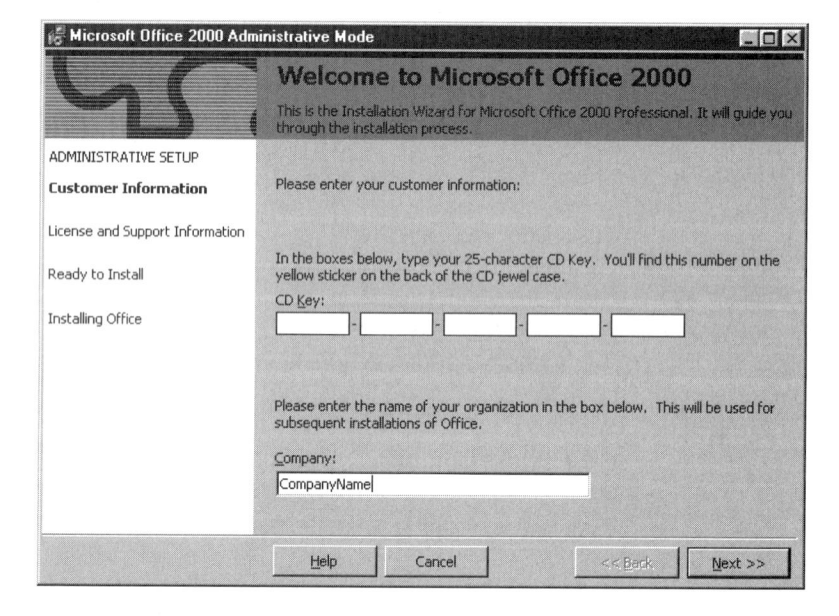

   - Type the **CD Key** numbers in the spaces provided—these are the SBS Pid numbers located on the Office 2000 CD.
   - In **Company**, type the name of the company.
   - Click **Next**, then read and accept the terms of the **End User License Agreement**.

- Click **Next**, to display the following **Microsoft Office 2000 Location** screen of the wizard.

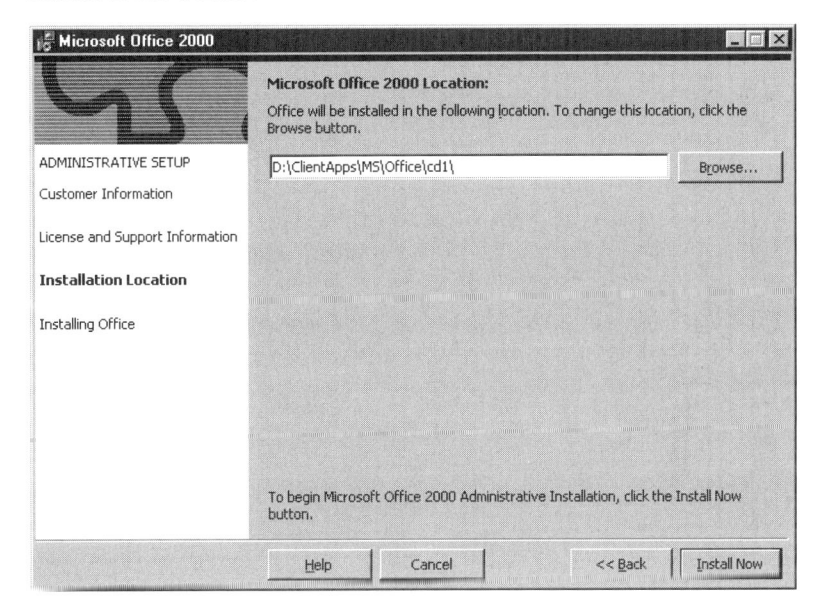

- Type the following location for the Office 2000 installation:

  *SBSServer**Clientapps**Ms**Office**CD1*, where *SBSServer* is the name of the Small Business Server.

Note Office 2000 Disc 1 must be installed in this location so the Set Up Computer Wizard can locate it.

- Click **Install Now** to begin the Office 2000 installation. When the installation is complete, click **Finish**, then remove Disc 1 from the CD-ROM drive.

5. Insert Disc 2 of Office 2000 into the CD-ROM drive.
6. Perform an administrative installation of Office 2000 Disc 2, as follows:
   - At the CD-ROM drive letter prompt (for example *E:*), type *Setup/A* to display the **Microsoft Office 2000 Administrative Mode** screen of the Microsoft Office 2000 Disc 2 Installation Wizard.
   - Type the **CD-Key** numbers in the spaces provided—these are the SBS Pid numbers located on the Office 2000 CD.
   - In **Company**, type the name of the company.
   - Click **Next**, then read and accept the terms of the **End User License Agreement**.

- Click **Next**, then type the following location for the Office 2000 installation:

  \\SBSServer\Clientapps\Ms\Office\CD2, where *SBSServer* is the name of the Small Business Server.

Note Office 2000 Disc 2 must be installed in this location so the Set Up Computer Wizard can locate it.

- Click **Install Now** to begin the Office 2000 installation. When the installation is complete, click **Finish**, then remove Disc 2 from the CD-ROM drive.
- In Windows NT Explorer, locate the Scw.ini file in the following path: SBSServer\SmallBusiness\Scw.ini. Rename this file to Scw.no.
- Locate the Scw.o file in the following path: SBSServer\SmallBusiness\Scw.o. Rename this file to Scw.ini.
- In Windows NT Explorer, locate the Clioc.inf file in the following path: SBSServer\SmallBusiness\Template\Clioc.inf. Rename this file to Clioc.no.
- Locate the Clioc.o file in the following path: SBSServer\SmallBusiness\Template\Clioc.o. Rename this file to Clioc.ini.

After completing these steps, you can then integrate Office 2000 applications into a new client computer setup with the Set Up Computer Wizard. Refer to *Chapter 20, Small Business Server Set Up Computer Wizard,* in *Part 3, Deployment,* for further information. You can also add Office 2000 applications to existing client computers via the **add software to a computer** taskpad on the **Manage Computers** page of the Small Business Server console.

Note If existing client computers already have Outlook 2000 installed, manually uninstall it on each client before installing the Office 2000 suite of applications; otherwise, clients will be unable to add certain features and components to Outlook.

Perform the steps below to remove Outlook 2000 from a client computer.

▶ **To remove Outlook 2000 from the client computer**

1. Click **Start**, point to **Settings**, and then click **Control Panel**.
2. Double-click **Add/Remove Programs** to display the following **Add/Remove Program Properties** dialog box.

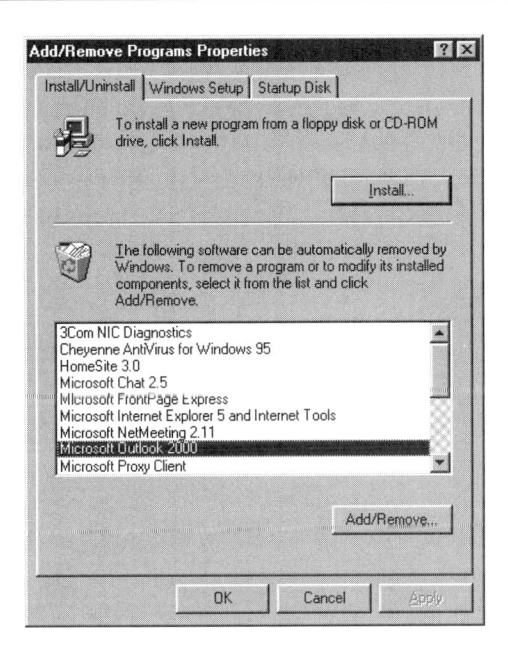

3. Highlight **Microsoft Outlook 2000**, and then click **Add/Remove** to display the following **Microsoft Outlook 2000 Maintenance Mode** utility screen.

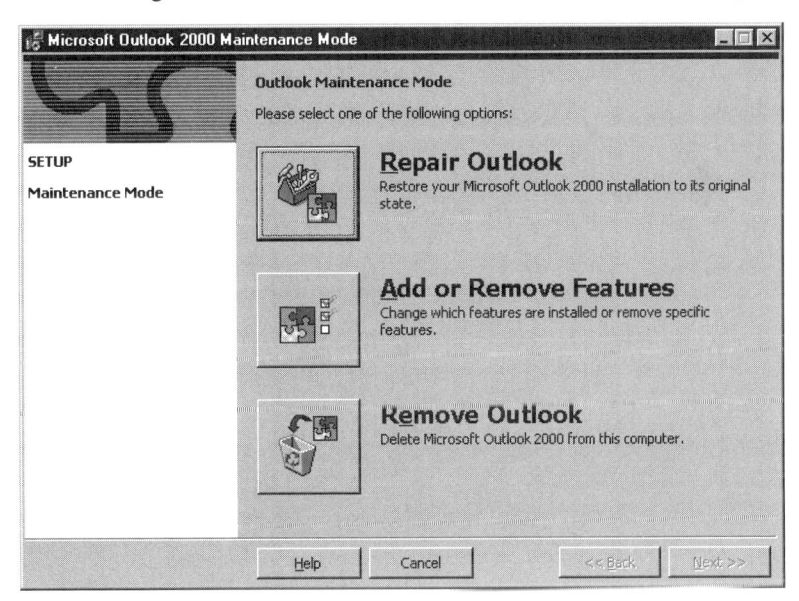

4. Click **Remove Outlook** to uninstall Outlook 2000 from the client computer.
5. Click **OK** when the uninstall is complete.

Integrating Office 2000 Applications in Custom Deployments

In Small Business Server 4.5, Office 2000 client applications are integrated with the Set Up Computer Wizard and then rolled out in a standard configuration. If you want to perform a custom deployment of Office 2000 with transforms, client applications cannot be integrated with the wizard. Refer to the *Office 2000 Resource Kit* for details on custom deployment scenarios. See *Chapter 24, Customizing Office 2000 Deployment,* in *Part 3, Deployment,* for a summary of the tools used to perform custom Office 2000 deployments.

CHAPTER 34

Client Interaction with the Server

Overview

The Windows NT® Server application of Microsoft® BackOffice® Small Business Server 4.5 has an open networking architecture for flexible communication with other network products, thus allowing client computers running operating systems other than Windows NT Workstation to interact with computers in the Windows NT Server domain. However, these clients do not have domain accounts and therefore do not have Windows NT Workstation logon security. Users running these other operating systems can have user accounts stored in the Windows NT Server directory database, but the computer itself does not have logon security to restrict access to its own resources.

Windows NT Workstation computers can also interact with servers and clients running other operating systems. Various protocols and software that allows interoperability are either native to Windows NT Server or are available separately.

Client Interactions

MS-DOS, Windows® 95/98, Windows 3.1, and Macintosh® clients interact with a Small Business Server 4.5 just as they would with a normal Windows NT Server 4.0. However, Small Business Server does not provide client setup software or client applications for MS-DOS, Windows 3.1, and Macintosh client operating systems.

MS-DOS Clients

MS-DOS clients running one of the following components can use shared network resources on the respective servers:

- Microsoft LAN Manager for MS-DOS version 2.2. Enables computers running MS-DOS to interact with Windows NT Server and LAN Manager 2.x domain controllers.
- Microsoft Network Client for MS-DOS version 3.0. Enables computers running MS-DOS to interact with a Windows NT Server domain controller and with computers running Windows NT Workstation and LAN Manager 2.x.

For information on installing and using Microsoft Network Client Version 3.0 for MS-DOS, refer to Chapter 16 of the *Windows NT Server 4.0 Networking Guide*.

Since MS-DOS-based computers cannot store user accounts, they do not participate in domains the way Windows NT-based computers do. Each MS-DOS computer usually has a default domain for browsing. An MS-DOS user with a domain account can be set up to browse any domain, not just the domain containing the user's account.

Windows 95/98 Clients

Access to Windows NT Server networking is built into the Windows 95/98 operating system. Windows 95/98 clients with domain accounts can log on to their accounts the same way Windows NT Workstation clients do. Windows 95/98 user account logons can be validated by both Windows NT Server or LAN Manager 2.x domain controllers.

Windows 3.1 and OS/2 Clients Running LAN Manager

Windows NT Server interoperates with Microsoft LAN Manager 2.x systems. Windows 3.1, OS/2, and MS-DOS computers running LAN Manager workstation software can connect to Windows NT Server.

Microsoft LAN Manager for OS/2 version 2.2 is a component of Windows NT Server that enables client computers running OS/2 version 1.3x to interact with Windows NT Server (and LAN Manager 2.x servers). This allows those client computers running OS/2 version 1.3x to share network resources.

Note LAN Manager 2.x servers (on OS/2 or UNIX® computers) can also work with Windows NT Server, but they must be backup domain controllers to interact with Small Business Server in the same domain.

Macintosh Clients

Microsoft Windows NT Server Services for Macintosh is a component of Windows NT Server that enables Windows and Apple Macintosh clients to share files and printers. This means that a Windows NT Server computer can act as a server for both these types of clients and that Macintosh computers can share resources with any client supported by Windows NT Server, including MS-DOS and LAN Manager client computers.

Note For complete information on planning and setting up a Macintosh network, refer to Part 5 of the *Microsoft Windows NT Server 4.0 Networking Supplement.*

Client Authentication

The sections that follow describe how MS-DOS, Windows 3.1, Windows 95, and Macintosh clients authenticate to a Windows NT Server.

MS-DOS Client Authentication

In order for an MS-DOS client to connect to a network, network software such as LAN Manager or Microsoft Networks must be installed and configured. Refer to the user documentation accompanying the network software for installation instructions.

When the network software is installed, the Autoexec file is modified. The network software then starts up automatically when the MS-DOS client is started. For the MS-DOS client to log onto Windows NT Server, the user account and appropriate permissions for the client must be created on the Small Business Server Console from the **Manager Users** page. After the user account and permissions are created and the network is started, the MS-DOS client types the **Net Use** command at the prompt. Then, the client types the server name and share to connect to. In the example below, the client is connecting to the payroll share on a payroll department server identified as *CAWPS30DPT01*:

Net Use * \\CAWPS30DPT01\Payroll

After typing this command, the client presses ENTER—then an available drive letter is assigned and a connection to the server is completed.

Windows 3.1 Client Authentication

In order for a Windows 3.1 client to connect to a Windows NT Server-based network, network software such as LAN Manager or Microsoft Networking Client must be installed and configured. Refer to the user documentation accompanying the network software for installation instructions.

When the network software is installed, the Config.sys and Windows\system.ini files are updated. This causes the network software to start up automatically when the Windows 3.1 client is started.

Note If LAN Manager network software is in use, the **LAN Manager Logon** screen is displayed every time the Windows 3.1 client starts up.

For a Windows 3.1 client to log onto Windows NT Server, the user account and appropriate permissions must be created on the Small Business Server console from the **Manager Users** page. Once the user account and permissions are set up, the Windows 3.1 client can logon and be authenticated on the Windows NT Server network. To access file and print services, the Windows 3.1 client must supply the network path to connect to the required Windows NT Server resources. Refer to Chapter 5, "Network Services: Enterprise Level" in the *Windows NT Server 4.0 Networking Guide* for procedures to connect a Windows 3.1 client to Windows NT Server resources.

Windows 95 Client Authentication

In order for a Windows 95 client to access a Windows NT Server domain, it must be configured properly. During Windows 95 client setup, the technology consultant supplies information that is reviewed later in the configuration process. This process also involves configuration of the Windows NT Server domain for the Windows 95 client. Refer to Chapter 5, "Network Services: Enterprise Level" in the *Windows NT Server 4.0 Networking Guide* for procedures to configure the Windows 95 client.

Note Before configuring Windows 95 clients, make sure you create a user account with appropriate permissions from the **Manage Users** page of the Small Business Server console.

After a user account, permissions, and the Windows 95 client are configured, the client may authenticate to the Windows NT Server at logon time.

Macintosh Client Authentication

Windows NT Server Services for Macintosh is a completely integrated component of Windows NT Server. This service makes it possible for Macintosh clients to share files and printers in the Windows NT Server domain. Macintosh clients only need their operating system software to function as a client. However, the optional Microsoft Authentication module, an extension to AppleShare, may be set up to provide additional security for Macintosh client logon to the Windows NT Server.

Microsoft Authentication encrypts (scrambles) passwords so they cannot be monitored when sent over the network. Microsoft Authentication also stores the passwords on the Windows NT Server. The Macintosh Authentication file may be set up by the technology consultant or the Macintosh client may do it across the network. With Microsoft Authentication, the Macintosh client can also specify the domain when they logon or change passwords.

Since Apple System software up to version 7.1 only has standard authentication modules, we recommend the installation of the Microsoft Authentication Module if increased security is necessary for Macintosh clients in the Windows NT Server domain.

More Information

For additional information about Macintosh client authentication, refer to Chapter 5, "Network Services: Enterprise Level" of the *Windows NT Server 4.0 Networking Guide*.

CHAPTER 35

Cross-Platform Interoperability

Overview

Many networks in use today were installed to provide basic file and printer sharing. As business requirements have expanded, so have the demands on computing infrastructures. These same networks must now support a growing number of new capabilities and services, such as electronic commerce, remote communications, web publishing, e-mail, and database applications in a client/server processing model.

To provide these services to small and large businesses, many information technology professionals are using Microsoft® Windows NT® Server-based computing environments. Windows NT Server 4.0 acts as a unifying foundation that does the following:

- Combines and enhances the capabilities of diverse server operating systems.
- Allows organizations to extend a consistent set of system services and user interfaces across the network.

The core server technology of Microsoft BackOffice® Small Business Server 4.5 is the Windows NT Server 4.0 operating system. This operating system is designed to work with many client network operating systems in use today. This protects the legacy investments of the small business organization and provides the flexibility to keep up with evolving business computing demands. This chapter describes the requirements for interoperability between Small Business Server 4.5 and other operating system environments.

Interoperability Layers

When assessing interoperability issues, think of your organization's computing infrastructure in terms of four layers: network, data, applications, and management. Depending on the platforms combined, one or more of these areas must be addressed:

- Network layer.

  Consists of low-level communication protocols, such as Internet Packet Exchange (IPX) and Transmission Control Protocol/Internet Protocol (TCP/IP), which are used to transport data. Also includes functionality such as terminal emulation or print services.

- Data layer.

  Provides access to both structured (primarily database) and unstructured (primarily file systems) data sources. In addition, includes access to other critical information, such as e-mail.

- Application layer.

  Addresses the way an organization's application infrastructure can allow applications running on different operating systems to work together. For example, this layer defines how two applications can participate in transactions, or how an application can be delivered to multiple client platforms.

- Management layer.

  Focuses on cross-platform user, system, and network management.

Operating System Environments Supported by Windows NT Server 4.0

Windows NT Server 4.0 supports all the standards required to interoperate with the following operating systems:

- NetWare 2.x/3.x/4.x
- UNIX® x.x
- Macintosh® System 6.0.7 or higher
- Windows NT Workstation
- Windows 95/98
- Windows 3.x
- MS-DOS
- OS/2®

The following current network protocols are also supported by Windows NT Server 4.0:

- TCP/IP
- Internet Packet Exchange/Sequenced Packet Exchange (IPX/SPX)
- Network Basic Enhanced User Interface (NetBEUI)
- AppleTalk
- Data Link Control (DLC)
- Hypertext Transfer Protocol (HTTP)
- Systems Network Architecture (SNA)
- Point-to-Point Protocol (PPP)
- Point-to-Point Tunneling Protocol (PPTP)

NetWare Interoperability

Small Business Server 4.5 integrates easily with the infrastructures of NetWare 2.x, 3.x, and 4.x (in bindery emulation mode). This helps to lower operating costs, increase resource utilization, and enables a platform for innovative client/server solutions. To ease the integration, Microsoft developed a set of utilities that allow the Windows NT Server application to fully integrate with most NetWare networks. These technologies address NetWare interoperability at the network, data, and management layers. The utilities listed immediately below are part of the Windows NT Server application in Small Business Server 4.5:

- Gateway Service for NetWare (GSNW)
- Client Services for NetWare (CSNW)
- NWLink (an IPX/SPX-compatible protocol)
- Migration Tool for NetWare

Also, the following add-on utilities may be purchased for further enhancements of Windows NT Server and NetWare interoperability:

- File and Print Services for NetWare (FPNW)
- Directory Service Manager for NetWare (DSMN)

Gateway Service for NetWare

GSNW is a Microsoft utility that allows a Windows NT Server-based computer to act as a gateway to resources on a NetWare LAN, as shown in the following illustration.

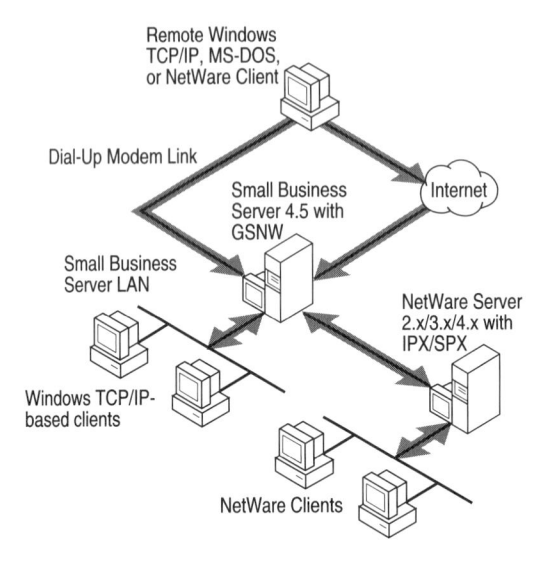

Figure 35.1 Gateway Service for NetWare configuration

GSNW offers the following features:

- Protocol availability.

    Allows the small business to use any protocol on client desktops without losing NetWare LAN connectivity. For example, Windows NT Workstation-based clients can access NetWare resources using TCP/IP without requiring a NetWare client redirector on an IPX/SPX protocol stack. The efficiency of GSNW reduces the administrative load for each client and thus improves network performance.

    GSNW also allows the technology consultant to deploy TCP/IP as the strategic protocol without incurring the additional costs of replacing older technologies.

- Remote access to NetWare file and print servers.

    Small Business Server can be deployed as a communications server to enable remote user access to the NetWare LAN. This feature of GSNW allows NetWare, MS-DOS, or Windows operating system-based clients to utilize the Windows NT Server Remote Access Service (RAS) to maintain a reliable and secure connection when connecting to the LAN.

- Novell Directory Services (NDS) support.

    This feature allows users to do the following:
    - Navigate NDS trees.
    - Authenticate with an NDS-aware server.
    - Print from NDS.
    - NetWare 4.x logon script support.

Client Services for NetWare

CSNW lets Windows NT Workstation-based clients access files and print resources on a NetWare 4.x server with a single logon and password. CSNW also supports Novell's NDS authentication to multiple NDS trees, and also provides full support for NDS property pages, passwords, and processing of NetWare login scripts.

NWLink

NWLink is an IPX/SPX-compatible protocol that provides NetWare clients with access to Windows NT Server-based applications. With this protocol, NetWare clients can access applications such as Microsoft SQL Server™ 7.0 or Exchange Server 5.5 without changing any client-side software. NWLink also establishes a means of communication for the tools that interoperate with NetWare.

Microsoft's implementation of IPX/SPX and Novell NetBIOS-compatible protocols can coexist with other protocols on the same network adapter card. This means you can have several networks running independently on the same network hardware connection. NWLink also supports Windows Sockets, Novell NetBIOS, and Named Pipes protocols.

Migration Tool for NetWare

This tool automatically ports NetWare 2.x/3.x resources to the Windows NT Server 4.0 application of Small Business Server. The migration of these resources can be accomplished with the Migration Tool for NetWare, without interruption to the NetWare server or clients. For more information about the Migration Tool for NetWare, refer to the "NetWare Migration Phase" section of *Chapter 39, Migrating From a NetWare Environment,* in *Part 8, Migration and Upgrade*, of this resource guide.

Add-On Utilities for NetWare

Microsoft created a bundle of add-on utilities for NetWare users to enhance their networks with Windows NT Server technology. This bundle of utilities is called Services for NetWare and consists of FPNW and DSMN. The sections that follow describe what can be done with these utilities.

File and Print Services for NetWare

The FPNW component allows Small Business Server to appear and act like a NetWare Server to all NetWare clients currently on the network. It supports NetWare 2.x, 3.x, and 4.x (in bindery emulation mode) clients without any changes to their configuration and allows Small Business Server to appear in each client's Windows Explorer list of NetWare-compatible servers. FPNW enables the Windows NT application of Small Business Server to emulate a NetWare file and print server while providing file and print resources that use the same dialogs as a NetWare Server.

With FPNW installed on Small Business Server 4.5, a NetWare client can do the following:

- Map to a shared volume and directory on Small Business Server.
- Connect to a Small Business Server printer.
- Log on to Small Business Server and have login scripts execute.
- Use Small Business Server applications and services.

Directory Service Manager for NetWare

This tool simplifies the management of NetWare clients on the network. Since Windows NT Server 4.0 offers global directory services, single network logon to all services, and a central administration point, DSMN allows the technology consultant to centrally manage the mixed Windows NT and NetWare environment with Windows NT Directory Services.

NetWare Account Administration Through Small Business Server

DSMN copies NetWare user and group accounts to the Windows NT Directory Service of Small Business Server and then propagates any account changes back to the NetWare Server. NetWare accounts are synchronized only once with Small Business Server, then all account administration changes can be done through Small Business Server (since the changes are propagated back to the NetWare Server).

Simplified Network Administration

Network administration tasks are simplified with DSMN since the technology consultant can manage both the Windows NT and NetWare account information with one user account and associated password for each end user. DSMN includes the following features:

- A point-and-click interface for propagating user and group accounts from NetWare 2.x, 3.x, and 4.x (in bindery emulation mode) to Windows NT Directory Services.
- Multiple options for setting up initial passwords, selecting user account propagation, handling account deletions, and performing a trial run to test propagation strategies.
- Account database backup and replication to any location on the network.

User access to the NetWare network is facilitated by DSMN in the following ways:

- Quick network access for new users.

    Since setup is done in Windows NT Directory Services and the user account is propagated back to all authorized NetWare servers, new users get on the network very quickly.

- Simplified logon.

    Each user's account name and password are identical on the NetWare and Windows NT Server 4.0, thus logon from either server is simplified. Logon with RAS also uses the same account name and password.

- Authentication of users to services running on Windows NT Server.

With a single logon, users have access to Small Business Server applications as well as file and print services.

More Information

For information on NetWare integration with Small Business Server 4.5, refer to *Chapter 39, Migrating From a NetWare Environment,* in *Part 8, Migration and Upgrade,* of this resource guide. Also, view the NetShow seminar "Microsoft Windows NT 4.0: Migration and Coexistence with Novell NetWare" at:
http://www.microsoft.com/seminar/1033/default.htm

UNIX Interoperability

Small Business Server 4.5 integrates easily with an existing UNIX infrastructure. This helps lower operating costs, increases resource utilization, and assures a smooth migration from legacy UNIX environments. To facilitate the integration of UNIX environments with the Windows NT Server application, Microsoft offers the Windows NT Services for UNIX Add-on Pack. The components of this package include technologies for resource sharing, remote administration, password synchronization, and common scripting across platforms. Support for these technologies is described in the following sections with respect to the network, data, application, and management layers.

Network Layer Interoperability

For basic integration with UNIX systems, Small Business Server 4.5 includes support for industry-standard protocols used by UNIX, such as TCP/IP and DNS. These and other common protocols found on UNIX systems are all included with the Windows NT Server 4.0 application. The sections that follow describe the interoperability characteristics of Windows NT Server and UNIX at the network layer.

TCP/IP

Windows NT Server 4.0 includes TCP/IP, the primary transport protocol for the Internet, intranets, and homogeneous or heterogeneous networks. With TCP/IP built into its operating system, Windows NT Server 4.0 can exchange data with both UNIX hosts and the Internet.

File Transfer and Hypertext Transfer Protocols

With File Transfer Protocol (FTP) and HTTP services, users can copy files across heterogeneous networks and then manipulate them locally as text files or Microsoft Word documents. PC users can also access character-based UNIX applications through Windows NT Server 4.0 support for remote logon. By running terminal emulation software built into Microsoft Windows 95/98 and Windows NT client operating systems, users can log on to a UNIX timesharing server in a dial-up connection manner. After entering an authorized user name and password, users can access character-based applications residing on the remote UNIX system as if they were logged on directly.

Domain Name Service

The Domain Name Service (DNS) is a set of protocols and services on a TCP/IP network that allows network users to employ hierarchical user-friendly names to find other computers rather than using IP addresses. Windows NT Server 4.0 has a built-in, standards-based DNS service. This allows the technology consultant to easily migrate an existing DNS to the Windows NT Server 4.0 DNS, or coexist with a non-Microsoft DNS.

Dynamic Host Configuration and Boot Protocols

Dynamic Host Configuration Protocol (DHCP) automatically configures a host during boot up on a TCP/IP network and can change IP settings while the host is attached. This allows storage of IP addresses in a central database along with associated configuration information, including the subnet mask, gateway IP address, and DNS server IP address. Since DHCP for Windows NT Server 4.0 is based on industry standards, requests from any type of client platform using these standards are supported. The Microsoft DHCP server also offers Boot Protocol (BOOTP) support, used for booting diskless workstations.

Network File System

The Network File System (NFS) is included in the Windows NT Services for UNIX Add-on Pack as a standard for sharing files and printers in the UNIX environment. The NFS client and server software add-on lets Windows NT Server 4.0 users access files on UNIX and lets UNIX users access files on Windows NT Server 4.0.

Advanced Server for UNIX

Advanced Server for UNIX (ASU) extends interoperability between Windows NT Server 4.0 and UNIX providing Windows NT domain controller support on UNIX. For interoperability in the Small Business Server 4.5 environment, the UNIX system is set up as a Backup Domain Controller. Then, users can log on to the Windows NT-based network and gain access to resources distributed between the UNIX and Windows NT Servers on the network.

AT&T® exclusively licenses the ASU technology to virtually all major UNIX suppliers, including Compaq®, Hewlett-Packard®, Data General®, Fujitsu-ICL®, and Siemens-Nixdorf®.

Data Layer Interoperability

At the data layer, Windows NT Server 4.0 includes support for data source interoperability with UNIX systems, as described in the sections that follow.

Oracle Database Access

The Microsoft Visual Studio® Enterprise Edition development system offers comprehensive support for Oracle 7.3 and later databases running on UNIX platforms. Using Visual Studio, developers can visually build or edit data-driven web pages quickly from multiple data sources. In addition, developers can use Visual Studio to build and edit stored procedures, database diagrams, triggers, and scripts.

Open Database Connectivity and Object Linking and Embedding Database

Open Database Connectivity (ODBC) is a software interface that separates data access from the data sources, in order to make it easier to access a database on a network. The ODBC database access interface lets programmers access data from a diverse set of sources using a standard series of functions and commands. This means an application developer using ODBC can create applications that connect to databases running on UNIX or Windows NT Server 4.0, and their application code will run exactly the same way on either platform. With ODBC, programmers avoid having to code to each specific data source's requirements—an efficiency that significantly increases productivity.

Object Linking and Embedding Database (OLE DB) takes ODBC a step further. Whereas ODBC is designed around accessing relational data sources using Structured Query Language (SQL), OLE DB is focused on providing access to *any* data, anywhere.

Application Layer Interoperability

At the application layer, Windows NT Server 4.0 supports interoperability with UNIX systems, as described in the sections that follow.

Microsoft Outlook Express for UNIX

This version of Outlook® Express lets you connect messaging solutions across both environments, such as retrieving mail from an Exchange Server on a UNIX workstation.

Microsoft Internet Explorer for UNIX

Using Microsoft Internet Explorer for UNIX, web applications and Internet or intranet access is now delivered to UNIX desktops in the familiar Internet Explorer interface. Also, client/server applications can be designed to operate within the browser, across multiple platforms.

Transaction Internet Protocol

Transaction Internet Protocol (TIP) describes a standard two-phase commit protocol that enables a UNIX transaction manager to coordinate distributed transactions. It can be used with any application protocol, but is especially important for the Internet HTTP protocol. For examples of TIP, use your browser and locate the following:
ftp://ftp.isi.edu/in-notes/rfc2371.txt

Microsoft Transaction Server 2.0 and Oracle 7.3 Support

Microsoft Transaction Server (MTS) is a component-based transaction processing system included with Small Business Server 4.5 that combines the features of a transaction processing monitor and an object request broker. MTS defines a programming model and provides a run-time environment as well as a graphical administration tool.

Microsoft has enhanced the Microsoft Oracle ODBC driver to work with MTS 2.0. In addition, Oracle version 7.3.3 for Windows NT Server supports the XA interface. As a result, Small Business Server users can access an Oracle database in a coexisting UNIX operating environment and the database can participate in MTS-based transactions.

For example, users can update a Microsoft SQL Server database in Small Business Server and an Oracle database on a UNIX system under a single atomic transaction. If the transaction commits, both databases are updated. If the transaction quits, all work performed on each database is backed out.

MTS interoperates with any Oracle platform accessible from Windows NT, Windows 95, or Windows 98. Microsoft Distributed Transaction Coordinator (DTC) does not have to be running on UNIX and other non-Windows NT platforms in order for an MTS component to update an Oracle database.

MTS also works with Oracle 8 databases. However, users must access the Oracle 8 database server by using the Oracle 7.3 client. Also, the Microsoft Oracle ODBC driver supplied with Microsoft Transaction Server version 2.0 must be used with the Oracle database because it is the only Oracle OBDC driver that works with MTS.

Distributed Component Object Model and UNIX

The Component Object Model (COM) is a Microsoft specification for developing distributed transaction-based applications and defining the manner by which objects interact through an exposed interface. Distributed Component Object Model (DCOM) extends the COM model and provides applications with a way to interact remotely over a network.

Microsoft is working with partners to port DCOM onto UNIX (and other) platforms. This enables the DCOM Application Programming Interface (API) of Windows NT Server to appear on UNIX servers. DCOM on a UNIX server enables consistent application behavior in a heterogeneous environment of Windows NT and UNIX clients. By employing DCOM on UNIX, users can do the following:

- Port DCOM server applications from Windows NT Server-based operating environments to UNIX operating environments.
- Create wrappers for existing UNIX applications, providing DCOM access to the applications by clients running Windows.
- Develop new distributed UNIX applications that take advantage of the DCOM distribution mechanism. These applications can make the most of the DCOM reuse, version independence, and language independence capabilities.

Management Layer Interoperability

At the management layer, Windows NT Server 4.0 supports interoperability with UNIX systems, as described in the sections that follow.

Simple Network Management Protocol

Simple Network Management Protocol (SNMP) service is included in the current versions of Windows NT Server and Windows NT Workstation operating systems. This means that SNMP management software, such as HP OpenView and IBM® NetView®, can be used to manage Windows systems. Using these products, the technology consultant can manage UNIX clients from the Windows NT Server application of Small Business Server 4.5.

Administrative Tools

The Windows NT Services for UNIX Add-on Pack offers three features that simplify the administration of combined Windows NT Server 4.0 and UNIX networks as follows:

- Password synchronization between Windows NT Server 4.0 and UNIX servers. This reduces user confusion and the technology consultant's workload.
- Services for UNIX offers Telnet administration of both UNIX and the Windows NT Server application. This provides access to network administration from a single client workstation.
- Services for UNIX provides Korn Shell (a UNIX command line interface) and common UNIX commands, thus allowing UNIX shell scripts to execute on Windows NT Server. This means UNIX administrators can use familiar UNIX commands on Windows NT Server.

More Information

For additional information about Windows NT Server and UNIX interoperability, use the resources listed below:

- Windows NT Services for UNIX Add-on Pack:
  http://www.microsoft.com/windows/news/november1998/sfurtm.asp
- Windows NT and UNIX Interoperability White Paper:
  http://www.microsoft.com/ntserver/zipdocs/ntinteropunix.exe
- Vendors providing UNIX Interoperability products and services:
  http://www.microsoft.com/ntserver/nts/exec/vendors/partners.asp
- UNIX and Windows NT interoperability online seminar:
  http://www.microsoft.com/seminar/1033/default.htm

MacIntosh Interoperability

Microsoft Windows NT Server Services for Macintosh is an integrated component of Windows NT Server 4.0 that enables Windows and Macintosh clients to collaborate and share information across the small business network. It allows Macintosh clients to connect to a Windows NT server in the same way they connect to an AppleShare® server. The service supports an unlimited number of simultaneous AFP connections to a Windows NT server, and the Macintosh sessions are integrated with Windows NT sessions.

Existing versions of LAN Manager Services for Macintosh can be easily upgraded to Windows NT Services for Macintosh. In the upgrade, graphical installation, administration, and configuration utilities are integrated with existing Windows NT administration tools. Windows NT Services for Macintosh requires System 6.0.7 or higher and is AFP 2.1-compliant, however, AFP 2.0 clients are also supported. AFP 2.1 compliance provides support for logon and server messages.

Windows NT Server is transparent to the Macintosh user—its presence is only known by the quickness and responsiveness of the network.

Graphics Performance

In the past, Macintosh clients used UNIX servers to facilitate the heavy performance requirements of moving large graphics files across a network. With optimization for high bandwidth networks like Fast Ethernet and its full-featured functionality, Windows NT Server 4.0 can handle the most demanding needs of Macintosh clients. Also, Windows NT Server is the ideal for the publishing marketplace since most of the top server applications are already running it.

File Sharing

Services for Macintosh allows Macintosh clients to access and share files on a Windows NT Server-based network. The service includes a full AFP 2.0 file server. All Macintosh file system attributes, such as resource data forks and 32-bit directory IDs are supported. As a file server, all filenames, icons, and access permissions are intelligently managed. For example, a Word for Windows file appears on the Macintosh machine with the correct Word for Windows icons. These applications can also be launched from the file server as Macintosh applications. When files are deleted, no orphaned resource forks remain for clean up.

Macintosh-accessible volumes can be created in My Computer. Services for Macintosh automatically creates a Public Files volume at installation time. At that time, Windows NT file and directory permissions are automatically translated into corresponding Macintosh permissions.

Printer Sharing

Windows NT Services for Macintosh has the same functionality as the LAN Manager Services for Macintosh 1.0 MacPrint. As such, it allows Macintosh clients to access and share printers on a Windows NT Server-based network. With Services for Macintosh, Macintosh users can access the print server through the familiar Chooser interface. Macintosh clients can print PostScript jobs to either PostScript or non-PostScript printers using the Windows NT Server print services.

Administration

Services for Macintosh can be administered from the Control Panel and can be started transparently if the technology consultant has configured the server to use it.

Connecting Macintosh Computers to the Internet

Windows NT Server 4.0 application has all the features necessary to connect Macintosh clients to the Internet or corporate intranet. With built-in DHCP, Small Business Server has full compatibility with Macintosh clients running Open Transport 1.1—which allows them to utilize dynamically assigned IP addresses. For example, a Macintosh PowerBook® can be moved anywhere in the network with no disruption to network services.

Security

With Microsoft Proxy Server 2.0, Macintosh clients have fast and secure access to the Internet. Also, Windows NT Services for Macintosh fully supports and complies with Windows NT security. It presents the AFP security model to Macintosh users and allows them to access files on volumes that reside on CD-ROM or other read-only media. The AFP server also supports both cleartext and encrypted passwords at logon time.

Note The technology consultant has the option to configure the server to not accept cleartext passwords.

Interoperability Benefit Summary of Windows NT Server 4.0 Services for Macintosh

The following table summarizes the interoperability benefits that Windows NT Server Services for Macintosh has for the Macintosh client.

Table 35.1 Services for Macintosh Interoperability Benefits

Feature	Benefit
Seamless connectivity for Macintosh clients	Macintosh clients can access the Windows NT Server as easily as an AppleShare server using the familiar Chooser interface.
High performance file and print services	Macintosh clients can utilize Windows NT Server performance with its ability to move larger graphics files faster than any other network operating system.
Full-featured AppleTalk® routing	With its built in Multi-Protocol Router, a Windows NT Server can replace a dedicated AppleTalk router.
Universal printing	Macintosh clients can print PostScript jobs to either PostScript or non-PostScript printers using the Windows NT print server. Server-side spooling means a faster return to the client application and increased client productivity.
	The Windows NT print subsystem handles AppleTalk despooling errors and uses the Windows NT Server built-in printer support. A PostScript-compatible engine allows Macintosh users to print to any Windows NT printer as if printing to a LaserWriter®.
AppleTalk/PostScript printing for Windows clients	Windows clients can send print jobs to PostScript printers on an AppleTalk network, which provides them with access to more network resources.
	A user interface in Services for Macintosh allows for publishing a print queue on AppleTalk and for choosing an AppleTalk printer as a destination device.

(continued)

Table 35.1 Services for Macintosh Interoperability Benefits *(continued)*

Feature	Benefit
User identification and directory permissions	Clients can log on to Small Business Server from either a Windows PC or a Macintosh computer using the same user identification. Windows NT Server directory permissions for Macintosh users can be set in exactly the same way as an AppleShare server. This eliminates the need for Macintosh clients to learn a new security model
High volume capacity	Macintosh clients can utilize Windows NT Server volume, which can hold 200 terabytes of data and supports up to 4 gigabytes of RAM.
Flexible server hardware options	Windows NT Server 4.0 supports more hardware options than any other network operating system. Therefore, Macintosh users can choose the server hardware platform that best suits their needs—including PowerPC platforms.

More Information

For additional information about setting up, configuring, and using Microsoft Windows NT Server Services for Macintosh, refer to Chapter 5, "Network Services: Enterprise Level" of the *Windows NT Server 4.0 Networking Guide*.

PART 7

Security

The Internet has opened vast new opportunities for businesses to benefit from information sharing. The number of companies connecting their internal networks to the Internet to improve productivity, customer service, and collaboration is increasing daily. Since the Internet serves as an open gateway to information sharing, sensitive or critical company resources can be exposed to unwanted solicitation or attacks. As a result of this situation, the security of data and resources in the private organizational network is a concern for small and large businesses alike.

With Microsoft® BackOffice® Small Business Server 4.5, the small business can take advantage of a broad range of leading edge security features and services that protect the network from unwanted intrusions. Part 7 discusses the features of the server applications in Small Business Server 4.5 that can provide this security to the small business network. Material discussed here includes:

Chapter 36   Firewall Security and Web Caching with Proxy Server 2.0   541

Chapter 37   Computer Security and Windows NT Server 4.0   587

Chapter 38   Internet Information Server 4.0 Security Model   599

CHAPTER 36

Firewall Security and Web Caching with Proxy Server 2.0

Microsoft® Proxy Server 2.0 is an extensible firewall and content cache server that delivers a compelling combination of security and performance. Proxy Server 2.0 integrates high performance content caching with firewall features for a complete small business solution. It provides an easy and secure way to bring Internet access to every desktop in the small business organization and renders an integrated network access management solution.

This chapter begins with an overview of Proxy Server 2.0, which includes a discussion on managed network access and descriptions of Proxy Server 2.0 features and services offered in the Microsoft BackOffice® Small Business Server 4.5 package. System architecture is presented next and the chapter concludes with descriptions of Proxy Server 2.0 firewall security, performance enhancing features, and their benefits to the small business.

Overview of Proxy Server 2.0

This section provides an overview of Microsoft Proxy Server 2.0, including:

- Managed network access background.
- Proxy as a secure gateway.
- Web content caching.
- Proxy services offered.
- Security features.
- Web Publishing support.
- Default configuration.
- Advantages of proxy connectivity.

Managed Network Access Background

Competition and the availability of greater Internet bandwidths is changing how business organizations share information on the Internet. The result is a need for managed network access for information sharing between local users, remote users, business partners, and customers. This need is driving the development of new solutions for connecting organizations to information systems. Some examples of broad information sharing solutions are listed below.

- **Content Caching Servers**. These are servers used to accelerate Hypertext Markup Language (HTML) page access by storing frequently used pages locally. This reduces the need to use slower Internet connections for commonly accessed information.

- **Application Proxies**. Servers that prevent direct attacks on corporate information servers by making requests to the servers on behalf of an Internet requestor, limiting operations to legitimate commands or service locations, and hiding the true location of either the requesting client or the target service.

- **Firewalls**. Systems that restrict access beyond typical routing features by limiting access based on protocols and port numbers. They sometimes inspect traffic for common service attacks.

- **Remote Access Service**. Provides authenticated, dial-up access for client systems so that corporate network services can be accessed as if the client were connected directly to the local area network (LAN).

- **Virtual Private Networking (VPN)**. Similar to Remote Access Service (RAS), this solution provides a secure, encrypted access to corporate networks from clients connecting through the Internet.

Each of these solutions serves an important function, however, none alone can adequately address managed network access requirements for information sharing in most companies. Almost without exception, a combination of caching, proxy, and firewall services is needed for secure access to and from the Internet. Most small businesses connecting to the Internet need these services integrated with a common management infrastructure and a common database for managing user access control, all installed on a single platform.

Proxy Server 2.0 Integrated Services on a Single Platform

While businesses of all sizes can benefit from a combination of proxy, caching, firewall, RAS, and VPN, the configurations used can vary depending on scale, information technology (IT) resources, budget, and the customer's approach to security and management. Small business managed network access needs can be as sophisticated as a large business, although on a smaller scale. With the Proxy Server 2.0 application integrated in Small Business Server 4.5, the small business achieves managed access services combined on a single platform. This reduces hardware capital expenses, complexity, and management costs for the small business.

Open Standards Platform

While information security and intrusion protection are as important to small businesses as they are to large, many small businesses have limited management resources to proactively review and track these issues. Without dedicated IT staff, sophisticated and complex reporting tools monitoring security cannot be utilized by smaller companies. The optimum solution for a small business in this situation is the employment of Proxy Server 2.0 on the Small Business Server 4.5 platform. The completeness, high performance capability, and the managed network access features of this application resolves security issues while requiring minimal administration after installation. Also, since Proxy Server 2.0 is an open system platform, it allows for the preservation of small business investments while still offering growth potential. This accommodates for the fact that the small business of today may become the large business of tomorrow.

By using an open standard platforms solution such as Proxy Server 2.0, customers can start small with consolidated services on a single system and then separate the services and expand them later for a scalable, partitioned deployment. For example, a small company can start by combining the features of Microsoft Proxy Server 2.0 with Windows NT® Server 4.0 to configure support for RAS, VPN, caching, proxy, and firewall needs. This results in a complete managed network access solution that offers a growth path for the small business.

Proxy Server 2.0 as a Secure Gateway

Proxy Server 2.0 acts as a secure gateway by controlling inbound access from the Internet to the small business network. It renders Internet security with packet filtering and proxies at the application and circuit layers, while also improving network response time and efficiency. By using a Proxy Server gateway, the small business network is secured against intrusion. Proxy Server acts as a barrier which allows outbound requests to the Internet and the reception of information, but it does not allow access to the small business network by unauthorized users. Proxy Server 2.0 also allows users on the Internet to access Web sites on the small business network through a feature called reverse proxy.

Web Content Caching

Proxy Server 2.0 has the most advanced set of scalable web content caching features available. With content caching, Proxy Server 2.0 accelerates the Internet experience for the user and reduces the cost of network communications. Proxy Server 2.0 increases the efficiency of Internet access by caching FTP text and HTTP objects on the server. This means network users can have access to popular Internet material quickly since it is loaded from a cache on their local network, rather than a distant Internet site. As a result, network traffic is reduced along with network costs.

Internet users who access popular material on your web site also benefit from faster access. Indirectly, all web servers to which the requests would have otherwise been sent, benefit from the decrease in load owing to the caching capability of Proxy Server 2.0.

Proxy Server 2.0 Services

Proxy Server provides the following three services:

- **Web Proxy**. This service supports HTTP, FTP, and Gopher for computers running TCP/IP.
- **Winsock Proxy**. This service supports Windows® Sockets client applications such as Telnet and RealAudio for computers running TCP/IP or IPX/SPX. IPX/SPX support enables any clients on the small business LAN using IPX/SPX to access the Internet without having TCP/IP on their computers.
- **SOCKS Proxy**. This service is a cross-platform mechanism that establishes secure communications between client and server computers. The SOCKS Proxy service supports SOCKS version 4.3a and allows users transparent access to the Internet by means of Proxy Server. The SOCKS Proxy service extends the redirection provided by the Winsock Proxy service to non-Windows platforms. It uses TCP/IP and can be used for Telnet, FTP, Gopher, and HTTP. The SOCKS Proxy service does not support applications that rely on the User Datagram Protocol (UDP), such as RealAudio, VDOLive, or Microsoft NetShow™.

SOCKS Proxy clients establish a connection to the Proxy Server computer, and the SOCKS Proxy service relays information between the client and the Internet server. Security is based on IP addresses, port numbers, and destination hosts. The SOCKS Proxy service does not perform client password authentication nor does it support the IPX/SPX protocol.

Security Overview

Proxy Server 2.0 provides firewall security to prevent unauthorized external access to the small business network.

Firewall Definition

The term Internet "firewall" commonly refers to hardware and software used to restrict entry to an organization's network from the Internet. Firewalls typically provide multilayered security—at the packet and application layers—although many routers that provide only packet filtering are often called firewalls. Also, firewalls usually provide alerting mechanisms to let network managers know if their networks are under attack by intruders. Some firewall products also support VPNs between locations.

Proxy Definition

The term *proxy* means "to act on behalf of another." In networking terms, a proxy server computer can act on behalf of several client PCs requesting content from the Internet or even on the small business intranet. The illustration that follows shows the proxy server as a secure gateway to the Internet interacting on behalf of client PCs.

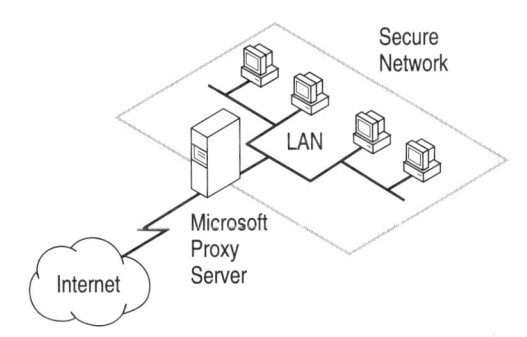

Figure 36.1 Proxy Server 2.0 and LAN configuration

The proxy server is relatively transparent to the parties in the communication path (the user and the Internet resource). The user interacting with the Internet from the desktop will not be able to tell that a proxy server is interceding—unless the user attempts to access a service or go to a site the proxy server is disallowing. The web server being accessed across the Internet interprets the requests from the proxy server as requests from a browser or FTP client.

LAN and Internet Isolation

The Small Business Server 4.5 computer in which Proxy Server 2.0 is installed is "dual-homed", which means the server has two network interface cards (NICs). One card connects the server computer to the small business network—the second card connects the computer to the Internet. This physically isolates the small business LAN from potential intruders on the Internet. Proxy Server 2.0 connects with the Internet through the second NIC which allows it to process and evaluate all interactions between the Internet and the small business LAN.

Protection of Internal IP Addresses from the Internet

With internal IP address forwarding disabled, the only IP address that can be externally recognized is that of the computer running Proxy Server 2.0. This reduces potential targets for intrusion and exposes only the most secure computer (the small business Proxy Server) to the Internet.

IP Packet Layer Filtering

Proxy Server 2.0 adds security through the dynamic packet filtering feature. This means that you can block or enable reception of certain packet types through certain ports. For instance, you can block small business network users from receiving Network News Transfer Protocol (NNTP) packets.

Kernel-mode packet filtering is integrated with Proxy services. Ports are only opened as necessary so that packets are allowed up the stack for the minimum duration necessary and only on ports in use. Proxy Server only filters external interfaces and the default state of received packets for all TCP/IP protocols and TCP/UDP ports is "drop".

Web Publishing Support

Proxy Server 2.0 supports web publishing, which is useful if the small business organization chooses to host a web site. Web publishing is the ability to place materials on a server that is accessible to users on the Internet. Proxy Server supports web publishing with the reverse proxy feature. Reverse proxy refers to the ability to monitor and respond to requests from the Internet on behalf of the small business web server (Internet Information Server). Essentially, Proxy Server impersonates the web server to the outside world.

Proxy Server 2.0 Default Configuration

By default, Proxy Server 2.0 is set up on the Small Business Server 4.5 platform for the optimum configuration for the small business, which includes basic protocol services, caching capabilities, and auto-dial setup for Internet access. The Proxy client side is also configured for all services by the Set Up Computer Wizard during installation of Small Business Server 4.5.

Advantages of Proxy Server 2.0 Connectivity

The small business organization that wants to extend Internet access to their client desktops is well positioned in using Proxy Server 2.0. Using Proxy Server 2.0 as a secure gateway from the small business intranet (LAN) out to the Internet has the following important advantages (over other possible methods):

- Sharing of the Internet connection resource among many users.
- Single, secure gateway to manage and monitor.
- Ability to offer Internet access appropriate to the individual or group.
- Ability to track usage by user.
- Much better performance—especially as the result of caching.
- Cost effective.

Disadvantages of Alternate Connection Methods

Typically, small organizations use the following two alternatives to provide Internet access to their users:

- Run phone lines directly to those users who want Internet access.
- Set up a few PCs and place them in locations where they can be shared resources among several people.

Both of these alternatives have serious drawbacks when compared to using Proxy Server. The disadvantages of using dedicated lines to each user include:

- Major security breach if modem-equipped PC is connected to the LAN.
- Extra hardware (for example, a modem) expense at each desktop.
- Recurring phone line charge for each user.
- No sharing of the phone line or Internet account resource.
- No network manager control over user Internet experience.
- Poor performance for the user due to modem connectivity.

The disadvantages of sharing Internet-ready PCs among several users are:

- User inconvenience.
- Frequent lack of availability (others using the computer).
- Everyone using the Internet on those PCs gets the same service—no ability to customize the Internet services to make them appropriate to the individual.
- Tracking and logging user usage is difficult to impossible.

Key Features of Proxy Server 2.0

This section describes key features of Proxy Server 2.0, including:

- Extensible security.
- Management.
- Security architecture.
- Access control.
- Web publishing support.
- Caching.
- Characteristics of other features including auto dial for Internet connections and the local address table (LAT).
- Proxy service architecture.

Extensible Security

Microsoft Proxy Server 2.0 acts as a gateway with firewall-class security between the small business LAN and the Internet. It plays an important role in enforcing the overall security policy of the small business organization. The basic firewall properties of the product are enabled by dynamic packet filtering and security at the application and circuit layers. Enhancements to the security properties of Proxy Server 2.0 are supported by the extensibility of the product. Third-party developers may therefore use Microsoft Proxy Server 2.0 as a platform for value-added development.

The small business customer can choose from a variety of third-party applications available for Proxy Server 2.0 including virus scanning, JavaScript and ActiveX® filters, site blocking enhancement products, and other security products built for the Proxy Server 2.0 platform. Proxy Server is also complementary to other security products such as high-end firewall solutions, if special security needs are required.

Management

Proxy Server 2.0 integrates with the networking, security, and administrative interfaces of the Microsoft Windows NT Server 4.0 operating system and Microsoft Internet Information Server (IIS) 4.0. This permits Proxy Server to take advantage of the ease of administration, performance, and scalability offered by these applications. Since Microsoft Proxy Server 2.0 is integrated with Windows NT Server 4.0, the technology consultant can use a single set of tools and services to manage small business intranets and Internet access. Among these services are the following:

- Windows NT Directory Service.
- Windows NT User Manager.
- Windows NT Performance Monitor.
- Windows NT Event Log.
- Internet Service Manager.
- Remote Access Service.
- Windows NT Security.

Proxy Server 2.0 management features also include HTML-based administration and command line support with scripting which complements graphical user interface-based support. In addition, management flexibility is provided by SOCKs v4.3 support, HTTP 1.1, and FTP caching which enables expanded use of Internet and intranet services to their users.

Windows NT Directory Services and User Manager

The integration of Microsoft Proxy Server 2.0 with the Windows NT Directory Service and User Manager enables a single user logon experience for all network services and applications, including Internet or intranet access through Proxy Server 2.0. This enables the technology consultant to utilize the user account information to allow or deny access to a wide range of Internet or intranet services accessed through Microsoft Proxy Server 2.0.

Windows NT 4.0 Performance Monitor and Event Log Tools

The Windows NT Server Performance Monitor supports several Microsoft Proxy Server real-time measurements. The Windows NT Event Log is also used to help track and troubleshoot Microsoft Proxy Server 2.0. These tools provide essential information to enable the technology consultant to monitor the disposition of Proxy Server 2.0.

Proxy Server 2.0 Management from IIS Console

Microsoft Proxy Server 2.0 is tightly integrated with IIS. For example, the extensibility of Proxy Server is related to the ISAPI support of IIS. All aspects of Proxy Server 2.0 management can be controlled from the IIS console shown in the following screen. The console may be accessed from the following path on Small Business Server:

Start/Programs/Microsoft Proxy Server/Microsoft Management Console.

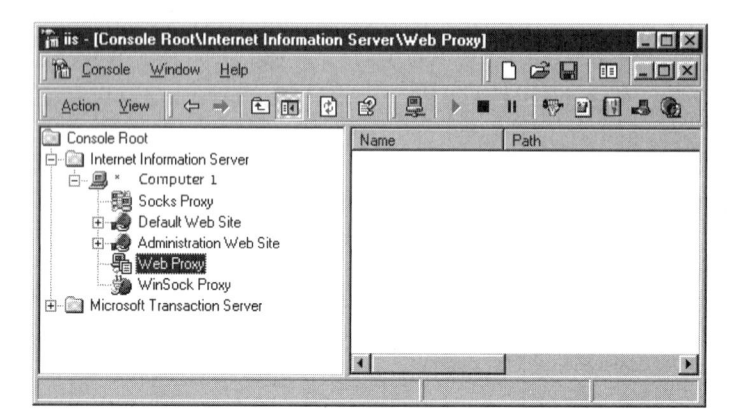

The Web Proxy, Winsock Proxy, and SOCKS Proxy services are all found in the Internet Information Server folder. By right-clicking on the icon of one of these services, you can access the **Service Properties** page for that service. For example, right-clicking on the **Web Proxy** icon brings up the **Web Proxy Service Properties** page shown in the following screen.

The buttons to the bottom left are shared services used by Proxy Server 2.0. On the bottom right are the common configuration options.

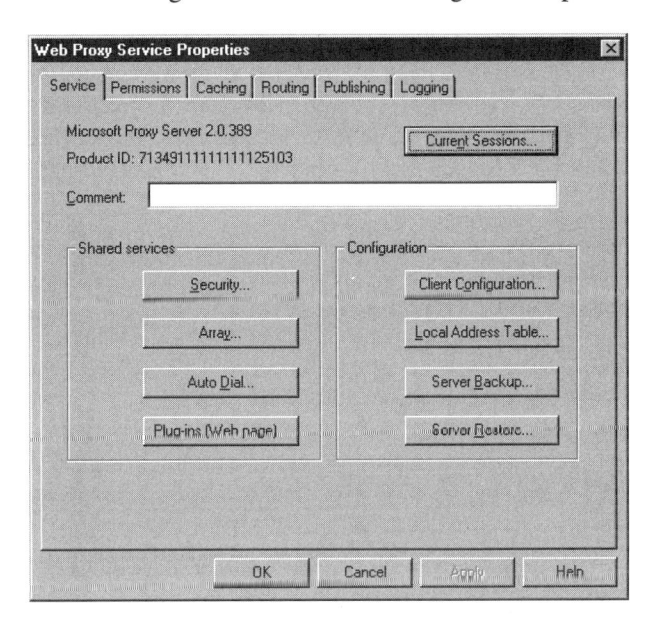

Proxy Server 2.0 administration procedures for Small Business Server 4.5 (which use screens such as the one above) are provided in *Part 4, Administering and Maintaining* of this resource guide.

Configuration Backup and Restore

From the **Services Properties** tab, the **Server Backup** and **Server Restore** buttons allow the technology consultant to save adjustments made to proxy settings or restore configurations, if necessary. Refer to the following screen.

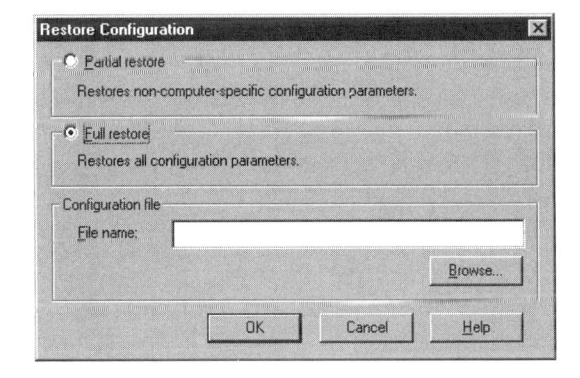

Windows NT Security

The basis of the security environment in Microsoft Proxy Server 2.0 lies in the security features and enabling technologies of Windows NT Server 4.0 which Proxy Server takes advantage of. The list below highlights some of the attributes making Windows NT Server 4.0 a secure network operating system and which can be managed for use with a firewall application such as Microsoft Proxy Server 2.0.

- Domains and accounts.
- Single logon and password management.
- Access control lists (ACLs).
- Security logs.
- Administration roles.
- Rights.
- Protocol security and C2 assurance.

The security features of Windows NT Server 4.0 (including RAS) are detailed in *Chapter 37, Computer Security and Windows NT Server 4.0,* of this resource guide.

Security Architecture

If the small business network only has outbound client access to the Internet, then this intermittent presence limits the security risk simply because Proxy Server 2.0 is not on the Internet at all times. However, if the small business hosts its presence on the Internet, Proxy Server will be constantly exposed to users on the Internet. Dynamic packet filtering should be used in all situations to create firewall security, but especially when the small business is hosting a web site.

This section describes the security architecture of Proxy Server 2.0 as implemented by the capabilities and inner workings of dynamic packet filtering. Also discussed is the default configuration of inbound access security for Small Business Server 4.5.

Capabilities of Dynamic Packet Filtering

The security features of Proxy Server allow for controlling the information flow to and from Proxy Server 2.0. Dynamic packet filtering is critical to establish firewall security. With dynamic packet filtering, you can do the following:

- Authenticate client requests.
- Intercept and either allow or block packets destined to specific proxy services on the Small Business Server computer. Proxy Server drops rejected IP packets on the external interface, thereby minimizing the number of exposed ports in either direction (as well as the duration that ports are open to the Internet).
- Send an alert when dropped packets or other suspicious events occur and either log the alert or send it by e-mail to a specific destination.

Packet Filtering Actions

Proxy Server offers the ability to apply predefined filters automatically, referred to as dynamic packet filtering. Packet filtering intercepts packets before they are passed to an application or to higher-levels in the protocol layers. Dynamic filtering helps Proxy Server act as a firewall by evaluating which TCP/IP packet types are accessible to specific internal network services.

Packet filters can be configured to deny certain packet types while passing other specified packet types through Proxy Server 2.0. This provides a high level of security for the small business network. Packet filtering can block packets originating from specific Internet hosts and reject packets associated with many common attacks, such as address spoof, SYN, and FRAG attacks. Packet filtering can also block packets that are destined to any server service on the small business internal network, such as the Web Proxy, Winsock Proxy, SOCKS Proxy, or Simple Mail Transfer Protocol (SMTP) services.

Dynamic and Static Filtering Modes

Proxy Server provides both dynamic and static packet filtering modes to control which protocol ports are opened for communication. With dynamic packet filtering, it is unnecessary for the technology consultant to explicitly unbind specific services from the external NIC connected to Proxy Server 2.0. Packets can automatically be blocked from reaching those services, regardless of whether they are bound or not. Ports are opened for either transmit, receive, or both directions. Ports are then immediately closed after any of the Proxy Server services terminates a connection. This offers a high degree of security and requires minimal administration since the Web Proxy, Winsock Proxy, and SOCKS Proxy services do all the work.

Note Proxy Server packet filtering only functions through the external network adapter. The internal network adapter is not affected and can still implement all Microsoft Windows NT® security measures, such as password authentication and user permissions. The Proxy Server 2.0 interface of Small Business Server 4.5 supports a single external network adapter.

The Inner Processes of Dynamic Packet Filtering

This section provides a brief explanation of the inner workings of dynamic packet filtering, to clarify the processes used. From an architecture perspective, dynamic packet filtering involves several components including the following:

- **Packet Filter Manager**. This provides the higher-level interface for Proxy Server 2.0 services to interact with the Packet Filter Driver.
- **Packet Filter Driver**. This is implemented deep within the Windows NT Server 4.0 networking architecture that communicates directly to the external network interface.

The section that immediately follows demonstrates how Proxy Services, Packet Filter Manager, and the Packet Filter Driver combine to create secure, dynamic packet filters. The illustration below is related to the Open Systems Interconnection (OSI) model architecture. The following explanation describes how the illustrated components interact to create packet filtering security.

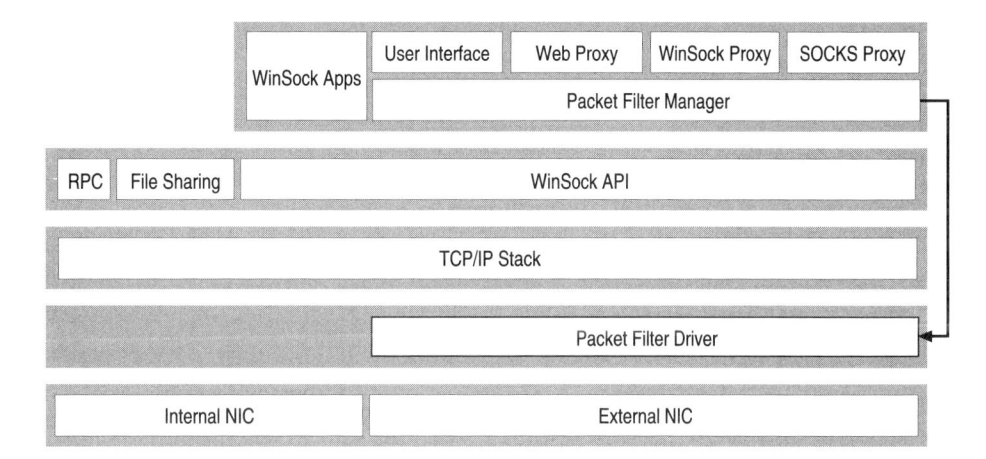

Figure 36.2 Component stack for Proxy dynamic filtering processes

The components of Proxy Server interact to create packet filtering security as described below. The result of these operations is a logical filter which allows packets from the approved communications path, but blocks other unapproved packets.

- A client with the Winsock Proxy client component launches a Telnet application and attempts to connect to an Internet server.
- The Winsock Proxy client component intercepts the Internet Telnet request and does a remote procedure call (RPC) connection request to the Winsock Proxy Server.
- The Winsock Proxy Server interrogates the client to ensure that the proper Windows NT User Directory Service permissions exist to access the telnet protocol on the Internet.
- If permissions are correct, the server instructs the Winsock API to create a local socket with, for example, a local port address of 6008.
- The Winsock Proxy Server then notifies the Packet Filter Manager that outbound connections from local port 6008 to a remote Telnet service have been approved by the Proxy service.
- The Packet Filter Manager instructs the Packet Filter Driver to open port 6008 for outbound Telnet connections and tells the Winsock Proxy Server to begin a Telnet session on behalf of the original client.
- The firewall port is opened only as long as necessary. As soon as the Winsock Proxy detects that the client has closed the Telnet session, it instructs the Packet Filter Manager to close the client's port (6008), blocking any further packets from the remote host.

The diagram that follows is the functional equivalent of dynamic packet filtering processes:

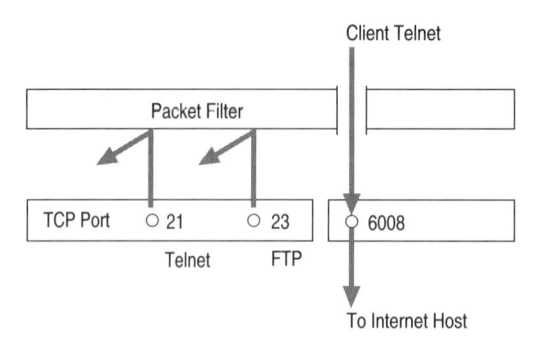

Figure 36.3 Packet filtering functional equivalent

Enabling Dynamic Packet Filtering

When the Small Business Server Internet Connection Wizard is run for Small Business Server 4.5, dynamic packet filtering is enabled and predefined filters are added for the Web Proxy service by default. The process can also be performed manually using the procedures and information in the paragraphs that follow.

The information that immediately follows shows how to manually set up a basic configuration for accessing Internet resources through the Winsock Proxy service, although the same procedure applies to the Web Proxy service. Additional information is also provided to allow for the modification or customization of packet filters.

▶ **To set up a dynamic packet filtering for basic Winsock Proxy service**

1. In the IIS console, right-click **Winsock Proxy Service**, then click **Properties**. The screen below appears.

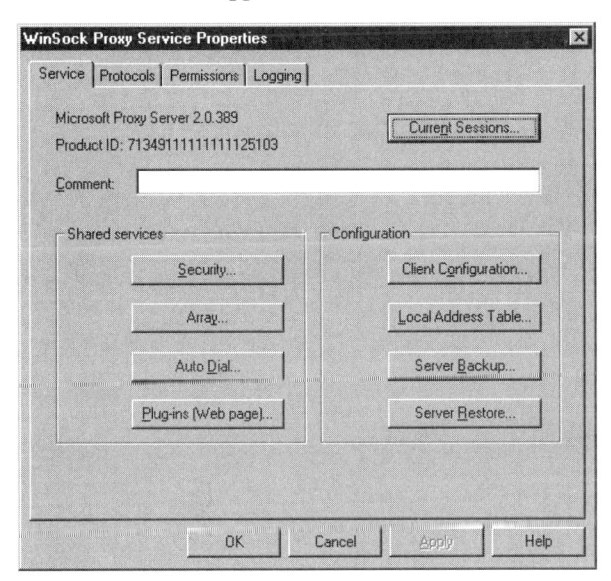

2. From the **Winsock Proxy Service Properties** screen, click **Security**.

3. When the **Security** screen appears, select all of the "Enable..." boxes on the **Packet Filters** tab. The internal network of the small business is now secured with predefined packet filters for the Winsock service.

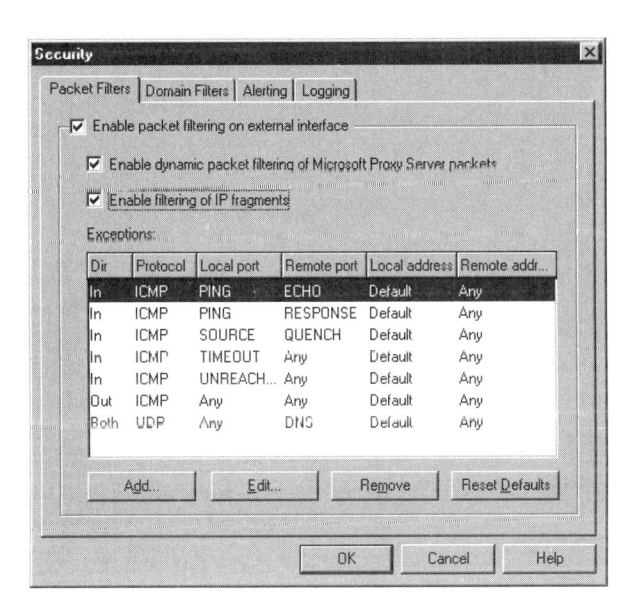

Packet Filter List

The packet types in the Exceptions list above apply to all requests issued to Proxy Server, whether the request originated from the Internet or from a small business network client. It is not possible to specify packet filtering on a user-level basis, however, ISAPI is extensible and provides a means for third parties to provide customized filtering.

Each entry in the Exceptions list consists of configuration parameters that specify a particular packet filter type. Packet type parameters include the direction of data flow, the transport protocol used, the local destination service port, the remote source IP address of the host, and the remote source service port.

Note Some protocols, such as Point-to-Point Tunneling Protocol (PPTP), require configuration of multiple filters (in the above Exceptions list) before they will work.

Predefined Packet Filters

Proxy Server 2.0 comes with a number of predefined packet filters in the Small Business Server 4.5 platform (shown in the Exceptions list of the previous screen). The technology consultant must determine if these filters are adequate to meet the security needs of the small business network. If not, then appropriate changes or additions should be made. It is important to remember that packet filters define exceptions, which means that all packet types will be blocked *except* for those in the **Exceptions** list. If a packet filter has not been enabled for a certain port, then listening on that port has been effectively disabled.

Note By default, packet filtering is enabled through the **Enable packet filtering on external interface** check box on the **Packet Filters** tab. This will block *all* packets on the external interface until an access request is made. To enable dynamic packet filtering, check the **Enable dynamic packet filtering of Microsoft Proxy Server packets** box. This will enable the filters in the **Exceptions** list. When an access request is made, service is enabled only for the type of packets allowed by the **Exceptions** list.

Customizing Packet Filters for Proxy Services

This section describes how to remove packet filters from a Proxy service, modify the parameters of a filter, or create a new filter. Use a combination of the procedures that follow to customize the packet filter list for Proxy services, if necessary. In order to support other services, new packet filters may need to be created.

Chapter 36 Firewall Security and Web Caching with Proxy Server 2.0

▶ **To remove a packet filter from a Proxy service**

1. In the IIS console, right-click a Proxy service, and then point to **Properties**.
2. In the **Service Properties** page, click **Security** to display the **Security** screen.
3. Select the **Packet Filters** tab.
4. To remove a filter from the list, select it in the **Exceptions** list and click **Remove**.
5. Click **OK** when finished.

▶ **To modify the properties of a packet filter**

1. In the **Exceptions** list on the **Packet Filters** tab, select the filter you want to modify.
2. Click **Edit** to display the current properties of the filter as shown in the following **Packet Filter Properties** page.

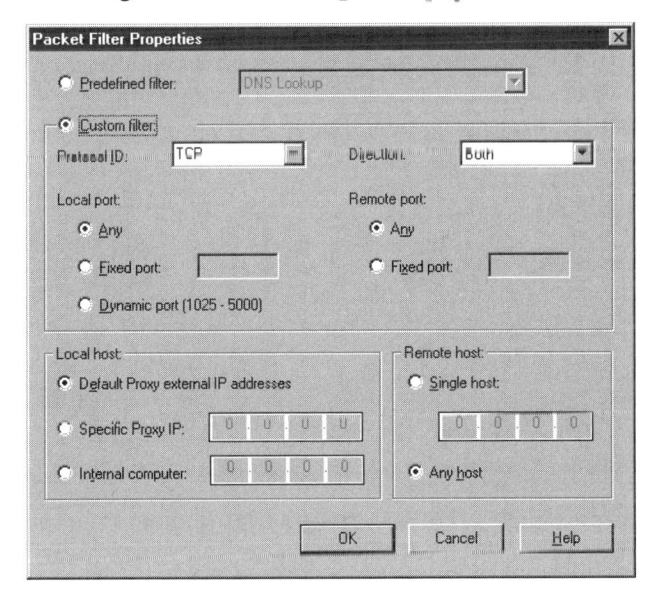

3. Modify the properties of the packet filter as required. Online Help may be consulted for assistance when making changes.
4. Click **OK** when finished.

▶ **To create a new packet filter using predefined protocol definitions**

1. In the **Security** screen, select the **Packet Filters** tab.
2. To enable packet filtering, select **Enable packet filtering on external interface**. This will block all packets.
3. To enable dynamic (automatic) packet filtering, select Enable dynamic packet filtering of Microsoft Proxy Server packets.

4. To add a filter, click **Add**.
5. Select **Predefined filter** and then select a protocol from the drop-down list.
6. Under **Local Host**, select the desired option to allow packet exchange with a specific host computer.
7. Under **Remote host**, define a single remote host, or select **Any host** to allow packet filter exchange with any host computer. Click **OK** when finished.
8. Repeat these steps until you have defined all packet filters needed for the Proxy service.

▶ **To create a new packet filter using custom protocol definitions**

1. Select the **Packet Filters** tab, and then click **Add**.
2. On the **Packet Filter Properties** page, click **Custom Filter**.
3. In **Protocol ID**, select a protocol from the drop-down list and in **Direction**, select a direction from the drop-down list.
4. Under **Local port**, select an appropriate option, or to have Proxy Server dynamically assign a port, click **Dynamic port**.
5. Under **Remote port**, select **Any** or **Fixed port**.
6. Under **Local host**, select the internal computer that exchanges packets with an Internet host computer.
7. Under **Remote host**, select **Single host** and enter a valid IP address if you want to allow packet exchange with a specific Internet host computer. To allow packet filter exchange with any host computer, click **Any host**.
8. Click **OK**.

Use the following procedure to restore all packet filters to their predefined default settings.

▶ **To restore the default packet filter parameters**

1. On the **Alerting** tab of the **Security** screen, click **Reset Defaults**.
2. Click **OK**.

Default Configuration of Inbound Access Security

This section discusses the default configuration of IP routing in Small Business Server 4.5. When Small Business Server is first installed, the network is fully secured from external users on the Internet in the following two ways:

- IP forwarding on the server is disabled. This forces all connections between the internal and external network to use the routing information from the Local Address Table (LAT). The LAT is discussed later in this chapter under the section entitled "Local Address Table".

Note When Microsoft Windows NT Server 4.0 RAS is installed, IP forwarding is enabled by default. IP forwarding should be disabled after installing RAS by using the procedure ahead entitled "To disable IP forwarding on Small Business Server."

- Listening on inbound service ports is enabled for only the specific application services in the packet filters **Exceptions** list of **Proxy Service Properties**. This causes packets originating from sources outside the applications on the **Exceptions** list to be dropped.

IP Routing

If IP forwarding is enabled, it allows packets to pass freely across the internal and external network interface. This effectively exposes the internal network to the Internet. An external user on the Internet could potentially exploit this exposure and devise a method that first accesses the internal network and then attacks higher-level services on the server or sensitive data on the network.

If your private network runs TCP/IP, you can ensure all packets are routed through the Proxy Server service and thus prevent unauthorized IP packets from infiltrating the small business network. To do this, follow the steps below.

▶ **To disable IP forwarding on Small Business Server**

1. Click **Start**, point to **Settings**, and then click **Control Panel**.
2. Double-click **Network** and select the **Protocols** tab.
3. Click Properties.
4. Select the **Routing** tab and then clear the **Enable IP Forwarding** box.
5. Click **OK** and exit all open screens.

Access Control

Proxy Server has several methods to control client outbound access to the Internet. The methods described in this section allow for a complete range of control over what a client can and cannot access on the Internet.

Control of Client Outbound Access to Internet Services

In general, only allow client or group access to those services used regularly. Otherwise, permissions for the service should not be given. The Web Proxy service allows for access control to only the basic Internet services as described in the list below:

- HTTP.
- FTP.
- Gopher.
- Secure Sockets Layer (SSL).

User permissions to access these services may be implemented via the **Permissions** tab in the following **Web Proxy Service Properties** screen. Select a service and click **Edit** to grant permissions to any user for the selected service.

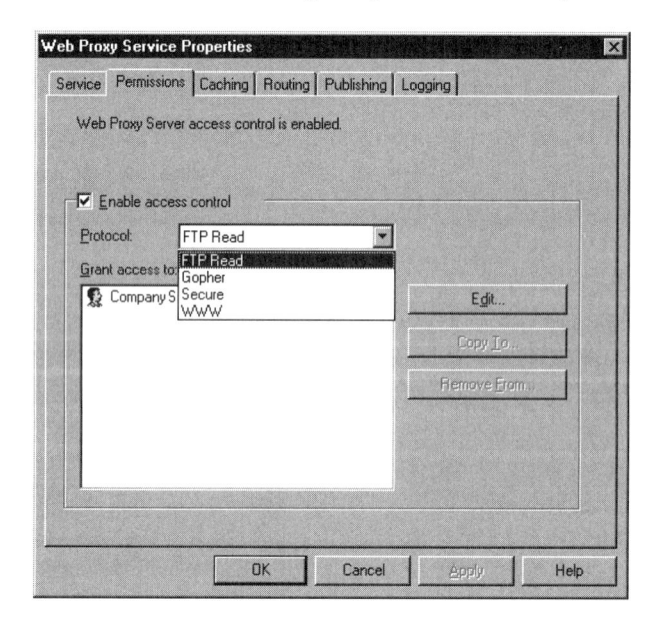

Access Control by Domain, IP Address, or Subnet Filtering

Microsoft Proxy Server 2.0 allows for the control of outbound access to a specific domain, IP address, or subnet. This is accomplished by enabling domain filtering and specifying the appropriate domain, IP address, or subnet mask. Refer to the following screen.

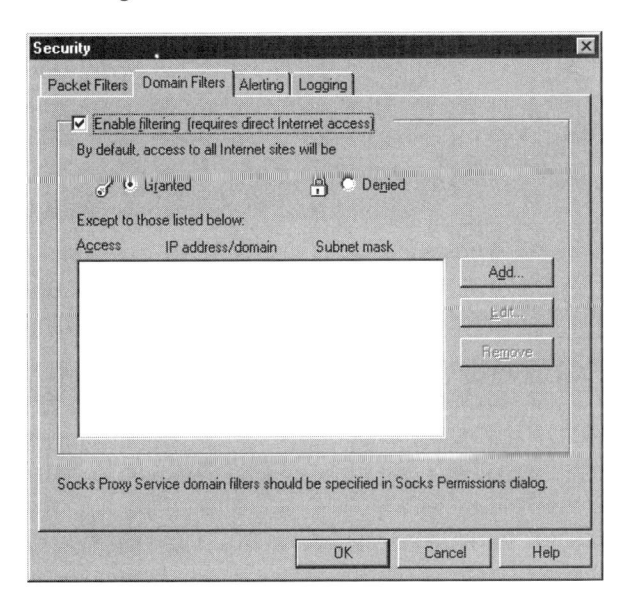

If you want everyone in the small business organization to have full access to the Internet, do not enable filtering. If you want to limit access to only specific computers, subnets, or domains, configure the server to deny access to all Internet sites and add only those which are to be accessible. If you want to prevent access to only a few specific computers, subnets, or domains, configure the server to grant access to all Internet sites and add those which are not to be accessed.

Note When granting or denying permissions, the specified IP address, subnet, or domain is the one that is *excepted* from the general rule; grant permission to all *except* those listed—or deny permission to all *except* those listed.

Access Control for Winsock Clients

Small Business Server 4.5 comes with a default set of protocol definitions for Windows Sockets client applications that access the Internet through the Winsock Proxy service. When using Winsock Proxy service, access to the Internet may be controlled in one of two ways. First, by specifying which users have permission to use the service, user access to specific Internet sites can be limited. This is configured on the **Permissions** tab of the **Winsock Proxy Service Properties** screen. Refer to the screen below.

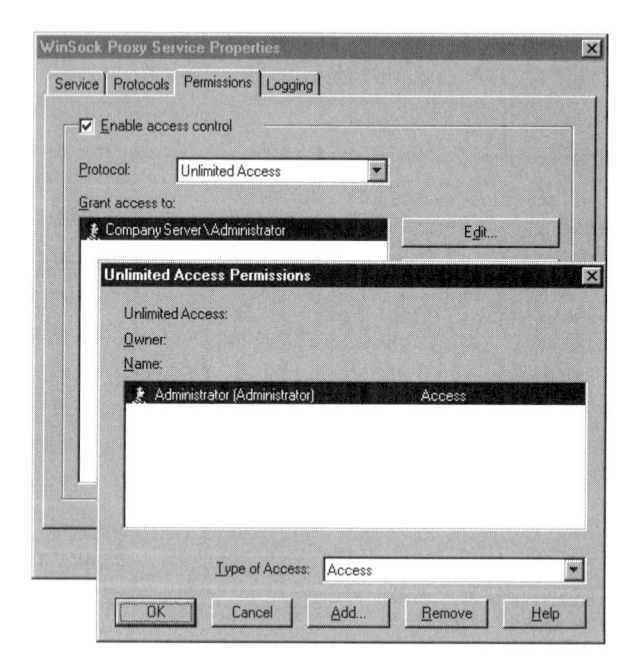

Second, if any predefined protocols are removed from the **Protocols definitions** list via the **Protocols** tab, then access to Internet services using that protocol is effectively removed for all users on the small business network. If you plan to use this feature, predefined protocols should be saved in a configuration file using the **Save** button on the **Protocols** tab, in case you need to restore the original protocol list later. Refer to the screen below.

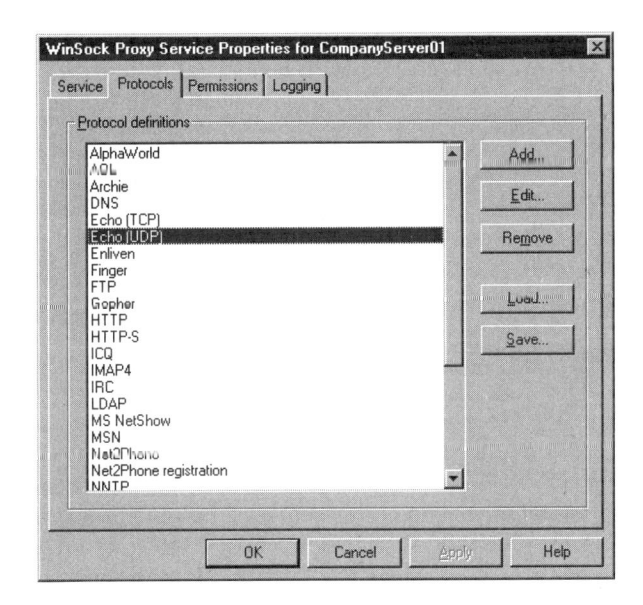

Access Control for Remote Users

If you assign permissions to remote users for the Winsock Proxy service, Web Proxy, or SOCKS Proxy service, follow the recommendations below to control their accessibility:

- Add users only when necessary.
- Enforce passwords and advise users to follow secure guidelines when choosing their passwords.
- Use default accounts whenever possible.
- You may want to offer individual or remote users secured individual connections to your internal web server. When this is the case, enforce passwords for all user logon attempts and recommend that users use a secure browser that supports Windows NT Challenge/Response, such as Microsoft Internet Explorer 4.0.
- Be conservative in enabling inbound protocol ports.
- Carefully set user permissions for protocol ports in Winsock Proxy service.

Never allow unlimited access for Internet users to application-level protocol ports. In most cases, HTTP or HTTP-S is the only permission that should be allowed. If you are enabling UDP protocols for RealAudio or VDOLive, use secured guest accounts to assign permissions and require full authentication for users of these protocol services.

Encryption

Proxy Server 2.0 takes advantage of the authentication and security architecture of Microsoft IIS. In addition, secure sockets layer (SSL) tunneling is enabled by default within Proxy Server 2.0 when a user is granted access to the Web Proxy service. The SSL supports data encryption and server authentication. All data sent to and from the client using SSL is encrypted. If HTTP authentication is used in conjunction with SSL, the user name and password are transmitted after client SSL encryption.

Also, when using the Internet Server Application Programming Interface (ISAPI) extensions, request authentication can be extended.

PPTP Supported

If you want to use PPTP protocol to provide additional security for remote clients, Proxy Server 2.0 can be configured to support PPTP-encrypted packets as described in earlier section of this chapter entitled "Customizing Packet Filters for Proxy Services."

Web Publishing Support

Web publishing in the small business network refers to the ability to place content on your web server (IIS) so it can be reached by Internet or intranet users. Publishing to the Internet using a web server increases the exposure of the small business internal network to external users and can thus potentially compromise network security.

When Proxy Server 2.0 is used for outbound proxy connections only, small business network exposure to Internet users is minimal. When web publishing is used, however, the small business web server will maintain a continuous presence on the World Wide Web. This creates the potential for unauthorized access the network.

Additionally, when interactive scripts or programming extensions, such as CGI or ISAPI (DLLs), are used to make dynamic changes in web-published content, external users may again be able to gain unauthorized network access if web server applications are inadequately or poorly designed.

This section describes security features of Proxy Server 2.0 that support web publishing for the small business organization.

Reverse Proxy

Reverse proxy describes the ability of a Proxy Server to process incoming requests to an internal web (HTTP) server and then respond on its behalf. Reverse proxy is *reverse* because requests are forwarded downstream to the small business internal web server (IIS) located behind Proxy Server 2.0, the opposite of forwarding internal requests out to the Internet.

With the web publishing features of Microsoft Proxy Server 2.0, the small business can publish to the Internet without compromising the security of the internal network. This is accomplished using the reverse proxy feature of Proxy Server 2.0.

Using Reverse Proxy, Proxy Server 2.0 impersonates a web server to the outside world. Proxy Server fulfills requests for web content from its cache and forwards them to the real web server only when the requests cannot be served from its cache. While this is happening, the real small business web server remains in a secure environment with access to other internal network services.

Server Proxying

Proxy Server 2.0 listens for incoming packets destined for applications and services in Small Business Server 4.5. Proxy Server forwards these packets to an application only if the protocol for that communication is supported by proxy services. For example, Microsoft Exchange Server can take advantage of the secure environment created by Proxy Server 2.0 since SMTP is supported by the Winsock Proxy Service, as shown in the following illustration.

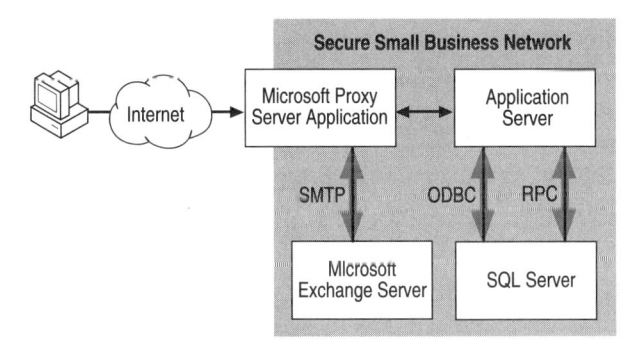

Figure 36.4 Running Internet applications behind secure network connection with server proxying

Configuring Reverse Proxy for Web Publishing

When implementing a web publishing plan, you first establish an overall policy and then make exceptions. Exceptions are displayed in the **Except for those listed below** list shown in the screen below. The entries display the incoming URL request and the URL to which it should be redirected.

▶ **To configure publishing parameters**

1. In the IIS console, right-click **Web Proxy**, then click **Properties**.
2. In the **Web Proxy Service Properties** box, select the **Publishing** tab.

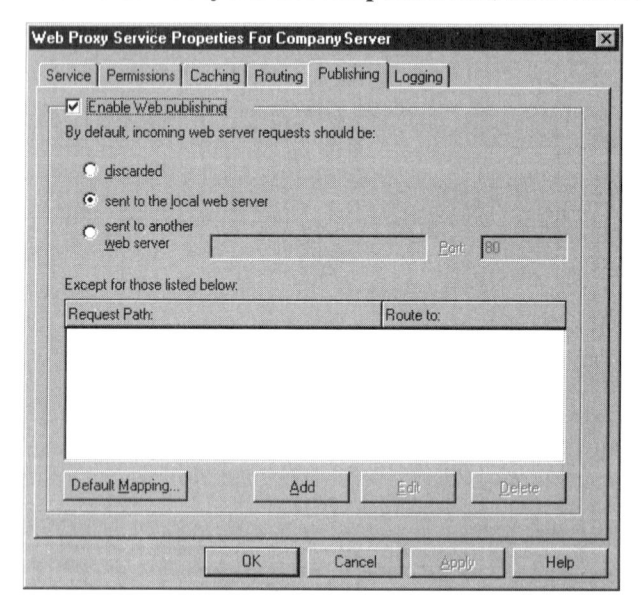

3. Select **Enable Web publishing**, and do one of the following:
   - To ignore all incoming web server requests, select **discarded**.
   - To forward incoming web server requests on Proxy Server to IIS, select **sent to the local web server**.
4. To set the default web server host, click **Default Mapping**. In the **Default Local Host Name** dialog box, enter the default server. The host name is the Small Business Server computer name.
5. Click **Apply** and then click **OK**.

Caching

Passive caching is the basic mode in which content caching functions. It is also known as *on-demand* caching. Proxy Server 2.0 intervenes between the client PC and a web site (either external or internal) and intercepts client requests. Before forwarding the request on to the web, Proxy Server determines if its cache can satisfy the request.

This Proxy Server 2.0 capability reduces network bandwidth by an average of 50%, improving response time for clients, reducing network congestion, and improving control over network resources, without burdening end users or the technology consultant.

This section describes passive caching and an enhancement to it called active caching. During the passive caching discussion, refer to the following illustration.

Passive Caching Process

With passive caching, Proxy Server 2.0 places an object in the cache and associates a Time-To-Live (TTL) function with that object. During this TTL, all requests for the object are serviced from the cache without generating traffic back to the web server. After the TTL has expired, the next client request for the object will generate traffic to and from the web server. Proxy Server 2.0 will then store the response from the web server in its cache and calculate a new TTL.

If the data is in its cache, Proxy Server 2.0 determines if the object is still usable (based on its TTL and other information). If the object is still valid, Proxy Server then returns the object to the client. If the object is not valid, Proxy Server updates the object and then returns the cached object to the client. If the data is not cached, Proxy Server retrieves the data from the web, returns it to the client, and then inserts it into the cache.

If the local disk space reserved for the cache is too full to hold new data, Proxy Server removes older objects from the cache using a formula that factors in the age, popularity, and size of the object. The caching process is shown below.

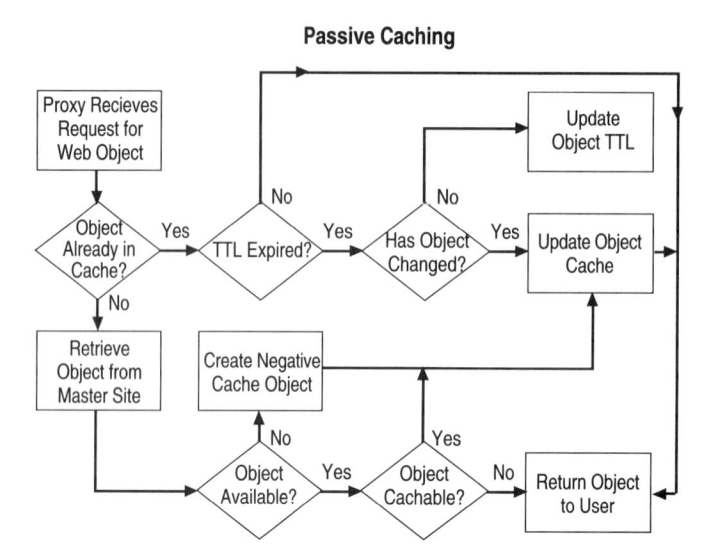

Figure 36.5 Passive caching process

Active Caching

Proxy Server 2.0 provides a unique way of assuring that Internet or intranet sites used the most by clients in the small business network are readily available for quick access. To do this, Proxy Server actively pre-caches web content. It automatically determines the most popular web sites visited by small business network clients. It then determines how often the content of those sites is refreshed and automatically goes out to pre-cache new content from the sites when the old content has expired. Once this feature is enabled, it works automatically without any network management intervention.

Important If active caching is enabled on Small Business Server 4.5, Proxy Server may initiate auto-dials to the Internet at an excessive rate. If this rate is inappropriate for the small business network, active caching should be disabled.

Active caching of Proxy Server augments the passive caching system by automatically generating requests for refreshed content. Proxy Server chooses the content it will actively cache on the following basis:

- **Popularity**. Ensures that requests made by Proxy Server are likely to be requested by clients as well.
- **TTL**. Longer TTLs are more valuable to cache than shorter TTLs; Proxy Server checks for content that is close to expiration.
- **Server load**. Proxy Server performs more aggressive active caching during periods of low server load than during periods of high server load.

Characteristics of Other Proxy Server 2.0 Features

Several other characteristics of Proxy Server 2.0 should be of interest in small business network applications, including the Auto Dial and LAT. These features are described in this section.

Proxy Auto Dial

Proxy Server 2.0 can be configured to automatically dial out to an ISP to establish an Internet connection. This feature is called Proxy Server Auto Dial. Proxy Server uses Windows NT Server 4.0 RAS and Dial-Up Networking to establish the ISP connection, as shown in the following illustration.

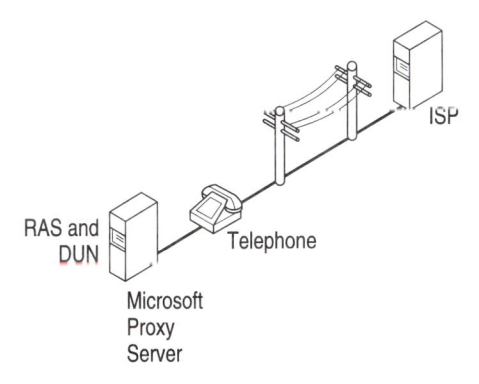

Figure 36.6 Proxy Auto Dial configuration

Proxy Server Auto Dial is event driven. It is activated only when needed. Auto Dial is initiated when the following service demands occur:

- **For Web Proxy service**—when a requested object cannot be located in the cache.
- **For Winsock Proxy service**—when any client request is made.
- **For SOCKS Proxy service**—when any client request is made.

Benefits of Proxy Server Auto Dial

Proxy Server Auto Dial can be used to reduce Internet connection time by connecting only when needed. This reduces costs since charges are incurred only when the Internet connection is active.

Proxy Server Auto Dial may also be used as a backup to provide limited fault tolerance to an existing continuous Internet link. The only direct costs of using this method of fault tolerance would be the hardware and the online time when the continuous Internet link is down. For example, a small business network may already have a T1 link to access the Internet. Proxy Server Auto Dial with RAS can be pre-configured to establish a dial-up link if the T1 link goes down.

Proxy Server Auto Dial can also regulate usage of the Internet by configuring the dialing hours to confine Internet access to specified time periods. For example, if an office is closed on weekends, Proxy Server Auto Dial can be configured so that dial-up connection to the Internet is only available on weekdays.

Configuration of Auto Dial

After Small Business Server 4.5 is installed, configure Auto Dial and the ISP DUN phonebook entry per the procedures provided in *Part 3, Deployment* of this resource guide.

Local Address Table

During Small Business Server 4.5 installation, the Setup program creates a list (by default) of the IP addresses that define the small business network (intranet). The information from the default setup is used to create a table in Proxy Server 2.0 called the LAT. IP addresses which are external to the small business internal network are specifically excluded from this table. This list spans the internal network address space used by the Dynamic Host Configuration Protocol Server (Windows NT Server 4.0) and includes the default TCP/IP address of Small Business Server 4.5 (10.0.0.2).

During Small Business Server client setup, the LAT file is copied to the client. In order to keep client LAT files current, it is regularly updated from the server. Each time a Windows Sockets application on the client attempts to establish a connection to an IP address, the LAT is used to determine whether that address is on the small business intranet or an external network (Internet). If the address is internal, the connection is made directly. If the address is external, the connection is made remotely, through the Winsock Proxy service.

The functions of the Proxy LAT causes it to act as an additional security feature, since it prevents direct client connection with Internet hosts other than those from which data is being returned in response to client requests. The only time the LAT may need to be changed is if the base IP address of Small Business Server 4.5 is changed. If this is necessary, follow the procedures in *Chapter 27, Administering Small Business Server Components,* in *Part 4, Administering and Maintaining,* of this resource guide.

Proxy Service Architecture

The three services of Proxy Server 2.0 that are used to gain access to Internet resources are Web Proxy, Winsock Proxy, and SOCKS Proxy. The architecture of these service components is described in detail in this section. An overview is provided below. These three services support the vast majority of Internet applications currently available.

- **Web Proxy**. This service is used by CERN-compliant applications. The Web Proxy service supports proxy requests from any CERN-compliant browser, such as Microsoft Internet Explorer or Netscape Communicator. This enables almost every type of desktop operating system to have web access, including Microsoft Windows 3.x, Microsoft Windows 95, Microsoft Windows NT, Macintosh, and UNIX® platforms.

- **Winsock Proxy**. This service is used by those Windows applications that use Windows Sockets. The Winsock Proxy service makes a Windows Sockets-compatible client application perform as if it were directly connected to the Internet. This enables applications such as Microsoft NetShow, RealAudio, and IRC to run from client computers.

- **SOCKS Proxy**. This service is used by applications that use SOCKS. The SOCKS Proxy service supports SOCKS version 4.3a. It provides a mechanism for establishing a secure proxy data channel between client and server computers, allowing transparent access to the Internet. SOCKS utilizes TCP so that applications such as Telnet, FTP, and Gopher can function on the client through the proxy server. It is a cross-platform service that supports many different types of client machines and operating systems.

Web Proxy Service

The Web Proxy service is accessed from the Internet Information Server folder in the Microsoft Management console. Web Proxy provides the following services for the small business network:

- HTTP, FTP, and Gopher Internet protocols.
- TCP/IP on the small business LAN.
- Disk caching.
- CERN-proxy compliance.
- Caching of HTTP and FTP objects.
- User-level security for each application protocol, including secure and encrypted logon capability for web browsers that support Windows NT Challenge/Response authentication.
- Data encryption using SSL tunneling.
- Support for all popular client operating systems and hardware platforms.
- Log information about Internet requests by Small Business Server network clients.

Functions of the Web Proxy Service

The Web Proxy service performs client and server functions. As a server, it receives World Wide Web requests from internal network clients. As a client, it responds to internal network client requests by issuing the appropriate requests to a server on the Internet.

The interface between the client and server components of the Web Proxy service provides opportunities to add value to the connections it services. By increasing security and functionality for client connections, the Web Proxy service can do much more than relay data between servers and clients.

HTTP and Client Communication

The majority of Internet applications such as FTP, World Wide Web, and Gopher use client/server architecture. These applications use the conventions established in HTTP for communication between client applications and server applications.

While most CERN-compliant web proxy services support WWW (HTTP), FTP, and Gopher requests, all communication between small business network clients and the Web Proxy service is through HTTP. HTTP defines a set of commands that a client can send to a server. The two most common commands are **Get** and **Post**.

- **Get** is used to forward a URL to a server for requesting the resource to which the URL refers.
- **Post** is used to forward a request that contains a URL and data. Typically, a user provides this data by completing an HTML form.

Web Proxy Service Components

The Web Proxy service runs as an extension to Microsoft IIS, a component of Microsoft Windows NT Server 4.0. The Web Proxy service consists of the following two primary components:

- Proxy Server ISAPI filter.
- Proxy Server ISAPI application.

Chapter 36 Firewall Security and Web Caching with Proxy Server 2.0

The Web Proxy service is implemented as a DLL that uses ISAPI. It therefore runs within the process of the IIS WWW service. The WWW service must be installed and running in order for Web Proxy requests to be processed. Since all proxy requests for HTTP, Gopher, or FTP resources are sent from the client to the proxy server using HTTP protocol, it is both convenient and efficient for the WWW service to receive these requests and pass them on to the Web Proxy service DLL by means of the ISAPI interface. The architecture of the Web Proxy service is shown in the following illustration.

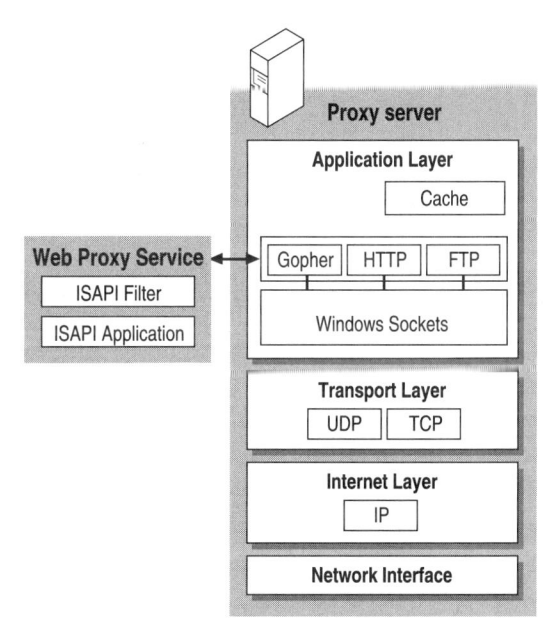

Figure 36.7 Web Proxy architecture

Proxy Server ISAPI Filter

The ISAPI filter interface is one of the two primary components of the Web Proxy service. This interface provides an extension that the web server calls upon whenever it receives a client HTTP request. An ISAPI filter is called for every request, regardless of the identity of the resource requested in the URL. An ISAPI filter can monitor, log, modify, redirect, or authenticate all requests received by the web server, illustrated as follows.

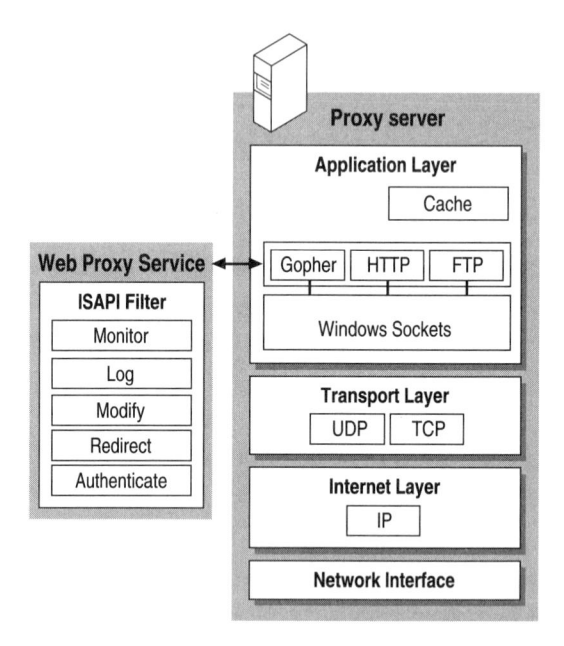

Figure 36.8 Web Proxy ISAPI filter

The web service can call an ISAPI filter DLL's entry point at various times in the processing of a request or response. When a filter is loaded, it registers the notification points in which it is interested, and the web service immediately starts calling the ISAPI filter DLL's entry point at each requested notification point for each HTTP request.

The Proxy Server ISAPI filter is contained in the W3proxy.dll file. This filter examines each request to determine if the request is a CERN-proxy request or a standard HTTP request.

If the request is a CERN-proxy request that contains a URL complete with protocol and domain name, then the Proxy Server ISAPI filter adds instructions to the request to route the response to the Proxy Server ISAPI application (W3proxy.dll). This causes the WWW service to forward the request to the Proxy Server ISAPI application for processing.

If the request is a standard HTTP request, which does not contain a protocol and a domain name, then the filter makes no change to the request and normal processing within the WWW server continues.

Proxy Server ISAPI Application

The other primary component of the Web Proxy service is the ISAPI application. ISAPI applications can create dynamic HTML and integrate the web with other service applications, such as databases. Unlike ISAPI filters, an ISAPI application is invoked for a request only if the request references that specific application. An ISAPI application does not initiate a new process for every request. The Proxy Server ISAPI application is also contained within W3proxy.dll.

ISAPI Requests

When the ISAPI receives a request, it does the following:

- Performs a client authentication.
- Does a domain filter check.
- Looks for the resource in the cache (and returns the resource from the cache if it is found and current).
- Gets the resource from the Internet, sends it to the client, and adds it to the cache if appropriate.

Refer to the following illustration.

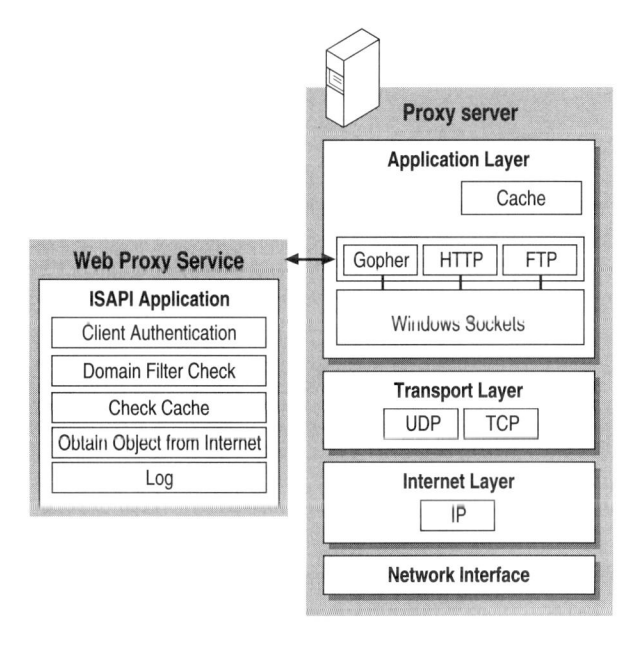

Figure 36.9 ISAPI application functions

If a request is valid and it is necessary to issue the request to an Internet site, the ISAPI application parses the URL to extract the protocol (HTTP, FTP, or Gopher) and the domain name. For HTTP requests, the ISAPI application calls the appropriate Windows Sockets Application Programming Interfaces (APIs) directly to process the requests.

HTTP Requests

For HTTP requests, all I/O is done asynchronously after the domain name has been resolved. When a request is issued to an Internet site, the Proxy Server ISAPI application does the following:

- Resolves the domain name to an IP address, using the Domain Name System (DNS) cache if possible.
- Connects to the remote site.
- Sends a request to the remote site.
- Receives a response header from the remote site.
- Reads data.
- Sends the content to the client and saves a copy in the Proxy Server cache.

From the standpoint of the web server, the Web Proxy service may require a relatively long period of time to process a request. This is impacted by periods in which the Web Proxy service is handling many clients. At these times, the Web Proxy service may forward many simultaneous requests to the Proxy Server ISAPI application.

Server Keep-Alives

By running as an ISAPI application, the Web Proxy service benefits from many other functions and performance features of IIS. One important feature is the web server's support for HTTP keep-alives. Keep-alives allow TCP connections to remain intact after the server has completed a request or response. This significantly improves performance when the same client makes another request to the same server within a certain time limit of the initial connection.

For example, Small Business Server 4.5 has a single Proxy Server application which handles all Internet access requests. Every attempt within the small business network to access Web, Gopher, and FTP sites requires a connection from a browser on a network client to one of these proxy services. The probability of reusing a connection between the same client and the same proxy services is very high. Keep-alives allow the initial connection to remain for a specified period of time until the server drops the connection.

Winsock Proxy Service

Winsock Proxy provides proxy service for Windows Sockets applications. Winsock Proxy allows a Windows Sockets application running on a small business network client to operate as if directly connected to the Internet—when in actuality, Proxy Server is acting as a gateway between the two networks.

The Winsock Proxy service is accessed from the Internet Information Server folder in the Microsoft Management Console. Winsock Proxy provides the following services for the small business network:

- Support for all Windows Sockets-compatible applications.
- TCP/IP on the LAN.
- Windows NT Challenge/Response authentication between the client and the server, whether or not the client application supports it.
- Control of inbound and outbound access by port number, protocol, and user or group.
- Restriction or filtering of access to Internet sites by domain name, IP address, and subnet mask.
- Blocking of external (Internet) users from access to internal (private network) computers.
- Logging of information about Internet requests made by clients.
- Compatibility with Microsoft Windows-based client computers.
- Data encryption by means of SSL tunneling.

Windows Sockets

Windows Sockets is a mechanism for interprocess communication between applications running on different computers, such as a client in the small business network and an Internet server. Windows Sockets defines a set of standard APIs that an application uses to communicate with one or more other applications. The APIs support the initiation of an outbound connection (for clients), accept an inbound connection (for servers), send and receive data on those connections, and then terminate the connections when finished.

The specifications for Windows Sockets includes a standard set of APIs supported by all Windows-based TCP/IP protocol stacks. Windows Sockets is a port of the Berkeley Sockets API that existed on UNIX, with extensions for integration into the Win16 and Microsoft Win32 message-based application environments. Windows Sockets also includes support for other transport protocols.

Windows Sockets supports point-to-point stream-oriented communications and point-to-point or multipoint connectionless communications (referred to as datagram-oriented). When using the TCP/IP protocol suite:

- Stream-oriented connections use the TCP protocol.
- Datagram-oriented communications use the UDP protocol.

Most Internet application protocols (HTTP, Gopher, FTP, and so on) are stream-oriented client/server protocols. A client typically initiates a connection to a server to process a user request. A server waits for connections initiated by clients, accepts those connections, and begins communicating with the client, following the rules of the specific application protocol.

Sockets Communication Channels

Windows Sockets communication channels are represented by data structures called sockets. A socket is identified by the following two components:

- An address.
- A port.

For example, a TCP/IP socket is associated with both an IP address and a TCP or UDP port. The port identifies the virtual channel used for communications at the TCP/UDP level. A stream-oriented (TCP) connection is associated with local and remote addresses and ports.

The following illustration shows a communication channel with a TCP/IP socket between a client socket application and a remote (Internet) server.

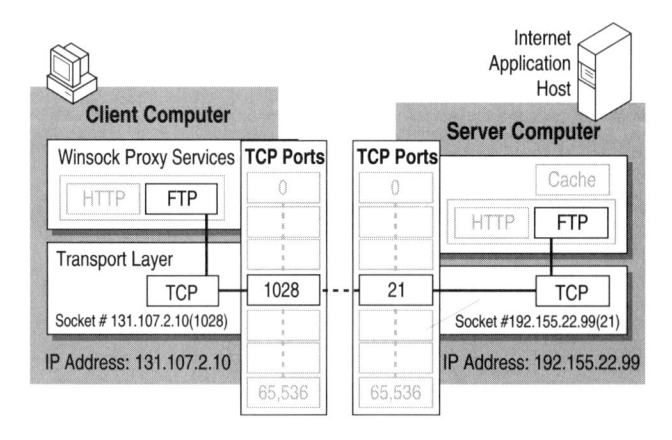

Figure 36.10   Windows socket communication channel

Winsock Proxy Client

The client application uses Windows Sockets APIs to communicate with another application running on an Internet computer. Winsock Proxy intercepts the Windows Sockets call and establishes a communication path from the internal application to the Internet application through Proxy Server 2.0. This process is totally transparent to the two applications. The illustration that follows shows the orientation of a client Windows Sockets call to Proxy Server and then a Winsock Proxy call made to an Internet server from Proxy Server.

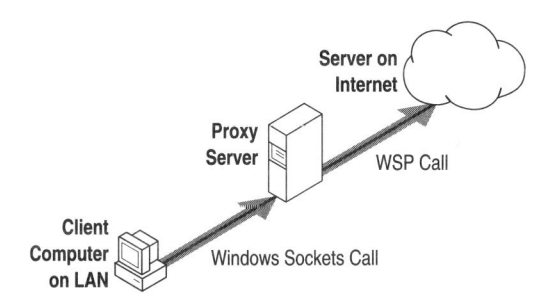

Figure 36.11 Winsock Proxy call to Internet host

The Winsock Proxy service works with Windows-based client computers. It offers client and server support for most standard and custom Internet applications that communicate through Windows Sockets.

Winsock Proxy Components

Winsock Proxy consists of the following components:

- A service running on Proxy Server.
- A DLL installed on each client computer.

Note On client computers, the Windows Sockets DLLs are renamed and the Winsock Proxy client DLL is given the name of the corresponding Windows Sockets DLL. This results in Windows Sockets applications linking to the Winsock Proxy client DLL and the Winsock Proxy client DLL linking to the renamed Windows Sockets DLL.

Service Running on Proxy Server

The Winsock Proxy service runs on Windows NT Server 4.0 only. It runs as a stand-alone Windows NT service and is responsible for the following:

- Creating virtual connections between internal applications and Internet applications.
- Transferring data between the two communications channels set up for a virtual connection.

Winsock Proxy Client DLL

The Winsock Proxy client DLL intercepts Windows Sockets API calls made by client computer applications. Depending on the API and the current socket status, the Winsock Proxy client DLL will do one of the following:

- Completely process the client's request.
- Pass the request to the actual (renamed) Windows Sockets DLL, after possibly making changes to the request, and/or
- Pass control information to the Winsock Proxy service of Proxy Server 2.0.

Note Network communication between applications on the internal network will continue to work if the Winsock Proxy client is installed on a computer that has a third-party TCP/IP stack and the Windows Sockets DLL.

There are two versions of the Winsock Proxy client DLL including:

- Winsock.dll for 16-bit Windows-based applications.
- Wsock32.dll for 32-bit Windows-based applications.

Winsock Proxy Control Channel

Winsock Proxy uses a control channel between the client and Proxy Server to manage the ability of Windows Sockets messages used remotely on the Internet. Ideally, the control channel will be used as little as possible and there is a minimum of Windows Sockets API calls that require special processing on the client computer. The control channel and the information it carries is illustrated as follows.

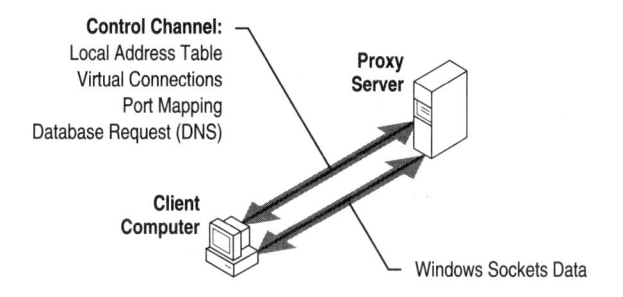

Chapter 36 Firewall Security and Web Caching with Proxy Server 2.0

Figure 36.12 Windows Sockets control channel

The control channel is set up when the Winsock Proxy client DLL is first loaded, and it uses the connectionless UDP protocol. The Winsock Proxy client and the Winsock Proxy service use a simple acknowledgment protocol to add reliability to the control channel. The control channel serves as a path for the following functions:

- Routing information from the Winsock Proxy server to the Winsock Proxy client. When the client first establishes the control channel, Proxy Server 2.0 sends the LAT to the client. The LAT contains a list of internal IP addresses and subnets, so the client will know which requests to send out to the Internet.
- Making TCP connections from the Winsock Proxy client to the Winsock Proxy server. When a client establishes a connection with a remote (Internet) application, Proxy Server 2.0 uses the control channel to establish the virtual connection. Once the connection is established, sending or receiving data will not require use of the control channel.
- Maintaining UDP communications between Winsock Proxy clients and Winsock Proxy servers. Winsock Proxy clients contact the Winsock Proxy server via the control channel when the UDP socket is bound. Additionally, in order to support multiple remote applications communicating with the internal application, port-mapping information is sent to the Winsock Proxy client DLL each time a new remote peer sends data. Sending and receiving data to and from known peers does not require the control channel.
- Handling the redirection of Windows Sockets database requests, such as DNS name resolution, by passing the client request to the Winsock Proxy service and forwarding the response to the Winsock Proxy client DLL via the control channel.

The architecture of Winsock Proxy requires special processing by the Winsock Proxy client DLL when establishing a connection with an Internet site. Once a communication channel or connection is established, however, the client can use standard Windows Sockets and Win32 APIs for reading and writing a socket or file with no special processing. The control channel currently uses UDP port number 1745 on the Winsock Proxy Server and client computers.

SOCKS Proxy Service

SOCKS Proxy service provides the following features:

- Compatibility with all popular client operating systems and client hardware platforms, including Windows, Macintosh, and UNIX.
- Support for SOCKS standard configuration file.
- Support of TCP/IP on the internal network.
- Support of the Identification Protocol (the Identd Simulation service) authentication to maintain communications with clients.
- Use of IP authentication to establish the communications channel.
- Logged information about SOCKS requests made by clients.
- Supports SOCKS Version 4.3a.

SOCKS Protocol

SOCKS is a protocol that functions as a proxy. It enables clients on one side of the SOCKS server to gain full access to hosts on the other side of the SOCKS server, without requiring direct IP accessibility. SOCKS protocol defines two operations—connect and bind. These are described below.

Connect Request

The SOCKS client sends a *connect* request when a connection to an Internet (SOCKS application) server is required. The client includes the following information in the request packet—SOCKS protocol version number, SOCKS command code, destination host IP address, destination host TCP port number, user ID, and null field. When the SOCKS application server receives and processes the request packet, it sends a reply packet to the client that indicates if the SOCKS request was granted, rejected, or failed—then the SOCKS server immediately closes the connection.

If the SOCKS application server grants the SOCKS client request, the client can immediately begin sending and receiving application data. If the SOCKS request was rejected or failed, the reply code may offer a reason or possible cause for the failure.

Bind Operation

The SOCKS *bind* operation provides access control based on TCP header information, such as IP addresses and port numbers of the source and destination hosts. For more information on SOCKS, refer to the NEC company web sites:
http://www.socks.nec.com/index.html
http://www.socks.nec.com/socks4.protocol

TCP/IP on the Small Business LAN

In Small Business Server 4.5, the internal network utilizes TCP/IP. Therefore, TCP/IP applications can communicate with a local (internal network) or remote (Internet) applications. When the Winsock Proxy client DLL initializes, it receives the LAT from the Winsock Proxy service through the control channel. The LAT contains a list of IP addresses and subnets located on the internal network.

When a client computer application attempts to communicate either locally or remotely, the Winsock Proxy client DLL does the routing with a specific IP address. If a client application attempts to communicate with a local IP address, the Winsock Proxy client DLL forwards the request to the original (renamed) Windows Sockets DLL, with no special processing.

In some cases, if an application attempts to communicate and the Winsock Proxy client DLL cannot determine if it wants to communicate with a local computer or a remote computer, Winsock Proxy assumes a local computer for the sake of security.

Using Web Proxy and Winsock Proxy Services Together

If the Winsock Proxy and Web Proxy services are used together, they can be configured so that service features are complementary to one and other. To do this, establish the following configuration:

- The client's Internet browser configured to use the Proxy Server 2.0 Web Proxy service.
- The client computer configured to use the Winsock Proxy service on the LAN.
- The LAT configured to specify that the Winsock Proxy server's internal IP address is not on the local network.

This forces the use of Winsock Proxy between the client and Proxy Server 2.0. Then, for HTTP, FTP, and Gopher requests from the client browser, the Winsock Proxy and Web Proxy services work together as follows:

- The browser sends a proxy request to the IP address of the proxy server.
- The Winsock Proxy client DLL intercepts the TCP connect process.
- The Winsock Proxy client DLL looks up the IP address in the LAT and determines if it needs to send the request remotely.
- The Winsock Proxy client DLL works with the Winsock Proxy service to set up a socket connection between the client and the service and another socket connection from the Winsock Proxy service (through IIS) to the Proxy Server ISAPI components.

- Client requests are sent from the client to the Winsock Proxy service, which provides Windows NT challenge/response authentication and support for TCP/IP (and IPX/SPX if in use) on the internal network.
- The Winsock Proxy service forwards the request to the Proxy Server components. The Proxy Server ISAPI application provides caching.
- The Proxy Server ISAPI application issues Internet requests for resources not found in the cache.

CHAPTER 37

Computer Security and Windows NT Server 4.0

Microsoft® Windows NT® Server 4.0 allows you a range of security levels to address the needs of the small business organization. In this chapter, different security levels are described along with some options for providing them. Since these levels are unique to the small business, the technology consultant may want to create a unique combination of the characteristics of security levels presented in this chapter.

Overview of Security Levels

Because sensitive data is stored on computers—anything from financial data, to personnel files, to employee correspondence—there is a need to protect these company resources. Small businesses also need to protect against accidental or deliberate changes to the way the computer is set up. At the same time, the technology consultant should factor in the need of small business network users to do their work without barriers to the resources they need.

In the small business organization, the level of security needed can vary depending on the specific requirements of the network. For example, maximum security may not be desirable at all times—since it poses access restriction to needed resources and also means additional work for the technology consultant to maintain maximum protections.

The first step in establishing security is to make an accurate assessment of needs in the small business network. Then, select the elements of security needed and implement them. Make sure that users know what they need to do to maintain security and why it is important. Lastly, monitor the small business network and make adjustments as needed.

Physical Security Considerations

This section describes standard and high-level physical security considerations and recommendations for the small business organization.

Standard Security

For standard security, the Small Business Server computer should be protected as any valuable equipment would be. Generally, this involves keeping the computer away from unauthorized users in a locked building. In some instances, you may want to use a cable and lock to secure the computer to its location. If the computer has a physical lock, lock it and store the key in a safe place for added security.

High-Level Security

Standard security precautions are sufficient for most installations. However, additional precautions are suggested for computers that contain sensitive data, or those with a high-risk of data theft or accidental (or unauthorized) disruption of the system. At a minimum, the physical security considerations described for standard security configurations should be followed. In addition, the physical link provided by your computer network should be examined. In some cases, it is wise to use controls built in to certain hardware platforms that restrict who can turn on the Small Business Server computer.

Networks and Security

When a computer is placed in a network, an access route to the server is created. Make sure this route is secured. For standard-level security, user validation and file protection are sufficient. However, for high-level security the network itself should be secure, and in some cases, the server must be completely isolated.

The risks to the server from the network include other network users and unauthorized network taps. If the network is entirely contained in a secure building, the risk of unauthorized taps is minimized or eliminated. If the cabling must pass through unsecured areas, use optical fiber links rather than twisted pair to foil any attempts at wire tapping to collect transmitted data.

If Small Business Server is connected to the Internet, be aware of the security issues involved in providing access to and from the Internet. For additional information on using network topology to provide security, consult *Chapter 3, Server Security on the Internet,* in the *Window NT Server Internet Guide*.

Controlling Access to the Computer

The Small Business Server computer is not completely secure if people other than authorized users can physically access it. For maximum security on a computer that is not physically secure (locked away), follow all or some of the following security measures:

- Disable floppy-based booting. If the computer doesn't require a floppy disk drive, remove it.
- The CPU should be in a case that cannot be opened without a key. Store the key away from the computer.
- The entire hard disk should be NTFS.
- If the computer doesn't require network access, remove the network card.

Controlling Access to the Power Switch

Keep unauthorized users away from the power and reset switches on the computer, particularly if your computer rights policy denies them the right to shut down the computer. The most secure computers (other than those in locked and guarded rooms) expose only the computer's keyboard, monitor, mouse, and printer to users. The CPU and removable media drives can be locked away where only authorized personnel have access to them.

On many hardware platforms, the system can be protected using a *power-on password*. A power-on password prevents unauthorized personnel from starting an operating system other than Windows NT, which would compromise system security. Power-on passwords are a function of the computer hardware, not the operating system software. Therefore the procedure for setting up a power-on password depends on the type of computer. Consult the computer vendor's documentation for additional information.

Standard Software Security Considerations

A secure system requires effort from both the technology consultant administering the system and network users. The technology consultant must maintain certain software settings and users must cultivate habits such as logging off at the end of the day and memorizing their passwords, rather than writing them down.

User Accounts

With standard security, a user account (user name) and password should be required in order to use the computer. User accounts can be managed with the Manage Users task on the Small Business Server console. The wizards of the Manager Users task allow you to set passwords and permissions; add, delete, or disconnect users; and manage e-mail distribution lists.

You can also configure users manually without the use of wizards via the NT User Manager for Domains, accessed from the **Start** menu, **Administrative Tools** program group. However, we recommend that you use the Small Business Server console wizards to simplify performance of these tasks.

> **Note** Changes to the Windows NT computer user rights policy take effect the next time the user logs on.

Administrative Accounts and User Accounts

Use separate accounts for administrative activity and general user activity. Individuals who do administrative work on the computer should have two user accounts, one for administrative tasks and one for general activity. To avoid accidental changes to protected resources, the user account with the least privileges should be used (as long as that user can perform the tasks at hand). For example, viruses can do much more damage if activated from an account with administrator privileges.

The Guest Account

Limited access can be permitted for visitors through the default Guest account. If the computer is for public use, the Guest account can be used for public logons. You should prohibit the Guest account from writing or deleting any files, directories, or registry keys, with the possible exception of a directory where information can be left.

In a standard security configuration, a computer that allows Guest access can also be used by regular users, for those files they don't want accessible to the general public. These users can log on with their own user names and access files in directories in which they have set the appropriate permissions. They should be especially careful to log off or lock the workstation before they leave. For more information, refer to *Chapter 2, Working with User and Group Accounts,* in the *Microsoft Windows NT Server Concepts and Planning* guide.

Logging On

All users should *always* press CTRL+ALT+DEL before logging on. Intrusive programs designed to collect account passwords can appear as a logon screen, waiting for user input. By pressing CTRL+ALT+DEL you get the secure log on screen provided by Windows NT and any intrusive programs are disabled.

Logging Off or Locking the Workstation

Users should always log off or lock their workstation when away from it for any length of time. Logging off allows other users to log on (if they know the password to an account) while locking the workstation does not. The workstation can be set to lock automatically if it is not used for a set period of time by using any 32-bit screen saver with the Password Protected option. For information about setting up screen savers, refer to Windows NT Server 4.0 Online Help.

Passwords

Anyone who knows a user name and the associated password can log on as that user. Users should be mindful about keeping their passwords secret. The list below provides a few additional tips:

- Change passwords frequently and avoid reusing passwords.
- Avoid using easily guessed words and words that appear in the dictionary. A phrase or a combination of letters and numbers works well.
- Don't write a password down—choose one that is easy for you to remember.

Enforcing Strong User Passwords

Windows NT Server 4.0 Service Pack 2 and later includes a password filter DLL file (Passfilt.dll) that lets you enforce stronger password requirements for users. Passfilt.dll provides enhanced security against *password guessing* or *dictionary attacks* by outside intruders. Passfilt.dll implements the following password policy:

- Passwords must be at least six characters long.
- The minimum password length can be increased further by setting a higher password policy value for the domain.

Passwords must contain characters from at least three of the four classes described in the following table:

Table 37.1 Password Characters for Passfilt.dll

Description	Examples
English uppercase letters	A, B, C, ... Z
English lowercase letters	a, b, c, ... z
Western arabic numerals	1, 2, 3, ... 9
Non-alphanumeric (special characters)	Punctuation symbols

Passwords may not contain the user name or any part of the full user name. These requirements are hard-coded in the Passfilt.dll file and cannot be changed through the user interface or registry. If these requirements need to be modified, the technology consultant or ISV may write a .dll and implement it in the same fashion as the Microsoft version available with the Windows NT 4.0 Service Pack 2.

To use Passfilt.dll, the technology consultant must configure the password filter DLL in the system registry on Small Business Server. This is done by setting up the following registry key values:

- **Hive**: HKEY_LOCAL_MACHINE\SYSTEM.
- **Key**: System\CurrentControlSet\Control\LSA.
- **Name**: Notification Packages.
- **Type**: REG_MULTI_SZ.
- **Value**: Add string "PASSFILT" (do not remove existing ones).

Protecting Files and Directories

Small Business Server 4.5 is installed on an NTFS partition. The NTFS file system provides more inherent security features than the FAT system. With NTFS, the technology consultant can assign a variety of protections to files and directories, specifying which groups or individual accounts can access these resources in which ways. By using the inherited permissions feature and by assigning permissions to groups rather than to individual accounts, you can simplify the chore of maintaining appropriate protections. For more information, see *Chapter 4, Managing Shared Resources and Resource Security,* in *Microsoft Windows NT Server Concepts and Planning*.

For example, a user might copy a sensitive document to a directory that is accessible to people who should not be allowed to read the document, thinking that the protections assigned to the document in its old location would still apply. In this case, the protections should be set on the document as soon as it is copied, or else it should be first moved to the new directory, then copied back to the original directory.

Conversely, if a file created in a protected directory is being placed in a shared directory so other users can read it, copy it to the new directory. If it is moved, change the protections on the file so other users can read it.

When permissions are changed on a file or directory, the new permissions apply any time the file or directory is subsequently opened. Users who already have the file or directory open when you change the permissions are still allowed access according to the permissions that were in effect when they opened the file or directory.

Protecting the Registry from Network Access

All the initialization and configuration information used by Windows NT Server 4.0 is stored in the registry. The registry can be altered directly with the Registry Editor, which supports remote access to the Windows NT registry. To restrict network access to the registry, use the Registry Editor to create the following registry key:

- **Hive**: HKEY_LOCAL_MACHINE.
- **Key**: \CurrentcontrolSet\Control\SecurePipeServers.
- **Name**: \winreg.

The security permissions set on this key define which users or groups can connect to the system for remote registry access. The default NT Workstation installation does not define this key and does not restrict the technology consultant's remote access to the registry.

Note The Registry Editor should be used only by individuals who thoroughly understand the tool, the registry itself, and the effects of changes to various keys. Mistakes made in the Registry Editor could render all or part of the system unusable.

Backups

Regular backups protect small business network data from hardware failures and honest mistakes, as well as from viruses and other malicious mischief. For more information about the Windows NT Backup Utility, refer to *Chapter 6, Backing Up and Restoring Network Files,* in *Microsoft Windows NT Server Concepts and Planning*.

You can access the backup utility from Small Business Server 4.5 console **Tasks**, or from the **Start** menu under **Administrative Tools**.

Obviously, files must be read to be backed up and they must be written to be restored. Backup privileges should be limited to administrators and backup operators. The latter are people with whom you are comfortable giving read and write access on all files.

Note The Backup Utility included with Windows NT Server 4.0 allows you to back up the registry in addition to files and directories.

Auditing

Auditing can inform the technology consultant of actions that pose a potential security risk and also identify the user accounts from which audited actions were taken. Note that auditing only identifies what user accounts were used for the audited events. If passwords are adequately protected, this in turn indicates which user attempted the audited events. However, if a password has been stolen or if actions were taken while a user was logged on but away from the computer, the action could have been initiated by someone other than the person to whom the user account is assigned.

When establishing an audit policy, the cost (in disk space and CPU cycles) of the various auditing options should be weighed against the advantages. At a minimum, failed logon attempts, attempts to access sensitive data, and changes to security settings should be audited. The following table describes some common security threats and the type of auditing that can help track them.

Table 37.2 Security Threats and Auditing

Threat	Action
Hacker-type break-in using random passwords	Enable failure auditing for logon and logoff events.
Break-in using stolen password	Enable success auditing for logon and logoff events. The log entries will not distinguish between the real users and the phony ones. What you are looking for here is unusual activity on user accounts, such as logons at odd hours or on days when you would not expect any activity.
Misuse of administrative privileges by authorized users	Enable success auditing for use of user rights; for user and group management; for security policy changes; and for restart, shutdown, and system events. Because of the high volume of events that would be recorded, Windows NT does not normally audit the use of the backup files and directories and the restore files and directories rights.

(continued)

Table 37.2 Security Threats and Auditing (*continued*)

Threat	Action
Virus outbreak	Enable success and failure write access auditing for program files such as files with .exe and .dll extensions. Enable success and failure process tracking auditing. Run suspect programs and examine the security log for unexpected attempts to modify program files or creation of unexpected processes. Note that these auditing settings generate a large number of event records during routine system use. You should use them only when you are actively monitoring the system log.
Improper access to sensitive files	Enable success and failure auditing for file- and object-access events and then use File Manager to enable success and failure auditing of read and write access by suspect users or groups for sensitive files.
Improper access to printers	Enable success and failure auditing for file and object-access events and then use Print Manager to enable success and failure auditing of print access by suspect users or groups for the printers.

Secure File Sharing

The native Windows NT Server 4.0 file sharing service is provided using the SMB-based server and redirector services. Even though only administrators can create shares, the default security placed on the share allows everyone full-control access. These permissions control access to files on down-level file systems, like FAT, that do not have built-in security mechanisms. Shares on NTFS enforce the security on the underlying directory to which the shares map. It is recommended that proper security be established with NTFS and not with the file sharing service. Service Pack 3 for Windows NT 4.0 includes several enhancements to SMB based file sharing protocol, as follows:

- Support for mutual authentication as a countermeasure to man-in-the-middle attacks.

- Support for message authentication to prevent active message attacks.

The above enhancements are provided by incorporating message signing into SMB packets—verified at both the server and client ends. There are registry key settings to enable SMB signatures on each side. To ensure that the SMB-based server responds to clients with message signing only, the two registry key values below should be configured on Small Business Server 4.5:

First key

- **Hive**: HKEY_LOCAL_MACHINE\SYSTEM.
- **Key**: System\CurrentControlSet\Services\LanManServer\Parameters.
- **Name**: RequireSecuritySignature.
- **Type**: REG_DWORD.
- **Value**: 1.

Second key

- **Hive**: HKEY_LOCAL_MACHINE\SYSTEM.
- **Key**: System\CurrentControlSet\Services\LanManServer\Parameters.
- **Name**: EnableSecuritySignature.
- **Type**: REG_DWORD.
- **Value**: 1.

Setting these values ensures that the Small Business Server communicates with only those clients that are aware of message signing. This means that for installations with multiple versions of client software, the older versions will fail to connect to servers with this configured key value.

> **Important** It is extremely important that *both* keys be changed. Setting RequireSecuritySignature while *not* setting EnableSecuritySignature will prevent all access to server SMB shares

It is extremely important that *both* keys be changed. Setting RequireSecuritySignature while *not* setting EnableSecuritySignature will prevent all access to server SMB shares

Similarly, security conscious clients can also decide to communicate with servers that support message signing and no one else. The following registry key should be configured on the client machine. Setting this key value implies that the client will not be able to connect to a server which does not have message signing support.

- **Hive**: HKEY_LOCAL_MACHINE\SYSTEM.
- **Key**: System\CurrentControlSet\Services\Rdr\Parameters.
- **Name**: RequireSecuritySignature.

- **Type**: REG_DWORD.
- **Value**: 1.

For more information on SMB message signing enhancements, refer to Microsoft Knowledge Base Article Q161372.

Controlling Access to Removable Media

By default, Windows NT Server 4.0 allows any program to access files on floppy disks and compact discs. For a highly secure and multi-user environment, the technology consultant should allow only the person logged on to access these devices. This allows the interactive user to write sensitive information to these drives, with confidence that no other user or program can see or modify that data.

When operating in this mode, the floppy disks and/or compact discs on the server computer are allocated to a user as part of the interactive logon process. These devices are automatically freed for general use or for reallocation when that user logs off. In this circumstance, it is important for the interactive user to remove sensitive data from the floppy or CD-ROM drives before logging off.

Note Windows NT Server 4.0 allows all users access to a tape drive installed on Small Business Server. Any user can therefore read and write the contents of any tape in the drive. In general this is not a concern, since only one user is interactively logged on at a time. However, in some rare instances, a program started by a user can continue running after the user logs off. When another user logs on and puts a tape in the tape drive, this program can secretly transfer sensitive data from the tape. If this is a concern, restart the computer before using the tape drive.

CHAPTER 38

Internet Information Server 4.0 Security Model

Microsoft® Internet Information Server (IIS) 4.0 is tightly integrated with the Microsoft Windows NT® Server 4.0 operating system to provide a powerful web server for the small business organization. This integration allows the small business to take advantage of Internet and intranet use, while maintaining the highest levels of security for applications and information. This chapter describes the security model used by IIS 4.0.

Overview of IIS Integrated Security Model

The robust security architecture of Windows NT Server 4.0 is used consistently across all system components, with authentication tied to controlled access to all system resources. IIS integrates with the Windows NT Server 4.0 security model and into operating system services such as the file system and directory. Since IIS uses the Windows NT Server 4.0 user database, the technology consultant does not have to create separate user accounts on the web server. IIS automatically uses the same common file, print, and group permissions set in the Small Business Server 4.5 console. Also, small business network clients only need to log on to the network once.

IIS does not install a separate security implementation on top of the network operating system as some Web servers do. This creates additional overhead and potential security exposure due to lack of integration and synchronization. Rather, IIS integrates into Windows NT Server 4.0, which is inherently secure by design. Files and system objects can only be accessed with the proper permissions. User and group accounts are managed by a globally unique identification. When accounts are deleted, all access permissions and group memberships are also deleted. So even if a new account is created using a previous user name, none of the permissions are inherited.

Central Management

Permissions to control access to files and directories can be set graphically since IIS uses the same Windows NT Server 4.0 Access Control Lists (ACLs) as all other Windows services—including such services as file sharing or Microsoft SQL Server™ 7.0 permissions. Permissions for IIS are not separate from other file services, so the same files can be securely accessed over other protocols including FTP, CIFS/SMB, or NFS without duplicating administration.

With IIS, it is unnecessary for the technology consultant to maintain multiple sets of user databases. All of the services for IIS can easily be managed from a single graphical tool. The integration of IIS with Windows NT Server 4.0 ensures that the technology consultant can give new network users access to valuable network resources (HTML pages, shared files, printers, corporate databases, etc.) with a few simple mouse clicks.

IIS produces standard Web server access logs to analyze usage. Integration with Windows NT Server 4.0 also means IIS can take advantage of system auditing for more secure monitoring of resource use. For example, failed attempts to access a secure file can be recorded in the Windows NT Event Log and audited with the same tools used for managing the server.

Comprehensive Security Solution

IIS takes full advantage of tight integration with Microsoft Proxy Server 2.0, Certificate Server, Site Server Express, and other applications to provide a comprehensive security platform with a rich spectrum of built-in functionality. This enables the small business to have a fully featured Web server that is secure for both public and intranet web sites. IIS allows for integration with existing solutions as well as delivering a new generation of Web applications.

Importance of Web Server Security

The Internet has created the opportunity for businesses of all sizes to have better access to information and improved business processes and models. However, the open nature of the Web and its role as an information gateway underscores the absolute need for using a Web server with a solid security foundation. It is also essential that the Web server be tightly integrated with the operating system which the network and applications run on. This security is vital for such things as:

- Application and database security
- Electronic commerce
- Business relationships and extranets
- Communicating with customers

Application and Database Security

Web browsers are increasingly being used to provide access to information and applications in databases and other existing business systems. For example, many businesses are allowing employees to manage their personal information and benefits plans through web browsers that link back to HR systems. These business systems must be protected so users are allowed to access only applications they have authorization for and so that employees can change only their personal information.

To do this, systems must be in place to first identify users, ascertain they are who they say they are, and determine if they have permission to view the information or to perform the requested task. This last step often requires integration with existing information systems. Also, the exchange between client and server must take place over a secure channel to ensure private information transfer. Windows NT Server 4.0 and IIS 4.0 provide integrated services to enable the small business to securely connect the Web with databases and business applications.

Electronic Commerce

Electronic commerce requires a greater degree of security than is often currently deployed on many corporate networks. The lack of acceptable protection, verification, and payment methods has prevented electronic commerce from realizing its potential. The Internet can be a safe place for business if used with care. The integrated security technologies and services of IIS 4.0 and Site Server Express 2.0 provide an infrastructure for building safe and secure applications using Windows NT Server 4.0.

Business Relationships and Extranets

Small business partnerships can benefit from the superior efficiency of using electronic information transfer and communication. Many small businesses like to make selective information available to third parties while still maintaining complete security. For example, a small business may allow resellers limited access to their internal customer information database to streamline the generation of sales leads. But when the small business opens its network to contractors, suppliers, and other business partners, security is a paramount concern.

When allowing outsiders access to information or applications, the server must be able to identify and authenticate users. Access control is also needed to allow the technology consultant to limit the areas a client can visit. Users must also have the ability to transfer information privately, so that confidential information cannot be intercepted over the network. By using public key cryptography, Challenge Access Protocol, and other advanced security features, IIS 4.0 provides the security required for opening parts of a corporate intranet to the outside world.

Note The secure zone between a corporate intranet and the public Internet is sometimes referred to as an extranet.

Communicating with Customers

A small business that provides services across the Internet presently has to manage multiple user names and passwords. Personal digital certificates can help streamline the process of customer service by providing a secure, efficient way to identify customers. Digital certificates can store data customized to the buying patterns and other important characteristics of each customer.

For example, each customer could be issued certificates based on services to which they subscribe. In the case of an online sports information service, one person might subscribe to football information only, while another subscribes to golf, and a third to all sports information offered. Customers can be issued personal digital certificates that are to be mapped to a Windows NT Server account group with access to certain portions of the site. With Microsoft Site Server Express, a Web site can also easily track usage and related information to personalize and enhance the user's experience.

Framework For Using Security

Microsoft designed IIS 4.0 and Windows NT Server 4.0 to provide the technology consultant with a powerful framework for deploying web servers. Above all, IIS and Windows NT Server provide the technology consultant with a single integrated security model. This gives it a number of advantages, including the ability to:

- Take full advantage of the strong, secure underpinnings of the U.S. Government C2 and ITSEC FC2-rated Windows NT Server 4.0 security.
- Eliminate possibilities for security weaknesses and holes by not having to add redundant security layers. This sets IIS 4.0 apart from other Web servers or operating systems with multiple security layers which increase their complexity and the subsequent possibility for security holes.

- Take advantage of existing Window NT Server knowledge, making it easy to learn and configure.
- Provide better performance by eliminating unnecessary overheads of additional security and access control layers.

This framework allows the technology consultant to determine everything from what type of end user authentication will be used on the web server, to how the web server itself will be physically locked down.

Access Control

One of the most important areas of focus for IIS 4.0 is providing powerful access control functionality for Web access to files and applications on Small Business Server. IIS 4.0 was designed to make it easy to use a wide range of mechanisms for access control to critical business data, depending on the needs of the small business organization. These include the following:

- Support for the Windows NT Challenge/Response (NTLM) authentication.
- IP address grant/deny restrictions.
- Ability to implement restrictions on virtual servers and directories.
- Support for the Windows NT File System (NTFS).
- Impersonation of users when running applications.
- Client and server digital certificates.
- Advanced security filters.

User Authentication and Authorization

IIS 4.0 security is integrated with the Windows NT Directory Service. This means only a user with a valid Windows NT user account can access all resources. This allows the technology consultant to use the full power of the Windows NT Directory Service account management, including the ability to audit and log all activity, set time of day restrictions, expire passwords, and force secure password policies.

Anonymous Access

When IIS 4.0 is set up, it creates an anonymous account for unauthenticated Web connections. When file security is not required, the request is processed by the server in the security context of this anonymous user account. The anonymous user account can access only files and applications for which permission has been granted.

User Name and Password

Files and applications can be restricted to access only by specific users or groups. This requires obtaining and verifying the user name. IIS 4.0 can be configured to require basic HTTP authentication. Users are prompted for a name and password, which are then compared to accounts in the Windows NT Server 4.0 directory. However, the name and password in basic authentication are passed as clear text over the network and can potentially be intercepted by a network packet sniffer.

Secure Windows Challenge/Response

IIS 4.0 also provides support for NTLM authentication, which uses a cryptographic technique to authenticate the password—the actual password is never sent across the network. Since every connection is mapped directly to a Windows NT Server user account, Internet users also receive the benefit of a single logon to all servers and services in the Small Business Server domain, just as they do on an intranet.

Currently, NTLM is supported by Microsoft Internet Explorer (version 3.0 and later). The IIS Software Development Kit includes documentation and sample source code so that other software vendors may include NTLM support in their browsers and applications.

Digital Certificates

IIS 4.0 supports the use of X.509 certificates for access control. A certificate verifies a user's identity in much the same way as a driver's license or corporate identification card. They are issued by a trusted certificate authority, either within an organization or a public company. How rigorously IIS 4.0 checks the user's identity or credentials when issuing a certificate depends upon the level of security required for the information or application being accessed. Users enter a password when signing their certificate—this password is required every time the certificate is activated for use. The possession of a certificate alone does not constitute proof of ownership. The password is the key to verifying access since only the owner of the certificate should know this information.

Certificate-based client authentication requires a protocol able to handle certificates at both the client and server ends in addition to the appropriate requests and replies. A server certificate is presented to a client so that the client may authenticate the identity of the server. When running Secure Sockets Layer (SSL) protocol, a server is required to have a server certificate. As an option, the server can ask for the client's certificate. The server certificate contains the web site name and the browser verifies that the web site is the name that was entered.

Access Control Using Custom Authentication Filters

IIS 4.0 provides a set of open APIs that developers can use to create filters that authenticate users based on custom rules. This gives the technology consultant the flexibility to control access using any authentication scheme or external directories.

Access Controls

Once users are authenticated, IIS 4.0 checks to see if they have permission to access the requested file or application.

IP Addresses

On the Internet, each server and client (or proxy for a group of clients) has a specific Internet address called the IP address. IIS 4.0 can be configured to grant or deny access to specified IP addresses. This gives the technology consultant the ability to exclude users by denying access from a particular IP address, or prevent entire networks from accessing the server. Conversely, the technology consultant can choose to allow only specific IP addresses to have service access.

NTFS File System Permissions

NTFS was designed to provide security features required for high-end web servers in both intranet and Internet scenarios. The NTFS file system supports discretionary access control and ownership privileges important for the integrity of critical small business data. NTFS allows the technology consultant to assign permission to individual files—not just to folders and directories. By using the NTFS file system for the content made available by IIS 4.0, the technology consultant can help ensure that only authorized individuals have access to individual files on the Web server.

Once the user's IP address restrictions are satisfied, user name or password is validated, and the service's virtual directory permissions are completed, IIS 4.0 will then attempt to access the specified resource (based on the URL) using the security context of the authenticated user. This allows Windows NT Server to enforce resource access control based on NTFS permissions, offering the technology consultant extremely granular control over sensitive resources and data.

Windows NT identifies each user by a globally unique security identification (SID), not by user name. This SID is mapped in the background to the user's account name, so file permissions and group accounts are managed using a friendly name but applied using the SID. When an account is deleted, all ACLs and group assignments for the account are also removed. SIDs and synchronization ensure that an account later created with the same user name cannot inherit permission to the old account.

Impersonation

IIS 4.0 accesses all files and runs all applications in the security context of the user requesting the file, restricting what can be accessed. This is either the anonymous user account specified in the server administration or an authenticated user account. This means that a CGI application or component in a user directory cannot access data or services restricted to other users or the server administrator. Moreover, application developers have much more flexibility in developing applications than they would if all codes were required to run in the security context of the server itself. Impersonation allows web-based applications to be used securely for applications or administrator-like functions to limit both who accesses the application and what they are allowed to do.

Permissions on IIS Services

IIS 4.0 allows the technology consultant to set read-only or execute-only permissions on the virtual directories. For every request, IIS 4.0 examines the URL and type of request to ensure the permissions set on the virtual directory or virtual root are honored. This ensures users cannot read files with execute-only permission or execute files with read-only permissions.

Auditing Access

Auditing security events is one of the few ways to determine if users are trying to gain access to secure content on your Web server. IIS 4.0 supports two forms of logging. The first is the standard Web server access log that records all file and object requests and errors. The second uses Windows NT Server capability to enable the technology consultant to log and audit all possible attempts to breach security through the Windows NT Server Event Viewer. For example, on a secure intranet web server, a technology consultant is able to log the following:

- All access to server files.
- Invalid logon attempts.
- All logons.

The audit log can be used in addition to the Web server access log for increased security monitoring as well as a duplicate log protected with different permissions. We recommend customers guard the audit logs generated by IIS, since some hackers try to cover their failed attempts to gain access to your Web server's secure information. Restrict access to the logs and periodically backup all files.

Confidentiality and Data Integrity

When a connection on the Internet between a Web browser and a Web server exists, the secure channel technology of IIS 4.0 provides privacy, integrity, and authentication in point-to-point communications for small business network users. SSL 2.0 and 3.0 and Private Communications Technology (PCT) for secure channel communication are included with Small Business Server 4.5 as a base feature of IIS 4.0.

Developers of Internet applications running on Windows NT Server 4.0 for the small business can provide SSL application support through the WinInet functions or through Winsock 2.0. The Transport Layer Security Protocol (TLS), now under consideration by IETF, will provide a single standard encompassing both SSL and PCT.

Confidentiality

Confidentiality prevents the content of a communication from being reached by unauthorized parties. In the case of a small business sales transaction, for example, it is important to guarantee that only the intended party has access to the information being transferred. Privacy mechanisms, such as an SSL-encrypted channel, are used to ensure that sales and other sensitive transactions are secure over the Internet or other carriers.

Data Integrity

Integrity assures that vital data has not been modified. Integrity is critical for conducting small business commerce over the Internet. Without assured integrity, things such as purchase orders, contracts, specifications, or stock purchase orders could be modified with devastating effects. This is why IIS 4.0 supports digital signatures and message authentication codes. Digital signatures provide fingerprints of a document to determine if data has been changed from the original signed document.

Digital Signatures

Digital signatures are used both to verify the identity of a user or server and to ensure that a message can be read only by the intended recipient. Digital signatures are used in e-mail and file transfers to verify identity and encrypt messages. They are also used by Web servers and browsers to provide mutual authentication, confidentiality of the pages transferred, and integrity of the information. Signing data does not alter it, but simply generates a string that is attached to the data.

Digital signatures are created using a public-key encryption algorithm such as the RSA public-key cipher. A public-key algorithm actually uses two different mathematically mated keys: the *public key* and the *private key*, which together are known as a key pair. A public key is available to anyone, while the private key is known only to its owner. Public-key algorithms are designed so that if one key is used for encryption, the other is necessary for decryption. Furthermore, the private key is virtually impossible to derive from the public key. IIS 4.0 certificate technology uses 1024-bit public key cryptography, which is extremely secure protection.

Secure Sockets Layer

IIS 4.0 supports SSL 3.0. SSL provides a security handshake that is used to initiate a TCP/IP connection, such as when communication between a Web browser and a Web server is initiated in the small business network. A browser and server with mutual authentication must be in agreement about the use of SSL security with TCP/IP connections. SSL provides privacy, integrity, and authentication in a private point-to-point communications channel. SSL also provides for selectable encryption and decryption of both request and response data being passed across network connections. An example is credit card information in a shopping-payment scenario.

Spontaneous communication on a worldwide basis is possible because SSL uses world standard cryptography from RSA, which is shipped in every Microsoft operating system and copy of Internet Explorer. Microsoft has proposed extensions to Winsock 2 in order to accommodate SSL as well as PCT and TLS. The goal is to make implementing an SSL-enabled application as easy as possible while still providing an adequate amount of flexibility. An application that uses these Winsock 2 extensions should be just as secure as one that implements the protocol internally.

SSL always provides authentication of the server—because if an SSL session is established, the server always provides a digital certificate to the client. Digital certificates are similar to an electronic license or notarizing a document, since they allow both parties to confirm they are talking with the server name that is being claimed. The browser will check the server name against the certificate and alert the user if they are different.

Secure Electronic Transport

Secure Electronic Transport (SET) is a secure message protocol for credit card transactions. SET is being developed by Visa and MasterCard with contributions from Microsoft, IBM®, GTE, Netscape®, and others. SET provides authentication for cardholders and merchants, and preserves the confidentiality of payment data without encrypting order descriptions or other non-confidential information. Unlike secure channel services such as SSL, SET uses 56-bit Data Encryption Standard (DES) encryption and requires digital signatures to verify the identities of all parties. By using multiparty messages that allow information to be encrypted directly to banks, SET will protect against misuse of credit card numbers.

To provide data integrity and ensure that the data coming through has not been tampered with, SSL uses the message digest MD-5 and the RC-4 stream cipher for privacy. The RC-4 encryption can be 128-bit for domestic use and 40-bit for use outside of North America.

Since the specification is license-free, interoperable, and open to all participants, it is anticipated that the majority of software firms will adopt SET for electronic commerce transactions. Microsoft will deliver tools to aid merchants, acquirers, and payment processors to create SET-compliant applications. Since the intention is to have all SET-compliant software able to obtain export and import approval easily, Visa and MasterCard are working to address any concerns the government may have regarding SET's use of cryptography.

Through the addition of digital certificates that associate the card holder and merchant with a financial institution and the Visa or MasterCard payment system, SET provides a higher level of security than is possible with today's technology. The integration of SET into the credit card processing system will give cardholders and small business merchants a high level of confidence that their transactions are secure.

Point-to-Point Tunneling Protocol (PPTP)

Microsoft Virtual Private Network (VPN) technology based on the Point-to-Point Tunneling Protocol (PPTP), was created to address secure, low-cost remote access to corporate local area networks (LANs) via public networks like the Internet. PPTP is a new networking technology that supports multiprotocol VPNs. Using PPTP, remote users of the small business network can employ Microsoft Windows® 9x and NT Workstation operating systems or other PPP-enabled client systems to dial a local Internet service provider and connect securely to the small business network via the Internet. VPN technology gives small business network users an economical and easy-to-implement solution for creating secure and encrypted communication across the Internet.

PPTP can also be used with dense and integrated communications solutions to support V.34 and integrated service digital network (ISDN) dial-up. Small businesses can also use a PPTP-enabled VPN over IP backbones to outsource dial-up access to their corporate networks in a manner that is cost-effective, hassle-free, protocol-independent, and secure, and requiring no changes to their existing network addressing.

Security Functionality for Developers

IIS 4.0 was designed to provide ISV developers with a powerful platform for designing web-based applications for the small business. In addition to the Internet Server API (ISAPI) and Active Server Pages for scripting the Web server, IIS makes the following secure technologies available to developers:

- Issuing Digital Certificates with Microsoft Certificate Server.
- CryptoAPI for cryptography.
- Using SSL certificates with Active Server Pages.

Issuing Digital Certificates with Microsoft Certificate Server 1.0

Certificate Server 1.0 enables the small business organization to easily manage the issuance, renewal, and revocation of certificates without having to rely on external certificate authorities. With Certificate Server 1.0, the small business organization also has full control over the policies associated with the issuance, management, and revocation of certificates, as well as the format and contents of the certificates themselves. In addition, Certificate Server 1.0 logs all transactions —this enables the technology consultant to track, audit, and manage certificate requests. The default policy automatically grants certificates to a trusted set of users based on a preset Windows NT Server 4.0 group of administrators and accounts. It can authenticate a user based on their Windows NT Server 4.0 logon and enables the technology consultant to approve or deny a certificate request directly.

The technology consultant can issue certificates in standard formats (X-509 versions 1 and 3) and add extensions to certificates as needed. Certificate Server 1.0 does the following:

- Accepts standard PKCS #10 certificate requests.
- Issues X-509 version 1 and version 3 certificates in PKCS #7 format.
- Issues SSL client and server certificates.
- Issues S/MIME certificates.
- Issues SET-compliant certificates.
- Supports open interfaces that enable writing of modules to support custom formats.

Certificate Server 1.0 functions with Microsoft and non-Microsoft clients, browsers, and web servers. The technology consultant can choose to distribute and request certificates in many ways, including transport mechanisms that may be customized to small business needs. The Certificate Server 1.0 can post certificates back to the user in e-mail, to a light directory access protocol (LDAP)-based directory service, or any other custom mechanism.

CryptoAPI

CryptoAPI, which is part of Windows NT Server 4.0 and Microsoft Internet Explorer 5.0, was designed to abstract the details of cryptography away from developers. It includes the Cryptographic Service Provider (CSP) interface, which makes accessing cryptography easier by allowing developers to change the strength and type of their cryptography without modifying application code.

CryptoAPI frees applications from having to do their own encryption. It provides extensible, exportable, system-level access to common cryptographic functions such as encryption, hashing, and digital signatures. Any application written with CryptoAPI can use certificates that support the standard X.509 standard. This enables any standards-compliant application or system to access the server from any platform, including those on UNIX and Macintosh platforms.

CryptoAPI provides a rich set of high-level APIs that make it easier for the developer to sign, seal, encrypt, and decrypt data. ISV developers will easily be able to integrate identity and authentication into their applications, thereby securing private communications and data transfers over intranets and the Internet. Examples of certificate services are: functions for generating requests to create certificates, functions for storing and retrieving certificates, and functions for parsing certificates.

Programmatically Interacting with Client Certificates

The scripting power of Microsoft Active Server Pages provides a programmatic way of interacting with client certificates. The certificate and its key fields can be exposed for scripting—thus allowing direct mapping, for example, into server-side databases. This also provides the ability to map client certificates to Windows NT Server 4.0 user accounts. In addition to specific client certificates being mapped on a many-to-one basis (multiple certificates mapping to the same Windows NT Server 4.0 user account), wildcard mapping is also included. For even greater security, Active Server Pages allow web masters to examine the content of a client-provided certificate.

PART 8

Migration and Upgrade

Part 8 presents information on how to plan, deploy, interoperate, and migrate Microsoft® BackOffice® Small Business Server 4.5 in the small business customer's existing NetWare environment. This part also discusses client licensing issues, upgrade paths for Small Business Server 4.5, and the process of migrating an Access database to Microsoft SQL Server™ 7.0. The following chapters are included in Part 8:

Chapter 39   Migrating from a NetWare Environment   615

Chapter 40   Small Business Server 4.5 Licensing and Upgrade   657

Chapter 41   Migrating from an Existing Windows NT Server   663

Chapter 42   Migrating an Access Database to SQL Server 7.0   667

CHAPTER 39

Migrating from a NetWare Environment

This chapter begins with the recommended basic planning to ease deployment and testing of Microsoft® BackOffice® Small Business Server 4.5 in an existing Novell® NetWare environment. The chapter continues with integration and procedures for migrating NetWare resources over to Small Business Server 4.5. Essentially, the migration process is completed in the following five phases:

- Planning and overview.
- Testing.
- Integration.
- Migration.
- Project review.

Note In this chapter, some references are made to Windows NT® Server—anything applicable to Windows NT Server 4.0 in this context is also applicable to Small Business Server 4.5.

Integration and Migration Planning

Since Small Business Server 4.5 contains the Windows NT Server 4.0 operating system, all the built-in NetWare migration and integration features of Windows NT Server 4.0 are included in Small Business Server 4.5. This also means that the Windows NT Server 4.0 add-on tools, which may be purchased separately to enhance integration and migration in a NetWare environment, will also work with Small Business Server 4.5. NetWare tools discussed in this chapter include:

- Migration Tool, Client Services, and Gateway Service included with Small Business Server 4.5.
- File and Print Services and Directory Service Manager may be purchased separately.

Note While these tools will help at many stages of deployment, they do not substitute for a rigorous deployment plan.

Deployment Plan

Considerable attention to the planning stage increases the prospect of successful deployment and assures that expected functionality is achieved within the allowable time constraints. If you are considering skipping all planning and immediately engaging the deployment process, please consider the time that could be wasted without a clearly defined approach and support information. Even the most rudimentary planning will help avert serious, costly, and time-consuming problems during deployment and migration.

General Agenda

The first step when planning for deployment and migration is to define your objectives. A clear, concise project objective will give the project focus. Before deploying Small Business Server 4.5 in a NetWare environment, the technology consultant should build a comprehensive deployment plan to describe the current small business network environment, any additional resources needed to deploy Small Business Server, and the necessary resources to migrate from NetWare to Small Business Server. The deployment plan should define the following:

- Proposed changes to the network.
- Plans for preliminary testing (proof of technology and pilot).
- Details for deployment.

Details of the Plan

The size and complexity of the migration project may dictate the scale of the evaluation and plan. However, the ability to predict events accurately and achieve success in all subsequent phases is dependent on the quality of work performed during the planning period. While the exact details of the plan may differ from one small business network to another, the outline of components for the plan remains fairly consistent. The details of the deployment plan rely heavily on the following:

- Current network architecture.
- Existing schedules or planned installation events.
- Integration plans outside the scope of the project.
- Future growth planned for the network.
- Business goals or objectives of the organization.
- Business expectations of local area network (LAN) service levels.

Pre-Installation Planning Checklist

As with any design, it is crucial that installations be highly controlled resulting in predictable server and workstation builds. A detailed step-by-step check and sign-off list should be used to control the process and order of the installation. Using the checklist technique also ensures that steps are not missed. The following is a typical checklist of items to be addressed during the planning stages of a NetWare to Windows NT Server deployment or migration:

- Ensure that all needed equipment and software have been ordered and are available.
- Run **Security** and **Modules** on the NetWare server to be migrated, in order to receive correct configuration information.
- Review the **Groups** and **Members** on the NetWare server.
- Review the **Security Equivalents** on the NetWare server.
- Determine if some or all groups are to be migrated.
- Decide whether clients will be migrated at the same time as the server conversion, before or after server migration, or whether they will be left as is.
- Determine if any applications will be migrated.
- Establish performance testing guidelines.
- Ensure sufficient database and file capacity requirements on Small Business Server.

Integration Overview

Successful deployment (or "rollout") depends on successful planning and execution. The deployment of Small Business Server 4.5 in a NetWare environment may consist of a NetWare and Small Business Server coexistence, a NetWare to Small Business Server migration, or a combination of the two. Whatever the case, the success of the deployment depends on demonstrating the following:

- The ability to implement the integration or migration.
- Being able to execute the deployment in a reasonable amount of time.
- Delivery of the expected business functionality.

In order to demonstrate the above, another issue must be considered. Since you are deploying Small Business Server 4.5—a tightly integrated suite of server applications for Windows NT—you must conduct testing in which the successful installation and basic usage of this software is demonstrated before trying to integrate it with the Novell NetWare environment. The scope of these tests and the instructions for executing them are included later in this chapter.

Implementation of Rollout

To ensure successful implementation of Small Business Server 4.5 into a NetWare environment, the rollout should be separated into two phases. While it is possible to abbreviate them, the technology consultant should plan on executing both of them in order to not increase any risks. These two phases are *test* and *integration*.

By modularizing the various steps of the rollout into these units, the technology consultant will be able to gauge progress more accurately and anticipate any potential problems after the rollout is complete. However, it should be noted that a trouble-free trial setup during the test phase does not guarantee there will be no problems during the actual rollout. The results for each phase are described in the following sections.

Test Phase

In the optimum situation, the deployment will progress exactly as anticipated with no unforeseen, technological snags that can halt the entire operation. However, when factoring in the complexities and imperfections of real-world experience, unexpected obstacles invariably arise. For this reason, it is advised to spend some time trying out the Small Business Server product and experimenting with its typical functionality before attempting integration into the network environment of the small business. Even a short test phase can uncover and resolve problems that would prove more costly when occurring in the integrated small business network.

Functionality Testing

The test phase is a relatively controlled environment where the technology consultant can demonstrate that the installation techniques and desired functionality described in the planning process works as expected. During the test phase, successful installation of all components and client connectivity should be demonstrated, as follows:

- Desktop workstations can access shared files on Small Business Server.
- Network printer(s) to be used with Small Business Server are set up and tested.
- Server applications to be used are tested, such as sending an e-mail through Microsoft Exchange Server.
- Third-party applications that are to be run on the Small Business Server operating system are tested.

Connectivity Testing

At this point in the test phase, testing the connectivity between Small Business Server and the NetWare server is appropriate, however, it may not be a practical option if there are limited or no resources available. For instance, you may not have assistant IT staffing or equipment ready to set up a NetWare server and conduct thorough tests.

A more feasible approach for testing NetWare connectivity may be to set up Small Business Server on the small business network during the *integration* phase. Then have a NetWare client access Small Business Server (after installing NetWare services). You can then add a Windows-based, Small Business Server client and have them access the NetWare server. This will show that both the Windows-based client and the NetWare client are able to see resources on both the NetWare Server and Small Business Server — which demonstrates the required connectivity between the two computers.

Configuration and Compatibility Issues

By utilizing the controlled and isolated environment of the test phase, configuration issues can be worked out before introducing an unknown platform or other variables into the existing environment. Successful testing in this area can eliminate most or all installation and hardware compatibility issues that could later impede the progress of the actual deployment. The downside is that only limited functionality can be tested in an isolated and controlled environment (of the test phase). The remainder of the functionality must be tested in the integration phase.

Note The test phase should be performed in an environment separate from the production network—any machines involved should be set up on an isolated hub. During this phase, test and document everything—and also note any unexpected behaviors.

Integration Phase

Once the initial testing of the new technology is complete, the next step is the integration of Small Business Server 4.5 in the production network environment. The same approach may be followed as in the test phase, as follows:

- Small Business Server is installed and applications are tested, including any third-party programs.
- The services for NetWare are installed and configured, and connectivity between Small Business Server and the NetWare operating system is verified.
- After Small Business Server to NetWare communication is established with test clients, have the actual users of the small business network begin using the Small Business Server 4.5.

Post-Integration Phase Considerations

The test and integration phases should demonstrate that the basic technology component is functional in the small business networking environment. Additional functionality of the Small Business Server operating system should work as expected, assuming there are no incorrect modifications to the system and that no hardware failures occur.

Note Although it may be necessary to perform other tasks in the small business network with Small Business Server 4.5, such as implementing a database with Microsoft SQL Server 7.0, this is beyond the scope of this chapter. Refer to *Part 4, Administering and Maintaining* in this resource guide.

Failures During the Integration Phase

If something goes wrong during the integration of Small Business Server 4.5 on the production network that did not occur during the testing phase (or that was not anticipated), the technology consultant should document the precise configuration details, attempt to recreate the scenario, and then troubleshoot the situation with Small Business Server 4.5 off the production network. In order to maintain a working environment, take Small Business Server offline and have office employees use the original network configuration.

A failure during the integration phase may be an indication that the test phase was not performed thoroughly enough, a configuration issue specific to the production network caused problems, or something was not installed or configured the same way as during the test phase. This is why a record of what was done during the test phase is highly encouraged.

The Test Phase

Before beginning the testing environment set up, prepare for the tests you will perform and determine their impact on equipment needs. The primary focus of the test phase is to verify that Microsoft Small Business Server 4.5 will install and function correctly on the hardware you have allocated for this project. However, the testing process should encompass at least some of the typical functionality you intend to implement on the actual small business network. Considering all details in advance should make deployment much easier.

Preparation Tasks

The sections that follow cover preparatory tasks for the test phase, including:

- Determining the physical location of the testing environment.
- Verifying hardware components.
- Determining the tests to be conducted.
- Securing the software needed.
- Hardware preparation tasks.
- Documentation.

Physical Location

The machines used in the testing process should not be connected to the small business network. The technology consultant should arrange for some office space dedicated to testing purposes and make sure there are enough power outlets for all the hardware being used in the test phase.

Verify Hardware Components

Before setting up Small Business Server, consult the Small Business Server Recommended Hardware List to verify that all hardware components you intend to use (network cards, modems, etc) appear on the list. The list may be found at the following web site:

http://www.microsoft.com/smallbusinessserver/deployadmin/Recommended.htm

If a hardware component does not appear on the list, you can try contacting the hardware manufacturer to see if you can get a Windows NT Server 4.0-compatible driver. In most cases, this will suffice. If a Windows NT Server 4.0-compatible driver is not available, you may have to obtain hardware and drivers referenced on the Small Business Server 4.5 recommended hardware lists. The correct hardware and drivers should then be installed in the appropriate machine.

Note The Recommended Hardware List in most cases provide links for downloads of device drivers.

In addition to the compatibility issues, make sure that the machine on which Small Business Server 4.5 is to be installed meets the capacities required for successfully installing and running the software. Confirm that the machine hardware meets or exceeds the specifications in the table below.

Table 39.1 Small Business Server Machine Hardware Requirements

Specification	Recommended Hardware
Processor:	Intel Pentium 120 Megahertz (MHz) (Microsoft recommends a Pentium 200 or above) or a reduced instruction set computing (RISC)-based processor such as the Digital Alpha.
Memory:	64 megabytes (MB) of random access memory (RAM).
Hard Disk:	2 gigabytes (GB) of free space. If Office 2000 is installed, a total of 3 GB of hard disk space is required.
Video:	Video Graphics Adapter (VGA) or higher resolution monitor and a VGA adapter are required; Super VGA with at least 800x600 resolution is recommended for both the monitor and adapter.
CD-ROM drive:	Double speed or higher is recommended.
Network Card:	Network adapters from the recommended hardware lists found on the Small Business Server web site should be used. Refer to: http://www.microsoft.com/smallbusinessserver/deployadmin/Recommended.htm
Fax/Modem:	A Class 1 Fax/Modem is required for a successful installation of
	Microsoft Fax Server. Class 1 capable fax-modems that will be detected by Small Business Server 4.5 are found on the Small Business Server web site at: http://www.microsoft.com/smallbusinessserver/deployadmin/Recommended.htm

Hardware for Client Connectivity Tests

Since client connectivity will be tested, make sure you have the correct components for at least one client machine. The client computer should run the same operating system as the majority of the end-user desktop computers. If the environment is fairly well mixed, set up one of each client type to be used on the network. It may be appropriate to set up one or more new client machines in order to prevent any disturbance to employees at work in the small business organization. If setting up new machines is necessary, the procedures listed in the operating system's manual for verifying compatible hardware components should be followed.

Windows 95 Client Setup

By using the Set Up Computer Wizard in the Small Business Server 4.5 console, you will be able to set up an existing Microsoft Windows® 95 installation for use with Small Business Server 4.5 without having to do some of the typical manual setup tasks. The Set Up Computer Wizard automates the reconfiguration of an existing Windows 95 installation, establishes network connectivity, and even sets up programs such as Microsoft Exchange, Microsoft Outlook® and Microsoft Internet Explorer.

Network Hub

An additional piece of hardware that should be considered is the network hub — a component that allows computers to be networked together. It is possible to connect a small number of computers together just by using cables attached to all of them, however, there will be less concerns and testing complications if a hub is used. In order to test client/server network connectivity with Small Business Server 4.5, at least a 4 or 5 port hub should be available. A port is a singular connection from a computer's network adapter card to the hub.

The only detail about the hub that requires attention is the transceiver type. You should identify whether the jacks on the hub are 10Base-T (also known as Twisted Pair or RJ-45) or 10Base-2 (also known as thinnet, BNC, or coaxial). Be sure that the network adapter cards for all the testing machines are of the same transceiver type (connection type) and that the hub used for testing matches that type.

In practice, a prudent implementation of the test environment will match that of the business network environment as closely as possible — the test hub connection type should be matched to what is actually used in the small business network. If the network uses a cabling scheme only, then it is most likely using thinnet cable. You may attempt to simulate this network setup if you wish, but be advised that it will be easier to use a hub configuration. 10Base-T tends to be a more popular connection type than 10Base-2 since it is the easiest to use. Appropriate networking cable to match the network adapter and hub will also be needed. Both the cable and hub can be purchased from a hardware vendor that merchandises networking products.

Determining Tests to be Conducted

In the test phase, the idea is to test the basic functionality required from the new server technology without yet involving the NetWare components. While it might be reassuring to test NetWare interoperability with a mock Novell server, the time required to do this may not make it a viable option. For this reason, during the integration phase, you should try to establish the required level of NetWare interoperability before deploying Small Business Server 4.5 to end users and employees in the small business organization.

If you do have the time and resources to spend on experimenting with Novell functionality in a test environment, proceed to the integration section of this chapter and follow the procedures. However, be aware that you will have to create the interoperability environment again during the actual integration phase. In either case, the following installation, configuration, and application/ functionality tests should be performed:

- Installation of Small Business Server.

  This is the essential part of the testing phase. As long as the hardware is correct and properly configured (where configuration is called for), everything should go smoothly. If not, consult the documentation provided with the software and double check all hardware components against the recommended hardware lists.

- Peripheral devices.

  If you have a printer or modem to be used in the small business network, the printing or communication goals of the deployment should be tested at this time. The To Do List of the Small Business Server console will allow you to install a printer and Manage Modems tool will guide you through all modem tasks.

- Adding and connecting users.

  Through the Manage Users tool, you will be able to add users to the system. Then you can test the ability to login to the server from a client machine and access shared files. Some shared folders are setup automatically by the installation.

- Small Business Server Applications.

  The test phase should also include a trial run for the Small Business Server 4.5 applications to be used the most in the small business organization, such as sending and receiving e-mail with Microsoft Exchange.

- Third-Party Applications.

  The test phase should include running any third-party software you intend to use on Small Business Server 4.5, from both the server and client machines.

Secure the Installation Software

Before proceeding with the test phase, make sure the following items are available:

- Small Business Server 4.5 Discs 1 - 5.
- Small Business Server 4.5 floppy diskettes 1, 2, and 3. These can be created from Disc 1, if necessary.
- Two blank floppy disks (for the Emergency Repair disk and user computer setup disk).
- Services for NetWare CD-ROM.
- Network adapter configuration diskette (if provided by the network card manufacturer). This disk may be necessary for saving modifications to settings on hardware memory, such as the transceiver type, before proceeding with the installation procedure.
- Drivers for network adapters, Class 1 Fax/modem, small computer system interface (SCSI) adapters, multiport serial devices, and the video adapter. Consult the Recommended Hardware List for Small Business Server 4.5.
- Any required workstation operating system software.
- Any third-party software.

Network Hardware Setup

Before beginning the test phase, some final hardware preparation tasks are required as described in the sections that follow.

Connect Computers to Hub

Once the location for the testing environment has been secured and all necessary materials are obtained, the connection from the computer to the hub must be set up. On the back of the computer are the interfaces for the adapter cards. The network adapter card interface will be either a large telephone jack or a round, protruding connector, depending on whether you have twisted pair cabling (10 Base-T) or thinnet coaxial cabling (10Base-2).

If you have a twisted pair, insert one end of the cable into the jack and the other into the hub. You should hear a click when each end is inserted properly. If you are using thinnet, verify that both ends have a round or conical terminator attached and insert the cable connector into each device. Make sure all test computers are connected to the hub in this way. If you are planning on not using a hub, make sure the thinnet cable used has the proper terminator on both ends of the wire and that all connecting pieces are inserted into all machines.

Configure Network Adapter Transceiver Type

The transceiver type for the network adapter in use is either a twisted pair or coaxial. Before you begin any software installation, power up all machines and boot from the network adapter configuration disk to verify that the setting on the network adapter matches the cabling scheme in use.

Documentation

During the test phase (and when preparing the testing environment), have a pen and paper ready in order to document the variables and settings chosen during the procedures. A legible record of what was done during this phase can be invaluable if something goes wrong and it is time to figure out what happened.

Installation of Small Business Server 4.5

For Small Business Server 4.5 installation procedures, refer to *Chapter 17, Installing on New Machines*, in *Part 3, Deployment*, of this resource guide or the *Getting Started* guide. The installation is guided by the Small Business Server Installation Wizard and requires a minimum of effort on the part of the installer (technology consultant). Small Business Server 4.5 will be optimized for the particular small business environment and, for the most part, the default information will be sufficient for a complete installation. This should help the installer understand what is happening on the machine and what information must be provided to complete the actual installation.

Client Setup

After Small Business Server installation is complete, you need to set up a new user account and test the functionality of the automated Set Up Computer Wizard for the client and server. The term *client* refers to the client in the client/server computing model, which in turn refers to an end-user machine. The purpose of the Set Up Computer Wizard is to do the following:

- Configure the server for the client.
- Configure client networking.
- Install and configure client portions of programs (such as Microsoft Outlook) on a machine that already has an installed operating system.

After creating the user account, you will be able to reconfigure an existing Windows 95 or Windows NT computer with a single setup disk.

Note If Small Business Server is to be used with other client operating systems, the Set Up Computer Wizard cannot be used for these clients.

Although adding a user can be done through the **To Do List**, the technology consultant should become accustomed to using the **Manage Users** tool available from the **Tasks** link on the Small Business Server console. Using the console is normally how Small Business Server 4.5 administration is conducted on the network. If you are still in the **To Do List**, click **Getting Started** to exit.

On the Tasks page of the Small Business Server console, click the **Manage Users** taskpad. Perform the steps of the next two procedures to set up a new user account and create a client setup disk.

▶ **To add a new user**

1. From the Small Business Server console, click **Add a User** to start the **User Account Wizard**. This will help you set up the user account. Click **Next**.

2. A dialog box appears asking you for the user's full name, account name, and an optional description. Since this is for the test phase only, you do not have to enter a description, but a full name and user name are required. Click **Next** to continue.

3. A dialog box appears asking you either to allow the wizard to generate a password automatically for the user or you may do so manually. If you select the wizard, it will create a secure password. Click **Next** to continue.

4. If you specified that you want to create your own password, a dialog box appears asking you to enter and confirm the password. Do so, then click **Next**.

5. The next three dialog boxes ask for company information for the user, company address for the user, and communication information. Enter values for what a typical user on the network might use. Click **Next**.

6. A dialog box appears to add the user to an e-mail distribution list. Select the list the user should be included on, click **Add**, then click **Next**.

7. The User Access Wizard is launched. The next dialog box to appear is for configuring user access to network resources, including setting access to shared folders and folder permissions. To accept the default options, click **Next**.

8. The **Shared Printer** dialog box appears. Make sure the printer you added earlier is included in the **Printers this user can print to** list. If it is not, click **Add** to add it.

9. Click **Next** to continue. If you installed a Class 1 fax-modem and it was detected properly, the **Select the Shared Fax Printers** screen of the wizard appears showing fax printers available to the user. Make sure the fax icon appears under the **Fax Printers this user can fax to** list. If it does not, click **Add** to add it. If no fax printers are in the list, refer to the Online Guide for more information.

10. A dialog box appears to add other user rights such as Internet access or server access from a dial-up modem (a remote user). Select the rights for a typical individual in the small business organization. Click **Next**.

11. The next dialog box allows you to determine whether the user has full administrative privileges or not. Granting a user full administrative privileges gives them full access to all server resources, they can use the console, and they may set permissions. In most situations, use the default setting, **No**. Click **Next**, and then **Finish**.

▶ **To create a client setup disk**

1. After clicking **Finish** in step 10, the Set Up Computer Wizard is launched.

   This allows you to connect a client to the small business network and select applications to install on the client machine. This is the recommended path for a thorough implementation of the test phase. Once the user's machine is setup, you can verify that the setup of client software functioned as expected and that user account creation and permission settings were successful.

   Click **Next** to continue.

2. A dialog box now appears asking you to select the type of computer the new user has, either a Windows 95/98 or NT Workstation client. Select the appropriate computer and then click **Next**.

3. If the user will be using a computer which is new to the network, a dialog box asks you to enter the computer name. Type the computer name and click **Next**.

4. In the next dialog box, select the operating system of the user machine, then click **Next**.

5. A dialog box appears for generating a list of applications to install on the client computer. Because applications may be added to the client at a later time from the console (or from the client), you may elect not to install any applications now. Otherwise, select the applications to install on the client computer, and then click **Next**. Next to each selected application, the total memory required for the application is displayed.

6. A dialog box appears allowing you to create a client set up disk. When opened on the client, this disk will instruct Small Business Server 4.5 which applications to download and setup on the client workstation. Label a high density floppy with the name of the user's computer and insert it into the floppy drive of Small Business Server.

   Click **Next**. Small Business Server formats the floppy disk and copies the necessary files to it.

7. The last screen of the Set Up Computer Wizard appears and provides instructions on how to set up the client computer with the set up disk you just created—refer to the following screen. Read and follow the instructions, then click **Finish**.

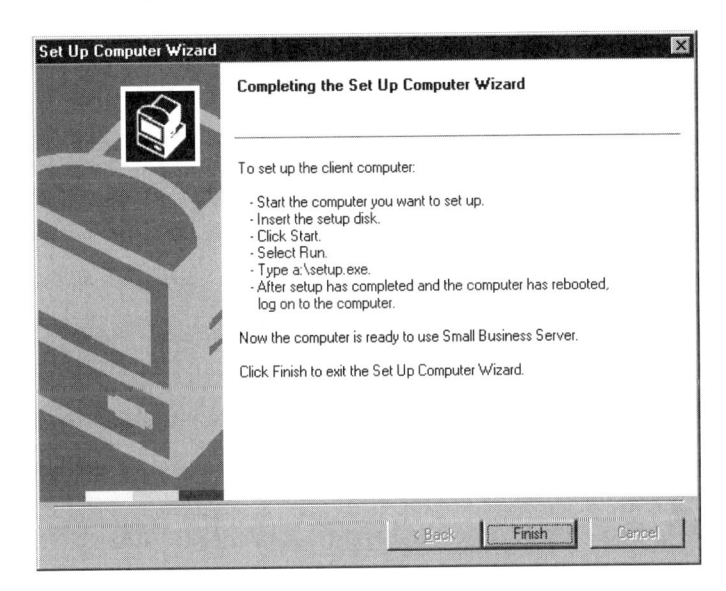

Client Software Installation

If the Set Up Computer Wizard client setup disk is having difficulty installing applications to the client computer, verify that the network adapter on the client computer is properly connected to the hub or other computers, and that the transceiver type is correctly set. The correctness of these physical network connections and settings is very important since the client software is installed over the network.

Client Machine Functionality Testing

After the client setup disk has successfully installed the client applications, a series of tests may now be run on the client machine. Testing begins with connecting to a share and then moves on to network printing and running client/server applications, such as Outlook 2000, for interaction with Small Business Server 4.5. Follow the steps below to run tests on the client. If you encounter any problems, consult the Troubleshooting section of the Online Guide.

▶ **To test share access and permissions on the client machine**

1. Log on to Windows with the proper user name and password.
2. On the desktop, double-click **Network Neighborhood**, then double-click **Small Business Server**.
3. A listing of all the shared file and print resources available on the Small Business Server appears. Double-click **Add-ins**, then double-click **Ins**.
4. Drag and drop the **Moderator** text document to your desktop.

5. Double-click the document to edit it, and do the following:
   - Go to the last line and type: **This is a test**.
   - Save the file.

   A message should appear that you are not able to save the document—this results from the security features that were configured during setup. This is what you want to happen because the Windows NT File System (NTFS) permissions are set up with read-only privileges on the **Add-ins** folder. This permission was retained when the folder was copied to the client machine where permissions were undefined.

6. Try saving the same file inside the folder with the same user name you are currently logged on as. Select the proper folder name from **Network Neighborhood** to do this. You should be able to save the file in this location because you have full access to the folder.

▶ **To test use of the network printer from the client**

1. The networked printer must first be set up on the client machine. On the **Start** menu, point to **Settings**, and then click **Printers**.

2. Double-click **Add Printer**. Click **Next**, then select **Network Printer**. Click **Next** again.

3. A screen appears asking you for the network path or queue name of the printer. Click **Browse** and then double-click the icons in the **Network Neighborhood** window, until you see the name of the printer you installed on Small Business Server. Select your printer, click **OK**, and then click **Next** to continue.

4. Select a printer name to use as the default printer for Windows programs. Select **Yes** to make this the default printer, and then click **Next** to continue.

5. Click **Yes** to print a test page, and then click **Finish**.

   The printer setup procedure should be able to locate the driver files automatically at this point. If not, you may be asked to supply driver files from the printer manufacturer.

6. If the test page printed correctly, click **Yes** on the pop-up dialog box. You should now be able to open up a document and print it out using the **Print** command from the **File** menu. If the test page did not print out correctly, click **No** to display the printer configuration troubleshooting guide.

▶ **To send a test e-mail with the Outlook client to Exchange Server**

In this test, you will attempt to connect to the Exchange Server from the Outlook client, assuming this is an installed application.

1. On the desktop, double-click the **Outlook** shortcut to start the program. If you are asked for a server name and mailbox name, you must re-enter this user information via the Small Business Server console, using the **Review or Change Information** task in the **Manage Users** screen.

2. Once Outlook starts, click **OK** on the assistant. Double-click the **Welcome** message in the Inbox to read it.

3. To test the functionality of the Exchange Server, compose a message with the Outlook client and send it back to the same user account. Check the Outlook Inbox to see if the mail was received. Continue on with the steps that follow.

> **Note** Since you are logged on to the client machine as the user you set up, and logged on to Small Business Server with the account used at the time of creation—you can send an e-mail from the Outlook client through Exchange and receive it back on the same client.

4. On the **Compose** menu of Outlook, select **New Mail Message**. In the window that appears, click **To...**, highlight the client name, and click **To->** in the **Select Names** dialog box. Click **OK**.

5. Next, type in a subject and a short message. Click **Send** to send the message.

If all goes well, you should be able to see the message in the Inbox on the client machine, assuming you are logged in as the recipient. The presence of this message in the Inbox verifies that the Small Business Server 4.5 and client software has been successfully set up. If not, make sure all physical network connections are being made and then review the steps of setup for possible problems.

Third-Party Application Testing

After Small Business Server 4.5 and client-side components have been verified to work as expected with the set up hardware, the functionality of any third-party applications you are planning to run should be tested. If these applications are designed to run on Windows NT Server 4.0, there should be no problems running them on Small Business Server 4.5. In any event, you should still verify successful installation and basic functionality of the software. If the software is designed to run in the client/server model, try performing the basic tasks it provides on a typical desktop machine, such as the client.

NetWare Functionality Testing

Before proceeding to the integration phase, consider whether you have the time and resources necessary to conduct testing of Small Business Server 4.5 with a Novell NetWare server in order to simulate the current small business environment. To do so, you'll need to set up a NetWare server, in addition to Services for NetWare installed on Small Business Server 4.5, as described in the following integration phase.

For the average small business, this may not be practical. However, if the time and resources are available, this is a good point to conduct the tests. The advantage of doing this now is that if anything unexpected happens, it can be documented, corrected, and prevented from happening on the actual business network. If the procedure is not viable at this time, it can be bypassed without any crucial consequences.

The Integration Phase

Integrating Microsoft Small Business Server 4.5 into the small business network involves following the procedures in the test phase and installing/configuring the various required services for NetWare. The procedures for setting up all of the NetWare services are documented, however it is possible you may not need to run all services. It depends on which functions are to be transferred to Small Business Server 4.5, as follows.

For example, the small business may want to continue using an existing NetWare print server for servicing printing needs to their client machines. In this case, the print functionality provided by File and Print Services for NetWare (FPNW) is not needed. In the integration phase, a summary of what each service does is provided before detailed installation instructions. This should help when making decisions about which services to run on Small Business Server.

During the integration phase, isolate Small Business Server 4.5 from users while it is being set up to interoperate with the NetWare server.

Integration of Small Business Server 4.5 in the NetWare Network

Begin the integration of Small Business Server in the NetWare environment by following the same procedures of the test phase to install and test functionality of the software. Set up and test a client machine, just as in the test phase, to ensure there are no communication problems in the small business network testing environment.

In the integration phase, physical network connectivity is important just as it was in the test phase. Make sure the network adapter cards are properly configured by using the manufacturer-supplied configuration utility. Check that physical links between computers and hubs are in place and that status indicators on the hub or network cards are signaling good connections.

Before installing Small Business Server 4.5, verify that no Dynamic Host Configuration Protocol (DHCP) servers are present on the small business network. DHCP is a method for assigning Internet Protocol (IP) addresses to computers automatically in a Transmission Control Protocol/Internet Protocol (TCP/IP) network. Since Small Business Server 4.5 uses DHCP by default, another DHCP server on the same network will cause interference. The presence of a DHCP server in the small business network is unlikely, especially since NetWare uses Internetwork Packet Exchange/Sequenced Packet Exchange (IPX/SPX)—but it should be checked.

After the above considerations are addressed, proceed with the Small Business Server 4.5 and client set up procedures described in the test phase. When complete, continue on as follows.

Installation of NWLink Protocol

After basic client/server functionality for Small Business Server has been proven on the small business network, the first component to be installed to provide NetWare interoperability is the NWLink protocol. NWLink is a network protocol for Small Business Server 4.5 compatible with IPX/SPX and it is the default protocol supported by NetWare. Although NWLink by itself does not provide a high degree of connectivity to NetWare servers, it is the core component that allows a Small Business Server-based computer to communicate with a NetWare client or server. NWLink protocol must be installed to provide a means of communicating with the tools that interoperate with NetWare.

▶ **To install the NWLink protocol**

1. On the Small Business Server computer, press **CTRL+ALT+DEL** (hold down all three keys) and examine the string "You are logged on as DOMAINNAME\username."

   Note Make sure you are logged on to the computer as the Administrator or with administrative privileges. If you are not, log off, then log on as Administrator.

2. Click **Start**, point to **Settings**, and then click **Control Panel**. Double-click **Network**.

3. Select the **Protocols** tab, and then click **Add**.

4. From the list that appears, select **NWLink IPX/SPX Compatible Transport**. Click **OK**.

   If a prompt appears to insert the NWLink installation files, insert the Small Business Server Disc 1 into the CD-ROM drive, and then click **OK**.

5. When the system is done copying files, click **OK** on the **Network** panel, and then click **Yes** to restart the computer.

Installation of Gateway Service for NetWare

Gateway Service for NetWare (GSNW) may be found on the Small Business Server compact Disc 1. It is installed using **Network** on the **Control Panel**. GSNW allows Small Business Server to function as a NetWare client. Once GSNW is installed, any NetWare servers configured for the same frame type as Small Business Server appear in a list under the heading "NetWare or Compatible Network." GSNW is required in order for the NetWare-to-Windows NT Server Conversion Utility to function.

Another feature of GSNW is the Windows NT Server to NetWare gateway. This provides Microsoft network clients with access to NetWare resources. This allows a user to access what appears to be a standard Microsoft server resource, although they are actually connected to the NetWare resource through a gateway service.

Uses of GSNW with Small Business Server 4.5

One of the practical uses of GSNW for the small business network is the ability to provide Small Business Server 4.5 and any connected client computers access to file and print resources on a NetWare server.

For example, using GSNW, Small Business Server can connect to a NetWare file server directory and share it as if the directory were on Small Business Server. The Small Business Server-based network clients can then access the directory on the NetWare server by connecting to the share created on Small Business Server.

Note GSNW is not intended to function as a full-service router for NetWare services. It is designed only for occasional access to the NetWare servers, or to serve as a migration path. Network performance will degrade if it is used for unlimited server access, since all clients are receiving services through one NetWare connection.

Locating a Preferred NetWare Server

During installation of GSNW, you will be asked to identify a preferred NetWare Server. This is the default NetWare Server a user will log on to from Small Business Server. If Small Business Server is unable to find the selected preferred server, check the following:

- Verify that the Novell server is physically on the network and that it is currently running. This server must be version 2.x, 3.x or 4.x and must be running in bindery emulation mode.

- Verify there is an unmatched frame type between the Windows NT Server and the Novell Server. The procedure to check this is given later.

Creating Duplicate Administrator Names

Before installing GSNW, it is advantageous to create duplicate administrator names (and passwords) on both the Windows NT Server domain and the NetWare server. You can either add an account called *Administrator* to the NetWare server and give it the same rights as the *Supervisor* account, or you can add an account called *Supervisor* to the Small Business Server 4.5 domain and make it a member of the Administrators group and the Domain Admins group. To do this, use the **Add a User** task in the **Manage Users** screen of the console (as in the test phase) but without setting up a new client machine with the Set Up Computer Wizard. Be sure to give the *Supervisor* account full permissions. Proceed on with installation of GSNW.

▶ **To install GSNW**

1. Click **Start**, point to **Settings**, and then click **Control Panel**. Double-click **Network**.

2. Select the **Services** tab, and then click **Add**.

3. From the list that appears, select **Gateway (and Client) Services for NetWare**, and then click **Continue**.

4. If you are prompted for a new location for distribution files, check the path shown and make sure it is correct. If it is not, and you are prompted to insert a disc containing the installation files, insert Small Business Server Disc 1 into the CD-ROM drive, and then click **OK**.

5. Once the system is finished copying files, click **OK** to close **Network** and then click **Yes** to restart the computer.

6. Log on again with the account you created that is recognized by both the NetWare server and Small Business Server. You will then be asked to select a **Preferred Server for NetWare** from a list that appears of all known Novell network servers.

After making a selection, you can log on to the Small Business Server with your Windows NT/NetWare account which will be automatically validated by the Windows NT Server domain and also authenticated by the preferred NetWare Server that was selected. If your password for the NetWare server is different from the Windows NT server domain password, you will be asked to provide the NetWare password. If the preferred server name was not found in step 4, perform the next procedure, "To check frame type," before proceeding to step 5.

7. To verify that the Gateway Service for NetWare has been installed, do the following:

   - Click **Start**, point to **Settings**, and then click **Control Panel**. A new icon for **GSNW** should appear.
   - If you start the **GSNW** applet, a dialog box appears asking you to change your preferred server and print options.

Note If you do not need to install the gateway feature of GSNW, then skip the next procedure, "To check for the frame type," and continue with installation of FPNW.

Be sure that the account under which you are logged on to Small Business Server has administrative rights and that it is a NetWare account. Make any necessary changes through the **Manage Users** task of the Small Business Server console.

▶ **To check the frame type**

1. From the **Control Panel**, double-click **Network**, select the **Protocols** tab, and then double-click **NWLink IPX/SPX Compatible Transport Properties**.

   If the frame type is set to manual, examine it and compare it to the frame type on the NetWare server. To do this, go to the NetWare server and type "load monitor" from the system prompt and place a check on "LAN Information" (or similar option on a NetWare version other than 3.x). The frame types should be listed here as 802.2 or 802.3.

2. If the settings between the two machines do not match, go back to Small Business Server and select **Auto Frame Type Detection**. Click **Apply**, and then click **OK**.

3. Click **Yes** to restart the Small Business Server.

4. If the NetWare server name is still not found, go back into the **NWLink** properties and set the frame type to match exactly what appears on the NetWare Server. Click **Apply**, **OK**, and reboot again.

5. If the connection is still not found at this point, check the network cables on both machines and make sure the hub indicator lights are showing active connections for the cables from each of the machines.

▶ **To install the gateway feature of GSNW**

1. Create a group called NTGATEWAY. From NWAdmin32, select **Group Information** and press ENTER.

2. Type the group name and press ENTER.

3. Create a shortcut to NWAdmin32. Refer to the Novell NetWare documentation for procedures.

4. From the NetWare Application Launcher (NAL), click **Application** to create a new group icon.

5. Create (or identify) a NetWare Gateway User Account, which is an account that the GSNW service uses to connect to the NetWare Server. To create an account for this purpose, use one of the existing NetWare clients on the network and run the **NWAdmin32** utility from the **public** directory on the **sys** volume.

6. Go to **User Information** and press ENTER. Press the INSERT key to create a new user.

7. Enter a user name for the gateway account (for example "gatewayuser") and press ENTER. Press ENTER again to accept the default home directory path.

8. Click **Yes** to verify creation of the new directory and press ENTER. ESC returns you to the main menu.

9. Make the user name of the Gateway User Account a member of the NTGATEWAY group.

10. From NWAdmin32, select **User Information**, and the user name you created, then press ENTER.

11. In the new menu that appears, select **Groups Belonged To** and press ENTER.

12. Press INSERT, highlight the **NTGATEWAY** group in the **Groups Not Belonged To** menu, and press ENTER.

13. Exit out of **NWAdmin**.

▶ **To configure the Small Business Server portion of GSNW**

1. Click **Start**, point to **Settings**, and then click **Control Panel**.

2. Double-click **GSNW**.

3. Click **Gateway**.

4. Select Enable Gateway and type the Gateway User Account and password in the appropriate text boxes. Retype the password in the Confirm Password box.

5. Click **Add** to add a Small Business Server shared folder to the NetWare volume.

   To do this, specify a name for the share, the network path to the NetWare volume you wish to map, and a drive letter. The network path must be specified in a syntax known as the Universal Naming Convention (UNC). For this syntax, specify the computer name and the directory name in the following format: *servername**sharename*. For example, if you want to map a drive letter to the **sys** volume of a NetWare server called "netware", type *netware**sys* for the UNC name.

6. Click **OK** on all the open windows when finished to save your changes and exit **GSNW**.

Testing GSNW Functionality

Next, test the functionality of the GSNW installation. Use the following steps to do so.

▶ **To test functionality of the GSNW installation**

1. On Small Business Server desktop, double-click **Network Neighborhood**, then the Small Business Server machine name.

2. Select the share created in Step 5 of the preceding procedure and then click **Map Network Drive** on the **File** menu.

3. Select a drive letter from the drop-down box and then click **OK**.

4. Click **Start**, point to **Programs**, and then click **Command Prompt**. At the prompt, type the following (press ENTER after each line and for N, substitute the selected drive letter):

   ```
   N:
   cd\public
   NWAdmin32
   ```

   This should start **NWAdmin32** on the NetWare Server, which means the GSNW installation was successful.

5. Press **ESC** to quit **NWAdmin32**. To see if you can access NetWare resources from a Small Business Server client, perform the following steps:
   - From the client machine's desktop, double-click **Network Neighborhood** and select the name of the Small Business Server computer.
   - Inside the new window, double-click the name of the share you created in **GSNW**. Open one of the folders until you see a list of files.
   - Copy a file to the desktop. If successful, the gateway feature of GSNW is functioning correctly.

Note GSNW is a powerful utility for accessing NetWare file and print resources from any Small Business Server client. If the small business owner is planning on converting all desktops in the office to Windows 95-based Small Business Server clients, GSNW should be installed on the server so clients can access NetWare resources without having to install or configure anything on their machines.

Installing File and Print Services for NetWare

FPNW is a separate, add-on product for Small Business Server 4.5. It is provided on the Services for NetWare (add-on) CD for Microsoft Windows NT Server 4.0.

The FPNW component allows the Small Business Server to act like a NetWare server to all NetWare clients currently on the small business network. Small Business Server will appear in the client's Windows Explorer list of NetWare and NetWare-compatible servers. A NetWare client can do the following with FPNW installed:

- Map to a shared volume and directory on an FPNW-enabled Small Business Server just as if it were a NetWare server.
- Connect to a printer on Small Business Server 4.5.
- Log on to the Small Business Server 4.5 and have configured system and personal login scripts execute.
- Use Small Business Server 4.5 applications services.

FPNW is a very valuable component of Small Business Server integration since it can provide a high degree of interoperability with the existing small business NetWare LAN, without the need to change the configuration of existing network computers.

Important If Directory Service Manager for NetWare is to be installed, be sure that you install it and propagate users before FPNW is installed. The procedures to do this are provided later in this chapter.

▶ **To install FPNW**

1. Click **Start**, point to **Settings**, and then click **Control Panel**.
2. Double-click **Network**. Select the **Services** tab, and then click **Add**.
3. From the new dialog box that appears, select **Have Disk**.
4. In the **Insert Disk** dialog box, type the path to the FPNW installation files and then click **OK**.

    The path to the FPNW files (for Intel processors) should be D:\FPNW\NT40\i386 (substitute the drive letter of your CD-ROM for D:). If the files are not here, browse the CD manually. Select **File and Print Services for NetWare** and click **OK**.

5. Once the files are copied, specify the Small Business Server directory to be used as the **SYS** volume. The default is C:\SYSVOL.

    > **Note** In most cases, you should rename the NetWare server—for example, rename it to OLD_NW312—and assign the previous NetWare server name to Small Business Server 4.5 configured with FPNW. This allows existing clients to run untouched.

6. A Small Business Server Supervisor account will be created. Supply and confirm the password for the Supervisor account.
7. In the NetWare Tuning section, select **Minimize Memory Usage** if the system is primarily used for applications, **Balance between Memory Usage and Performance** if the server is both an applications server and file and print server, or **Maximize Performance** to provide the best file and print sharing performance (this will use additional system memory). Click **OK** when finished.
8. A special Small Business Server account called FPNW Service Account will be created for running the FPNW services. Supply and confirm a password for the account. Click **OK**. Click **OK** on the **Network Settings** dialog box and restart the computer.
9. Log on to the system under the user name that created the Small Business Server.
10. Click **Start**, point to **Settings**, and then click **Control Panel**. If there is a new **FPNW** icon, the FPNW installation was successful.

    A successful installation of FPNW will also create an FPNW menu in the File Manager (run "winfile" from **Run** under the **Start menu**) which allows you to manage the NetWare partitions. If you browse C:\winnt.sbs\system32 with Windows NT Explorer, you will find a help icon with the file name "fpnw." This icon is a book with a question mark. When opened, it provides help for using FPNW.

After successfully completing the last step of the FPNW installation procedure, you have achieved Small Business Server 4.5 coexistence in the NetWare environment. At this point, migration can be accomplished easily in order to replace the functionality of the NetWare servers and decommission them—if the deployment calls for it.

Note Make sure you have documented all the actions taken up to this point to set everything up. Also document any problems encountered, along with the resolution.

Installing Directory Service Manager for NetWare

Even though Directory Service Manager for NetWare is a tool intended for large corporate environments, there may be some circumstances where this tool can be useful in a smaller environment. If the intention is to maintain a mixed environment of a NetWare Server along side Small Business Server, Microsoft Directory Service Manager for NetWare (DSMN) is a utility that might make the network easier to manage. With DSMN, the technology consultant can centrally manage NetWare 2.x/3.x systems and enable a single login, user account, and password for end users.

DSMN 4.0 has been enhanced to support the Windows 95 graphical user interface which allows the technology consultant to administer Small Business Server 4.5 from a Windows 95 machine. DSMN copies NetWare user and group account information to Small Business Server 4.5 and then propagates any changes to the accounts back to the NetWare servers. NetWare accounts only need to be synchronized once with the Small Business Server 4.5. Then all account administration changes can be done through Small Business Server, since those changes will be propagated back to the NetWare side. Take note however, that using DSMN in a relatively small environment can often be more difficult than other solutions.

▶ **To install Directory Service Manager for NetWare**

1. The first step is to be sure that each NetWare account has a full name. For a NetWare 3.x server, run **syscon**, go to **User Information**, highlight a user and then press ENTER. Go to the **Full Name** option and give the user a full name—usually the same as the account name. This will be the name that Small Business Server uses for the user when the propagation is complete.

2. Click **Start**, point to **Settings**, and then click **Control Panel**.

3. Double-click **Network**, select the **Services** tab, and then click **Add**.

4. Click **Have Disk**. Insert the Services for NetWare CD-ROM in the CD-ROM drive. Type the path to the DSMN installation files, and then click **OK**. The path to these files should be D:\DSMN\NT40\i386, where D: is substituted by the letter of your CD-ROM drive.

5. Select the **Directory Service Manager** for NetWare and click **OK**. When asked, enter a password for the service account automatically created to start the DSMN service and then close the **Network**. Click **Yes** to restart the computer.

> **Note** If File and Print Services for NetWare is loaded ahead of DSMN, a warning appears stating that any user accounts enabled with NetWare compatibility will not be transported automatically to the NetWare Server. If you receive this warning, go to the User Manager for Domains (under **Programs** in the **Start** menu) and select **Maintain NetWare Compatibility** for each user propagated from the NetWare Server. Do this immediately after propagation.

6. Click **Start**, point to **Programs**, and then click **Administrative Tools**. Double-click **Directory Service Manager Utility**. On the **Synchronization Manager** screen, select **Add Server to Manage** from the **NetWare Server** drop-down menu, and type the name of the NetWare Server you wish to manage. When asked, type the user name and password.

7. Select the users and groups to be propagated, a password scheme, the **Supervisors** group, and the **Console Operators** group. Select **Trial Run**, which will not commit the changes, but will allow you to view the log files (shown below) in a similar way as the Migration Tool.

   Printing out the log files here is useful since it helps when assigning permissions. You can create or edit a file mapped to resolve any conflicts reflected in the logs, or change any other parameters you see fit.

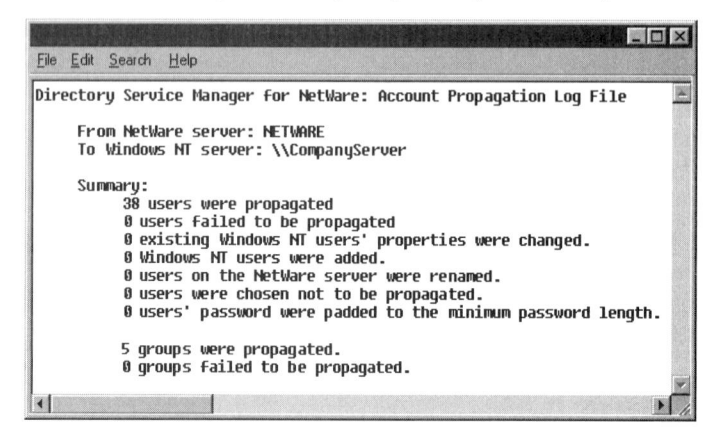

```
Directory Service Manager for NetWare: Account Propagation Log File

    From NetWare server: NETWARE
    To Windows NT server: \\CompanyServer

    Summary:
        38 users were propagated.
        0 users failed to be propagated
        0 existing Windows NT users' properties were changed.
        0 Windows NT users were added.
        0 users on the NetWare server were renamed.
        0 users were chosen not to be propagated.
        0 users' password were padded to the minimum password length.

        5 groups were propagated.
        0 groups failed to be propagated.
```

8. When you feel confident that the propagation of NetWare accounts to Small Business Server will execute smoothly, and after being reminded to back up the NetWare Server, you can commit the changes.

9. Next, select the Small Business Server domain accounts to be propagated to the NetWare Server. Remove the NetWare Servers you don't want. Refer to the following illustration. Click **OK**.

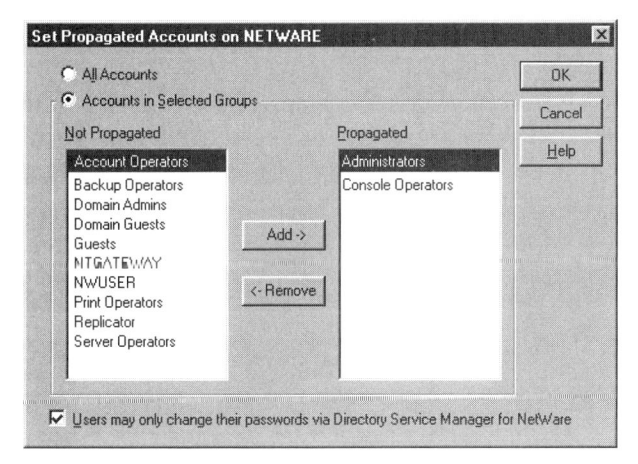

10. Exit the Synchronization Manager or select another NetWare Server to manage.

Mailboxes for Propagated Accounts

After accounts have been propagated across the operating systems, mailboxes for the propagated accounts should be created. This may be done in the Microsoft Exchange Server Administrator. It is only necessary to do this if the propagated accounts require e-mail functionality. Perform the following steps to create the required Exchange mailboxes.

▶ **To create Exchange mailboxes for propagated user accounts**

1. Click **Start**, point to **Programs**, point to **Microsoft Exchange**, and then click **Microsoft Exchange Administrator**.

2. The following **Connect to server** dialog box appears. Click **Browse** and select the Small Business Server computer. Select **Set as default**, and then click **OK**.

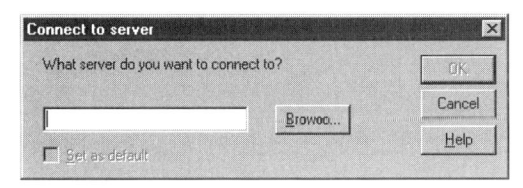

3. The following screen appears with the server domain name selected in the left pane and **Configuration** in the right. Click on the + next to the server domain name, and then double-click **Recipients**.

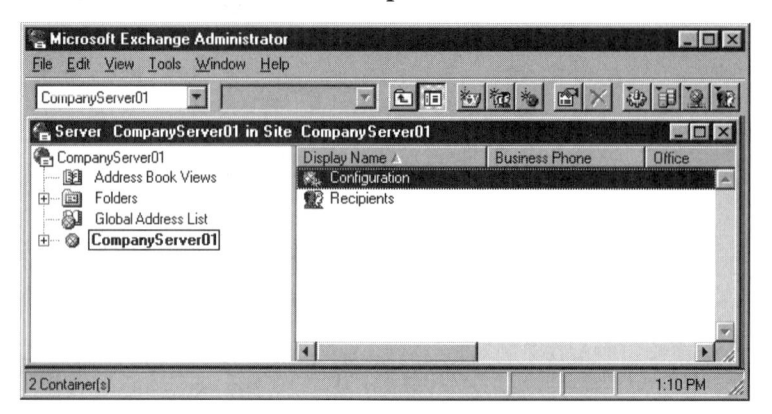

4. The following screen appears. Highlight a recipient from the list and on the **File** menu, and then click **New Mailbox**.

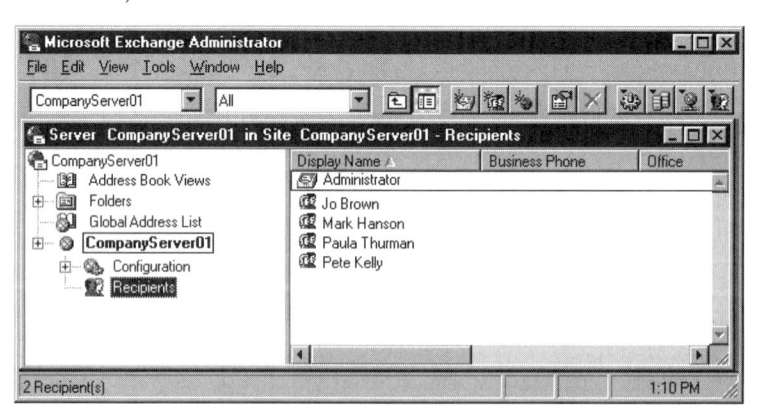

5. The following **Properties** dialog box appears. From here, a user mailbox may be created by filling in all the information on the **General** tab.

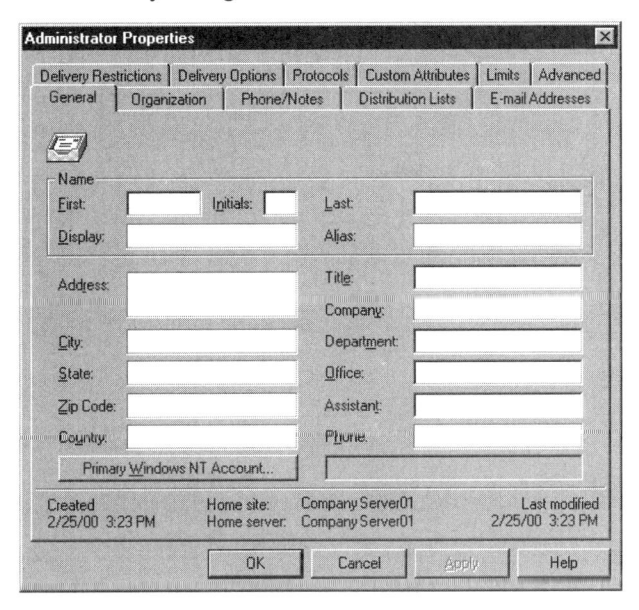

6. Link the new mailbox to the Small Business Server account. On the **General** tab, click **Primary Windows NT Account**. The following dialog box appears. Select **Select an existing Windows NT account**, and then click **OK**.

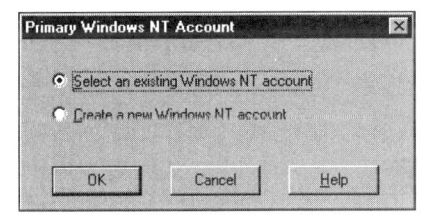

7. The following **Add User or Group** dialog box appears. Scroll down the list to the appropriate user, select the user, then click **Add**. The new mailbox appears in **Add Name**. Click **OK**.

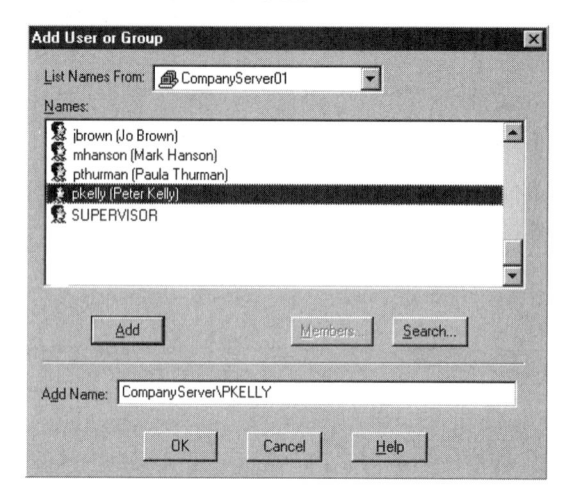

8. A confirmation dialog box appears displaying all the data entered for the user. Click **OK** and repeat the process for each new user account propagated from the NetWare Server.

Create Login Scripts

Login scripts are used to automate a number of tasks and perform initialization of variables when a user first logs in to a system. For the NetWare clients who will be running login scripts on the FPNW-enabled Small Business Server, the first step is to make sure the corresponding user subdirectories in the \MAIL directory were migrated to the same location (SYS volume and \MAIL directory) of Small Business Server.

▶ **To find which subdirectory is associated with a user**

1. Click **Start**, point to **Programs**, **Administrative Tools**, and then click **User Manager for Domains** to open the User Manager.

2. On the **User** menu, click **Properties** to display the **User Properties** dialog box.

3. Click **NW Compatible**.

4. The resulting dialog box includes a user Object ID that corresponds to the user's script directory in the \MAIL directory. Click **Edit Login Script** to modify the LOGIN text file in the user's home directory.

5. If you need to create a system login script, create and/or modify the file NET$LOG.DAT, located in the SYS:\PUBLIC directory.

   During the login process, the system login script runs first followed by the personal login script.

> **Note** The user and/or system login scripts that load special initialization programs (called "TSRs") or device drivers with the "#" or "EXIT" logon script commands will not work properly on Windows 95-based clients. There is no need for concern about this.

Client Configuration Assumption

In many cases, workstations in the small business network will be NetWare clients. This means they were already configured with a NetWare client service and have the IPX/SPX protocol loaded. There are two options with these clients, as follows:

- The first option is to make no changes to the client at all. Just rename the NetWare Server (if it is to remain in service) and adopt the old NetWare server name as the name for Small Business Server 4.5. By doing this, changes on the NetWare client machines can be avoided altogether.

- The second option is to leave the NetWare server name unchanged and to assign a new name to the FPNW-enabled Small Business Server 4.5. In this case, additional changes may be required for the NetWare clients to enable access to shared resources and applications on Small Business Server 4.5. These changes are described in the following section.

NetWare Migration Phase

In most cases, migrating off the NetWare platform is preferable to coexistence with Small Business Server 4.5. The migration from the NetWare Server to Small Business Server 4.5 is completed in the following four phases.

- Create users and group accounts on the Small Business Server 4.5, using the console **Manage Users** task and the Set Up Computer Wizard.

- Migrate all data from the NetWare Server directories to the Small Business Server, using the Migration Tool for NetWare.

- Configure clients on the new network. Clients running Windows for Workgroups 3.11, Windows NT Workstation, or Windows 95 may require some minor reconfiguration.

- Test network connectivity. Several tests should be run before users in the small business organization can start to use the new network.

Creating New User Accounts

By creating new user accounts, rather than migrating the NetWare accounts to Small Business Server 4.5, the small business can take advantage of full-featured Small Business Server 4.5 accounts. Also, creating new group accounts is an opportunity to reorganize company data in a more intuitive manner.

Before migrating data, new user accounts must be created on Small Business Server 4.5 using the Manage Users task on the Small Business Server console. The Set Up Computer Wizard runs as part of this process. When adding a new user, the Set Up Computer Wizard creates a setup disk for the client configuration. Refer to the Online Guide for further information.

Migrating the Data

Copy all user home files to the new user directories and all company shared data on the NetWare Server to the Company Shared Data folder on Small Business Server. With the Small Business Server Shared Folder Wizard, you can reorganize company data in any directory structure and permissions configuration desired.

If user logon scripts will be running from an FPNW-enabled Small Business Server instead of the NetWare Server, then migrate and modify logon scripts as necessary. The logon scripts will need to be associated with the user accounts.

Starting the Migration Utility

This section describes how to start up and configure the Migration Tool for NetWare in preparation for migrating data from the NetWare Server to Small Business Server.

▶ **To start up and configure the Migration Tool for NetWare**

1. Logon to the Small Business Server 4.5 with the full-privileges account on both Small Business Server and NetWare Server. Verify that the NetWare Server can be seen in **Network Neighborhood**. You may have to click **Entire Network** to see the NetWare Server list.

2. Click **Start**, point to **Programs**, point to **Administrative Tools**, and then click **Migration Tool for NetWare**. The NetWare Migration Utility is launched.

3. Select the servers to be migrated using the elliptical buttons next to the NetWare Server and Windows NT Server, as in the following illustration.

   Note If FPNW is installed on the Small Business Server, a second NetWare server will appear in the list (for example, servername_FPNW). **Do not select this server.**

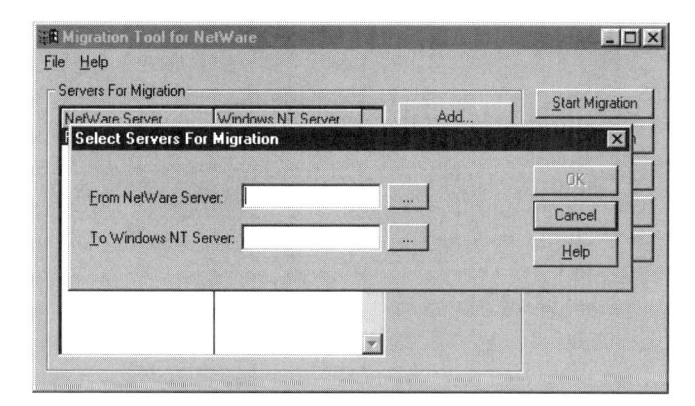

4. Click **OK**. The following **Migration Tool for NetWare** dialog box appears.

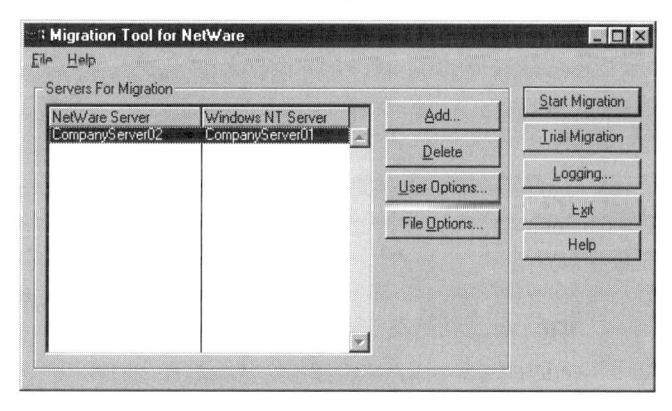

5. Click **User Options** and deselect the **Transfer Users and Groups** on the following **User and Group Options** dialog box. Click **OK**.

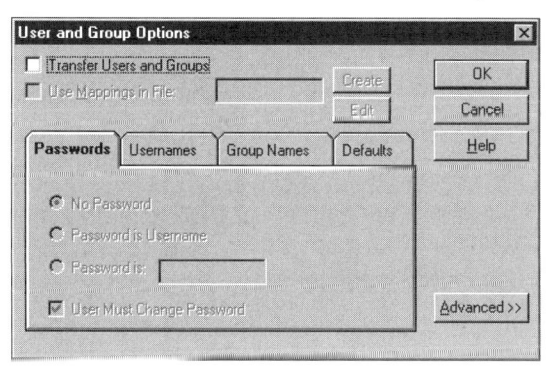

6. When the home screen of the **Migration Tool for NetWare** appears, click **File Options**, then **Modify**. The following **Modify Destinations** dialog box appears. Change the share to **company** from the Share drop-down box. Click **OK**.

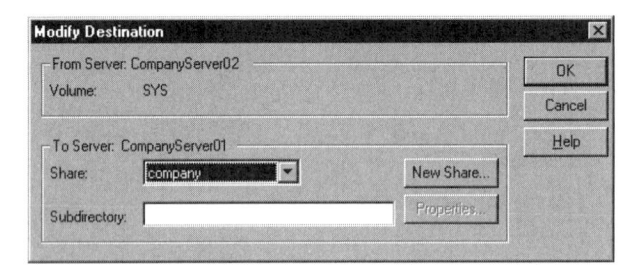

7. Click **Files** on the screen that follows. The following **Files to Transfer** dialog box appears. Use this box to select the directories you will migrate in the following section.

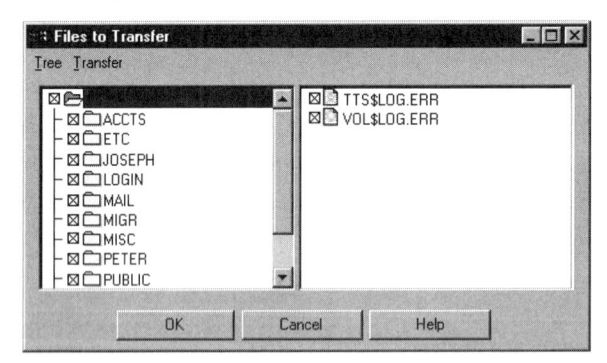

Moving Directories and Files

The next task is to move the NetWare data according to the procedure below.

▶ **To move NetWare data**

1. On the **Files to Transfer** dialog box, check the box for each directory you want to migrate. Make sure to check every directory that contains information the small business organization needs, including all personal user directories.
2. Click **OK** to begin the migration process.

Before you move NetWare data, run a trial migration of the data to generate useful statistics. When you do so, a log file is created with the number and size of the files and directories. If there is not enough disk space on the destination Small Business Server for the files and directories, a warning appears.

When the log file results from the trial run are satisfactory, start the actual migration process. When the move is complete, review all of the resulting log files and document number, size, and time statistics to maintain a record.

Note If errors occur while trying to move data, ensure that you are properly logged in to both the NetWare and Small Business Server. Then attempt to migrate data again.

Moving Migrated User Data to the New Directories

In the migration, all data will be moved to the **Company shared folder** sharepoint on Small Business Server 4.5. To move migrated user data into the appropriate user directories, open Microsoft Windows NT Explorer, and drag-and-drop user files from the migrated directories to their Small Business Server 4.5 personal directories. These files will now be protected for the user, since they inherit the rights and permissions applied by the new Small Business Server user account.

At this point of the migration, there is an opportunity to reorganize the company directories in order to make small business information structuring more efficient. For example, you may want to separate all accounting information from all project information. Then you can make the former available only to company accountants and the latter available to everyone in the organization.

Configuring the Clients

This section provides some optional reconfiguration information for different client platforms, to be performed after user data is migrated.

Configure Windows for Workgroups NetWare Clients

If there are Windows for Workgroups 3.11-based NetWare clients in the small business network who will still use a NetWare Server as the preferred server, then no changes are needed to enable the client to access an FPNW-enabled server. However, you may elect to alter the workstation configuration, depending on the access these workstations require to Small Business Server 4.5, even though no changes are required. Additionally, consider installing the TCP/IP protocol since this is the default Small Business Server 4.5 network protocol.

Note TCP/IP is not provided with Windows for Workgroups and must be obtained from a software vendor.

Configure Windows NT Workstation Clients

Windows NT Workstation-based NetWare clients already have the IPX protocol installed and should also have the Client Services for NetWare (CSNW) service installed and running. No changes are necessary in order to access resources and applications on the FPNW-enabled Small Business Server.

Configure Windows 95 NetWare Clients

If you keep the current NetWare preferred server, no changes are necessary. However, if the preferred login server is to be changed to the FPNW-enabled Small Business Server, perform the following steps.

▶ **To change the preferred server**

1. Click **Start**, point to **Settings**, and then click **Control Panel**.
2. Double-click **Network**. On the Configuration tab, select **Client for NetWare Networks**.
3. Click **Properties**. The general properties tab appears (the default) from the drop-down list. Select the **Preferred Server**. From here, you may also allow NetWare login script processing and you can set the **First Network Drive**.

Note The Microsoft Windows 95 operating system does not check for a duplicate computer name on the network. If someone duplicates computer names on the network, serious problems may result. All users on the small business network should be told not to change their computer name unless absolutely necessary.

Testing Basic Connectivity

Several tests should be conducted before the users in the small business organization start using the new network setup. There are no extensive instructions for carrying out the connectivity tests, however, document the ones you plan to perform ahead of time. Depending on the NetWare services you selected for configuring, you may run some or all of the following tests.

Note These tests are required for a Small Business Server replacement of the NetWare preferred server. In an environment where the Small Business Server will coexist with current NetWare servers, these tests may not be necessary.

- **Tests for basic connectivity**
  - Login from (NetWare) client to Small Business Server with no login script.
  - Login from (NetWare) client to Small Business Server with system login script.
  - Connect (MAP) to a shared volume on the Small Business Server (the SYS volume is created during the FPNW installation).
  - Copy a large file (5 MB) from the workstation to the mapped drive on the Small Business Server.
  - Copy a large file (5 MB) from the mapped drive on the Small Business Server to the workstation.
  - Test file-level security. Check a user's permissions settings from the Small Business Server 4.5 Console User Manager task. Then login to the user workstation as a user with different permissions and try to access the same resources.
  - Connect to a Small Business Server printer that has been configured as a NetWare printer queue.
  - Send output to the attached printer. Since this part of the deployment is not application testing, you can simply use Notepad or some other accessory to generate the print.
  - Use the setpass utility that comes with the File and Print Services for NetWare to change the NetWare Login password and the Small Business Server password. Do not use the standard setpass that is provided with the NetWare client software. Note that the FPNW clients have both a Small Business Server domain user account and an FPNW account, each with separate passwords.
  - Use the chngpass utility that comes with the File and Print Services for NetWare. Note that the Small Business Server Change Password Wizard does the same thing as setpass.

Documenting Migration Results

Summarize the success or failure of the various components used in the migration, including each NetWare service or tool used in the process. Note problems and their respective resolutions.

Project Review Phase

Compile all the information into a concise format for a formal project review with the small business owner. A project review will not only serve as a project summary for the small business, but will also provide a solid base for any further company network upgrades. Include the following in the project review document:

- Executive summary
- Project objective
- Schedule analysis

Executive Summary

The executive summary should not be longer than one page and should cover at least the following topics:

- Project objective
- High-level summary of changes performed
- Project schedule versus summary of actual results
- Project budget versus summary of actual results (by division)

Project Objective

This section should discuss in detail the specific problems that the upgrade was intended to resolve and the plan used to accomplish this. A quick summary of the plan used to address the issues will clearly identify your strategies to solve the problems. Where appropriate, include actual network diagrams used in analyzing the network.

Also include how this objective fits into the overall small business organization computing strategy, according to one-, three-, and five-year network objectives. You may address factors such as scalability and upgrade paths as the small business grows beyond the 50-user limit.

Clearly specify issues that were decided to be excluded from the scope of the project, as they will likely be identified and discussed during the project-review process. If the items are clearly documented, it saves time and also demonstrates you and your team are aware of the issues—and that you decided not to include them in the project.

Schedule Analysis

A significant part of the review process is an analysis of the scheduling, including any unexpected events that caused a schedule slip. This information is critical to planning project schedules. You can use a Microsoft Project colored chart to compare the schedule with the actual results. The chart will highlight the areas of the project ahead of schedule and those that went beyond the target date. This provides the small business owner with a comprehensive overview of project scheduling.

CHAPTER 40

Small Business Server 4.5 Licensing and Upgrade

This chapter covers the following topics:

- Licensing requirements to expand the user base of Microsoft® BackOffice® Small Business Server 4.5 up to 50 users and beyond.
- Client Access Licenses.
- Installation of Client Add Packs.
- Integrated application upgrade scenarios.
- Upgrading to BackOffice Server to accommodate small business growth.

Licensing Issues

Since many small businesses have more users than PCs, the Small Business Server 4.5 licensing model provides maximum flexibility and value. There is no limit to the number of user accounts that can be created on Small Business Server 4.5. However, the maximum number of client computers that can be connected is 50. A Client Access License is required for each client computer accessing Small Business Server 4.5—this includes clients running Microsoft Windows® 3.x, Windows for Workgroups, Windows NT® Workstation, Windows 95, and Windows 98.

Client Access Licenses

Small Business Server 4.5 Client Access Licenses (or Client Add Packs) are available in increments of 5 or 20 users, and allow for expansion of the small business network up to a maximum of 50-users. These Client Add Packs are unique to Small Business Server since they cannot be used with any other BackOffice products, for example, a stand-alone Microsoft Windows NT Server machine. In addition, users may not apply Client Access Licenses for any other BackOffice products to Small Business Server 4.5.

A Client Access License is needed by a client to access any service from the Small Business Server such as file, print, or the SQL Server™ 7.0 database.

Adding Client Access Licenses

Client Access Licenses are added via the Client Add Pack Setup program. Client Add Packs add users in 5 and 20 user increments, up to the allowed maximum. Attempting to install users beyond the maximum number permitted will result in an installation error.

Note The number of licenses for a given machine is recorded in the registry. This registry key is protected and cannot be changed by the user. It can only be changed using the Client Add Pack.

To add licenses, the installer begins on the Small Business Server **About** page accessed from the **Home** page of the Small Business Server console and performs the steps below.

▶ **To add client access licenses**

1. Click **Add licenses** to open the Online Guide.
2. Read and follow the instructions in the Online Guide for adding licenses.
3. When finished, click **OK**.
4. Make sure to mark the disk with installation order of Client Add Packs.
5. Reboot the machine.
6. You'll be given the option to set up additional Client Add Packs. Install the Client Add Packs according to the Online Guide instructions.
7. Click OK to finish the process and restart the machine.

Note If at any time, you have to reinstall Small Business Server software, Client Add Packs must be reinstalled in the same order they were installed originally. For example, Client Add Pack 5-10 must be installed before 10-15. For this reason, it is important to mark the disks with the appropriate installation order.

Upgrading the Server Machine

If you are doing an upgrade to your server machine and re-installing Small Business Server software along with CALs, the technology consultant or installer will be prompted for a password. A System ID number appears on the screen along with a message to call Microsoft Technical Support for the new password. In order to unlock the diskette and allow the full number of licenses to be added, a newly supplied password from Technical Support is required.

Windows NT License Manager Disabled

Adding or changing client licenses can only be done at the Small Business Server 4.5 Console. The Windows NT Server 4.0 license manager is disabled in Small Business Server 4.5. If you attempt to launch the license manager from the Control Panel, Small Business Server 4.5 will display an error message and instruction to use the Small Business Server console.

Upgrading Small Business Server 4.5

Small Business Server runs on a single-server computer and supports a maximum of 50 connected client computers. If the small business organization outgrows this limitation, one of the following upgrade scenarios is recommended:

- Upgrade of integrated applications, depending on which services require expansion.
- Upgrade to full BackOffice Server 4.5 or later.

The sections that follow describe the upgrade scenarios.

Upgrading Integrated Applications

This section covers upgrade scenarios for Windows NT Server 4.0, Exchange 5.5, SQL Server 7.0, and Proxy Server 2.0 along with the requirements for licensing in each case. For information on SKUs and pricing for upgrades, refer to the following web site:
http://www.microsoft.com/smallbusinessserver

Windows NT Server 4.0 Upgrade

If the small business requires more than 50 client computers accessing file and print services or needs to establish a trust relationship, an upgrade to the full version of Windows NT Server 4.0 is recommended, to break the limitations imposed by Small Business Server 4.5. To do this, the Windows NT Server 4.0 upgrade disk is required along with the purchase of Windows NT CALs for file and print access, and Small Business Server CALs for the remaining applications. The Windows NT Server 4.0 upgrade includes 25 CALs. For more than 25 users, the purchase of new Windows NT Server CALs is required.

Windows NT 4.0 and Exchange Server 5.5 Upgrades

If the small business requires more than 50 client computers accessing file and print services and needs to support more e-mail clients, an upgrade of Windows NT Server and Exchange Server are recommended. In this scenario, the Windows NT portion is upgraded with the upgrade disk and the limits on Exchange are broken. To do this, the technology consultant must provide Windows NT CALs for file and print access, Exchange CALs for e-mail, and SBS CALs for the remaining applications.

Note Exchange Server 5.5 cannot be upgraded without also upgrading Windows NT Server 4.0.

The following example illustrates what is required—if the small business currently has 25 CALs and is upgrading to full versions of Windows NT Server 4.0 and Exchange Server 5.5, they will receive 25 Windows NT CALs. Next, they should purchase an Exchange upgrade with 5 CALs and then 20 upgrade Exchange CALs. When expanding beyond these limits and adding new users, additional Windows NT and Exchange CALs are required.

SQL Server 7.0 Upgrade

If growth in the small business exceeds the limits of the integrated SQL Server 7.0 application, typically from high SQL database usage, then the full version of SQL Server should be installed (along with the existing database application) on a member server. In order to do this you must also purchase the Windows NT Server 4.0 upgrade. The same licensing scenario described in the Exchange upgrade above applies in this scenario.

Proxy Server 2.0 Upgrade

If you want to install Proxy Server 2.0 as a member server on a separate machine, the small business must purchase Windows NT Server 4.0 and Proxy Server 2.0 upgrades. CALs are not required for Proxy Server, but CALs for NT Server are required as described earlier.

Upgrade to BackOffice Server 4.5

When expansion of the small business organization beyond the Small Business Server limit of 50 client computers occurs, or when the integrated applications are in intensive use, upgrading to BackOffice Server is recommended. This upgrade provides greater scalability and a broader base of BackOffice components, while also retaining the usability of Small Business Server data. When expanding to BackOffice Server, the small business is required to purchase BackOffice Server and the appropriate number of CALs. For more information on upgrading to BackOffice Server, refer to the following Microsoft web site:
http://www.microsoft.com/backofficeserver

CHAPTER 41

Migrating from an Existing Windows NT Server

This chapter discusses how to migrate user accounts from an existing Windows NT® Server 4.0 to Microsoft® BackOffice® Small Business Server 4.5 using the Microsoft Migrate User Wizard.

Migrating Users to Small Business Server 4.5

User accounts on an existing Windows NT Server 4.0 installation can be transferred to Small Business Server 4.5 in a two-phase process. These correspond to the following two modes of the Migrate User Wizard.

- Export mode—An information file is created based on existing Windows NT Server 4.0 user account data.
- Import mode—User accounts are created on Small Business Server using the information file.

Migrate User Wizard Export Mode Processes

The Migrate User Wizard is launched in the export mode from the Autorun page of Small Business Server Disc 1. The wizard performs the following:

- Detects the operating system on which it is running.

  If the operating system is not Windows NT 4.0 Server, an error message appears. The wizard can only be run on a Windows NT 4.0 Server.

- If the operating system is Windows NT 4.0 Server, the wizard will be displayed with the More Information button enabled. Click this button to read more information about migrating users.

- The wizard then collects data from NT User Manager, RAS, and Exchange to create the information text file and the user account file.

If Exchange does not exist on the machine, the Exchange fields are left blank in the user account file.

The user account file is created by default as a:\users.txt, however the technology consultant may specify another location.

Migrate User Wizard Import Mode Processes

The Migrate User Wizard is launched in the import mode from the Small Business Server console's **To Do List**. The wizard takes the information from the user account file and creates all of the user accounts, groups, and mailboxes. The following tasks are performed for each user:

- A user account is created if it does not already exist. If the wizard encounters an existing user account with the same user name it is trying to create, it moves on to the next user in the user account file; the information is not overwritten.
- An Exchange mailbox is created (unless it already exists) and the user's global address list information is entered. If no Exchange information is present in the user.txt file, a mailbox is still created but the GAL information is blank.
- The user password is set to blank.
- RAS permissions are set.
- If specified, the user is added to an existing group (if the group already exists).
- The wizard creates the user's shared folder and adds the user to the default company distribution list. It also sets the logon script so the Set Up Computer Wizard will run. With respect to these tasks, the wizard mimics the functions of the Add User Wizard.

Migrate User Wizard Information File

Access the Migrate User Wizard from the Autorun screen of Small Business Server Disc 1, by clicking **Migrate Users**. The Migrate User Wizard is then launched in the export mode.

The Migrate User Wizard surveys the Windows NT Server 4.0 installation and creates a text file with the following information on all user accounts for the server.

- User ID
- Full name
- Remote Access Service (RAS) permissions
- Group information

If Microsoft Exchange Server is installed on the machine from which you export the users, the following information will also be migrated:

- Exchange mailbox.
- Global address list (GAL) information (telephone numbers, addresses, and so on).

Note If an Exchange Server does not exist, a mailbox is still created in the import mode, however, the GAL information will be blank.

The above information collected by the Migrate User Wizard is then used in the import mode. The Migrate User Wizard will not export the following to information file:

- Internet access permissions
- Exchange distribution lists
- Passwords

Note If you are replacing your Windows NT Server 4.0 installation, make sure to use the default and place the information file on floppy disk. Do not place the file on the hard drive of the machine receiving the Small Business Server installation, since Setup configures the memory partition to NTFS and all data will be lost.

Note The data not included in the information file must be re-entered once the user accounts are imported to Small Business Server. For example, since passwords are specifically left blank, users are required to enter new passwords the first time they log on to Small Business Server 4.5. As an alternative, the Change Password Wizard may be used to set user passwords after user accounts are created.

Modifying the Information File

The Information file, user.txt, can be modified to delete certain users you may not want to migrate, since Migrate User Wizard exports *all* users to the information file. Since the file is an ASCII text file, you can edit it in Microsoft Notepad.

Note You can also delete users after user accounts are imported via the **Remove a User** option in the **Manage Users** task of the Small Business Server console.

Import Users Task

Launch the Migrate User Wizard in the import mode by clicking **Import Users** on the Small Business Server console's **To Do List**. This allows for the migration of users from the Windows NT Server 4.0 installation to Small Business Server using the information file created by the wizard in export mode. To complete the migration, follow the steps of the Migrate User Wizard.

Additional Tasks

After the Migrate User Wizard runs in the import mode, the following tasks can be performed from the Small Business Server console, to create the items not exported by the Migrate User Wizard.

- Set Internet permissions.

    To set Internet access permissions, launch the Internet Access Wizard from the Small Business Server console's **Manage Internet Access** page, using the **control access to the Internet** taskpad.

- Enter GAL information (if Exchange GAL information was not exported).

    To enter GAL information, launch the User Account Wizard from the Small Business Server console's **Manage Users** page, using the **review or change user information** taskpad.

- Create distribution lists.

    To create a distribution list, launch the E-mail Distribution List Wizard from the Small Business Server console's **E-mail Distribution Lists** page, using the **create a distribution list** taskpad.

- Change and set passwords.

    To change and set passwords, launch the Change Password Wizard from the Small Business Server console's **Manage Users** page, using the **change password** taskpad.

More Information

For further descriptions on the Migrate User Wizard, see *Chapter 25, Small Business Server Wizard Processes,* in *Part 4, Administering and Maintaining*, of this resource guide.

CHAPTER 42

Migrating an Access Database to SQL Server 7.0

As the needs of the small business organization grow and the demand for a high-performance database increases, it may be necessary to migrate from the file-server environment of the Microsoft® Access Jet engine to the client/server environment of Microsoft SQL Server™ 7.0. The Access 2000 Upsizing Wizard included with Microsoft Office 2000, moves Access tables and queries into SQL Server 7.0. If the small business has used an earlier version of Access, applications may be migrated to SQL Server 7.0 by upgrading to Access 2000 and then using the Upsizing Wizard.

If the technology consultant prefers not to use Access 2000 and the Upsizing Wizard to migrate, the material presented in this chapter still serves as a general guide for moving an Access application to SQL Server 7.0. Moving an Access application requires moving the data into SQL Server 7.0 and then migrating the Access queries into the database or into SQL files for execution at a later time. The last step is migrating and optimizing the applications.

SQL Server 7.0 Tools Used in Migration

Several tools in SQL Server 7.0 assist in the migration of Access data and applications. These tools are described in the sections that follow.

SQL Server Enterprise Manager

SQL Server Enterprise Manager allows for enterprise-wide configuration and management of SQL Server 7.0 and SQL Server objects. SQL Server Enterprise Manager provides a powerful scheduling engine, administrative alert capabilities, and a built-in replication management interface. You can also use SQL Server Enterprise Manager to do the following:

- Manage logins and user permissions
- Create scripts
- Manage backup of SQL Server objects

- Back up databases and transaction logs
- Manage tables, views, stored procedures, triggers, indexes, rules, defaults, and user-defined data types
- Create full-text indexes, database diagrams, and database maintenance plans
- Import and export data
- Transform data
- Perform various web administration tasks

SQL Server Enterprise Manager is included in the SQL Server 7.0 application installed with Microsoft BackOffice® Small Business Server 4.5. It may be accessed in the Program group of the **Start** menu. In migration procedures, Data Transformation Services (DTS) will be launched from the SQL Server 7.0 Enterprise Manager interface.

Data Transformation Services

DTS allows you to import and export data between multiple heterogeneous sources that use an object linking and embedding database (OLE DB)-based architecture such as Microsoft Excel spreadsheets. It also allows for transferring databases and database objects (for example, indexes and stored procedures) between multiple computers running SQL Server 7.0. You can also use DTS to transform data so it can be used more easily to build data warehouses and data marts from an online transaction processing (OLTP) system.

The DTS Import Wizard and DTS Export Wizard allow you to interactively create DTS packages that use OLE DB and open database connectivity (ODBC) to import, export, validate, and transform heterogeneous data. The wizards also allow you to copy schema and data between relational databases.

SQL Server Query Analyzer

SQL Server 7.0 Query Analyzer is a graphical query tool that allows for visual analysis of the plan of a query, execution of multiple queries simultaneously, viewing data, and obtaining index recommendations. SQL Server Query Analyzer provides the Showplan option, which is used to report data retrieval methods chosen by the SQL Server 7.0 Query Optimizer.

SQL Server Profiler

SQL Server 7.0 Profiler captures a continuous record of server activity in real time. SQL Server 7.0 Profiler allows you to monitor events produced through SQL Server 7.0, filter events based on user-specified criteria, and direct the trace output to the screen, a file, or a table. Using SQL Server 7.0 Profiler, you can replay previously captured traces.

The Profiler Tool also helps application developers identify transactions that might be deteriorating the performance of an application. This can be useful when migrating an application from a file-based architecture to a client/server architecture, since the last step involves optimizing the application for its new client/server environment.

Migration Phase

This section covers the migration procedures using the tools previously described.

Access Database Backup

Before migrating tables and queries to SQL Server 7.0, it is strongly advised to work from a backup of the Access database since using the Upsizing Wizard will change it. In order to obtain the best possible SQL Server database, you will probably need to run the wizard through a few trial passes before performing the actual migration. You can experiment on the backup copy of the Access database until the best configuration is obtained, at which time the actual migration should be performed on the production database.

Moving Tables and Data

Access data may be transferred to SQL Server 7.0 using the DTS Import Wizard. Follow these steps:

▶ **To transfer Access data to SQL Server 7.0**

1. In SQL Server Enterprise Manager, on the **Tools** menu, point to **Data Transformation Services**, and then click **Import Data**.

2. In the **Choose a Data Source** dialog box, select **Microsoft Access as the Source**. Next, type the file name of your .mdb database (.mdb file extension) or browse for the file.

3. In the **Choose a Destination** dialog box, select **Microsoft OLE DB Provider for SQL Server**, select the database server, and then click the required authentication mode.

4. In the **Specify Table Copy or Query** dialog box, click **Copy tables**.

5. In the **Select Source Tables** dialog box, click **Select All**. Click **OK** when finished.

Migrating Access Queries

Existing Access queries must be moved into SQL Server 7.0 in one of the formats described in the following sections.

Transact-SQL Scripts

Transact-SQL statements are usually called from database programs, but you can use SQL Server 7.0 Query Analyzer to run them against the database directly. SQL Server 7.0 Query Analyzer helps developers to test Transact-SQL statements against development databases and run Transact-SQL statements that perform queries, data manipulation (INSERT, UPDATE, DELETE), or data definition (CREATE TABLE).

Stored Procedures

Most Transact-SQL statements that originate from Access queries (SELECT, INSERT, UPDATE, and DELETE) can be moved into stored procedures. Stored procedures written in Transact-SQL can be used to encapsulate and standardize your data access, and are actually stored within the database. Stored procedures can run with or without parameters and are called from database programs or manually from the Query Analyzer. The following table below describes Access queries.

Table 42.1 Access Queries

Access query type	SQL Server migration options and comments
SELECT	A SELECT statement can be stored in a Transact-SQL file, a stored procedure, or a view. Creating stored procedures is the best way to separate the database application development from the physical implementation of the database design. Stored procedures are created in one place, and are called from the application. Calls to stored procedures will not "break" if the underlying database changes and the stored procedure is carefully modified to reflect these changes.
CROSSTAB	Crosstabs are used for summary reports. An Access CROSSTAB can be implemented as a Transact-SQL SELECT statement in a SQL script, a stored procedure, or a view. The data join is re-executed each time a query is issued, ensuring that the latest data is always used. Depending on the application, it might be appropriate to store data from the crosstab as a temporary table (see MAKE TABLE in the next row). The temporary table requires fewer resources, but offers only a snapshot of the data at the time the temporary table is created.

(continued)

Table 42.1 Access Queries *(continued)*

Access query type	SQL Server migration options and comments
MAKE TABLE	An Access MAKE TABLE can be implemented as a Transact-SQL CREATE TABLE statement in a Transact-SQL script or stored procedure. The syntax follows: `SELECT [ALL	DISTINCT]` `[{TOP integer	TOP integer PERCENT}` `[WITH TIES]]` `<select_list>` `[INTO new_table]` `[FROM {<table_source>} [,…n]]` `[WHERE <search_condition>]` `[GROUP BY [ALL] group_by_expression [,…n]` `[WITH { CUBE	ROLLUP }]`  `CREATE TABLE mytable (low int, high int)`
UPDATE	An UPDATE statement can be stored in a Transact-SQL script. However, the recommended way to implement an UPDATE statement is to create a stored procedure.
APPEND	An APPEND statement can be stored in a Transact-SQL script. However, the recommended way to implement an APPEND statement is to create a stored procedure.
DELETE	A DELETE statement can be stored in a Transact-SQL script. However, the recommended way to implement a DELETE statement is to create a stored procedure.

Views

Views are used as virtual tables that expose specific rows and columns from one or more tables. They enable users to create queries without directly implementing the complex joins that underlie the query. Views do not support the use of parameters. Views that join more than one table cannot be modified using INSERT, UPDATE, or DELETE statements. Views are called from Transact-SQL statements, and can also be used in *.scripts that are run in SQL Server Query Analyzer. SQL Server views and the SQL-92 standard do not support ORDER BY clauses in views.

For more information about Transact-SQL, stored procedures, or views, refer to the SQL Server Web site at:
http://www.microsoft.com/sql

Migrating Access Queries into Stored Procedures and Views

Each Access query must be placed into the set of statements described below.

```
CREATE PROCEDURE <NAME_HERE> AS
< SELECT, UPDATE, DELETE, INSERT, CREATE TABLE statement from Microsoft
Access >
GO
CREATE VIEW <NAME_HERE> AS
<Place (SELECT only, with no parameters) Microsoft Access Query>
GO
```

For each Access query, perform the following steps.

▶ **To migrate Access queries into stored procedures and views**

1. Open Access, and then open the SQL Server 7.0 Query Analyzer.
2. In the **Database** window of Access, select the **Queries** tab, and then click **Design**.
3. On the **View** menu, click **SQL**.
4. Paste the entire query into SQL Server Query Analyzer.
5. Either test the syntax and save the Transact-SQL statement for later use, or run the statement in the database. Transact-SQL may also be saved to a script, as described in the next section.

Migrating Access Queries into Transact-SQL Scripts

Most Access queries should be translated into stored procedures and views. Nevertheless, some statements that are run infrequently by an application developer can be stored as a Transact-SQL script, which is a text file that ends in the file extension .sql. These files can be run from within SQL Server Query Analyzer.

If you plan to transfer some of the small business Access queries into .sql files, consider separating the Transact-SQL statements into several scripts, depending on how they are used. For example, those Transact-SQL statements that must be run with the same frequency may be grouped together into a script. Another script might contain all Transact-SQL statements that are run only under certain conditions. Also, Transact-SQL statements that must be run in a specific order should be grouped together in a discrete script.

▶ **To move a statement from Access to a Transact-SQL file**

1. Copy the statement into SQL Server Query Analyzer.
2. Use the blue check mark icon to parse the statement.
3. Execute the statement if appropriate.

If there are MAKE TABLE Access queries, two options are available for SQL Server. Either of the following can be created:

- **A view**. A view creates the effect of having a dynamic, virtual temporary table that provides the latest information. This is input/output (I/O) intensive since it requires the rejoining of the data tables each time a query is issued.

- **A temporary table**. A temporary table creates a snapshot of data for a connected user's session. You can create local and global temporary tables. Local temporary tables are visible only in the current session and global temporary tables are visible to all sessions.

Prefix local temporary table names with single number sign (#table_name), and prefix global temporary table names with double number sign (##table_name). Queries run quickly against temporary tables because they generally use only one table rather than dynamically joining together several tables to obtain a result set. For more information about temporary tables, see the SQL Server web site at:
http://www.microsoft.com/sql

The DTS in SQL Server 7.0 allows you to standardize, automate, and schedule the creation of temporary tables by creating packages. For example, when you migrate the Access 2.0 **Northwind** sample database, the crosstab created for reporting quarterly data becomes either a view, or a data transformation creating a temporary table on a regular basis.

Other Migration Considerations

The following section describes other issues to consider when migrating the Access database to SQL Server 7.0.

Using Parameters

SQL Server 7.0 stored procedures that have parameters need a different syntax from Access queries, as described in the following table. In the section following the table, an example is given of the syntax changes of an Access 2.0 query versus the equivalent SQL Server 7.0 stored procedure syntax.

Table 42.2   Differences Between SQL Server 7.0 and Access Syntax

Access	SQL Server
ORDER BY in queries	ORDER BY in views not supported
DISTINCTROW	DISTINCT
String concatenation with "&"	String concatenation with "+"
Supported clauses/operators:	Supported clauses/operators:
SELECT	SELECT
SELECT TOP N	SELECT TOP N
INTO	INTO
FROM	FROM
WHERE	WHERE
GROUP BY	GROUP BY
HAVING	HAVING
UNION (ALL)	UNION (ALL)
ORDER BY	ORDER BY
WITH OWNER ACCESS	COMPUTE
	FOR BROWSE
	OPTION
Not Supported: COMPUTE, FOR BROWSE, OPTION	Not Supported: WITH OWNERACCESS
Aggregate functions:	Aggregate functions:
AVG	AVG([ALL | DISTINCT] expression)
COUNT(column)	COUNT([ALL | DISTINCT] expression)
COUNT(*)	COUNT(*)
	GROUPING (column_name)
MAX	MAX(expression)

(continued)

Table 42.2 Differences Between SQL Server 7.0 and Access Syntax *(continued)*

Access	SQL Server
MIN	MIN(expression)
STDEV, STDEVP	STDEV, STDEVP
SUM	SUM([ALL | DISTINCT] expression)
VAR, VARP	VAR, VARP
FIRST, LAST	Not supported: FIRST, LAST
TRANSFORM (SELECT statement)	WITH ROLLUP, WITH CUBE on SELECT statements
PIVOT	?
MAKE TABLE, ALTER TABLE	CREATE TABLE, ALTER TABLE
Other supported clauses:	Other supported clauses:
CONSTRAINT	CONSTRAINT
ADD COLUMN	ADD COLUMN
DROP COLUMN	DROP COLUMN
DROP INDEX	?
Also, stand-alone statement: DROP INDEX	Stand-alone statement: DROP INDEX

Access and SQL Server Syntax

Below is a syntax example of an Access 2.0 query and the equivalent for a SQL Server 4.0 stored procedure.

Access Query Name: Employee Sales By Country, in NWIND.mdb:

```
PARAMETERS [Beginning Date] DateTime, [Ending Date] DateTime;
SELECT Orders.[Order ID], [Last Name] & ", " & [First Name] AS
Salesperson, Employees.Country, Orders.[Shipped Date], [Order
Subtotals].Subtotal AS [Sale Amount]
FROM Employees INNER JOIN (Orders INNER JOIN [Order Subtotals] ON
Orders.[Order ID] = [Order Subtotals].[Order ID]) ON Employees.[Employee
ID] = Orders.[Employee ID]
WHERE (((Orders.[Shipped Date]) Between [Beginning Date] And [Ending
Date]))
ORDER BY [Last Name] & ", " & [First Name], Employees.Country,
Orders.[Shipped Date];
```

SQL Server stored procedure syntax:

```
CREATE PROCEDURE EMP_SALES_BY_COUNTRY
@BeginningDate datetime,
@EndingDate datetime
AS
SELECT Orders.[Order ID], [Last Name] + ", " + [First Name] AS
Salesperson, Employees.Country,
Orders.[Shipped Date], [Order Subtotals].Subtotal AS [Sale Amount]
FROM Employees INNER JOIN (Orders INNER JOIN [Order Subtotals] ON
Orders.[Order ID] = [Order Subtotals].[Order ID]) ON Employees.[Employee
ID] = Orders.[Employee ID]
WHERE (((Orders.[Shipped Date]) Between @BeginningDate And @EndingDate))
ORDER BY [Last Name] + ", " + [First Name], Employees.Country,
Orders.[Shipped Date]
GO
```

Nested Queries

Some Access queries are created on top of other queries in a nested fashion. Nested queries in Access become nested views in SQL Server. The ORDER BY clauses cannot be part of a view definition but are appended to the SELECT statement that queries the VIEW. If you have nested Access queries, create several views and then create stored procedures that perform both a SELECT operation on the view and append an ORDER BY clause to the SELECT statement.

For example, the following Access query:

```
SELECT *
FROM STUDENTS
WHERE COUNTRY = "USA"
ORDER BY LAST_NAME
```

becomes the SQL Server view and a stored procedure:

```
CREATE VIEW US_STUDENTS AS
SELECT * FROM STUDENTS
WHERE COUNTRY = "USA"
CREATE PROCEDURE US_STUDENTS_ORDER AS
SELECT * FROM US_STUDENTS_ORDER BY LAST NAME
```

Verifying SQL Server 7.0–Compliant Syntax

You can use the **Parse** command on the **Query** menu in SQL Server 7.0 Query Analyzer to verify whether a view or stored procedure functions in SQL Server 7.0. In the example below, the Access query uses the word "DISTINCTROW." SQL Server 7.0 uses the Transact-SQL command DISTINCT to perform the same operation. The **Parse** command allows the technology consultant to isolate and modify syntax problems in Access queries.

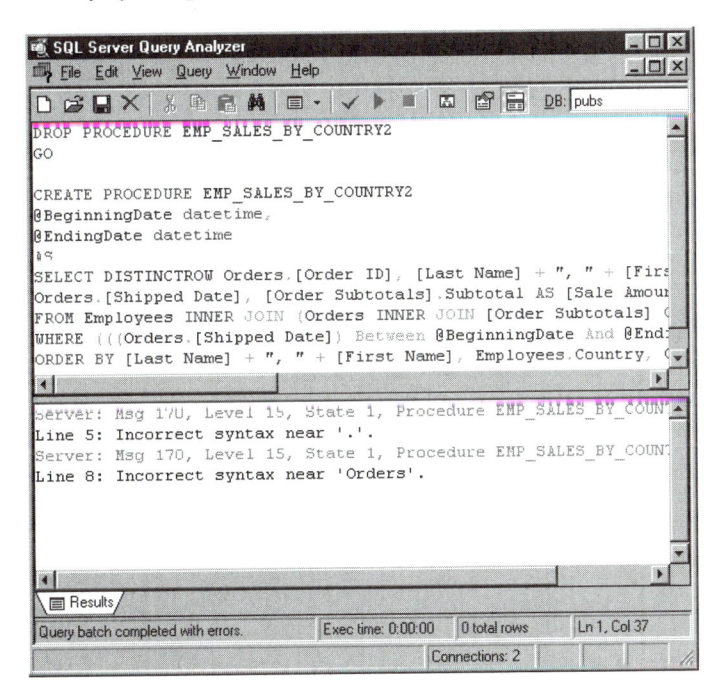

Connecting the Applications

Many Access applications predating Office 2000 were written by using Microsoft Visual Basic® for Applications or the Visual Basic for Applications Access user interface. Applications that use Visual Basic for Applications as the development environment can run against SQL Server 7.0, using the Jet ODBC driver. Applications that use the forms and reports found in the Access user interface can access SQL Server 7.0 using linked tables.

If the small business application is to use linked tables, make sure that all Access tables get moved to SQL Server 7.0 to increase performance. Creating queries against a mix of Access (Jet) and SQL Server using linked tables can be very resource-intensive.

Optimizing the Application

The Access application may now be optimized for the client/server environment as follows:

- Monitor Transact-SQL statements being sent to the server
- Implement efficient indexes

Monitoring Transact SQL-Statements

SQL Server Profiler is a useful tool for monitoring how Transact-SQL statements are sent to the database. If you run an unmodified Access application on SQL Server 7.0, you might send less than optimum Transact-SQL statements to the database by using Data Access Objects (DAO) with the Jet/ODBC driver. For example, a DELETE statement that uses the Jet/ODBC driver to delete 1,000 rows makes 1,000 calls to the database—this negatively impacts the performance of a production database. In this example, SQL Server Profiler displays 1,000 DELETE statements, allowing you to modify the application to use Microsoft ActiveX® Data Objects (ADO) with the Microsoft OLE DB Provider for SQL Server 7.0, and thereby improve the application's efficiency.

Implementing Efficient Indexes

After determining that the Transact-SQL statements being sent to the database are efficient, you can fine-tune those statements by using indexes more effectively. The Index Tuning Wizard allows you to find bottlenecks and then makes recommendations to resolve them. Your Transact-SQL statements are not modified, but their performance improves with the correct use of indexes.

Note For additional information about optimizing the Access application for client/server performance, refer to Knowledge Base article Q128808 in the support section on the Microsoft web site at:
http://support.microsoft.com

PART 9

Developing Small Business Server Solutions

Microsoft® BackOffice® Small Business Server 4.5 has several extensible features that allow the technology consultant to deliver solutions specifically tailored for their small business customer. In addition, extensibility of components such as the Small Business Server console, allows the independent software vendor (ISV) to seamlessly integrate their applications into server functionality.

Part 9 presents architectural background, mechanisms, and/or procedural information for extending the following features of Small Business Server:

- Small Business Server console
- Set Up Computer Wizard
- Server Status Tool

Other information supporting solution development and enhancements is also included to assist the technology consultant and third-party application developers in extending the functionality of Small Business Server. The chapters covered in this Part include:

Chapter 43   Customizing and Extending the Small Business Server Console   681

Chapter 44   Extension Mechanism for the Set Up Computer Wizard   713

Chapter 45   Using the MSDE Solution with Microsoft Access 2000   725

Chapter 46   Other Extensions and Solutions   735

Chapter 47   Enhancing Office 2000 Functionality   743

Chapter 48   Office 2000 Customer Manager   757

Chapter 49   Application Communication with MSMQ   759

Chapter 50   TAPI Solutions for Small Business Server   761

CHAPTER 43

Customizing and Extending the Small Business Server Console

This chapter outlines the rationale behind the design of the Microsoft® BackOffice® Small Business Server console, including console layout, placement of buttons, and organization. The importance of a consistent interface is highlighted. Sample code and the mechanism used to extend the Small Business Server console are also given. The information in this chapter is presented to support the technology consultant or ISV in extending the functionality of the Small Business Server console.

Important To extend the Small Business Server console, the server must be fully installed. Third-party software vendors will need to write an application that performs the necessary steps to extend the Small Business Server console after the server is set up, as outlined in this chapter. The technology consultant should test-run the application after completion of Small Business Server setup.

Note The technology consultant may also add console links for new applications using the Small Business Server Customization Tool described in *Part 10, "Tools and Utilities,"* of this resource guide.

Console Extension Philosophy

The key concept behind Small Business Server console extension is to make everything very easy for users. Everything users need to do should be intuitively and visually obvious. Thus, the console should serve as a guide for users by directing them to the correct actions for solving problems and performing tasks.

Extension Organization

Extensions to the console should be well thought out for organization and design simplicity. Tasks should be grouped in a logical manner and navigation should be intuitive. Avoid the confusion a user experiences in trying to identify what task should be done next and then trying to complete that task independently.

User Success

User success is very important. When users set out to perform a task, the console should let them do so quickly. For this reason, multiple ways of doing things are provided for the user throughout the console. Although there are multiple paths, each path provides a consistent and intuitive interface for the user. This consistency, coupled with a clean and concise interface, improves the user success rate.

While designing for ease-of-use and user success, keep in mind the user profile and the type of business the console is targeting. The typical small business scenario is one in which there is no dedicated system administrator. The person responsible for the network may be the person with the most interest in computers, the most experience, or possibly the one who uses the server as their computer. This user typically has some Windows experience but is in no way a network expert. Network administration is likely only one of their responsibilities in the company. The faster the user can accomplish administration tasks, the more quickly they can return to other tasks, and the more satisfied they are with personal performance and the product.

Console Organization

The organization of the console is discussed in the following sections.

High-Level Pages

The high-level pages of the console breaks the tasks related to managing Small Business Server into the three functional groups listed below.

- Home. A high-level overview of server status including free disk space, service errors, etc., and important links—such as Favorites—are provided on the Home page. The purpose of this page is to help the user monitor the health of their server, as well as be able to navigate to important links quickly.
- Tasks. The individual tasks a user needs to perform are listed on the Tasks and More Tasks pages, including Manage Users, Manage E-mail, etc. From here, the user can navigate to sub pages to perform specific tasks such as Add a User, Create a Distribution List, and so on.
- Online Guide. All help-related actions are exposed through the Online Guide.

Sub-Level Pages

The sub-level pages are accessed from the **Tasks** or **More Tasks** page. Sub pages contain status information and actions relevant to the selected task.

> **Note** Specific page layout is covered in the next section, "Page Layout and Design."

Use sub pages sparingly in instances such as the following:

- When selection of an item on a sub page is required to provide information on that item. For example, use a sub page to select a printer and display print jobs.
- When you want an immediate response. For example, use a sub page to launch a help topic.

The idea of the sub pages and overall console design is to get users to the point where they can complete what they need to do in as few steps as possible. With this hierarchy, the user is required to navigate only through two levels to complete the desired action—selecting the appropriate task on the **Tasks** or **More Tasks** page, and then selecting the specific action.

Secondary Sub Pages

In some cases, a secondary sub page is needed to outline further tasks related to an object chosen on a sub page. These pages are typically necessary when an immediate action is required. For example, consider the **Manage Printer Jobs** page. The actions listed on this page are **Pause**, **Resume**, and **Cancel a Print Job**. These are actions that should be completed immediately upon selection. It is not appropriate or efficient to have the user select a printer from the **Manage Printers** page, work through a wizard to select a print job, and then take a corresponding action.

Another example is the **Manage Folder Size** page. The actions are again immediate —**Compress and Uncompress** — rather than actions that are completed through a wizard started from the **Manage Shared Folders** page.

In the above cases, it is appropriate to have a secondary sub page. This secondary sub page, like the sub page, contains status information and actions relevant to the selected task. Actions that appear on the sub page are typically completed with an immediate action, as discussed earlier.

Page Layout and Design

This section describes the concepts behind console page layout and design.

Home Page

When the Small Business Server Console is launched from the **Start** menu, the **Home** page appears. This page is designed as a central navigation point from which all Small Business Server administration tasks, online support, and the preliminary tasks of the **To Do List** can be found. The **Home** page shown below also provides the user with access to the following:

- Product and licensing information
- Small Business Server web site
- Disk space and usage information
- Service error indicator
- Link to the To Do List

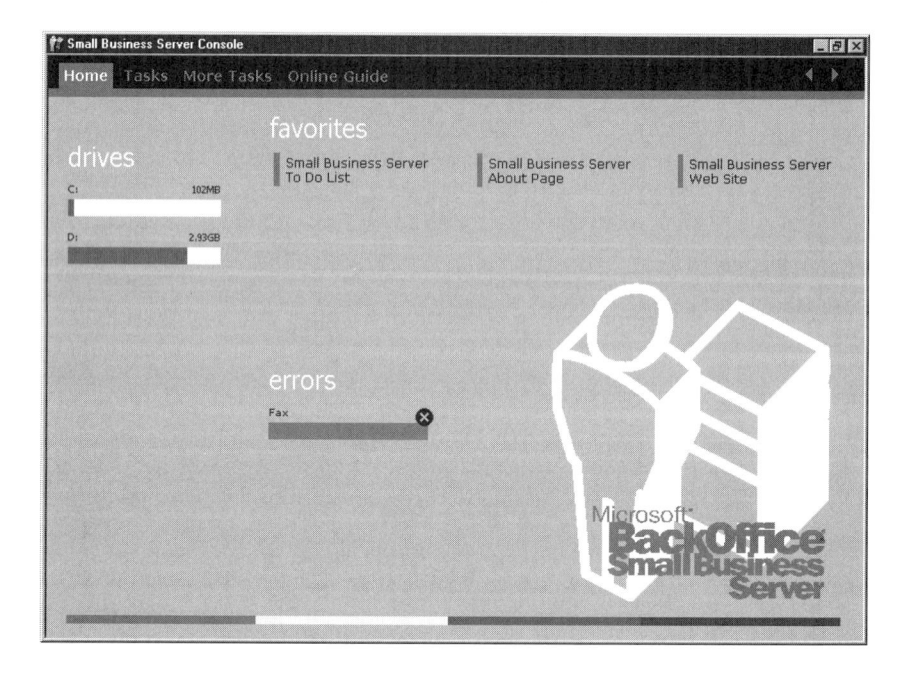

Tasks and More Tasks Pages

The **Tasks** and **More Tasks** pages single out the main tasks the user is trying to complete without overwhelming them with too much information. The title of the link tells the user the main task to be performed.

If more information is required for the user to make the decision, a tool tip provides a description of the types of actions that can be performed there when the user places the mouse pointer over the button.

For example, the button for managing users has the title **Managing Users**. If the user need more information, the tool tip descriptive text says, "Add new users, change user accounts and passwords, manage user permissions." The additional text provides the user with more information with which to make a selection. Ensure that the descriptive text in your extension describes *actions* the user will perform on that sub page. In the example, the tool tip text uses action verbs such as *add, change,* and *manage* to inform users of the tasks they can expect to perform via that button.

The layout of the page groups the task links into three columns. Additional links are added from top to bottom, moving from left to right as shown in the illustration below.

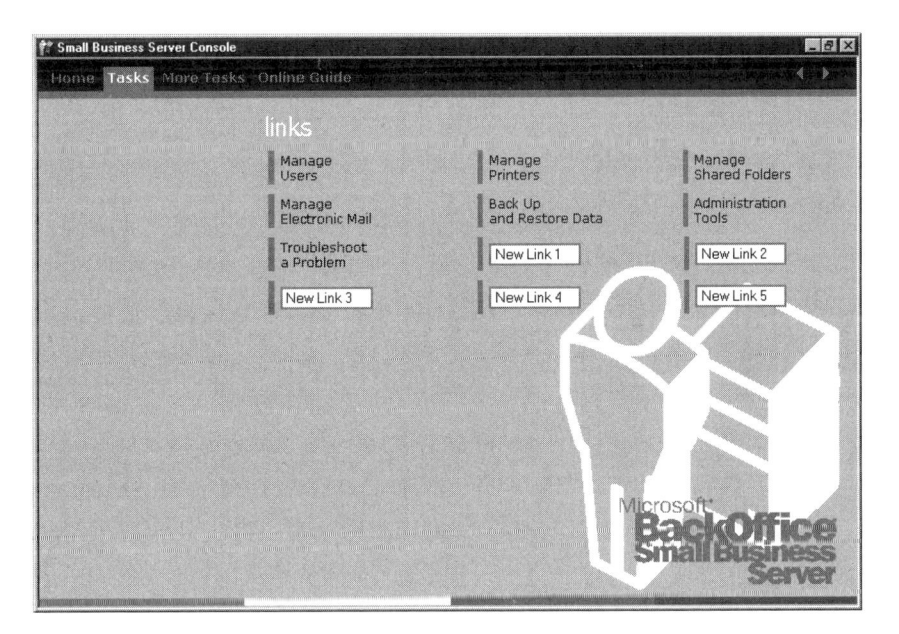

Figure 43.1 Task link arrangement on the console

Important The extension of the **Task** and **More Task** pages is **based on a first-come, first-placement method**. Once a task position has been taken, use the next available position. This may mean that your button will not occur in the same place in every installation. Your extension code should handle placing the button in the next available position, regardless of where this is on the page.

Sub Pages

The function of sub pages is to allow the user to quickly determine the selection they need to make to complete the desired task. For this reason, symbols are used to guide the user's attention to the actions on the page.

Watermarks and Symbols

Each sub page has an associated watermark used in the background to symbolize the noun associated with the page (for example—Users, E-mail, etc.). Symbols used on the page are characterized by a verb (for example—Add, Remove, etc.). The title under the symbol indicates the action performed when you click on it. For example, on the **Manage Users** page, the watermark is a **User** and the text under the **Add** symbol is **add a user**, thus combining **Add** and **User**.

Note The exception to this is the **Troubleshooting** page. Since this page is associated with a verb, troubleshooting, the background watermark is the verb and all of the symbols are the nouns.

Tool Tips

Tool tips display descriptive text when the mouse is moved over the task symbol. Tool tips should always be used to provide additional information that helps the user make a selection. As in the case of the tool tip for the **Tasks** and **More Tasks** pages, have your tool tip text on the sub pages indicate the actions that selecting the symbol will perform. For example, **Create a New Distribution List** has the tool tip descriptive text "Select users for a new distribution list," indicating to users what they will do if they click this symbol. This helps them make the appropriate decision.

Sub Page Content

The overall layout of the sub pages is clean and concise. The goal is to direct users to the actions they need to perform. As a result, any explanatory information about the page or general information about what the page manages is not shown. Information of this sort was placed in an overview help topic to avoid cluttering the page. When extending the console with a sub page, all unnecessary or general explanatory text should be avoided. Furthermore, many of the pages in the console have links to other related pages, in case the user misnavigates through the console. Users should never have to backtrack through a page but always continue to move forward. This increases their chances of success and reassures them with the sense that they are doing the right thing.

Typical Layout

The typical layout of a sub page includes both important status information about the task on the left, and the various actions related to the high-level task on the right. This layout is used because the user's attention is usually directed from left to right. The status information provides users with an indication of *what they are managing* and the actions show *how they manage it*.

On the sub pages, selecting an action typically requires users to select an object in the status area and then click the action they want to perform. For example, on the **Manage Users** page, to change the password of a user, a user is first selected from the list of users on the left, and the action **Change Password for a User** on the right is then selected.

While the layout maps to the users actions, from left to right, consideration was also given to placing actions that require the user to select a status item before the action in the positions closest to the status information.

Default Layouts

Four default layouts may be used on the sub pages, depending on the type of data to be displayed, as described ahead.

Vertical List View

Use this view when there are a lot of items to display without much information. The following **Manage Users** page is a good example of this. On the **Manage Users** page, the list of users can be quite long, but only the full user name is shown. Other data about each user does not appear on this page.

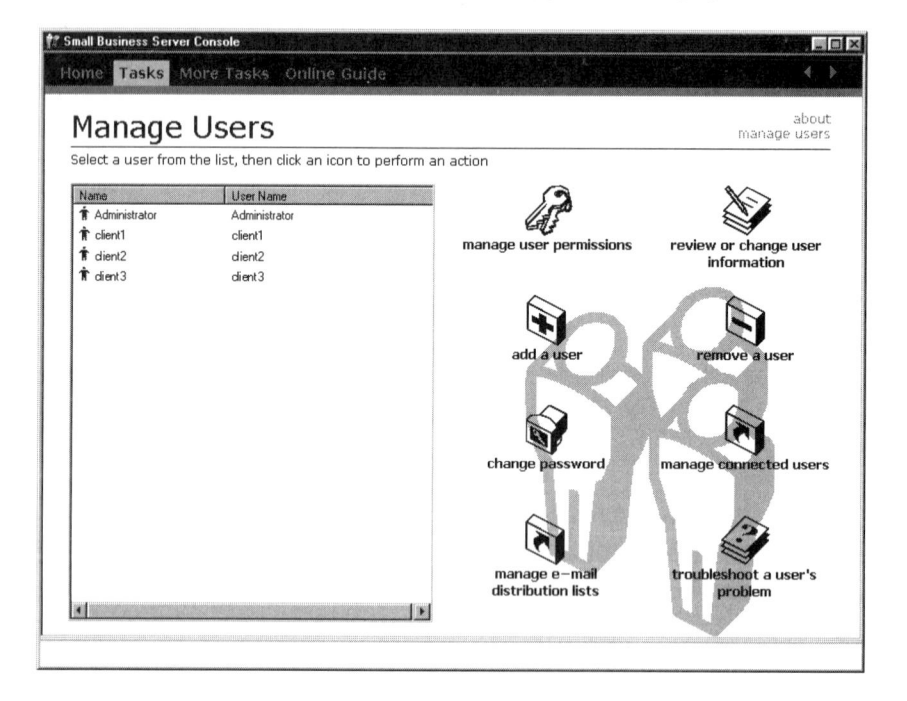

Horizontal List View

Use this view when there are not many items to display, but each item has a lot of associated information. The **Manage Printer Jobs** page, where there are not many printer jobs but all jobs have an associated user name, document name, status, etc., is a good example of this, as follows.

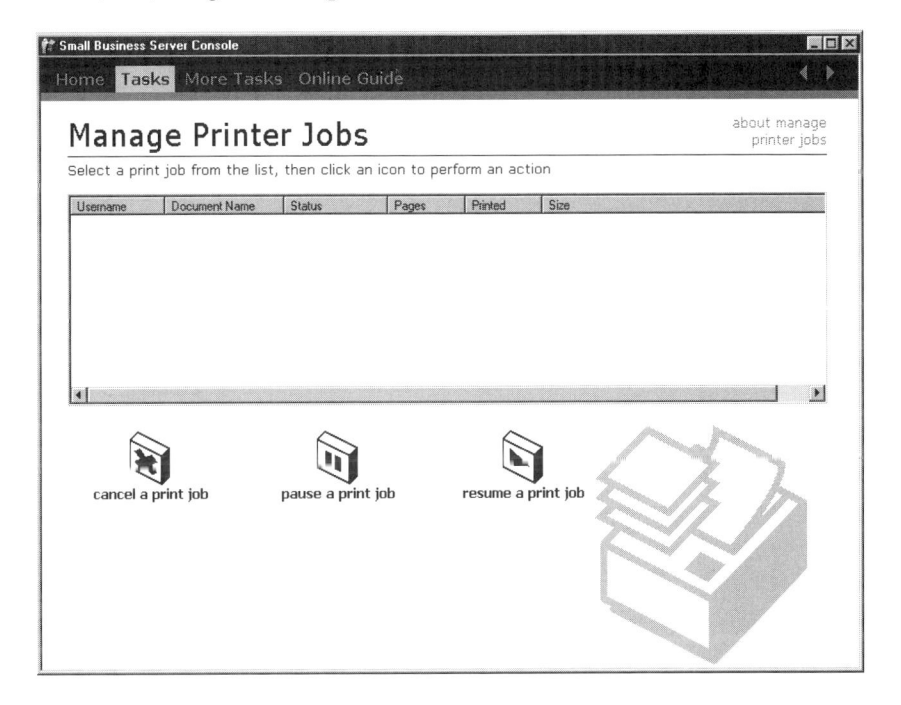

Status

Use this when the status information to display does not lend itself to a list control, and no user interaction with the status is necessary to complete the actions listed on the page. An example of this is the **Publish on the Internet** page, where the page displays the various uniform resource locators (URLs) associated with the server, as follows.

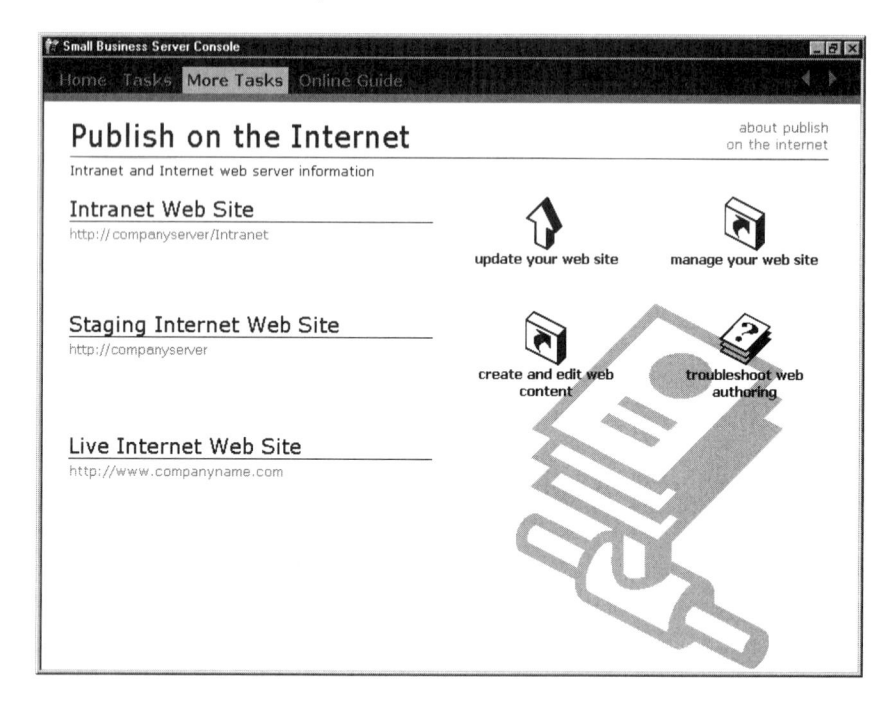

No List View

Use this view when there is not an appropriate status metric to display. An example of this is the **Back Up or Restore Data** page, as follows.

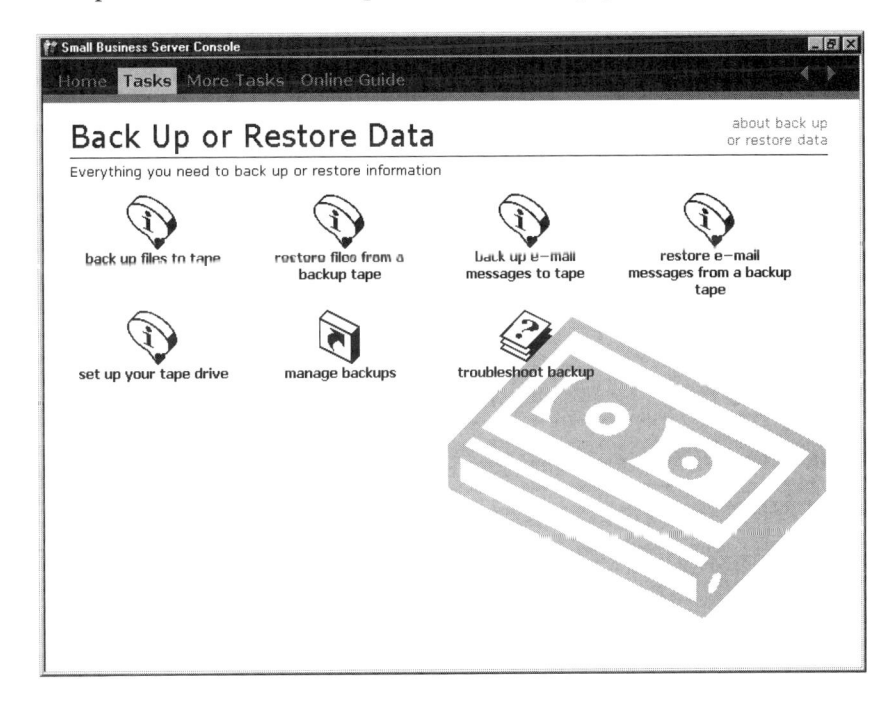

Sub Page Action Capacity

All sub pages will support eight actions (the Status page will support 16) without scrolling. Although the page will scroll beyond this number, it is recommended not to exceed these values since then the user may be overwhelmed by the page.

Important The extension of a sub page is not supported in this version of Small Business Server.

Consistency

Consistency plays a major role in console design. If users observe a similar layout of pages, placement of actions, flow of wizards, and design of icons throughout the console, they will know what to expect and learning becomes more intuitive. Experience helps them to quickly find the next thing to do.

In designing the console, special consideration was given to ensure the points of consistency described in the sections that follow.

Text in Lower Case

Text for new console tasks items, except for words which require capitalization (like Internet), should be in lower case for consistency with existing console text.

Similar Tasks on Various Sub Pages Should Be Placed in the Same Location

The order of the following list of tasks defines the sequence in which they were placed on sub pages. Up to eight tasks can be included on a sub page.

- **Wizards**. Actions that start wizards.
- **Online Guide**. Actions that link to Help topics.
- **Links**. Actions that navigate or link to other console pages.
- **Troubleshooting**. Actions that link to troubleshooting topics.

For consistency with the existing console design, keep action pairs together—for example, **Add** and **Remove** should be next to one another. The sequence described above is reflected in task placements on the following **Manage Printers** screen.

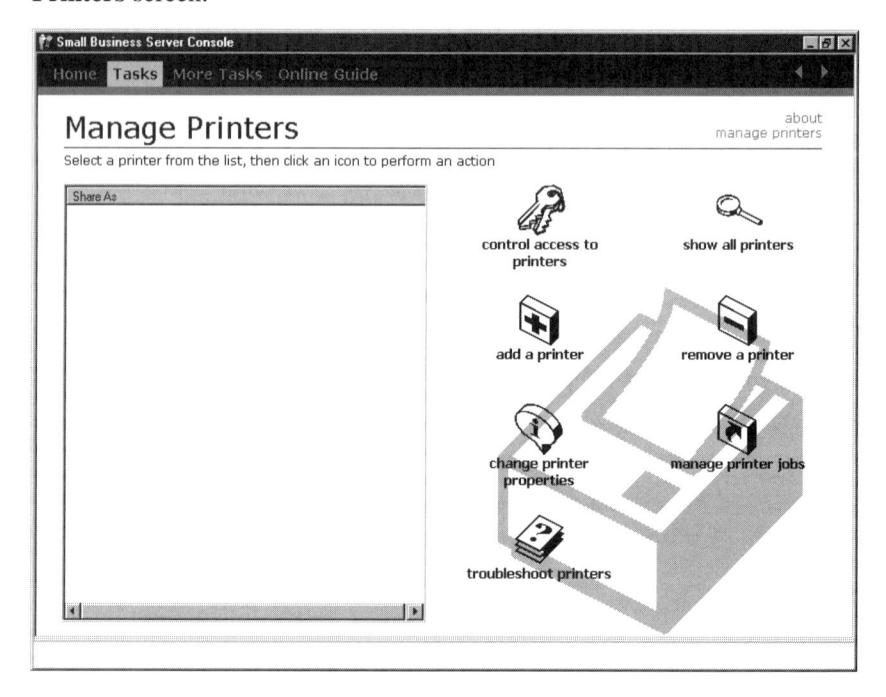

Sub Page Left Column Content

The left column should contain activities or selections that interact with status area tasks.

Similar Tasks Should Have the Same Background Watermarks

This is to impress the noun represented by the watermark symbol on the user.

All Actions with the Same Associated Verb Should Have the Same Symbol

Each action that performs the same verb-action should have the same symbol. For example, all "add" actions should use the following symbol:

Figure 43.2 Add symbol

Background, Content, and Links Should be Consistent

- Other consistency features include:
- Each sub page contains a link to the appropriate overview topic in the Online Guide. Explanations of the page or general information is in the Help. The Online Guide overview topic for that subject then contains a link to the corresponding console page. The phrase "about _____" is used for the link title, since users recognize the word about to mean either help or a description.
- If an extension is consistent with what already exists in the console, users will more likely be successful completing their desired tasks.
    - The Online Guide uses two distinct icons to indicate whether the topic is an online guide or troubleshooting topic, as shown below. Throughout the console, these icons have been adopted to inform the user that the action is a help topic and to indicate the type of help.

Online Guide   Troubleshooting

Figure 43.3 Online Guide topic icons

Extension Mechanism for Console Pages

This section provides information about extending the console as follows:

- Add links to the Home page.
- Add tasks to the Tasks and More Tasks pages.
- Add sub and secondary sub pages to the console.

Adding Favorite Links to the Home Page

To support the extension of the **Home** page to include additional "Favorite" links, the page is implemented as an active server page (ASP). When loaded, the ASP page checks the registry to determine the links that should be placed on the **Home** page. For each link that should appear on the page, the registry contains the following information:

- URL
- Description text
- Enabled dword
- Target dword
- Title text

To add a link to the **Home** page, the registry entry for that link must be created. Use the steps below to create additional links.

Chapter 43 Customizing and Extending the Small Business Server Console 695

▶ **To create additional links on the Home page**

1. Click **Start**, and then click **Run**. Type **regedit** in the dialog box to open the Registry Editor.

2. Navigate the following registry path:

   HKEY_LOCAL_MACHINE\Software\Microsoft\SmallBusiness\Console\Favorites

3. At this location there are registry keys for the default links entitled "Microsoft" and custom links to be added to the **Home** page entitled "Custom." Find the Custom key in the following location:

   HKEY_LOCAL_MACHINE\Software\Microsoft\SmallBusiness\Console\Favorites\Custom

   Note Under this key is a string that corresponds to the number of custom links that have been added to the **Home** page. This string is "LinkCount"=dword:00000000 by default. This value is in hexadecimal and must be incremented each time a custom link is added.

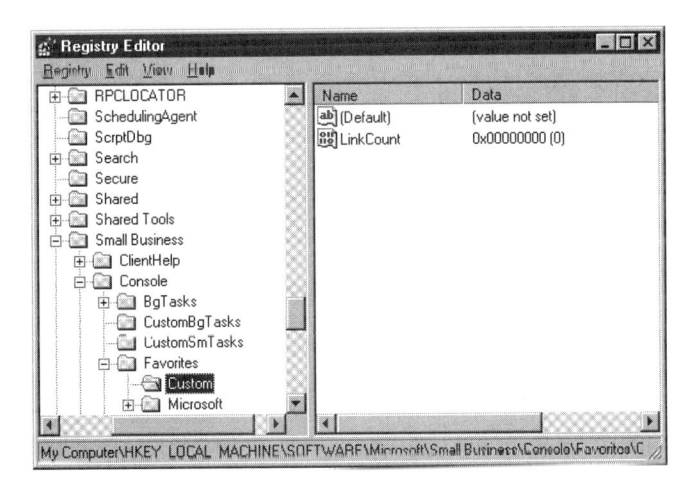

4. For each custom link to be added, create a sub key under the Custom key. This sub key must have the format "Link#" where the "#" corresponds to current (incremented) value of the "LinkCount". For example:

HKEY_LOCAL_MACHINE\Software\Microsoft\SmallBusiness\Console\Favorites\Custom\Link#

The ASP page reads the sub keys in the format "Link#" for the number of sub keys specified by "LinkCount." These links will then be displayed on the **Home** page in the order they are found.

> **Important** There is no way to guarantee the position of the custom link will be the same on all Small Business Server machines. In order for the extension mechanism to work, custom links must be added programmatically to the registry following the steps above.

5. For each sub key added, create the following strings as shown in the screen that follows:

   - URL. The target page to open. This should be in URL format only. Any special actions should be handled by ASP code on the target page.
   - DescriptionText. The tooltip text that describes what the task does. It should be in HTML.
   - "Enabled"=dword:00000001
   - "Target"=dword:00000000 The value of the dword can be as follows:

     00000000 – this will open the URL in a separate window. Use to navigate to web pages.

     00000001 – this will open the URL under the navigation bar (below the Home, Tasks, More Tasks, Online Guide links). Use to navigate to sub pages.
   - Product. The product name.
   - TitleText. The title of the link as it should appear on the page. It should be formatted in HTML.

> **Note** The custom link may be removed by setting the "Enabled" dword as follows: "Enabled"=dword:00000000. Do not remove the key itself.

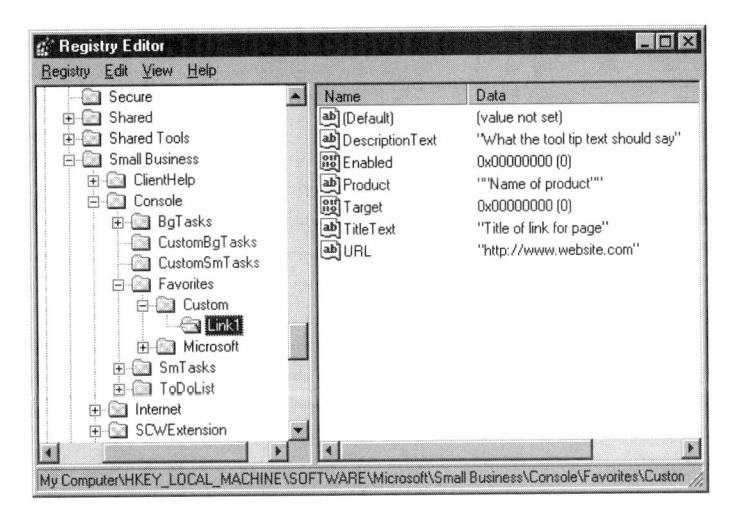

Adding Tasks to the Tasks and More Tasks Pages

To support extension of the **Tasks** and **More Tasks** pages with additional tasks, the pages are implemented as ASP pages. When loaded, the ASP pages check the registry to determine the tasks that should be placed on each page. For each task that should appear on the page, the registry contains the following information:

- URL
- Description text
- Enabled dword
- Target dword
- Product
- Title text

To add a task to a page, the registry entry for that task must be created. Use the steps below to create additional tasks.

▶ **To create additional tasks on the Tasks or More Tasks pages**

1. Click **Start**, and then click **Run**. Type **regedit** in the dialog box to open the Registry Editor.

2. For each page (**Tasks** or **More Tasks**) find the corresponding Custom key under their respective registry locations:

    - **Tasks page**:

      HKEY_LOCAL_MACHINE\Software\Microsoft\Small Business\Console\CustomSmTasks

- **More Tasks page**:

    HKEY_LOCAL_MACHINE\Software\Microsoft\Small Business\Console\CustomBgTasks

> **Note** Under each of these keys is a string that corresponds to the number of custom tasks that have been added to the page (**Tasks** or **More Tasks**). This string is: "LinkCount"=dword:00000000. This value is in hexadecimal and must be incremented each time a custom task is added.

3. For each custom task to be added, create a sub key under the appropriate customization key. This sub key must have the format "Link#" where the "#" corresponds to current (incremented) value of "LinkCount" from above. For example, to add a task to the **Tasks** page, create the following:

    HKEY_LOCAL_MACHINE\Software\Microsoft\Small Business\Console\CustomSmTasks\Link#

    The ASP page reads the sub keys in the format "Link#" for the number of sub keys specified by "LinkCount." These tasks will then be displayed on the **Tasks** or **More Tasks** page in the order they are found.

> **Important** There is no way to guarantee the position of the custom task will be the same on all Small Business Server machines. In order for the extension mechanism to work, custom tasks must be added programmatically to the registry following the steps above.

4. For each sub key added, create the following strings:

    - **URL**. The target page to open. This should be in URL format only. Any special actions should be handled by ASP code on the target page.
    - **Description Text**. The tooltip text that describes what the task does. It should be in HTML.
    - "Enabled"=dword:00000001
    - "Target"=dword:00000001
    - **Product**. This is the name of the product installing the customization. This should be a user-friendly and informative name that can be recognized in the user interface, for example, "Bob's technology consultant backup", not just "backup extension."
    - **Title Text**. The title of the link as it should appear on the page. It should be formatted in HTML.

> **Note** A sub key may be removed by setting the "Enabled" dword as follows: "Enabled"=dword:00000000. Do not remove the key itself.

▶ **To replace an existing page**

1. Click **Start**, and then click **Run**. Type **regedit** in the dialog box to open the Registry Editor.

2. For each item that appears on the **Tasks** and **More Tasks** page, find the corresponding key under the respective registry locations:

   - **More Tasks page**:

     HKEY_LOCAL_MACHINE\Software\Microsoft\Small Business\Console\BgTasks

   - **Tasks page**:

     HKEY_LOCAL_MACHINE\Software\Microsoft\Small Business\Console\SmTasks

   Each key has the following string: "Enabled"=dword:00000001.

3. If the value of the "Enabled" dword is 00000001, then the link will appear on the **Tasks** or **More Tasks** page. In order to replace this link, set the value of the dword as follows: "Enabled"=dword:00000000.

4. Create your own custom task following the steps in the previous procedure, "To create additional tasks on the Tasks or More Tasks pages."

Note To uninstall the link, the "Enabled" dword for the page that was replaced is reset as follows: "Enabled"=dword:00000001. Do not remove the key itself.

Adding Tasks with the Small Business Server Customization Tool

The Small Business Server Customization Tool, which may be installed from the *Small Business Server 4.5 Resource Kit CD*, can be used to automatically add links to the following Small Business Server console pages:

- Home
- Tasks
- More Tasks

If you do not want to perform manual configuration of the registry to add links to console pages, as specified in the previous paragraphs, you can use a Small Business Server Customization Tool feature called **Customize SBS Console** to automatically configure the links to be added to the console pages. Refer to *Part 10, Tools and Utilities*, of this resource guide for information on how to install and use the Customization Tool.

Adding Sub Pages and Secondary Sub Pages

The sub page can be created once the **Tasks** or **More Tasks** page has been extended, so the tasks navigates to it when selected. A new sub page can easily be created by deciding which style is appropriate and then making the necessary changes. When doing this, observe the guidelines outlined in the "Page Layout and Design" section discussed earlier.

> **Note** An easy way to create a new sub page is to use an existing sub page and change the values to reflect your custom task.

Sub Page Requirements

- Sub pages must meet the following requirements:
- DHTML is used for the sub page.
- Jscript is the primary scripting language.
- ActiveX® can be contained on the sub page.

Sub Page Components

There are five major components of a sub page as follows.

- **Title**. The title of the page should be the same as the title of the link on the **Tasks** or **More Tasks** page. In the Small Business Server sub pages, it is defined by the following variable:

    L_szTaskpadTitle_StaticText

- **Description**. If on a **Status** page, the description should provide an overview of the page. If on a **List View** page, it should provide details on the list. In the Small Business Server sub pages, this is defined by the following variable:

    L_szTaskpadDescription_StaticText

- **Task Buttons**. Eight task buttons are allowed on a page before scrolling occurs (16 for the Status layout). Task buttons should perform an action. For example, the task button should launch a wizard, complete the specified task, or open a help procedure to guide the user through the completion of the specified task. In the Small Business Server sub pages, the titles of these task buttons are defined by the following variable:

    L_szBtnCaptions_Button[#]

    where # is the number of the task button

The tooltips for these task buttons are defined by the following variable:

L_szBtnTooltips_Tooltip[#]

where # is the number of the task button

The symbol for these task buttons are defined by the following variable:

gaszBtnSymbols[#]

where # is the number of the task button

Important For more information on how symbols are referenced and defined, see the "Symbols" section later in this chapter.

The action these task buttons perform are then defined using a case statement.

```
case '0':
    jscript;
    break;
case '1':
    etc.
```

- **About Link.** The link to the appropriate overview topic in the Online Guide. It should appear in the upper right-hand corner of the page. In the Small Business Server sub pages, the text of this link is defined by the following variable:

  L_szTaskpadAbout_Address

  The HTML page this link should load in the Online Guide is defined by the following variable:

  gszAboutLink

- **Status.** An ActiveX control that displays various status information pertaining to the page. In List View styles, this is typically a list box that lists the items the page manages. The status information is meant to be a quick reference to the items in question.

For example, on the **Manage Users** page, the list box displays the users. The list box could also display full user name, their descriptions, and countless other pieces of information. At a quick glance, however, the user's full name is the most useful. We recommend that, in deciding what information to display as status information, you follow these guidelines:

- What does the user need to know?
- What will the user be looking for?
- What will the user understand?

You can omit status information if it doesn't seem applicable. In this case, use the No List View style.

Symbols

Each button on a sub page should have a corresponding symbol. The symbol used for a button should correspond to the verb associated with the task the button performs. For example, if the button adds a user, use the "add" symbol.

A symbol is also used for the watermark on the sub page. Here it corresponds to the noun associated with the sub page. For example, if the sub page deals with managing users, use the "user" symbol.

To view the symbols supplied with the Small Business Server, install the following fonts from the Symbols directory on the *Microsoft BackOffice Small Business Server Resource Kit CD:*

- Glyph100.ttf
- Glyph110.ttf
- Glyph_map.html

Then use the Glyph_map.html file to view the various symbols and find the corresponding value of the symbols.

Important It is possible to create your own symbols by creating your own font. However, the Small Business Server sub pages provided reference Small Business Server fonts and associated symbols.

Installation Mechanism

You can manually extend the Small Business Server console with additional pages as described below, or you can create an installation application to perform the steps in the order shown.

▶ **To extend the console with an installation application**

1. Copy your HTML files to the server. The preferred directory is:

    %SBS%\SmallBusiness\Html

2. Copy any files needed by your console page to the server.

3. Create your custom key in the registry by following the procedures outlined in the "Extension Mechanism for Console Pages" section, earlier in this chapter.

The installation application could also have an uninstallation procedure which does the following.

▶ **To remove the installation application**

1. Remove all HTML and other associate files from the appropriate directory on the server.

2. Disable your extension by changing the value of the Enabled field in the registry.

Console Page Extension Changes From SBS 4.0a

The following summarizes the changes in extension implementation from SBS 4.0a to SBS 4.5:

- Changes to the registry are no longer made directly to the SmTasks and BgTasks keys. Instead, changes are made to the CustomSmTasks and CustomBgTasks keys to determine what extensions exist.

- These registry entries are no longer used:

   Action. This has been changed to **URL**. Previously, this entry supported specifying the Visual Basic Script to execute the button click. In order to provide backwards compatibility moving forward, this entry has been limited to an HTML target in the 4.5 release. The HTML file can be an ASP page which executes JScript®.

   ImageFile and **ImageID**. Icons are no longer displayed on the **Tasks** and **More Tasks** pages in the console.

- These registry entries are now required:

   Target

   Enabled

   LinkCount

- These requirements are no longer true of sub pages:

   Back Button. The back button functionality is built into the navigation bar across the top of the console. As a result it is not needed on the sub page.

   Icons. Icons are no longer used on sub pages.

- These requirements are now true for sub pages:

   DHTML must be used for the sub page.

   Jscript must be the primary scripting language.

   Scalable sub pages must use symbols or another form of scalable art to support the scalability of the console.

Upgrading From Small Business Server 4.0(a)

During the upgrade from Small Business Server 4.0(a) to 4.5, the SmallBusiness key in the registry is updated. As a result, extensions made to the Small Business Server 4.0(a) machine will not automatically be preserved. The Small Business Server 4.0(a) SmallBusiness key will however, be copied to SmallBusinessOld. All of the changes made to the Small Business Server 4.0(a) registry can then be manually moved to the new format described in the previous sections.

Extension Mechanism for the Online Guide

The *Online Guide* is made up of HTML files and is easily extended by creating the appropriate HTML files and linking them into the existing structure. If the extension is performed correctly, these new topics can be accessed from the following locations:

- Directly from the console
- From the Find tab
- From the Table Of Contents tab

The following sections provide details about how to add files to the *Online Guide* and make the appropriate modifications to integrate the new topics.

Topic Files

There are several different types of *Online Guide* help topics. The type you use depends on the type of information you want to convey to the user. In addition to selecting the appropriate type of topic, present the information in each topic in a similar fashion.

> **Note** The best way to see how these topics are structured and used, study the Online Guide files in the following server directory location: %systemdrive%\Winnt.sbs\Help\Sbs.srv\htm.

Overview Topics

Overview topics contain a general overview of key concepts and features. Typically they are associated with the About link on a console page. They should begin with a brief introduction (one to three sentences) that concisely explains the benefits and relevance of the topic. This overview should be followed with everything (from end-to-end) required for each feature or concept in the topic. The idea is to get users to the point where they are able to enjoy the benefits of the topic. This may include explanatory information, planning information, or recommendations. The overview topics are made up of three HTM files:

- **Top-level container file**. Sets up the frame structure for the left and right content files. This file typically ends in 000.htm.
- **Left-frame file**. Contains the symbol corresponding to the content described in the right-frame file and a link to the related console page. This file typically ends in 00L.htm.
- **Right-frame file**. Contains the overview information on the topic. This file typically ends in 00R.htm.

Manage Topics

Manage topics contain a general overview of the procedures that can be performed for the given topic. Manage topics should begin with a brief introduction to the topic. The procedures should be grouped and listed with an introduction included for each group. Like overview topics, manage topics are made up of three HTM files:

- **Top-level container file**. Sets up the frame structure for the left and right content files. This file typically ends in 000.htm
- **Left-frame file**. Contains the symbol corresponding to the content described in the right-frame file and a link to the related console page. This file typically ends in 00L.htm
- **Right-frame file**. Acts as an index to all of the procedural topics, related to the general topic, grouped by task. This file typically ends in 00R.htm.

Procedure Topics

Procedural topics should open in a separate window from the Small Business Server console and provide step-by-step information on how to complete a specific task. These topics should have a title that describes the task or the task goal. The rest of the topic should contain essential steps to achieve the goal. Procedural topics should always be in their own windows and therefore should link only to other procedural topics.

Troubleshooting Topics

Troubleshooting topics should open in a separate window from the Small Business Server console. These topics should have a title that describes the problem or the symptom a user experiences. The topic itself contains solutions to the problem.

Adding Topic Files

To add new HTML to the *Online Guide*, copy the new files into the following directory:

%systemdrive%\Winnt.sbs\Help\Sbs.srv\Htm

This ensures the new pages can be accessed from the console and that those files will be included in searches from the **Find** tab.

It is important to ensure that the new *Online Guide* files use the same style sheet used by all the other *Online Guide* topics. Doing so provides the user with a familiar interface and maintains consistency throughout the *Online Guide*. The style sheets used by the *Online Guide* are found in the following directory:

%systemdrive%\Winnt.sbs\Help\Sbs.srv\Htm

Elements Inside Topic Files

The following sections describe various elements available within an Online Guide HTML file.

Console Page Links

The left-frame and right-frame files in the Overview topics may contain links directly to the Small Business Server console. The syntax for the link is:

```
<A HREF="javascript:top.Frame_Taskpad.location.href =
'http://localhost/Admin/consolepage.htm',1)">Link Title</A>
```

Topic Links

The various *Online Guide* topic files can contain links to other topic files. Overview or Manage topics can link to the same type of topic. To link to another overview or manage topic, the syntax for the link is:

```
<A HREF="filename.htm" target="_parent">Link Title</A>
```

To link to a procedure topic from within an Overview or Manage topic, the syntax for the link is:

```
<A HREF="javascript:ShowHelpWrapper('http:/localhost/help/sbs.srv/htm/
filename.htm')">Link Title</A>
```

Procedure or Troubleshooting topics should only link to other procedure or troubleshooting topics, since the topic will appear in the same pop-up window as the original procedure topic. To link to another procedure or troubleshooting topic the syntax for the link is:

```
<A HREF="filename.htm">Link Title</A>
```

Extending the Table of Contents

To add new topics to the *Online Guide* table of contents, you must create a table of contents file (.hhc) and add your table of contents file to OEM.hhc.

OEM.hhc

OEM.hhc, will need to be created the first time the table of contents is extended and should be placed in the following directory:

%systemdrive%\Winnt.sbs\Help\Sbs.srv\Misc

The template file for OEM.hhc can be found on Small Business Server installation CD 3, in the following location:

SBSadmin\i386\Help\Sbs.srv\Extend

To add your table of contents file to OEM.hhc, the following addition must be made to the OEM.hhc file:

```
<OBJECT type="text/sitemap">
<param name="merge" value="../misc/myextension.hhc">
</OBJECT>
```

This entry should be made just before the </HTML> tag.

Important There is no way to guarantee the position of the table of contents entry in the table of contents. In order for the extension mechanism to work, table of contents entries must be added programmatically to the OEM.hhc file following the outline above.

Additionally, there is no way to disable the table of contents entry for files included with the Small Business Server. For example, if you were to disable one of the console pages, the associated table of contents entry and help files would still remain available.

Table of Contents File

The OEM.hhc file can be used as a template for your table of contents file. To add content to this file, insert the following section:

```
<UL>
<LI>
<OBJECT type="Text/sitemap">
<param name="Name" value="Title of Section to Appear in TOC">
<param name="Local" value="">
```

```
</OBJECT>
<A HREF="myextension.hhc"> Title of Section to Appear in TOC</A>
</LI>
<UL>
    Insert Help File Entries Here.
</UL>
</UL>
```

This section should be added just before the </HTML> tag. Then, for each Help topic to appear in the table of contents, the appropriate list item must be added. The following sections outline the entries that should be made for each Help file, organized by topic file type.

Overview and Manage Topic

Overview and Manage topics require the following entry:

```
<LI>
<OBJECT type="Text/sitemap">
<param name="Name" value="Title of Topic">
<param name="Local"value="http://localhost/help/sbs.srv/htm/filename000.htm">
<param name="ImageNumber" value="13">
</OBJECT>
<A HREF="http://localhost/help/sbs.srv/htm/filename000.htm">Title of Topic</A>
</LI>
```

Procedure Topics

Procedure Topics links require the following entry:

```
<LI>
<OBJECT type="Text/sitemap">
<param name="Name" value="Title of Topic">
<param name="Local" value="">
<param name="ImageNumber" value="11">
<param name="SendEvent" value=
"*http://Localhost/Help/Sbs.srv/htm/filename.htm">
</OBJECT>
<A HREF="http://localhost/help/sbs.srv/htm/filename000.htm">Title of Topic</A>
</LI>
```

Troubleshooting Links

Troubleshooting topics require the following entry:

```
<LI>
<OBJECT type="Text/sitemap">
<param name="Name" value="Title of Topic">
<param name="Local" value="">
<param name="ImageNumber" value="9">
<param name="SendEvent" value=
"*http://Localhost/Help/Sbs.srv/htm/filename.htm">
</OBJECT>
<A HREF="http://localhost/help/sbs.srv/htm/filenamc000.htm">Title of
Topic</A>
</LI>
```

Integrating with Console Sub Pages

There are several different types of Help links that can be used to access Help topics in the *Online Guide*. The type depends on the nature of the topic.

About Links

Every console page has an About link that gives an overview of what is on the page, why it is important, and what actions can be performed there. This is also where additional information is placed not specific to the tasks on the page.

The About link is located at the top right of each console page. All that is required to be specified on the sub page is the title of the About link and the HTML page.

Overview Links

In addition to the About link, some tasks may need to open an overview topic that switches to the *Online Guide*. Overview topics usually correspond to a task that is extra long, requires planning, or needs additional information such as graphics, as opposed to step-by-step instructions.

Links to Overview topics are implemented from a button on a sub page. The button must be defined on the sub page and the necessary parameters specified.

Procedure Links

For actions on sub pages where no programmatic interface is available to create a wizard, a procedure topic window should be used. When a button is clicked, the procedure topic window opens and creates a window with instructions on how to complete the task. In addition to the instructions, the window usually contains one or more shortcuts to start any applications needed to complete the task.

Procedure topics are linked-to from a sub page button. The button must be defined on the sub page and the necessary parameters specified.

Troubleshooting Links

Throughout the Small Business Server console, there are many troubleshooting topics. On each sub page, a button launches a help window with related troubleshooting topics. The troubleshooting links are scripted the same way as procedure links.

Installation

Perform the following steps in general to manually extend the Small Business Server console subpages for Online Guide integration, or create an installation application that can perform the steps listed in the order shown.

▶ **To extend the Online Guide with an installation application**

1. Copy your HTML files to the server. The preferred directory is :

   %SBS%\Winnt.sbs\Help\Sbs.srv\Htm

2. Add a reference to your .hhc file to OEM.hhc.

3. Copy your extension .hhc file to the server. The preferred directory is:

   %SBS%\Winnt.sbs\Help\Sbs.srv\Misc

The installation application could also have an uninstallation procedure which does the following:

- Remove your entry in the OEM.hhc file from the server.
- Removes all associated HTML files.

Important Integrating with the *Online Guide* is not recommended without a corresponding extension to the Small Business Server console.

Online Guide Integration Changes From SBS 4.0a

The following summarizes the changes in extension implementation from Small Business Server 4.0(a) to Small Business Server version 4.5:

- The style sheets and scripting used to launch procedural topics and overview topics have been updated. Use the templates provided to transfer your content into the new files with the updated scripting.
- The table of contents can now be extended. Follow the information in "Extending the Table of Contents" to add your help files.
- There is no separate troubleshooting search, so the meta tag required for the troubleshooting search is no longer necessary.
- All files in the %systemdrive%\Winnt.sbs\Help\Sbs.srv\Htm directory will be searched, so the meta tag required to exclude files from the search is no longer necessary.

CHAPTER 44

Extension Mechanism for the Set Up Computer Wizard

The details of installing a third-party application on the Microsoft® BackOffice® Small Business Server can be simplified by extending the Set Up Computer Wizard application list. By integrating with the Set Up Computer Wizard, the third-party application then becomes available for deployment and installation on client computers throughout the Small Business Server network.

Extension of the Application List in the Set Up Computer Wizard

To extend the application list in the Set Up Computer Wizard, the following three things need to be done:

- Make sure your setup program can perform an unattended installation and suppress its reboot requirement, thereby enabling it to integrate with the Set Up Computer Wizard.
- Create an information file (INF) detailing how to install your application. The Set Up Computer Wizard will use this INF file to run the setup program on the client computer.
- Modify existing Set Up Computer Wizard client setup files to include your application.

The following sections outline the information necessary to extend the Set Up Computer Wizard application list with your application.

Integration Requirement

To integrate with the Set Up Computer Wizard, your application setup program must support the following:

- An unattended or automated install mode, enabling Small Business Server to automate installations on Small Business Server clients.
- No order dependencies for installing multiple applications.
- The option to eliminate the reboot prompt.

> **Important** If your application uses InstallShield for setup, you must use the –SMS option on the install command line. Without this option, the silent install will start another process to complete the installation, thus the Set Up Computer Wizard continues installing remaining applications without waiting for your application to finish its installation. The end result may be that Set Up Computer Wizard asks the user to reboot before your application has fully installed.

Creating Your Application INF File

To add your application to the Set Up Computer Wizard, a standard setup INF file is required. This section details the INF file entries required to integrate with Set Up Computer Wizard. For more information on the INF file and setting up your application, see the documentation that accompanied your setup management software.

Along with standard required information in your application's INF file, you must provide the following for the Set Up Computer Wizard:

- The INF section name that provides information about your setup application.
- The command line text to install your application on the client workstation.
- The amount of disk space in megabytes your application needs during installation, including temporary files and directories.
- Message strings your application may need to display during installation.

To create the INF file for your setup application, perform the following steps.

> **Note** Only one application per INF file is allowed.

▶ **To create the INF file for your setup application**

1. Include the required **[Version]** section.
2. Under the **[Version]** section, include the Signature parameter with the value **$WINDOWS NT$**.
3. Include the **[Optional Components]** section.
4. In the **[Optional Components]** section, include the INF section name that provides the information about your setup application.
5. In your **[application]** section, you can use the optional **OptionDesc and Tip** parameters to provide explanatory text about your application to Set Up Computer Wizard. The values for these optional parameters must be string parameters defined in the **[Strings]** section.
6. In your **[application]** section, add the **IconIndex** parameter with the index number of 0 for an extension application.
7. In your **[application]** section, add the **InstallCmd** parameter with the actual quoted text required to run your setup program in unattended mode. Do not use a value from the **[String]** section.

   Use the **%SBSServer%** environment variable for the path to the server, and construct the install command from that location. Small Business Server shares the %SBSServer%\Clients directory that you can use for this purpose. If you don't use the %SBSServer%\Clients directory, then you will have to make sure that users who install your application have permission to run programs in the %SBSServer%\Clients directory.

8. In your **[application]** section, add the **DiskSpaceEstimate** parameter with the number of megabytes your setup application needs on the client computer during installation. This includes temporary directories.
9. In the **[Strings]** section, add the string parameters for the optional messages you need.

Example of INF File

The following example shows a fictional INF file by the developer of the fictional Bob's Time Card Application.

```
;
; myapp.inf
;
; Component INF for installing My Application. This example includes
; only the sections necessary to integrate with the Set Up Computer
Wizard.
;
; The Version section is required for all INF files. See the SDK for
; other legal values.
;
```

```
[Version]
Signature = "$Windows NT$"
;
; This section contains the name of the section that
; contains your application setup information.
;
[Optional Components]
myapp
;
; This is the application section.
;
[myapp]
;
; Optional 'application description' and 'tip' to be displayed in the
Set Up Computer Wizard.
; The myapp_desc and myapp_tip strings are defined in the [Strings]
section.
;
OptionDesc = %myapp_desc%
Tip = %myapp_tip%
;
; Required icon definition for the extension application setup program.
;
IconIndex = 0
;
; Required value for the command-prompt unattended installation.
; The %SBSServer% variable is the location of the small business
; server software.
;
InstallCmd = "\\%SBSServer%\clients\myapp\setup /q"
;
; Required value for the amount of disk space required on the client
; computer during installation, specified in MB.
;
DiskSpaceEstimate = 7
;
; Standard section. Required when you use string parameters.
;
[Strings]
;
; This value is used in the OptionDesc parameter
;
myapp_desc = "My Application"
;
; This value is used in the Tip parameter
;
myapp_tip = "Allows users to use my application."
```

Response File Requirements

If your setup program uses a response file during its unattended mode, you must do the following:

- Create a master copy (template) of the response file to be used for all client installations of your application. This template file should be stored in the location specified in the Set Up Computer Wizard by your application.
- Within this master copy, use Set Up Computer Wizard variable names for fields that need to be substituted during installation. For example, HomeDir=%SBSServer%

Note The use of a response file is not a requirement of integrating with the Set Up Computer Wizard.

Note At present, **%SBSServer%** is the only Set Up Computer Wizard variable name defined. Future versions of Set Up Computer Wizard will provide others.

Adding Your Application to Scw.ini

The Set Up Computer Wizard file (Scw.ini) is located in the following directory:

%SBS%\SmallBusiness\

This file is used by Set Up Computer Wizard to determine the application that should be displayed in the application list. The following sections outline the requirements for adding your application to the Small Business Server scw.ini file.

Increment the Number of Applications

The number of applications is identified under the [**SCW_OptionalApplications**] section with the **SCW_NumberOfApps** entry. The current value of the number will be the number your application uses when adding information to Scw.ini. This number must be incremented. For example, if prior to modification, the Scw.ini file contains the following lines:

```
[SCW_OptionalApplications]
SCW_NumberOfApps=6
```

then the identification number for your application will be 6. Your pre-installation program must increment this to the next greatest number (in this case, to 7) before it adds the information about your application.

Add Application Information

Once you have determined your application number, your preinstallation program needs to add the following information to the **[SCW_OptionalApplications]** section of the scw.ini file.

Note You must append the number of your application to each key name (represented in the example below by *x*).

SCW_AppName*x*=<*application symbol name*>
Internal name Set Up Computer Wizard uses to identify your application. Do not use spaces in the application symbol name. This value is required and will be used later when modifying Clioc.inf.

SCW_AppDisplayString*x*=<*message display name*>
This is the string Set Up Computer Wizard displays in message boxes and log files. You can use spaces in the message display name. This value is required.

SCW_AppSelectedByDefault*x*=[NO|YES]
If Yes, the Set Up Computer Wizard enables the check box to set up your application. If No, the Set Up Computer Wizard clears the check box. Either Yes or No is required.

SCW_AppRequiresUnattendedTextFile*x*=[NO|YES]
If Yes, your application requires a response file for unattended mode. (You must also provide the response file.) If No, your application requires no response file. Either Yes or No is required.

SCW_AppTemplatePath*x*=<*appUnattend/ResponsePath*>
Path and name of the application file. This path must be relative to the %SBSServer%\SmallBusiness directory. The Template directory is the preferred location.

SCW_AppTemplateSourceName*x*=<*appTemplateSourceName*>
Initial name of the unattend/response file template at the location specified in SCW_AppTemplatePath*x*.

SCW_AppTemplateDestName*x*=<*appTemplateDestName*>
The name to which the SCW_AppTemplateSourceName*x* file must be changed when it is copied to the client response directory.

Note This can be the same as the Source name or different from it, depending on what your setup requires.

SCW_AppSetupInfPathx=*Template*
Path to your application INF file. This path must be relative to the %SBSServer%\SmallBusiness directory. The Template directory is the preferred location.

SCW_AppSetupInfSourceNamex=*<appSetupInfSource>*
This is the initial name of your application INF file.

SCW_AppSetupInfDestNamex=*<appSetupInfDest>*
The name to which the SCW_AppSetupInfSourceNamex file must be changed when it is copied to the client response directory.

SCW ArchitectureListx=*[win95|i386]*
If your applications run on Windows 95 only, specify **win95**. If your application runs on Windows NT, specify **i386**. If your application runs on Windows 95 and Windows NT, specify both **win95** and **i386**.

Example of Scw.ini Modification

The following excerpt details how "My Application" would be defined in the Scw.ini file **[SCW_OptionalApplications]** section.

```
[SCW_OptionalApplications]
;
; The value for SCW_NumberOfApps is read and then incremented for the
next application
;
SCW_NumberOfApps=7
;
; The following lines reflect the new fields that need to be created
when
; adding an application to Set Up Computer Wizard.
;
; The following entry is the name of your application to be used by the
Set Up Computer Wizard (not displayed).
;
SCW_AppName6=myapp
;
; The following entries define how your application is displayed in
; the applications list, and whether or not an unattended file is
; required.
;
SCW_AppDisplayString6=My Application
SCW_AppSelectedByDefault6=YES
SCW_AppRequiresUnattendedTextFile6= NO
;
; The following three entries are unused options, since no
; unattended/response file is required for installation. Had one been
; required, these would have been specified.
;
```

```
SCW_AppTemplatePath6=
SCW_AppTemplateSourceName6=
SCW_AppTemplateDestName6=
;
; The following entries inform the Set Up Computer Wizard of the
; location of the INF file and what operating system your
;application will install on.
;
SCW_AppSetupInfPath6=Template
SCW_AppSetupInfSourceName6=myapp.inf
SCW_AppSetupInfDestName6= myapp.inf
SCW_AppArchitectureList6=win95
```

Set Up Computer Wizard detects the end of your entry when it encounters the next SCW_AppNamex= entry.

Adding Your Application to Clioc.inf

The client optional component file (Clioc.inf) is located in the following directory:

%SBS%\SmallBusiness\Template

This file is used by the Set Up Computer Wizard to determine the INF files required for each application listed. The name and identifier of your application setup INF file must be added to the **[Components]** section of Clioc.inf.

Entries in the **[Components]** section have the following format:

```
"","",<inf-file-name>
```

where *inf-file-name* is the name of the information file you supply with your setup program.

Note The first two quote-enclosed null fields in the line are required.

The following shows the contents of the default Clioc.inf file.

```
[Components.w95]
proxy = "","",cliproxy.inf
outlook = "","",clioutl.inf
clifax = "","",clifax.inf
mshare = "","",climshr.inf
ie3 = "","",cliie3.inf
myapp = ,"",myapp.inf
client = ..\..\setup\win95\ocsam.dll,OcEntry,client.inf
```

```
[Components.x86]
proxy   = "","",cliproxy.inf
outlook = "","",clioutl.inf
clifax  = "","",ntfax.inf
mshare  = "","",ntmshr.inf
ie3     = "","",cliie3.inf
myapp   = ,"",myapp.inf
client  = ..\..\setup\i386\ocsam.dll,OcEntry,client.inf
```

The entry for your application should be placed immediately before the client entry, like the entry created for *myapp* in italics.

Note Do not change the order of any of the applications already listed. It is not possible to specify the order in which your application will be installed. In order for this extension model to work, additions to this file must be made in a programmatic manner. Furthermore, if your installation program places the entry for your application setup INF file in another location within Clioc.inf, Set Up Computer Wizard will ignore that entry. Users will not be able to install your application.

If your application runs on both the Windows NT and Windows 95 platforms, you must add the line describing your application to both the Components.w95 and Components.x86 blocks. If the application runs only on Windows 95, then add your application to the Components.w95 section only.

In addition, you must add a register key and value so Set Up Computer Wizard can detect whether your application is already installed. You do this by adding a section to the end of the Clioc.inf file in the following format:

```
HKLM="<register key>","<value>"
```

For example:

```
[myapp]
HKLM="SOFTWARE\MyCompany\MyApp\Installed","YES"
```

Installation

The steps to add your application to the Set Up Computer Wizard application list can be performed manually as described in the following steps, or you can also create an installation application to perform these steps in the order specified.

▶ **To add your application to the Set Up Computer Wizard application list**

1. Copy the INF file for your application to the directory you specify in Scw.ini. The preferred directory is:

   %SBS%\SmallBusiness\Template.

2. Copy all the files needed by your actual client setup program to the server location specified in the INF file.
3. Modify the Set Up Computer Wizard initialization file, Scw.ini.
4. Modify the client optional component file, Clioc.inf.

Your installation application could also include an uninstallation routine to perform the steps discussed in the next section.

Removing Your Application from the Set Up Computer Wizard

If you choose to remove your application from the Set Up Computer Wizard there are a series of steps that must be followed. Your application uninstallation must back out all the changes that were made to both Scw.ini and Clioc.inf. To do this, perform the following steps:

▶ **To remove your application from the Set Up Computer Wizard**

1. Decrement the number of Optional Applications in Scw.ini by decrementing the following lines:

   [SCW_OptionalApplications]

   SCW_NumberOfApps=6

2. Remove your application section from Scw.ini.
3. Decrement the application number for each section that appears after your application in Scw.ini. For example, if your application section was numbered 4 after removing it, check to see if other applications were added below yours. If there is an application 5, all references to it must be changed to 4, and so on for any remaining applications. In the following section, this would involve changing every occurrence of the number 5 to 4.

   ```
   SCW_AppName5=NextApp
   SCW_AppDisplayString5=Next Application
   SCW_AppSelectedByDefault5=NO
   SCW_AppRequiresUnattendedTextFile5=NO
   ;
   SCW_AppTemplatePath5=
   SCW_AppTemplateSourceName5=
   SCW_AppTemplateDestName5=
   ```

```
;
SCW_AppSetupInfPath5=Template
SCW_AppSetupInfSourceName5=nextapp.inf
SCW_AppSetupInfDestName5=nextapp.inf
SCW_AppArchitectureList5=win95
```

4. Remove your application section from Clioc.inf.

Set Up Computer Wizard Extension Changes from SBS 4.0a

The following summarizes the changes in extension implementation from Small Business Server 4.0(a) to Small Business Server version 4.5.

- The client installation no longer provides a mechanism for uninstalling applications. As a result, the uninstall command line is no longer needed for integration with the Set Up Computer Wizard in your application's INF.

- You no longer need to create a safe copy of Scw.ini and Clioc.inf. If the Small Business Server Setup is executed to add an application that was not initially installed, these files will remain untouched.

- It is no longer possible to specify the icon to be displayed during the client installation program for your application. The default IconIndex of 0 should be used.

Upgrading from Small Business Server 4.0(a)

During the upgrade from Small Business Server 4.0(a) to version 4.5, Scw.ini and Clioc.inf will be updated. As a result, extensions made to Set Up Computer Wizard on a Small Business Server 4.0(a) machine will not be automatically preserved. The Scw.ini and Clioc.inf files will, however, be copied to Scw.old and Clioc.old. All of the changes made to Small Business Server 4.0(a) files can then be manually moved to the new files on the Small Business Server 4.5 machine.

CHAPTER 45

Using the MSDE Solution with Microsoft Access 2000

With the release of Microsoft® Access 2000, users and developers have the choice of utilizing two data engines in the product—an improved version of the existing Access engine called the Jet Database Engine, or the Microsoft Data Engine (MSDE), which is compatible with Microsoft SQL Server™ 7.0.

MSDE is an enabling technology that provides local data storage and offers compatibility with SQL Server 7.0. This is similar to the Jet Database Engine, which is the data engine that currently exists in Microsoft Access. Although Access 2000 uses and installs the Jet Database Engine data engine by default, developers who want to develop a single application that is also compatible with Microsoft SQL Server 7.0 should use MSDE.

The information in this chapter is intended to help the technology consultant understand the advantages of using the MSDE solution with Access for SQL Server 7.0 compatibility, in comparison to the limitations of the Jet Database Engine. The data engines are compared in the following three ways:

- Organizational requirements
- Usage analysis
- Feature analysis

Generally speaking, the Jet Database Engine works best for the greatest compatibility with Access 97 or earlier versions. MSDE works best if you want to develop from a single code base, from a single user to thousands of users, or if a future need for scalability is anticipated.

Microsoft Access Features

Microsoft Access 2000 is a powerful relational database application which a desktop user can use to efficiently create and manipulate database systems. Access targets the desktop category and works best for individuals and workgroups managing megabytes of data. For multiuser access to the same database, Access uses file-server architecture, rather than client-server architecture. Access is included in the Professional and Developer Editions of Microsoft Office 2000.

Microsoft Access makes it easy for users to find and manage their data to make better business decisions. Access 2000 is strongly integrated with Microsoft Office 2000, offering a similar appearance and functionality to other applications in the Office 2000 suite.

Access provides ease-of-use wizards throughout, such as the Database Wizard for getting up and running quickly, and the Simple Query Wizard for easily finding information from the data. More advanced features include Microsoft Visual Basic® for Applications programming language, programmable toolbars, and the freely distributable runtime version of Access 2000 available with the Office 2000 Developer Edition.

Access Components

Access has two major components. The first is the application development environment for Visual Basic for Applications programmers that include forms technology, reports, and database administration. In addition, there is also the User Interface (UI) common to both Access and the other Office 2000 applications. The second component in Access 2000 is the data engine—the main topic of this chapter. Before Access 2000, users and developers were using the Jet Database Engine, the only data engine provided with earlier versions of Access. In Access 2000, users and developers are given a choice of data engines. They can continue to use the improved version of the Access default data engine, Jet Database Engine 4.0, or they can use the new option, MSDE.

Overview of Jet Database Engine 4.0 and MSDE

The sections that follow describe enhancements made to the Jet Database Engine and introduce the functionality of MSDE.

Jet Database Engine

The Jet Database Engine 4.0 is the default data engine for Access 2000. It is a new and improved version of Jet 3.51, the data engine in Access 97. The Jet Database Engine 4.0 contains the following enhancements:

- Full Unicode support.
- Sorting compatibility with the Windows NT®, Windows® 95, and Windows 98 operating systems.
- Row-level locking.
- Enhanced support for American National Standards Institute (ANSI) SQL92 and compatibility with SQL Server (examples include GRANT/REVOKE, DECIMAL type data type, and Declarative Referential Integrity).
- Jet database /SQL Server 7 bi-directional replication.
- Enhanced replication-conflict resolution.
- Native object linking and embedding database (OLE DB) provider.

Microsoft Data Engine

MSDE is the new data engine for Access 2000 which is completely compatible with the SQL Server version 7.0 code base. This enables customers to write one application that scales from a PC running the Windows 95 operating system to multiprocessor clusters running Windows NT Server, Enterprise Edition. Some of the technologies included in MSDE are:

- **Dynamic Locking** Automatically selects the optimal level of lock (row, key range page, or table) for all database operations. It maximizes the trade-off between concurrency and performance, resulting in optimal usage. No tuning is required.
- **Unicode**. Improves multilingual support.
- **Dynamic Self-Management**. Enables the server to monitor and manage itself, allowing for hands-off standard operations.
- **Merge Replication**. Allows users to modify distributed copies of a database at different times, online or offline, and the work is later combined into a single uniform result.

MSDE incorporates technology from SQL Server 7. By using MSDE, developers can later enable hundreds or even thousands of users to use SQL Server 7.0 features like:

- **Data Transformation Services**. Makes it easy to import data from any source, for example OLE databases, Windows NT Directory Services, and spreadsheets, and transform or export the data to any other data source.
- **Microsoft SQL Server OLAP Services**. Enables fast, efficient analysis of complex information by optimizing data access. This enables your organization to quickly retrieve the specific data it needs. The PivotTable® Services run on client workstations and provide desktop multidimensional analysis by making the PivotTable dynamic views more intuitive and putting all of the PivotTable options on the screen for your use. For the first time, Excel users can analyze gigabytes and terabytes of data by using Microsoft SQL Server 7.0.
- **English Query**. Allows users to ask questions in English instead of forming queries with complex SQL statements.
- **Parallel Queries**. Allows steps in a single query to be executed in parallel, delivering optimal response time.

Comparing the Jet Database Engine and MSDE

This section compares the two data engines in three different ways—by organizational requirements, usage, and features. This should help you determine which database to use for the small business organization.

Organizational Requirements

If you are developing or using Access in a small business organization (a maximum of 50 users), MSDE is the recommended data engine. At this level, the needs of the small business do not approach the enterprise level, but by using the Access front-end with the MSDE back-end, it is assured that your database will be in the optimal position for scaling to SQL Server 7.0 as the needs of the small business grow.

Enterprise-level applications require scalability, security, and robustness which can be implemented with MSDE or SQL Server, but not with the Jet Database Engine. For example, if your application needs transaction support or you want to be prepared for a network, server, client computer, or client application crash, MSDE or SQL Server should be used. Conversely, the Jet Database Engine does not support atomic transactions. It does not guarantee that all changes performed within a transaction boundary are committed or rolled back.

Another important issue to corporate environments is security. MSDE and SQL Server 7.0 are integrated with Windows NT security, while the Jet Database Engine is not.

The table that follows shows how each of the data engines compare in relation to organizational needs. If your business has any of the needs listed in the left column, you will want to implement MSDE. If it does not, continue on to the next section to determine the right data engine for you.

Table 45.1 Organizational Needs for MSDE and the Jet Database Engine

Requirement	SQL Server (use MSDE if these are future requirements)	Jet Database Engine
Scalability	SMP Support	No SMP support
	Virtually unlimited number of concurrent users	Maximum of 255 users
		2 GB of data
	Terabyte levels of data	No transaction logging
	Transaction Logging	
Business critical support	7x24 support and quick fix engineering (QFE)	No 7x24 support or QFE
		Recoverable to last backup
	Point-in-time recovery	No transaction logging
	Guaranteed transaction integrity	No integrated security with Windows NT
	Built-in fault tolerance	
	Security integrated with Windows NT	

Jet Database Engine and MSDE Usage Analysis

There are four key-usage criteria to consider when choosing the most appropriate database engine. This criteria is provided below in order of priority.

Simplicity of the Jet Database Engine 4.0

The Jet Database Engine 4.0 clearly has the highest compatibility with Access 97 and earlier versions. If you have existing applications developed for Access, the Jet Database Engine is your easiest and probably best option given its compatibility with Access 97 and earlier.

The Jet Database Engine is easier to use and administer than MSDE, making it a good choice for new and relatively simple database applications that do not have compatibility concerns with SQL Server. It has low resources for memory and disk and requires nearly zero administration. The Jet Database Engine is also the default database option for Access 2000. A database created using the Jet Database Engine can always be upsized later to SQL Server using the Upsizing Wizard, although some additional modification may be required.

Data Integrity Advantage of MSDE

MSDE incorporates technology from SQL Server 7.0. SQL Server delivers a single code base, which scales from a PC running Windows 95 to multiprocessor clusters running Windows NT Server, Enterprise Edition, offering 100 percent application compatibility. The Jet Database Engine does not have this type of scalability since it is confined to the Access product.

MSDE is a client/server data engine. The Jet Database Engine is a file/server data engine. The greatest advantage that MSDE has over the Jet Database Engine is that MSDE is a process that runs queries and logs transactions. If anything should go wrong during a write to the database, such as a disk error, network failure, or power failure, MSDE can recover since it logs transactions. After the system comes back up, MSDE will revert back to the last consistent state. This gives MSDE greater reliability than the Jet Database Engine. If the system were to go down with the Jet Database Engine, the database could become corrupt and you may need to revert back to your last backup copy.

MSDE is the better alternative for systems that involve important transactions, such as financial applications, or for mission-critical applications that need to be up 24 hours per day, seven days a week, such as the Internet. The more important the database, the more likely it is that MSDE is the right choice.

Performance Advantages of MSDE

SQL Server 7.0, the basis for MSDE technology, can handle a very large number of simultaneous users. Both the Jet Database Engine and MSDE are optimized for individual or small workgroup solutions.

MSDE outperforms the Jet Database Engine for large sets of data and multiple simultaneous users. Because the Jet Database Engine is a file-server system, the query processing must happen on the client. This involves moving a lot of data over the network for large databases. MSDE runs that same query on the server. This loads the server more, but can reduce network traffic substantially, especially if the users are selecting a small subset of the data. If you are creating a new application for a small group of users, MSDE or SQL Server will help your application scale in the future.

Amount of Data Handling

The Jet Database Engine can handle up to 2 GB of data per .mdb file. MSDE also supports 2 GB of data.

Jet Database Engine and MSDE Feature Analysis

The third criteria for deciding which engine is best for the small business organization rests upon analyzing features of both engines. The table that follows should assist Microsoft Access users in deciding between the Jet Database Engine and MSDE, on the basis of features.

Table 45.2 Jet Database Engine and MSDE Feature Comparison

Features	Jet Database Engine	MSDE
Heterogeneous joins	X	X
Top n and top n% queries	X	X
Validation rules	X	X
Default values	X	X
Triggers and stored procedures		X
Referential integrity through triggers		X
Declarative referential integrity	X	X
Engine-level cascading updates and deletes	X	
Basic locking unit	Row	Row
Row locking on insert	X	X
Field-level replication	X	X
Custom code for replication-conflict resolution	X	X
Scheduled replication	X (requires the Microsoft Office 97, Developer Edition)	X
Built-in security	X (file level read/write password or permissions via OS)	X

(continued)

Table 45.2 Jet Database Engine and MSDE Feature Comparison *(continued)*

Features	Jet Database Engine	MSDE
Built-in encryption	X	X
Distributed transactions		X
Dynamic backup and restore		X
Transaction log backups		X
Automatic Recovery		X
32-bit engine	X	X
Data capacity	2 GB per database	2 GB per database. SQL Server supports TBs per database.

Microsoft Access Upsizing Wizard

The Microsoft Access Upsizing Wizard takes a Jet database and creates an equivalent database on SQL Server. It will recreate table structures, data, indexes, validation rules, defaults, autonumbers, and relationships. It also creates other attributes of the original database and takes advantage of the latest SQL Server functionality wherever possible. However, there are no modifications made to reports, queries, macros, or security. This Upsizing Wizard is included with Office 2000 Professional Edition.

Functions of the Upsizing Wizard

The Upsizing Wizard has three main functions, as follows:

- Migrating databases from Jet to SQL Server.
- Creating Access and SQL Server applications via Jet-linked tables.
- Creating Access and SQL Server applications via Access Projects (new development model that uses an Access project file connected directly to a SQL Server database).

The Upsizing Wizard allows developers who design client-server applications on their desktop in Access to generate a SQL Server database from their prototype. Also, developers who have existing Jet Database Engine-based applications will be able to grow those applications to SQL Server and take advantage of its technology.

The wizard will run from a read-only share and use a temporary database to store information about the upsizing process. All user-preferences will be stored in the registry on a per-user basis.

Summary

The conditions under which each database engine is the most effective with Access 2000 in the small business organization is as follows.

The Jet Database Engine should be used if:

- You want the highest compatibility with Access 97 or earlier versions.
- Your environment has a small number of simultaneous users.
- You have very low resources, such as memory or disk.
- Ease-of-use is a premium.

Use the MSDE database engine if:

- You want to develop from a single code base, from a single user to thousands of users.
- You expect a future need for greater scalability.
- You require easy merge replication with the central server.
- You need the best security.
- You need greater reliability, such as transaction logging.
- Your system is online 24 hours a day, 7 days a week.
- You need stored procedures and triggers.

CHAPTER 46

Other Extensions and Solutions

This chapter covers extensions and solutions that allow the technology consultant to expand Microsoft® BackOffice® Small Business Server 4.5 functionality in the following areas:

- Extending the Server Status Tool to include other application logs in server status reports.
- Creating a team intranet site with the Microsoft Office 60 Minute Intranet Kit.

Extending the Server Status Tool

The Server Status Tool is preconfigured to send five Small Business Server application logs/reports to the technology consultant, as described in *Chapter 26, Administrative Tools*, in *Part 4, Administering and Maintaining* of this resource guide. However, the Server Status Tool may also be extended to include reports for other Small Business Server applications, including those developed by an Independent Software Vendor (ISV). The technology consultant can do this with the Small Business Server Customization Tool. If the Small Business Server Resource Kit is not yet installed on the server, performing the following steps to install the kit and access the Small Business Server Customization Tool.

▶ **To install the Small Business Server Resource Kit**

1. Insert the *Small Business Server 4.5 Resource Kit CD* into your CD-ROM drive on the server computer. The **BackOffice Small Business Server 4.5 Resource Kit CD-ROM** screen is displayed.
2. Click **Explore the CD** to display the CD directory contents.
3. In the CD directory, double-click the **SBS45rk** icon to launch the Small Business Server 4.5 Resource Kit Setup Wizard.

4. Click **Next**, read the end-user agreement, then click **I Agree** when you accept the agreement terms.
5. Click **Install** to begin the installation.
6. When installation is complete, remove the *Small Business Server Resource Kit CD* from the CD-ROM drive. The Resource Kit components and tools are now accessible from the **Start** menu of Small Business Server.

▶ **To extend the Server Status Tool**

1. Log on to Small Business Server as Administrator.
2. On the **Start** menu, point to **Programs**, point to **Resource Kit**, and then click **Tools Management Console** to launch the following RKtmc console.

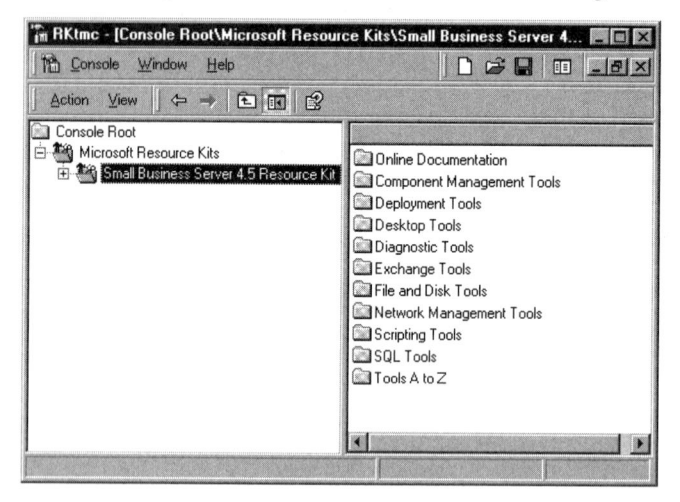

3. Double-click **Microsoft Resource Kits** and then double-click **Small Business Server 4.5 Resource Kit** to display the tool category folders.
4. In the right pane, double-click the **Component Management Tools** folder and then double-click the **SBS Console Extension Tool** to display the following **Small Business Server Customization Tool** dialog box.

| Small Business Server Customization Tool |
| Menu | Adding reports to the Server Status Tool |

Instructions

Customize SBS Console

Configure Server Status Tool

List of Custom Reports: NT Event Viewer

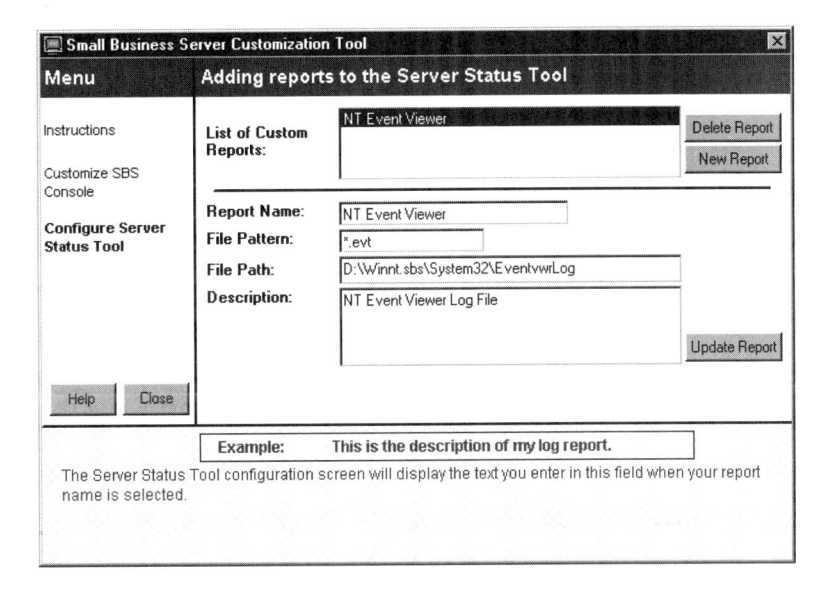

Report Name: NT Event Viewer
File Pattern: *.evt
File Path: D:\Winnt.sbs\System32\EventvwrLog
Description: NT Event Viewer Log File

[Delete Report] [New Report] [Update Report] [Help] [Close]

Example: This is the description of my log report.

The Server Status Tool configuration screen will display the text you enter in this field when your report name is selected.

5. Under **Menu**, click **Configure Server Status Tool**.

Note When the cursor is in an information field, a description of the field function is displayed in the lower pane of the **Customization Tool** dialog box. The NT Event Viewer is used as an example above, although it could also be an ISV application.

6. Click **New Report** to clear all text fields.

Note To remove a report from the **List of Custom Reports**, select the report and click **Delete Report**.

7. In **Report Name**, type the name of the report you are adding.
8. In **File Pattern**, type the kind of file, for example, back*.log.

Note The Server Status Tool queries the directory you specify in the **File Path** field looking for the most recently created log file, based on the information you enter in **File Pattern**.

For example, if the application creates a file called back*.log and you know the file always ends with .log, then the file pattern you should enter is back*.log. The wildcard character (*) represents a variable such as the date of the most recent file, as in back*0101*.log, back*0108*.log, and so on. If your log file will always have the same name, the wildcard character is not needed.

9. In **File Path**, type the location of the log file you want to include in the server status report.
10. In **Description**, type a brief description of the application you are reporting.
11. Click **Add Report** to automatically configure the registry with the appropriate settings that facilitate locating and sending the application log.

> **Note** If you edited existing report information, click **Update Report** to commit the changes to the registry.

12. Click **Close** when finished.

▶ **To verify the application log is included in server status reporting**

1. On the Small Business Server Console, click **configure server status tool** on the **Administration Tools** page.
2. In the displayed online Help, click **Server Status Configuration** to launch the **Server Status Configuration** dialog box.
3. Select the **Reports** tab and verify that your new report is listed there.

Registry Configuration by the Customization Tool

When ISV applications are added to Small Business Server 4.5 using the Small Business Server Customization Tool, the required registry settings are automatically configured. This section describes how the registry is configured by the tool so the application log files may be located and sent. The technology consultant may also use this information to manually configure the registry.

The Small Business Server Customization Tool creates a registry key for the log to be added to the Server Status Tool, and then creates the appropriate values in the key. The registry key created is HKLM//Software/Microsoft/SmallBusiness/VapReporting/LogFiles/*xxxx*, where *xxxx* represents the name of the log. This key informs the Server Status Tool that there is a log file to be added.

The following values are created in the registry key:

- DisplayName.

  The information from the **Report Name** field of the Small Business Server Customization Tool is the display name string used to identify the report name. After registry configuration, the report name is displayed on the **Reports** tab of the **Server Status Configuration** dialog box. If no DisplayName value is found in the registry, the name used defaults to the key name.

- LogFileNamePattern.

  The information from the **File Pattern** field of the Small Business Server Customization Tool is used to specify the LogFileNamePattern. This determines which files are to be sent.

- LogFilePath.

  The information from the **File Path** field of the Small Business Server Customization Tool is used to specify the directory path where the logs can be found, for example, %systemroot%\\System32\\Logfiles. Regedit uses two backslashes (\\) instead of just a one (\).

- Description

  The information from the **Description** field of the Small Business Server Customization Tool is the description string used to explain what the log/report does. After registry configuration, the description string is displayed on the **Reports** tab of the **Server Status Configuration** dialog box.

The following DWORDS are created:

- REG_DWORD SendLog

  SendLog=dword:00000000. 1 is to enable sending the log; 0 is for not sending the log. When viewing in Regedit, the value will look like 0x00000000 (0). The first is the hex representation and the number in the parenthesis is the decimal representation. The values are determined by whether sending the report is enabled or disabled on the **Send Options** tab of the **Server Status Configuration** dialog box.

- REG_DWORD LastSentFileTime

  LastSentFileTime=dword:00000000. The time the log was last sent. Used when checking for the presence of new log files. All new logs occurring after the last log file sending, will be sent to the technology consultant. This DWORD is added when the Server Status Tool runs and is not created by the Customization Tool.

Note If the Small Business Server Customization Tool is used to add ISV applications to the Server Status Tool, it overwrites any previous registry entries with the same report name that were made manually or added with a third-party tool. For example, if the customization tool finds a registry key with the same name as the one it is trying to create, it will be overwritten.

Locating and Sending New Application Log Files

When scheduling is set up in the Server Status Configuration dialog box, the Server Status Tool appears on the **Task Scheduler** in **My Computer**. After a new report is added in the Server Status Configuration dialog box, it is automatically added to this schedule. When the server status report is generated, the new application log is located and sent as follows:

- **Task Scheduler** launches the Vaprt.exe application to gather the log/report information for the new application.
- The configured registry values point Vaprt.exe to the location of the new application's log file.
- The files latest logs are collected and added to the server status report.
- The server status report is sent to the technology consultant either as an e-mail attachment, a fax, or through use of a command line.

Creating a Team Intranet Site

Using the Microsoft Office 60 Minute Intranet Kit, you can quickly create and customize an intranet site for small business workgroups or teams. The kit configures the intranet site to take advantage of Office 2000 features, thus allowing team members to communicate ideas, analyze information, collaborate by publishing documents to the web, and track team news and events. You can download the kit from the following web site:
http://officeupdate.microsoft.com/2000/downloaddetails/60minute.htm

Microsoft Office 60 Minute Intranet Kit Features

The features of the Microsoft Office 60 Minute Intranet Kit make it easy to create, customize, and use the team intranet site, as described in the following section.

FrontPage 60 Minute Intranet Site Wizard

A team web site can be created using the FrontPage® 60 Minute Intranet Site Wizard, which contains startup tutorials and the following customized departmental templates:

- Sales and Marketing
- Information Systems
- Human Resources
- Finance or Product Development

The wizard uses the Microsoft FrontPage Web Site Management tool to walk you through creation of the team web site. Since the wizard creates a FrontPage-based web, you can easily modify its design and navigation features using FrontPage. You can also do the following:

- Import existing web content to the team site.
- Integrate the team site into the small business intranet.
- Design custom site themes to match the small business corporate image.

Team Web Home Page

When small business intranet users first open the team home page, they can add the team site to their list of web folders and set up their discussion server. This allows team members to begin participating in the team web immediately.

Document Library

Whenever a user publishes a document to the team site, a hyperlink to that file is automatically created. This allows users to browse, search, and conduct discussions on documents from their web browsers. The library also notifies users when a document is added or modified.

Auto Updating News Engine

This database-driven news engine updates the team site so that site visitors are always kept informed of the latest team news. It also allows any member of the team to add, edit, or delete news items using their web browser.

Event Calendar

By publishing the Outlook® 2000 calendar as a web page, the Event Calendar allows a small business team to stay informed of upcoming company events or key project dates.

Online Applications

The Microsoft Office 60 Minute Intranet Kit includes samples of interactive web-based applications that show how to use Office 2000 to interact with data, from the web browser. Samples include time-tracking and sales-analysis applications.

Search Feature

The team site is enabled with search features that permit users to quickly locate any document on the team web.

Help

The Microsoft Office 60 Minute Intranet Kit includes Help on using the new web collaboration features of Office 2000, with topics that include:

- Publishing documents to a web server.
- Participating in web discussions.
- Working with data from inside your web browser.

More Information

You can find more information about the Microsoft Office 60 Minute Intranet Kit at the following web site:
http://www.microsoft.com/office/intranet/

CHAPTER 47

Enhancing Office 2000 Functionality

In direct response to customer feedback, design priorities for Microsoft® Office 2000 included reducing the cost of ownership, increasing integration with the web, and improving support for organizational software. Although Microsoft Office 2000 already offers significant advances, even greater functionality is enabled by combining Microsoft Office 2000 with other Microsoft software—such as Microsoft FrontPage®, and Microsoft Internet Explorer. This chapter addresses Microsoft Office 2000 functionality enhancements.

Enhancements of Office 2000

The sections that follow include descriptions of enhancements to Office 2000 that may be implemented in the small business organization through collaboration with other applications.

File Format Compatibilities

File formats between Microsoft Office 2000 and Microsoft Office 97 are compatible, which means that Office 97 and Office 2000 users can exchange documents natively. Office 97 will be able to open any Office 2000 file without a converter. However, certain formatting options available in Office 2000 will not be compatible since Office 97 does not recognize the new features. The only exception is Access, due to the new support of Unicode (Access did not previously support this file format). Access 2000 will be able to do downward revision saves to Access 97.

File Error Detection and Fix

Microsoft Office 2000 includes an executable that can be installed on Microsoft Windows operating systems to automatically detect and fix errors to files or registry settings needed for successful application launch. The Microsoft Office Custom Installation Wizard and Microsoft Office Profile Wizard make it simple and efficient to customize how Microsoft Office 2000 installs in your organization. Better support for roaming profiles makes it possible for Office 2000 users to work using their own preferences and settings, regardless of what computer they are working on, as long as it uses the same operating system.

Reduced Cost of Ownership

One of the most commonly discussed information technology topics today is the overall cost of personal computing ownership and how to reduce it. Reducing the cost of ownership of Microsoft Office is a top priority for Office 2000. It is reflected in new administrative capabilities and in features that make computing with Microsoft BackOffice® Small Business Server 4.5 as easy as possible.

Office 2000 features help reduce the cost of supporting operating system features such as security, customizable Help, and other usability improvements. All of these features are available to all users, regardless of the Microsoft applications in use.

Some capabilities are better implemented at the desktop or server operating system level. If typical system administration problems are fixed at the operating system level, the administrator has an entire desktop easier to administer, as opposed to just four or five applications.

The following sections include descriptions of features that enhance Office 2000 functions and also further reduce the cost of ownership when Microsoft Office 2000 is combined with other Microsoft software.

Operating System Shell Update

Windows 98 and Microsoft Internet Explorer 4.01 all include an updated shell that supports additional functionality in Office 2000. A service pack will be available for updating the shell in Windows 95 and Windows NT Workstation 4.0. The functionality enhancements are discussed in the sections that follow.

Install on Demand

Install on Demand automatically installs an Office 2000 feature or application when necessary. For example, if a user has installed some, but not all of the Office components, the missing components will be installed when the user first tries to access them. Install on Demand is activated in the following three ways.

- From within an Office application
- From the Start menu (the shell)
- From within another application, such as a Word document attached to an e-mail message

The first method works with any operating system on which Office 2000 runs. With the combination of Office 2000 and Windows 9x or Windows NT 4.0 with Internet Explorer 4.01 and the shell update, both the first and second methods work. The Windows installer service is installed when any one of these products is present. If the Windows installer service is available, it handles the request for installing the application and can install it from a variety of locations rather than from just one hard-coded location. The last method requires a Windows 2000 Professional client. This improves the resiliency of this feature over the lifetime of the Office 2000 product.

Single Document Interface

With Office 2000 applications, each open document appears on the Windows taskbar. In the past, only the active document appeared. Word for Windows will show individual documents on the taskbar on every operating system on which Office 2000 runs. Microsoft Excel, PowerPoint, and Access make use of the shell update to make this feature possible. This enhancement makes it easier to drag and drop contents from one document to another document using the taskbar.

Web Folders

Web folders allow you to view web servers from the Windows Explorer just as you would view network servers or local hard drives. Office 2000 supports the ability to cut, copy, and paste (or drag-and-drop) documents from a web server to a network server or local hard drive, or from a local hard drive or network server to a web server. This makes it easier to use content found on the Internet or an intranet, or to have average users post content to an intranet site or Internet staging server.

Increased Integration with the Web

Microsoft Office 2000 increases integration with the web by providing tools for easy creation of web content, easy publication to the web, and simplified retrieval of web content. Many of these features are enabled entirely by Microsoft Office 2000 and are independent of the browser or server software your organization is using. Some of these features include:

- **HTML File Format**. Saving files to HTML format is as easy as saving to the native application file format. This has greatly improved fidelity. In addition, information is stored in the file to improve using it again in the original application. For example, if the user creates a spreadsheet and saves it to HTML, all of the elements will look right in a browser. In addition, if the user opens that file again in Microsoft Excel 2000, formulas will recalculate, PivotTable® dynamic views will pivot and other features will work as if the file had remained in Microsoft Excel format. In other words, the Excel spreadsheet will "round-trip" to its binary format (*.xls), to HTML, and back to its binary format with full fidelity.

- **Enhanced Application Features**. Some applications have added features to support commonly used HTML formats. For example, Microsoft Word has added support for using frames in creating a table of contents, with a linking table of contents in the left-hand frame rather than embedded within a document as appropriate for a printed document.

- **Save to the web**. Not only is it easier to save to the HTML format, but it is also easier to save a document as a web page on a web server. Simply navigate a web server as you would a network server, and save your file. This means that Office 2000 users can more easily share documents with people creating web sites using FrontPage 2000. For example, save a Word document as HTML in a FrontPage-based Internet or intranet site.

Office 2000 Enhanced by Browser and Web Server Functionalities

Some of the new functionality in Microsoft Office 2000 is actually enabled by combining Office with either a specific level of browser functionality, web server functionality, or both. The following sections describe these features.

Creating and Managing Intranets

Microsoft Office 2000 and FrontPage 2000 together provide organizations with a comprehensive solution for creating and managing workgroup webs or intranets. FrontPage 2000 lets users create exactly the site they want, makes updating web sites easy, and works great with Office. Office 2000 users can now save HTML documents directly to a FrontPage-based web site. Features such as shared Office menus and toolbars make Office users feel immediately comfortable using FrontPage 2000.

Robust web collaboration features such as check-in and check-out, as well as control over security at multiple levels, enable teams to work together with confidence. Since web sites (both intranet and Internet) are global in nature, FrontPage 2000 integrates with the new worldwide deployment features found in Office 2000, making it easy to deploy throughout your organization.

Features Enabled by Browsers

Some Microsoft Office 2000 functionality is enabled by having an Internet browser view content created by the Office application. Different versions of browsers support different versions of HTML and other web features. While users with any Netscape or Microsoft browser (version 3 or later) will have a good experience with the features described in this section, those with Internet Explorer 5.0 will have the best experience. Internet Explorer 5.0 currently provides the best fidelity — a result of support for more advanced features and layouts of the HTML specification.

Microsoft Internet Explorer 5.0

Users with Internet Explorer 5.0 will have access to all of the features available to users with earlier versions of Internet Explorer, with the following additional features.

Best Viewing of HTML File Format

Users who have Internet Explorer version 5.0 will have the best fidelity viewing Office-generated HTML files. Internet Explorer 5.0 will display and scale vector graphics natively, providing better display and smaller files for Office–generated HTML documents, including PowerPoint presentations. Features such as small caps and vertical text in Word, which will not appear correctly in other browsers, look the same as they would in the Office application that created them.

Solutions with Data Access Pages

Although similar in function to classic Access forms and reports, Data Access Pages are specifically designed to view, edit, and report on data within a browser. Users design pages in much the same way they create forms and reports, yet they can now use new web-enabled features and easy drag-and-drop capabilities. The resulting Data Access Pages are essentially HTML pages that have the ability to maintain a live link (are bound) to data which can be in the form of a Microsoft Access database or even a Microsoft SQL Server™ store.

These Data Access Pages are stored as HTML files outside the Access database .mdb file. This allows users to easily send Data Access Pages through e-mail or post them on the web as an HTML page. The result is that anyone with Microsoft Internet Explorer 5.0 can now use an Access database without having Microsoft Access installed on their computer.

Web Features Enabled through Server Software

Some of the new functionality in Microsoft Office 2000 actually capitalizes on web server functionality as well as browser functionality. Where existing functionality was available, Microsoft Office 2000 built upon it. If no equivalent server functionality existed, the Microsoft Office group wrote server extensions (known as Microsoft Office Server Extensions) as needed. The enhancements to Office 2000 created by server functionalities are described in the sections that follow.

Windows NT Server 4.0

The features described immediately below are enabled by the functionality of Windows NT Server 4.0.

PowerPoint Presentation Broadcast Support for Large Audiences

With Microsoft Windows NT Server 4.0 and the NetShow server installed, users can deliver a presentation over an intranet, displaying the presentation slides in HTML along with the narration as streaming audio and video. NetShow Services uses streaming multicast technology to distribute a live or recorded audio and/or video broadcast over an intranet.

PowerPoint 2000 adds ease of use to the technology by broadcasting presentations directly from within PowerPoint. A camera is not required but video is supported if used. Since the presentation is sent in HTML format, the audience needs only a compatible browser to view it on PC, Macintosh®, or UNIX® workstations. For example, this feature may be used for company meetings, presentations to remote groups, or a team meeting at several different locations. No browser is needed by the presenter, but Microsoft Internet Explorer 4.0 or higher is required for the audience, with exception of the Macintosh users who will need Internet Explorer 5.0 or later. NetShow Services are not required for presentations with fewer than 16 viewers and no video.

HTTP 1.1 Servers with PUT Protocol

Web servers that do not have the PUT protocol can only use hypertext transfer protocol (HTTP) to send documents to a client computer. HTTP 1.1 PUT-enabled servers allow Microsoft Office 2000 applications to save files on these servers. This includes any server that can support FrontPage extensions, including the Windows NT Server Internet Information Services (IIS), *Unix* servers, *Apache*, *Netscape*, and *Sun* web servers. FrontPage extensions are not required for this feature.

Since most servers today support this, almost everyone can have this additional functionality due to Office 2000.

Save to the Web

Users can publish any HTML content created by an Office 2000 application from within that application. In the past, users had to use a method outside of Office to publish files to a web server, but now users can accomplish this using menu commands from within the application.

HTTP-DAV Servers

DAV (distributed authoring and versioning) is a new, open Internet standard that was created to make two-way communication possible on a web server. This allows users to send and retrieve or publish documents to a web server using open Internet standards. DAV will be integrated into future versions of server products.

Web Site Navigation

For any client computer with the operating system shell update mentioned earlier in this chapter (Microsoft Windows 9x, Internet Explorer 4.01, and Windows NT 4.0), Microsoft Office 2000 makes it possible to navigate a web server just as a user would a file server. By using the "File, Open" dialog box in Microsoft Word —or by using the Windows Explorer—a user can click on a web server, expanding and collapsing folders to view their contents without having to know the full HTTP path. The difference between this and the Save to the Web defined above is that Save to the Web requires that the user know the fully qualified HTTP path.

Office 2000 Enhanced Web Functionality with Microsoft Internet Information Services

All of the features mentioned previously are enabled in addition to those described in the sections that follow.

Remote Data Services

Remote Data Services (RDS) is a way of retrieving data from a web page supported by Microsoft Access. There are two main components to RDS–a client component which is an ActiveX® control, and a server component which is an ActiveX server component and an RDS application.

Integrated Security

Because IIS runs on Windows NT 4.0 in Small Business Server, the security is integrated with Windows NT security. Therefore, any of the Microsoft Office 2000 features implemented via web functionality will benefit from Windows NT security.

IIS with FrontPage Extensions

Organizations using IIS with FrontPage extensions benefit from all the previously mentioned server enhancements and can also utilize the functionality described in the following.

Managing Embedded Files

The HTML format does not actually embed objects within it, rather it maintains links to files such as graphics. When users move, delete, or copy HTML files, those other embedded objects normally remain where they are and are not treated in the same way as the HTML file. With Windows 2000, IIS, and FrontPage extensions, the files that go with the HTML file are moved, copied, or deleted along with it.

IIS with Office Server Extensions

Microsoft Office 2000 actually ships with server extensions that run only on IIS with Windows NT. These Office Server Extensions enable new collaboration features that would not otherwise be possible and exploit the existing functionality in Microsoft Office 2000, as described in the following sections.

AutoNavigation

AutoNavigation is a feature that displays the contents of a web server, including Office documents, in a web page. It is a hierarchical view similar to a file directory and allows users to open, print, copy, and paste web files easily.

Web Discussions with Comments

With the Office Server Extensions, users can have discussions in both native Office 2000 documents and HTML files within the browser. Discussions can be added either through an Office application or through the browser using a special toolbar supplied by the Office 2000 client. With a level 3 browser (Netscape Navigator 3 or Internet Explorer 3.0), the discussions can only be incorporated at the document level, not imbedded or integrated into the document, and are viewed in the discussion pane at the bottom of the page. With a level 4 browser or higher, the discussions can be made in-line or integrated directly into the document. The toolbar has buttons for inserting new comments, navigating through existing comments, editing and replying to comments, and viewing or hiding the discussion pane.

The comments themselves are actually stored in a database, the MSDE (Microsoft Data Engine), which ships with Office 2000, and has the same architecture as Microsoft SQL Server 7.0. In fact, if you expect that the volume of comments will be very large, you can substitute SQL Server 7.0 for the MSDE. Since the comments are stored separately, the speed of viewing the document and the size of the document are not affected, and the number and length of the comments can be almost unlimited. Also, users only need permission to write to the server that stores the database, not the actual site itself. This allows users to comment on any site on the Internet since they are not limited to the company's intranet. Users can also choose to subscribe to a document and its discussions so that they can read it offline. New comments, however, cannot be added offline.

The following is an example that illustrates the business benefits of these discussions: Imagine that you have written a new document or proposed a product specification or standard. It's important that users on *any* platform provide feedback, but you don't want anyone editing or changing the original proposal. With threaded discussions, the size and integrity of the original document are maintained. At the same time, valuable feedback is gathered and concerns are aired.

Web Subscriptions and Notifications

Web Subscriptions and Notifications improve collaboration between people on the web by keeping users up-to-date. Users subscribe to a particular document or set of documents on a web server with Microsoft Office Server Extensions, and they are notified by e-mail when the status of any selected document changes. Users can choose to be notified when a document is changed, created, or deleted. Users can be notified of changes immediately, or in the case of a document undergoing frequent revisions, can choose to be notified on a daily or weekly basis.

NetMeeting Conferencing Software

NetMeeting is an exciting collaboration tool that makes it easy and engaging to work together without being in the same room. When combined with Office 2000, users are able to consult with coworkers without having to fly across the country or book a large capacity conference room.

NetMeeting Conferencing and Collaborative Editing

Integration with Microsoft NetMeeting conferencing software lets users start a conference and share any Office document with others for collaborative editing. With NetMeeting conferencing and collaborative editing, users can use all of the creation and editing tools of Microsoft Office together, online and in real-time. For example, an author and a technical expert can review and make changes to a document together at their own desks on opposite ends of the country (or the world).

Microsoft NetMeeting Integration

Users can easily schedule real-time meetings using Outlook 2000 and automatically start the NetMeeting conferencing software with an Office document to share during the NetMeeting-based conference.

Presenters can schedule a broadcast just as they would any other meeting, using Outlook 2000. A "Lobby" page is automatically generated and available when the audience is ready to tune in. When the presenter is ready to start the broadcast, the presentation is saved in HTML format and copied out to the specified server location. If a NetShow Services server is set up, the pages will be multicast automatically. As the audience tunes in to the Lobby page for the event, the HTML pages will be cached on the machines of each member. When the presenter begins a separate multicast stream with audio and video (if present), the slide navigation commands are sent to the audience. Viewers are also free to join in even after the meeting has started.

Presentation on Demand

PowerPoint 2000 records the live presentation, allowing anyone who missed it to see and hear it later, as the presenter gave it. If the presenter has a microphone, PowerPoint 2000 can even record the audio portion, or the presenter can use the new voice narration feature in PowerPoint 2000 to add the audio portion of the presentation.

Enterprise Integration and Support with Office 2000

Over the years, Microsoft Office has often been first to embrace standards that allow it to be a client in the enterprise and not just a personal productivity tool. Office 4, which shipped in 1993, supported Object Linking and Embedding (OLE), so it could be programmed by other applications, and also supported other enterprise standards such as Open Database Connectivity (ODBC), Microsoft Mail, and Lotus Notes. Microsoft Office 2000 is continuing the tradition of being an enterprise client by providing enhancements or improvements in the following areas:

- Data access
- Corporate reporting tools
- Ability to create custom solutions with Office 2000

Data Access

All of the enterprise support mentioned above is available in Microsoft Office 2000, with additions and improvements for all customers that include improved Microsoft Excel text import. Many Microsoft BackOffice family customers have requested that Office improve its integration and support for SQL Server, including the improved performance and new capabilities of SQL Server 7.0.

OLE DB

Access 2000 supports Object Linking and Embedding Database (OLE DB), a recent standard for data access. By using OLE DB, Access 2000 databases can connect directly to Microsoft SQL Server 7.0 instead of going through the Jet engine, the traditional default database engine in Access. Power users and developers can now create solutions that combine the ease-of-use and speedy development of the Access interface (client) with the scalability, performance, and reliability of Microsoft SQL Server 7.0. Processing occurs in Microsoft SQL Server for a true client/server solution. Power users and developers appreciate developing using the Access interface, and end users performing data entry find it as easy to use as other Office applications. Support for OLE DB in Microsoft Office has been tested with Microsoft SQL Server, ORACLE®, Thor, and IOLT

Microsoft SQL Server OLAP Services Support

Office 2000 provides support for SQL Server OLAP Services, a new Online Analytical Processing (OLAP) capability in SQL Server 7.0 that allows users to perform sophisticated analysis on large volumes of data with exceptional performance. Since Office works tightly with SQL Server-based data warehouses, this allows a broader audience of users to access corporate information. For example, users can use a PivotTable dynamic view in Microsoft Excel 2000 to create persistent local cubes of data from a SQL Server via the SQL Server OLAP Services feature. This provides a new method for high-performance data analysis of large amounts of data, right from the familiar interface of Microsoft Excel 2000. This eliminates the limitations of working with data in PivotTable dynamic views that existed with the previous version of Excel. The Office Web Components also support OLAP to provide browsing and charting functionality within a browser.

Access 2000 Client Server Tools

Because Access is renowned for its easy-to-use wizards, this functionality has been extended to the client/server realm. A variety of wizards make it easier for Access power users and developers to create a client/server database.

Access users will appreciate the ability to use popular Access wizards, such as the Report Wizard, Form Wizard, Control Wizard and Button Wizard against a back end in Microsoft SQL Server 7.0. These wizards have been updated to support the new client/server architecture.

Client/Server Design Tools

With a Microsoft Access Project, new design tools allow users to create and manage Microsoft SQL Server 7.0 objects from the design view, including tables, views, stored procedures, and database diagrams. This makes it easier for current Access power users and developers to extend their database knowledge to the client/server environment.

Microsoft SQL Server-Based Administration Tools

Microsoft Access 2000 allows users to perform and manage common administration tasks in Microsoft SQL Server 7.0, such as replication, backup and restore, and security. This means that users can use Access 2000 on the client to perform SQL administrative tasks.

Corporate Reporting

Microsoft Excel has been a premier corporate reporting tool for years. Its financial analysis capabilities, combined with unique tools such as PivotTable dynamic views, have provided the basis for corporate reporting systems for many organizations. Included in Microsoft Office 2000 are enhancements that make Pivot Table dynamic views easier to use and provide PivotChart dynamic views that update each time a PivotTable view is changed. The following section details features that are improved for users who combine Office 2000 with other technologies such as intranets or databases.

Enhanced Web Queries

For those organizations with connectivity to the web or an intranet, Microsoft has enhanced the Microsoft Excel Web Queries feature. The new Web Query Wizard makes it much easier to get data from the web into Microsoft Excel. This wizard walks users through the process of bringing data from a web page into Microsoft Excel 2000, and helps create the query file as they choose the web page, the desired content for importing, and the type of formatting. Web query pages can be refreshed automatically on a scheduled basis.

Office Web Components

Office 2000 includes three new Office Web Components — a spreadsheet component, a chart component, and a PivotTable component. These new components make corporate data available through any browser.

The spreadsheet component provides basic spreadsheet functionality in the browser, allowing users to enter text and numbers, create formulas, recalculate, sort, filter, and perform basic formatting. It supports frozen panes for keeping header rows and columns visible while scrolling through data, as well as in-cell editing and resizable rows and columns. With the Office Web Components, the Office Spreadsheet component allows users to interact with Microsoft Excel 2000 data in a browser, as in the following illustration.

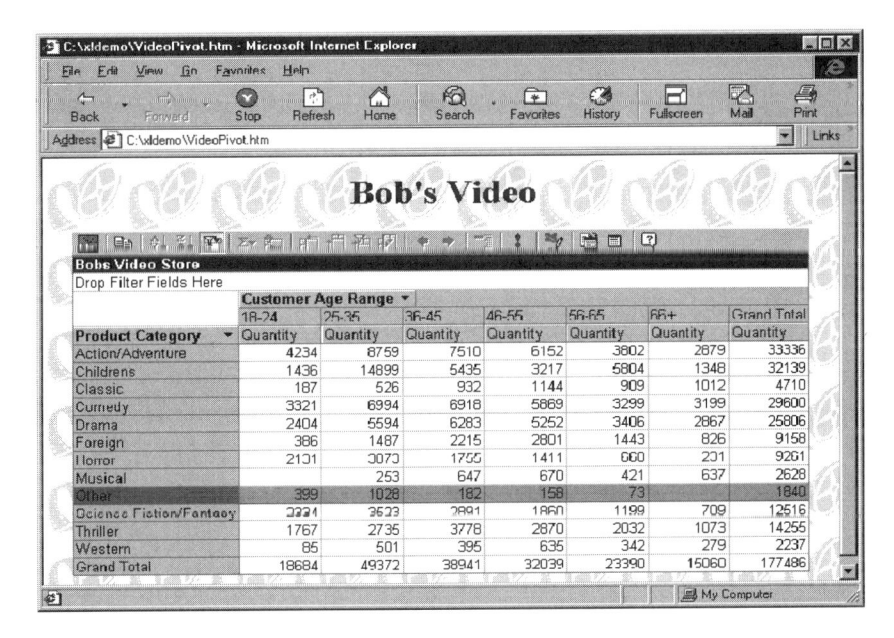

The chart component provides interactivity and automatic updates as the underlying data changes.

The PivotTable component is similar to PivotTable views in Microsoft Excel 2000 and provides a dynamic way to view and analyze database information in the browser. The PivotTable component is created in either Microsoft Access or Microsoft Excel and resides on a Data Access Page. This component lets users browse data, dynamically sort and filter it, group it by rows or columns, create totals and focus on the details behind the totals. It helps users work efficiently with large or small amounts of data. Although the author of the Data Access Page determines the initial view, the user can access the Field List Chooser to drag-and-drop the dynamically linked fields directly onto the page.

Conclusion

Microsoft Office 2000 has met its design goals of reducing the cost of ownership, increasing integration with the web, and improving support for the web and the enterprise. Users of Office 2000 will benefit from these improvements regardless of what environment they work within. However, users who work in an environment that supports Microsoft Internet Explorer 5.0, Windows 2000 Professional, Microsoft IIS, NetMeeting, NetShow Services, and SQL Server 7.0 will find that Microsoft Office 2000 offers solutions to today's computing problems that are far beyond those of a traditional desktop productivity application suite.

More Information

For information on creating custom Office 2000 solutions using add-ins, templates, wizards, and libraries, refer to Chapter 11 of the *Microsoft Office 2000 Visual Basic Programmer's Guide*.

CHAPTER 48

Office 2000 Customer Manager

Microsoft® Office Small Business Customer Manager (SBCM) is an application that maintains a central database for importing and storing contact management and accounting information from other source applications running on Small Business Server. To import data, SBCM uses software components called import filters to retrieve data from these source applications—it then converts the data to native SBCM format. SBCM databases may also be customized if you do the following:

- Add data tables using a supplementary customer database.
- Display added data in the SBCM interface.
- Automate data export and import into added tables.

Information and Resources

For technical information on customizing SBCM databases, refer to the following web site:
http://www.microsoft.com/directaccess

CHAPTER 49

Application Communication with MSMQ

Microsoft® Message Queue Server (MSMQ) is a feature of the Windows NT 4.0 operating system which can be installed on Microsoft BackOffice® Small Business Server 4.5. MSMQ provides loosely coupled and reliable network communication services based on a messaging queuing model. MSMQ enables the integration of applications, the implementation of a push style business event delivery environment between applications, and building reliable applications that work over unreliable, cost effective networks.

If you wish to use MSMQ, you must install the application since it is not installed by default with Small Business Server setup. You can locate this service in the Windows NT Option Pack setup using the following path on Small Business Server installation Disc 2:

<Diskdrive>\Ntoptpak\En\Winnt.srv\Setup

Information Sources

For further information on MSMQ, refer to the following web site:
http://www.microsoft.com/ntserver/appservice/exec/overview/MSMQ_Overview.asp

At this site, you can find information describing the benefits of message queuing technologies, the important features and functions of MSMQ 1.0, and examples of ways that you can realize benefits by using MSMQ in the small business network. Developer resources may also be found at this location.

CHAPTER 50

TAPI Solutions for Small Business Server

The Microsoft® Windows® Telephony Applications Programming Interface (TAPI) 2.1 included with Windows NT® Server 4.0, provides a powerful and flexible platform for developing and using computer telephony applications. TAPI 2.1 isolates the hardware layer (OSI model) by allowing the Windows telephony API to communicate with any type of telephony hardware device. This frees the developer and user from network and device dependence. TAPI 2.1 is the only platform that enables applications for use on analog telephone, Integrated Services Digital Network (ISDN), Private Branch Exchange (PBX)-based, and Internet Protocol (IP) networks.

Information Sources

For further information on TAPI 2.1, you can download white papers and the TAPI 2.1 SKD from the following web site:
http://www.microsoft.com/ntserver

PART 10

Tools and Utilities

In addition to tool help, various utilities, and online documentation, the *Microsoft® BackOffice® Small Business Server 4.5 Resource Kit CD* contains tools for the following:

- Client computers
- Computer administrative
- Desktop
- Diagnostic and troubleshooting
- File and disk
- Microsoft Exchange Server 5.5 (server and client tools)
- Network management and diagnostics
- Registry
- Scripting
- Small Business Server 4.5
- SQL™ Server 7.0

The resource kit tools may be used to simplify certain Small Business Server administrative and extensibility tasks. Part 10 describes how to install and access resource kit tools and what you can do with the new tools specifically developed for Small Business Server 4.5. The material is presented in the following two chapters:

Chapter 51   Small Business Server 4.5 Tool Installation and Access   765
Chapter 52   Small Business Server 4.5 Tool Descriptions   771

CHAPTER 51

Small Business Server 4.5 Tool Installation and Access

Overview

This chapter describes how to install and access the tools and utilities supplied on the *Microsoft® BackOffice® Small Business Server 4.5 Resource Kit CD*, including those specifically developed for Small Business Server 4.5. The installation process is automated by the Small Business Server Resource Kit Setup Wizard.

The material for this chapter is presented in the following two sections:

- Installing the Small Business Server Resource Kit.
- Accessing Small Business Server Tools.

Installing the Small Business Server Resource Kit

Perform the following steps to install the Small Business Server 4.5 Resource Kit on the server computer.

▶ **To install the Small Business Server 4.5 Resource Kit**

1. Insert the *Small Business Server 4.5 Resource Kit CD* into your CD-ROM drive on the server computer. The following **BackOffice Small Business Server 4.5 Resource Kit CD-ROM** screen is displayed.

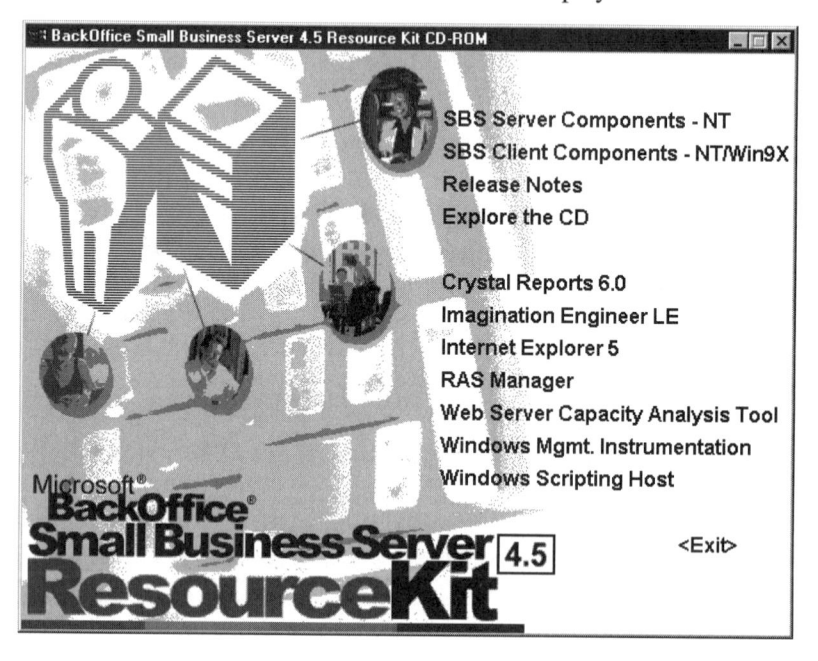

2. Click **Explore the CD** to display the CD directory contents.

3. In the CD directory, double-click the **SBS45rk** icon to launch the following Small Business Server 4.5 Resource Kit Setup Wizard.

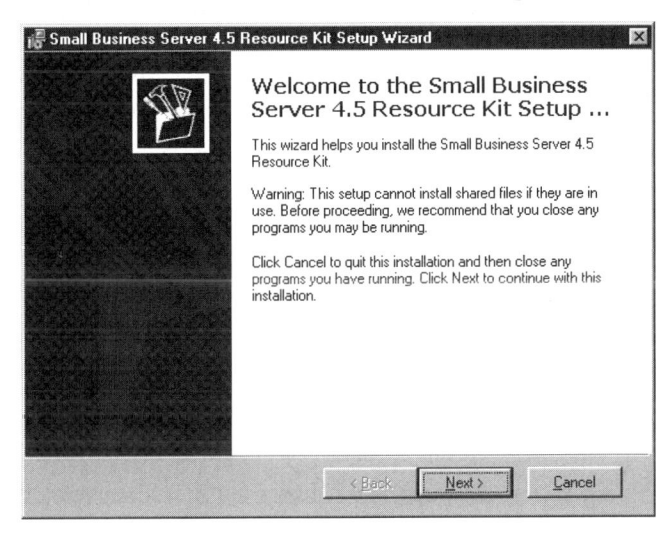

4. Click **Next**, read the end-user agreement, then click **I Agree** when you accept the agreement terms.
5. Click **Install** to begin the installation.
6. When installation is complete, remove the *Small Business Server Resource Kit CD* from the CD-ROM drive. The Resource Kit components are now accessible from the **Start** menu of Small Business Server.

Accessing Small Business Server Tools

After installing the Small Business Server 4.5 Resource Kit, tools and utilities are accessed and launched from the Tools Management Console, as discussed in the following sections.

Tools Management Console

The Tools Management Console (TMC) is an integrated Microsoft Management Console (MMC) snap-in for exploring and running Resource Kit tools or utilities, and for linking to online documentation. The TMC is installed by default when you install a Resource Kit on your server. After installation, the Resource Kit appears as a folder in the left-hand contents pane of the TMC, under the **Microsoft Resource Kits** folder. Within this folder are the following sub-folders.

- Online Documentation.

    Contains HTML Help versions of the online books and tool documentation for the Resource Kit

- Tool category folders.

    Contains folders for each category of tools in the Resource Kit
- Tools A - Z.

    Contains the tools presented in an alphabetical list.

Running Tools

The TMC provides a convenient interface from which to launch the Resource Kit tools. In general, tools listed in the TMC can be run directly by double-clicking on the tool name or icon. However, some tools cannot be run this way, including tools which (1) are not installed by the Resource Kit setup program, (2) might cause unacceptable results when used in the wrong context, or (3) must be run from a command-line or within the context of another program or service.

For these reasons, the TMC exposes the tools in the TMC content pane by identifying them with an associated icon, as follows:

- Tool icon. Graphical User Interface (GUI) executables and other tools which can be executed directly.

    These tools are identified by the tool's icon. Double-clicking on the tool name or icon runs the tool. Right-clicking the tool icon brings up a context menu with help on the tool.
- Command window icon. Tools launched by a command line.

    These tools are identified by a command window icon. Double-clicking runs the command with the /? parameter, and opens an MS-DOS window that displays the syntax for the tool. Right-clicking the tool name opens a context menu with a selection for tool help.
- Help icon. Tools which cannot be run from the TMC.

    These tools are identified by a help icon next to the tool name. Double-clicking the tool name or icon opens a help topic for the tool.

Accessing the Tools

To access Small Business Server tools, perform the following steps.

▶ **To access the Small Business Server 4.5 tools and utilities**

1. Click **Start**, point to **Programs**, point to **Resource Kit**, and then click **Tools Management Console** to launch the following **RKtmc Console**.

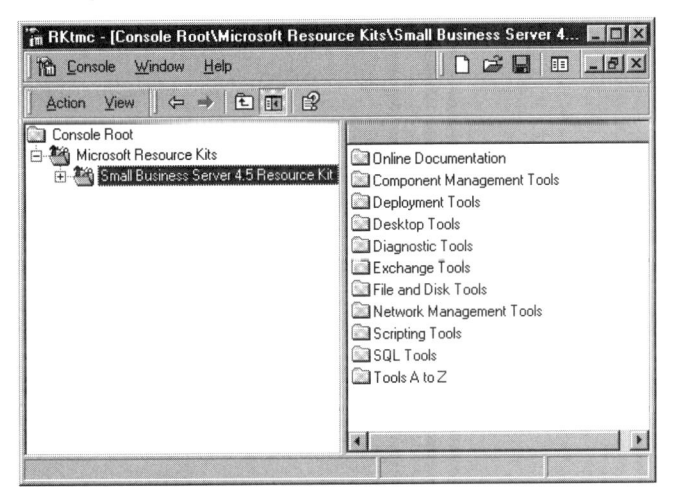

2. In the left content pane of the **RKtmc Console**, double-click the **Microsoft Resource Kits** folder.

3. Double-click the **Small Business Server 4.5 Resource Kit** folder to display the tool category folders.

4. Locate the tool you want to use in the category folders or use the alphabetical listing.

5. Launch the tool in accordance with the information presented in the "Running Tools" section above.

CHAPTER 52

Small Business Server 4.5 Tool Descriptions

Introduction

The following tools were developed specifically for Microsoft® BackOffice® Small Business Server 4.5:

- Small Business Server Start Menu Tool
- Batch User Add Tool
- Modem Status Tools
- Small Business Server Customization Tool
- Small Business Server Client Setup Integration Wizard
- Fax Monitoring and Performance Tools

This chapter describes tool functions and what you can do with them on Small Business Server 4.5.

Small Business Server Start Menu Tool

Use the Small Business Server **Start Menu Tool** to create a Small Business Server 4.5 **Start** menu program group containing the Small Business Server console and wizards. When the tool is launched, the following **Start Menu Tool** dialog box appears to the user.

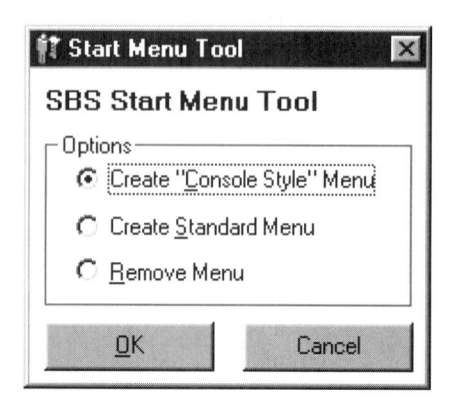

The following three options are available:

- **Create "Console Style" Menu**. Creates a program group divided into sections similar to the way Small Business Server console tasks are arranged, such as **Manage Email** or **Manage Folders**.
- **Create Standard Menu**. Places all shortcuts into one group.
- **Remove Menu**. Removes the Small Business Server **Start** menu program group.

After selecting the option you want, click **OK** to create the program group.

Accessing Tasks on the Start Menu

After the program group is created, it may be accessed from the server **Start** menu. For example, if you choose to create a console style menu, then on the **Start** menu, the following Small Business Server tasks and components appear by pointing to **Programs** and **Microsoft Small Business Server 4.5**:

- **Manage E-Mail**. Tasks include creating, editing, or deleting an e-mail distribution list.
- **Manage Folders**. Tasks include changing folder permissions, creating a new shared folder, or moving a shared folder.
- **Manage Internet Access**. Allows you to launch the Internet Connection Wizard or set Internet access permissions.
- **Manage Other**. Allows you to run the Set Up Computer Wizard, change printer and fax printer permissions, or configure and send server status reports.

- **Manage Users**. Tasks include adding or deleting a user, changing a user's password, editing user access to resources, or editing user account information.
- **SBS Console**. Launches the Small Business Server console.
- **Setup Small Business Server 4.5**. Launches Small Business Server setup for installing Small Business Server components.
- **Welcome to Small Business Server 4.5**. Launches Internet Explorer displaying the Small Business Server Client Help page.

If you choose to create a standard menu, all the tasks and components described above will appear in a single pop-up menu accessed from the same path on the **Start** menu.

Batch User Add Tool

Use the Batch User Add Tool to add multiple users at once to Small Business Server 4.5. The tool gathers data for a user account text file containing the specific user information, using the following features:

- A **Configure Defaults** button to enter default company information.
- An Excel spreadsheet to enter specific user information.
- A **Create File** button to create the c:\users.txt file, which can be viewed in Notepad.

After all the user information is gathered and the user account text file is created, save it to a floppy disk on the Small Business Server 4.5 computer. From there, click **Import Users** on the Small Business Server console **To Do List** to launch the Migrate User Wizard. The wizard prompts for the user account text file and the floppy disk, imports the user information to Small Business Server, and creates the new user accounts. For more information on the Migrate User Wizard, see *Chapter 25, Small Business Server Wizard Processes,* in *Part 4, Administering and Maintaining,* of this resource guide.

Modem Status Tools

The Modem Status Tools include the following three tools that allow viewing Telephony Application Programming Interface (TAPI) line status when monitoring modems:

- TAPI.Exe
- Timon
- TAPIstate

TAPI.Exe Tool

Identifies the state of the TAPI lines—idle, connected, dialing, or offering. Since TAPI associates numbers to lines, by supplying the device number, the tool can identify the state of a specific line only. Device numbers range from 0 to the total number of devices—this is not a fixed number since it can change when TAPI restarts.

Run TAPI.exe by double-clicking the tool and typing *TAPI* at the DOS command prompt that appears. When you type *TAPI* with no arguments added, you display the state of the TAPI lines. When you add an argument from the list below to the *TAPI* command, for example *TAPI_/c*, the associated functions are implemented:

- _/c—Displays the TAPI configuration.
- _/?—Displays help message.
- _/k—Displays the TAPI configuration in a different style.
- _<number>—Displays the state of a specified TAPI line.

Note The underscore character in the arguments above represents a space.

Timon Tool

Timon is a Windows NT® service that enables Component Object Modeling (COM) access to TAPI functions and data. In order to start the service, you register it by running Timon.exe/Service from the **Services** utility in **Control Panel** or type *Net Start Timon* at a Small Business Server DOS command prompt. After the service is registered, Timon is ready to service client requests. To program Timon to service client requests, refer to the Timon.htm file in the Small Business Server 4.5 Resource Kit.

TAPIstate Tool

The TAPIstate application is a Timon client that monitors the state of the TAPI lines. To use it, make sure Timon is running and then start TAPIstate.exe by typing *TAPIstate* at a Small Business Server DOS command prompt. The TAPIstate user interface lets you select the TAPI line you want to monitor and will display the calls and their state on that line.

Small Business Server Customization Tool

The Small Business Server Customization Tool is an application called SBSCustom.exe. It is written in Visual Basic and designed to simplify certain extension tasks for the technology consultant. It is accessed from the Tools Management Console on Small Business Server, as described in *Chapter 51, Small Business Server 4.5 Tool Installation and Access,* in *Part 10, Tools and Utilities,* of this resource guide. When you launch SBSCustom.exe, it displays the following **Small Business Server Customization Tool** screen.

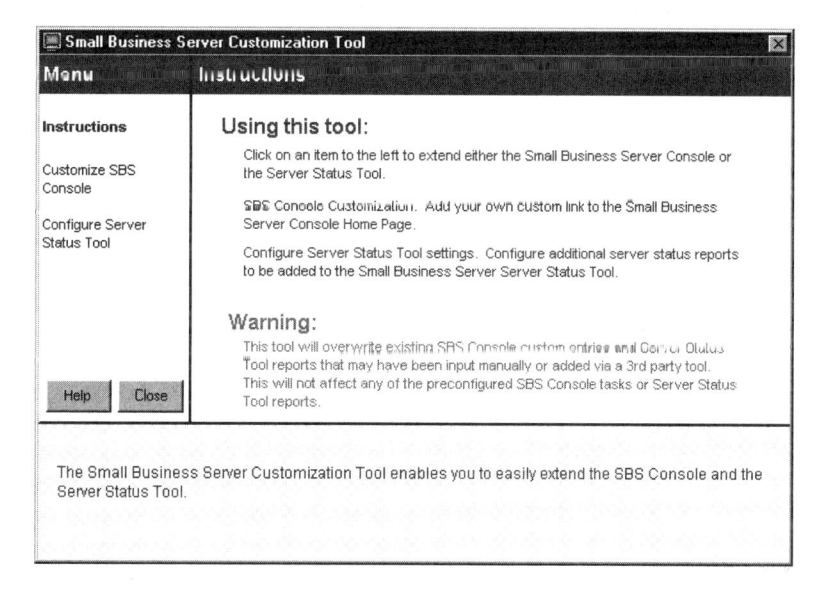

From this opening screen, you can launch the following tasks:

- **Customize SBS Console**. Gathers the information necessary to add custom links to the Small Business Server console.
- **Configure Server Status Tool**. Gathers the information necessary to extend the Server Status Tool by adding new application logs to the server status report.

The following section describes how to add custom links to the Small Business Server console using the **Customize SBS Console** task. A description of Customization Tool features for extending the Server Status Tool is also provided.

Note For Server Status Tool extension procedures, refer to *Chapter 46, Other Extensions and Solutions,* in *Part 9, Developing Small Business Server Solutions,* of this resource guide.

Customize SBS Console

The Small Business Server console is a single administrative interface that consolidates management tasks of several server applications and services into one unified console. The console is extensible by manual configuration of registry keys and values as described in *Chapter 43, Customizing and Extending the Console*, in *Part 9, Developing Small Business Server Solutions,* of this resource guide. However, the **Customize SBS Console** task of the Small Business Server Customization Tool may also be used to add task links to the console, by automating the entry of the registry values. The extensibility model of the console allows you to add links that launch either customized HTM pages or external Internet Unified Resource Locators (URLs).

Customization Process

When using the Small Business Server Customization Tool to extend the console, Hyper Text Markup Language (HTML) links are added to one of the three console pages. This link can either point to a local .htm file, an Active Server Page (ASP), or an Internet URL. The initial steps of the customization process depend on whether you are linking locally or to an Internet URL, as described later in this section.

Linking to Local HTM File

If you are linking to a local file, create the HTM file or ASP with an HTML editor such as Microsoft FrontPage® and place it in the following folder:

%systemdrive%\SmallBusiness\HTML

Once this file is in place, run Internet Explorer 5.0 from Small Business Server and type the following in the **Address** field of the browser:

http://Localhost/Admin/Yourfile.htm

where *Yourfile.htm* is the name of the file you placed in the folder above. If the browser displays this file, you are ready to use the Customization Tool. If it does not display this file, make sure you placed it in the correct folder.

Linking to an Internet Address

If you are linking to an Internet address, launch Internet Explorer 5.0 and type in the **Address** field of the browser the URL you want to add to the Small Business Server Console. If the browser displays the correct web page, you are ready to use the Customization Tool. If the browser does not display the web page, make sure you entered a valid URL.

Adding Links

When you want to add links to the Small Business Server Console, consider the following three pages where a user initiates tasks:

- **Home**. The first page displayed when the console is launched—designed to give the user quick status on server health and to provide a location for placing links to other customized information. A good location to place a link to the company Internet web page or to add a locally stored custom information page.

- **Tasks**. Includes user tasks most frequently performed on the server. Add a link to the **Tasks** page to place newly created custom applications requiring server administration or to include your own troubleshooting page.

- **More Tasks**. Designed for tasks used on an irregular basis or for one-time setup tasks and administrative wizards. Add a link to the **More Tasks** page to create a page with links to Internet resources or information about a custom administration tool.

Adding Links with the Customization Tool

When you want to add a link to the console, click the **Customize SBS Console** task to display the following **Extending the Small Business Server Console** dialog box.

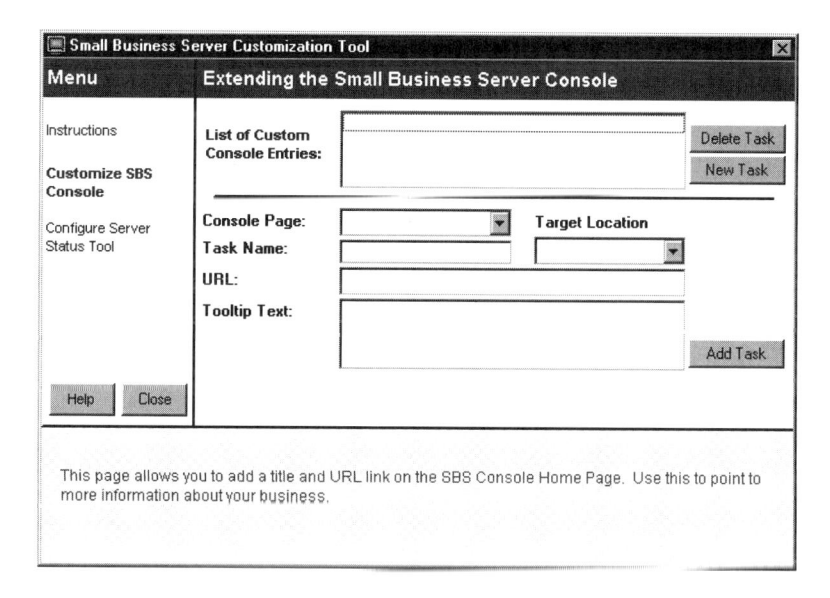

Information Fields

When you place the cursor in an information field of the **Extending the Small Business Server Console** dialog box, a *description* appears in the detail field (lower pane of the dialog box). After a new link is configured, placing the cursor in the information field causes the *values* of the configured item to appear. Information field definitions for the required entries are listed below.

- **Console Page**. A drop-down list allowing you to select the Small Business Server console page where your task item will be displayed. Selections include **Home Page**, **Tasks**, and **More Tasks**. Use **Home Page** for Internet links or for support information, **Tasks** for frequent or daily tasks, and **More Tasks** for less frequent tasks.
- **Task Name**. Name of the task to be displayed on the Small Business Server Console.
- **Target Location**. A drop-down list which applies only when **Home Page** is selected in **Console Page**, although the items in this information field are always visible. Selections include **In Frame**, which displays the linked page within the active Small Business Server console frame, and **New Window**, which starts a new instance of the browser pointing to the URL defined in **URL**. Use **New Window** if you are linking to an external URL, otherwise select **In Frame**.
- **URL**. The local or Internet link to the task page. The information typed in this field must be in the format of either *http://www.yourcompany.com* or *Yourfile.htm*, where Y*ourfile.htm* is located in the %systemdrive%\SmallBusiness\htm directory.

Caution If you input an incorrect link in this field, the Small Business Server Console may not load correctly.

- **Tooltip Text**. Text that appears when the cursor hovers over the task name. Briefly describe where the user will go or what they will be doing after selecting the link.

Controls

The following buttons (controls) are also provided on the **Extending the Small Business Server Console** dialog box, for use when configuring new links on the console:

- **Delete Task**. Click to remove configured tasks appearing in the **List of Custom Console Entries**.
- **New Task**. Click to clear all information fields when configuring a new console task.

- **Add Task**. Click to automatically configure the registry and add the newly configured task to the **List of Custom Console Entries**.
- **Help**. Click to display the opening screen of the Small Business Server Customization Tool with Help on using this tool.
- **Close**. Click to exit after completing console extension.

Running the Customization Tool

When you are ready to add a link to the console using the Customization Tool, perform the following steps.

▶ **To add a custom console link with the Small Business Server Customization Tool**

1. Logon to Small Business Server as the Administrator.
2. Launch the Small Business Server Customization Tool as described in *Chapter 51, Small Business Server 4.5 Tool Installation and Access*.
3. Click **Customize SBS Console** to display the following **Extending the Small Business Server Console** dialog box.

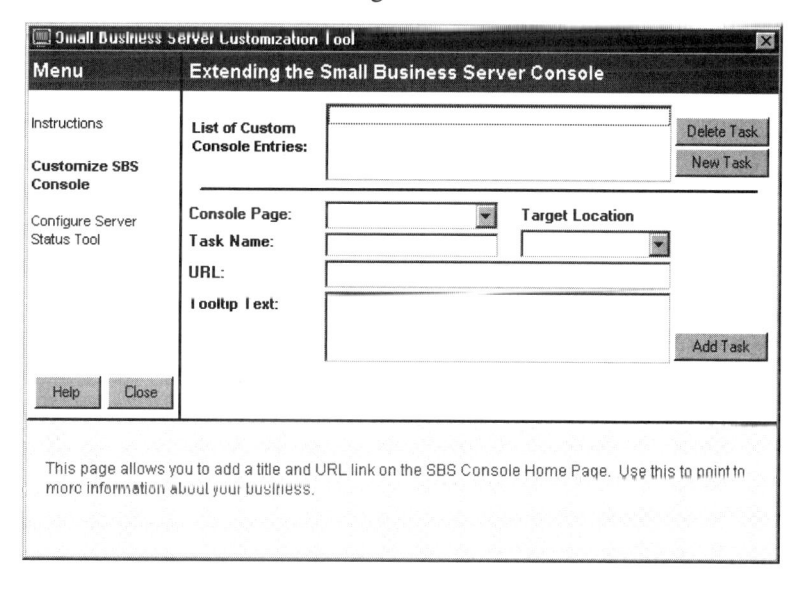

4. Click **New Task** to clear all information fields.
5. From the **Console Page** drop-down list, select the appropriate page where the link is to appear.
6. Type the appropriate information in the remaining information fields.
7. Click **Add Task** to enter the information into the registry.
8. Click **Close** when finished.

Checking the New Link

After adding the new link with the Small Business Server Customization Tool, launch the Small Business Server console and verify the task item appears on the correct console page with the link working properly.

Configure Server Status Tool

The Server Status Tool is a monitoring application that enables the technology consultant to send e-mail or faxes with various server status reports to either a machine on the local network or an external Internet address. The Server Status Tool is preconfigured to send the following reports:

- Hard disk space
- Service Status
- Internet Information Server (IIS) Logs
- Web Proxy Logs
- Winsock Proxy Logs

With the **Configure Server Status Tool** task of the Small Business Server Customization Tool, the Server Status Tool may be extended to include status reports for other Small Business Server applications, including third-party applications. The following section describes the Small Business Server Customization Tool features used for Server Status Tool extension. For Server Status Tool extension procedures, refer to *Chapter 46, Other Extensions and Solutions*, in *Part 9, Developing Small Business Server Solutions*, of this resource guide. For further Server Status Tool descriptions, refer to *Chapter 26, Administrative Tools*, in *Part 4, Administering and Maintaining*, of this resource guide.

Extending the Server Status Tool

When extending the Server Status Tool report list, a registry entry is added to include the profile information of your custom report. The Small Business Server Customization Tool automatically configures this registry entry. To gather the required profile information, the Small Business Server Customization Tool provides specific information fields as shown in the following **Adding reports to the Server Status Tool** dialog box.

Information Fields

When you place the cursor in an information field of the **Adding reports to the Server Status Tool** dialog box, a *description* appears in the detail field (lower pane of the dialog box). After a new report is configured, placing the cursor in the information field causes the *values* of the configured item to appear. Information field definitions for the required entries are listed below.

- **Report Name**. The report name to be displayed in the Server Status Tool administration screen.

- **File Pattern**. The file pattern of the server logs created, based on the specified report name. The Server Status Tool searches the file path specified in **File Path** for the most up-to-date file matching the pattern specified in this field. For example, a pattern could be *xxx**.log, where *xxx* is a constant and * is a variable. This causes a search for all files with the .log extension. See *Chapter 46, Other Extensions and Solutions,* in *Part 9, Developing Small Business Server Solutions,* of this resource guide.

- **File Path**. The location on the server where the log files associated with this report are stored. Enter the full path, including drive name and folder location. There is no validation for this field—if you enter an incorrect path or use the wrong slashes, the Server Status Tool will not work.

- **Description**. The full description of the report. Appears within the Server Status Tool administration screen.
- **List of Custom Reports**. A list of all configured reports added to the Server Status Tool. Newly configured reports appear after you click **Add Report**.

Note Make sure the log files gathered under the specified report name are smaller than 1 MB. Since reports are sent by either fax or e-mail, transmission problems may occur if the report logs are larger than 1 MB.

Controls

The following buttons (controls) are also provided on the **Adding reports to the Server Status Tool** dialog box, for use when configuring new Server Status Tool reports:

- **Delete Report**. Click to remove configured reports appearing in the **List of Custom Reports**.
- **New Report**. Click to clear all information fields when configuring a new report.
- **Add Report**. Click to automatically configure the registry and add the newly configured report to the **List of Custom Reports**.
- **Update Report**. Click to update fields in a configured report. After changes are made, click **Update Report** to commit the changes to the registry.
- **Help**. Click to display the opening screen of the Small Business Server Customization Tool with Help on using this tool.
- **Close**. Click to close the dialog box after completing report configuration.

Small Business Server Client Setup Integration Wizard

One of the functions of Small Business Server's Set Up Computer Wizard is to facilitate installation of its application list components onto client computers. The Small Business Server Client Setup Integration Wizard extends the Setup Computer Wizard application list, thus providing an easy way of integrating third-party applications into client computer setup.

When the Small Business Server Client Setup Integration Wizard is launched, the following two options appear in the wizard's **Welcome** screen:

- Add an application to client setup.
- Remove an application from client setup.

The following section describes how to add and remove applications from the Set Up Computer Wizard using the Small Business Server Client Setup Integration Wizard.

Note The Set Up Computer Wizard application list may be extended manually, as described in *Chapter 44, Extension Mechanism for the Set Up Computer Wizard,* in *Part 9, Developing Small Business Server Solutions,* of this resource guide.

Information Fields

When running the Client Setup Integration Wizard, you will be prompted for information about the application you wish to add to the Set Up Computer Wizard. Information field definitions for the required entries are described below.

- **Enter the name of the application as you would like it to appear in client setup**. Name of the application as it will appear in the Set Up Computer Wizard's list of applications to install, and in log files.

- **Enter a short name for the application**. Name used internally by the Set Up Computer Wizard to track your application. This short name may be a maximum of 8 characters.

- **What operating system does the application run on**. A drop-down list, used to select the operating system the application can be installed on. Select **Both**, if the application will run on Windows NT 4.0 Workstation, Windows 95 and Windows 98—select **NT4.0**, if the application only runs on Windows NT 4.0 Workstation—or select **Win9x** if the application only runs on Windows 95 and Windows 98.

  Note If your application uses a different install command or package to install on Windows NT 4.0 Workstation versus Window 95 and Window 98, you will need to add the application to the Set Up Computer Wizard by doing *both* of the following:

  - Select **NT4.0** in the drop-down list and specify the information for the Windows NT 4.0 Workstation installation.
  - Select **Win9x** and specify the information for the Windows 95 and Windows 98 installation.

- **Should the application be selected by default in client setup**. A drop-down list, used to select whether the application should appear selected or unselected in the Set Up Computer Wizard application list. Select **Yes** or **No**.

- **Description of application**. Text describing the application and used by the Client Installation Wizard (the Set Up Computer Wizard running on the client side).

- **Disk space estimate in megabytes.** Number specifying the amount of disk space required by your application on the client computer to complete installation.
- **Installation command.** Command line needed to complete unattended installation of your application. The default value is the following:

    \\%SBSServer%\ClientApps

    You must append the folder name you created for your application in the above share location along with the install command, as shown in the following example:

    %SBSServer%\ClientApps\YourApplicationName\Setup.exe

    where *%SBSServer%* is your server name.
- **Installation key.** The registry key and string used by the Client Installation Wizard to detect whether your application is already installed. This must be specified in the following format:

    "<Registry key>","<String name>"

    where <Registry key> is replaced with the path to the registry key that needs to be checked to determine if the application is already installed on the client machine, and where <String name> is replaced with the value name of the string. For example:

    "SOFTWARE\Microsoft\Windows\CurrentVersion\Uninstall\YourApplication Name","DisplayName"
- **Does the application require an unattend file for setup.** A drop-down list used to select whether the application requires an unattend file to complete installation. Select **Yes** if your application requires a response file for unattended more (you must also provide the response file); select **No** if your application does not require a response file.
- **Location of the unattend file.** The path to your application's INF file. This path must be relative to the %SBSServer%\SmallBusiness directory. The Template directory is the preferred location.
- **Source Name.** Initial name of the unattend/response file template at the location specified in **Location of the unattend file**.
- **Destination Name.** The name to which the **Source Name** file must be changed after it is installed.

Customization Process

When using the Client Setup Integration Wizard to extend the Set Up Computer Wizard, the Set Up Computer Wizard application list is customized to include your application for set up to client computers. In order for the Set Up Computer Wizard to locate your application, the installation files for the application must be installed on the server, as described in the following section.

Copying Your Application Installation Files to the Server

To enable Set Up Computer Wizard installation of your application to client machines, copy your application installation files to the server as follows:

- Create a folder for your application in the following share:

    %servername%\ClientApps

- Copy your application installation files to that folder.

Copying Your Unattend File to the Server

To enable Set Up Computer Wizard installation of your application to the client machine when your application is using an unattend file, you must also copy the unattend file to the server, preferably to the following share:

%sbsroot%\SmallBusiness\Template

Running the Small Business Server Client Setup Integration Wizard

To add or remove an application from the Set Up Computer Wizard using the Small Business Server Client Setup Integration Wizard, perform the following steps.

▶ **To add an application to the Set Up Computer Wizard application list**

1. Log on to Small Business Server as the Administrator.
2. Launch the SBS Client Setup Integration Wizard as described in *Chapter 51, Small Business Server 4.5 Tool Installation and Access.*
3. Select **Add an application to client setup**, and then click **Next**.
4. Type the required information for your application in the appropriate fields. For a description of the required information, refer to the "Information Fields" section discussed earlier. Click **Next** when complete.
5. If your application requires an unattend file, enter the required information for the unattend file. For a description of required information, refer to the "Information Fields" section discussed earlier. Click **Next** when complete.
6. Click **Finish**.

▶ **To remove an application from the Set Up Computer Wizard application list**
1. Log on to Small Business Server as the Administrator.
2. Launch the SBS Client Setup Integration Wizard as described in *Chapter 51, Small Business Server 4.5 Tool Installation and Access*.
3. Select **Remove an application from client setup**, and then click **Next**.

   Note Only the applications integrated into client setup by the Small Business Server Client Setup Integration Wizard can be removed by it.

4. From the **What application would you like to remove?** list, select the application you wish to remove from client setup. Click **Next** when complete.
5. Click **Finish**.

   Note This will not remove your application installation files from the server.

Checking the Set Up Computer Wizard Application List

If you added or removed an application from the Set Up Computer Wizard, you can check the content of the wizard's application list as follows:

▶ **To check the Set Up Computer Wizard application list**
1. Click **Start**, and then click **SBS Console** to launch the Small Business Server console.
2. Click **More Tasks** and then click **Manage Computers** to display the **Manage Computers** page.
3. Click the **set up a computer** taskpad to launch the **Set Up Computer Wizard**.
4. Confirm that your application was added or removed from the wizard's application list.

Fax Monitoring and Performance Tools

The following Fax Monitoring and Performance Tools are graphical user interfaces (GUIs) used to observe fax status and performance data:

- FaxMon
- FaxPerf

FaxMon

FaxMon provides real-time status of all fax devices and displays histories of fax job and fax device status. Also, this tool logs fax job histories to the faxhistory.log file and the fax device status history to the devicehistory.log file. When the **Fax Monitoring Tool** is double-clicked from the Resource Kit's Tools Management Console (TMC), it launches the **FaxMon** GUI containing displays for fax devices, faxes, and history.

FaxPerf

FaxPerf lists the initial (from the time FaxPerf started), current (present moment), and difference (current minus initial) numbers for the following fax performance data:

- Inbound: bytes, faxes, pages, minutes, and failed receptions
- Outbound: bytes, faxes, pages, minutes, failed connections, and failed transmissions
- Total: bytes, faxes, pages, and minutes

The data is updated every minute and logged to the faxperf.log file. When the **Fax Performance Monitoring Tool** is double-clicked from the TMC, it launches the FaxPerf GUI containing a display of the above fax performance categories.

PART 11

Troubleshooting

Part 11 contains troubleshooting techniques and procedures for the following Microsoft® BackOffice® Small Business Server 4.5 components or services:

Chapter 53   Small Business Server Setup Troubleshooting   791

Chapter 54   Client Setup Troubleshooting   799

Chapter 55   Fax Service Troubleshooting   809

Chapter 56   Modem Sharing Service Troubleshooting   827

Chapter 57   E-mail and Internet Troubleshooting   833

CHAPTER 53

Small Business Server Setup Troubleshooting

Overview

This chapter outlines common error messages and problems encountered while installing or upgrading the Microsoft® BackOffice® Small Business Server. Troubleshooting assistance is provided.

Troubleshooting during Setup

The following outlines some common setup problems and upgrade issues, with their potential cause and probable solution.

Problem   **Small Business Server components are not updated during upgrade**

Solution   If you installed Small Business Server 4.5 beta software, you must uninstall each individual beta version application before you install the retail version of Small Business Server 4.5. If you do not uninstall the beta versions, Setup will fail and the beta version of the application will remain on your server computer.

Problem   **Programs interrupting Small Business Server 4.5 Setup**

Solution   Small Business Server 4.5 Setup will restart your computer a number of times. To avoid potential problems during setup, you should remove all shortcuts from the **Startup Programs** group.

Problem   **SQL Server 6.5 uninstall doesn't finish**

Solution   Once you have upgraded from Small Business Server 4.0 to Small Business Server 4.5 and uninstall SQL Server 6.5, a pop-up message appears slightly hidden behind the **Modifying Services** dialog box. Click **OK** to finish uninstalling SQL Server.

Problem	**Internet Explorer 5.0 Favorites and Homepage are not updated after the Small Business Server 4.5 upgrade**
Solution	If you installed Internet Explorer 5.0 on your Small Business Server 4.0x computer, and then upgraded to Small Business Server version 4.5, Internet Explorer will retain all previous settings. Some of these settings are no longer applicable to Small Business Server 4.5.

The following adjustments need to be made for Internet Explorer on the Small Business Server computer. Add the following web site Favorites to the Favorites menu in Internet Explorer:

- Microsoft Small Business web site:
  http://www.microsoft.com/smallbusinessserver
- My Internet Home Page:
  http://LocalHost
- My Intranet Home Page:
  http://LocalHost/Intranet
- Small Business Server Client User Guide:
  http://LocalHost/Intranet/SBSClientHelp/Default.asp

▶ **To set the default home page to the Client User Guide**

1. Open **Internet Explorer**.
2. On the **Tools** menu, click **Internet Options**.
3. Select the **General** tab.
4. Under **Home Page**, type the following in the **Address** box:
   http://LocalHost/Intranet/SBSClientHelp/Default.asp
5. Click **OK**.

Chapter 53 Small Business Server Setup Troubleshooting

Problem Small Business Server does not automatically detect 8255x Intel network interface cards

Solution If you have an Intel 82557, 82558, or 82559-based network interface card installed on your Small Business Server computer, Small Business Server Setup will not detect and install the card. You must install the card manually from the **Hardware Confirmation** screen during Small Business Server Setup.

▶ **To manually install the 8255x Intel network interface cards**

1. On the **Hardware Confirmation** page, click **Change**, and then select **Network**.
2. Select the **Adapters** tab.
3. Select **MS Loopback Adapter**, and then click **Remove**.
4. A message asking to confirm your action appears. Click **OK**.
5. Click **Add**, and then click **Have Disk**.
6. Insert the disk containing the network adapter driver.
7. Click **OK**, and then select the adapter type from the drop-down list. Acknowledge any vendor-specific messages that appear.
8. Select the **Bindings** tab, and then expand the tree view so you can see the network adapter listed under each binding type. Move your network adapter to the top of each list.
9. Click **Close**. The **TCP/IP Properties** dialog box appears.
10. Select **Specify an IP address**.
11. Type **10.0.0.2** for the **IP Address**.
12. Type **255.255.255.0** for the **Subnet Mask**.
13. Select the **WINS Address** tab.
14. Type **10.0.0.2** for the **Primary** and **Secondary WINS Server**.
15. Click **OK** and then click **Yes** to restart your computer. After the computer restarts, Small Business Server setup will continue automatically.

Problem Event Viewer Log Errors that do not cause problems

Solution A number of known errors can appear in the Event Viewer logs under certain circumstances, but they do not cause problems in your applications. Some of these errors occur when Performance Monitor counters are not properly implemented by the applications that are running.

Table 53.1 Known Errors

Error ID	Source	Description
1005	MSExchangeSA	network preventing connection to the Microsoft Exchange
4320	NetBT	duplicate WINS names
1008	Perflib	open MSSQLServer failed
1008	Perflib	open ISAPIsearch in QPerf.dll failed
1008	Perflib	open ContentIndex in QPerf.dll failed
1008	Perflib	open ContentFilter in QPerf.dll failed
1008	Perflib	buffer size problems in modemshr.dll
1001	SQLCTR70	unable to open shared memory segment
1001	SQLCTR70	SQL Performance DLL open function failed
1001	SQLCTR70	cannot open the registry key
14	W3Svc	HTTP Filter DLL failed to load, data error

Problem Small Business Server Setup fails and displays a blank dialog box entitled *Csvroot.exe*

Solution If Remote Access Service (RAS) is not properly configured, it can cause the program csvroot.exe to fail. This condition will also prevent the Small Business Server console from running correctly.

▶ **To correct this problem**

1. Close the blank **csvroot.exe** dialog box.
2. Close the Small Business Server console (it may display as a blank screen without icons or text).
3. Click **Start**, point to **Settings**, click **Control Panel**, and then double-click **Network**.

4. Select the **Services** tab.
5. Select **Remote Access Server**, and then click **Remove**.
6. Follow the on-screen instructions to complete the removal. Click **Yes** to restart the server.
7. After the restart, click **Start**, point to **Settings**, click **Control Panel**, and then double-click **Network**.
8. Select the **Services** tab.
9. Click **Add**.
10. Select **Remote Access Service**.
11. Click **OK**.
12. On the **Add RAS Device** dialog box, verify that your modem is listed and then click **OK**.
13. Click **Configure**.
14. Under **Port Usage**, select **Dial out and Receive calls** and then click **OK**.
15. Click **Network**.
16. Under **Server Settings**, click **Configure**.
17. Under **Allow remote TCP/IP clients to access**, select **This computer only**, and then click **OK**.
18. Click **OK**, click **Continue**, click **OK**, and then **Close**.
19. Click **Yes** to restart the computer.

Problem   Uninstalling SQL Server 7.0 may cause the Content Indexer to fail

Solution   Before you uninstall SQL Server 7.0, verify two registry values. Any time you modify registry values manually, back up your system first as a protection against inadvertently corrupting a critical entry.

Caution Do not edit your registry unless it is absolutely necessary. If there is an error in your registry, your computer may become nonfunctional. Before you edit the registry, make sure you understand how to restore it if a problem occurs. For information on how to restore the system registry, see "Restoring the Registry" in the online Help for Regedit.exe or "Restoring a Registry Key" in the online Help for Regedt32.exe.

▶ **To back up the Windows NT® registry to a tape drive**

1. Click **Start**, point to **Programs**, **Administrative Tools (Common)**, and then click **Backup**.
2. On the **Operations** menu, click **Backup**. The **Backup Information** dialog box appears.
3. Select **Backup Local Registry** and follow the on-screen instructions.

Note If the **Backup Local Registry** checkbox is not available, the hard drive that contains the registry has not been selected prior to opening the **Backup Information** dialog box. Cancel out of the dialog box and in the **Drives** dialog box make sure that your system drive is selected.

▶ **To check the Windows registry**

1. Click **Start**, click **Run**, type *regedit.exe*, and then click **OK**.
2. Expand **HKEY_LOCAL_MACHINE**, **SOFTWARE**, **Microsoft**, **Windows**, **CurrentVersion**.
3. Click **SharedDlls**.
4. Scroll down the list until you find SystemDrive:\WINNT.SBS\System32\qperf.dll.
5. Double-click SystemDrive:\WINNT.SBS\System32\qperf.dll and make sure the **Value Data** is 2 or greater. If not, change the value in the **Value Data** box, and then click **OK**.
6. Find SystemDrive:\WINNT.SBS\System32\query.dll. It should be just below qperf.dll.
7. Double-click SystemDrive:\WINNT.SBS\System32\query.dll and make sure the **Value Data** is 2 or greater. If not, change the value in the **Value Data** box, and then click **OK**.
8. Close the **Registry Editor**.
9. Uninstall SQL Server.

Problem	SQL 6.5 database did not automatically upgrade to SQL Server 7.0 during Small Business Server 4.5 upgrade
Solution	This behavior is by design. The Small Business Server 4.5 Version Upgrade setup application will install SQL Server 7.0 into a new folder and will not migrate your existing SQL Server 6.5 database to SQL Server 7.0. Many third-party software applications might have a dependency on SQL Server 6.5 so you should consult the appropriate software vendor to ensure their software is compatible with SQL Server 7.0.

If you want to migrate your own SQL Server 6.5 databases to SQL Server 7.0, run the SQL Server Upgrade Wizard, which walks you through the process of migrating an existing SQL Server 6.5 database to the new SQL Server 7.0 format. This wizard is accessible from the Small Business Server **To Do List**.

Related Troubleshooting Knowledge Base Articles

The following knowledge base articles contain information on troubleshooting server setup and upgrades. The articles are located at:
http://support.microsoft.com

Article Number	Title
196098	*Microsoft Installer is Installed on the Small Business Server*
195146	*FTP Not Installed by Default in Small Business Server 4.5*
217914	*INTL Non-Office Canceling Outlook Install in OC Manager: Prevents Installing in the Future*
217999	*Services Installed by Default On Small Business Server 4.5*
218013	*Install Screen - Directories are not Listed for all Items*
218038	*Small Business Server 4.5 Install Appears to Hang during Modem Detection Phase of RAS Install*
218064	*Setup Does Not Prompt User to Remove Disk 3 and Reboot*
218076	*NTOP Setup: Small Business Server Does Not Let Customer Pick Components*
222489	*Setting Up Small Business Server Without a Network Adapter Being Detected*
225101	*Reinstalling the Small Business Server 4.5 Console Deletes all MAPI Profiles from the Server*
225309	*Disk Partitions Created with Non-Microsoft Utilities May Cause Setup to Fail*

CHAPTER 54

Client Setup Troubleshooting

Overview

This chapter outlines common error messages and problems encountered while using the Small Business Server Set Up Computer Wizard and when installing applications on the client with the Client Setup Wizard. Troubleshooting assistance is provided.

Troubleshooting during Client Setup

The following outlines some common client setup problems, with their potential cause and probable solution.

Problem — **When creating the client setup disk on Small Business Server, the following message appears:**
"Error 3 occurred attempting to open c:\smallbusiness\floppy\netpurum.ini for writing"

Solution — The Set Up Computer Wizard creates a client setup floppy diskette using files from the following directory on Small Business Server:

%systemroot%\Clients\Floppy

If the files within the Floppy directory or the Floppy directory itself is missing, Set Up Computer Wizard may display this error message. To resolve the error, the Floppy directory for the Set Up Computer Wizard must be reinstalled.

▶ **To reinstall the Floppy directory for the Set Up Computer Wizard**

1. Insert Disc 3 into the compact disk drive of Small Business Server.
2. Locate the Floppy directory using the path:

   \SbsAdmin\i386\Scw

3. Copy the Floppy directory to the following directory on Small Business Server:

   %systemroot%\SmallBusiness

4. Restart the Set Up Computer Wizard.

Problem   **When reinstalling the Floppy directory, the following message appears:**
"Error 5 occurred attempting to open c:\smallbusiness\floppy\netparam.ini for writing"

Solution   If the user account performing this operation does not have Read/Write access to the files within the Floppy directory on Small Business Server, the error message may be displayed, preventing the directory from being copied. To resolve the error, the permissions on the %systemroot%\SmallBusiness\Clients\Floppy directory of Small Business Server must be modified.

▶ **To grant full access permission to the user account performing the copy operation**

1. Click **Start**, point to **Programs**, and then click **Windows NT Explorer**.
2. Right-click on the SmallBusiness folder and then click **Properties**.
3. Select the **Sharing** tab, and then click **Shared as**.
4. Click **Permissions**, and then click **Add**.
5. Select the user account to which you want to add permissions. Click **Show Users** if necessary.
6. Click **Add**, and then click **OK**.
7. From the **Type of Access** drop-down menu, select **Full Control**.
8. Click **OK** and **Apply**. Click **OK** again.
9. Perform the steps of the procedure "To reinstall the floppy directory for the Set Up Computer Wizard" again.

Problem   **The Set Up Computer Wizard will not launch from the Small Business Server Console**
OR
The Set Up Computer Wizard crashes with a fatal error message

Solution   These problems may arise if any Set Up Computer Wizard files are missing or corrupted. All the files necessary for the Set Up Computer Wizard to run are located within the SmallBusiness directory. To remedy this problem, the Set Up Computer Wizard must be reinstalled.

▶ To reinstall the Set Up Computer Wizard files

1. Insert Disc 3 into the compact disk drive of Small Business Server.
2. Locate the following directory:

    \Sbsadmin\i386\Scw

3. Copy the files within the Bin subdirectory to %systemroot%\SmallBusiness on Small Business Server.
4. Copy the Floppy and Template directories to %systemroot%\SmallBusiness on Small Business Server.

Problem   The login script does not run when the user logs on to the client computer

Solution   Small Business Server uses a logon script to initiate the installation of the client applications. If the organization has a backup domain controller (BDC), the login scripts should be copied manually from Small Business Server, the primary domain controller (PDC), in order to ensure that the client login script will execute at all times.

▶ To copy login scripts to the BDC's

1. Locate the login scripts in the following directory on the Small Business Server:

    %systemroot%\Winnt.sbs\System32\Repl\Import\Scripts\SmallBusiness

2. Copy the SmallBusiness directory from Small Business Server to the %systemroot%\Winnt.sbs\System32\Repl\Import\Scripts directory on the BDCs.

If further troubleshooting is required, observe error messages that occur during the login process. To do this, make a network connection to the Small Business Server and run the login script manually according to the steps that follow.

▶ To run the login script manually

1. Open a command prompt or an MS-DOS prompt on the client computer.
2. Type *Net Use Z:\\sbsserver\netlogon*, where *sbsserver* is the name of Small Business Server.
3. Type *Z:* and then press ENTER.
4. Locate the SmallBusiness directory and run the batch file named *username*.bat, where *username* is the name of the user currently logged on.
5. If an error message appears, record the error message and search the Microsoft Knowledge Base for assistance in troubleshooting the error.

Problem	**The Client Installation Wizard does not startup for client application installation**
Solution	When the client login script executes, it checks whether or not it has run the Client Installation Wizard previously. Failure to run the Client Installation Wizard may indicate that the client login script thinks that it has previously run the wizard. To force the Client Installation Wizard to run, the "Installed" file in the client computer's response directory must be renamed.

▶ **To rename the "Installed" file**

1. Check the server for the "Installed" file using the following path: %systemroot%\SmallBusiness\Clients\Response*ClientComputer*, where *clientcomputer* is the client computer name.
2. If you locate the file, rename it to installed.old.
3. Log off the client machine and then log back on.
4. If the Client Installation Wizard still fails to run, create a new client setup diskette and run it on the client computer.

Problem	**The Client Installation Wizard terminates with** *"Setup was unable to open the information file \\%sbsserver%\clients\response\clientcomputername\clioc.inf. Contact your system administrator"* **error message (error code: 0x3 at line 1373780)**
Solution	A missing or incomplete client response directory typically causes this error. To resolve this error, the client response directory must be reinstalled.

▶ **To reinstall the client response directory**

1. From the Small Business Server console **More Tasks** page, click **Manage Computers** to setup a client computer with the Set Up Computer Wizard.
2. Follow the steps of the Set Up Computer Wizard.
3. When the Set Up Computer Wizard prompts for **computername**, type the name of the client computer.
4. When the wizard is finished, log off the client and log back in. The login script should run and the Client Installation Wizard should start.

Note The Set Up Computer Wizard creates a client setup diskette. It is not necessary to apply this diskette to the client computer to resolve this error message.

Problem	**The Client Installation Wizard starts to install client applications, but applications fail to install**
Solution	The Client Installation Wizard is designed to install all applications silently. The wizard does not display error messages encountered during application installation. If the specific application setup program encounters a fatal error, then the application installation will terminate and the Client Installation Wizard will skip to the next application.

Each application creates an associated log file on the client computer. The log file for Office 2000 (office.log) is stored in the following directories:

- Windows 95/98:
  %windir%\System\Setup
- Windows NT Workstation:
  %systemroot%\System32\Setup

All other application log files are stored in the root of the C: drive. The log files are named after the application and contain information about the installation. Analyzing the log files may be helpful in determining the cause of installation failure. If this approach does not isolate the cause of failure, you can install applications manually on the client to expose the installation dialog boxes and allow error messages to be displayed on the screen when they occur.

▶ **To install client applications manually and observe error messages**

1. Insert the client setup diskette created by the Set Up Computer Wizard, into the client machine floppy drive.
2. Open a command prompt on the client machine and type in a command line listed below to manually install an application.
3. If any error messages appear during the installation, record the error message and search the Microsoft Knowledge Base for assistance in troubleshooting the error.

The list below describes the command strings for installing each application manually. In each case, %sbsserver% refers to the name of Small Business Server. Use the procedure that follows to install client applications manually.

- NT Service Pack 4:
  \\%sbsserver%\Clientapps\MS\Winntsp4\Sp4i386.exe
- Internet Explorer:
  \\%sbsserver%\Clientapps\MS\Office\Cd1\Ie5\En\Ie5setup.exe
- Proxy Client:
  \\%sbsserver%\Mspclnt\Setup.exe

- Microsoft Office 2000 CD1: \\%sbsserver%\Clientapps\MS\Office\Cd1\Setup.exe
- Microsoft Office 2000 CD2: \\%sbsserver%\Clientapps\MS\Office\Cd2\Setup.exe
- Fax Client (Windows 95/98): \\%sbsserver%\Clientapps\MS\Fax\Win95\Setup.exe
- Fax Client (Windows NT): \\%sbsserver%\Clientapps\MS\Fax\i386\Faxsetup.exe
- Microsoft Outlook: \\%sbsserver%\Clientapps\MS\Office\Cd1\Setup.exe
- Modem Sharing Client (Windows 95/98): \\%sbsserver%\Clientapps\MS\Modemshr\Win95\Setup.exe

▶ **To install the Modem Sharing Client on Windows NT Workstation**

1. From **My Computer**, double-click **Control Panel** and then **Network**.
2. Select the **Services** tab and then click **Add**.
3. Select the **Modem Sharing service** and click **Have Disk** to change the installation path to :\\%sbsserver%\Clientapps\MS\Modemshr\Winnt\i386
4. Follow the on-screen instructions of the installation.

Problem   Windows 95/98 Client Computer with a 3Com 3C905b network interface adapter can't access the Small Business Server computer

Solution   Some versions of the Windows 95/98 driver for the 3Com 3C905b network interface card may not function correctly in 32-bit NDIS mode. If you have this network card in a client computer, and you cannot see the server following the network configuration, you need to use the 16-bit NDIS mode.

▶ **To change NDIS modes**

1. On the client computer, click **Start**, point to **Settings**, click **Control Panel**, and then double-click **Network**.
2. Select the network interface card, and then click **Properties**.
3. Select the **Driver Type** tab.
4. Select **Real Mode (16 bit) NDIS driver**.
5. Restart the computer.

Chapter 54 Client Setup Troubleshooting

Problem	**Small Business Server Client Setup installs incorrect Intel network interface card**
Solution	If you have an Intel 82558 network interface card installed on your client computer, Small Business Server Client Setup will detect and install it as an Intel 82557 network interface card, which does not work.
	To correct this problem, install the Intel 82558 network interface card on your client computer before you run Setup from the disk created using the Set Up Computer Wizard.

▶ **To install the correct network interface card on a client computer**

1. Click **Start**, point to **Settings**, click **Control Panel**, and then double-click **Network**.
2. Select the **Configuration** tab, and then click **Add**.
3. Click **Adapter**, and then click **Add**.
4. Click **Have Disk**, and insert the disk containing the network adapter driver.
5. Click **OK**, and follow the on-screen instructions to complete the installation.

Problem	**Client computer cannot read the client setup disk**
Solution	Some computers have trouble reading the Set Up Computer Wizard disks.
	If this occurs, copy the Setup.exe, Ipdetect.exe, Ipdx86.exe, and Netparam.ini files on the client setup disk to a temporary folder on the server. Next, copy the files to a 3.5-inch disk that was formatted by the client computer.
Problem	**The Set Up Computer Wizard did not create the configuration files for a client computer or user**
Solution	The Set Up Computer Wizard copies the configuration files to a folder on the server in systemdrive:\SmallBusiness\Clients\Response\ClientComputerName for each client computer it sets up.
	Verify that this folder exists. If it was not created, check the permissions for the Response folder. The Administrator account should have full control.
	Also confirm that the Administrator account has full control for the folder systemdrive:\Winnt.sbs\System32\Repl\Import\Scripts\SmallBusiness.
	The wizard copies the SBSUser.bat file to this location.
	Once you have confirmed the above items, run the Set Up Computer Wizard again.

Problem	**After running the client setup disk and restarting, the client computer cannot connect to the server**
Solution	If the client computer is not physically connected to the network, or its network adapter is not correctly configured, the client computer cannot gain access to the Small Business Server network.
	Confirm that the client computer is physically connected to the network, that the network adapter is installed and configured properly, and that TCP/IP and the client networking components are installed.
	If the client computer is running Windows NT Workstation 4.0, check the system event log for errors.
Problem	**No Small Business Server client applications are installed on the client computer**
Solution	Client applications should be installed when the user logs on to the client computer for the first time.
	Verify that the user logs on to the computer by using the correct user account, and that the client computer has available hard disk space.
	Run the Client Installation Wizard to add the client applications to the computer.
Problem	**No client applications are available to a new user on a client computer running Windows NT Workstation already set up on the network**
Solution	If the user who first installs the Small Business Server client applications on a client computer running Windows NT Workstation did not have administrative rights, the client applications may not be available to other users.
	Uninstall the client applications, and then use the Set Up Computer Wizard to add the client applications to the computer.
Problem	**A user is unable to access any modem-based resources from a client computer**
Solution	After setting up the client computer, you must configure its modem sharing port to use the modems attached to the server computer.
	On the client computer, run the Modems program in **Control Panel**. If the program does not detect a modem driver, configure it manually by using the same type of modem as those installed on the server.

Related Troubleshooting Knowledge Base Articles

The following knowledge base articles contain information on troubleshooting client setup and the Set Up Computer Wizard. The articles are located at: **http://support.microsoft.com**

Article Number	Title
214688	*How to Troubleshoot Small Business Server Setup Computer Wizard*
215721	*How to Troubleshoot Client Application Installation*
183234	*Small Business Server Client Applications Cannot be Installed Over a Modem*
184454	*No Restart after Client Setup Causes Invalid Password*
217943	*Cannot Install Proxy Client from CD*
216106	*What the Client Setup Disk Does*
218072	*Fax Client and Modem Sharing Client will not Install on Windows 2000 Professional*
218112	*Client Setup won't Run for Proper User when More than One User Shares Computer*
225272	*Client Applications do not Finish Installing on Windows 95 client*
225499	*Preventing Multiple User's Icons from Appearing on Small Business Server Clients*

CHAPTER 55

Fax Service Troubleshooting

Overview

This chapter outlines common error messages and problems encountered when installing and using Microsoft® Fax Service. Troubleshooting assistance is provided.

Troubleshooting Fax Service

The following outlines some common faxing problems, their potential cause and probable solution.

Problem — **Microsoft Fax Service fails during installation and the following error message appears:**
"At least on Class 1 modem must be installed for the Fax Service to install"

Solution — Microsoft Fax Service installation may fail if an unsupported modem is installed during Small Business Server Setup. At least one Class 1 modem must be installed during the Small Business Server Setup or the fax and modem services will not install correctly. If the modem is a data-only modem, error messages may occur.

If fax or modem services fail to install, perform the procedure below to determine if Small Business Server supports the modem you are using.

▶ To check for Small Business Server modem support and reinstall services

1. Check the Recommended Hardware List at:
   http://www.microsoft.com/smallbusinessserver
   for your modem. This list contains modems specifically tested to work with Small Business Server 4.5.

2. If the modem appears on the Recommended Hardware List, make sure the modem is connected securely to the correct COM port and then reinstall the Fax Service by running the Small Business Server Setup again, from **Add/Remove Programs** in **Control Panel**.

3. If the Fax Service still fails to install, check that the modem firmware and Modem.inf file is the latest version available from the manufacturer. If necessary, obtain the latest versions and then repeat step 2.

Note If you are uncertain whether you have a Class 1 modem, use the procedure outlined in the "Troubleshoot the Modem with HyperTerminal" section in *Chapter 56, Modem Sharing Service Troubleshooting* to determine modem class.

Problem	Problems sending faxes — server configuration problems
Solution	If faxes cannot be sent, this may be a symptom of one of the following problems:

Improperly connected modem

Use the procedure outlined in the "Troubleshoot the Modem with HyperTerminal" section in *Chapter 56, Modem Sharing Service Troubleshooting* to determine if the modem is correctly connected to the computer.

▶ To verify the Fax Server sends a test fax

1. Click **Start**, point to **Programs**, **Fax (Common)**, and then click **Fax Send Utility**. The **Compose New Fax** dialog box appears.

2. Enter the recipient name and all other information necessary to send a test fax.

3. Click **Start**, point to **Settings**, and then click **Printers** to open the **Printers** dialog box.

4. Double click the **Fax** icon. The **Fax queue** dialog box appears.

5. Verify that the fax was sent by the status in the Fax queue.

Note If the fax entered and left the queue when sent, the problem may be on the client end. In that case, see "Problems sending faxes: client configuration problems" later in this chapter.

Faulty fax device registry setting incurred from modem removal/reinstalls

When modems are removed and reinstalled, a problem occurs if entries under fax devices in the registry are not cleared automatically as the modems are removed. This may result in a faulty device list which shows entries for devices that are not actually attached to the system. This can cause several fax problems, including the inability to send a fax. To correct this, perform the procedure below.

▶ **To correct the registry key for fax devices**

1. From **My Computer**, double-click **Control Panel**.
2. Double-click **Services** to open the **Services** dialog box.
3. Select **Microsoft Fax Service** and then click **Stop**.
4. Click **Start** and then click **Run**.
5. Type *Regedt32*. The **Registry Editor** appears.
6. Delete all entries under the following registry key: HKEY-LOCAL-MACHINE/Software/Microsoft/Fax/Fax devices
7. Exit the **Registry Editor** and restart Small Business Server.
8. Perform the procedure earlier in this section entitled "To verify the Fax Server sends a test fax."

Note If the fax entered and left the queue when sent, the problem may be on the client end. In that case, see "Problems sending faxes: client configuration problems" later in this chapter.

Improperly configured fax client

If a test fax is sent and it does not appear in the fax printer queue, the Fax client installation may be at fault. See "Problems sending faxes: client configuration problems" next in this chapter.

Problem **Problems sending faxes — client configuration problems**

Solution When troubleshooting the fax sending process on the client computer, you must identify where the process is failing. The process starts with creating a fax on the client computer, and sending it to the shared fax printer on the server computer for transmission.

If the fax never appears in the server's fax printer queue, but does appear in the local fax printer's queue, then you should:

- Verify the client computer is connected to the server computer, and is using the correct shared fax printer.

Because Fax Service uses the Windows NT print services to send a fax to the shared fax printer on the Small Business Server computer, try printing a document to a shared printer on the server computer. If you can print a document successfully, then the fax printer on the client computer and the shared fax printer can communicate successfully.

- Verify that the user has permission to send a fax to the shared fax printer.

▶ **To verify the fax client permissions are properly configured**

1. Send test faxes to multiple clients to determine if only one client is at fault. Use the procedure earlier in this section entitled "To verify the Fax Server sends a test fax."
2. If only one client is not receiving the test fax, go to the **Manage Faxes** page on the Small Business Server console and highlight the fax printer in the list.
3. Click **Control access to fax printers** to launch the Printer Access Wizard.
4. Verify that the client appears in **Users who can fax** list in the right pane of the wizard to determine if the client has fax printer permissions.
5. If the client does not have permissions, add them to the list by highlighting the user name in the left pane and then click **Add**.
6. Click **Next** and then **Finish** to update fax permissions.
7. Resend a test fax using the procedure "To verify the Fax Server sends a test fax" and verify the fax was received.

- Try sending a fax from another client computer to determine if the problem is specific to the computer or to the network.
- Log on to the client computer as another user to determine if the problem is specific to that user or to the client computer.
- If you are using Outlook to send the fax, verify that the Fax Mail Transport service is installed. In Outlook, on the **Tools** menu, click **Services**. The Fax Mail Transport service should appear in the **Services** list box.
- Verify that the Fax Client program exists in **Control Panel**. If not, the client computer was set up incorrectly. You will need to run the Set Up Computer Wizard and reinstall the Fax Service Client.
- If the other client computers can send faxes, reinstall Fax Service Client on the problem client computer by using the Set Up Computer Wizard.

If reinstalling Fax Service Client does not resolve the problem, you may need to remove Fax Service Client by using **Add/Remove Programs** in **Control Panel**, then you can reinstall Fax Service Client.

Problem Problems with fax jobs entering and staying in the fax queue

Solution If fax jobs are entering and staying in the fax queue, the problem may be with connectivity. The following are troubleshooting steps to test the connectivity and isolate the problem.

- First, retry the fax job, and then check the System log and the Application log for any fax-related events.
- If the Application log lists line-busy or no-dial-tone errors, check the physical telephone connection. Plug an analog telephone into the fax line, and dial the destination fax machine. Be sure to enter any necessary dialing prefixes. If the destination fax machine answers, the physical connection between your fax server and the destination machine is good.
- If the physical telephone connection is working, the problem may be the numbers the Fax Service is dialing:

Some non-local telephone numbers are preceded by "1" to dial correctly. In the **Dialing** tab of the **Fax Server Administrator** utility, you can identify which telephone numbers must be preceded by "1" by selecting their three-digit prefixes.

If your area code uses 10-digit dialing for several different area codes, then numbers need to be entered differently in the Fax Client, depending on whether the number is local or long distance. If the fax number is a true long-distance number, specify the appropriate country, area code, and fax number, such as *United States, 212, 555-1212*. The number will then be dialed correctly as 1 212 555-1212. If the fax number is a 10-digit number, the fax number is dialed as entered. In that case, the user just needs to enter the digits to be dialed, such as *206, 555-1212*.

If the analog telephone line used for the fax modem requires a dialing prefix (the most common prefix is "9,"), then TAPI Dialing Location needs to reflect this. This dialing location can be configured in **Control Panel**, **Modems**, **Dialing Properties**.

Note The dialing location properties (such as the prefix) are not used if the **Dial as Entered** box is checked when entering a contact's fax number. This means that for a 10-digit fax number, the entire dialing string must be entered in the fax number dialog box, i.e., "9,2065551212."

If the telephone line does not work, check for these problems:

- The telephone line may only allow dial-in. Some telephone lines especially RAS lines or members of a rollover group, are not enabled for outbound dialing. Be sure that all outbound telephone lines can dial both locally and long distance. Being able to obtain a dial tone by itself is not is not proof that outbound dialing works.
- The telephone may not have long-distance access or may require an access code. Telephone lines can be disabled for long-distance access or require an authorization code.
- The telephone may be digital. The telephone line must be analog because modems require analog lines. Most business telephone systems that have more than three lines are digital. Some digital telephones have an analog-out jack that can be used by modems.

Once the telephone line is confirmed to be configured correctly, check the server installation as follows:

▶ **To ensure that the Fax Service was correctly installed**

1. In **Control Panel** on the server, double-click **Services**. Make sure the Microsoft Fax and Telephony Services are started.
2. Check the startup account for the Fax Service, as follows:
   - Select **Microsoft Fax Service**, and then click **Startup**.
   - Verify that the account this service is using is an administrator account.

   Note If the password for this account has recently been changed, it must also be changed here

   Note In order for Exchange routing to work, the Exchange profile referenced in the **Routing** tab must be for the same Windows NT account as the Fax Server Service Account. By default, this is the Administrator account, and the profile is called the Administrator profile.

3. Double-click **Telephony**. Make sure the TAPI and Unimodem drivers are installed on the **Telephony Drivers** tab.
4. Double-click **Modems**. Make sure the modem is installed and attached to the correct COM port. Verify the properties of the device, and make sure the settings are correct for the modem type.
5. Double-click **Fax Server**. Check the following:
   - Is a fax printer listed? Try assigning and testing another fax printer.
   - Is a device name (modem) selected in the fax printer properties?

6. Check cables for fuzzy connection. Put an analog telephone on the fax line, and listen to the dial tone and to the number tones as they are dialed. If the line has noticeable static, replace the telephone cable with a new one, and check again. If there still is a noticeable amount of static, the problem may be with the telephone line itself.
7. Verify that the telephone line is plugged into the correct port on the modem. The correct jack typically is labeled "telco" or has a small picture of a wall jack.
8. If the modem is external, make sure it is connected properly and powered on. Turn the modem off and on again, and try sending the fax again. You can also check the status in the Fax Server application in **Control Panel** via the **Status** tab.
9. If necessary, replace the modem, and remove and reinstall the fax and modem services.

Problem

Failures receiving faxes

Solution

The best way to troubleshoot fax reception is to check each step of fax reception and isolate the error. Arrange for a fax to be sent to the Fax Server, and listen to your Fax Server answer. If the modem speaker is enabled on your server, you will hear a modem handshake tone, similar to the handshake of a dial-up networking session. If the Fax Server does not answer, select the **Receive** tab in **Fax Administrator**, and check the following:

- Is a device name (modem) selected?
- Is the correct telephone number specified for the receiving device?
- Is the number of rings set to 1 or 2? If the number of rings is set to 0, then the Fax Server may not answer. The preferred settings are 1 or 2.

If the modem answers with a handshake, or the handshake does not complete correctly, then RAS may be interfering with Microsoft Fax Service. This happens most often with modems that do not support Adaptive Answer. If this is the case, in **Control Panel**, under **Services**, stop the Remote Access Server Service and retry the fax. If the fax comes through, you will need to either install a separate modem for Remote Access, disable one service or the other, or replace the existing modem with a modem that supports Adaptive Answer.

If faxes are arriving but are not being delivered to a network storage point, verify permissions, as follows:

- In Explorer, verify that Everyone is set to have at least the permission Change on the following folders:

    %systemroot%\FaxReceive

    %systemroot%\FaxStore

If faxes are not being routed to the correct Exchange account, then check that the profile specified under the **Routing** and **Receive** tabs of **Fax Server Administrator** is for the startup account of the Microsoft Fax Server Service. Microsoft Fax Service routes faxes through the fax printer queue. When Microsoft Fax Service is unable to route an incoming fax (for example, if a shared directory is unavailable), it keeps the fax in the fax jobs list until it successfully delivers the fax. You can open the fax jobs list for any fax printer and restart the print job for the incoming fax once the destination is available.

- In **Fax Server Administrator**, click the **Receive** tab, and check the following:

    Is a device name (modem) selected?

    Is the correct telephone number specified for the receiving device?

- If the inbound device is a printer, make sure the printer is online and can successfully print a test page.

- If the inbound device is a folder, check the NTFS permissions on the folder in Explorer.

- If the inbound device is a local Inbox, make sure the Profile Name selected is the currently logged-in user and that the user has Administrator rights. This user must also be the user who started the Fax Service.

Problem   **A fax print job is hung in the print queue**

Solution   Delete all pending print jobs on the fax printer, then stop and restart the spooler service in **Control Panel**, under **Services**.

If this does not fix the problem, the fax job may be hung in the queue because of a stuck print job.

▶ **To clear the print queue**

1. Stop the Fax Service (from **Control Panel**, under **Services**).
2. Stop the Spooler service (from **Control Panel**, under **Services**).
3. Go to C:\Winnt.sbs\System32\Spool\Printers and delete everything in the directory.

   Note This will delete all pending print and fax jobs, thus users need to reprint all jobs not printed or faxed.

4. Restart the Spooler service (from **Control Panel**, under **Services**).

Chapter 55 Fax Service Troubleshooting 817

5. Restart the Fax Service (from **Control Panel**, under **Services**).
6. Send the fax again.

> **Note** The above procedure is especially useful for print jobs that can't be deleted from the queue through Explorer.

Problem
One of the following messages appears in the Applications Event Log:
"The description for Event ID (8199) in Source (NT Fax) could not be found. It contains the following insertion string(s):
c:\Winnt.sbs\FaxReceive\<MsgNo.tif>,<MailboxName/Alias>"
OR
"Unable to route c:\Winnt.sbs\FaxReceive\<MsgNo.tif> to local inbox:<MailboxName/Alias>. The following error occurred: MAPI Error."

Solution
This problem results from installing Small Business Server, including its Exchange and Fax components, then uninstalling the Exchange component of Small Business Server and reinstalling the Enterprise Edition of Microsoft Exchange on the Small Business Server.

The error stems from the difference in the default installation behavior of Small Business Server compared to Windows NT® 4.0 or Windows NT 4.0 Enterprise Edition and Microsoft Exchange Server. Unlike Standard Windows NT and Exchange, Small Business Server automatically creates the Windows NT Service Account for Exchange Server and creates the Administrator mailbox and profile. When the Small Business Server version of Exchange is uninstalled and the Enterprise Edition of Exchange is reinstalled, the Administrator mailbox is not recreated. This means that the Administrator profile is pointing to a non-existent account. Therefore, faxes can no longer be routed to the Administrator profile as configured in Fax Server Administrator.

In order to correct the problem, in Exchange Server Administrator, create a mailbox for the Administrator account. Then, delete and recreate the profile for the Administrator account, being sure to name the profile "Administrator." Open **Fax Server Administrator** in **Control Panel**, and verify that the Administrator profile is set under the **Routing** tab.

Problem
When attempting to install Fax Server after the initial Small Business Server installation, the following message appears:
"Unable to create fax printer"

Solution
When you are trying to reinstall the Fax Server Service and permissions to the initial fax printers have been changed, this error may occur.

To correct the problem, the "Administrator" account must be given Full Control of all fax printers. Check the properties of existing fax printers, and ensure that Administrator is set to Full Control, then reinstall the fax server.

Problem When trying to administer printers, the following message appears:
"Delete Port, Fax device can't be used for Printer folder, Please use the appropriate Fax Configuration applet in the Control Panel."

Solution This error occurs when trying to go to **File**, **Server Properties** in the Printers folder or when trying to configure printer ports. It may be caused by corrupted or nonsupported third-party drivers corrupting the print monitors.

▶ **To resolve the problem, do the following**

1. Delete the fax device from within Fax Server Properties or Task Manager.
2. Stop the Spooler and Fax Server services in **Control Panel**, under **Services**.
3. Run the Windows NT Registry Editor (Regedt32.exe) and open the following key:

   HKEY_LOCAL_MACHINE\System\CurrentControlSet\Control\Print\Monitor

> **Important** The next steps involve editing the registry. Before you edit the registry, make sure you understand how to restore it if a problem occurs. For more information, view the Help topic "Restoring the Registry" in Regedit.exe or the Help topic "Restoring a Registry Key" in Regedt32.exe.

4. Delete the subkey Microsoft Fax Monitor.
5. Go to the following key:
   KEY_LOCAL_MACHINE\System\CurrentControlSet\Control\Print\Printer
6. Delete the subkey call FAX.
7. Exit the Registry and restart the Spooler and Fax Server services.

At this point, you can manage the printers without getting an error message. It is highly recommended the customer obtains and installs a supported modem before you reinstall the fax printer.

Problem The following messages appear:
Event ID 2510, *"Server unable to map error code 1797"*
OR
"The Server Service was unable to map error code 1797"

Solution This error occurs on fax client setup when the login fax client cannot see the client applications subdirectory.

If a subdirectory is shared out with the name "clients," then the fax client installation will fail with this message.

Look in the \\<servername>\Clients\MS\Fax\<OS> subdirectory for the fax client setup programs. If a different subdirectory has been shared out with the name clients, then that subdirectory's share name will need to be changed, and the %systemdrive%\Clientapps subdirectory will need to be reshared as clients.

Chapter 55 Fax Service Troubleshooting

Problem When attempting to connect to the Fax share, the following message appears: *"Access is Denied."*

Solution Small Business Server Fax Service clients may receive the error message when attempting to connect to the Small Business Server Fax Service from a client. This error occurs primarily when the number of client licenses has been exceeded in one of two ways:

- The Small Business Server Not for Resale version comes with a six client licenses. A seventh client receives the *Access is Denied* error message.
- The Small Business Server 4.5 full version comes with licenses ranging from a five client licenses to 50 client licenses. Additional clients receive the *Access is Denied* error message.

To determine if you have more clients than licenses, run the **Server** applet in **Control Panel**, and check the user connections. Compare the number of connected users with the number of client licenses for Small Business Server. You can check the number of licensed users for Small Business Server by selecting About Microsoft Small Business Server in the **Manage Server** console. If the number of users exceeds the number of client licenses, then either add client licenses or disconnect users.

Users do not need to have their accounts deleted; they just need to be disconnected from the server. Click **Disconnect User** in the **Server** applet in **Control Panel**, or have the user log off from the network.

Problem Event ID 8199 message:
"Unable to route d:\ SBS <file> to the local inbox admin. MAPI error occurred."

Solution The Exchange profile used for fax routing must be for the same Windows NT account as the Microsoft Fax Server service account. By default, this account is the Administrator Windows NT account, and the Exchange profile is named Administrator.

If the Fax Server service account is changed, then a new Exchange profile needs to be created for that account, and that profile needs to be specified in Fax Properties.

If the profile is correctly configured, enable the Fax Server to route faxes to a printer, then send a test fax to verify that inbound routing to a printer works.

If inbound fax routing to a printer is working, reconfigure fax routing to route to the service account e-mail profile, and test again.

Problem	**Small Business Server Fax does not retain Receive tab settings.**
Solution	If the **Receive** tab in **Fax Service Administrator** can be configured, but inbound faxes are not saved, routed or printed according to the updated configuration, the options set in the **Receive** tab are not being saved.
	To resolve this problem, delete the **Receive** values from the registry. The next time the fax service is started it will recreate these values correctly.

▶ **To delete the Receive values from the registry**

1. Using Regedt32.exe, delete the following key:

    HKEY_LOCAL_MACHINE\Software\Microsoft\Fax\Devices\<device number>\Routing

2. Reboot the Small Business Server, and configure the **Receive** tab in **Fax Administrator**.

> **Note** Another method to resolve this problem without a reboot may be preferred. Delete all devices listed below the devices key, stop and restart the fax service, and reconfigure the **Receive** tab, as follows:
> HKEY_LOCAL_MACHINE\Software\Microsoft\Fax\Devices\<device number>

Problem	**Incoming faxes are routed only to the Administrator, and you want other users to be able to view them**
Solution	Inbound faxes in Microsoft Fax Service can only be routed to a single Inbox. This Inbox is by default the Administrator Inbox. Routed faxes can be routed to other domain users (such as an Office Administrator) by granting permission for the users to view the Administrator's mailbox or by routing faxes directly to the users. The recommended way to allow other users to view incoming faxes is for the Administrator to give them permission to view the Administrator mailbox. These users then have the ability to view and forward any faxes that are routed to the Administrator mailbox, without the administrator having to change the fax routing or fax service account settings.

▶ **To grant domain users the ability to view the Administrator mailbox**

1. While logged onto the server as Administrator, open the Microsoft Exchange client. The Administrator profile is automatically configured during Small Business Server setup. Click **View**, click **Folders**, right-click **Inbox**, then click **Properties**.

2. Select the **Permissions** tab, add the users who need to forward or view incoming faxes, and select an appropriate role. For help with selecting user roles, click **Help**.

3. On the users' machines, open the Exchange client application. Under **Tools**, under **Services**, select properties of the Microsoft Exchange Service.

4. Select the **Advanced** tab and add the Administrator mailbox. The Administrator mailbox is now available to the user, and incoming faxes can be viewed, sorted, and forwarded.

Another way to change the user who receives routed faxes it to configure the Fax Server to route messages to an e-mail account other than Administrator. This method is not recommended for inexperienced users. Some important considerations need to be taken into account when using this method:

- The account that is routed to (the route-to user) must be the Fax Server service account.
- Because the route-to account must be a service account, the route-to account must have Domain Administrator privileges. Domain Administrator privileges give the user full access to the server.
- A Mail profile must be configured on the server for the route-to user.

▶ **To configure a route-to account other than Administrator**

1. Grant the Domain Admin privileges to the route-to user in **User Manager for Domains**.

2. In **Control Panel**, under **Services**, select **Microsoft Fax Service**, click **Startup**, and then enter the route-to user and password in the **Account** section. The user's account will be granted the "logon as service" right.

3. Stop and start the Microsoft Fax Service.

4. In **Control Panel**, **Mail**, create a new profile for the route-to user that contains only the Microsoft Exchange Service.

5. Note the name of the new profile, and select it as the **Route-To** profile in **Fax Administrator**.

▶ **To route faxes to a public mailbox**

1. Open Exchange Administrator (by default this is c:\Exchsrvr\Bin\Admin, unless the install location was changed during setup.)

2. Create a new mailbox named FAX.

3. For the user account, chose the **Everyone** group from the **Domain** list.

4. Create a new mail profile for the Administrator account that points to the FAX mailbox.

5. Have the fax routing option use the new profile.

This will allow all users to see the faxes, but not the Administrators mail. However, if the Administrator starts Outlook, or any MAPI mail client, on the server, incoming faxes will be sent to the Administrator mailbox while Outlook is open. This is because only one MAPI profile can be used at a time. As soon as the Administrator closes Outlook, faxes will be routed to the FAX mailbox.

Problem   **Windows 95/98 clients are unable to see a fax printer**

Solution   If you have created a fax printer on Small Business Server and your Windows NT Workstation 4.0 clients are able to see it, however, your Windows 95 and 98 clients are unable to see it, you should shorten the share name of the fax printer. The maximum share name length that can be seen by Windows 95 and 98 clients is between 6 and 12 characters, depending upon the character set being used.

▶ **To shorten the share name of a fax printer**

1. From Small Business Server, click **Start**, point to **Settings**, and then click **Printers**.
2. Select the fax printer your clients are unable to see.
3. Right-click the fax printer and click **Sharing**.
4. Shorten the **Share Name**.
5. Click **Close**.

Problem   **The e-mail "Subject Line" was not sent when faxing from Outlook**

Solution   When faxing an e-mail message from Outlook on a Windows NT client computer, the subject line will not be sent by Fax Service. If you want the subject line to appear on the fax, you must enable cover page for Fax Mail Transport.

See the Small Business Server Online Guide for steps on how to add and configure the Fax Mail Transport for a Windows NT client computer.

Problem   **Problems sending documents as Outlook attachments**

Solution   To attach a document, the application that the document is registered to must be able to render the document. This involves the following two important components:

- The document must have a properly registered file type. If an attached file is not registered to an application, then the document will not be registered.
- The application must support the shell "PrintTo" verb. This verb allows you to print a specified document to a specified printer. To see if a program supports PrintTo, make the fax printer non-default, and then drag a document onto the fax printer. If the fax printer processes the document, then the application supports PrintTo.

Problem — **Sending Attachments from Outlook prompts you with the Fax Send Utility**

Solution — If you are sending a file attachment to a fax recipient in Outlook, you may be required to use the Fax Send Utility in order to send the attachment. This occurs when the attachment is a file type that uses DDE to print. In this case, if the application corresponding to the file type is open, the Fax Send Utility will appear. If the application is closed, the mail will be sent directly.

The most common applications that use this file type are Office 97 and Office 2000 applications.

▶ **To identify other files types that use DDE to print**

1. Double-click **My Computer**.
2. On the **View** menu, click **Options**.
3. Select the **File Types** tab.
4. Under **Registered File Types**, double-click the file type you are interested in (e.g., Microsoft Word document).
5. Under **Actions**, double-click **print** or **print to**.
6. Look at the **Use DDE** checkbox. If this is selected, the file type uses DDE to print.

Problem — **Sending Attachments from Outlook on Windows 95/98 clients results in multiple fax calls**

Solution — The behavior is by design. If you are sending a file attachment to a fax recipient in Outlook from a Windows 95/98 client, Fax Service will place a separate call for each attachment.

Problem — **Fax Messages from Outlook are not being sent**

Solution — Failure to deliver fax messages from Outlook could leave the fax transport in an unstable state. If no fax messages can be sent from Outlook, you must close and log out of Outlook, or restart the computer in order to reset the fax transport. You may run into this problem when attempting to send large fax jobs (such as bitmaps) on a Windows 95/98 client with low memory, or when attempting to fax from an application by printing to the fax printer while Outlook delivers a job to the printer spooler.

Problem	**Fax Send Utility does not display Outlook contacts when used on the Small Business Server computer**
Solution	The Fax Send Utility uses the Windows Address Book and not the Outlook Address Book, when used on the Small Business Server computer. In order to create a fax address in Outlook, you must add the Fax Address Book and the Personal Address Book to Outlook. You will then be able to create a fax address in Outlook that will be visible in the Windows Address Book.

▶ **To add Fax Address Book and Personal Address Book to Outlook**

1. Click **Start**, point to **Settings**, click **Control Panel**, and then double-click **Mail**.
2. Click **Add**.
3. Select the **Personal Address Book**, and then click **OK**.
4. Click **Add**.
5. Select the **Fax Address Book**, and then click **OK**.
6. Click **OK** to close.

▶ **To create a fax address in Outlook**

1. Open Outlook.
2. On the **Tools** menu, click **Address Book**.
3. On the **File** menu, click **New Entry**.
4. Select **Personal Address Book** from the **Put this entry** in the drop-down list.
5. Select **Fax Address** from the **Select the Entry Type** box and then click **OK**.
6. Enter the recipients' name and fax numbers and then click **OK**.
7. Close the **Address Book**.

Problem	**Fax Client Installer attempts to find the Fax Server**
Solution	During the installation of the client applications on a Windows NT Workstation client computer, the Fax Client will attempt to locate the Fax Server even if the Fax Server was not installed on the Small Business Server computer. The Fax Client installer will prompt for the name of the Fax Server. Click **Cancel** and Setup will continue to install the client applications.

Related Troubleshooting Knowledge Base Articles

The following knowledge base articles contain information on troubleshooting the Fax Service. The articles are located at:
http://support.microsoft.com

Article Number	Title
Q225101	Reinstalling Small Business Server 4.5 Console Deletes all MAPI Profiles on Server
Q222532	Small Business Server: Recommended Practices with Fax Service
Q225327	Small Business Server: Incomplete Print Job Listed in Queue when Fax Send Canceled
Q224433	Duplicate Modems Ports Appear in Fax Printer Properties
Q217977	Area Code is not Dialed Using Small Business Server Fax Wizard
Q225384	Small Business Server: Fax Does Not Use Second Modem when the First One is Busy
Q225461	Outlook Contacts are not Accessible from Fax Send Utility on Small Business Server
Q222616	Unable to Send Attachments by Fax When Source Program Is Open
Q217947	"Client Must Use These Cover Pages" Doesn't Work w/Windows 95/98
Q225374	Fax E-mail Confirmation may not Work if You Reinstall Fax Client
Q217948	Cover Page Note Field Cannot Handle Large Amount of Text
Q217907	Err Msg: "Wangimg.exe Has Been Changed" Opening Fax Doc Viewer

CHAPTER 56

Modem Sharing Service Troubleshooting

Overview

This chapter outlines common error messages and problems encountered when installing or using the Modem Sharing Service. Troubleshooting assistance is provided.

Troubleshooting Modem Sharing Service

The following outlines some common client setup problems, their potential cause and probable solution.

Problem Modem detection fails on a shared port

Solution Modem detection may fail on a shared port if the modem is in use by another client, or by another application on the server. Wait until the modem becomes available, and try again, or install the modem manually.

Problem Unable to share TAPI devices that do not have a serial-port interface

Solution The Modem Sharing Service can only share serial ports or TAPI devices that use serial ports. It cannot share TAPI devices that do not use a serial port, such as ISDN adapters. ISDN modems may be shared, as with any other device that connects to a serial port.

Problem Modem is inaccessible to users for a long period of time

Solution Modem-sharing clients that connect to Small Business Server allocate a modem on the server for exclusive use. The modem remains allocated as long as the client's application keeps the connection open. Modem-sharing connections are not timed out. If the user does not disconnect from the server or close the communication application, the modem remains inaccessible to other users. A common scenario is a client running a communication application that waits for an incoming call. This allocates a modem exclusively for this purpose and no one can use the modem as long as the communication application is waiting for a call.

Instruct users to disconnect the modem-sharing connection or terminate the communication application when they have finished using the shared modem.

Problem **Error message:** *"Open port error 100D (Server Not Found)"*

Solution When manually installing a modem for a Windows 95-based machine to be used on a Modem Sharing Communications port, a session may not be established. When you try to dial out using the shared modem port, you will see the Modem Sharing Event Viewer appear in the Systray. Double-clicking the icon pulls up the Viewer and displays any error messages. You will typically receive the error message *"Open port error 100D (Server Not Found)."*

To correct this problem, first make sure that you have network connectivity by performing a UNC connect to the Small Business Server. Verify the following settings:

1. Determine if the Modem Sharing Settings within Device Manager\Ports\ModemSharingPort(x) specifies the correct UNC path (i.e., \\SBSServerName\ModemPool)
2. Make sure that the modem is set to use the Modem Sharing COM port within **Control Panel**, **Modems** on the Windows 95-based machine.
3. Make sure that the Modem Sharing Configuration settings (i.e., Modem Pool Name and COM Port) are correctly set within the **Control Panel**, **Modem Sharing**, **Configuration** tab.

If all above settings are correct and the Windows 95-based machine is still unable to use the shared modems, do the following:

1. Stop the Small Business Server Modem Sharing Service in **Control Panel**, **Services**, **Modem Sharing**.
2. In **Control Panel**, **Modem Sharing**, **Configuration**, remove the Modem Pool name, and then add the Modem Pool name again, assigning an appropriate COM port to the new pool.
3. Start the Small Business Server Modem Sharing Service in **Control Panel**, **Services**, **Modem Sharing**.

The Windows 95-based machine should now be able to connect successfully to the Small Business Server shared modem.

Problem	**A Small Business Server client cannot browse the Internet when using a shared modem to connect to an ISP**
Solution	When a workstation is added to a Small Business Server domain using the installation floppy disk, the workstation's proxy settings are configured to use the Small Business Server as a Proxy Server. However, the modem-sharing client bypasses the Proxy Server and makes a direct connection to the Internet. The Proxy Server settings need to be removed from the client browser configuration in order to connect to the Internet using the Modem Sharing Service.

To use the Modem Sharing software on the Small Business Server to make a direct connection to the Internet via the ISP, make the following adjustments:

1. In **Control Panel**, **Internet**, select the **Connection** tab.
2. Deselect **Access the Internet Using a Proxy Server**.
3. Click **OK**.
4. In **Control Panel**, **WSP Client**, deselect **Enable WinSock Proxy Client**.
5. Click **OK** and restart the computer.

> **Note** The Web Proxy and Winsock Proxy settings will need to be reenabled if the client wishes to connect to the Internet through the Proxy Server at a later time.

Problem	**When using modem pooling, the following message appears:** *"COM port already in use"*
Solution	This occurs when the Fax Server is using the modem for other services, such as for a Remote Access Session or to send a fax. If these other services are not using the modem, then reset the modem by using HyperTerminal and entering *ATZ!*.
Problem	**Problems with external modems**
Solution	If you are having problems with an external modem, verify the following settings:

1. The COM port is on the motherboard or is provided by a serial card, make sure the port is not disabled in the BIOS (also called the CMOS) setup of the computer. Refer to the documentation for your computer to obtain information about configuring options in the BIOS setup.
2. Make sure that no other adapters or devices are configured for the same Base I/O Address or IRQ as the COM port to which the modem is attached.
3. Verify that the serial port is not defective. If the modem and any other serial devices fail on the COM port but work on other COM ports, and you have verified the two steps above, the serial port may be defective.
4. Verify that the serial cable is not defective by using a new standard serial cable.

Problem	**Problems with internal modems**
Solution	If you are having problems with an external modem, verify the following settings:

1. If the COM port is defined by an internal modem, make sure the jumpers on the modem are configured properly. Non PnP internal modems usually have a jumper on the adapter that configures the modem as a particular COM port. There may or may not be jumpers that allow you to set the Base I/O Address and IRQ to be used by the modem as well.

2. If the modem is configured for a COM port number that is assigned to a COM port on the motherboard or a serial card (physical port), you must either set the modem to use a different COM port or use the BIOS setup to disable the COM port with the same number as the internal modem. For example, if both the internal modem and the physical COM port are set to COM1, you must set the internal modem to a different, unused COM port, or the physical COM1 port must be disabled in the BIOS setup.

3. Make sure that no other adapters or devices are configured for the same Base I/O Address or IRQ as the internal modem. Usually COM3, using IRQ 5, is a good choice for an internal modem. However, if you have a sound card, you may need to choose an IRQ number other than 5, since many sound cards use 5 as their interrupt number.

4. In the **Ports** component of **Control Panel**, verify that the IRQ settings and the I/O addresses are correct. Check the System log with the Event Viewer for I/O or IRQ conflict errors.

5. When possible, use standard settings for COM ports, which are as follows:
   - SERIAL 1 COM1: I/O Address = 3F8h IRQ = 4
   - SERIAL 2 COM2: I/O Address = 2F8h IRQ = 3
   - SERIAL 3 COM3: I/O Address = 3E8h, IRQ = 4
   - SERIAL 4 COM4: I/O Address = 2E8h, IRQ = 3

6. You do not need to add a new port in **Control Panel**, **Ports** to add support for an internal modem. NTDETECT detects the internal modem and the COM port it is configured to use. If a duplicate port was added via the **Add** button in **Control Panel**, **Ports**, use the **Delete** button to remove the duplicate port.

7. Verify that the internal modem is not defective. It may also be a good idea to check with the vendor of your modem to see if a flash upgrade is available for your modem.

Troubleshoot the Modem with HyperTerminal

The HyperTerminal program can be used to verify that Windows NT recognizes your modem and that you can dial out. To do so, perform the following steps:

Note Before attempting to use HyperTerminal, verify that the Remote Access Server service is not running. Double-click **Control Panel**, **Services** and verify that the **Status** column next to **Remote Access Server** is blank. If it displays "Started," click **Stop** to disable the Remote Access Server service before continuing. Also verify that the **Status** column next to **Microsoft Fax Service** is blank. If it displays "Started," click **Stop** to disable the Fax Service before continuing.

▶ **To verify that Windows NT recognizes your modem and can dial out**

1. Click **Start**, point to **Programs**, **Accessories**, **HyperTerminal**, then click **HyperTerminal**.
2. When the **New Connection Wizard** appears, click **Cancel**.
3. On the **File** menu, click **Properties**, and then select the modem you want to test from the **Connect Using** drop-down list.
4. Click **Configure**, verify that your modem is set to use the correct port, then click **OK**.
5. Type *AT* in the **HyperTerminal** dialog box, and then press ENTER.
6. If *AT* is displayed in the **HyperTerminal** dialog box as you type it, and *OK* is displayed after you press ENTER, HyperTerminal recognizes the modem properly. If *AT* is not displayed as you type it or if *OK* is not displayed after you press ENTER, then HyperTerminal does not recognize the modem.
7. Verify that your modem can dial out using HyperTerminal. On the **File** menu, click **New Connection**, and then follow the on-screen instructions.
8. Click **Dial**. If the modem's speaker is enabled, you should hear a dial tone and the sound of the modem dialing the telephone number.

To determine if your modem is a Class 1 modem, perform steps 1 through 6 above and then:

1. Type *AT | FCLASS=?* and press ENTER.
2. If the reply includes the digit "1," then your modem is a Class 1 modem.

Related Troubleshooting Knowledge Base Articles

The following knowledge base articles contain information on troubleshooting the Modem Sharing Service. The articles are located at:
http://support.microsoft.com

Article Number	Title
Q218105	*Small Business Server Modem Sharing Displays Port w/UPS as Available Modem Pool*
Q218081	*Small Business Server: Remote Port not Created with Manual Modem Sharing Install*
Q218072	*Cannot Install Both Small Business Server Fax and Modem Sharing Clients on Windows 2000*
Q225260	*Problems Installing Modem Sharing Service with Two Network Cards*
Q224504	*Modem Sharing Installs the Netmodem Tool*
Q225298	*Modem Sharing Service Does Not Display User Account Connection*
Q222522	*Unable to View Modem Sharing Port in Ports Tool*

CHAPTER 57

E-mail and Internet Troubleshooting

Overview

This chapter outlines common error messages and problems encountered while using e-mail and Internet related features in the Microsoft® BackOffice® Small Business Server. Troubleshooting assistance is provided.

Troubleshooting E-mail and Internet

The following outlines some common e-mail and Internet-related problems, their potential cause and probable solution.

Problem Starting Internet Explorer 5 prompts users for a password

Solution If users are prompted to enter a password when starting Internet Explorer 5 or when attempting to access an Internet site, they may not have permission to access the Internet.

▶ **To grant a user Internet access permission**

1. Open the Small Business Server Management console.
2. Click **More Tasks**, and then **Manage Internet Access**.
3. Click **Control Access to the Internet**.
4. Follow the on-screen instructions to grant a user Internet access permission.

Problem Exchange Administrator exits unexpectedly after configuring TURN

Solution Exchange Administrator may exit unexpectedly while running the Small Business Server Internet Connection Wizard if you choose to use TURN with Secure Sockets Layer (SSL) to dequeue mail. To correct this problem, disable SSL.

▶ **To disable SSL**

1. From the **More Tasks** page in the Small Business Server console, click **Manage Internet Access**.

2. Click **Configure Internet Hardware**. The Small Business Server Internet Connection Wizard starts.

3. On the **Receive Exchange Mail** screen of the wizard, disable **SSL**.

Problem   Internet mail delivery does not occur before demand-dial router disconnects from the Internet

Solution   Small Business Server uses a program called Sbsetrn.exe to retrieve mail. By default, Sbsetrn will run every hour to retrieve mail. When Sbsetrn runs, the demand-dial router will connect to the Internet. Under some circumstances the demand-dial router will connect, but it will take over a minute for Sbsetrn to send the signal to retrieve mail. Other custom commands may do the same thing.

Demand-dial routers will disconnect after a period of inactivity. The router may disconnect before mail is delivered if that period is less than one minute. To correct this problem, configure your router to wait for more than one minute of inactivity.

Problem   When Using Outlook Web Access, the following error appears: *"Failed to Access Inbox"*

Solution   This error occurs when a user attempts to open their mailbox with a web browser, in an attempt to connect to Outlook Web Access. Typically this error represents a permissions problem when logging onto the mailbox. To correct this problem, give the **Everyone** group permission to log on locally.

▶ **To give the Everyone group permission to log on locally**

1. Click **Start**, point to **Programs, Administrative Tools (Common)**, and then click **User Manager for Domains**.

2. On the **Policies** menu, click **User Rights**. The **User Rights Policy** dialog box appears.

3. Select **Log on locally** and then click **Add**. The **Add Users and Groups** dialog box appears.

4. Under **Names**, select **Everyone** and then click **Add**.
5. Click **OK** twice to save your changes and close the **User Rights Policy** dialog box.

Caution Setting **Log on locally** for the **Everyone** group may have security repercussions. If your server is connected to the Internet, make sure that you have enabled the Proxy Server firewall features. A simple way to enable the firewall is to use the Small Business Server Internet Connection Wizard. This wizard can be accessed from the **Manage Internet Access** link on the **More Tasks** page of the Small Business Server console.

Problem Unable to use Telnet

Solution If Packet Filtering is enabled in Microsoft Proxy Server, Telnet will not work.

▶ **To modify Telnet settings**

1. Click **Start**, point to **Programs**, **Microsoft Proxy Server**, and then click **Microsoft Management Console**.
2. Expand **Internet Information Server**.
3. Expand the name of your Small Business Server computer.
4. Right-click **Web Proxy**, and then click **Properties**.
5. Under **Shared services**, click **Security**.
6. On the **Security properties** page, click **Add**.
7. Under **Exceptions**, select **Telnet: custom filter**, and then click **Edit**.
8. Modify the settings as follows:

Protocol ID:	TCP
Direction:	both
Local port:	any
Remote port:	23
Local Host:	Default proxy external IP addresses
Remote Host:	any host

Problem	**Configure Firewall Settings box doesn't appear when using Router, DSL, Cable Modem, or other Broadband Connection in the Internet Connection Wizard**
Solution	When a second network interface card is used to connect to the Internet, the Small Business Server Internet Connection Wizard will display the **Configure Firewall Settings** dialog box. This dialog box appears because Small Business Server assumes it will route Internet traffic. This dialog box will not appear if the second network interface card is using a non-routable IP scheme.

To correct the problem you must remove the non-routable IP scheme from the Proxy Server's Local Address Table (LAT). For example, if your Small Business Server has a second network interface card that is connected to a router, and the router's IP address is 192.168.16.x, you must remove the 192.168.16.x range from the Proxy Server's LAT or you must change the IP address of the router.

▶ **To modify the Proxy Server's LAT**

1. Click **Start**, point to **Programs**, **Microsoft Proxy Server**, and then click **Microsoft Management Console**.
2. Expand **Internet Information Server**, and then expand the name of your server computer.
3. Click **Web Proxy**.
4. On the **Action** menu, click **Properties**.
5. On the **Web Proxy Service Properties** dialog box, select the **Service** tab.
6. Under **Configuration**, click **Local Address Table**.
7. From the **Internal IP ranges** list select the IP range to be removed, and then click **Remove**.
8. Click **OK** twice to save your changes and close the **Web Proxy Service Properties** dialog box.

Problem	**Change Password is grayed out in the Small Business Server Internet Connection Wizard**
Solution	Following the upgrade from Small Business Server 4.0/4.0a to Small Business Server 4.5, the **Change Password** option in the **Change Internet Settings** screen of the Small Business Server Internet Connection Wizard is grayed out. After an upgrade the Small Business Server is unable to determine which RAS phonebook entry is used for connecting to your ISP. Without knowing the correct phonebook entry, it is impossible to change the password correctly. To correct this problem, use the Small Business Server Internet Connection Wizard to set the phonebook entry and password.

▶ **To access the Small Business Server Internet Connection Wizard**

1. From your Small Business Server console, **More Tasks** page, click **Manage Internet Access**, and then click **Connect to the Internet**.
2. Click **Next**.
3. Select **Connect to the Internet**, and then click **Next**.
4. Select **Modem or terminal adapter**, and then click **Next**.
5. Select a phonebook entry (or create a new one), type a **Password**, type it again in **Confirm password**, and then click **Next**.
6. Follow the on-screen instructions to complete the wizard.

Problem Web Publishing Wizard is unable to post web pages and the following message appears:
"The Web Publishing Wizard was unable to publish your file(s) to the Web server for the following reason: The operation timed out."

Solution If Proxy Server Dynamic Packet Filtering has been enabled, the Web Publishing Wizard will be unable to publish web pages.

This error occurs because the Web Publishing Wizard uses FTP to post web pages. Dynamic Packet Filtering will block FTP. In order to publish using the Web Publishing Wizard, you must open the FTP ports.

▶ **To open the ports used by FTP**

1. Click **Start**, point to **Programs**, **Microsoft Proxy Server**, and then click **Microsoft Management Console**.
2. Expand **Internet Information Server** and then the name of your Small Business Server computer.
3. Right-click **Web Proxy**, and then click **Properties**.
4. Under **Shared services**, click **Security**.
5. On the **Security** tab, click **Add**.
6. Select **Custom Filter** and then set the following:

Protocol ID:	TCP
Direction:	both
Local Port:	any
Fixed Port:	20
Local Host:	Default proxy external IP address
Remote Host:	any host

7. Click **OK**, and then click **Add**.

8. Select **Custom Filter** and then set the following:

Protocol ID:	TCP
Direction:	both
Local Port:	any
Fixed Port:	21
Local Host:	Default proxy external IP address
Remote Host:	any host

9. Click **OK** three times.

Problem — When browsing directories and files in Internet Service Manager (HTML), the following message appears:
"Microsoft VBScript runtime error '800a000d'
Type mismatch: '[String: "IE"]'
/iisadmin/JSBrowser/JSBrwLs.asp, line 9"

Solution — When using Internet Service Manager (HTML) to browse directories and files, you may receive this error.

To correct the error, replace the file Jsbrwls.asp located in the \Winnt\System32\Inetsrv\Iisadmin\Jsbrowser\ folder of your Small Business Server computer with the updated file located in the Ntoptpak\%Language%\%Platform%\Winnt.srv\ folder of Small Business Server CD 2.

Problem — IMS Queue Bottleneck

Solution — Delete messages from the IMS queue

Related Troubleshooting Knowledge Base Articles

The following knowledge base articles contain information on troubleshooting the e-mail and Internet-related problems. The articles are located at:
http://support.microsoft.com

Article Number	Title
Q181407	*Troubleshooting Proxy RAS Autodial and Autodisconnect*

Glossary

A

ACL access control list.

Active Server Pages (ASP) A server-side scripting environment that runs ActiveX scripts and ActiveX components on a server. Developers can combine scripts and components to create web-based applications.

.Adm files Administrative files, which are hierarchical templates with categories and subcategories that dictate the settings available through the user interface.

Administrator account The user account created during Windows NT Sever Installation. This account has all rights and permissions to administer the server.

ADO ActiveX Data Objects.

ADSL *See* asynchronous digital subscriber line.

alias An easily remembered name used in place of an IP address, directory path, a user's name, or other identifier; also called a *friendly name*.

American National Standards Institute (ANSI) A quasi-national standards organization that provides area charters for groups that establish standards in specific fields. Standards approved by ANSI are often called ANSI standards. Additionally, ANSI is commonly used to refer to a low-level table of codes used by a computer.

American Standard Code for Information Interchange (ASCII) A coding scheme using seven or eight bits that assigns numeric values to up to 256 characters, including letters, numerals, punctuation marks, control characters, and other symbols. ASCII was developed in 1968 to standardize data transmission among disparate hardware and software systems and is built into most minicomputers and all personal computers.

ANSI *See* American National Standards Institute.

AOL America Online.

APIs Application Programming Interfaces.

application A program designed to assist in the performance of a specific task, such as word processing, accounting, or database management.

argument A constant, variable, or expression passed to a procedure or subprogram.

ASCII *See* American Standard Code for Information Interchange.

ASP *See* Active Server Pages.

asynchronous digital subscriber line Technology and equipment allowing high-speed digital communication, including video signals, across an ordinary twisted-pair copper phone line, with speeds up to 9 megabits per second downstream (to the customer) and up to 800 kilobits per second upstream. Also called asymmetric digital subscriber loop.

ASU Advanced Server for UNIX.

attribute 1. Information that indicates whether a file is read-only, hidden, system, or compressed, and whether the file has been changed since a backup copy of it was made. 2. In object-oriented software, the individual characteristics of the object.

B

Backup Domain Controller In a Windows NT Server domain, a computer running Windows NT Server that receives a copy of the domains directory database, which contains all account and security policy information for the domain. The copy is synchronized periodically and automatically with the copy on the primary domain controller (PDC). BDCs also authenticate user logons and can be promoted to function as a PDC as needed. Multiple BDCs can exist on a domain. In a Small Business Server network, the Small Business Server is the PDC.

bandwidth The data transfer capacity of a digital communications system.

BDC *See* Backup Domain Controller.

BIOS basic input/output system. A critical series of software routines that test PC-compatible hardware upon startup, and support data transfer between hardware devices.

BOOTP Boot Protocol. A protocol used for booting diskless workstations.

bps bits per second.

BRI Basic Rate Interface. A common ISDN bandwidth.

browser A client application that enables a user to view HTML documents, follow the hyperlinks among them, transfer files, and execute some programs. Most current Web browsers permit users to send and receive e-mail, read newsgroups, play audio and video files, download files, and execute small programs, such as Java applets or ActiveX components, that can be embedded in HTML documents. Some Web browsers require helper applications or plug-ins to accomplish one or more of these tasks. Also known as *web browser*.

C

cache 1. A special memory subsystem in which frequently-used data values are duplicated for quick access. A memory cache stores the contents of frequently-accessed RAM locations and the addresses where these data items are stored. When the processor references an address in memory, the cache checks to see whether it holds that address. If it does hold the address, the data is returned to the processor; if it does not, a regular memory access occurs. A cache is useful when RAM accesses are slow compared with the microprocessor speed, because cache memory is always faster than main RAM memory. 2. Some applications designate a certain amount of hard disk space as a disk cache. The application uses this space as a temporary storage for files and data.

CALs client access licenses. Special licenses required to allow client computers to access Small Business Server. Five licenses are provided with the initial Small Business Server installation. To allow more client computers to access the Small Business Server network, more client access licenses must be purchased from Microsoft.

CD compact disc.

CGI Common Gateway Interface.

CIFS/SMB protocol Common Internet File System.

clean installation On a LAN or the Internet, a computer that accesses shared network resources provided by a server computer.

client computer On a LAN or the Internet, a computer that accesses shared network resources provided by a server computer.

Clioc.inf file The client optional component file.

CM Microsoft Connection Manager. A component of Microsoft Internet Connection Services (ICS). Connection Manager runs on top of Dial-Up Networking and simplifies the network access experience for remote clients. Manages the user access configuration, including dial-in and VPN access numbers.

CMAK Connection Manager Administration Kit. A component of Microsoft Internet Connection Services (ICS). A step-by-step wizard that creates a service profile (custom tailored connection information) for Connection Manager clients, for connecting to a public or private network.

CMOS Complementary Metal Oxide Semiconductor.

C.O. Central Office. The central office of the public switched telephone network that handles the routing of calls in a specified area.

COM Component Object Model. Also stands for *communication port*, as in COM port: an RS232 serial interface for computer communications.

component Part of a larger system or structure. In Small Business Server, the various services and servers (such as Exchange Server) are sometimes referred to as component applications.

connectivity 1. The nature of the connection between a user's computer and another computer, such as a server or a host computer on the Internet or a network. This may describe the quality of the circuit or telephone line, the degree of freedom from noise, or the bandwidth of the communications devices. 2. The ability of hardware devices and/or software packages to transmit data between other hardware devices and/or software packages. 3. The ability of hardware devices, software packages, or a computer itself to work with network devices or work with other hardware devices, software packages, or a computer over a network connection.

console A control unit through which a user communicates with a computer via primary input devices (keyboard and mouse) and a primary output device (screen). A console integrates all the tools, information, and web pages an administrator needs to perform specific tasks.

CPS Connection Point Services.

CSNW Client Services for NetWare.

CSLIP Compressed version of SLIP (Serial Line Internet protocol).

CSP Cryptographic Service Provider.

CSS cascading style sheets.

CSV files comma separated value files. CSV is a parsing format for the files that store information from Small Business Server Fax Service and Proxy Server logs. When Fax Service and Proxy Server reports are launched from the console, the CSV file is parsed and then ASP pages display the report information on the console.

D

DAO Data Access Object.

database A file composed of information. Usually there are also methods for searching, sorting, recombining, organizing, and extracting the information in various ways.

DAV distributed authoring and versioning.

DCOM Distributed Component Object Model.

default gateway The gateway used to connect to the rest of the network. *See also* gateway.

DES Data Encryption Standard.

DHCP *See* Dynamic Host Configuration Protocol.

dial-up networking A connection that uses the public switched telephone network rather than a dedicated circuit or some other type of private network.

DID Direct Inward Dialing. A feature of modern PBXs that allows outside callers to ring an extension inside an organization's telephone network directly, while bypassing the PBX voice mail system.

digital certificate An encrypted file containing user or server identification information, used to verify identity and establish a secure link; it is called a client certificate when issued to a server administrator.

distribution list A group of recipients created to expedite mass-mailing of messages and other information. When mail is sent to a distribution list, all members of that list receive a copy.

DIT Direct Information Tree.

DLC Data Link Control.

DNS Domain Name System. The system by which hosts on the Internet have both domain name addresses and IP addresses. The domain name address is automatically translated into the numerical IP address, which is used by the packet routing software.

domain A group of computers that share a database and have a common security policy; the basic unit of Windows NT Server LAN. This term can also be used to refer to an Internet domain name.

DOS Disk Operating System.

DS Directory Services.

DSMN Directory Service Manager for NetWare.

DTC Microsoft Distributed Transaction Coordinator.

DTS Data Transformation Services.

dual-boot system A computer configuration that allows a user to start one of a choice of two operating systems on a PC.

DUN Dial-Up Networking.

Dynamic Occurring immediately and concurrently.

Dynamic Host Configuration Protocol (DHCP) In a Small Business Server network, Small Business Server is also a DHCP server. The DHCP server uses a TCP/IP protocol that enables a client computer connected to the Small Business Server network to be assigned a temporary IP address automatically when the client computer connects to the network.

E

EULA End-User License Agreement.

extensibility The ability to add functionality to an existing program. For example, the Small Business Server console is extensible in that additional features and help files can be added and integrated by value-added providers and end users.

F

FAT *See* file allocation table.

FEP front-end processor. The input processing equipment at an Internet service provider site.

file allocation table (FAT) A table or list maintained by some operating systems, (such as MS-DOS) to manage disk space used for file storage. Files on a disk are stored, as space allows, in fixed-size groups of bytes (characters) rather than from beginning to end as contiguous strings of text or numbers. A single file can thus be scattered in pieces over many separate storage areas. A file allocation table maps available disk storage space so that it can mark flawed segments that should not be used and can find and link the pieces of a file.

file sharing The use of computer files on networks where files are stored in, on a central computer or a server, and are accessed by more than one user. When a single file is shared by many people, access can be regulated through such means as password protection, security clearances, or file locking to prohibit changes to a file by more than one person at a time.

filter **1.** A program or set of features within a program that reads its standard or designated input, transforms the input in some desired way, and then writes the output to its standard or designated output destination. A database filter, for example, might flag information of a certain age. **2.** A pattern or mask that data is passed through to isolate specified data. For instance, a filter used in e-mail or in retrieving newsgroup messages can allow users to filter out messages from other users. **3.** In Internet Information Server (IIS), a feature of ISAPI that allows pre-processing of requests and post-processing of responses, permitting site-specific handling of HTTP requests and responses.

firewall A security system intended to protect an organization's network against external threats, such as hackers, coming from another network, such as the Internet. A firewall prevents computers in the organization's network from communicating directly with computers external to the network and vice versa. Instead, all communication is routed through a proxy server outside of the organization's network, and the proxy server decides whether it is safe to let a particular message or file pass through to the organization's network.

FPNW File and Print Services for NetWare.

FTP file transfer protocol.

G

gateway A device that connects networks using different communications protocols so that information can be passed from one network to the other. A gateway transfers information and converts it to a form compatible with the protocols used by the receiving network.

GB gigabyte.

graphical user interface (GUI) An environment that represents programs, files, and options by icons, menus, and dialog boxes on the screen. The graphical user interface provides standard software routines to handle and report user's actions (such as a mouse click or a key press); applications call these routines with specific parameters rather attempting to reproduce them from scratch.

GSNW Gateway Service for NetWare. This server allows the Windows NT Server to function as a NetWare client.

GUI *See* graphical user interface.

H

HAL hardware abstraction layer.

hardware The physical components of a computer system, including any peripheral equipment such as printers, modems, and mouse devices.

HCL Hardware Compatibility List.

host The main computer in a system of computers or terminals connected by communications links.

HTML hypertext markup language. The markup language used for documents on the World Wide Web and private intranets. An HTML document is an ASCII text file with delineated character tags that create the format of the document. Web browsers interpret the tags to produce how the document appears.

HTTP Hypertext Transport Protocol. The client/server protocol used to access information on the World Wide Web.

I

IAS Internet Authentication Services.

ICS Internet Connection Services.

IEAK Internet Explorer Administration Kit.

IETF Internet Engineering Task Force.

IIS Internet Information Server.

IMS Internet Mail Service.

.Inf files Device information files, containing scripts used to control hardware operations.

.Ini files Initialization files used by Windows-based applications to store per-user information that controls application startup.

Internet Protocol (IP) The protocol within TCP/IP that governs the breakup of data messages into packets, the routing of the packets from sender to destination network and station, and the reassembly of the packets into the original data messages at the destination.

Internet service provider (ISP) A business that supplies Internet connectivity services to individuals, businesses, and other organizations.

Internetwork Packet Exchange (IPX) The protocol in Novell NetWare that governs addressing and routing of packets within and between LANs.

intranet A network designed for information processing only within a company or organization.

I/O input/output.

IP *See* Internet Protocol.

IPX *See* Internetwork Packet Exchange.

IPX/SPX Internetwork Packet Exchange/Sequenced Packet Exchange.

IRQ interrupt request.

IS information store.

ISAPI Internet Server Application Programming Interface.

ISDN Integrated Services Digital Network. A completely digital telephone/telecommunications network that carries voice, data, and video information over the existing telephone network infrastructure. It is designed to provide a single interface for hooking up a telephone, fax machine, computer, and so on.

ISP Internet service provider. A business that supplies Internet connectivity services to individuals, businesses, and other organizations.

ISV independent software vendor. An individual or organization that independently creates computer software.

IT information technology.

J, K, L

KB Knowledge Base.

Kbps kilobits per second.

KBps kilobytes per second.

LAN local area network. A group of computers and other devices dispersed over a relatively limited area and connected by a communications link that enables the devices to interact together.

LAT Local Address Table. An IP address table defining the internal network address space for Proxy Server. When filling client URL requests, the LAT tells Proxy Server to go the internal network and not to the Internet for the IP addresses specified in this table.

legacy Pertaining to documents, data, or systems that existed prior to a certain time.

M

MAPI Messaging Application Programming Interface.

MB megabyte.

MBps megabytes per second.

MHTML MIME (Multipurpose Internet Mail Extensions) encapsulation of aggregate HTML (hypertext markup language) documents.

MHz megahertz.

Microsoft Management Console A general-purpose management display framework for hosting administration tools or snap-ins.

message queuing An ordered list of messages awaiting transmission, from which they are taken up on a first in, first out (FIFO) basis.

Migration The process of making existing applications and data work on different computers or operating systems.

MPPC Microsoft Point-to-Point Compression.

MSDE Microsoft Data Engine. The data engine used with Microsoft Access to develop databases that can seamlessly migrate to SQL Server 7.0.

MSMQ Microsoft Message Queue Server. A Microsoft server application which is part of the NT Options Pack (NTOP). Provides application integration and allows them to communicate with each other reliably and asynchronously.

MSN Microsoft Network.

MTS Microsoft Transaction Server.

MX Mail eXchange.

N

NAS network access switch.

NAT network address translation. The ability of a device such as a router to convert IP addresses from one network to those of another.

NDS Novell Directory Services.

NetBEUI NetBIOS Enhanced User Interface.

network interface card (NIC) An expansion card or other device used to connect a computer to a local area network.

NFS Network File System.

NIC *See* network interface card.

NNTP Network News Transfer Protocol. The NNTP connector on an Exchange Server that supports Internet newsreaders.

node In local area networks, a device that is connected to the network and is capable of communicating with other network devices.

NSF National Science Foundation.

NT1 network terminating. A unit that conditions signals in an ISDN basic rate interface configuration.

NTFS file system The file system designed for use specifically with the Windows NT operating system. NTFS supports file system recovery and extremely large storage media. It also supports object-oriented applications by treating all files as objects with user-defined and system-defined attributes.

NTLM Windows NT License Manager.

NTOP Windows NT Options Pack.

NWLink – part 6 An IPX/SPX-compatible protocol.

O

ODBC Open Database Connectivity.

OLE DB object linking and embedding database.

OLTP online transaction processing.

optimize To improve the performance of a computer, network, or other device or system.

OSI Open Systems Interconnection. A layered architecture that standardizes levels of service and types of interaction for computers exchanging information through a communications network.

P

PAP Password Authentication Protocol.

parameter In programming, a value that is given to a variable, either at the beginning of an operation or before an expression is evaluated by a program. Until the operation is completed, a parameter is effectively treated as a constant value by the program. A parameter can be text, a number, or an argument name assigned to a value that is passed from one routine to another. Parameters are used as a means of customizing program operation.

partition **1.** A logically distinct portion of memory or a storage device that functions as though it were a physically separate unit. **2.** In database programming, a subset of a database table or file.

PBX Private Branch Exchange. A call processing and routing device that interfaces an organization's internal telephone network with the Public Switched Telephone Network (PSTN).

PC personal computer.

PCT Private Communications Technology.

PDC Primary Domain Controller.

PID product identification number.

.Pif files program information files.

PKCS public key cryptography standards.

Point-to-Point Protocol (PPP) A data link protocol developed by the Internet Engineering Task Force (IETF) for dial-up telephone connections, such as between a computer and the Internet. PPP provides greater protection for data integrity and security than does SLIP, at a cost of greater overhead.

POP Post Office Protocol.

Post Office Protocol 3 (POP 3) This is the current version of the Post Office Protocol standard in common use for e-mail transmission on TCP/IP networks.

PPP *See* Point-to-Point Protocol.

PPTP Point-to-Point Tunneling Protocol. An encryption protocol used for remote computers to securely access other computer networks across an Internet connection.

Primary Domain Controller In Windows NT, a database providing a centralized administration site for resources and user accounts. The database allows users to log on to the domain, rather than a specific host machine. A separate account database keeps track of the machines in the domain and allocates the domain's resources to users.

PRI primary rate interface. An ISDN bandwidth.

PRMD private management domain.

protocol A set of rules and conventions by which two computers pass messages across a network. Networking software usually implements multiple levels of protocols layered one on top of another.

PSTN public switched telephone network.

Q

QFE quick fix engineering. A patch or hot fix to correct a bug.

query **1.** The process of extracting data from a database and presenting it for use. **2.** A specific set of instructions for extracting particular data repetitively.

R

RADIUS Remote Authentication Dial-In User Service.

RAID redundant array of independent disks.

RAM random access memory.

RAS Remote Access Service. On a local area network, a host that is equipped with modems to enable users to connect to the network over telephone lines. Works with dial-up networking to allow one computer to connect to another through a modem to access shared resources, such as drives or files.

remote administration Administering a computer or network from another computer.

RDS Remote Data Service.

Regedit.exe Windows 95 Registry Editor.

Regedt32.exe Windows NT Registry Editor.

RHL Recommended Hardware List.

RISC A reduced instruction set computing-based processor, such as the Digital Alpha.

robust Able to function or to continue functioning well in unexpected situations.

rollout Successful deployment of a server in a small business environment.

RPC remote procedure call.

run time 1. The time period during which a program is running. 2. The amount of time needed to execute a given program.

S

SAP Service Advertising Protocol.

scalable Relating to the characteristic of a piece of hardware or software that makes it possible for it to expand to meet future needs.

script A program consisting of a set of instructions to an application or utility program. The instructions usually use the rules and syntax of the application or utility.

SCSI Small Computer System Interface.

service In reference to software, a program that provides support to other programs, particularly at a low (close to the hardware) level.

SET Secure Electronics Transactions.

SID security identification.

Simple Mail Transport Protocol (SMTP)
A TCP/IP protocol for sending messages from one computer to another on a network. This protocol is used on the Internet to route e-mail.

SLIP Serial Line Internet Protocol.

S/MIME Secure/Multipurpose Internet Mail Extensions.

SMP symmetric multiprocessing.

SMS Systems Management Server.

SMTP *See* Simple Mail Transport Protocol.

SNA Systems Network Architecture.

SNMP Simple Network Management Protocol.

SP service pack. A Microsoft software package containing additional applications and services.

SP4 Windows NT Service Pack 4.

SQL *See* Structured Query Language.

SSL Secure Sockets Layer protocol.

Structured Query Language (SQL)
A database sublanguage used in querying, updating, and managing relational databases; the de facto standard for database products.

swap file A hidden file on the disk drive that an operating system uses to hold parts of programs and data files that do not fit in memory.

system partition In terms of Small Business Server 4.5, the system partition is the disk drive partition where the main Windows NT Server files are located. This partition will also contain the files of those server applications that must be located on the system partition.

T

TAPI Telephony Applications Programming Interface.

TCP/IP *See* Transmission Control Protocol/Internet Protocol.

technology consultant A business or individual that supplies services, such as consulting or system troubleshooting, in addition to selling computer hardware and software.

Telnet A protocol used for interactive logon to a remote computer.

thread 1. In programming, a process that is part of a larger process or program. 2. In e-mail and Internet newsgroups, a series of messages and replies related to a specific topic.

throughput A measure of the data transfer rate through a typically complex communications system or of the data processing rate in a computer system.

TIFF Tagged Image File Format.

TIP Transaction Internet Protocol.

TLS Transport Layer Security protocol.

Transmission Control Protocol/Internet Protocol (TCP/IP)
A protocol developed by the Department of Defense for communications between computers. It is built into the UNIX system and has become the de facto standard for data transmission over networks, including the Internet.

TTL Time to Live. A header field for a packet sent over the Internet indicating how long the packet should be held.

turnkey Finished and complete; ready to be used.

U

UDP User Datagram Protocol.

UI user interface.

UNC universal naming convention.

Unicode A 16-bit character encoding standard developed by the Unicode Consortium. By using two bytes to represent each character, Unicode enables almost all of the written languages of the world to be represented in the form of text files. (By contrast, even 8-bit ASCII is not capable of representing even all of the combinations of letters and diacritical marks that are used with the Roman alphabet.) Approximately 28,000 of the 65,536 possible combinations have been assigned to date, 21,000 of them being used for Chinese. The remaining combinations are open for expansion.

uninterruptible power supply (UPS)
A device, connected between a computer (or other electronic equipment) and a power source (usually an outlet receptacle), that ensures that electrical flow to the computer is not interrupted because of a blackout and, in most cases, protects the computer against potentially damaging events, such as power surges and brownouts. All UPS units are equipped with a battery and a loss-of-power sensor; if the sensor detects a loss of power, it switches over to the battery so that the user has time to save any work and shut off the computer.

UPS *See* uninterruptable power supply.

URL Uniform Resource Locator. An address for a resource on the Internet. URLs are used by web browsers to locate Internet resources. A URL specifies the protocol to be used in accessing the resource, the name of the server on which the resource resides, and, optionally, the path to a resource (such as an HTML document or a file on that server).

user account An established means for an individual to gain access to a system and its resources. Usually, created by a system administrator, a user account consists of information about the user, such as password, rights, and permissions.

V

VAR value-added reseller. Typically, a company recognized as an official seller of computer hardware or software. A VAR usually supplies custom or specialized services to enhance the functionality of the systems.

variable In programming, a named storage location capable of containing data that can be modified during program execution.

VGA Video Graphics Adapter.

virtual directory A directory name, used in an address, which corresponds to a physical directory on the server.

VPN virtual private network. Similar to RAS, this solution provides a secure, encrypted access to corporate networks from clients connecting through the Internet.

W

WAN wide area network. A communications network that connects geographically separated areas.

Windows NT A portable and secure, 32-bit, preemptive-multitasking operating system. Windows NT Server provides centralized management and security, advanced fault tolerance, and additional connectivity.

Windows Internet Naming Service (WINS)
A Windows NT Server method for associating a computer's host name with its address.

WINS provides a distributed database for registering and querying dynamic NetBIOS computer names to IP address mapping in a routed network environment. It is designed to solve the problems that occur with name resolution in complex internetworks.

WINS *See* Windows Internet Naming Service.

wizard An interactive help utility within an application that guides users through each step of a task.

World Wide Web (WWW) The total set of interlinked hypertext documents residing on Web or HTTP servers all around the world. Documents on the World Wide Web, called pages or Web pages, are written in HTML, identified by URLs that specify the particular computer and path by which a file can be accessed, and transmitted from node to node to the user under HTTP. Codes, called tags, embedded in an HTML document associate particular words and images in the document with URLs so that a user can access another file, which may be halfway around the world, at the press of a key or the click of a mouse.

WWW *See* World Wide Web.

WYSIWYG what-you-see-is-what-you-get.

X, Y, Z

Index

.adm files 292
.csv files 317 – 322
.hhc files 707
.inf files 153, 156, 714 – 716
.ins files 80 – 81
.isp files 79
.job files 331 – 332
.lnk files 303
.mdb files 731
.msi files 244
.mst files 244
.ops files 244
.ost files 357
.pif files 303

1

16-bit operating systems 137

5

56-bit Data Encryption Standard (DES) 609

6

60 Minute Intranet Kit 740 – 742

A

A (Address) records 161
Access 2000
    client/server tools 753 – 754
    components 726
    Data Access Pages 747
    database engines See Microsoft Data Engine (MSDE); Microsoft Jet 4.0
    enterprise integration and support 753 – 754
    features 726
    migrating See migrating to SQL Server
    OLE DB 753
    overview 725
    Upsizing Wizard 422 – 423, 732 – 733
access control
    client outbound access to Internet services 562
    computers 589
    custom authentication filters 605
    directories 600
    domains 563
    encryption 566
    files 600, 603 – 606
    Internet 561 – 566
    Internet Information Server (IIS) 4.0 security model 603 – 606
    IP addresses 563, 605
    overview 561
    power-on-password 589
    Proxy Server 390 – 394, 561 – 566
    remote users 565 – 566
    removable media 597
    security 561 – 566, 603 – 606
    subnet filtering 563
    user authentication and authorization 603 – 605
    users 390 – 394
    Web access to files and applications 603 – 606
    Web Proxy service 390, 562
    Winsock clients 564 – 565
    Winsock Proxy service 390
    X.509 certificates 604
Access Control Lists (ACLs) 600
Access Wizards 266 – 268
accessing the Internet directly 70
accounts
    administrative 590
    anonymous 603
    creating for remote users 214
    exporting existing user accounts 251
    Guest 590
    machine 157, 275 – 276
    security 589 – 590
    user account files 253 – 255
    User Account Wizard See User Account Wizard
    users 589 – 590
ACLs (Access Control Lists) 600
Active Caching 102, 570
Add User Wizard 480
adding applications to Clioc.inf 720 – 721
adding applications to Scw.ini 717 – 720
adding favorite links to Home page 694 – 697
adding Online Guide topic files 706
adding secondary sub pages 700 – 702
adding sub pages 700 – 702

854 Index

adding task pages 42
adding tasks to Tasks and More Tasks pages 697 – 699
adding tasks with Customization Tool 699
additional information
   See also web sites
   BackOffice Server 661
   Btrieve database migration 423
   caching 450
   dequeuing methods 166, 185
   Digiboard multiport serial cards 99
   e-mail 838
   Exchange Server disaster recovery 65
   fault tolerant disk configurations 64
   Fax Service 825
   firewalls 450
   Internet 838
   InterNIC database 160
   ISP connectivity 168
   Knowledge Base 797, 807, 825, 832, 838
   Macintosh 519, 537
   Microsoft Office 60 Minute Intranet Kit 742
   Modem Sharing Service 832
   MSMQ 759
   NetMeeting 281
   NetWare networks 527
   Office 2000 756
   optimization 678
   Outlook 442
   Outlook Web Access 438
   Performance Monitor 369
   policy templates 245
   PPTP 96
   Proxy Server 102
   publishing resources 163
   Recommended Hardware List 11
   SBCM 757
   Scheduled Task utility 335
   security 592
   Set Up Computer Wizard 807
   Setup 797
   Small Business Server 45
   SMB message signing enhancements 597
   SOCKS 584
   SQL Server 422, 423, 671, 673
   SQL Server disaster recovery 65
   System Policy 286, 313
   TAPI 761
   training 43
   troubleshooting Outlook Web Access 438
   UNIX 533
   Upsizing Wizard 423
   user profiles 302 – 303, 313
   Web Publishing Wizard 163
   web site development 74
   Windows 95 user profiles 302 – 303

add-on sales 39
Address (A) records 161
Address Book views 355 – 356
addresses
   Exchange Server 354 – 356
   fax 346
   foreign e-mail 106
   IP *See* IP addresses
   protecting internal IP addresses from the Internet 546
   TCP/IP 400
   X.400 106 – 107
adm files 292
administration of Small Business Server 281
administrative accounts 590
administrative tools *See* utilities
Advanced Server for UNIX (ASU) 529
alerts
   configuring 323 – 329
   creating 324 – 325, 329, 418 – 420
   modifying 326 – 327
   Performance Monitor 323 – 329, 377 – 378, 387 – 388
   Proxy Server 396 – 397
   Web Proxy service 416
   Winsock Proxy service 417 – 418
alternatives for ISP connectivity
   Exchange Server 501
   Modem Sharing Service 499 – 501
   overview 493
   POP3 501 – 507
   Proxy Server 494 – 499
   SMTP 507
   web browsing 493
anonymous access to public folders 435 – 438
anonymous accounts 603
application layer
   described 522
   interoperability 530 – 532
application service components 31 – 32
applications
   access control 603 – 606
   adding to Clioc.inf 720 – 721
   adding to Scw.ini 717 – 720
   adding to Set Up Computer Wizard 714 – 716, 721 – 722
   backing up 66, 593
   communicating with MSMQ 759
   installing on clients 158, 277
   integration 42
   manually installing on client computers 215 – 217
   optimization 468
   optimization during installation 464
   removing from Set Up Computer Wizard 722 – 723
   security 601
ASU (Advanced Server for UNIX) 529
auditing 594 – 595, 606

Index

authentication
    CHAP 87
    client computers 517–519
    filters 605
    IAS 449
    Macintosh clients 519
    MS-CHAP 87
    MS-DOS clients 517
    NTLM 604
    PPTP 226–227
    RAS 87
    setting up 186–187
    users 603–605
    Windows 3.1 clients 518
    Windows 95 clients 518
authorization for users 603–605
Auto Dial 102, 571–572
automatic setup 9–13
AutoNavigation 750
auto-updating news engines 741

B

backing up applications 66, 593
BackOffice Server 4.5
    Fax Service 347
    upgrading 661
    web sites 661
backup systems 54–55
Backup utility
    disaster recovery 66
    registry 593
    tape device support 54
bandwidth 75–76
basic rate interface (BRI) 71–72
Batch User Add Tool 773
benefits of Small Business Server 4, 7–8, 37–39
Berkeley Sockets API 579
boot partitions 57
Boot Protocol (BOOTP) 529
bottlenecks
    disk subsystems 115–116
    memory 115
    performance 113–116
    processor 115
BRI (basic rate interface) 71–72
broadband connections *See* full-time/broadband connections
Btrieve database migration to SQL Server 423
Business Class fax modems 124

C

caching 102, 413–414, 450, 544, 569–570
capacity
    controller devices 54
    disk space consumption 118
    networks 118–119
    planning 109
    sub page actions 691
Certificate Server 1.0 610–611
certificates 602, 604, 610–611
Challenge Handshake Authentication Protocol (CHAP)
    authentication 87
Change Password Wizard 262–263
CHAP authentication 87
Class 1 fax modems 124
Client Access Licenses 657–659
Client Add Packs 657–659
client computers
    access control 589
    adding VPN devices 229–230
    application configuration files 156
    authentication 517–519
    certificates 611
    changing registries 285
    configuring Dial-Up Networking 230–232, 235–238
    configuring networking 157–158, 276–277
    configuring to use Dial-Up Networking 217–219
    creating alerts for 329
    disk defragmentation 453–456
    hardware requirements 52–53
    installing applications 158, 277
    installing policy templates 295–296
    installing PPTP 228–229, 235
    installing System Policy Editor 295–296
    manually installing applications 215–217
    optimization 468
    outbound access control to the Internet 561–566
    performance test configurations 112–113
    PPTP 227, 228–242
    recommended operating systems 53
    remote *See* remote client computers
    running Set Up Computer Wizard 155
    server interactions 515–517
    setup 13
    software requirements 52–53
    Windows 95/98 217–218
    Windows NT Workstation 218–219, 234–241
Client Installation Wizard 13
Client Services for NetWare (CSNW) 525

856 Index

Client Setup Integration Wizard
    adding applications 785 – 786
    application list 786
    customization process 784 – 785
    information fields 783 – 784
    overview 782
    removing applications 785 – 786
Client User Guide 18 – 19, 34
client/server
    Access 2000 753 – 754
    model network 4
    Office 2000 design tools 754
Clioc.inf 158, 720 – 721, 723
Clioc.old 723
CM (Connection Manager) 444 – 445
CMAK (Connection Manager Administration Kit) 89, 445 – 448
code optimization 477 – 478
COM (Component Object Model)
    interoperability 532
    Scheduled Task utility 335
comma separated value (CSV) files 317 – 322
Common.adm 286
communicating
    confidentiality 607
    customers 602
    MSMQ 759
    overview 21 – 29
communication components 32, 51 – 52
compatibility
    control devices with Windows NT Server 54
    hardware 52, 63, 123 – 125
    operating systems 53
Component Object Model (COM)
    interoperability 532
    Scheduled Task utility 335
components
    Access 2000 726
    application services 31 – 32
    client setup 13
    communications 32, 51 – 52
    file services 31 – 32
    FPNW 143 – 145
    ICS 444
    Internet access supporting 33
    Office Web Components 755
    print services 31 – 32
    RAS 90
    sub pages 700 – 702
    Web Proxy service 574 – 577
    Winsock Proxy service 581 – 582
compressed serial line Internet protocol (CSLIP) 71
computers *See* client computers; server computers
confidentiality 607 – 610
Configure Server Status Tool 780 – 782

configuring alerts 323 – 329
configuring client networking 157 – 158, 276 – 277
configuring clients to use Dial-Up Networking 217 – 219
configuring Dial-Up Networking on clients 230 – 232, 235 – 238
configuring disks 482
configuring DNS domain names 194
configuring Exchange Server 5.5 165 – 168
configuring Exchange Server clients for POP3 mail 208 – 212
configuring Exchange Server IMS connectors 200 – 208
configuring for ISP connectivity
    Internet connection issues 159 – 163
    non-dialup connections 163 – 168
configuring hardware to connect to the Internet 175 – 176
configuring Internet domain names 188 – 189
configuring Internet mail settings 182 – 183
configuring ISP dial-up networking phonebook entries 193
configuring ISP DNS 80, 161
configuring NICs 180 – 182
configuring Outlook Express clients for POP3 mail 208 – 212
configuring PPTP 228 – 241
configuring Proxy Server 2.0 165, 195 – 199
configuring Proxy Server LAT 199, 408 – 412
configuring Proxy Server packet filtering 199
configuring RAS 26
configuring remote client computers 214 – 219
configuring reverse proxy for web publishing 568
configuring server applications for Internet connectivity
    domain names 194
    Exchange Server 200 – 208
    ISP dial-up networking phonebook entries 193
    overview 193
    POP3 mail 208 – 212
    Proxy Server Internet connectivity 195 – 199
    Proxy Server LAT 199
    Proxy Server packet filtering 199
    Web Publishing Wizard 199 – 200
configuring server for clients 156 – 157, 274 – 276
configuring SMTP mail delivery 183 – 184
configuring Small Business Server 9 – 13
configuring System Policy settings 293
configuring tasks 334
configuring to use existing second-level domains 160
configuring VPN devices 225 – 226
configuring Web Publishing Wizard 165, 199 – 200
configuring Windows NT Server 4.0 164
configuring Winsock Proxy service 391 – 394
Connection Manager (CM) 444 – 445
Connection Manager Administration Kit (CMAK) 89, 445 – 448
Connection Point Services (CPS) 90, 450 – 451
connection requirements 487 – 488

console
    consistency 691 – 694
    customizing See extending Small Business Server console
    described 33, 34
    extending See extending Small Business Server console
    extension changes from Small Business Server 4.0a 703
    high-level pages 682
    IIS 550 – 551
    optimization 479
    organization 682 – 683
    overview 14 – 16
    page layout and design 684 – 694
    secondary sub pages 683
    sharing remotely 282
    sub pages 683, 686 – 693
    utilities 776 – 780
    wizards 256
control channels 582 – 583
controller devices
    capacity 54
    compatibility with Windows NT Server 4.0 54
    installing 55
controlling user environments 283 – 295
counters
    Exchange Server 361 – 362
    Interrupts/Second 328 – 329
    overview 323
    Processor Queue Length 327 – 328
    testing 325
    thresholds 363
CPS (Connection Point Services) 90, 450 – 451
CPU
    access control 589
    bottlenecks 115
    performance 117
    Performance Monitor 367 – 368
creating alerts 324 – 325, 329, 418 – 420
creating application INF files 714 – 716
creating default System Policy 297 – 299
creating new mandatory profiles 309 – 313
creating new roaming profiles 306 – 309, 311 – 312
creating Office 2000 profiles 244
creating packet filters for Proxy services 395, 558 – 560
creating performance monitors 376 – 381
creating phonebook entries 220 – 221, 230 – 234
creating Proxy performance monitors 418 – 420
creating Setup boot diskettes 126
creating shared folders 299
creating System Policy 286 – 291
creating task pages 42
creating team intranet sites 740 – 742
creating user accounts 214
creating user profiles 301
credit card transactions 609

cross-platform interoperability See interoperability
CryptoAPI 611
Cryptographic Service Provider (CSP) 611
CSLIP (compressed serial line Internet protocol) 71
CSNW (Client Services for NetWare) 525
CSP (Cryptographic Service Provider) 611
CSV (comma separated value) files 317 – 322
custom authentication filters 605
custom deployments of Office 2000 514
Custom Installation Wizard 244 – 245
custom recipients 354 – 356
custom tasks 698
customers
    benefits of Small Business Server 4, 7 – 8, 38
    communicating with 602
    personal digital certificates 602
    profiles 3
    requirements 3 – 4
Customization Tool 699, 738 – 739, 775 – 782
Customize Small Business Server console 699, 776 – 780
customizing Office 2000 deployments
    Custom Installation Wizard 244 – 245
    installing 243 – 245
    Network Installation Wizard 244 – 245
    Office Profile Wizard 243 – 244
    overview 243
    System Policy Editor 245
customizing packet filters for Proxy services 395, 558 – 560
customizing SBCM databases 757
customizing Small Business Server console 41
customizing System Policy 285
Cyrillic keyboard 127

D

Data Access Pages 747
Data Encryption Standard (DES) 609
data integrity 607 – 610, 730
data layer
    described 522
    interoperability 530
Data Transformation Services (DTS) 668
database security 601
database-driven news engines 741
DAV (distributed authoring and versioning) 749
DCOM (Distributed Component Object Model) 532
dedicated connections 83, 166 – 168
Default Computer 285, 287
default layouts 688 – 691
default logging 381
Default User 287
DEFRAG.EXE 455
defragmenting disks 453 – 456
deleting tasks 335

dequeuing methods 166, 185
DES (Data Encryption Standard) 609
design philosophy of Small Business Server 7 – 8
development of web sites 73 – 74
DHCP *See* Dynamic Host Configuration Protocol
diagnostics logging 381
dial-on-demand 164 – 166
dial-up e-mail accounts 82
dial-up modem connections 71, 169, 170
Dial-Up Networking
    configuring clients 230 – 232, 235 – 238
    configuring Exchange Server 165 – 166
    configuring ISP phonebook entries 193
    configuring remote client computers to use 217 – 219
    connecting remote client computers to Small Business Server 220 – 222
    cost-effective connectivity 28
    overview 25
    server access requirements 53
    upgrading 234 – 235
Digiboard multiport serial cards 99
digital certificates 602, 604, 610 – 611
digital signatures 607 – 608
Direct Access web site 45
Directory Service Manager for NetWare (DSMN)
    installing 641 – 646
    interoperability 526 – 527
Directory Services 549
disaster recovery
    Exchange Server 5.5 65
    NT Backup 66
    overview 65
    SQL Server 7.0 65
    Windows NT Server 4.0 65
discussion groups 430 – 435
disk configurations 482
disk controllers 56
disk defragmentation 453 – 456
disk duplexing 59
disk mirroring
    advantages of 58
    boot and system partitions 57
    disadvantages of 58 – 59
    disk stripe sets with parity comparison 63 – 64
    duplexing 59
    I/O requests 57
    overview 56
    partition size 57
Disk Mix suite 112
disk space consumption guidelines 118

disk stripe sets 60 – 64
disk subsystems 115 – 117
Distinguished Names 103 – 104
distributed authoring and versioning (DAV) 749
Distributed Component Object Model (DCOM) 532
DNS
    configuration issues 85
    configuring 80, 161
    interoperability 529
    second-level domain names 85
DNS A (Address) records 161
DNS MX (Mail eXchange) records 161
document libraries 741
Domain Name Server *See* DNS
Domain Name Service *See* DNS
Domain Name System *See* DNS
domain trusts 461
domains
    access control 563
    configuring to use existing second-level domains 160
    filters 397 – 398
    names 85, 160, 188 – 189, 194
DOS *See* MS-DOS
DSMN *See* Directory Service Manager for NetWare
DTS (Data Transformation Services) 668
DTS Export Wizard 668
DTS Import Wizard 668
dual-homed 546
DUN *See* Dial-Up Networking
duplexing 59
Dynamic Host Configuration Protocol (DHCP)
    interoperability 529
    optimization 462 – 463
    overview 161
    performance tuning 488 – 489
dynamic IP addressing 161 – 162
dynamic packet filtering
    capabilities of 553
    configuring 199
    creating packet filters for Proxy services 395, 558 – 560
    customizing packet filters for Proxy services 395, 558 – 560
    enabling 556 – 558
    inner processes of 554 – 556
    overview 546
    packet filter lists 558
    predefined packet filters 558
    removing packet filters from Proxy services 395, 558 – 560

E

editing registries using System Policy Editor 291 – 295
electronic commerce 601
e-mail
    automatic forwarding 358
    dial-up accounts 82
    fax integration 343 – 344
    foreign addresses 106
    internal 501
    Internet connection issues 162
    ISP DNS entries 161
    overview 23
    troubleshooting 833 – 838
    web sites 838
E-mail Addresses property page 106
E-mail Distribution List Wizard
    Create a Distribution List mode 271 – 272
    modes described 271
    Remove a Distribution List mode 273
    Review or Change Distribution List mode 272 – 273
encryption
    access control 566
    CryptoAPI 611
    DES 609
    PPTP 226 – 227
    RAS 88
    VPN devices 226 – 227
Enterprise Manager 667 – 668
estimating bandwidth 75 – 76
ETRN 165
evaluating performance *See* performance
evaluation tests 110 – 112
Event Calendar 741
Event Log 549
Event Viewer 378 – 381
examples
    Access vs. SQL Server syntax 675 – 676
    Distinguished Names 104
Excel 2000
    corporate reporting 754 – 755
    PivotTable dynamic views 754
    Web Query Wizard 754
Exchange Directory 103
Exchange Server 5.5
    additional information 65
    Address Book views 355 – 356
    addresses 354 – 356
    Administrator program 352 – 353
    alternatives for ISP connectivity 501
    automating e-mail forwarding 358
    configuring 165 – 168
    configuring for POP3 mail 208 – 212
    configuring IMS connectors 200 – 208
    custom recipients 354 – 356
    described 21, 32
    disaster recovery 65
    disk I/O 366 – 367
    Distinguished Name example 104
    distribution lists 353 – 354
    domain name changes 160
    end-user objects 357
    fax integration 343 – 344
    faxing from 345 – 346
    foreign e-mail addresses 106
    internal e-mail 501
    IS 368 – 369
    mailboxes 105 – 106, 353
    naming scheme details 104 – 108
    naming strategies 103
    new users 354
    off-line synchronization 356 – 357
    optimization 465 – 466
    organization names 104
    overview 29, 352
    Performance Monitor *See* Performance Monitor
    performance tests 111
    performance tuning 485
    planning 103
    predefined performance monitors 370
    processor performance 117
    public folders 356 – 357
    server names 105
    site names 104
    SMTP restrictions 108
    upgrading 660
    usage characteristics 362
    Web Access 359
    web browsing 501
    Windows NT Backup 357 – 358
    X.400 addresses 106 – 107
exporting existing user accounts 251
extending Online Guide
    About links 709
    adding topic files 706
    console page links 706
    elements inside topic files 706
    installation 710
    integrating with console sub pages 709 – 710
    integration changes from Small Business Server 4.0a 711
    manage topics 705
    overview 704
    overview links 709
    overview topics 704 – 705
    procedure links 710

procedure topics 705
table of contents 707 – 709
topic file types 704 – 705
topic links 706
troubleshooting links 710
troubleshooting topics 705
extending Server Status Tool 317, 735 – 740, 780 – 781
extending Set Up Computer Wizard
adding applications to Clioc.inf 720 – 721
adding applications to Scw.ini 717 – 720
changes from Small Business Server 4.0a 723
creating application INF files 714 – 716
installing applications 721 – 722
integration requirements 714
overview 42, 713
removing applications 722 – 723
response file requirements 717
upgrading from Small Business Server 4.0a 723
extending Small Business Server console
adding favorite links to Home page 694 – 697
adding sub pages and secondary sub pages 700 – 702
adding tasks to Tasks and More Tasks pages 697 – 699
adding tasks with Customization Tool 699
changes from Small Business Server 4.0a 703
facilitating add-on management 39
installation mechanisms 702 – 703
Online Guide 704 – 711
organization of console 682 – 683
overview 41, 681, 694
page layout and design 684 – 694
philosophy 681 – 682
extensible console feature 39, 41
extensible firewall 541
extensible security 548
extranets 601 – 602

F

failures of disks in stripe sets with parity 61 – 62
FAT (file allocation table) 424
fault tolerance 468
fault-tolerant disk configurations
additional information 64
backup hardware 64
disk duplexing 59
disk mirroring 56 – 59
disk stripe sets 60 – 64
overview 55 – 56
using identical hardware 64
favorites
adding links to Home page 694 – 697
optimization 476
setup 469
Fax Access Wizard 266

Fax client
installing on remote client computers 216
optimization 468
fax modems 124
Fax Monitoring Tool (FaxMon) 787
Fax Performance Monitoring Tool (FaxPerf) 787
fax reports 317 – 322
Fax Server 4.5
described 22, 32
e-mail integration 343 – 344
optimization 467
overview 24
Fax Server Properties page 338 – 339
Fax Service
adding devices 339 – 340
adding fax printers 340
BackOffice Server 347
canceling 342
configuring fax printers 340
cover pages 340 – 341
described 337
e-mail integration 343 – 344
introduction 97
modem requirements 99
monitoring 343
notifications 342
pausing 342
planning 100
pre-deployment 97 – 100
properties 338 – 339
receiving and routing faxes 341 – 342
restarting 342
sending and resending faxes 342
tasks 338
troubleshooting 809 – 825
user access 340
Web sites 825
Windows NT Workstation clients 340
faxing
See also Fax Service
addresses 346
benefits of Small Business Server 22
e-mail integration 343 – 344
from Office 2000 347
from Outlook or Exchange 345 – 346
overview 24
Print command 344 – 345
FaxMon (Fax Monitoring Tool) 787
FaxPerf (Fax Performance Monitoring Tool) 787
features
Access 2000 726
administration 34 – 35
application service components 31 – 32
client application integration 34
Client User Guide 34

Index 861

communication components 32
consistent solutions 35
extensible console 39
file service components 31 – 32
Integrated Server Setup 33
Internet access supporting components 33
Microsoft Jet 727, 731 – 732
Microsoft Office 60 Minute Intranet Kit 740 – 742
MSDE 727 – 728, 731 – 732
Office 2000 743 – 752
Online Guide 34
overview 3, 8, 31
print service components 31 – 32
Remote Server Administration 35
Server Status Tool 35
Set Up Computer 34
Small Business Server console 33, 34
solution development 34 – 35
To Do List 33
upgrading Small Business Server 34
wizards 34
FEP (front end processor) 93
file allocation table (FAT) 424
File and Print Services for NetWare (FPNW)
    client capabilities with 144 – 145
    installing 144 – 145, 639 – 641
    interoperability 526
    overview 143
file service components 31 – 32
File Transfer Protocol (FTP) 415, 528
files
    access control 600, 603 – 606
    adm 292
    client application configuration 156
    Clioc.inf 158, 720 – 721, 723
    Clioc.old 723
    comma separated value (CSV) 317 – 322
    Common.adm 286
    compression 425
    csv 317 – 322
    DEFRAG.EXE 455
    Glyph_map.html 702
    Glyph100.ttf 702
    Glyph110.ttf 702
    hhc 707
    I/O bottlenecks 115 – 116
    I/O performance 117
    I/O throughput 112
    inf 153, 156, 714 – 716
    information files 153, 156, 664 – 665, 714 – 716
    ins 80 – 81
    Install.ins 470
    Installed 158

Ipdetect.exe 157, 276
Ipdx86.exe 157, 276
isp 79
job 331 – 332
lnk 303
locating and sending application log files 740
log 381 – 386, 399 – 400, 421, 740
mdb 731
Msdun.exe 235
Msdun12.exe 235
msi 244
mst 244
Netparam.ini 157, 276
NTConfig.pol 284, 297
NTuser.dat 285, 301 – 302
OEM.hhc 707 – 709
Office 2000 and Office 97 format compatibilities 743
Office 2000 error detection and correction 744
ops 244
ost 357
Passfilt.dll 591
pif 303
Poledit.exe 295 – 296
Program Information (.pif) 303
SBSCustom.exe 775 – 782
Schema.ini 321 – 322
Scw.exe 157
Scw.ini 156, 717 – 720, 723
Scw.old 723
Scwfiles.inf 157
setup (.msi) 244
Setup.exe 157, 276
sharing 595 – 597
shortcut (.lnk) 303
Startcli.exe 277
table of contents 707 – 709
TAPI.exe 774
TAPIstate.exe 774
task (job) 331 – 332
Template.bat 156, 274 – 275
transform 244
Unattend.txt 10
user account 253 – 255
user.txt 665
Windows.adm 286
Winnt.adm 286
firewalls
    additional information 450
    configuring settings 190 – 192
    described 545
    security 541
fonts 702

862 Index

foreign e-mail addresses 106
FPNW *See* File and Print Services for NetWare
front end processor (FEP) 93
FrontPage 2000
    creating intranets 746 – 747
    described 33
    extensions 750
    IIS 750
    managing intranets 746 – 747
    web site development 73
FrontPage 60 Minute Intranet Site Wizard 740
FrontPage Web Site Management tool 741
FtDisk 57
FTP (File Transfer Protocol) 415, 528
full-time/broadband connections
    overview 82, 169
    performance tuning 488
    required information 171
    requirements 488

G

Gateway Service for NetWare (GSNW)
    installation issues 139 – 143
    installing 634 – 638
    interoperability 524 – 525
    overview 138
    preferred NetWare Servers 139
    testing 638 – 639
    Windows NT Server to NetWare gateway 139
gateways 543
Glyph_map.html 702
Glyph100.ttf 702
Glyph110.ttf 702
Gopher services 74
group scheduling 22
GSNW *See* Gateway Service for NetWare
Guest account 590

H

Hard Disk Space report 315
hard page faults 115
hardware
    backup 64
    client computer requirements 52 – 53
    client computer test configurations 113
    compatibility 52, 63, 123 – 125
    configuring 175 – 176
    detection problems 147 – 153
    fax modems 124
    Internet connection requirements 51 – 52
    multiport serial adapter boards 125
    network adapter cards 124, 148 – 150

    performance recommendations 118 – 119
    performance tuning 482
    Recommended Hardware List 11, 52, 54, 100, 124
    requirements for PPTP clients 94 – 95
    server computer requirements 51 – 52
    server computer test configurations 112 – 113
    Windows NT Hardware Compatibility List 55, 63
Help *See* Online Guide
hhc files 707
high-level pages 682
high-level security 588 – 589
Home page 682, 684, 694 – 697, 741
horizontal list views 689
HTTP *See* Hypertext Transfer Protocol
HTTP 1.1 servers with PUT protocol 748 – 749
HTTP-DAV servers 749
HyperTerminal 831
Hypertext Transfer Protocol (HTTP)
    interoperability 528
    keep-alives 578
    PUT protocol 748 – 749
    requests 578

I

I/O *See* input/output
IAS (Internet Authentication Services) 449
ICS *See* Internet Connection Services
IIS *See* Internet Information Server
impersonation 606
import filters 757
IMS *See* Internet Mail Service
inbound access security 561
independent software vendors (ISVs) 610 – 611
Index Server 2.0 17
Index Tuning Wizard 678
inf files 153, 156, 714 – 716
information files 153, 156, 664 – 665, 714 – 716
Information Store (IS) 368 – 369
input/output (I/O)
    bottlenecks 115 – 116
    disk mirroring 57
    file throughput 112
    performance 117
ins files 80 – 81
Install on Demand 745
Install.ins 470
Installed files 158
installing client applications 158, 215 – 217, 277
installing controller devices 55
installing Fax client on remote client computers 216
installing File and Print Services for NetWare (FPNW) 144 – 145, 639 – 641

Index

installing Gateway Service for NetWare (GSNW) 139 – 143, 634 – 638
installing in existing environments
    16-bit operating systems 137
    decisions made automatically 7 – 8
    migrating data 136
    migrating users 135 – 136
    NetWare networks 5, 137 – 145
    overview 135
    replacing existing Windows NT 135 – 136
    Windows 95 137
    Windows 98 137
    Windows NT 4.0 Server 135 – 136
installing Internet Explorer on remote client computers 215
installing modem drivers 153
installing modems manually 151 – 152
installing network adapters 150
installing on new machines
    completing Setup using To Do List 131 – 133
    decisions made automatically 7 – 8
    hardware compatibility 123 – 125
    installing applications 129 – 131
    materials required 125
    overview 123
    performing 125 – 133
    procedure 126 – 131
    server requirements 123 – 125
    Setup boot diskettes 125 – 126
    Setup Wizard 129 – 131
    Windows NT Server GUI Mode portion of Setup 127 – 129
    Windows NT Server Text Mode portion of Setup 126 – 127
installing Outlook on remote client computers 215
installing PPTP
    adding VPN devices as RAS ports 225 – 226, 229 – 230
    authentication 226 – 227
    client connections to Small Business Server 227
    configuring on Small Business Server 224
    connecting to Small Business Server 242
    dialing an ISP 242
    Dial-Up Networking 230 – 232, 235 – 238
    encryption 226 – 227
    overview 223
    procedure 224 – 225, 228 – 229, 235
    requirements 223
    Windows 95-based remote clients 234 – 241
    Windows NT Workstation-based remote clients 228 – 234
installing RAS 26
installing Resource Kit 766 – 767
installing Small Business Server *See* installing on new machines; installing in existing environments
installing System Policy Editor on clients 295 – 296
installing Windows NT Server 10, 126 – 129, 460 – 464

Integrated Server Setup 33
Integrated Services Digital Network (ISDN)
    connections 163
    overview 71 – 72
    routers 164
    terminal adapters 163
integrating e-mail and fax 343 – 344
integrating Office 2000 509 – 514
interfaces, BRI and PRI 71 – 72
internal e-mail 501
Internet
    See also web
    access control 561 – 566
    access protocols 74
    access supporting components 33
    accessing directly 70
    addresses *See* IP addresses
    browsing 29
    configuring domain names 188 – 189
    configuring IMS connectors 200 – 208
    configuring mail settings 182 – 183
    configuring Proxy Server connectivity 195 – 199
    configuring server applications for connectivity *See* configuring server applications for Internet connectivity
    connecting 28 – 29
    connection hardware requirements 51 – 52
    connection issues 159 – 163
    connection process 79 – 85
    connection specifications 69 – 78
    connection topologies 168
    connection types 70 – 72, 169
    connectivity modes and security 101 – 102
    controlling access 28 – 29
    dedicated connections 83
    dial-up modem connections 71
    dynamic IP addressing and mail issues 161 – 162
    firewalls 545
    full-time connections 82
    impact of connectivity on server hardware 78
    isolation from LANs 546
    ISP capabilities 69
    line protocols 71
    Macintosh connections 535
    optimization of site location 476
    performance tuning 485 – 489
    planning for presence on 67
    proposal for access 68 – 69
    reports 317 – 322
    security 21
    sites *See* web sites
    troubleshooting 833 – 838
    viewing active sessions 412 – 413
    web sites 838
Internet Access Wizard 266 – 268
Internet Authentication Services (IAS) 449

Internet Connection Services (ICS)
  benefits 444
  CM 444 – 445
  CMAK 445 – 448
  component list 444
  CPS 450 – 451
  IAS 449
  overview 443
Internet Connection Wizard
  add-on sales 39
  automating ISP connectivity tasks 21
  Configure Firewall Settings screen 190 – 192
  Configure Hardware screen 175 – 176
  Configure Internet Domain Name screen 188 – 189
  Configure Internet Mail Settings screen 182 – 183
  Configure SMTP Mail Delivery screen 183 – 184
  Configure Web Site Information screen 189 – 190
  described 33, 279
  dynamic packet filtering 556
  finishing 192
  information required 170 – 171
  Internet connection topologies 168
  Internet connection types 169
  Network Interface Card Configuration screen 180 – 181
  optimization 480
  overview 22 – 23, 168
  Prepare to Sign Up Online screen 176 – 177
  Receive Exchange Mail screen 184 – 186
  running 173 – 192
  Send and Receive POP3 Mail screen 187 – 188
  Set Up Authentication screen 186 – 187
  Set Up Connection to Your ISP screen 174 – 175
  Set Up Modem Connection to ISP screen 177 – 178
  Set Up Router Connection to ISP screen 179 – 180
  Set Up Second Network Adapter screen 181 – 182
  starting 172
Internet Explorer 5.0
  described 33
  installing on remote client computers 215
  Office 2000 747
  optimization 469 – 470
Internet Explorer for UNIX interoperability 531
Internet Information Server (IIS) 4.0
  console 550 – 551
  described 32
  FrontPage extensions 750
  integrated with Proxy Server 550 – 551
  Office 2000 749
  Office Server Extensions 750 – 751
  optimization 467
  security See Internet Information Server (IIS) 4.0 security model
  services 74
  web site hosting 73

Internet Information Server (IIS) 4.0 security model
  access control 603 – 606
  ACLs 600
  advantages 602 – 603
  auditing access 606
  central management 600
  confidentiality 607 – 610
  data integrity 607 – 610
  framework for using security 602 – 603
  functionality for developers 610 – 611
  logging 606
  NTLM authentication 604
  overview 599 – 600
  PCT 607
  permissions 600, 606
  SSL 608
  user authentication and authorization 603 – 605
  web server security 600 – 602
  X.509 certificates 604
Internet Information Server Logs report 315
Internet Mail Service (IMS)
  configuring connectors 200 – 208
  queue monitoring 370 – 371
Internet Protocol (IP)
  access control by IP addresses 563, 605
  addresses See IP addresses
  dynamic packet filtering 553 – 560
  forwarding 561
  overview 71
  packet layer filtering 546
  protecting internal addresses from the Internet 546
  routing default configuration 561
  static packet filtering 554
Internet Referral Server 23, 177
Internet Server Application Programming Interface (ISAPI) 576 – 578
Internet Service Provider (ISP)
  automated server configuring 80
  capabilities 69
  configuring DNS 80, 161
  connectivity See Internet Service Provider (ISP) connectivity
  dial-up networking phonebook entries 193
  functions required for Small Business Server compliance 81
  information required from 84
  locations 70
  offline sign-up and configuration 81
  referral program 79 – 80
  selecting 23
  setting up connections to 174 – 175
  sign-up scripts 80
  types of services 82 – 83
  web site hosting requirements 73

Internet Service Provider (ISP) connectivity
    See also alternatives for ISP connectivity
    additional resources for 168
    automating tasks 21
    configuring for non-dialup connections 163 – 168
    Internet connection issues 159 – 163
    overview 159
    planning 81 – 84
    troubleshooting 81 – 84
InterNIC database 160
interoperability
    application layer 522, 530 – 532
    ASU 529
    BOOTP 529
    COM 532
    CSNW 525
    data layer 522, 530
    DCOM 532
    DHCP 529
    Domain Name Service 529
    DSMN 526 – 527
    FPNW 526
    FTP 528
    GSNW 524, 525
    HTTP 528
    Internet Explorer for UNIX 531
    Macintosh 533 – 537
    management layer 522, 532 – 533
    Migration Tool for NetWare 525
    MTS 531
    NetWare 523 – 527
    network layer 522, 528 – 529
    NFS 529
    NWLink 525
    ODBC 530
    OLE DB 530
    operating systems 522 – 523
    Oracle 530, 531
    Outlook Express 530
    overview 521
    protocols 523
    SNMP 532
    TCP/IP 528
    TIP 531
    UNIX 528 – 533
    Visual Studio 530
    Windows NT Services for UNIX 533
Interrupts/Second counter 328 – 329
intranets
    advantages of 76 – 77
    creating and customizing sites 740 – 742
    document libraries 741
    extending the default page 19, 77
    Office 2000 746 – 747
    optimization of page and content 476

overview 19
security precautions 77
site relationships 77
IntranetWare networks 5
introduction 3
IP *See* Internet Protocol
IP addresses
    access control by 563, 605
    changes 401 – 408
    configuring network adapters 150
    default range 400
    dynamically assigning to clients 161 – 162
    optimization 462 – 463
    performance tuning 486
    protecting from the Internet 546
Ipdetect.exe 157, 276
Ipdx86.exe 157, 276
IS (Information Store) 368 – 369
ISAPI (Internet Server Application Programming
    Interface) 576 – 578
ISDN *See* Integrated Services Digital Network
ISP *See* Internet Service Provider
isp files 79
issuing digital certificates 610 – 611

J

Jet 4.0 *See* Microsoft Jet 4.0
job files 331 – 332

K

K56Flex modems 100
keep-alives 578
kernel-mode packet filtering 546
key pairs 608
keyboard layouts 127
Knowledge Base *See* additional information

L

LAN (local area network) performance tuning 489
LAT *See* Local Address Table
layers
    application 522, 530 – 532
    data 522, 530
    management 522, 532 – 533
    network 522, 528 – 529
layouts
    default 688 – 691
    horizontal list view 689
    no list view 691
    status 690
    vertical list view 688

leased line connections 164, 166 – 168
leveraging BackOffice skills and solutions 39
libraries 741
licensing 657 – 659
line protocols 71
links
    About 709
    console page 706
    overview 709
    procedure 710
    topic 706
    troubleshooting 710
lnk files 303
load simulation tools 111
LoadSim tool 111
Local Address Table (LAT)
    configuring 199, 408 – 412
    overview 400, 572
    updating 408 – 412
local area network (LAN) performance tuning 489
local profiles 300
log files 381 – 386, 399 – 400, 421, 740
logon scripts 156, 274 – 275, 646 – 647

M

machine accounts 157, 275 – 276
Macintosh
    additional information 519, 537
    administration 535
    authentication 519
    benefits 536 – 537
    file sharing 534
    graphics 534
    Internet connections 535
    interoperability 533 – 537
    printer sharing 535
    resources 519, 537
    security 535
    server interactions 517
Mail eXchange (MX) records 161
mailboxes 105 – 106, 353
mailings 22
Manage Faxes page 24, 338
Manage Modems page 26
Manage Server 214
Manage Users page 15 – 16, 26
managed network access 542
management layer
    described 522
    interoperability 532 – 533
mandatory profiles 300, 309 – 313
mass mailings 22
mdb files 731

memory
    bottlenecks 115
    optimization 478
    performance 117 – 118
    Performance Monitor 365 – 366
message signing 596 – 597
Microsoft Access 2000 *See* Access 2000
Microsoft Access Upsizing Wizard *See* Upsizing Wizard
Microsoft Certificate Server 1.0 610 – 611
Microsoft Connection Manager (CM) 444 – 445
Microsoft Data Engine (MSDE)
    comparing to Microsoft Jet 728 – 732
    data handling 731
    data integrity 730
    features 727 – 728, 731 – 732
    organizational requirements 728 – 729
    overview 725, 727 – 728
    performance 730
    usage analysis 729 – 731
    when to use 733
Microsoft Direct Access web site 45
Microsoft Excel 2000 *See* Excel 2000
Microsoft Exchange Server 5.5 *See* Exchange Server 5.5
Microsoft Fax Server 4.5 *See* Fax Server 4.5
Microsoft Fax Service *See* Fax Service
Microsoft FrontPage 2000 *See* FrontPage 2000
Microsoft FrontPage Web Site Management tool 741
Microsoft Internet Explorer 5.0 *See* Internet Explorer 5.0
Microsoft Internet Explorer for UNIX interoperability 531
Microsoft Internet Information Server 4.0 *See* Internet Information Server (IIS) 4.0
Microsoft Internet Referral Server 23, 177
Microsoft Jet 4.0
    comparing to MSDE 728 – 732
    compatibility with Access 97 729 – 730
    data handling 731
    features 731 – 732
    new features 727
    organizational requirements 728 – 729
    overview 725, 727 – 728
    simplicity of 729 – 730
    usage analysis 729 – 731
    when to use 733
Microsoft Knowledge Base *See* additional information
Microsoft Message Queue Server (MSMQ) 759
Microsoft Migrate User Wizard *See* Migrate User Wizard
Microsoft Modem Sharing Service *See* Modem Sharing Service
Microsoft NetMeeting *See* NetMeeting
Microsoft Office 2000 *See* Office 2000
Microsoft Office 60 Minute Intranet Kit 740 – 742
Microsoft Office Server Extensions 748, 750 – 751
Microsoft Office Small Business Customer Manager *See* Small Business Customer Manager
Microsoft Outlook 2000 *See* Outlook 2000

Microsoft Outlook Express *See* Outlook Express
Microsoft Point-to-Point Compression 88
Microsoft PowerPoint 2000 748, 752
Microsoft Proxy Server 2.0 *See* Proxy Server 2.0
Microsoft Remote Access Service *See* Remote Access Service (RAS)
Microsoft Site Server Express 601 – 602
Microsoft SQL Server 7.0 *See* SQL Server 7.0
Microsoft TechNet 45
Microsoft Transaction Server (MTS) interoperability 531
Microsoft Upsizing Wizard *See* Upsizing Wizard
Microsoft virtual private network *See* virtual private network
Microsoft Visual Studio interoperability 530
Microsoft Web Publishing Wizard *See* Web Publishing Wizard
Microsoft Windows NT *See* Windows NT
Microsoft Windows Telephony Applications Programming Interface (TAPI) 761
Microsoft Windows NT Services for Macintosh *See* Macintosh
Migrate User Wizard
    default file location 255
    editing user account files 254
    export mode 250 – 255, 663 – 664
    exporting existing user accounts 251
    exporting existing user groups 251 – 252
    import mode 255, 664
    Import Users task 666
    information file 664 – 665
    information not exported 252
    modes described 136, 663
    overview 135 – 136, 249 – 250
    tasks 666
    user account files 253 – 255
migrating from NetWare
    client configurations 647, 651 – 652
    client setup 626 – 629
    client setup testing 629 631
    connectivity tests 652 – 653
    creating new accounts 648
    data migration 648 – 651
    documentation 626, 653
    executive summary 654
    functionality testing 632
    GSNW testing 638 – 639
    hardware setup 625 – 626
    hardware verification 622 – 623
    installation software 625
    installing DSMN 641 – 646
    installing FPNW 639 – 641
    installing GSNW 634 – 638
    installing NWLink protocol 633
    installing Small Business Server 626 – 632
    integration overview 618
    integration phase 632 – 647
    integration phase overview 620
    login scripts 646 – 647
    migration phase 647 – 653
    Migration Tool 648 – 650
    moving directories and files 650 – 651
    overview 615 – 616
    planning 616 – 617
    post-integration phase overview 620 – 621
    project objectives 654
    project review phase 654 – 655
    rollout overview 618 – 621
    schedule analysis 655
    test computer location 621
    test phase 621 – 632
    test phase overview 619 – 620
    test preparation tasks 621 – 626
    test types 624
    third-party application testing 631
    Windows 95 clients 652
    Windows for Workgroups clients 651
    Windows NT Workstation clients 652
migrating from Windows NT Server 663 – 666
migrating to SQL Server
    Access data transfer 669
    Access database backup 669
    Access queries 670 – 672, 676
    applications predating Office 2000 677
    DTS 668
    Enterprise Manager 667 – 668
    Index Tuning Wizard 678
    nested queries 676
    optimizing applications 678
    overview 422, 667
    parameters 674 – 676
    Profiler 668 – 669, 678
    Query Analyzer 668
    stored procedures 670 – 672, 674 – 676
    syntax example 675 676
    syntax verification 676 – 677
    tools 667 – 669
    Transact-SQL statements 670, 672 – 673, 678
    views 671 – 672
migrating users when replacing existing Windows NT 135 – 136
Migration Tool for NetWare 525, 648, 650
minimum computer configurations 51 – 53
mirroring *See* disk mirroring
Modem Sharing Service
    alternatives for ISP connectivity 499 – 501
    configuring clients 350
    configuring modem pools 349 – 350
    connecting Windows 95 clients 350 – 351
    connecting Windows NT Workstation clients 351
    described 32
    introduction 97

monitoring 352
multiple accounts 499 – 501
optimization 467
overview 26 – 27, 347 – 348
pre-deployment 97 – 100
properties 348
troubleshooting 827 – 832
viewing modem pools 349
web browsing 499 – 501
web sites 832
Modem Status Tools 352, 773 – 774
modems
   See also Modem Sharing Service
   communication standards 100
   connections 71
   information files 153
   installing 124
   multiple usage scenarios 98 – 99
   multiport serial cards 99
   planning 98 – 100
   pools 349 – 351
   Recommended Hardware List 100
   requirements for Fax Service 99
   requirements for RAS 99
   setting up connections to ISP 177 – 178
   sharing 26 – 27
   troubleshooting 150 – 153, 827 – 832
Modprof 471 – 473
More Tasks page 15 – 16, 684 – 685, 697 – 699
Move Folder Wizard 270
MS Loopback Adapter 148 – 149
MS-CHAP authentication 87
MSDE *See* Microsoft Data Engine
MS-DOS
   authentication 517
   installing Small Business Server on existing environments 137
   server interactions 516
Msdun.exe 235
Msdun12.exe 235
msi files 244
MSMQ (Microsoft Message Queue Server) 759
mst files 244
MTS (Microsoft Transaction Server) interoperability 531
multi-link PPP 88
multiport serial adapter boards 125
multiport serial cards 99
MX (Mail eXchange) records 161

N

names
   domains 160, 188 – 189, 194
   example of Distinguished Names 104
   mailbox 105 – 106
   optimization 460 – 461
   organization 104
   second-level domain 85, 160
   server 105
   site 104
   users 333, 604
naming strategies for Exchange Server 103
NAT (Network Address Translation) 169
NetBench tool 112
NetMeeting 38, 42, 281 – 282, 751 – 752
Netparam.ini 157, 276
nets 70
NetShow 748
NetWare networks
   CSNW 525
   DSMN 526 – 527
   FPNW 143 – 145, 526
   GSNW 138 – 143, 524 – 525
   installing Small Business Server on existing environments 5, 137 – 145
   interoperability 523 – 527
   migrating *See* migrating from NetWare
   Migration Tool 525
   NWLink 138, 525
   web sites 527
NetWare-to-Windows NT Server Conversion Utility 138
network adapter cards 124, 148 – 150
Network Address Translation (NAT) 169
Network File System (NFS) interoperability 529
Network Installation Wizard 244 – 245
network interface cards (NICs) 164, 180 – 182, 546
network layer
   described 522
   interoperability 528 – 529
network terminating (NT1) units 72
networks
   adapter cards 124, 148 – 150
   capacity guidelines 118 – 119
   characteristics of 49
   client/server model 4
   configurations 49 – 50
   IntranetWare 5
   managed access 542
   NetWare 5, *See* NetWare networks
   peer-to-peer 4
   protocols 94
   reducing traffic on 544
   restricting access to the registry 593
   security 101, 588

news engines 741
newsgroups 45
NFS (Network File System) interoperability 529
NICs (network interface cards) 164, 180 – 182, 546
no list views 691
non-Office 2000 versions 509 – 513
Novell NetWare *See* NetWare
NT *See* Windows NT
NT Backup utility
    disaster recovery 66
    registry 593
    Scheduled Task utility 335
    tape device support 54
NT Event Viewer 378 – 381
NT Performance Monitor *See* Performance Monitor
NT1 (network terminating) units 72
NTConfig.pol 284, 297
NTFS
    optimization 460
    overview 424
    permissions 304 – 305, 424, 605
    security 592
    volumes 425
NTLM authentication 604
NTuser.dat 285, 301 – 302
NWLink protocol
    installing 633
    overview 138, 525

O

Object Linking and Embedding Database (OLE DB) 530, 753
ODBC (Open Database Connectivity) interoperability 530
OEM.hhc 707 – 709
Office 2000
    Access 2000 client/server tools 753 – 754
    additional information 756
    AutoNavigation 750
    client/server design tools 754
    corporate reporting 754 – 755
    creating intranets 746 – 747
    creating profiles 244
    custom deployments 243 – 245, 514
    Custom Installation Wizard 244 – 245
    Customer Manager *See* Small Business Customer Manager
    data access 753 – 754
    document interfaces 745
    enhanced web queries 754
    enhancements 743 – 752
    enterprise integration and support 752 – 755
    faxing from 347
    features enabled by browsers 747
    file error detection and correction 744
    file format compatibilities 743
    HTTP 1.1 servers with PUT protocol 748 – 749
    HTTP-DAV servers 749
    IIS 749
    Install on Demand 745
    integrated security 749
    integration issues 509 – 514
    Internet Explorer 5.0 features 747
    managing intranets 746 – 747
    Microsoft Office Server Extensions 748, 750 – 751
    NetMeeting 751 – 752
    Network Installation Wizard 244 – 245
    Office Profile Wizard 243 – 244
    Office Web Components 755
    OLE DB 753
    operating system shell updates 744 – 745
    optimization 471
    overview 743
    policy templates 245
    reducing cost of ownership 744
    SQL Server OLAP Services support 753
    SQL Server-based administration tools 754
    summary of enhancements 756
    System Policy Editor 245
    transforms 244
    web browser and web server functionality 746 – 752
    web folders 745
    web integration 746
Office 60 Minute Intranet Kit 740 – 742
office networks *See* networks
Office Profile Wizard 243 – 244
Office Server Extensions 748, 750 – 751
Office Small Business Customer Manager (SBCM) 757
Office Web Components 755
off-line synchronization 356 – 357
OLAP (Online Analytical Processing) 753
OLE DB (Object Linking and Embedding Database) 530, 753
on-demand caching 569
Online Analytical Processing (OLAP) 753
Online Guide
    console page links 706
    described 34
    elements inside topic files 706
    extending *See* extending Online Guide
    high-level console pages 682
    manage topics 705
    overview 17 – 18
    overview topics 704 – 705
    procedure topics 705
    topic file types 704 – 705
    topic links 706
    troubleshooting topics 705
Open Database Connectivity (ODBC) interoperability 530

Open Systems Interconnection (OSI) model architecture 554
operating systems
  16-bit 137
  compatibilities 53
  interoperability 522 – 523
  recommendations for client computers 53
ops files 244
optimization
  See also performance tuning
  Add User Wizard 480
  application installations 464
  client applications 468
  code 477 – 478
  console 479
  DHCP 462 – 463
  domain trusts 461
  Exchange Server 5.5 465 – 466
  fault tolerance 468
  favorites 476
  Fax client 468
  Fax Server 467
  IIS 467
  Internet Connection Wizard 480
  Internet Explorer 5.0 469 – 470
  Internet site 476
  intranet page and content 476
  IP addresses 462 – 463
  memory 478
  Modem Sharing Service 467
  Modprof 471 – 473
  names 460 – 461
  NTFS 460
  Office 2000 471
  Outlook 2000 470 – 471
  overview 459 – 460
  PDC 461
  permissions 474 – 475
  Proxy Server 2.0 464, 467
  RAID 468
  RAS 464
  security groups 461
  Set Up Computer Wizard 479 – 480
  shared folders 461, 473, 479
  single platform 477 – 479
  SQL Server 466
  SQL Server migration 678
  TCP/IP 462
  user limitations 478 – 479
  version number 468
  web sites 678
  Windows NT Server 460 – 464
  WINS 462
Oracle 530 – 531
organization names for Exchange Server 104
OS/2 server interactions 516

OSI (Open Systems Interconnection) model architecture 554
ost files 357
Outlook 2000
  anonymous access 435 – 438
  contact databases 438 – 442
  described 21, 32
  discussion groups 430 – 435
  Event Calendar 741
  faxing from 345 – 346
  group task lists 438 – 442
  installing on remote client computers 215
  optimization 470 – 471
  overview 426
  POP3 503 – 507
  public folders 426 – 430
  web sites 442
Outlook Express
  clients 208 – 212
  interoperability 530
Outlook Web Access 359, 438
overview 3

P

Packet Filter Driver 554
Packet Filter Manager 554
packet filtering *See* dynamic packet filtering; static packet filtering
pages
  adding secondary sub pages 700 – 702
  adding sub pages 700 – 702
  Data Access Pages 747
  E-mail Addresses property 106
  extension mechanism for 694 – 704
  Fax Server Properties 338 – 339
  high-level 682
  Home 682, 684, 694 – 697, 741
  layout and design 684 – 694
  Manage Faxes 24, 338
  Manage Modems 26
  Manage Users 15 – 16, 26
  More Tasks 15 – 16, 684 – 685, 697 – 699
  Publish on the Internet 73, 77
  secondary sub 683, 700 – 702
  sub 683, 686 – 693, 700 – 702
  symbols 686, 693, 702
  Tasks 15 – 16, 42, 682, 684 – 685, 697 – 699
  watermarks 686, 693
PAP (Password Authentication Protocol) 87
parity 60 – 64
partitions
  boot 57
  disk mirroring 56
  disk stripe sets with parity 61

Index

sizes 57
system 57
Passfilt.dll 591
passive caching 569
Password Authentication Protocol (PAP) 87
passwords 262 – 263, 316 – 317, 333, 591 – 592, 604
pausing tasks 335
PCT (Private Communications Technology) 607
PDC (Primary Domain Controller) 461
peer-to-peer networks 4
performance
   See also Performance Monitor
   analysis 116 – 118
   bottlenecks 113 – 116
   client computer test configurations 112 – 113
   disk space consumption 118
   disk subsystems 117
   evaluating 109 – 112
   Exchange Server 111
   file I/O throughput 112
   hardware recommendations 118 – 119
   memory 117
   monitoring 113 – 118
   MSDE vs. Microsoft Jet 730
   optimization 477 – 479
   processor 117
   RAM 117 – 118
   response time test results 116
   server computer test configurations 112 – 113
   SQL Server 110 – 111
   test results 113 – 118
   tests 110 – 112
Performance Monitor
   additional information 369
   alerts 323 – 329, 377 – 378, 387 – 388
   baselines 362
   bookmarks 383
   chart options 377
   Chart view 383
   configuring alerts 323 – 329
   counters 323, 361 – 363
   CPU utilization 367 – 368
   creating alerts 324 – 325, 329
   creating monitors 376 – 381
   data collection and analysis 361, 364 – 369
   default logging 381
   diagnostics logging 381
   disk I/O 366 – 367
   disk space 389
   Event Viewer 378 – 381
   Exchange server processes 360
   features 360
   IMS queues 370 – 371
   Interrupts/Second 328 – 329
   IS 368 – 369
   knowledge required 369
   log files 381 – 386
   memory 365 – 366
   modifying existing alerts 326 – 327
   monitoring phase 370
   overview 323, 359
   predefined monitors 370
   problem analysis 361
   Processor Queue Length 327 – 328
   Proxy Server 415 – 421, 549
   queue monitoring 370 – 372
   reports 388
   server health 372 – 373
   server history 373 – 374
   server load 374 – 375
   server queues 371 – 372
   server users 375
   service levels 362
   subsystem monitors 364
   testing counters 325
   testing Small Business Server performance 114 – 115
   thresholds 361, 363
   usage characteristics 362
performance tuning
   See also optimization
   connection requirements 487 – 488
   DHCP 488, 489
   disk configurations 482
   Exchange Server 5.5 485
   full-time/broadband connections 488
   hardware 482
   Internet 485 – 489
   IP addresses 486
   LAN 489
   overview 481
   RAID 482
   routers 485 – 489
   SQL Server 7.0 485
   TCP/IP vs. Named Pipes 485
   Windows NT Server 4.0 483 – 485
permissions
   IIS 606
   NTFS 424, 605
   optimization 474 – 475
   protecting files and directories 592
   resource access 265
   setting graphically 600
   user profiles 304 – 305
   users 265
personal digital certificates 602, 604, 610 – 611
phonebook entries 193, 220 – 221, 230 – 234
Phonebook Wizard 230
pif files 303
PivotTable dynamic views 754

872 Index

planning
    backup systems 54 – 55
    capacity 109
    disaster recovery 65 – 66
    Exchange Server 5.5 103
    fault-tolerant disk configurations 55 – 64
    Fax Service 97, 100
    Internet presence 67
    migrating from NetWare 616 – 617
    Modem Sharing Service 97
    modems 98 – 100
    Proxy Server 2.0 101
    remote access users 87
    Small Business Server networks 49
    user profiles 304 – 306
Point-to-Point Compression 88
Point-to-Point Protocol (PPP) 71, 88, 226 – 227
Point-to-Point Tunneling Protocol (PPTP)
    access control 566
    additional information 96
    advantages of 91
    authentication 226 – 227
    configuring 226 – 241
    connecting to Small Business Server 242
    deployment issues 95 – 96
    dialing an ISP 242
    encryption 226 – 227
    hardware requirements 94 – 95
    illustration of 91
    installing *See* installing Point-to-Point Tunneling Protocol
    network protocols 94
    overview 91, 609 – 610
    uses of 92
    VPNs 93 – 94
    web sites 96
    when used 93
Poledit.exe 295 – 296
policy templates 245, 286, 292, 295 – 296
POP (Post Office Protocol) mail 83, 166
POP3
    alternatives for ISP connectivity 501 – 507
    configuring for 208 – 212
    multiple accounts 503
    Outlook 2000 503 – 507
    overview 166
    sending and receiving mail 187 – 188
    single accounts 502
    SMTP vs. POP3 167
    web browsing 501 – 507
Post Office Protocol (POP) mail 83, 166
power-on-password 589
PowerPoint 2000 748, 752
PPP *See* Point-to-Point Protocol
PPTP *See* Point-to-Point Tunneling Protocol

preferred NetWare Servers 139
PRI (primary rate interface) 71 – 72
primary disk partitions 56
Primary Domain Controller (PDC) 461
primary rate interface (PRI) 71 – 72
print service components 31 – 32
Printer Access Wizard 266
Private Communications Technology (PCT) 607
private keys 608
processor
    access control 589
    bottlenecks 115
    performance 117
    Performance Monitor 367 – 368
Processor Queue Length counter 327 – 328
profile evaluation for clients and computers 285
Profiler 668 – 669, 678
Program Information Files (.pif) 303
programmatically interacting with client certificates 611
protocols
    accessing the Internet 71
    list of supported 523
proxy
    addresses 106
    creating performance monitors 418 – 420
    described 545
    reports 317 – 322
    viewing performance monitors 420 – 421
Proxy Server 2.0
    access control 390 – 394, 561 – 566
    additional information 102
    alerting 396 – 397
    alternatives for ISP connectivity 494 – 499
    architecture 572 – 586
    Auto Dial 102, 571 – 572
    caching 413 – 414, 569 – 570
    configuring 165
    configuring for dial-up Internet connectivity 102
    configuring for Internet connectivity 195 – 199
    configuring LAT 199, 408 – 412
    configuring packet filtering 199
    connectivity advantages 547
    default configuration 546
    described 21, 33
    disk space 399 – 400
    domain filters 397 – 398
    dynamic packet filtering 395, 546, 553 – 560
    extensible security 548
    features 394, 548, 571 – 572
    firewall security and Web caching 541
    FTP 415
    inbound access security 561
    integrated services 543
    integrated with IIS 550 – 551
    LAT 400, 408 – 412, 572

log files 399 – 400
managed network access 542
management features 549 – 552
network security 101
open standards platform 543
optimization 464, 467
overview 28 – 29, 389 – 390, 541
Performance Monitor 415 – 421, 549
planning 101
planning resources 102
reports 399
secure gateways 543
security 395 – 400, 545 – 546
security architecture 552 – 561
server proxying 567
services described 544
single accounts 494
SOCKS Proxy service 584
static packet filtering 554
TCP/IP on the small business LAN 585
third-party filtering services 399
updating LAT 408 – 412
upgrading 660
using Web Proxy and Winsock Proxy services
 together 585 – 586
value-added filtering services 398
viewing Internet sessions 412 – 413
web browsing 29, 494 – 499
web content caching 544
Web Proxy service 390, 416, 573 – 578
web publishing support 546, 566 – 568
Windows NT security 552
Winsock Proxy service 390 – 394, 417 – 418, 579 – 583
Proxy Server ISAPI applications 577
Proxy Server ISAPI filters 576
PSTN (Public Switched Telephone Network) 71, 236
PTR records 161
public folders 356   357, 426 – 430, 435 – 438
public keys 608
Public Switched Telephone Network (PSTN) 71, 236
Publish on the Internet page 73, 77
PUT protocol 748 – 749

Q

Query Analyzer 668
Quick Defrag 454 – 456

R

RAID *See* Redundant Array of Independent Disks
RAM (random access memory) 117 – 118

random access memory (RAM) 117 – 118
RAS *See* Remote Access Service
RDS (Remote Data Services) 749
recommended computer configurations 51 – 53
Recommended Hardware List (RHL) 11, 52, 54, 100, 124
recommended operating systems 53
records
 A (Address) 161
 MX (Mail eXchange) 161
 PTR 161
Redundant Array of Independent Disks (RAID)
 optimization 468
 overview 55 – 56
 performance tuning 482
redundant disk partitions 56
referral program for ISPs 79 – 80
Referral Server 23, 177
registering second-level domain names 85, 160
registry
 changing client computers 285
 configuration by Customization Tool 738 – 739
 connecting to remote 291
 editing using System Policy Editor 291 – 295
 System Policy 283
 user profile configuration preferences 301 – 302
Registry Editor 593
remote access
 overview 91
 planning 87
 PPTP 91 – 96
 security 91
Remote Access Service (RAS)
 adding VPN devices as RAS ports 225 – 226, 229 – 230
 authentication 87
 client support 88
 compression 88
 Connection Manager Administration Kit 89
 Connection Point Services 90
 connectivity options 88
 described 33
 encryption 88
 features 87 – 90
 ICS *See* Internet Connection Services
 installing and configuring 26
 low cost hardware and systems 89
 modem requirements 99
 multi-link 88
 open and extensible platform 89
 optimization 464
 overview 25 – 26, 87, 443
 protocol support 88
 requirements for implementing 90
 scalability 88

Index

remote client computers
    adding VPN devices 229 – 230
    configuring 214 – 219
    configuring Dial-Up Networking 230 – 232, 235 – 238
    connecting to Small Business Server 220 – 222
    creating user accounts 214
    installing PPTP 228 – 229, 235
    manually installing applications 215 – 217
    overview 213
    PPTP 227, 228 – 242
    preliminary setup 213
Remote Data Services (RDS) 749
Remote Server Administration
    client and server interactions 282
    described 35
    overview 38, 42, 281
    remote connections 282
remote users
    access control for 565 – 566
    creating accounts 214
removable media security 597
removing MS Loopback Adapter 149
removing packet filters from Proxy services 395, 558 – 560
removing undetected modems 151 – 152
replacing existing Windows NT 135 – 136
replacing task pages 42
replicating solutions 37
reports
    fax 317 – 322
    generating 318, 388
    Internet 317 – 322
    preconfigured 315
    proxy 317 – 322, 399
    sending 314 – 317
requirements for connections 487 – 488
requirements of Small Business Server 51 – 53
resources
    BackOffice Server 661
    Btrieve database migration 423
    caching 450
    dequeuing methods 166, 185
    Digiboard multiport serial cards 99
    e-mail 838
    Exchange Server disaster recovery 65
    fault tolerant disk configurations 64
    Fax Service 825
    firewalls 450
    Internet 838
    InterNIC database 160
    ISP connectivity 168
    Macintosh 519, 537
    Microsoft Office 60 Minute Intranet Kit 742
    Modem Sharing Service 832

    MSMQ 759
    NetMeeting 281
    NetWare networks 527
    Office 2000 756
    optimization 678
    Outlook 442
    Outlook Web Access 438
    Performance Monitor 369
    policy templates 245
    PPTP 96
    Proxy Server 102
    publishing 163
    Recommended Hardware List 11
    SBCM 757
    Scheduled Task utility 335
    security 592
    Set Up Computer Wizard 807
    Setup 797
    Small Business Server 45
    SMB message signing enhancements 597
    SOCKS 584
    SQL Server 422, 423, 671, 673
    SQL Server disaster recovery 65
    System Policy 286, 313
    TAPI 761
    training 43
    troubleshooting Outlook Web Access 438
    UNIX 533
    Upsizing Wizard 423
    user profiles 313
    Web Publishing Wizard 163
    web site development 74
    web sites 45
    Windows 95 user profiles 302, 303
response folders 156, 275
restoring server applications 66
restricting network access to the registry 593
restrictions to performance 113 – 116
reverse proxy 546, 567, 568
RHL *See* Recommended Hardware List
roaming profiles 300, 306 – 309, 311 – 312
routers
    connections 164, 169 – 171, 179 – 180
    performance tuning 485 – 489

S

sales add-ons 39
SBCM (Small Business Customer Manager) 757
SBS 4.0a *See* Small Business Server 4.0a
SBSCustom.exe 775 – 782
scalability *See* performance tuning
Scheduled Task utility 330, 334 – 335
Scheduled Task Wizard 331

Index 875

scheduling
    backups 55
    communications 22
    tasks 330 – 335
Schema.ini files 321 – 322
Scw.exe 157
Scw.ini 156, 717 – 720, 723
Scw.old 723
Scwfiles.inf 157
secondary disk partitions 56
secondary sub pages 683, 700 – 702
second-level domain names 85, 160
Secure Electronic Transport (SET) 609
secure file sharing 595 – 597
secure gateways 543
secure sockets layer (SSL)
    confidentiality and data integrity 607
    digital certificates 604
    encryption 566
    overview 608
security
    access control 561 – 566, 603 – 606
    accounts 589 – 590
    additional information 592
    applications 601
    architecture 552 – 561
    auditing 606
    business relationships 601 – 602
    communicating with customers 602
    confidentiality 607 – 610
    configuring firewall settings 190 – 192
    data integrity 607 – 610
    databases 601
    digital signatures 607 – 608
    dynamic packet filtering 553 – 560
    electronic commerce 601
    extensibility 548
    extranets 601 – 602
    firewalls 545
    framework for using 602 – 603
    functionality for developers 610 – 611
    groups 461
    high-level 588 – 589
    IIS *See* Internet Information Server (IIS) 4.0 security model
    Internet 21
    Internet connectivity modes 101 – 102
    intranet 77
    IP packet layer filtering 546
    IP routing 561
    LAN and Internet isolation 546
    levels described 587
    Macintosh 535
    networks 101, 588
    Office 2000 749
    overview 545
    physical 587 – 589
    protecting internal IP addresses from the Internet 546
    proxy 545
    Proxy Server 395 – 400, 545 – 546
    remote access 91
    scheduled tasks 331 – 333
    standard *See* standard security
    static packet filtering 554
    user authentication and authorization 603 – 605
    user credentials 332
    user names and passwords 333
    web caching 102, 541, 544
    web publishing support 566 – 568
    web servers 600 – 602
    web sites 21
    Windows NT 552, 587, 599 – 600
security identification (SID) 605
serial line Internet protocol (SLIP) 71
server applications
    backing up 66
    restoring 66
server certificates 604
server computers
    access control 589
    adding VPN devices 225 – 226
    client interactions 515 – 517
    configuring for clients 156 – 157, 274 – 276
    configuring PPTP 224, 226 – 227
    CPU architecture 78
    creating alerts 324 – 325
    hardware requirements 51 – 52
    impact of Internet connectivity 78
    installing PPTP 224 – 225
    installing Resource Kit 766 – 767
    names for Exchange Server 105
    performance test configurations 112 – 113
    RAM requirements 78
    requirements for installation 123 – 125
server extensions 748, 750 – 751
server interactions
    Macintosh clients 517
    MS-DOS clients 516
    OS/2 clients 516
    overview 515
    Windows 3.1 clients 516
    Windows 95/98 clients 516
Server Status report 315

876 Index

Server Status Tool
    controls 782
    described 35
    extending 317, 735 – 740, 780 – 781
    information fields 781 – 782
    operation 314
    overview 38, 314, 780
    report contents 315
    sending reports 314 – 317
    setting passwords 316 – 317
Service Pack 2 (SP2) 591
Service Pack 3 (SP3) 595
Service Pack 4 (SP4) 157, 277
Services for Macintosh *See* Macintosh
SET (Secure Electronic Transport) 609
Set Up Computer Wizard
    See also Setup; Setup Wizard
    Add a New Computer to your Network mode 274 – 277
    Add a User to an Existing Client mode 278
    Add Software to an Existing Client mode 278
    adding applications to 714 – 716, 721 – 722
    client application configuration files 156
    configuring client networking 157 – 158, 276 – 277
    configuring server for clients 156 – 157, 274 – 276
    described 34
    extending *See* extending Set Up Computer Wizard
    installing add-on applications 39
    installing client applications 158, 277
    Ipdetect.exe 276
    Ipdx86.exe 276
    logon scripts 156, 274 – 275
    machine accounts 275 – 276
    modes described 273
    Netparam.ini 276
    optimization 479 – 480
    overview 12 – 13, 155
    Proxy client configuring 546
    Remove a Computer from your Network mode 278
    removing applications from 722 – 723
    response folders 156, 275
    running 155
    Scw.ini 156
    Setup.exe 276
    Startcli.exe 277
    Template.bat 274 – 275
    troubleshooting 799 – 807
    web sites 807
Setup
    See also Set Up Computer Wizard; Setup Wizard
    boot diskettes 125 – 126
    completing Setup using To Do List 131 – 133
    hardware detection problems 147 – 153
    installing applications 129 – 131
    modems not detected 150 – 153
    MS Loopback Adapter 148 – 149
    troubleshooting 147 – 153, 791 – 797
    unable to verify modems 152 – 153
    web sites 797
    Windows NT Server GUI Mode 127 – 129
    Windows NT Server Text Mode 126 – 127
setup files (.msi) 244
setup of Small Business Server 9 – 13
Setup Wizard
    See also Set Up Computer Wizard; Setup
    completing Setup using To Do List 131 – 133
    installing Resource Kit 766 – 767
    installing server applications 129 – 131
Setup.exe 157, 276
shadow partitions 56
Share a Folder Wizard 268 – 269
Shared Folder Access Wizard 266 – 267
shared folders
    creating 299
    optimization 461, 473, 479
shortcut files (.lnk) 303
SID (security identification) 605
sign-up scripts for ISPs 80
Simple Mail Transfer Protocol (SMTP)
    alternatives for ISP connectivity 507
    benefits of using 167 – 168, 507
    configuring mail delivery 183 – 184
    dial-up mail 83
    ETRN 165
    overview 161, 167
    POP3 vs. SMTP 167
    restrictions 108
Simple Network Management Protocol (SNMP)
  interoperability 532
single platform optimization 477 – 479
site names for Exchange Server 104
Site Server Express 601, 602
SLIP (serial line Internet protocol) 71
Small Business Customer Manager (SBCM) 757
Small Business Server 4.0a
    console page extension changes from 703
    Online Guide integration changes from 711
    Set Up Computer Wizard 723
    upgrading 509 – 513, 704
Small Business Server Client Setup Integration Wizard *See* Client Setup Integration Wizard
Small Business Server console *See* console
Small Business Server Customization Tool 699, 738 – 739, 775 – 782
Small Business Server Recommended Hardware List 11, 52, 54, 100, 124
Small Business Server Set Up Computer Wizard *See* Set Up Computer Wizard

Index 877

Small Business Server Setup Wizard
    See also Set Up Computer Wizard; Setup
    completing Setup using To Do List 131 – 133
    installing Resource Kit 766 – 767
    installing server applications 129 – 131
Small Business Server Start Menu Tool 772 – 773
Small Business Server Web Publishing Wizard See Web Publishing Wizard
SMB-based services 595 – 597
SMTP See Simple Mail Transfer Protocol
SNMP (Simple Network Management Protocol)
  interoperability 532
sockets 580
Sockets communication channels 580
SOCKS protocol 584
SOCKS Proxy service 544, 573, 584
software
    client computer requirements 52 – 53
    client computer test configurations 113
    server computer test configurations 113
solution development 41 – 42
SP2 (Service Pack 2) 591
SP3 (Service Pack 3) 595
SP4 (Service Pack 4) 137, 277
SQL Server 7.0
    additional information 65, 423
    client/server design tools 754
    database planning 422 – 423
    described 32
    disaster recovery 65
    enterprise integration and support 753 – 754
    memory performance 117
    migrating See migrating to SQL Server
    OLAP Services support 753
    optimization 466
    overview 421
    performance tests 110 – 111
    performance tuning 485
    processor performance 117
    upgrading 660
    web sites 422, 671, 673
SQL Server Enterprise Manager 667 – 668
SQL Server Profiler 668 – 669, 678
SQL Server Query Analyzer 668
SSL See secure sockets layer
standard security
    administrative accounts 590
    auditing 594 – 595
    backups 593
    directory protection 592
    file protection 592
    file sharing 595 – 597
    Guest account 590
    logging on or off 590 – 591
    overview 588 – 589
    passwords 591 – 592
    permissions 592
    registry 593
    removable media 597
    user accounts 589 – 590
Start Menu Tool 772 – 773
Startcli.exe 277
static packet filtering 199, 554
status views 690
stopping tasks 335
stripe sets 60 – 64
sub pages 683, 686 – 693, 700 – 702
subnet filtering 563
support 19
symbols 686, 693, 702
system partitions 57
System Policy
    See also System Policy Editor
    additional information 286, 313
    changing default 298
    controlling user environments 283 – 295
    creating 286 – 291
    creating default 297 – 299
    customizing 285
    operation of 284 – 285
    overview 245, 282 – 283
    restoring default 298 – 299
    revision methods 292
    Small Business Server 283
    templates 286
System Policy Editor
    See also System Policy
    application of policies 293 – 294
    changing client computer registries 285
    changing default user policy 298
    check box selection levels 287
    Common.adm 286
    configuring policy settings 293
    connecting to remote registries 291
    controlling user profile settings 287
    creating shared folders 299
    creating System Policy 286 – 291
    disabled commands 287
    editing registries 291 – 295
    hidden items 287
    installing on clients 295 – 296
    managing user desktops 284
    NTConfig.pol 284
    overview 245
    Poledit.exe 295 – 296
    removed commands or items 287
    restoring default user policy 298 – 299
    template files 292
    Windows.adm 286
    Winnt.adm 286

T

table of contents file 707 – 709
TAPI (Telephony Applications Programming Interface) 761
TAPI.exe 774
TAPIstate.exe 774
tasks
    configuring 334
    deleting 335
    editing 334
    files 331 – 332
    mobility and accessibility of files 331
    pausing 335
    running 333
    Scheduled Task utility 330, 334 – 335
    Scheduled Task Wizard 331
    scheduling 330 – 335
    security 331 – 333
    stopping 335
Tasks page 15 – 16, 42, 682, 684 – 685, 697 – 699
TCP/IP (Transmission Control Protocol/Internet Protocol)
    address changes 401 – 408
    default address 400
    interoperability 528
    optimization 462
    performance tuning 485
team home page 741
TechNet 45
technical support 19
Telephony Applications Programming Interface (TAPI) 761
Template.bat 156, 274 – 275
terminal adapter cards 163
testing web sites 79
tests of Small Business Server performance 110 – 112
third-party filtering services 399
thresholds 361, 363
Time-To-Live (TTL) function 569
Timon 774
TIP (Transaction Internet Protocol) interoperability 531
TLS (Transport Layer Security Protocol) 607
TMC (Tools Management Console) 767 – 769
To Do List
    completing Setup using 131 – 133
    described 33
    overview 12
tool tips 686
tools *See* utilities
Tools Management Console (TMC) 767 – 769
TPC-C Benchmark 110 – 111
training
    Online Guide 17
    resources 43

Transaction Internet Protocol (TIP) interoperability 531
Transact-SQL statements 670, 672 – 673, 678
transform files 244
Transmission Control Protocol/Internet Protocol *See* TCP/IP
Transport Layer Security Protocol (TLS) 607
troubleshooting
    additional information 797, 807, 825, 832, 838
    e-mail 833 – 838
    Fax Service 809 – 825
    hard page faults 115
    hardware 147 – 153
    HyperTerminal 831
    Internet 833 – 838
    ISP connectivity 81 – 84
    Modem Sharing Service 827 – 832
    modems 150 – 153, 827 – 832
    MS Loopback Adapter 148 – 149
    network adapter cards 148 – 150
    Outlook Web Access 438
    Set Up Computer Wizard 799 – 807
    Setup 147 – 153, 791 – 797
    tips 19
TTL (Time-To-Live) function 569
tutorials 19

U

Unattend.txt 10
UNC (Uniform Naming Convention) 142, 302
undetected modems 151 – 152
Uniform Naming Convention (UNC) 142, 302
UNIX
    application layer interoperability 530 – 532
    data layer interoperability 530
    interoperability overview 528
    management layer interoperability 532 – 533
    network layer interoperability 528 – 529
    web sites 533
upgrading BackOffice Server 4.5 661
upgrading Exchange Server 5.5 660
upgrading networks 5
upgrading Proxy Server 2.0 660
upgrading Small Business Server 4.0a 509 – 513, 704
upgrading Small Business Server 4.5 34, 659 – 661
upgrading SQL Server 7.0 660
upgrading Windows NT Server 4.0 659 – 660
Upsizing Wizard 422 – 423, 732 – 733
User Access Wizard 264 – 266
User Account Wizard
    Add a User mode 257 – 260
    modes described 256
    Remove a User mode 261 – 262
    Review or Change User Information mode 260 – 261
    user access control 26

User Manager 549
user profiles
    additional information 302, 303, 313
    administering 301
    configuration preferences stored in profile directories 302
    configuration preferences stored in registry hives 301 – 302
    content 300
    creating 301
    creating new mandatory user profiles 309 – 313
    creating new roaming user profiles 306 – 309, 311 – 312
    implementation 304 – 306
    logging on to Small Business Server 285
    overview 300
    paths 305 – 306
    planning 304 – 306
    saving 305 – 306
    selecting locations for 305 – 306
    setting permissions for 304 – 305
    structure 301 – 302
    types of 300
    Windows 95 vs. Windows NT 302 – 303
user.txt 665
users
    access control 390 – 394
    access control for remote users 565 – 566
    accessing fax printers 340
    account files 253 – 255
    accounts 589 – 590
    adding 257 – 260
    anonymous access to public folders 435 – 438
    anonymous accounts 603
    authentication and authorization 603 – 605
    changing information 260 – 261
    controlling environment 283 – 295
    creating accounts 214
    credentials 332
    customizing System Policy 285
    exporting existing accounts 251
    exporting existing groups 251 – 252
    limitations 178 – 179
    Migrate User Wizard *See* Migrate User Wizard
    migrating when replacing existing Windows NT 135 – 136
    modifying parameters with wizards 256
    names 333, 604
    optimization 478 – 479
    passwords 333, 591 – 592, 604
    permissions 265
    personal digital certificates 604
    planning for remote access 87
    profiles *See* user profiles
    removing 261 – 262
    reviewing information 260 – 261
    User Access Wizard *See* User Access Wizard
    User Account Wizard *See* User Account Wizard
utilities
    accessing 767 – 769
    Batch User Add Tool 773
    Configure Server Status Tool 780 – 782
    console 776 – 780
    CSNW 525
    Customization Tool 699, 738 – 739, 775 – 782
    DSMN 526 – 527, 641 – 646
    DTS 668
    Enterprise Manager 667 – 668
    FaxMon 787
    FaxPerf 787
    FPNW 639 – 641
    GSNW 138 – 143, 524 – 525, 634 – 639
    installing 765 – 767
    list of 771
    Migration Tool for NetWare 525, 648 – 650
    Modem Status Tools 352, 773 – 774
    Modprof 471 – 473
    NetWare-to-Windows NT Server Conversion 138
    NWLink 138, 525, 633
    Performance Monitor *See* Performance Monitor
    Profiler 668 – 669, 678
    Query Analyzer 668
    SBSCustom.exe 775 – 782
    Scheduled Task 330, 334 – 335
    Server Status Tool 314 – 317, 780 – 782
    Start Menu Tool 772 – 773
    TAPI.exe 774
    TAPIstate.exe 774
    Timon 774
    Windows NT Backup 54, 66, 335, 357 – 358, 593

V

value-added filtering services 398
value-added service opportunities 39
version number optimization 468
vertical list views 688
views
    Address Book 355 – 356
    Chart 383
    horizontal list 689
    no list 691
    queries 671 – 672
    status 690
    vertical list 688

880   Index

virtual private network (VPN)
    adding as RAS ports 225 – 226, 229 – 230
    creating connections to PPTP servers 239 – 241
    encryption 226 – 227
    features 92
    network protocols 94
    overview 93, 609 – 610
Visual Studio interoperability 530
VPN *See* virtual private network

W

watermarks 686, 693
web
    See also Internet
    access to files and applications 603 – 606
    browsers 747
    caching 102, 541, 544
    connecting to 28 – 29
    controlling access 28 – 29
    discussions with comments 750
    features enabled through server software 748
    folders 745
    hosting information 162 – 163
    hosting services 83, 507
    Office 2000 enhancements 746 – 752
    Office 2000 integration with 746
    publishing 546
    publishing support 566 – 568
    server security 600 – 602
    site navigation 749
    Subscriptions and Notifications 751
Web Access 359
web browsing
    alternatives for ISP connectivity 493
    Exchange Server 5.5 501
    Modem Sharing Service 499 – 501
    POP3 501 – 507
    Proxy Server 2.0 29, 494 – 499
Web Proxy Logs report 315
Web Proxy service
    access control 390, 562
    alerts 416
    components 574 – 577
    described 544
    functions of 573 – 574
    HTTP requests 578
    ISAPI requests 577 – 578
    keep-alives 578
    overview 573
    using with Winsock Proxy service 585 – 586

Web Publishing Wizard
    additional information 163
    configuring 165, 199 – 200
    overview 162 – 163
    web site development 73
Web Query Wizard 754
web sites
    60 Minute Intranet Kit 740 – 742
    BackOffice Server 661
    Btrieve database migration 423
    caching 450
    configuring information 189 – 190
    dequeuing methods 166, 185
    development 73 – 74
    Dial-Up Networking 53
    Dial-Up Networking 1.2 Upgrade 234 – 235
    Digiboard multiport serial cards 99
    Direct Access 45
    e-mail 838
    Exchange Server 5.5 disaster recovery planning 65
    Fax Service 825
    firewalls 450
    FrontPage Web Site Management tool 741
    hosting requirements for ISPs 73
    hosting with IIS 4.0 73
    Internet 838
    InterNIC database 160
    ISP connectivity 168
    Microsoft Direct Access 45
    Microsoft Office 60 Minute Intranet Kit 740, 742
    Modem Sharing Service 832
    MSMQ 759
    NetWare networks 527
    optimization 678
    Outlook 442
    Outlook Web Access 438
    PPTP 96
    publishing resources 163
    SBCM 757
    Scheduled Task utility 335
    security 21
    Set Up Computer Wizard 807
    Setup 797
    Small Business Server Recommended Hardware List 11, 52, 54, 100, 124
    Small Business Server resources 45
    SOCKS 584
    SQL Server 422, 671, 673
    System Policy 313
    TAPI 761
    TechNet 45
    testing 79
    training 43
    troubleshooting Outlook Web Access 438

UNIX 533
upgrade information 659
Upsizing Wizard 423
user profiles 313
VPN 234 – 235
Web Publishing Wizard 163
Windows NT Hardware Compatibility List 55, 63
Windows 3.x
    authentication 518
    installing Small Business Server on existing
        environments 137
    server interactions 516
Windows 95
    authentication 518
    Common.adm 286
    configuring client computers 217 – 218, 234 – 241
    connecting client computers to Small Business
        Server 220 – 221
    Disk Defragmenter 453
    installing Small Business Server on existing
        environments 137
    installing System Policy Editor 296
    mandatory profiles 312 – 313
    Modem Sharing Service 350 – 351
    PPTP 234 – 241
    roaming profiles 311 – 312
    server interactions 516
    upgrading Dial-Up Networking 234 – 235
    Windows NT profile differences 302 – 303
    Windows.adm 286
Windows 98
    configuring client computers 217 – 218
    connecting client computers to Small Business
        Server 220 – 221
    installing Small Business Server on existing
        environments 137
    server interactions 516
Windows Internet Naming Service (WINS) 462
Windows NT Backup utility
    disaster recovery 66
    Exchange Server 357 – 358
    registry 593
    Scheduled Task utility 335
    tape device support 54
Windows NT Directory Services 549
Windows NT Event Log 549
Windows NT Event Viewer 378 – 381
Windows NT File System *See* NTFS
Windows NT Hardware Compatibility List 55, 63
Windows NT Performance Monitor *See* Performance
    Monitor
Windows NT Remote Access Service *See* Remote Access
    Service (RAS)

Windows NT Server 4.0
    See also server interactions
    Access Control Lists (ACLs) 600
    Backup utility 593
    compatibility with control devices 54
    configuring 164
    CryptoAPI 611
    described 31
    disaster recovery 65
    fault-tolerant disk drivers 57
    file sharing service 595 – 597
    FPNW 143 – 145
    FtDisk 57
    Hardware Compatibility List 55, 63
    ICS *See* Internet Connection Services
    installing 10, 126 – 129, 460 – 464
    installing Small Business Server on existing
        environments 135 – 136
    interoperability *See* interoperability
    machine accounts 157
    migrating from an existing server 663 – 666
    MSMQ 759
    Office 2000 748
    operating systems 522 – 523
    performance tuning 483 – 485
    protocols 523
    RAS *See* Remote Access Service
    security 552, 587, 599 – 600
    Service Pack 2 591
    Service Pack 3 595
    TAPI 761
    upgrading 659 – 660
Windows NT Server GUI Mode 127 – 129
Windows NT Server Text Mode 126 – 127
Windows NT Services for Macintosh *See* Macintosh
Windows NT Services for UNIX 533
Windows NT User Manager 549
Windows NT Workstation
    Common.adm 286
    configuring client computers 218 – 219, 228 – 234
    connecting client computers to Small Business
        Server 221 – 222
    creating alerts for clients 329
    Disk Defragmenter 453
    Fax Service 340
    installing System Policy Editor 295
    mandatory profiles 309 – 311
    Modem Sharing Service 351
    PPTP 228 – 234
    roaming profiles 306 – 309
    Service Pack 4 157
    storing profiles 305
    Windows 95 profile differences 302 – 303
    Winnt.adm 286

Windows Sockets 579 – 580, 582
Windows Telephony Applications Programming Interface (TAPI) 761
Windows.adm 286
Winnt.adm 286
WINS (Windows Internet Naming Service) 462
Winsock Proxy client DLL 582
Winsock Proxy Logs report 315
Winsock Proxy service
    access control 390, 564 – 565
    alerts 417 – 418
    components 581 – 582
    configuring 391 – 394
    control channels 582 – 583
    described 544
    overview 573, 579
    using with Web Proxy service 585 – 586
    Windows Sockets 579 – 581
wizards
    Access 266 – 268
    Add User 480
    Change Password 262 – 263
    Client Installation 13
    Client Setup Integration 782 – 786
    CMAK 89, 445 – 448
    console 256
    Custom Installation 244 – 245
    described 34
    DTS Export 668
    DTS Import 668
    E-mail Distribution List 271 – 273
    Fax Access 266
    FrontPage 60 Minute Intranet Site 740
    Index Tuning 678
    Internet Access 266 – 268
    Internet Connection *See* Internet Connection Wizard
    Migrate User 135 – 136, 249 – 256, 663 – 666
    modifying user parameters 256
    Move Folder 270
    Network Installation 244 – 245
    Office Profile 243 – 244
    overview 249
    Phonebook 230
    Printer Access 266
    Scheduled Task 331
    Set Up Computer *See* Set Up Computer Wizard
    Share a Folder 268 – 269
    Shared Folder Access 266 – 267
    Upsizing 422 – 423, 732 – 733
    User Access 264 – 266
    User Account 26, 256 – 262
    Web Publishing 73, 162 – 163, 165, 199 – 200
    Web Query 754
World Wide Web *See* web

X

X.400 addresses 106 – 107
X.509 certificates 604
x2 modems 100

Z

Ziff-Davis NetBench tool 112

System Requirements

To use the *Microsoft BackOffice Small Business Server 4.5 Resource Kit* compact disc, you need a computer equipped with the following minimum configuration.

For server:

- System with a Pentium 120-MHz or higher processor (Pentium 200 or higher recommended)
- 64 MB of RAM
- CD-ROM drive
- 3.5" high-density disk drive (must be configured as drive A)
- Super VGA monitor and video adapter (800 x 600 or higher resolution; 16 colors)

For desktop:

- Client operating system with Microsoft Windows 95 or later, or Windows NT Workstation 4.0
- PC with a Pentium 90-MHz or higher processor recommended
- 32 MB of RAM recommended
- 3.5" high-density disk drive
- VGA or higher-resolution monitor and video adapter
- Microsoft Mouse or compatible pointing device

The *intelligent* way to practice for the **MCP exam**

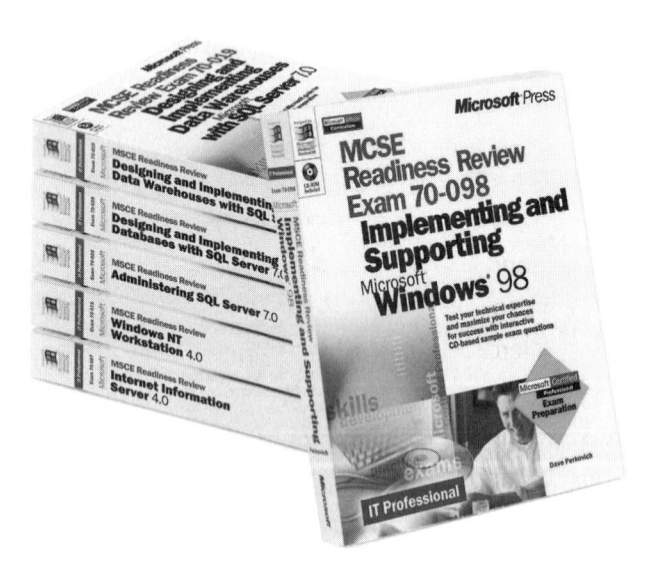

If you took the Microsoft Certified Professional (MCP) exam today, would you pass? With the *Readiness Review* MCP exam simulation on CD-ROM, you get a low-risk, low-cost way to find out! Use this electronic assessment tool to take randomly generated, 60-question practice tests, covering actual MCP objectives. Test and retest with different question sets each time, and then consult the companion study guide to review all featured exam items and identify areas for further study. *Readiness Review*—it's the smart way to prep!

MCSE Readiness Review—Exam 70-058: Networking Essentials
U.S.A. $29.99
U.K. $27.99 [V.A.T. included]
Canada $42.99
ISBN 0-7356-0536-X

MCSE Readiness Review—Exam 70-067: Microsoft® Windows NT® Server 4.0
U.S.A. $29.99
U.K. $27.99 [V.A.T. included]
Canada $42.99
ISBN 0-7356-0538-6

MCSE Readiness Review—Exam 70-073: Microsoft Windows NT Workstation 4.0
U.S.A. $29.99
U.K. $27.99 [V.A.T. included]
Canada $42.99
ISBN 0-7356-0537-8

MCSE Readiness Review—Exam 70-087: Microsoft Internet Information Server 4.0
U.S.A. $29.99
U.K. $27.99 [V.A.T. included]
Canada $44.99
ISBN 0-7356-0541-6

MCSE Readiness Review—Exam 70-098: Implementing and Supporting Microsoft Windows
U.S.A. $29.99
U.K. $27.99 [V.A.T. included]
Canada $44.99
ISBN 0-7356-0671-4

Microsoft Press® products are available worldwide wherever quality computer books are sold. For more information, contact your book or computer retailer, software reseller, or local Microsoft Sales Office, or visit our Web site at mspress.microsoft.com. To locate your nearest source for Microsoft Press products, or to order directly, call 1-800-MSPRESS in the U.S. (in Canada, call 1-800-268-2222).

Prices and availability dates are subject to change.

Microsoft®
mspress.microsoft.com

There's no *substitute* for *experience.*

Now you can apply the best practices from real-world implementations of Microsoft technologies with *Notes from the Field*. Based on the extensive field experiences of Microsoft Consulting Services, these valuable technical references outline tried-and-tested solutions you can use in your own company, right now.

Deploying Microsoft SQL Server™ 7.0
(Notes from the Field)
U.S.A. $39.99
U.K. £37.49
Canada $59.99
ISBN 0-7356-0726-5

Optimizing Network Traffic
(Notes from the Field)
U.S.A. $39.99
U.K. £37.49 [V.A.T. included]
Canada $59.99
ISBN 0-7356-0648-X

Managing a Microsoft Windows NT®
Network (Notes from the Field)
U.S.A. $39.99
U.K. £37.49 [V.A.T. included]
Canada $59.99
ISBN 0-7356-0647-1

Coming Soon!
Deploying Microsoft® Office 2000
(Notes from the Field)
U.S.A. $39.99
U.K. £37.49
Canada $59.99
ISBN 0-7356-0727-3

Microsoft Press® products are available worldwide wherever quality computer books are sold. For more information, contact your book or computer retailer, software reseller, or local Microsoft Sales Office, or visit our Web site at mspress.microsoft.com. To locate your nearest source for Microsoft Press products, or to order directly, call 1-800-MSPRESS in the U.S. (in Canada, call 1-800-268-2222).

Prices and availability dates are subject to change.

Microsoft®
mspress.microsoft.com